Systems and Policies for the Global Learning Economy

INTERNATIONAL SERIES ON TECHNOLOGY POLICY AND INNOVATION

a joint initiative of
The IC² Institute, The University of Texas at Austin
http://www.utexas.edu/depts/ic2
and
the Center for Innovation, Technology and Policy Research
Instituto Superior Técnico, Lisbon
http://in3.dem.ist.utl.pt

The main objectives of this series are (1) to publish leading scholarly work representing academic, business, and government sectors world-wide on technology policy and innovation; and (2) to present current and future issues of critical importance for using science and technology to foster regional economic development and shared prosperity.

Series Editors: Manuel V. Heitor, David V. Gibson, and Pedro Conceição

Systems and Policies for the Global Learning Economy

Edited by
David V. Gibson, Chandler Stolp,
Pedro Conceição, and Manuel V. Heitor

Foreword by George Kozmetsky

INTERNATIONAL SERIES ON TECHNOLOGY POLICY AND INNOVATION

Manuel V. Heitor, David V. Gibson, and Pedro Conceição, Series Editors

IC² Institute, The University of Texas at Austin, Texas and
The Center for Innovation, Technology and Policy Research,
Instituto Superior Técnico, Lisbon, Portugal

Westport, Connecticut
London

Library of Congress Cataloging-in-Publication Data

Systems and policies for the global learning economy / edited by David V. Gibson...[et al.] ; foreword by George Kozmetsky.
   p. cm.—(International series on technology policy and innovation, ISSN 1528–1698)
   Includes bibliographical references and index.
   ISBN 1–56720–476–7 (alk. paper)
   1. Economic development—Congresses. 2. Information technology—Economic aspects—Congresses. 3. Technological innovations—Economic aspects—Congresses I. Gibson, David V. II. Series.
HD73.S97   2003
338—dc21   2002030748

British Library Cataloguing in Publication Data is available.

Library of Congress Catalog Card Number: 2002030748
ISBN: 1–56720–476–7
ISSN: 1528–1698

First published in 2003

Praeger Publishers, 88 Post Road West, Westport, CT 06881
An imprint of Greenwood Publishing Group, Inc.
www.praeger.com

Printed in the United States of America

The paper used in this book complies with the Permanent Paper Standard issued by the National Information Standards Organization (Z39.48–1984).

10 9 8 7 6 5 4 3 2 1

Contents

PART III: TRENDS AND OPPORTUNITIES FOR SCIENCE, TECHNOLOGY, AND INNOVATION POLICIES

PART IV: CORPORATE STRATEGIES FOR THE KNOWLEDGE-BASED ECONOMY

Foreword: Perspectives on Creating Value Through Global Knowledge Partnerships

George Kozmetsky

The 21st century is a time for creating value based on knowledge and human capital. The early part of the 21st century is a period of transformation to a "new economy." The term new economy is at best a controversial phrase. I have always felt it hard to justify using the word "new." It has been my experience that someone has already discovered or identified what others thought was new. What I mean by the "new economy" is to recognize early the reality of changes that are happening. There is not much question in my mind that national and global economies have been going through radical evolutionary changes. In the 1960s to 1980s it was common to refer to the developed nations' economies as postindustrial. In a postindustrial society a community's, state's, or nation's advantage was based on its natural endowments such as land, minerals, climate, and other factors related to comparatively "simple" technologies. On the other hand, the new economy for the 21st century will be based on advanced technologies that are both complex and digitally based. Economic historians refer to these technologies as the 4th industrial revolution; more commonly they are known as digital/knowledge innovations. The 4th industrial revolution technologies have made production and services factors move toward knowledge and human resources-based investments, dependent on highly skilled personnel across the human capacity spectrum and abundant financial assets. Key productive factors no longer rely on natural endowments or the value-added chain but more on how technologies, the economy and society are integrated and partnered in all sectors—academic, business, government, foundations, and not-for-profit organizations. It is also clear that the new economy is also undergoing a newer power shift. Jessica T. Mathews defined "power shift" as follows: "A competing notion of 'human security' is creeping around the edges of official thinking, suggesting that the security be viewed as emerging from the conditions of daily life—food, shelter, employment, health, public safety—rather than flowing downward from a country's foreign relations and military strength."[1]

Creating value for the 21st century requires utilizing knowledge and innovation as the prime drivers. In short, all communities, regions, and nations and their respective sectorial entities need to determine their own status and various futures. This calls for newer forms of leadership as well as organization to create and attain their own knowledge and innovation for wealth and prosperity creation.

The most significant lesson for the 21st century that I have learned is that generating wealth and prosperity is based on knowledge and innovation. Knowledge consists of science and technology and "know-how"—what is in people's heads. Innovation is to successfully utilize knowledge to create value. Key lessons in knowledge and innovation are as follows:

1. Technology is a type of wealth—one that we do not yet know how to measure for economic purposes. It is not the number of patents or refereed articles or books. Wealth, of course, is a means of attaining economic, social, and cultural status for individuals, as well as a way of achieving institutional objectives and ensuring the general welfare of society.
2. Technological innovation is a prime factor in stimulating productive capacity and ensuring competitive international trade.
3. Each nation's technological needs are linked with other nations' commercial needs. In no case is one market wholly insulated from what happens to other markets.
4. All nations—industrialized or emerging or underdeveloped—need effective technological management and entrepreneurial training at all levels in both the private and public sectors and in operations as well as in research.
5. It is feasible to develop a technology road map for innovations that are drivers for venture creation and expansion.
6. Technology commercialization is not a simple transfer of a product or service. It is a process that integrates all the partners involved with the existing means of design, production, distribution, and maintenance as well as developing applications new to the world.
7. Contemporary issues for creating value from knowledge in the 21st century require a newer class of research than the traditional scientific approach generally associated with an academic discipline.

Application-driven research is centered around a concrete problem but is also coupled with a test of adequacy as well as relevance. In other words application research goes beyond simply solving a problem, it also goes on to test for adequacy and relevance and comes up with generalized lessons learned to be adapted to other specific and localized applications before developing a research base or discipline.

Referring to generation of knowledge by Mode 1 and Mode 2 has a lot to commend the usage of these terms. The critical distinctions are as follows: Mode 1 has an academic focus and relies more on the specialization of disciplines, while Mode 2 is more transdisciplinary and relies on the context and need for successful innovative applications. Mode 1 relies on peer review for quality control. Mode 2 quality control is based more on social accountability and acceptance from a set of heterogeneous practitioners and ultimate consumers. Diffusion paths differ sharply. Mode 1 relies more on specialization and disciplinary professionals that are to be found in multiple institutions. Mode 2 relies more on advanced information technologies and rapid communication.

The IC² Institute studies—both "think" and "do"—have made it clear that a different type of leadership is required for the 21st-century digital/knowledge new economy and society. In transforming from a postindustrial society to a high technology or information technology economy and society, technology entrepreneurship was required during the period of the 1970s through the 1990s. Technology entrepreneurship was rooted in the private sector—entrepreneurs who started technology-based firms or who transformed companies to utilize the newer technologies and concepts. However, for the 21st century, technology entrepreneurship by itself is not enough. It must be integrated with civic entrepreneurship.

Civic entrepreneurship is a collaborative partnership of community leaders in academia, business, government, and the nonprofit sector. Until there is such a cooperative partnership there is little transformation even while each sector is within itself excellent or world class. Under sectorial excellence, at best there can be only a gradual transition. What many of us have observed in the past is that it takes a community, state, or region some twenty to forty years to develop technology-based industries. For example, it took at least thirty to forty years under a hot/cold war for California to develop Silicon Valley.

It is my belief that in the 21st century economy creating value will require global knowledge networking entrepreneurship. How firms in one country share with firms and society in other countries and share risks and rewards with each other will be key to global knowledge partnerships. The means of sharing risks and rewards globally is part of the knowledge economy. Wealth in the 21st century will be "liquid paper," for example, stocks and bonds. Investors have participated globally in such sharing in the past. How to partner in the 21st century to share such rewards with all stakeholders will be the challenge and opportunity. There are many examples and experiments towards such efforts. Stock options are provided to employees at various levels in globally based firms on their subsidiarys' countries stock exchanges. Some global firms establish stock-pacing firms in various countries. There is not much question in my mind that in the next ten to twenty years there will be more and more regional stock markets and eventually a global stock market.

In "Global Economic Competition: Today's Warfare in Global Electronics Industries and Companies" IC² researcher Dr. Piyu Yue and I reached an early conclusion that global national competition was driving the technology chain from a high technology business with large gross margins to a low-gross-margin commodity business.[2] In other words the life cycle of technology products is short. As new and advanced products are launched on the market, the earlier generations become technologically and economically obsolete. What we have observed is that while the technology-based product/service cycle is short—under two years—in the 21st century nations can't take some twenty to forty years to develop their digital/knowledge innovation-based industries.

Those corporations that successfully market and sell digital/knowledge innovations at any given in time will experience spectacular growth rates—so-called hypergrowth—for example, 50 percent/year or more. Economists have been late in recognizing this phenomenon, so characteristic of the digital/knowledge economy. Conversely, corporations clinging to product laggards can see their markets collapse overnight, with disastrous results. The 21st-century economy can become polarized into two camps: swarms of small start-up companies growing at phenomenal rates, and stumbling giants.

The high tech corporation is typically embarked on a dynamic path that is located far from equilibrium all the time. The orbit is nonlinear. It harbors the possibility of chaos. In the resulting setting of industrial turmoil, there will occur rapid technological evolution. A kind of balance will be established between creativity and oblivion, between the commercialization of new products, the launching of new start-up companies, mergers and acquisitions, and bankruptcies.

> In a quite technical sense, the balance of attention of the society as it approached and went beyond maturity shifted from supply to demand, from problems of production to problems of consumption, and of welfare in the widest sense.
>
> W. W. Rostow, IC^2 Fellow

For the 21st century, knowledge is creating value by integration of newer technology advances with consumer services that become the drivers for economic growth. World economies and societies have been transforming and restructuring dramatically. We are moving forward toward a newer stage of economic growth: the age of digital/knowledge technology. Knowledge innovation based on integration of technologies with services will continue to create newer hybrid industries. This, in turn, will require new kinds of workers with continuous updated knowledge, special skills, and competencies to fulfill new missions. Education and training to meet the challenges of raising productivity have become critical in the 21st century knowledge economy. If demand for skilled and competent workers is not met due to poor education and training, corporations will seek such workers on a global basis.

> The richness of a community is no longer tied to natural resources or the industrial base, but to how well its leadership takes advantage of human potential. A community's ability to learn not only how to create technology, but also how to turn it into a product and gain value from it will be the test that determines success in the 21st century.
>
> Dr. Skip Porter, Vice President of Research and Dean of Engineering at the University of Oklahoma

IC² Institute, The University of Texas at Austin, along with other leading universities worldwide is developing knowledge for understanding as well as incubating centers (such as the Austin Technology Incubator) for creating ventures and partnerships in communities, regions, nations, and globally. The technologies of the 4th industrial revolution as well as the newer digital-knowledge economy will continue to transform the role and scope of the universities in venture creation. Providing graduates with traditional degrees and sustained discipline-specific (Mode 1) research is valued and needed, but it is not sufficient for current and future needs. What is also needed is more transdisciplinary research and education (Mode 2) that relies more on the context and need for successful innovative applications to develop human capital that can think globally as well as act locally to seek peaceful coexistence and prosperity.

NOTES

1. Jessica T. Mathews (1997). *Foreign Affairs Magazine*, Vol. 76, No. 1, January/February.

2. George Kozmetsky and Piyu Yue (1997), *Global Economic Competition: Today's Warfare in Global Electronics Industries and Companies*. Boston: Kluwer Academic Publishers.

Acknowledgments

The editors of *Systems and Policies for the Global Learning Economy* thank the organizers and sponsors of the 3rd International Conference on Science and Technology Policy and Innovation (ICTPI), which was held in Austin, Texas, August 30-September 2, 1999. The two sponsoring academic institutions were The Instituto Superior Tecnico (IST), Lisbon, Portugal, through the Center for Innovation, Technology and Policy Research, IN+, and The University of Texas at Austin including the IC^2 Institute; the Lyndon B. Johnson School of Public Affairs; the College and Graduate School of Business; the Colleges of Liberal Arts, Communication, and Engineering; and the Graduate School of Library and Information Science. Austin-based corporate sponsors were Motorola, 3M, Microelectronics and Computer Technology Corporation, Radian International, Vinson & Elkins LLP, Gray Cary Ware & Freidenrich LLP, Triton Ventures, Angelou Economic Advisors, the Greater Austin Chamber of Commerce, and JETRO (The Japan External Trade Organization, Houston). Thanks are also due to the Portuguese Science and Technology Foundation for cosponsorship.

We are also grateful to the conference's International Organizing Committee and Program Committee for planning the conference and for reviewing and selecting papers to be presented. And we are grateful to those who so effectively managed the three-day event, in particular the staff at the IC^2 Institute that included Coral Franke, Wesley Cole, Susie Brown, Li Eckert, and staff at the Lyndon B. Johnson School of Public Affairs.

The editors thank the chapter authors for sharing their insights and regional perspectives on a range of important topics regarding science and technology policy and innovation. Finally, the editors are especially grateful for the dedicated and excellent publication effort including Miguel Silveiro, Publications Coordinator at the Center for Innovation, Technology, and Policy Research, IST, Lisbon, Portugal, and Katie Chase, Project Editor, Greenwood Publishing Group, for successfully bringing this volume to publication.

PART I:
INTRODUCTION

Outline of the Book

The recognition that knowledge networks and learning are key to the global economy motivated the organization of this book, which reviews and extends select papers of the 3rd International Conference on Technology Policy and Innovation. Under the broad designation of "Creating Value for the 21st Century: Global Knowledge Partnerships," the Conference brought together 340 academic, business, and government experts from 34 countries to present a range of perspectives and to contribute to a better understanding of worldwide assets and challenges for accelerated knowledge-based growth in developed, developing, and emerging regions.

The three volumes published, to date, in this International Series on Technology Policy and Innovation share several general themes. One is the notion of a "learning economy" in which knowledge is created, stored, updated, transmitted, diffused, and applied. Key elements of the learning economy include universities and research organizations, private firms, foundations, the public sector, and networks of communication flows that link these institutions regionally, nationally, and globally. A second general theme concerns "metrics for knowledge" and the challenge of measuring critical but elusive concepts such as "technology," "knowledge," "innovation," and "productivity." A third theme is the concept of "inclusive development." To be sustainable, strategies for economic development not only have to consider humankind's relationship with physical environments, they also need to adapt to and be integrated with the particular social and cultural characteristics of different regional settings.

Two questions link the chapters collected in this volume:

- What are the most important challenges facing knowledge-processing and policy-making institutions in a world in which innovation is becoming the key driving force for economic growth and development?
- How can institutions best develop and exploit science, technology, and engineering to meet these challenges in light of specific social, political, and economic conditions at regional, national, and global levels of analysis?

In part, to answer these questions, the chapters in this volume are presented under four broad headings. Part I includes an introductory chapter and individual essays on Latin America, Europe, and Japan. Part II includes a set of ten papers examining regional economic development, learning networks, and systems of innovation. Part III includes seven studies that consider trends and opportunities for science, technology, and innovation policy. Part IV highlights four studies that examine corporate strategies for the knowledge-based economy.

Chapter 1, "Knowledge and Innovation for the Global Learning Economy: Building Capacity for Development," by Pedro Conceição, David Gibson, Manuel Heitor, and Chandler Stolp presents a combination of broad themes and specific topics that set the stage for the other chapters that follow. These themes and topics include contexts for innovation, trends and challenges for S&T policy, metrics for knowledge, and thoughts for an inclusive learning society. Each of the three essays that follow concern important challenges for Latin America, Europe, and Asia. Lawrence Graham compares Brazil's history of regionalism with patterns of "new regionalism" elsewhere in the world with an eye to how these contexts shape, and are shaped by, technology policies. Graham concludes with a look at the particularly successful case of the Brazilian state of Paraná. Robin Miège follows with a discussion of European efforts to coordinate the promotion of regionally based innovation. He argues that the complexities and interconnectivities that attend innovation policy call for integrated measures and coordination at the highest levels of European Union government. In the third essay, Akio Nishizawa discusses steps that Japan has taken, or could potentially take, to stimulate innovation and economic development through university spin-off companies.

The chapters in Part II emphasize regional economic development, learning networks, and systems of innovation in Europe, Korea, Latin America, Canada, Australia, and India. Latin America provides a set of particularly instructive examples of innovation and development in light of reforms adopted since the late 1980s to open and integrate national economies and in light of the special, and sometimes conflictive, relationships these countries have historically had with the United States. The chapters on the European Union (EU) and Korea provide a set of interesting insights and lessons learned based on government-directed policies targeted to foster innovation and economic development. The chapter on India emphasizes that a nation's innovation capacity benefits from promoting entrepreneurship in traditional and low-tech industries as well as new and emerging industries.

"Learning Regions in Europe: Theory, Policy, and Practice through the RIS (Regional Innovation Strategies) Experience," by Mikel Landabaso, Christine Oughton, and Kevin Morgan suggest that a new kind of regional policy is emerging in the EU in which the emphasis is on collective learning and institutional innovation or "social capital" rather then on "physical capital." These innovative forms of economic governance are network based and characterized by strong public-private partnerships whose actions are concerned not with the scale of state intervention, but with the framework for effective interaction. The authors argue for innovation strategies involving key regional actors, projects, and policy objectives.

In Chapter 3, Claudia Salas, Gabriel Susunaga, and Ismael Aguilar-Barajas emphasize the role of knowledge in development processes in "The Role of Innovation in Regional Economic Development: Some Lessons and Experiences for Policy Making." The authors emphasize several challenges for regional transformation towards the information economy. The importance of knowledge generation and access must be appreciated, they state, as should beneficial interrelationships between firms, universities, local government, labor markets, communities, entrepreneurs, infrastructure, and financial resources. And they emphasize the increasing integration of regional and global networks. The authors suggest that strategies based on high technology are not viable for all regions, and increasing innovation in regionally based firms does not require the construction of science parks; instead, they argue for two critical and complementary conditions for the generation of knowledge and innovation: imagination and creativity, and analytical ability.

"Characteristics of Innovation in a Non-Metropolitan Area: The Okanagan Valley of British Columbia," by J. Adam Holbrook and Lindsay Hughes contend that policy makers need information on the state of investment in knowledge and how this investment flows through the regional and national systems of innovation. They suggest that, in general, the direct role of government is relatively unimportant. What is important is the firm's internal environment and customer feedback or signals from the marketplace. However, in non-metropolitan regions the role of government as a "knowledge supplier" needs to be enhanced since institutions and networks are less developed for fostering innovation. Additional research needs to be focused on how smaller economies over time augment or depreciate technical knowledge and human capital.

Chapter 5, "Incubating and Sustaining Learning and Innovation Poles in Latin America and the Caribbean," by David V. Gibson, Pedro Conceição, and Julie Nordskog contends that less-developed countries worldwide can leap ahead in regionally based economic development by regional, national, and international relationship building and enhanced knowledge transfer using computer and information technologies (CIT). On the one hand, economic development strategies that built such successful "technopoles" as Silicon Valley, California; Route 128 in Boston, Massachusetts; and Austin, Texas, argued for the local agglomeration of talent, technology, capital, and business know-how along with access to local markets. The development of such physical and "smart" infrastructures required co-located financial resources, human capital, and physical infrastructure. Learning and innovation poles, on the other hand, emphasize the importance of building and maintaining regional and international networks to facilitate knowledge sharing and access to global markets for accelerated technology-based growth.

Scott Tiffin, Gabriela Couto, and Tomas Gabriel Bas in "Venture Capital in Latin America for New Technology-Based Firms" draw on the research projects and experiences of Canada's International Development Research Center (IDRC) in Montevideo, Uruguay. The authors discuss why venture capital is important to the development of new technology-based firms (NTBFs) in Latin America, with particular reference to Southern Cone countries of Argentina, Brazil, Chile, and Uruguay. The authors conclude that major challenges to funding and growing more NTBFs in Latin America include (1) burdensome regulations, (2) the necessity for small enterprises to operate, to some degree, outside legal norms, (3) the lack of an appropriate stock exchange to facilitate initial public offerings, (4) the largely untested and often ambiguous protection of intellectual property, and (5) a business culture that relies, to a great extent, on personal and family relationships. The authors suggest that public policy professionals should be more involved in creating an environment that fosters the growth of NTBFs, including regulatory structures relating to intellectual property rights, business formation, and tax incentives for creating venture capital pools.

Carlos Quandt in "Mapping Knowledge Flows in Clusters and Networks: Case Studies of Technology-Based Firms in Brazil" emphasizes that the divide between more- and less-developed regions is likely to be increasingly defined in terms of relative ability to innovate, diffuse, and apply knowledge rather than on a region's other more physical endowments. Technology-intensive firms in Latin America and the Caribbean typically face great obstacles in their successful access of new technology and to markets within and outside the region. Quandt emphasizes the importance of coordinating industrial and technological policy to create an environment of innovation and competition for local firms. This includes the establishment of decentralized support mechanisms such as adequate and accessible financing, education and training, and technological services that build on regional strengths.

Chapter 8, "Regional Innovation Systems in Korea," by Sunyang Chung reviews a number of regional innovation systems in Korea and concludes that they are weak and that innovation actors and institutions are unevenly distributed and poorly networked. Chung suggests that regional governments need to be more proactive in the funding of science and technology and in the development of local networks, and Korea's central government needs to support this decentralization and accept regional governments as important partners in enhancing the national innovation system. Chung also argues for the importance of building on a region's existing industrial structures, universities, and public research institutes.

Chapter 9, "The Third Generation Technopoleis in Korea," by Tae Kyung Sung states that Korean technopolis development can be characterized into three distinct generations: first, the 1970 and 1980 development of select science towns or regions; second, the 1980 and mid-1990 focus on building local economies; and third, mid-1990 the increased involvement of local economies supported by the national government. This chapter reviews the successes and failures of each of these strategies while highlighting profiles of six Korean technopoleis with a focus on the configuration, participating sectors, operation, and funding. Finally, future directions for Korea's technopolis development are suggested.

"Weak and Strong Ties, Individualism, Collectivism, and the Diffusion of Technological Knowledge" by Paul Robertson, Thomas Keil, and Erkko Autio contends that while firms need to acquire technological knowledge from both external and internal sources, there are substantial barriers to acquiring knowledge from outside a firm's immediate environment. These barriers are often the result of knowledge being generated in a decentralized and chaotic manner, which makes it difficult for firms to locate partners that can help them solve their problems. The authors develop a case study on individualism among Australian and Finnish firms and suggest that strong ties between organizations with low levels of expertise may be of less value in diffusing knowledge than weak ties between knowledgeable and less-knowledgeable firms. The authors suggest that appropriate government action might facilitate technological networking especially among organizations with weak ties, and they suggest that "brokering institutions" such as industry research boards facilitate the process.

Successful innovation and entrepreneurship to facilitate a region's innovation capacity is not always associated with high tech as elaborated in "Enterprise Innovativeness and Farm-Level Technical Change: A Case Study of Floriculture Sector in India," by Kavita Mehra. "Floriculture" (the world trade in flowers and ornamentals) is a profitable global business that increased from $2.5 billion (U.S.) in 1985 to $6 billion in 1996. Capturing market demand and introducing production and marking innovations based on the skill of local entrepreneurs has been a key factor accelerating technological change in this industry in India. Mehra emphasizes innovation as "learning by doing" rather than through formal education. Innovations in the increased quality of products, preservation of planting material, maximization of flowering and manipulation of the growing period, and changes in harvesting time and packaging have all contributed to the increased international competitiveness of India's Floriculture industry.

The chapters in Part III—Trends and Opportunities for Science, Technology, and Innovation Policies—draw insights from specific policies designed to promote systems of innovation. The first four (Chapters 12-15) share a common concern with both the transfer and commercialization of technology. All highlight the difficulties that typically lie in transferring knowledge from one setting to another. This emphasizes the point that local circumstances play a critical role in determining the ultimate viability of specific instances of technology transfer. The lessons offered are amplified by the fact that these four chapters examine the transfer and commercialization of technology from the vantage point of different levels of governance. Giesecke and Cramer et al. focus on national policies, Rogers et al. consider a specific instance of subnational policy, while Windsor takes a look at the framework of supranational policies governing intellectual property rights. The last three chapters in Part III carry these general themes forward in a set of country-specific studies of national science and technology policy in Hungary (Inzelt), Russia (Rogalev), and Japan (Tamada et al.).

In Chapter 12, Susanne Giesecke leads off Part III with a comparative study of innovation in biotechnology in the United States and Germany. "Determinants of Successful S&T Policy in a National System of Innovation" explains why the United States outperforms Germany (and all other countries) in pharmaceutical biotech innovation despite the fact that Germany was among the first to adopt coordinated science and technology policies specifically targeting biotechnology. The central concern of this study is the degree to which national innovation systems can learn from one another. However, Giesecke concludes that institutional characteristics of national innovation systems are so unique that to attempt to transfer and adopt national strategies across regions is highly problematic.

Reid Cramer, John Horrigan, Chuck Wessner, and Robert H. Wilson follow with a study of the U.S. Department of Defense's Small Business Innovation Research Fast Track Program (SBIR) that draws on a nationwide survey conducted by the National Research Council. The SBIR represents an effort by the U.S. federal government to direct funds for research and development and for technology commercialization to small innovative firms throughout the United States. While small businesses in the United States have consistently been shown to be the most prolific source of new technologies, they have historically been at a disadvantage with respect to larger firms in their ability to attract private capital to commercialize these technologies. The SBIR program is an attempt to tap into this tremendous potential by compensating for difficulties in attracting private capital. While the authors find that the short-lived SBIR Fast Track Program was successful in promoting technology commercialization, this focus also led to negative impacts on the competing goals of basic research and innovation.

In "Lessons Learned About Technology Transfer" Everett Rogers, Shiro Takegami, and Jing Yin turn the discussion to what is today the most popular issue in local economic development, namely how to harness technology transfer to replicate the successes of regions like Silicon Valley. The setting for this chapter is the northern portion of the state of New Mexico, a part of the United States that enjoys a long history of hosting important national research laboratories, most of them linked to the defense industry. At the same time, New Mexico suffers serious handicaps. It is remote from metropolitan centers of capital and from large consumer markets, it is the poorest state in the United States in terms of per capita income, and it must contend with the reality that weapons-related defense research is difficult to commercialize. Among the several mechanisms of technology transfer that Rogers et al. examine, they identify spin-offs as the most crucial to local economic development. These are new companies formed around a core technology by former employees of a parent organization. Citing Austin, Texas, as a particularly relevant success story, the authors discuss how in New Mexico the slow, but accelerating, agglomeration of spin-offs is capable of reaching the critical mass required for accelerated technology-based growth.

In Chapter 15, Duane Windsor addresses the supranational dimension of technology transfer in "The Global Regime for Intellectual Property Rights." Embodied in the World Intellectual Property Organization (WIPO) and the World Trade Organization (WTO), this framework was established by, and is largely enforced by, the advanced industrial countries who are themselves the sources of a great percentage of intellectual property. In light of this, Windsor questions the appropriateness of the WIPO-WTO system for furthering the normative goal of maximizing global social welfare over the goal of defending owners' rights to profits per se. There exists, he points out, a clear trade-off between promoting and protecting innovation on the one hand and facilitating economic development in less technologically advanced countries on the other. The distinctly positive spillover effects to innovation favor pricing at or near the low marginal costs of knowledge production, yet setting low prices to maximize these social returns tends to retard innovation by reducing private investment in dynamic knowledge sectors. To balance these concerns, Windsor advocates a "stakeholder management" approach that recognizes that there are circumstances in which there should be exceptions to the strict protection of intellectual property rights. Practical examples of this line of thinking include recent agreements by multinational pharmaceutical firms to provide drugs, at reduced price, to counter the HIV/AIDS epidemic to developing countries.

In chapter 16, "Restructuring and Financing R&D: New Partnerships," Annamária Inzelt discusses the case of Hungary, a country whose Cold War political-economic system continues to define the institutional setting in which innovation takes place. Dr. Inzelt points to the need to foster closer partnerships between universities and industry and between regional industry and foreign industry.

Nikolay Rogalev looks to Russia in chapter 17 with a focus on the Moscow Power Engineering Institute (MPEI), a technical university and one of Moscow's most innovative and successful centers of technological innovation in a country that continues to undergo dramatic political and economic change. At the heart of the study is a survey-based comparison and contrast of experiences of technology commercialization through spin-off ventures at MPEI and at the University of Texas at Austin.

Schumpeter Tamada, Robin E. Sowden, Manabu Eto, and Kenzo Fujisue conclude Part III with a study of Japan's need, after a decade of recession, to shift from static centralized science and technology policy to a more dynamic model of innovation policy. The instrument on which the authors focus is Japan's incremental R&D tax credit program. The authors' survey-based analysis provides detailed suggestions for redesigning the existing system of tax incentives to render it more widely accessible and more in tune with the realities of the knowledge economy.

Part IV includes four chapters that consider corporate strategies for the knowledge-based economy. Chapter 19, "The Cognocratic Organization: Toward a Knowledge Theory of the Firm," by Filipe Santos and Manuel Heitor emphasizes the key importance of knowledge and technological change in contesting a traditional, neoclassical understanding of the firm and the economy. A knowledge-based theory of the firm includes natural systems and institutional theory while embracing global perspectives. The authors suggest that a knowledge-based view of the firm encourages multidisciplinary perspectives to better explore the meaning of competitive advantage in developing, acquiring, and using knowledge for enhanced products and processes and in better understanding the interaction between organizations and the economy in which they are embedded.

"Restructuring to Build Knowledge-Integration Capabilities for Innovation" by Simon Collinson is also concerned with how firms organize and manage knowledge and expertise for innovation. Collinson suggests that understanding specialization in technologies, products, and markets is central to improving knowledge-based approaches to the firm, for it is such specialization that provides corporate advantage. He develops his ideas through a comparative study of R&D and innovation management in eight large Japanese and British manufacturing firms. Through this comparison, Simon explores a range of cross-sector and cross-national differences, and how these differences resist transfer because they are often embedded in broader contexts. The chapter concludes with a review of new forms of organization introduced by British firms with implications for firms that are looking to improve their knowledge management capabilities.

"Knowledge Assets in Global Services Strategy" by Pedro Oliveira, Aleda Roth, Von Conley, and Chris Voss stresses how the emerging knowledge-based, global economy highlights the importance of innovation and business services. The authors discuss how advances in information and computer technologies is revolutionizing how individuals and organizations collect, store, and transmit knowledge at home and abroad. The authors suggest "transnational organizational capabilities" will be an increasingly important determinant of firm performance. Services most based on codified knowledge are likely to become more global than those based most on tacit knowledge. The authors conclude with a call for more research on how to accelerate economic development in less developed economies and to promote more inclusive development.

"Problems of Learning in Organizations Producing Complex Product Systems," by Tim Brady and Gillian Shapiro, the final chapter in this volume, centers its attention on the challenges of knowledge management given the number of firms involved in the design and development of complex products and systems (CoPS) in limited numbers. The authors also focus much of their discussion on the importance of understanding the role of codified and tacit knowledge involving different actors and representing different communities of interest. They conclude with the following thoughts for producing complex product systems: (1) adequate organizational resources need to be dedicated to the development of learning tools and processes, (2) learning mechanisms and systems should be appropriate to the people who are expected to use them and at different stages of the innovation process, (3) an open learning culture needs to be encouraged, and (4) it is important to use different techniques, at different stages of the innovation process, to capture and store knowledge.

1

Knowledge and Innovation for the Global Learning Economy: Building Capacity for Development

Pedro Conceição, David V. Gibson, Manuel V. Heitor, and Chandler Stolp

INTRODUCTION

In this introductory chapter, we discuss possible roles for technology policy and innovation in the global learning economy. *Technology policy* focuses on the development of *systems of innovation* at regional, national, and global levels of analysis, policy that influences the environment in which firms and institutions operate, and, consequently, determines the conditions and opportunities for innovation.

Innovation adopted encompasses *the way in which firms and entrepreneurs create value by exploiting change.* The world is changing at a dramatic and accelerated pace and all of this is driven, in one way or another, by advances in technology. Robert Fogel (1999) illustrates the unprecedented rate of change by contrasting the development of the plow, around 4000 B.C., with the development of flight. While it took 2,000 years to diffuse the invention of the plow across the shores of the Mediterranean Sea, it took only 66 years from the first airplane flight in 1903 to place a man on the moon.

Change can be associated with technological advances, but also with modifications of the regulatory framework of an industry, change in organizational structure and processes, shifts in consumers tastes, changes in the demographics of a region, or major alterations of global geopolitics. In this context, our approach is to discuss important trends in the development of *systems of innovation* and on regional, national, and international policies that are likely to influence the environment in which firms conduct their business, and, consequently, determine the conditions and opportunities for innovation.

This chapter includes four main parts. First we look at the international context and dynamics of innovation. Second, we analyze current trends and challenges for science, technology, and innovation policy, which provide us with the necessary empirical evidence to discuss the need for new indicators and, in general, new metrics for knowledge, which we discuss in the third section. We conclude by discussing avenues for innovation policy towards an *inclusive learning society*.

The following discussion frames the need to promote *inclusive development*, which implies shared prosperity in developed, developing, and emerging regions worldwide. A key challenge concerns the *sharing and diffusion of knowledge* and efforts channeled towards the understanding of the conditions for globally integrated learning processes. *Learning*, in this context, reflects the idea of knowledge creation and diffusion and we contend a central component of the global economy. National or regional learning depends on the existence of social capital, which is largely defined by networks and influencers and by institutions—influencers and institutions that govern the interactions among the nodes of the networks, be the nodes composed of people or of organizations—small and large firms, colleges and universities, and local and federal governments.

THE CONTEXT FOR INNOVATION

In this section we discuss three critical determinants of regional economic development: (1) globalization, (2) technological change and the growing importance of knowledge, and (3) institutional change including the changing role of the state. Worldwide, countries and regions have followed a range of economic development strategies within the context of existing technoeconomic paradigms and innovation systems. We look now at the economic performance of different countries beginning with an interpretation of five major paradigms from the late 18th to the late 20th centuries, in Table 1.1.

With some empirical evidence, these paradigms serve to illustrate the main features of five technoeconomic paradigms. Let us consider, for example, the first, "Early Mechanization," which corresponds to the emergence of the industrial revolution as mechanization was increasingly incorporated in manufacturing, especially in industries such as textiles. Technologies that were well diffused and used within this paradigm presented some important limitations for the increase of the scale and output of productive activity. Most firms remained small and local. Process control was poor and hand-operated machines did not allow for output of reliable quality. Naturally, advances in steam-engine technologies and machinery were already taking place, but it took a long time until they were ready for fruition. When these important technologies matured to the level that made their economic utilization possible, they became the core technologies of the second technoeconomic paradigm.

Table 1.1
Tentative Sketch of Major Technoeconomic Paradigms

Approximate Period	Description	Key Sectors	Economic Organization
1770s to 1840s	Early Mechanization	Textiles, Canals, Turnpike Roads	Individual entrepreneurs and small firms; local capital and individual wealth
1830s to 1890s	Steam Power and Railway	Steam Engines, Railways, World Shipping	Small firm competition, but emergence of large firms with unprecedented size; limited liability corporations and joint stock ownership
1880s to 1940s	Electrical and Heavy Engineering	Electrical Engineering, Chemical Process Industries, Steel Ships, Heavy Armaments	Giant firms, cartels, trusts; mergers and acquisitions; state regulation and enforcement of antitrust; professional management teams
1930s to 1980s	Fordist Mass Production	Automobiles, Aircraft, Consumer Durables, Synthetic Materials	Oligopolistic competition; emergence of multinational corporations; rise of foreign direct investment; vertical integration; technocratic management styles and approaches
1970s to …	Information and Communication	Computers, Software, Telecommunications, Digital Technologies	Networks of large and small firms based increasingly on computer networks; wave of entrepreneurial activity associated with new technologies; strong regional clusters of innovative and entrepreneurial firms

Source: Adapted from Freeman and Soete (1997: Table 3.5).

The new technoeconomic paradigm based on the steam engine and machinery ameliorated some of the previous limitations, and created in itself the germ for new types of economic organization, as the table details.

If we cross the technoeconomic paradigms with geography, then we start joining together the ideas of technological trajectory and national innovation system. The two first technoeconomic paradigms were led by Britain. In this context, the United States and Germany, for example, were "latecomers." Still, they became leaders in the third technoeconomic paradigm, with Japan also leading in the fourth and the United States arguably retaining the lead in the fifth. Therefore, the concept of *latecomer* is strongly influenced by the challenges brought through the emergence of globalization and technical change.

Globalization

Globalization corresponds to the growing integration of the world's economies—enhanced by institutional and technological change. This integration has led to a growth in world trade, more open global financial transactions, higher levels of international investment flows, and growing interdependency of large firms, among other economic factors. Importantly the distribution of wealth remains unequal and the gap is indeed increasing, which has contributed to a backlash against the trend towards globalization and against some of the international institutions that are perceived as symbolizing and championing globalization. Complicating these issues is the reality that increasingly important global challenges—such as the environment, health care, cyber- and other forms of terrorism—are calling for higher international coordination and are beyond the national self-interest of the richest countries.

Productivity, in a way, is probably the best indicator of the extent to which a nation takes full advantage of the conditions provided by the existing technoeconomic paradigm. In this context, a recent study by Ark and McGuckin (1999) tackles international comparisons of productivity and income in a particularly careful way, especially in finding comparable measures across countries. They also link labor productivity with output per capita following a common decomposition procedure. While the relationship between these two variables may seem obvious, in fact there are many subtleties involved. For example, a country that is very productive but where workers engage in productive activities for fewer hours than a less-productive country can result in an output per capita that is higher in the second country. Table 1.2 shows the results presented in this work. Column (1) indicates labor productivity and column (8) provides the level of GDP per capita.

Portugal and Turkey have the lowest hourly labor productivity rate of the OECD. Portuguese hourly productivity is about half of the OECD average. Productivity in Greece is 19 points above Portugal's, and Spain's productivity is 28 points above the Portuguese hourly labor productivity. Still, when one looks at column (8) Greece's GDP per capita is actually lower than Portugal's by two points, and Spain's GDP is only 11 points above Portugal's.

Table 1.2 shows the variety of effects involved. Column (2) shows the impact of the number of hours worked. The summation of columns (1) and (2) produces the GDP per person employed. We see that the Spanish and Japanese work longer hours than in most of the other countries. Per worker productivity in Spain, measured as GDP per worker, raises almost to the OECD level. Portuguese workers also work long hours, adding 2 points to the per-hour productivity measures. In Italy, France, The Netherlands, Norway, and the United Kingdom less hours of work reduce per-employee productivity. Standards of living are determined not only by the number of hours worked and the productivity of each hour of work, but also by the "number of mouths to feed." The effect of labor force participation connects per worker productivity and GDP per person. It is the effect of labor force participation, for example, that brings down the income per capita of the productive and hard-working Spanish workers: the combined effect of unemployment and the low level of labor force in the working-age population take 26 points to the per worker productivity. The same happens in Greece, where 12 points are taken to the per worker GDP. In Portugal, both the effects of hours worked and labor force participation are small and positive.

It is therefore clear that the real challenge to increase the level of GDP per capita in Portugal is not so much a reduction of unemployment or, more generally, an increase in labor force participation (as in Spain, for example), but that it is really the increase in the fundamental hourly labor productivity. To understand these differences it is important to look at the existing dominant technoeconomic paradigm, to which we will now turn.

In conclusion, while globalization is an unavoidable trend, both theory and practice suggest that there is no assurance that economies that engage in open trade are driven to promote innovation. Indeed trade and growth models show that if a country specializes (and may be driven to increase that specialization by comparative advantage incentives) in nondynamic sectors that lag behind the technological frontier, it is likely to remain locked-in to low-growth or stagnant industries. As Grossman and Helpman (1991) indicate, innovation can indeed be promoted only if the forces of comparative advantage push the economy's resources towards activities that enable and enhance growth in R&D and product variety, better quality of products and services, and investments in human capital.

Table 1.2
Decomposition of GDP per Hour Worked into Effects of Working Hours, Labor Force Participation, and GDP Per Per Capita, 1997

	GDP per hour worked as a % of the OECD Average	Effect of working hours	GDP per person employed as a % of the OECD Average	Effect of unemployment	Effect of labor force as a % of the working age population	Effect of working age population as a % of the total population	Total effect of labor force participation	GDP per person as a % of the OECD Average
	(1)	(2)	(3)=(1)+(2)	(4)	(5)	(6)	(7)=(4)+(5)+(6)	(8)=(3)+(7)
Australia	96	0	96	-1	2	0	1	97
Austria	102	-4	98	3	-2	1	2	100
Belgium	128	-5	123	-3	-19	-1	-22	101
Canada	97	2	98	-2	2	2	2	100
Denmark	92	0	92	1	9	1	11	103
Finland	93	0	94	-7	2	0	-5	88
France	123	-9	113	-6	-9	-2	-17	97
Germany	105	-5	100	-3	-4	2	-4	96
Greece	75	-4	71	-2	-11	1	-12	58
Ireland	108	5	113	-4	-12	-3	-18	95
Italy	106	-11	96	-5	-1	2	-5	91
Japan	82	10	92	4	6	4	14	106
The Netherlands	121	-26	95	2	-4	2	0	96
New Zealand	69	8	77	1	3	-1	2	79
Norway	126	-17	109	4	12	-4	12	122
Portugal	56	2	58	0	1	1	2	60
Spain	84	13	97	-14	-13	2	-26	71
Sweden	93	-3	89	-3	6	-4	-1	88
Switzerland	94	0	94	3	12	1	17	111
Turkey	36	2	38	0	-8	-1	-9	29
United Kingdom	100	-9	91	0	3	-2	0	92
United States	120	-1	118	3	9	-2	10	128
EU-14	103	-5	98	-4	-4	0	-8	90

Source: Ark and McGuckin (1999). Summations may not add exactly due to rounding errors.

Knowledge, Technology, and the Digital Chimera

The advent of new digital technologies has captured the minds of businessmen, policy makers and many academics alike. The computer, new telecommunications devices, and, more recently, the Internet are, indeed, powerful and impressive technologies. They are affecting people and firms in fundamental and permanent ways. Within this context, it is not surprising that many countries, regions, and cities around the world are attempting to "catch the wave" of the Internet and of digital technologies. By most accounts, regional economic development based on new information technologies (IT) results from a combination of efforts from both private and public sectors. Recently, public officials and decision makers have been heavily pushing the development of initiatives geared towards the enhancement of the conditions that can lead to IT-driven prosperity. The European Commission, for example, through its Commissioner for Enterprise and the Information Society, said in a recent speech: "Europe is in the middle of an economic revolution. This is the time for a call for action to both the private and the public sectors in Europe. We must work for a strong European e-economy which realizes electronic services for the benefit of all"[1].

While the United States took the lead in the development and diffusion of digital technologies, and especially in finding and promoting ways to derive economic benefits from its usage[2], Europe is catching up; however, with the exception of mobile phones, by almost any measure digital technologies are not as diffused and are not used with the intensity that occurs in the United States. But still, the growth rate in Europe is attracting investors (see Cornet, Milcent and Roussel, 2000). Indeed, the European advantage in mobile telephony is seen as a major one since wireless Internet applications are forecasted to increase in importance.

But the emergence of the "information society" should clearly be understood from a deeper understanding of its role for development. Gordon (1999) concludes:

> There has been no productivity growth acceleration in the 99 percent of the [US] economy located outside the sector which manufactures computer hardware, beyond which can be explained by price remeasurement and by a normal (and modest) procyclical response. Indeed, far from exhibiting a productivity acceleration, the productivity slowdown in manufacturing has gotten worse; when computers are stripped out of the durable manufacturing sector, there has been a further productivity slowdown in durable manufacturing in 1995-00 as compared to 1972-95, and no acceleration at all in non-durable manufacturing.

It will take time for such benefits to reveal themselves statistically in other industries, but a spillover to other industries is likely to arise. Anecdotal evidence suggests that digital technologies are gaining momentum in terms of their economic weight and in the changes they are driving in people's and firm's behavior. According to some, the computer and its associated digital technologies are part of a regime transition, following the pioneering formulation of Freeman and Perez (1986). This hypothesis suggests that *the emergence of a new radical technology requires a number of minor technological improvements, as well as institutional and social adjustments, to make its impact noted in the economy.* In a word, the emergence of a radical technology requires time. Historical analysis proposed, among others, by Paul David (1990) shows that previous important technological breakthroughs took decades until they had a measurable economic effect. David focused on the substitution of electric motors for steam engines while noting an historical equivalence with the computer. David (2000) suggests that the same type of "delaying" mechanisms is at work today with digital technologies and the Internet[3].

In summary, while much attention has been devoted to digital technologies, the association between information technologies and augments in productivity remains ambiguous. Still, it is undeniable that the spread of the computer and the Internet is changing in profound ways how people and firms behave and interact, with important consequences for policy and strategy. A more fundamental change at the start of the new millennium is the increasing importance of knowledge for economic prosperity. This feature of current developed countries corresponds to the continuing trend of accelerating the importance of the creation and diffusion of knowledge throughout the century. Beyond digital technologies, other technological breakthroughs, in many areas from the life sciences to the many fields of engineering, are likely to be seen in the future.

In broad terms, Figure 1.1 provides a first illustration with the horizontal axis representing the intensity of knowledge-based industries in the mid-1990s and the vertical axis the growth rate of these industries in the previous decade. Most countries are clustered at the bottom of the figure, with growth rates between 2% and 4% a year. The horizontal distribution of the countries shows Germany, the United States, Japan, and other leading developed countries to the right, with Spain and Greece to the left. In this context, Portugal and Korea stand out. The intensity of the knowledge-based industries in these countries is relatively low, especially for Portugal, which has the lowest level of knowledge-based industries. However, the growth rates for Portugal and Korea are remarkably higher, with the knowledge-based industries in Portugal growing close to 7% a year, and in Korea at more than 12% a year. The rate of growth of knowledge-based industries in comparable periods was 3.1% for the European Union and 3.5% for the entire OECD. The difference between the growth rates of Portugal and Korea is not as extraordinary as it may seem. In fact, the business sector as a whole rose in Korea at 9.1% a year, while in Portugal the growth rate of the entire business sector was 4.6%. Consequently, the difference between knowledge-industries' growth rate and the entire business sector growth was 2.3% for Portugal (or 50% of the business sector growth rate) while in Korea the difference was 3.4% (a higher difference, but only 37% of the entire business growth rate).

Figure 1.1
Knowledge-Based Industries' Intensity and Growth

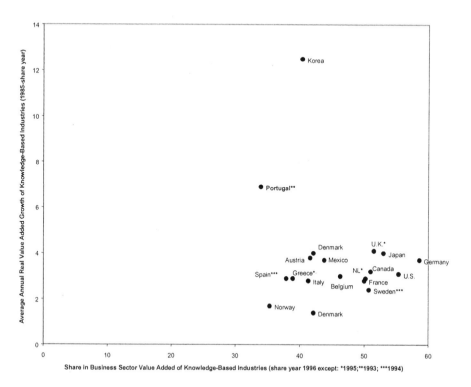

Source: OECD (2000).

If we turn our attention only to those technologies that are more relevant for the information society: information and communication technologies (ICT), again, most countries show growth rates below 4%, with the expenditures on ICT as a percentage of GDP in the United States about 2% above the European average. Individual countries, such as Sweden, outperform the United States, but most countries lag behind.

Going back to the conceptualization of the knowledge-based or learning economy that we presented above, it can be said that, fundamentally, the performance in this knowledge-rich competitive environment depends on the *quality of human resources* (skills, competencies, education level, learning capability) and on the activities and incentives that are oriented towards the *generation and diffusion of knowledge*. We will first look at some indicators associated with the quality of human resources, and then at others associated with knowledge-generation activities.

According to the OECD (1999), Portugal has, after Turkey, the lowest share of the population aged 25-64 with at least an upper secondary education level.

This share is about 20% for Portugal, while the OECD average is three times larger, at 60%. In the United States it is 76%, in Finland it is 67%, and in Ireland it is 50%. In the Czech Republic almost three-fourths of the population aged 25-64 have at least an upper secondary education level. It is important to note that the deficiency is not so much on university or tertiary education. While the share of the Portuguese population with university education is also low (about 7%), it is only about half of the OECD average, and is comparable to that of countries such as Italy and Austria.

Equally problematic is the flow of graduates in science and engineering, measured as the percentage of the labor force. In the mid-1990s the European Union average of the share of graduates in science and engineering was, according to OECD (1999), around 0.12%. Countries such as the United States had shares equal to the EU average, and Ireland had a share more than double the European Union average, at 0.25%. In 1996 the value for Portugal and other south European zones was 0.03%, or one-fourth of the EU average.

Equating the quality of human resources with educational levels is clearly an incomplete characterization. Still, it is reasonable to expect the educational level to be associated with the quality of human resources and with human capital[4]. But beyond human capital, which corresponds to the aggregation of an individual capacity for knowledge accumulation, developing a collective capacity for learning—as suggested by Wright (1999) in the context of the United States—is as if not more important than individual learning. Instead of individual or even aggregated human capital, a further important concept for learning seems to be social capital. The importance of social capital, while still controversial, is increasingly being seen as an important determinant of economic performance and, especially, of innovation and creativity. Temple (2000) discusses the impact of education and social capital together as determinants of growth; noting that evidence is still thin, Temple argues that there is a growing number of works suggesting that social capital is at least as important as education as a driver of economic growth. The relationship of social capital for the economic performance of nations was recognized by Olson (1982) and North (1990), in broad descriptions of the process of development, and was framed explicitly in terms of social capital by Putnam (1993). Bruton (1998: 904) wrote: "There is increasing doubt that growth is as simple as it appears in [simple] arguments, and renewed emphasis is being placed on more basic characteristics of an economy, especially entrepreneurship, institutions, and knowledge accumulation and application."

The next question is, then, to find out what are the determinants of social capital. Glaeser (2000) suggests that education is strongly associated with social capital, which indicates that an important component of policies aimed at increasing social capital necessarily needs to go hand in hand with policies aimed at increasing the educational level.

The analysis in the paragraphs above has been driven by our perception that one other important dimension of the knowledge economy that must be considered in the analysis includes the activities expressly oriented towards the *generation and diffusion of knowledge*. It is, as with education, risky to reduce a complex set of activities to a single educator, but the national *effort on research and development* provides an indication of the commitment, at the country level, to activities explicitly oriented towards the generation of new knowledge. These activities tend to occur in institutions, such as universities and research labs, or within institutional settings, such as the R&D unit within a firm, that provide incentives that foster the specialization on exploration and discovery, as well as exchange of knowledge.

Figure 1.2 shows both the *scale* and *intensity* of national expenditures on R&D for several OECD countries, with the horizontal axis, representing the scale of the expenditure, having a logarithmic scale. The relationship between scale and intensity shows *decreasing returns*: as the scale of the investment grows, the increase in intensity also grows but at a decreasing (in fact, logarithmic) rate. The results also suggest that there are three different "paths" in which this relationship is expressed.

The thick line represents a simple fitting of the position of most countries. Nordic countries have a path of their own, with a much higher responsive intensity to increases in scale, while Southern European countries are shown in the lower left-hand corner of the figure. Ireland is a particularly interesting example, since the scale of R&D expenditure is almost the same as for Portugal, but the intensity for Ireland is comparatively much higher. The large intensity of R&D expenditures in Ireland is largely due to the R&D that is performed in the business sector, which in 1997 accounted for almost three-fourths of the total R&D expenditure in Ireland (the share of R&D expenditure in Portugal was 22.4%). Ireland showed the largest increase in business R&D expenditure of all OECD countries in the 1990s, at an annual growth rate of close to 20%. However, most of this growth is being driven by foreign affiliates doing business in Ireland. The share of foreign affiliates in manufacturing R&D in Ireland in 1995 was close to 70%. This large share indicates a very low capacity of domestic firms to innovate. Ireland is, in this regard, an exception, since for most OECD countries domestic firms take the largest share of R&D performed in the business sector.

R&D expenditure is an important indication of the commitment and resources a country devotes to knowledge production and diffusion, but the growing importance of knowledge extends beyond those activities traditionally associated with creativity and learning. Innovation performance, in particular, depends on conditions that foster *technology-based entrepreneurship*. Mechanisms such as venture capital and high growth start-up stock markets (like the NASDAQ) are ways to mobilize private capital for investment in knowledge economies (Soete, 2000). Gompers and Lerner (1999) show that venture-capital-backed start-ups appear to have a disproportionate positive impact on innovation. The question, which we must also consider, is the *institutional framework* necessary for their development.

Figure 1.2
Intensity and Scale of R&D Expenditure in the OECD (1997)

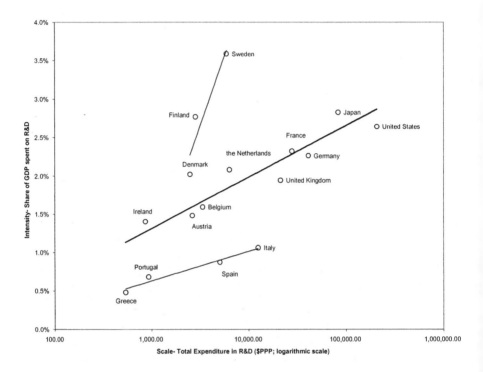

Source: OECD (2000).

Institutional Development: A Regulatory System, the Changing Role of the State, and Social Dynamics

The OECD has called to our attention that from the diffusion of information technology and the growth of the knowledge economy to the globalization of markets and radical managerial innovations, the factors driving and being driven by social change are both wide-ranging and deep. It is a tide of pervasive transformation that is simultaneously washing away and reshaping the social foundations provided by cultural traditions, social symbols, and institutions of authority and security. From the family and school to the firm and parliamentary fora, long-standing social reference points are being called into question, reformed, and reinvented. Exploring the challenges posed by this transition to new, more dynamic social foundations are critical to promote innovation for Portugal, as in most late-industrialized countries.

In this context, Petit and Soete (2000) provide insight into the impact of globalization and technical change on social cohesion and exclusion in the European Union. The most important insight relates to the fields of the *regulatory system* (where it is argued the European policy makers take the lead in setting up appropriate frameworks in emerging science-based industries), *science and technology policy* (where user-learning could be more central), *territorial policy* (where the notion of knowledge capital could be much more central in the Structural Funds), and *labor market policy* (where a twin strategy of targeting small sectors with relatively large spillovers, together with boosting jobs in areas such as personal services is proposed).

Again, we believe that we learn by comparing the regulatory framework among OECD countries, mainly because in the past two decades an increasing number of countries have been reforming their regulatory environments in both the labor and product markets. It should be noted that regulation is essentially aimed at improving the functioning of market economies, by establishing the "rules of game" in areas such as market competition, business conduct, labor market, consumer protection, public safety and health, and the environment. In this context, many national reforms have been driven by comparisons with the policies implemented and the results obtained by other countries. In addition, cross-country comparisons allow identifying and analyzing to what extent regulatory arrangements and their economic implications are country-specific or can apply more generally.

Figure 1.3 shows sample results collected in OECD countries making use of *formal* economic (i.e., constraints and incentive mechanisms concerning market access, the use of inputs, output choices, pricing, and incremental trade and investment) and administrative regulations (i.e., interface between government agencies and economic agents) that affect product markets, but ignore other important regulatory areas, such as environmental, health, and safety regulations. Also, provisions concerning financial markets and land use, which are likely to affect entrepreneurship, are not considered. The analyses do not assess the overall quality of regulations, focusing exclusively on the relative friendliness of regulations to market mechanisms in terms of the impact on the intensity of product market competition. Although it is clear that a market-oriented and administrative regulatory environment is only a necessary condition for enhancing product market competition, the analysis is particularly important to extract lessons for Southern European countries, namely in terms of apparent relations established among *product market regulations* and *employment protection*. In fact, based on a simple average of the summary indicators for regular and temporary contracts through factor analysis, the Mediterranean countries appear with the tightest regulations.

Figure 1.3
Product Market Regulation and Employment Protection Legislation in the OECD

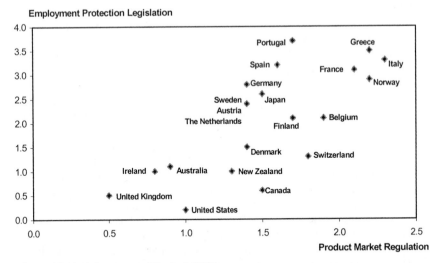

Source: Nicoletti, Scarpetta, and Boylaud (2000)

The evidence from the results above is that restrictive product market regulations are matched by analogous employment protection legislation restrictions to generate a *tight overall regulatory environment* for firms in their product market as well as in the allocation of labor inputs. In addition, the analysis suggests the possible existence of compounded effects on labor market outcomes, making regulatory reform in one market less effective than simultaneous reform in many markets. Making use of selected summary indicators for product market regulations (state control, barriers to entrepreneurship, and barriers to international trade and investment) and employment protection legislation (regular and temporary employment), Figure 1.3 identifies *three clusters of countries*, as follows: a) the United States, United Kingdom, and commonwealth countries characterized by a relatively liberal approach; b) continental European countries with relatively restrictive product market regulations; and c) Mediterranean countries characterized by a tight overall regulatory framework. This raises fundamental issues for European policies, namely in terms of the economic effects as product market regulations and employment protections interact.

The question that thus arises is, how far does the impact of deregulation depend upon the broad socioeconomic context and overall institutional framework? For example, the strong regulatory framework of Norway, together with the expected high levels of social capital of the Nordic countries, at least as measured by the levels of "thrust," clearly result in a context which differs from that found in Mediterranean countries. Certainly "unemployment protection" for the former may represent a risk incentive, so that regulatory frameworks are not directly comparable. Anyway, there are a number of implications for innovation, but in general the analysis calls for a renewed attention for deregulation, which should definitely be accompanied by the development of new competencies and complementary actions at the levels of knowledge creation and diffusion.

It is also clear that the question of regulation must be considered within a more complex and ambiguous tendency that is emerging at the outset of the 21st century—that is, the perception that there is a changing role for the state. This is a controversial area, since it involves ideology and issues associated with personal beliefs on the effectiveness and fairness of social and political systems. In very broad terms, the changing role of the state can be characterized by an increased detachment from holding economic assets and from shying away from determining the direct allocation of economic resources. Yergin and Stanislaw (1998), in a popular book, framed this trend as a "battle" between the state and the marketplace, where the marketplace has been gaining further advantages.

CHALLENGES FOR SCIENCE AND TECHNOLOGY POLICY

Following the analysis above, it is clear that the U.S. ability to generate knowledge emerged with any significance only almost one century after the industrial revolution, which was born in Europe. Thus, as Gavin Wright (1999) points out, for U.S. development "what mattered most was the emergence in the nineteenth century of an indigenous American technological community, pursuing a learning trajectory to adapt European technologies to the American setting." The challenge before us, if we want to achieve a stage of *inclusive development*, is to globally promote similar "learning trajectories". Beyond every single country, where local/regional-based learning networks emerge, it is important to extend these learning networks and trajectories beyond a single country, so that they reach the entire humanity.

Clearly, these issues are too broad to be addressed in a context where we are looking for specific policy suggestions. In the broadest sense, any discussion of these issues must include a treatment of the need for the promotion of democracy, peace, and the rule of law. These are the preconditions that we so strongly emphasized in Conceição et al. (2001) as being essential in the case of the poorest countries. However, we will constrain ourselves to suggestions for questions to be addressed in the context of science and technology policy.

Requirements for Science and Technology Policy

As we emphasized earlier, learning can occur in many shapes and forms, some of which are informal, and other formal. The institutions and organizations that comprise the national and regional systems of science and technology attempt largely to formalize and accelerate the learning process for individuals, firms, and nations. Thus, by looking at this particular set of organizations, their networks, and institutions, we could be able to suggest routes for policy that can positively influence the conditions for inclusive development through learning.

The challenges for policy in order to move towards inclusive development are really twofold. First, *what can be done* at the regional and national levels *to start and sustain learning networks and trajectories* that can lead to development? Second, *how can the overall global learning processes be made more inclusive*, so that fewer countries are excluded, extending the reach of the learning networks globally?

At the national level, it is increasingly clear that innovation is not a direct consequence of R&D. In the academic literature, the lack of validity of the linear model of innovation has been repeated *ad nauseum*, but the fact remains that it still informs much of the policy rationale for investing in R&D. There is no question that the ideas that result from formalized knowledge exploration activities lead, in the long run, to innovations, but to expect this to be so in the short run is misguided both for firms and governments. Kortum and Lerner (1998), for example, show that venture capital is probably much more effective in promoting innovation than R&D at the firm level.

This does not mean that firms and governments should stop doing R&D, but rather that they should do it for the right reasons. And there are many reasons, from promoting human capital, to extending the frontier of knowledge. But in terms of public policy, the realization that innovation and R&D are not as connected as once thought is particularly important. This realization means the firms may lack even more incentives to perform their own R&D as previously thought, and thus require a stronger intervention of the public sector. This may be particularly important for late industrializing countries, with scientific and technological systems not yet fully developed and matured. Often these countries, such as Portugal, show very low levels of private commitments to R&D, with disproportionate high government expenditures in R&D.

With the hindsight gained from the discussion of Conceição et al. (1998), we can also "explain" the increased need of public intervention for science and technology policies, as resulting from the *nonrival character of software*. Market mechanisms do not yield the allocation efficiency to be expected from competitive exchange. Expanding on the ideas proposed by Nelson (1996), Dasgupta and David (1994) suggest three ways to yield the conditions for the effective production of nonrival software. The first is *patronage*, consisting of a mechanism by which the government gives direct subsidies to producers of nonrival software, on the condition that it becomes publicly available at virtually zero cost after it has been produced. The competitive research grants awarded by any national science and technology foundation are an example.

The second, *procurement*, is based on the direct production of goods by the government, awarding specific contracts to private agents whenever necessary. The case of state labs in many countries, illustrates this feature. Finally, the third, *property*, is associated with the privatization of the nonrival software, awarding the producer monopolistic rights that yield returns large enough to cover the total costs of production. Specific legal instruments include patents, copyrights, and trade secrets. Both patronage and procurement rely on a direct intervention of the government, by which the nonrival software remains nonexcluded, and, therefore, effectively a public good. Property grants private producers of new knowledge exclusive property rights in the use of their creations. This yields the private incentives in which markets operate efficiently. In the current political and economic context in which governments are increasingly called to reduce public expenses, the property mechanism may seem a suitable way to foster the development of new software

It is clear from the analysis above that it is crucial not only to make available financial resources (namely public resources), but to do so *in a way* that provides the right incentives for S&T organizations *to hook up in learning networks* that can generate localized social capital and endogenous growth dynamics. That *way* is definitely *not unique* and depends on local conditions, roots and trajectories, which raise the question of *inclusive development*.

At the global level, growing trade liberalization and the increasing reliance of information and communications technologies will certainly contribute to a wider and faster diffusion of knowledge, amplifying the reach of successful learning trajectories. Wolf et al. (1999) show how financial flows from the United States into Europe have helped to foster the launching of biotechnology start-ups in Europe. This is a typical example of the broadening of the scope of a learning network that we have been mentioning. Financial resources and management expertise from the United States, coupled with public support for R&D and education in Europe, help to implement creative firms in Europe. Financial returns will go to the United States, but human capital and knowledge will remain in Europe.

A critically overlooked aspect to enhance knowledge flows around the world is associated with the free movement of people. Although possible in large regional contexts, such as the European Union, the United States and Canada, and MERCOSUL (South America's Common Market), there are still major barriers to the movement of people, crucial bearers of knowledge.

Whether we are interested in enhancing local and regional learning networks, or globalizing the reach of successful learning networks, it is crucial to understand the local reality, according to different angles. The Comprehensive Development Framework, the World Bank strategy to guide its development policies for the 21st century, clearly identifies the forces of globalization and localization[5]: "*globalization*, reflecting the integration of the world, will require the nation-state to reach out to international partners in order to manage changes affecting trade, financial flows, and the global environment; *localization*, reflecting the assertion of regional identities, will push the nation-state to reach down to regions and cities in order to manage changes affecting domestic politics and patterns of growth." The chapters in this book attempt precisely to provide some of these more local perspectives in a context of globalization. Mostly from country-level studies, the various chapters give us a perspective on relevant issues to move towards learning-based inclusive development.

Challenges for Research

This section introduces challenges for future research in *technology policy and innovation*, framed in the context of the emerging importance of learning for development.

Balancing Innovation and Diffusion

Establishing intellectual property rights makes software excludable, yielding to private incentives to production. This strategy is obviously implemented often in commercial computer software programs, books, and music CDs. However, there are two difficulties with this strategy. First, it is sometimes difficult to implement and enforce intellectual property rights, especially at the international level, due to the ease of copying and reproducing software. Second, and most important, establishing property rights on software may have perverse effects, since if the benefits are given only to an inventor-turned-monopolist they will not spread society-wide.

In other words, too much emphasis may be being given to innovation at the expense of diffusion, which can slow the overall rate of technological change, or knowledge diffusion and adoption. To illustrate this, Nelson and Romer (1996) ask, what would have happened if the concept behind a worksheet, first introduced by Lotus, would have been given exclusive rights? The competition between Lotus, Microsoft, and Borland (with their products Lotus 123, Excel, and QuattroPro), which entailed significant improvements in worksheets, might never have happened. Therefore, technology policy should not only focus on promoting innovation by restricting access to information, so that innovative firms accrue monopolistic profits temporarily. Since diffusion is just as important, there is a need to promote measures that allow the rapid distribution of knowledge. Ways to achieve this aim consist of continuing to channel public funds to R&D, giving incentives to the monopolistic firms to share their information sooner, and promoting networks.

Beyond the Excludable/Nonexcludable Dichotomy for Software

The solutions described by Dasgupta and David (1994) for solving the allocation problem with software in a competitive market represent a significant advance in relation to the early ideas of Nelson (1997). They acknowledge the possibility for private incentives to produce software, once this is made excludable through intellectual property rights; whereas Nelson, and most of the Solownian formulation of growth, viewed software (or technology) as a pure public good. New growth theories, as discussed by Conceição et al. (1998), also take the view in some models that private incentives can exist to produce software, once it is made excludable.

However, the second challenge that we will pose will force us to go even further. Establishing intellectual property rights makes software excludable, yielding to private incentives to production. This may be appropriate when the software under analysis is, say, a new formula for Coca-Cola. The new software will benefit only one company. When the software under consideration has a potential society-wide impact, as for example, the cure for cancer would have, then this software production should be induced through patronage or procurement. It is in the public interest that the results be available society-wide.

This is the dichotomy between making software excludable or nonexcludable. However, there is a large gray area, in which the decision to make software excludable may not be that easy. As Kyriakou (1997) has pointed out, some software may not benefit only a firm, nor the entire society. It can benefit an industry, a region, a group of citizens, a number of countries. In this case, the incentives for collective action should be focused on the subjects affected. To subsidize through general taxation such an effort may not be justifiable. Kyriakou proposes a couple of instances by which focused mechanisms for collective action within the group of subjects that would benefit from the software may be generated. However, the field here is wide open for innovative institutional settings that need to go beyond the pure public/private approach for giving incentives for software production.

Policies Based on the Interactive Models of Innovation

The relation between science and technology, in general, and R&D, in particular, and economic growth is widely acknowledged to be very complex, as we have seen in this chapter. One way to structure this complexity is through the traditional linear models of innovation. In these models, successful commercialization of R&D was understood as being the result of a linear process beginning with scientific research, through development, financing, manufacturing, to marketing. Connections between academia, business, and government were downplayed.

From a conceptual point of view, the linear models have long been replaced. Today the relationships between technological innovation and economic wealth generation are understood as part of an integrated and interactive process that blends scientific, technological, socioeconomic and cultural aspects in rapidly moving environments. Myers and Rosenbloom (1996), expanding on the seminal work of Kline and Rosenberg (1986), argue that there are complex links and feedback relations between firms (where the innovation takes place) and the society in general, and the scientific system in particular. Innovation determines and is determined by the market. Organizational capabilities are seen as the foundations of competitive advantage in innovation and include firm-specific knowledge, communities of practice, and technology of platforms.

Firm-specific knowledge represents the accumulated learning of the organization, which is pertinent to the business. This is to be distinguished from the body of generally accessible knowledge. The specific knowledge of a firm is embodied in the firm's workforce and its technology platforms, products, and processes. Communities of practice are ensembles of skilled technical people with expertise on working across the organization. These communities span organizational divisions and provide both a repository for the firm's expertise and a medium for communication and application of new knowledge.

Technology platforms are an output of the design process, which provide a framework on which families of specific products and services can be created over time. A platform comprises an ensemble of technologies configured in a system or subsystem that creates opportunities for a variety of outputs. The fundamental message here is that the complexity and interactive engagement of the different components of the innovation process at the firm level go much beyond the linear models of innovation. However, as David (1993) notes, we still have separate policies for research, education, innovation, industry, trade, and so on. A mix of policies, or a *policy portfolio*, is needed in order to make effective innovation policies, making justice to the complexity of the process. This may require interministry (or interagency) projects, or even coordination at the top executive and legislative levels, as the importance of the production, distribution, and usage of knowledge for growth and development becomes increasingly clear to public opinion.

Promoting Wetware and Software Interaction

A particularly important policy area that needs to be integrated, according to the framework provided above, is education. As discussed by Conceição et al. (1998), *wetware*, also thought of as human capital, results from the natural endowments with which each person is born, but also from the accumulation of experience and from education. Although formally a rival good, we saw that *software* may be useless without adequate levels of *wetware*. And without adequate levels of *wetware*, *software* production may even stagnate. This observation leads us to question the true relevance of treating *wetware* as a purely private good or, as the new growth theorists say, a thing-like type of good. Depending on the importance of *wetware* to render a specific type of software economically useful, *wetware* may be so closely linked with software that it, in itself, may acquire public good characteristics. Whether this is the case or not, the close linkage between software and *wetware*, revealed also in the learning processes as noted by Soete (1996), calls for a special attention for coordinating technology policy with educational policy.

Institutional Development and Renewal

Another important policy aspect that needs careful research and education is related with the extent to which *institutions* do matter to promote and establish socioeconomic development. The process of liberalization, including privatization, restructuring, and the introduction of competition, have become more and more marked internationally in the former state-owned network industries, especially in electricity and gas, but also in telecommunications, transport, water, and waste management. These *critical infrastructures* determine to a great extent the design of our physical environment and our practical way of living, while they provide a favorable climate for the development of a more service-oriented economy. New technologies, and especially information and telecommunication technologies, have helped promoted many changes, but liberalization also has had profound effects on the technologies used. The complex interactions between technology and institutions in shaping the technological trajectories of large technical systems may require the restructuring of industries, and this needs to be accompanied by clearer policies and legislation.

Another clear example of the need for new institutional developments is in the area *environmental protection*, namely in a context of sustainability, which requires integrated approaches over the entire life cycle of products. Policy measures that will encourage the adoption of technologies and practices that are both sustainable and competitive have become an important source of innovation, requiring the correct design of institutions responsible for the interpretation, implementation, and enforcement of policy. Such measures employ systems-based analysis tools and seek to change the behavior of business and consumers, implying complex and timely processes.

The Need for an Inclusive Development

Our last challenge refers to the specific problems posed by specific regional contexts, including late industrialized zones and developing countries. The emerging importance of knowledge has a potential for widening the gap between rich and poor within and between countries. An illustration of the potential for increasing inequality between countries can be found in Pritchett (1995), which shows the shares of return from human capital for different regions of the world. The shares vary from .26 to .62, which, assuming that the contribution for growth of total wages is .6, means that the contribution of human capital to growth is between .16 in Sub-Saharan Africa, and .37 in the OECD.

However, not everything is bleak. As we noted, software is extremely cheap to transfer, and is subject to increasing returns and lock-in. Therefore, even minor and rather inexpensive transfers of software, through, say, an investment from a multinational corporation in a developing country, may have significant, expanding, and long-lasting effects. Romer (1996) has advocated for such a type of approach to economic development. Also, since the value of software is directly related with the scale of its market, expanding markets is also of interest to the holders of software. In some sense, the development of the knowledge-based economy is strongly interlinked, calling for an *inclusive development*. The opportunities are huge, due to the cheapness of software and the advantages of expanding the markets, but there are also difficulties. Wetware is costly to transfer, and takes time. Nonetheless, as the World Bank suggests (1997), the opportunities clearly out-balance the difficulties, and it is time to bring the developing countries to the community of the knowledge-based economies, in an inclusive manner.

METRICS FOR KNOWLEDGE

Beyond the specific topics for research and education, the challenge to ultimately consider in the development of an *Agenda for Innovation and Technology Policy* is on the acquisition and use of data. In fact, the availability of specific data showing the growing importance of knowledge is still scarce, as analyzed throughout this book. The empirical advances have not accompanied the important theoretical advances in a better understanding of knowledge-based growth, much less the reality of the on-going processes of learning-based development. This is also due to the characteristics of knowledge, which are extremely difficult to measure quantitatively. Howitt (1996) provides an excellent overview of the difficulties with the measurement of knowledge in the context of growth models.

Knowledge is certainly not the only area where economics has measurement problems. Thus Fogel (1999) claims that economics needs to catch up with the economy, in the sense that much is happening that is unaccounted for and not understood at all. Specifically, in terms of measurement, Fogel (1999: 1) points out that "the root of the problem is the difficulty in measuring output in the service sector which now represents two-thirds of the economy"; moreover, the continuous proliferation of new services, and the processes of commodization, industrialization, and reorganization of services on a global scale suggest that services are at the core of current structural changes in modern economies.

Technology and innovation activities represent major forces behind such structural processes, with information and communication technologies playing a pivotal role in revolutionizing the ways most "traditional" services are produced, traded, and delivered, as well as offering opportunities for the generation of new ones in a variety of service industries. This already suggests that the old view according to which service industries are technologically backward could be misleading. An increasing amount of empirical evidence is showing that this is the case.

Until recently, the bulk of investment in scientific research and experimental development of the business sector has been carried out by manufacturing firms, but the picture is changing. Recent estimates show that service industries now perform in most industrialized countries almost a fourth of total business R&D (25% in 1991 compared to a share of 4% in 1981). Also with respect to the adoption and diffusion of new technologies, the service sector does not seem to be backward relative to manufacturing. Service industries are heavy users of information technologies, and the bulk of information technology investment is actually used by services—around 80% in the United Kingdom and United States.

One problem with defining the stock of knowledge is that access to knowledge is limited and therefore steps should be taken in order to increase its diffusion across people, institutions, and countries. Another problem consists of separating economically useful from irrelevant knowledge, even though this distinction is extremely difficult to be done in practice: some piece of information may sit on the shelves for a long time until it becomes crucial for solving a problem, while some knowledge at the basis of a technological paradigm may suddenly become obsolete.

Economists used to solve the problem of measuring knowledge by looking at indicators that reflected the rate of return on intellectual assets and used them to calculate the present value of intellectual capital, that is, human capital. Such calculations imply a number of simplifying assumptions, including the definition of the depreciation rate. A more general methodological approach is the focus on processes and flows rather than on states and stocks. This is basically the choice made in the calculation of science and technology indicators.

Intangible Investment

At present various indicators are used to illustrate the structure and changes of the science and technology system and its impact on the economy and society: R&D, patents, innovation surveys, the technological balance of payments, trade of high tech products, intangible investment, surveys on production technologies, the analysis of innovations, human resources, bibliometrics, the diffusion of information, and communication technologies (Sirilli, 1997). The analysis of intangible investment and innovation surveys shows that knowledge is deeply socially embedded in institutions and in the socioeconomic environment in which they operate.

The knowledge content of products and production processes is becoming more and more important, and investment is rapidly evolving towards the acquisition of services and the carrying out of activities that pay off over a long period of time. Intangible investment includes a series of items such as R&D, training of personnel, software, marketing, as well as goodwill, mineral exploration, development of organizations, rights to use intellectual property or concessions.

Taking the experience of Finland and the Netherlands, four components— research and development, education and training, software, and marketing— make up about 80% of the total intangible investment, which, in turn, represents between 20 and 50% of tangible investment. In Austria it has been calculated that intangible investment is 43% of all business investment.

Innovation surveys, as discussed below, conducted in some thirty countries tell a similar story: half of the innovation expenditure of manufacturing firms is linked to the generation and acquisition of new knowledge through design, R&D, trial production, acquisition of know-how, training, and marketing, the other half being spent for new machinery and equipment. Looking at the activities that are most often carried out for introducing new products and processes in service firms, the most frequent ones are R&D, development or acquisition of software, investment in machinery, and training of personnel. The data from innovation surveys show also that innovation in firms is a quite diffused phenomenon, with about one-third of firms introducing innovations over a three-year period (Sirilli and Evangelista, 1998).

The metrics for knowledge have to face at least three challenges. First, a comprehensive view encompassing many areas such as science, technology, knowledge, economic growth, employment, the environment, firm and social organization, education, and institutions is more and more required. While no single model can as yet cover such a vast territory, certainly a new cross-disciplinary understanding can create a new way of looking at indicators and innovation systems. Second, we have learned that national and local institutions and institutional cultures do matter and therefore indicators of these "intangible" aspects need to be devised. Third, we need to be able to capture the dimensions of knowledge (tacit and codified) as well as how the diffusion process takes place in competitive environments (markets) and in noncompetitive settings (in education or in the health sector in countries where it is mostly public).

Measuring the Innovation Performance

How to measure the innovative performance of an entire country? Furthermore, *how to measure this performance in a way that is comparable across the diverse realities of many countries?* These demanding challenges have been addressed by a joint effort of OECD and Eurostat, who have promoted the development of innovation surveys at the country level according to a set of criteria that values cross-country comparability of results. Portugal has been an integral part of this effort, for which there are results for several European countries. This European effort is designated by Community Innovation Surveys (CIS), and its framework of inquiry has been adopted in both official and autonomous research surveys in many countries, from Eastern Europe to Latin America.

By giving more importance to cross-country comparability, the CIS loses somewhat of its potential ability to probe into the dynamics of innovation within each country, since it asks only broad and generic questions, which can be accepted to have similar meanings in different economies. However, it provides a reliable way to compare national innovation performance across countries. Figure 1.4 shows the overall innovation performance of countries in Europe measured by the shares of firms that have introduced innovations over a two-year period.

The horizontal axis indicates the innovative performance in manufacturing, and the vertical axis in services. There is a close relationship between innovation in services and manufacturing, since countries are located across a 45-degree diagonal. In general, innovation rates are lower in services than in manufacturing.

The concept of *resources for innovation* is broadly understood in this section as the financial and human inputs that can contribute to further the innovative performance of national firms. Among these, it is natural to look, first, to the resources that firms themselves allocate to innovative activities. The analysis shows that more expenditure on innovation does not guarantee better innovation performance. For example, for manufacturing firms, Ireland and the United Kingdom spend almost the same on average, but Ireland's innovation performance is substantially higher. Sweden and Finland are the highest spenders, but are surpassed by many countries in terms of innovation performance.

Figure 1.4
Cross-Country Comparisons of Innovation Performance in Europe (2001)

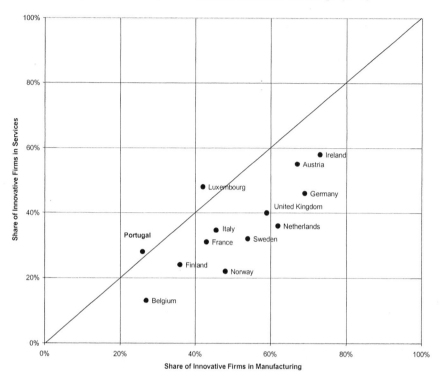

Source: Conceição and Ávila (2001).

While more expenditure is no assurance of a higher innovation rate, it is also true that countries with the lowest share of innovating firms are also among those where firms spend less on innovative activities. Firms' expenditure on innovation activities is important, but equally relevant is the scale of overall national resources that are committed to science and technology. In fact, most *investments in science and technology create spillovers that benefit people and organizations beyond those that initiated the investment*. In fact, the analysis shows that two factors are important when considering R&D expenditure at the national level: the *total amount spent* (which gives a measure of the scale of the investment) and the *resources allocated to R&D* as a share of the overall resources available to the country.

BUILDING INCLUSIVE SYSTEMS OF INNOVATION AND COMPETENCE BUILDING

The analysis presented above considers a context in which the wealth and well-being of individuals, organizations, and nations is increasingly based on the *creation, dissemination, and use of knowledge*. This fact is reflected in the trend in developed economies towards an increasing investment in advanced technology, research and development, education, and culture. As a consequence, concepts such as *learning ability, creativity, and sustainable flexibility* gain greater importance as guiding principles for the conduct of individuals, institutions, nations, and regions. Against this background, and emphasizing concepts such as the *nonrivalry of information* and the *externalities* associated with education and research and development, this chapter builds on the notion of *localized technological change* and the need to develop an agenda to promote inclusive development. This is particularly appropriated to understanding the dynamics of innovation in much of Portuguese industry, which is heavily characterized by so-called traditional sectors.

In these terms, although there is an emerging set of literature on technological innovation and industrial economics looking at the distinctive features and institutional characteristics of European regions (e.g., Wolfe and Gertler, 1999; Gambardella and Malerba, 1999), there have been few attempts to build analytical frameworks to improve understanding and to allow the development of well-sustained technology policies for less-favored zones and late-industrialized European regions. In fact, the *neoclassical approaches in industrial economics* have emphasized the analysis of the microeconomic behavior of firms and built theories specialized in the American and Anglo-Saxon systems and related market dynamics. On the other hand, *evolutionary economics* have attempted to improve our understanding of *learning* processes and the role of institutions in economic development, but have not specialized on the specific historical context of European regions, namely those characterized by late industrialization (e.g., Cooke and Morgan, 1998). Building on the evolutionary approaches and in system theory, the concept of a *national system of innovation* (e.g., Lundvall, 1992; Nelson, 1993; Edquist, 1997) has led to numerous studies of individual European countries, but there is still a long way to go in order to assess the specificity of transition economies and late industrialized regions and countries.

The various aspects above include heterogeneous approaches to technological innovation, but consider *change* at the center of the analysis. This has been considered throughout the entire chapter, but taking into account that firms' competencies are characterized by *stability and inertia* and, therefore, *lock-ins and competence traps* are expected to occur, in that successful firms may be driven by their success in existing technologies to disregard new alternatives. Another important aspect to take into consideration is that the phenomena of *increasing returns* and *path-dependence* affect the nature of the innovation processes and the dynamics of industries in Europe.

Among the various aspects raised above, it should also be noted that the *sectoral specificity* in the organization of innovative activities, on one hand, and the *specific characteristics of local systems of innovation*, on the other hand, are expected to play a significant role in shaping the organization of innovative activity in every nation. The prevalence of one effect over another depends on history and competitiveness of firms and their degree of internationalization.

The Dynamics of Localized Technological Change

Following Antonelli and Calderini (1999), "the internal bottom-up learning process based upon the improvement of design and technological processes plays a major role in feeding the continual introduction of technological and organizational innovations". In this respect, the authors conclude *that technological knowledge is embedded in the specific circumstances in which the firms operate,* and *its generation is the result of a joint process of production, learning and communication,* of which R&D activities are only a part. In these terms, current evolutionary economics have shown the importance of path dependence of economic processes, in that it is at the core of selection mechanisms between competitive firms and technologies (Metcalfe, 1994). Competition is therefore the result of *the rate of change of market share,* apart from being dependent on differences in the rates of growth of individual firms. The result is a fully endogenous process, which, in the presence of increasing returns, gives rise to a strong interdependence between *specialization and diversification.*

The direct implication for innovation policies in transition and developing economies is the important but limited role of demand at the firm level in assessing the amount of incentives for firms to introduce technological innovations. In more general terms, the analysis call for the need to feed all the processes of learning ("formal" and "informal", as defined by Conceição and Heitor, 1999), implement technological cooperation among firms and between firms and research institutions, and on the process of on-the-job training of the workforce. Technological centers specifically designed to sustain localized processes of technological change might play an important role in this context. However, it is important to clearly emphasize the important role of the science and technology system (S&T) in fostering innovation, as well as the related implications for public policy.

Building a Dynamic National Science Base

Following Pavitt (1998), "innovation studies confirm Tocqueville's prediction that continuous technical change in business firms in modern society would require the development in close proximity of publicly funded basic research and associated training". In this context, analysis has shown that the main practical benefits of academic-based research are not "easily transmissible information," but involve the transmission of tacit and noncodifiable knowledge, with a tendency for geographically localized benefits (e.g., Katz, 1994). Furthermore, following Hicks (1995), countries and firms benefit academically and economically from basic research performed elsewhere *only* if they belong to the international professional networks that exchange knowledge. This requires high-quality foreign research training and a strong presence in basic research, mainly because *academic research is certainly not a "free good"*, although it has some attributes of a "public good". In this context, Pavitt, among others (e.g., Narin et al., 1997; Mowery and Rosenberg, 1998), conclude that *"public expenditure on academic research is a necessary investment in a modern country's capacity for technical change"*. The analysis suggests the coevolution of scientific performance with national technology and economy, in that "the rate and direction of the development of a country's science base is strongly influenced by its level of economic development" (Pavitt, 1996).

Casual observations have shown, however, that patterns of scientific strength and weakness are strongly influenced by the nature of the societal and technological problems to be solved. In any case, current understanding of the complexities of the knowledge bases that underlie future technological knowledge base is very limited, what led Pavitt (1998) to conclude that "policies advocating more central management and choice based on foresight should be resisted. ...The aim of policy should be to create a broad and productive science base, closely linked to higher (and particularly post-graduate) education, and looking outward both to applications and to developments in other parts of the world". If any conclusion can be taken with direct application to transition and developing economies, it is that allocation to resources between broad fields of science should remain incremental, and that inadequacies in the rate of technological change should not be claimed to academic research. However, important questions remain to be solved, mainly in terms of the way academic governance influences the performance of basic research activities, and the linkages between basic and applied disciplines. Also, the way that demands for knowledge influence research policies remain to be examined.

It is clear that one important dimension of the knowledge economy includes the activities expressly oriented towards the generation and diffusion of knowledge. It is, as with education, risky to reduce a complex set of activities to a single educator, but the national *effort on research and development* provides an indication of the commitment, at the country level, to activities explicitly oriented towards the generation of new knowledge. These activities tend to occur in institutions, such as universities and research labs, or within institutional settings, such as the R&D unit within a firm, that provide incentives that foster the specialization on exploration and discovery, as well as exchange of knowledge. If the critical role of the national S&T systems is unquestionable today, it is also clear that they do not represent by themselves a true measure of innovation, namely in socioeconomic terms. This has led us to broaden our analysis and to attempt to relate current practices for the evaluation of S&T with innovation measurements and other social measures.

Promoting Innovation in Hetereogeneous Contexts

Recent work within the framework of the OECD International Futures Program suggests two broad policy-related conclusions which apply not only to OECD countries in general but, to a large extent, also to late industrialized countries. The first is that if one is to build on the opportunities offered by the considerable progress that has been made in key technological sectors; if one is to reap to the full the economic benefits of rapidly integrating markets and the emerging knowledge society, and if solutions are to be found to tackle the challenges that the management of such a rapidly changing world raises, then what is needed are *innovative, creative societies*. The second is that in achieving that higher degree of innovativeness and creativity, *policy* will matter. The way ahead does not necessarily mean less government, not less policy but—certainly in some key areas—different policy.

The reservation "in some key areas" is important. Just because we are headed into a rapidly changing world in the coming decades does not mean that we have to throw out all policies and make a completely fresh start. Indeed, some policies that have proved their worth in the past may well continue to do so in the future. However, it is clear that in other policy areas at least incremental adjustments are called for, and in yet others some radical new thinking is required. This provides, in fact, a simple but convenient framework for looking at the role of general policies in the future and their implications for innovation: (1) policy continuity, (2) policy reform, (3) policy breakthroughs.

In this context, we present below four main groups of *strategies* to be considered for innovation, which, *per se*, reinforce the need to develop an *Agenda for Innovation and Technology Policy*:

- *Human capital for Innovation*: Substantial investments in human capital, mainly at the basic and secondary levels, will continue to be a main target to promote and nurture innovation if the skill and qualification requirements of future jobs are to be met. This will require imaginative new ways of organizing education and validating people's knowledge. Regarding the higher education system, our work suggests two important ideas. First, we propose that the *institutional integrity* of the university needs to be preserved. Universities are a special type of learning organization specialized in producing and diffusing knowledge in unique ways. Second, we argue that, important as universities are, they are not enough to guarantee prosperity, and there is a need to promote a *diversity of organizational arrangements*, even at the higher education level. Indeed, this organizational diversity could be a major contributor to ensure the institutional integrity of the university. In addition, it is concluded that the allocation of resources between broad fields of science should remain incremental, in a way that the aim of policy should be to create a broad and productive science base.
- *Institutional Renewal for Innovation*: The evidence from OECD suggests the value of structural and regulatory reforms in supporting the development of innovative and creative societies and economic growth. Among dominant factors, we envisage the role of market liberalization, and market opening, including the privatization of *critical infrastructures*. The process is to be implemented together with a comprehensive program of *organizational renewal*, namely at the state level, and in

a way to promote the establishment of cooperative agreements towards the establishment of *social capital*. Fiscal incentives for *network organizations* and a new regulatory framework for employment protection and market regulation should be attempted.

- *Networking and Corporate Strategies for Innovation*: A framework for devising and implementing strategies in business environments typical of transitional economies is to be considered, taking into account clustering effects. The low level of "thrust" typical of the Portuguese society is a major barrier, which is to be overcome along the enterprise value chain and making use of aggressive *product development strategies*, together with specific factors as time to market, market and technology, product and process innovation, increasing returns markets, managing environmental complexity, managing organizational change, and devising knowledge strategies.

- *Alternative Forms of Financing Innovation*: Different funding forms to be used, including offset and countertrade tools, are conceived in order to promote and develop different approaches to innovation within national companies. Traditional means in financial innovation tend to be "outdated" on the "new" economy context. Beyond offsets in processes for buying military equipment, countertrade should be considered as well for purchase of civil goods and *critical infrastructures*. The research carried out aims to provide guidelines to benefit local economies on the innovative use of tools as offset and countertrade to increment new forms of cooperation between existing firms and new technology-based firms, creating multipolar, interdisciplinary, and market-driven networks.

NOTES

1. Cited in Cordis Focus, March 13, 2000. Cordis is available at www.cordis.lu

2. In reality, two European researchers at CERN, the large European research lab for particle physics, invented the World Wide Web.

3. There have been attempts to formalize these hypotheses, under the emerging field of the study of General Purpose Technologies. The collection of essays in Helpman (1998) provides a snapshot of the literature in this area.

4. Human capital includes, beyond education, features associated with health quality among others.

5. Available on the Internet at http://www.worldbank.org/wdr/2000/overview.html

REFERENCES

Antonelli, C., and Calderini, M. (1999). "The Dynamics of Localized Technological Change", in Gambardella, A., and Malerba, F. (eds.), *The Organization of Economic Innovation in Europe*, pp. 158-176. Cambridge: Cambridge University Press.

Ark, B. van, and McGuckin, R. H. (1999). "International Comparisons of Labor Productivity and Per Capita Income", *Monthly Labor Review*, July, pp. 33-41.

Bruton, H. J. (1998). "A Reconsideration of Import Substitution", *The Journal of Economic Literature*, 36 (June), pp. 903-936.

Conceição, P., and Ávila, P. (2001). *A Inovação em Portugal* (in portuguese). Lisbon: Celta Books.

Conceição, P., Gibson, D. V., Heitor, M. V., and Shariq, S. (1998). "The Emerging Importance of Knowledge for Development: Management and Policy Implications", *Technological Forecasting and Social Change*, 58(3), pp. 181-202.

Conceição, P., Gibson, D. V., Heitor, M. V., and Sirilli, G. (2001). "Knowledge for Inclusive Development: The Challenge of Globally Integrated Learning and Implications for Science and Technology Policy", *Technological Forecasting and Social Change*, 66(1), pp. 1-29.

Conceição, P., and Heitor, M. V. (1999). "On the Role of the University in the Knowledge Economy", *Science and Public Policy*, 26(1), pp. 37-51.

Cooke, P., and Morgan, K. (1998). *The Associational Economy*. New York: Oxford University Press.

Cornet, P., Milcent, P., and Roussel, P.-Y. (2000). "From e-Commerce to Euro-Commerce", *The McKinsey Quarterly*, 2, pp. 31-45.

Dasgupta, P., and David, P. (1994). "Toward a New Economics of Science", *Research Policy*, 23, pp. 487-521.

David, P. (1990). "The Dynamo and the Computer: An Historical Perspective on the Productivity Paradox", *American Economic Review*, 80(2), pp. 355-361.

David, P. (1993). "Knowledge, Property, and the System Dynamics of Technological Change", in Summers, L. H., and Shah, S. (eds.), *Proceedings of the World Bank Annual Conference on Development Economics 1992, Supplement to the World Bank Economic Review*.

David, P. (2000). "Understanding Digital Technology's Evolution and the Path of Measured Productivity Growth: Present and Future in the Mirror of the Past," in Brynolfsson, E., and Kahin, B. (eds.), *Understanding the Digital Economy*. Cambridge, MA: MIT Press.

Edquist, C. (1997). *Systems of Innovation—Technologies, Institutions and Organizations*. London: Pinter Publishers.

Fogel, R. W. (1999). "Catching Up with the Economy," *American Economic Review*, 89(1), pp. 1-21.

Freeman, C., and Perez, C. (1986). "The Diffusion of Technical Innovations and Changes in Techno-economic Paradigm", mimeo.

Gambardella, A., and Malerba, F. (1999). *The Organization of Economic Innovation in Europe*. Cambridge: Cambridge University Press.

Glaeser, E. L. (2000). "The Formation of Social Capital," presented at the International Symposium on the Contribution of Human and Social Capital to Sustained Economic Growth and Well-being, Québec City, Canada, 19-21 March.

Gompers, P. A., and Lerner, J. (1999). *The Venture Capital Cycle*. Cambridge, MA: MIT Press.

Gordon, R. (1999). "Has the 'New Economy' Rendered the Productivity Slowdown Obsolete?", mimeo.

Grossman, G. M., and Helpman, E. (1991). *Innovation and Growth in the Global Economy*. Cambridge, MA: MIT Press.

Helpman, E. (1998) (ed.). *General Purpose Technologies and Economic Growth*. Cambridge, MA: MIT Press.

Hicks, D. (1995). "Published Papers, Tacit Competencies and Corporate Management of the Public/Private Character of Knowledge", *Industrial and Corporate Change*, 4, pp. 401-424.

Howitt, P. (1996). "On Some Problems in Measuring Knowledge-Based Growth", in Howitt, P. (ed.), *The Implications of Knowledge-Based Growth for Micro-Economic Policies*. Calgary, Canada: University of Calgary Press.

Katz, J. (1994). "Geographical Proximity and Scientific Collaboration", *Scientometrics*, 31(1), pp. 31-43.

Kline, S. J., and Rosenberg, N. (1986). "An Overview of Innovation", in Landau, R., and Rosenberg, N. (eds.), *The Positive Sum Strategy: Harnessing Technology for Economic Growth*. Washington, DC: The National Academy Press.

Kortum, S., and Lerner, J. (1998). *Does Venture Capital Spur Innovation?*, NBER Working Paper 6846. Cambridge, MA: National Bureau of Economic Research, Inc.

Kyriakou, D. (1997). "Technology Policy Strategy: Between Research and Development", *The IPTS Report*, no. 12, pp. 12-18.

Lundvall, B. A. (1992). *National System of Innovation—Towards a Theory of Innovation and Interactive Learning*. London: Pinter Publishers.

Metcalfe, J. S. (1994). "Competition, Fisher's Principle and Increasing Returns to Selection", *Journal of Evolutionary Economics*, no. 4, pp. 327-349.

Mowery, D. C., and Rosenberg, N. (1998). *Paths of Innovation—Technological Change in the 20th Century America*. Cambridge: Cambridge University Press.

Myers, M. B., and Rosenbloom, R. S. (1996). "Rethinking the Role of Industrial Research", in Rosenbloom, R.S., and Spencer, W.J. (eds.), *Engines of Innovation*. Boston: Harvard Business School Press, pp. 209-228.

Narin, F., Hamilton, K., and Olivastro, D. (1997). "The Increase Linkage Between Us Technology and Public Science", *Research Policy*, 26, pp. 317-330.

Nelson, R. (1993). *National Innovation Systems*. Oxford: Oxford University Press.

Nelson, R. R. (1996). "What Is 'Commercial' and What Is 'Public' about Technology, and What Should Be?", in Rosenberg, N., Landau, R., and Mowery, D. C. (eds.), *Technology and the Wealth of Nations*. Stanford, CA: Stanford University Press.

Nelson, R. R. (1997). "How New Is Growth Theory?", *Challenge*, 40(5), pp. 29-58.

Nelson, R. R., and Romer, P. (1996). "Science, Economic Growth, and Public Policy", in Smith, B.L.R., and Barfield, C. E. (eds.), *Technology, R&D, and the Economy*. Washington, DC: Brookings Institution.

Nicoletti, G., Scarpetta, S., and Boylaud, O. (2000). "Summary Indicators of Product Market Regulation with an Extension to Employment Protection Legislation", *OECD Economic Dept. Working Paper*, 226, ECO/WKP(99)18.

North, D. C. (1990). *Institutions, Institutional Change and Economic Performance*. Cambridge: Cambridge University Press.

OECD (1999). *Science, Technology and Industry Scoreboard—Benchmarking Knowledge-Based Economies*. Paris: OECD.

OECD (2000). *Information Technology Outlook*. Paris: OECD.

Olson, M. (1982). *The Rise and Decline of Nations—Economic Growth, Stagflation, and Social Rigidities*. New Haven, CT: Yale University Press.

Pavitt, K. (1996). "National Policies for Technical Change: Where Are the Increasing Returns to Economic Research?", *Proceedings of the National Academy of Sciences*, Issue 23, Nov. 12, Washington, DC.

Pavitt, K. (1998). "The Social Shaping of the National Science Base", *Research Policy*, 27(8), pp.793-805.

Petit, P., and Soete, L. (2000). *Technology and the Future of European Employment*. Cheltenham: Edward Elgar Publishing Ltd.

Pritchett, L. (1995). *Where Has All the Education Gone*, World Bank working paper no. 1581. Washington, DC: The World Bank.

Putnam, R. D. (1993). *Making Democracy Work: Civic Traditions in Modern Italy*. Princeton, NJ: Princeton University Press.

Romer, P. (1996). "Why, Indeed, in America? Theory, History, and the Origins of Modern Economic Growth", *American Economic Review*, 86(2), pp. 202-206.

Sirilli, G. (1997). "Science and Technology Indicators: The State of the Art and Prospects for the Future", in Antonelli G., and De Liso, N. (eds.), *Economics of Structural and Technological Change*. London: Routledge.

Sirilli, G., and Evangelista R. (1998). "Technological Innovation in Services and Manufacturing: Results from Italian Surveys", *Research Policy*, no. 27, pp. 881-899.

Soete, L. (1996). "The Challenges of Innovation", *The IPTS Report*, no. 7, pp. 7-13.

Soete, L. (2000). "The Challenges and the Potential of the Knowledge Based Economy in a Globalised World," presented at the International Hearing within the Portuguese Presidency of the European Union, mimeo.

Temple, J. (2000). "Growth Effects of Education and Social Capital in the OECD," presented at the *International Symposium on the Contribution of Human and Social Capital to Sustained Economic Growth and Well-being*, Québec City, Canada, 19-21 March.

Wolf, O., Hemmelskamp, J., and Malsch, I. (1999). "Transatlantic Investments and Human Capital Formation: The Case of Biotech Firms," *The IPTS Report*, no. 33 (April), pp. 34-40.

Wolfe, D., and Gertler, M. (1999). *Innovation and Social Learning*. London: Macmillan/New York: St. Martin's Press.

World Bank (1997). "World Development Report 1998: Knowledge for Development", (Annotated Outline). Mimeo.

Wright, G. (1999). "Can a Nation Learn? American Technology as a Network Phenomenon," in Lamoreaux, N., Raff, D.M.G., and Temin, P. (eds.), *Learning by Doing in Markets, Firms, and Countries*. Chicago: The University of Chicago Press.

Yergin, D., and Stanislaw, J. (1998). *The Commanding Heights—The Battle Between Government and the Marketplace That Is Remaking the Modern World*. New York: Simon and Schuster.

Introductory Note 1

New Dynamics in Economic Restructuring: Cross-National Patterns in Regional Accommodation and the Brazilian Response

Lawrence S. Graham

INTRODUCTION

All around the world, the increasing globalization of economic life has been reshaping relations between the private and public sectors, as well as redefining the characteristics of each. For essentially structural reasons, this dual process has imposed new constraints on economic policy, producing a greater degree of openness, and nullifying many of the policy instruments previously in vogue. Concurrently, there has been a notable growth in the number of regional economies that see their economic destinies as being linked dynamically with markets beyond the borders of the nations in which they are embedded.

Brazil constitutes a case where both developments are having great impact on the capacity of government to set a development agenda that can deal effectively with the realities of the distribution of political and economic resources in a federalized presidential system. Brazil's 1988 constitution has coupled redemocratization with the decentralization of political power in such a way that much of the capacity to act in public policy has shifted from the center to state and local governments. In assessing the prospects in Brazil for the development of a networked economy based on knowledge exchanges and the necessary institutions in a specific regional setting, one must take into account how shifting political alignments affect the prospects for new policy initiatives and how changes in government at the federal, state, and local levels shape these development options in tangible and direct ways.

THE CONTEXTUAL SETTING FOR TECHNOLOGY POLICY AND INNOVATION IN BRAZIL

The first set of pressures, the increasing globalization of development issues, and Brazil's capacity to respond to them can best be seen in Brazil's 2020 Project. While analysis of the policy context facing a particular set of decision makers does not guarantee effective response to such pressures, it can constitute an important first step in policy development. In Brazil's case this initiative can best be categorized as an exercise in strategic planning focused on how networks of public- and private-sector organizations and individuals within them might best create portfolios of public and private investments in accord with the identification of specific axes for national integration and development. In this project the leading public-sector actors have consisted of the presidency of the Republic, the BNDES (the National Bank for Economic and Social Development), and the Ministry of Planning, in cooperation with Brazilian private-sector firms and international partners.[1]

External contractors developed four scenarios as particularly relevant to the debate within Brazil over how best to allocate available public- and private-sector resources for development initiatives during the next 20 years. While these scenarios focused attention in 1998 on the international pressures to which government would have to respond, there is no necessary link with specific policy responses on the part of government since then. This is because what is involved are political choices and decisions responding to political and economic realities. Embraced within these political realities are a divided government in a federal system and the difficulties the Cardoso government has encountered, in moving from its first to second administration, in reconstituting a coalition in congress supporting reform initiatives. In economics they consist of structural adjustments linked to devaluation and the inability of the federal government to impose fiscal austerity on the state governments. Regardless of the current political impasse, these scenarios provide a useful way of analyzing external pressures and identifying long-term policy options.

The international policy scenarios affecting Brazil can best be summed up in terms of four key drivers that influence the choices Brazil has to make in engendering economic growth. Under the first scenario, one must confront a setting in which global corporate capitalism driven by national and transnational corporations is producing a situation in which government must concede far more control over commerce, trade, exchanges rates, and currency flows than has been the case in the past. In this setting, the capacity of national governments, be they First World or Third World, to act is much more likely to be weakened due to a variety of external and internal political and economic forces working against government's use of regulatory policy.

Alternatively, in a second scenario, information technology advancement and the development of knowledge-based industries and networks become the key external factors influencing economic growth. In this setting, alliances involving private-sector firms focused on information technology advancement, regional and local governments, and educational institutions become the crucial ingredients in the construction of knowledge-based networks. But what is required for a response to this scenario to work is major investment in education. For countries like Brazil with a weak educational infrastructure, the setting of educational priorities, extending from the primary level through postgraduate education, over and above other competing demands for limited economic resources, imposes constraints that are extremely difficult to supersede.

In the third scenario, decision makers are more likely to be faced with situations in the years ahead where certain irreversible ecological thresholds affecting larger and larger numbers of people are going to be crossed. In these instances, both natural disasters and disturbing regional and global trends affecting the physical well-being of millions of people are likely to generate conditions beyond the ability of individual national states to act. While it is relatively easy to reach the conclusion that such developments should generate outcomes which require concerted international action, to date it has proven to be very difficult to establish effective international agreements and organizations capable of responding to these situations. Ozone depletion, biological warming, deforestation, desertification, and fresh water depletion all constitute developmental issues which are requiring that attention be given to social and political priorities over economic development. States and nations faced with environmental issues of this magnitude find their policy agendas dominated by questions related to sustainable development and the human condition. For example, the debate over priorities in so many of the sub-Saharan African states has come to be centered around desertification, public health problems stemming from epidemics beyond the control of national governments, and natural disasters in instances involving sustained drought.

The fourth scenario projects a world setting in which regional conflicts centered around opposing ideologies and belief systems, ethnic and religious conflicts emerge and accelerate the development of an international setting that is increasingly multipolar and multicivilizational where modernization and not Westernization is the motivating force. Considerations of this nature are especially salient in such world areas as the Balkans, the Caucasus, and the Indian subcontinent.[2] In the Brazilian setting it was generally concluded in discussing these scenarios that it was the first two scenarios which were the most relevant to the country as a whole, that the third scenario was more regional in nature, being especially relevant to the Amazon region, and that the fourth was not likely to have impact on the Brazilian subcontinent.

THE NEW REGIONALISM IN THE GLOBAL ECONOMY

Against these international scenarios that call attention to different developments or trends in the international context, which have a bearing on economic planning and strategic choices, stand growth in the number of regional economies that see their economic destinies as being linked dynamically with markets beyond the borders of the nations in which they are lodged. This development is particularly relevant to Brazil, where regions historically have enjoyed far more autonomy and freedom of action than is the case elsewhere in Latin America and where under current structural arrangements many individual Brazilian states have the capacity to initiate development policy initiatives which will permit them to decide how best to situate themselves in the global economy. Cross-nationally one can identify a search for new ways of achieving various social objectives and growing interest in exploring the degree to which emergent regionalisms, at the supranational and subnational levels, can enhance the capacity of national societies to deal with the political, socioeconomic, and cultural tensions facing them. Within Brazil, these wider cross-national trends can be seen in the shift of political power away from Brasília, where it was centralized during authoritarian rule (1964-84), to the various states; the revival of gubernatorial politics, at a level of intensity not seen since the First Republic (1891-1930); and the war over fiscal incentives among the states, which are competing with each other openly and directly in their efforts to attract new foreign investments (for example, Ford's recent decision to build a new plant in the state of Bahia rather than Rio Grande do Sul) and to influence transnationals already situated within Brazil to move plant operations from one state to another (as in the case of Philips International, in relocating many of its assembly operations in electronics and small appliances from São Paulo to Minas Gerais).

One way of tapping into these developments and to show how these patterns in Brazil fit into a larger international trend is to sum up the findings of an international collaborative project involving the assembling of seven country teams in Europe and the Western Hemisphere, entitled "The Political Economy of Regional Accommodation: A New Dynamic in Restructuring." The expectation of this conference group was that, through the comparative analysis of theoretically relevant case studies in Europe and the Western Hemisphere, and within this framework inclusion of Brazil, participants would be better able to ascertain what regional development questions need to be asked and what can be said—in light of the most recent social science research on regional development—about appropriate public policy at different levels of government, with particular reference to the management of growth and the accommodation of regional diversity.[3]

In assessing Brazil and the options available to it in terms of generating new economic growth, it is just as important to understand these countervailing pressures which are linked to globalization but which were not included in global scenario building under the Brazil 2020 project: the emergence of a new regionalism beyond the confines of existing national states. This new regionalism is making many small regional states viable in the new world economy, redefining center-periphery relations in older medium-size and larger national states, and contributing to the breakup of other national entities. It is also a phenomenon that is leading in some instances to the emergence of transborder regional economies, while in others it is accelerating the process of differentiation within larger national states whereby one encounters markedly different responses in leading and lagging regions as a function of how these areas insert themselves into the world economy. In yet others it is enhancing the development of micro states.

To sample this diversity, the Regional Accommodation conference group selected countries in Europe and the Western Hemisphere which reflected these developments, on the basis of those cases which were the most relevant theoretically and the most different comparatively. In Europe it selected France (as a leading example of an old unitary state developing new patterns in its economic regions), Spain (as a leading example of a country which had abandoned the unitary state model for one facilitating the development of autonomous regions), Poland (as a leading example where economic convergence had led to a new regionalism on the basic of historic demarcations identified with how Poland was governed prior to its reconstitution as an independent national state in 1918), and the ex-Yugoslavia (as the leading example on how the convergence of nationalism and globalization led to the breakup of a prior national state along the fault line of historic regional identities). In the Western Hemisphere the conference group decided on Canada, Mexico, and Brazil. The first of this group constitutes a leading instance where older developments in federalism are requiring major reconfiguration for an existing national state to survive under the shift to continental markets in North America. The second, Mexico, is a leading example of a cohesive national society in which globalization has created new strains in hitherto unitary state structures by encouraging one leading region (Nuevo León) to respond to economic restructuring by collaborating in the creation of new transborder relationships, while other regions have reaffirmed their ethnic identities in such a way as to create further obstacles to their economic development in an increasingly global economy (viz., the case of Chiapas). While Mexico is a federal republic constitutionally, de facto it remained a unitary state until authoritarian government linked to presidential dominance began to disintegrate in the 1990s and a democratic transition emerged in 1997 in which there has been movement toward state and local autonomy within the context of making federalism function for the first time. The third, Brazil, is the focal point for this chapter.

What is most significant in this context is that Brazil is a country of continental dimensions where historic regional identities in individual states in a federal republic have found in decentralization and a revamped federal system new opportunities for leading and lagging regions alike to accelerate their economic development, while reaffirming their identities as historic regions. The findings of this project thus are particularly relevant to Brazil. Two different explanatory theories accounted for the variations found in these studies of regional development: local entrepreneurship and leadership versus location theory. Each of these speaks directly to the development options pursued in Paraná and Ceará and explains in large part why these two states, the former from Brazil's developed South and the latter from its historically underdeveloped Northeast, have encountered in Brazil's new policy context opportunities for accelerating their own regional development independently of the cycle at the national level of successful reform-mongering during the first Cardoso administration and stasis and stalemate in the second administration.

Generally speaking, the conference papers on dynamic regions argued that "development-inducing innovation" was above all else a consequence of local entrepreneurship. These papers called attention to how different networks of local entrepreneurs and local political leaders had taken the initiative by marshaling the necessary resources from within the region, through the innovation and creativity of the local leadership, coupled with their ability to secure the necessary capital either locally or externally. There were two types of cases which followed this pattern: either historic leading regions which had restructured their regional economies to respond to new patterns of globalization, or historic lagging regions that found in the new political economy the opportunity to restructure and insert themselves into supranational markets. The case studies which confirmed these patterns were Rhône-Alpes (a leading region) and Languedoc-Roussillon (a lagging region) in France, Slovenia (a leading region in the former Yugoslavia), Catalonia (a leading region) in Spain, Nuevo León (a leading region) in Mexico, and Paraná and Ceará (leading and lagging regions) in Brazil. Those cases where the authors explained the dynamics of leading and lagging regions primarily in terms of location theory (their proximity to or distance from established centers of sustained economic growth) were Wielkopolska (a leading region) and Upper Silesia (a lagging region) in Poland, Andalucía (a lagging region) in Spain, the Federal Republic of Yugoslavia—Serbia and Montenegro (a lagging region) in the former Yugoslavia, and Québec (a leading region) and the Maritime Provinces (a lagging region) in Canada. In the latter cases, the authors of these regional studies explained the success or failure of these regions to respond to globalization in terms of their dependency on external resources and their spatial location. Either growth had occurred as a spin-off from their nearness to major centers of already established economic growth or they found themselves faced with growing problems linked to their increasing marginalization as a function of their isolation from such centers.

Nevertheless, there was no single pattern of relationships which explained either of these outcomes; what this finding points to is the importance of identifying policy options and the ability of regional and local leaders to build new partnership arrangements. Local entrepreneurship and leadership varied widely according to how local leaders marshaled available economic and political resources, and in the Paraná case proximity to São Paulo state and city had a lot to do with its initial growth. Three different patterns emerged in terms of innovative solutions either to restructuring regional economies in historic leading regions that had slipped or achieving economic breakthrough in lagging regions.

First are those cases where local leadership has demonstrated a sustained capacity across time to respond to external shifts in markets and opportunities to acquire new technology (Lyon in France and Monterrey in Mexico). In the face of economic dislocations and especially regional economic collapse, which was the case of Monterrey in the 1980s, what proved to be crucial in economic restructuring was local entrepreneurship coupled with a solid set of educational institutions producing new generations of individuals with the technical capacity to respond to new economic initiatives linked to knowledge-intensive work and the tools and technologies identified with revitalizing local industries, engineering, and the computer sciences.

Second are those areas where the decision of the local political leadership to push either for autonomy or independence as a way to break loose from the constraints imposed by central government authorities (Catalonia, with its regional capital Barcelona, and Slovenia in the former Yugoslavia) served to create new political communities. There the reconstitution of viable regional governments and autonomous regional political communities served as the basis from which successful economic restructuring could then occur by working from the manufacturing basis established in these regions earlier and by obtaining new external financing internationally.

Yet another pattern is to be found in regions where the local leadership focused attention on the building of strategic alliances whereby the local leadership saw in the combined forces of globalization and decentralization in national governments the opportunity to build new partnership arrangements (Curitiba and Fortaleza in Brazil). In the case of Brazil, the specific development options pursued varied greatly in terms of local resources in that Curitiba is the capital of a state that this is the center of new economic growth derived from immigration and natural resources that made possible the construction of a rapidly growing agroindustry, whereas the latter is centered in a historic lagging region that is poorer in natural resources and had to restructure itself around small and medium-sized industries based on textiles, shoes, and apparel, commercialization of cashew nuts, and tourism. Through the effective use of negotiation skills, regional leaders also have been able to secure location of an oil refinery outside Fortaleza and, through this initiative, attract anchor investments in steel and related downstream industries.

In the two cases of leading regions taken from French and Mexican experiences (the Rhône-Alpes region in France and Monterrey in northwestern Mexico), regional centers constituted the growth poles and served as the location of innovation, creativity, and capital accumulation. An even more interesting case confirming the importance of local entrepreneurship as the source of dynamic regional development is Languedoc-Roussillon with its core city of Montpellier, in France—historically a lagging region. Despite a regional identity of long-standing on a par with Catalonia and Slovenia, Niles Hansen (the author of the paper on this case) argues that it was not this historic identity that was the source of its economic take-off, but the appearance of an entrepreneurial elite, displaced from Algeria which was more readily accepted in Montpellier than elsewhere in France, who focused their energies on securing local development.

To this base Hansen adds two additional factors: the location of an IBM factory in Montpellier, with the subsequent impact of expanding the local basis for innovation through identification with high technology-based growth, and Montpellier's proximity to what the author identifies as a larger emerging European economic region linking together Languedoc-Roussillon, Midi-Pyrénées, and Catalonia into a larger region more competitive within the single EU market, as a consequence of transnational economic developments in the European Union.[4]

The Brazilian cases signal yet another pattern in local entrepreneurship and leadership: the building of new strategic alliances linking regional elites with national elites and international actors. While the current emphasis on markets in Brazil is very much a part of how that country is inserting itself in the global economy (in accord with the first scenario identified above), the regional economic strategies pursued constitute a reworking of the economic choices made during the 1970s. In that period, the linking of local entrepreneurs with state and national officials and the securing of new capital and technology from abroad provided a basis for stimulating new economic growth which lasted approximately a decade, but did not necessarily create the conditions for continuing new growth beyond that point.

The difference in the present setting is how new emphasis on political decentralization and the revitalization of Brazilian federalism, combined with the push toward a free market economy, has created new economic opportunities for lagging as well as leading regions in that country and generated conditions which are much more likely to be sustained than was the case in the earlier regional development model, which depended heavily on public-sector initiatives. In this setting the state of Paraná has been able to capitalize on its strategic location as the entrance point in Brazil into wider regional markets in Argentina, Uruguay, and Paraguay under Mercosur and its earlier development of agroindustries to create a platform in Curitiba linked to the development of knowledge-based industries. But this has not kept a state like Ceará in Northeastern Brazil from innovating. Far removed from the dynamic regional economies of the South, its local leadership has made enormous strides by building and maintaining a strategic regional alliance with national and international actors and capitalizing on its comparative advantage in the Northeast. As a consequence, Ceará has found sufficient space in a decentralized Brazil to achieve a significant development breakthrough in what was hitherto an underdeveloped Northeastern state.[5]

THE CASE OF PARANÁ IN COMPARATIVE PERSPECTIVE

What is of particular relevance from the Regional Accommodation project for technology policy and the development of knowledge networks in a global economy are comparison of the case studies of Languedoc-Roussillon and Paraná. In both cases, albeit working with different physical and human resources, there has been a concerted effort on the part of local entrepreneurs and political leaders to change conditions within the core city in each subnational region and the surrounding area. By maximizing their strategic advantages and building appropriate networks and partnerships that could maximize the use of available physical, human, and economic resources, regional and local leaders have made use of existing economic and institutional platforms to respond to the conditions for new economic growth through taking advantage of the second scenario identified above as the option most likely to facilitate their insertion into the global economy over the next several decades.

Since the objective in the Regional Accommodation project was to identify theoretically relevant cases in Europe and the Western Hemisphere which would permit analysis of cross-national trends in what can be called the new regionalism, it is important to see how Paraná and its state capital, Curitiba, fit into the broader, cross-national setting before looking at the specifics surrounding this case as outlined by Wilson, Magalhães, and Cuttino.

Contrasting Curitiba and Paraná with Montpellier and Languedoc-Roussillon calls attention to local entrepreneurship as the key variable in initiating change, rather than pre-existing conditions and location. What is particularly interesting about Languedoc-Roussillon is the fact that this was a historic lagging region in France where earlier development policies emphasizing central government transfers to the region and top-down assistance programs did little to overcome the region's long-standing underdevelopment.

In his paper, Hansen relates how this region and its capital, Montpellier, evolved from economic stagnation to a path of sustained economic development through making use of available high-technology resources.[6] In this instance local authorities and entrepreneurs developed a technopole strategy whereby beginning with the attraction of IBM to Montpellier to open a major manufacturing facility, they were able to build a network of small and medium firms oriented to high technology in other localities in Languedoc-Roussillon. As Hansen points out, this development was facilitated by the transformation of Montpellier into a regional capital, through the transfer to that locale of regional branches of national governmental agencies located elsewhere within the region, in accord with the restructuring of subnational governance to match more closely older historic regions that had had their regional identities suppressed in the earlier emphasis on building a centralized state.

Equally important in securing an autonomous base for development initiatives in Montpellier was the presence of local entrepreneurs, stemming largely from the resettlement there of French Algerians after the independence of Algeria in 1962. Operating outward from Montpellier (where attention has focused on developing more effective working relationships among private-sector high tech firms, the regional government and regional offices of central governmental organizations, and the regional university), development initiatives have expanded throughout the Languedoc-Roussillon region. As this base has been secured, attention has been turned more recently towards linking up this area with the previously mentioned development corridor that has been emerging along the border.

Paralleling these developments is the state of Paraná and its capital of Curitiba. There, despite the fact that location was a key factor in its initial development, in policy choices made more recently by regional elites—both in terms of developing a coherent strategy for socioeconomic development and in the partnership arrangements developed among the local business community, subnational governmental agencies, and educational institutions to enhance productive activities—local entrepreneurship has become the crucial ingredient. Certainly, external resources, financial and otherwise, have been essential, but what stands out is the opening up of a different dynamic with development policies being created from the bottom-up, rather than the top-down. To this base must be added the initiatives by local leadership to secure a cooperative pattern of intergovernmental relations as well as to attract new private-sector funding, domestically and internationally.

To sum matters up, the significant local ingredients in these cases were the successful combination of innovation, creativity, and capital at the regional level and the securing of successful partnership arrangements among the private sector, the public sector, and local educational institutions. Where these developments have been tied to effective and meaningful political and administrative decentralization, an appropriate context has been created for the successful design and implementation of development-oriented policies and programs.

Finally, whereas Montpellier already has an established base in high technology, Curitiba is in the process of developing such a base. The overall conclusions reached from these comparative studies and from a field trip focused on local organizations and institutions during July 1999, is that all the crucial ingredients are present for establishing a successful technopole there, and from this base for moving on to establish an effective learning and innovation pole linked to the development of knowledge-based industries. However, in terms of external linkages, Europeans in the high tech field have been much more sensitive to the importance of the interfacing present there among critical subnational governmental organizations and actors, private-sector firms, and local educational institutions and the advantages accruing to foreign transnationals by situating their personnel in Curitiba and the immediate surrounding regions rather than elsewhere in Brazil. Whereas Dell responded essentially to a more limited set of fiscal incentives provided by the state of Rio Grande do Sul in deciding to locate its plant there, Siemens looked at a broader range of factors.

Beyond the fiscal incentives provided by the various states, the quality of life in Curitiba (which has the reputation of being the best in Brazil); the overall economic, social, and political development of the city and the state; the range provided in its educational institutions; and the city's ability to attract new professional and technical personnel were crucial in its decision to center its Western Hemisphere operations in Curitiba and to integrate its operations with other firms in the high technology park being developed there under new partnership arrangements linking together government, private-sector interests, and technical schools and universities in the city and the surrounding region.

NOTES

1. The U.S. contractors in this project were Booz, Allen, and Hamilton and Bechtel.

2. In developing each of these global trends, the contractors participating in this project singled out a particular publication in each case that was particularly influential in drawing attention to the importance of these diverse developments in the contemporary world. These books are, in the order of the above scenarios, Daniel Yergin and Joseph Stanislaw, *Commanding Heights: The Battle Between Government and the Marketplace That Is Remaking the Modern World* (New York: Simon and Schuster, 1998); Manuel Castells, *The Rise of the Network Society* (Malden, MA: Blackwell Publishers, 1998); Daniel Sitarz (ed.), *Agenda 21: The Earth Summit Strategy To Save our Planet* (Boulder, CO: Earthpress, 1994); and Samuel Huntington, *The Clash of Civilizations and the Remaking of World Order* (New York: Simon and Schuster, 1996).

3. This is an edited version of the statement drafted principally by William P. Glade with the assistance of Lawrence S. Graham for the program of a working conference, "The Political Economy of Regional Accommodation: A New Dynamic in Restructuring in Europe and the Americas" (Austin: University of Texas at Austin, May 27-29, 1998), a collaborative research project involving seven country teams studying regionalism in France, Spain, Poland, the ex-Yugoslavia, Canada, Mexico, and Brazil.

4. Niles Hansen, "Languedoc-Roussillon and Montpellier: How a New Dynamic Economy Emerged from Long-Term Stagnation" (Austin: Center for the Study of Western Hemispheric Trade, Institute of Latin American Studies, May 1998), p. 19.

5. For a fuller development of a comparative study of these two cases for the regional accommodations project, see the paper prepared for the Regional Accommodation project by Robert H. Wilson, Antônio Rocha Magalhães, and John Cuttino, "Redefining Regional Development in Brazil: State Development Policy and International Markets in Paraná and Ceará" (Austin: Center for the Study of Western Hemispheric Trade, Institute of Latin American Studies, May 1998). See also a shorter version of this paper prepared for the 2nd International Conference on Technology Policy and Innovation (Lisbon 1998), "Redefining Regional Development: State Development and International Markets in Two Brazilian States," by Robert H. Wilson.

6. Hansen, pp. 1-2.

Introductory Note 2

Technological Innovation in the European Union

Robin Miège

INNOVATION POLICY

What do we mean by innovation policy[1]? It can be defined as the policy measures needed to promote the generation, diffusion and absorption of new technologies, including so-called soft technologies in the area of management and organisation. It is broader than research and technology policy stricto sensu, although science and technology play an increasingly important part in it. In addition to technology policy, it encompasses activity like legal and regulatory measures in the area of intellectual property, norms and standards, public procurement, competition and financing as well as specific actions to support small and medium sized enterprises, to promote entrepreneurship and so on.

Given the variety of domains covered, it calls for an integrated set of measures and a coordinated approach to be effective. This intrinsic need for coordination and integration is one of the major difficulties it faces. It also means that it should be run from as high a level as possible in governmental hierarchy.

TECHNOLOGICAL INNOVATION: A GROWING CONCERN AT THE EUROPEAN LEVEL

For several years, technological innovation has been a growing concern at the European level, for mainly two reasons:

- the recognition that innovation and technology are main drivers for growth and competitiveness
- the feeling that we may not be as good at it as the Americans and that we have to strive to catch up.

What is somewhat reassuring is the fact that the same preoccupation is present on the U.S. side. According to Michael Porter, in the recent report he drafted for the Competitiveness Council, the United States should be wary of increasing competition from European countries especially Nordic states, and has to take decisive actions to recover its supremacy in technological innovation[2]. However, we Europeans believe that we are the ones lagging behind and that we must take remedial action.

TECHNOLOGICAL INNOVATION IN THE UNITED STATES AND EUROPE COMPARED

There are a number of indicators that support this view. To quote but a few:

- Investment in R&D (one of the critical factors highly and positively correlated with the success of a nation's innovation system, according to the Council of Competitiveness' Innovation Index Report) is lagging behind in Europe. In 1997 the European Union devoted 1.83% of its GDP to research and technological development (RTD), while the United States spent 2.55% and Japan 2.8%. Moreover, during the past five years, the United States has steadily increased its efforts and is continuing, while Europe barely managed to maintain it at the same level.
- Patents statistics also signal that Europe's position is eroding: the share of patents filed by residents dropped from 38% in 1981 to 19% in 1993. That year the corresponding figures were 57% in the United States and 83% in Japan.
- The rapidity of technology diffusion and uptake is one of the main differentiating factors in the competitive performance of countries. This is all the more true in today's knowledge sectors like the information society, where value and economic importance increases with connection rates (cf. the "Metcalfe Law"[3]). Therefore Europe's lag is even more worrying.
- The Internet is one of the main drivers of growth: capitalisation of Internet-based companies overtakes that of the automobile sector. Twenty-four% of U.S. households are connected to the Web vs. only 7% of their European counterparts. This trend will continue for some time. In a recent estimate the U.S. Department of Trade forecasts that by 2006 almost half of the American work force will be directly or indirectly employed in the IT sector.
- An estimate of e-commerce in 2001 gives the following figures for the European Union and the United States:

	EU	US
e-commerce	$64 Billion	$206 Billion
Proportion of GDP	0.9%	2.7%
Connected individuals	53 Million	98 Million
Annual expenditure per cap.	$1,217	$2,101

- As regards the use of PCs, the situation in 1998 was as follows:

	EU	US	Japan
Professional PCs per 100 staff	54	103	18
PCs per 100 inhabitants	16	46	12

- Biotechnology is another field where competition is fierce and stakes very high. There again Europe lags behind the United States and companies as well as public authorities at national and European levels strive to invest and catch up.
- In the United States, entrepreneurship is strongly supported by the regulatory and administrative framework, financial markets, education and culture. According to a recent Gallup poll, seven out of ten high-school students (and 50% of the general public) want to start their own business. In the European Union, in contrast, the interest in entrepreneurship as a career is in general lower, and there is a substantial lack of business creation and of growth of new businesses. In addition there is a cultural bias that concentrates on failure rather than on opportunity.

TOWARDS A EUROPEAN INNOVATION POLICY, A CONSTRUCTION OVER 15 YEARS

The first mention of measures in favour of innovation (distinct from R&D policy) at the European level stems back to the mid-1980s. It took several steps and around 10 years to turn it into an explicit "European innovation policy." In the course of the process and reflecting changes in the overall environment, the objectives have also evolved.

In the beginning the focus was on intermediary organisations, and interlinking them at the European level to support innovative small and medium-sized enterprises (SMEs) efforts in entering the single market. Later the emphasis was put on helping regional and local actors in setting up proper support mechanisms and in exchanging good practice. More recently the accent has been put on the integration of the different aspects of innovation policy, with priority on job creation, new technology-based firms and spin-offs from research and academia.

Innovation and technology policies are influenced by a number of changes that affect their "praxis". Multidisciplinarity, the reduction of the cost of accessing and processing information are impacting upon them. They also have to adapt to the drivers of change in the broader environment in which they operate: increasing market pressures, globalisation and deregulation, changing patterns of demand, new societal needs.

As a consequence, policies try to act on the main elements that enable us to create and retain value out of technology advances: intellectual property rights, ability to finance innovation, technology absorption capacity, entrepreneurship. The main European innovation programs since 1984 are:

- A pilot program in 1984 (already focusing on technology transfer, pan-European networking and venture capital).
- A more structured set of measures 1989-1994: the SPRINT programme (integrated set of measures, including support to local and regional initiatives, demonstration projects, organisational innovation, venture capital, focus on SMEs). But it had a limited budget and was not closely linked to mainstream RTD policies.
- A larger program, included into the 4th Framework Programme for RTD (the INNOVATION programme 1994-1998).
- A broad consultation on a Green Paper on Innovation, published in December 1995.
- A First Community Action Plan for Innovation in November 1996.
- A more focussed consultation on spin off creation from academia and R&D in 1998.
- New features introduced in the 5th Framework Programme 1999-2002.

GENERAL POLICY GUIDELINES FOR THE EUROPEAN COMMISSION (EC)

A lead assumption is that innovation depends more on private actors and the marketplace than on measures or programs decided by the public authorities. Where public policy is concerned, it is recognised as being mostly a national or regional prerogative: competence of the different Member States rather than at the Union level.

One of the now commonly admitted guidelines is that, at the community level, in addition to direct investment in RTD, technological innovation can be best promoted through indirect actions, in two areas:

- creating a favourable economic, legal, regulatory and administrative environment (competition rules, internal market defragmentation, intellectual property rights [IPR])
- spreading good practice and promoting networking.

Measures in favour of innovation involve several Commission departments, each having its own specific policy agenda (e.g., research, industry, enterprise, training policies). The European Union is therefore confronted with the problem of coordinating the different instruments, avoiding duplication of efforts and reaching critical mass, common to all national innovation policies. In addition it is faced with a specific challenge in articulating regional, national and European activities in that field.

As time does not allow for a comprehensive picture of all facets of European innovation policy, I will restrict myself to describing specific measures in four priority areas. These are the protection of intellectual property, risk capital, new orientations of the RTD policy, and the promotion of innovative spin-off companies from research establishments and universities.

SPECIFIC MEASURES IN FOUR PRIORITY AREAS

The Protection of Intellectual Property Rights

This is perhaps the most basic policy affecting a country's innovative potential. IPRs at the same time provide rewards for innovation by private inventors, and encourage the diffusion of knowledge throughout the economy through public disclosure of information describing the innovation. However, the European patent system is complex, expensive and fragmented along national lines.

Three systems coexist: national, Union (never entered into force as not ratified by all countries) and European patents. In practice, the European Patent Office acts as a one-stop-shop for filing a patent in the countries designated. However, thereafter national laws apply (and national courts are competent). A European patent may cost as much as six times the cost of a U.S. one. Translation costs amount on average to €10,000. Total translation costs per year at the European level may reach €400 million.

In addition or as a result, there is both a lack of awareness of the possibility and importance of IPR protection and a failure to take advantage of existing possibilities in the EU. It is estimated that two-thirds of European SMEs which produce innovations do not apply for patents.

The EC made significant progress in 1998 on two outstanding issues:

- the legal protection of biotechnological inventions was finally settled through the adoption of the related Directive.
- The harmonisation of the protection of utility models (proposed Directive).

Following the wide consultation on the Green Paper on "the Community Patent and European patent system", in February 1999, the Commission defined the actions it has the intention to undertake by mid-2000. [4] These include:

- The proposal to introduce before the end of 1999 a regulation concerning the creation of a Union Patent system. This aims at reducing the cost of patenting and unifying the still-fragmented European patent system. However, adoption will require unanimity of the Member States.
- A complementary proposal for a directive concerning the patentability of computer programmes.
- An "interpretative communication" concerning patent agents, particularly in relation to the right of establishment and the free provision of services.
- A concerted effort to promote patent information (on-line access through the European Patent Office esp@cenet server) and to support national patent office endeavours to explore how patent information can be more comprehensible, accessible and practical to SMEs.
- Measures in R&D programmes to sensitize researchers to the importance of protection and to facilitate this process (e.g., setting up an IPR help desk for participants in framework programme, patent filing cost eligible for support, possibility of granting exclusive licenses).

Financing

European venture capital has grown rapidly over the past five years, but remains significantly smaller than in the United States and insufficiently oriented towards young and innovative companies. A few figures illustrate Europe's position as compared to the United States in the area of private equity:

1998	USA	Europe
Private equity raised	€ 80 Billion	€ 20 Billion
Private equity invested	> € 60 Billion	€14.5 Billion
Invested in VC	€ 12 Billion	€ 7 Billion
Early stage	€ 4.5 Billion	€1.6 Billion
High tech (healthcare and IT)	80% of VC	• <28% of private equity • doubled between 97 and 98 from € 2.3 to € 4 Billion

- Investment in the early stage is much smaller in Europe than in the United States, but is increasing and the trend can be expected to accelerate in the years to come as the performance of the European venture capital funds improves.
- The European stock markets dedicated to high growth companies[5], created in 1995 are still dwarfed by the American NASDAQ: they quote 8 times fewer companies (600 in total as opposed to almost 5,000), their total market capitalisation is 33 times lower than NASDAQ's and they remain extremely fragmented.
- There are 31 different national and cross-border clearing and settlement systems.
- Despite recent developments and moves from private operators and stock exchanges alike, Europe still is way behind as regards the development of electronic share trading (today more than 5 million on-line brokerage accounts in the United States and Electronic Communication Networks already account for nearly 30% of trading volume on NASDAQ).
- In Europe, pension funds have a limited development and institutional investors show a relatively low interest for venture capital. American pension funds (which account for more than half of the venture capital investments in the United States) are currently the largest investor in the U.K. venture capital industry. A similar situation exists as regard business angels.

European action in regard to financing includes:

- On April 21, 1998, the Commission presented to the European Ministers of Economy and Finance a communication entitled "Risk Capital, a key for job creation in the European Union", which included an action plan to remove existing legal and cultural barriers, both from the point of view of the supply of risk capital and of the demand for it. Covering also items such as market fragmentation (since the action plan, a number of initiatives have been undertaken by main actors to try to establish links between the respective stock markets) barriers are being removed. For instance the EC tabled on July 17, 1998, two proposals modifying Directive 85/611/EEC, the first concerning cross-border marketing of UCITS-units of collective investment funds, widening the scope of assets in which these funds can invest, and, second, providing a European passport to fund management companies. A political agreement is expected before the end of 1999.

In June 1998, the Cardiff Summit endorsed the Risk-Capital Action Plan and invited the Commission to table a framework for action in order to "improve the single market in financial services" against the backdrop of the incoming introduction of the Euro. In response to this, the Commission, after extensive consultation, adopted a communication in May 1999, later endorsed by the Cologne Summit of June 1999. This communication contains a detailed action plan made up of 43 measures which would constitute the main Commission work programme for the next five years in the financial services area (e.g., by mid-2000 the EC will propose a Directive on the prudential supervision of pension funds, which would relax existing rules in some Member States governing investment in unlisted SMEs, etc.).

- Specific measures are being implemented by the European Investment Bank (EIB), the European Investment Fund and the Commission to boost the supply of risk capital to technologically innovative companies. Thus several hundred million Euros are or will be made available to private venture capital companies (either through investment, coinvestment or guarantee mechanisms). At the Cologne Summit the heads of states and governments have decided to increase the effort: an extra 1 billion Euros will be devoted to investments in venture capital funds by the EIB, from its operating surplus, over the next few years.

The problem is no longer the amount of money available, it is the number of quality projects.

User- and Result-Oriented Research

The consultation on the Green Paper on Innovation confirmed the diagnosis that one of the main deficiencies of the European Union lay in its relative inability to transform excellent research results into economic and commercial successes. European action in this area includes:

- The Community 5th Framework Programme for RTD, which came into operation on January 1, 1999, introduces a number of changes to gear more effectively the European research effort towards innovation. These include focusing the €15 billion (approx. $15 billion) research efforts on societal or economically important issues through, for instance, the so-called key actions. These 23 key actions cater to a multidisciplinary approach and the involvement of all parties concerned in the resolution of an issue (regulator, research and academia, industry, user groups). Nonhomogeneous, often competing, actors work together to identify the strategic skills of the future (i.e., the nature of future products, processes or services and the knowledge needed to develop and produce them) and promote initiatives to acquire or develop these competencies.
- In each of the four main thematic programmes "innovation cells" have been set up to coordinate the innovation and exploitation activities.
- A horizontal programme "Innovation & SME Participation" provides common infrastructures (the network of Innovation Relay Centres and the Cordis information service) and services (innovation trend chart, financing and IPR help desks) and runs

pilot actions, which can serve as a test bed for wider application in the thematic programmes (technology transfer projects, regional innovation strategies).

- Its SME component aims to provide a one-stop shop for SME participation in the different thematic programmmes. The participation of smaller companies, usually considered as more inclined to innovate, strongly increased throughout the previous 4th Framework Programme. The current measures (feasibility studies, two-step procedure) aim to still improve that score.
- As regards administrative rules, the orientation towards exploitation has been reinforced with the introduction of a "technology implementation plan" in research project deliverables. Furthermore, costs related to the protection of intellectual property rights are now eligible for support, the granting of exclusive licenses is now possible and various measures to inform and advise participants on such rights have been put in place (in particular the setting up of an on-line IPR help desk).

The tools are in place to augment the number of innovative projects. But what about people to bring them to successful completion? What about entrepreneurs?

Creation and Development of Hi-Tech Companies

One of the relative weaknesses of the European Union at large (spread unequally among its Member States) is the difficulty it has in nurturing new hi-tech companies and helping them grow into world leaders. There are obviously a number of success stories such as SAP, Gemplus, Genset, but these are not numerous nor sufficiently large.

In the United States, up to 19% of the medium-sized companies belong to what David Birch has named the "gazelles" of the economy (rapidly growing companies) as opposed to only 4% in Europe.[6]

Concern has gradually been growing among Member States, and the more advanced ones have undertaken a number of integrated measures. They cover a vast array of initiatives, including:

- administrative simplification (formalities to set up a company still may take several weeks and cost several hundred Euros according to the country and the legal form chosen);
- setting up of technology incubators close to universities or research centres;
- fostering private seed capital funds or business angels networks;
- encouraging local public-private partnerships and university spin-off schemes.

Examples of recent measures in that field include the U.K. University Challenge, the Exist initiative in Germany, a national contest for university incubators in France and a number of integrated schemes in Scandinavian countries such as SPINNO in Finland, and the like. European action has involved:

- Promotion of entrepreneurship has been highlighted as a key policy measure to restore growth and create jobs (Luxembourg and Cardiff European Council meetings, guidelines for employment policy of the Member States, etc.)
- Various incentive mechanisms in SME, training and innovation policy.
- Diffusion of good practice through European networks of "innovative regions".

In summary, initially, I argued that innovation policy calls for an integrated set of measures, including many nontechnological aspects, and a coordinated approach. Europe is lagging behind in a number of areas but it has realised the importance of the challenge and has, in the last few years, taken vigorous steps at regional, national and Union level, which will help it catch up and hopefully lead in its turn.

Now, I will briefly describe the corresponding measures undertaken by the Joint Research Centre of the European Commission.

TECHNOLOGY TRANSFER AT THE JOINT RESEARCH CENTRE

Introducing the JRC

The Joint Research Centre (JRC) is the corporate research centre of the European Commission. It employs 2,500 multinational staff, on five sites (in as many different countries), in eight Institutes. Its mission is to provide scientific and technical support to the Commission to and in policy making, implementing and monitoring. It functions as a network organisation with more than 1,000 partners throughout the world. Its main competencies are in the area of measurement, testing and validation of methods, where it acts as a reference centre for the EU. Its scientific competence covers nuclear energy, materials, environment, information technology, life sciences and advanced materials.

Some of its recent achievements include validating tests to detect the BSE, producing reference materials for the detection of GMOs, advances in nuclear medicine (main European producer of radio-isotopes, alpha-immunotherapy being submitted to phase 1 clinical testing at Sloan Kettering Hospital, New York), in land mine detection, nuclear safeguards, water and air quality management, dependability of e-commerce and so on.

Budget for the next four years amounts to €1 billion (three-fourths nonnuclear, one-fourth nuclear). In addition an extra €150 to 200 million are to be gained from so-called competitive activities from research contracts, third party work or technology transfer.

A Pro-Active Technology Transfer Programme

Since 1998 the JRC has set up and implements a pro-active Technology Transfer Programme, which includes:

- Strategic partnerships with industry and national labs with the aim of creating a sort of "extended laboratory" with "accredited partners" in the Member States, to be able to respond more rapidly to the requests of policy makers and to be in a position to mobilize the best available expertise on subjects of policy concern. (e.g., BSE, dioxin, global change, emission-related measures, etc.)

- Active participation in research consortia (e.g., collaborative research projects under Framework Program Five) and at the international level (many partnerships with lead U.S. organisations such as NASA, NIST, Los Alamos or Oakridge Labs, etc. and in domains like dependability of e-commerce, seismic research, endocrine disrupters, reference materials, etc.).
- A technology transfer unit with a network of correspondents in the eight institutes and several professional technology brokers under contract.
- A pilot in-service course on entrepreneurship on the main site in Ispra, Italy (start January 1999, 6 months, 20 attendees selected from 35 candidates, mainly staff on short-term contracts, 15 business ideas, 3 start-ups being formed, course to be repeated on other sites, with local partners and possibly including a "virtual" component).
- A privately operated dedicated technology transfer fund, raised entirely on the market (target €20 million, 50% dedicated to JRC technologies, both for start-ups and for technology transfer to existing SMEs, multisite, multitechnology. Call for expression of interest in July, selection in September 1999).
- A virtual technology park/incubation mechanism—the European Technology Transfer Network—providing a test-bed for over 50 technology transfer and SME support organisations in the Member States to use modern communication technologies, in particular the Internet, to trade and transfer technologies and innovations.
- A knowledge management programme and infrastructure is being studied.

These efforts are recent. It is too soon to provide evaluation or indicators of success. However, already the number of patents filed has increased threefold since 1996, but more important, attitudes have changed, and new managerial methods are being introduced and accepted. The challenge is to maintain the effort over the coming years to make the change a durable one.

FINAL REMARKS

Technological innovation has become a key policy priority in the European Union, at national as well as Union levels. European Commission President Romano Prodi, in his first address to the European Parliament, made it clear that it will constitute one of the main thrusts of his programme. Instruments have been developed and progress is being made.

Yet there are a number of pressing challenges for European policy makers.

- The first challenge is to maintain and strengthen European cohesion. This is a difficult task ahead, particularly when one considers the very diverse situation from country to country in the European Union (for instance, in 1996, R&D investment ranged from 0.8% of GDP in Portugal to 3.5% in Sweden) and the challenges of the Union's enlargement (soon to be a Union of 20 or 25 Member States).
- The second challenge is to determine what degree of international opening is the more appropriate for Europe, while one should acknowledge the already important international opening of the European economy and research (The 5th Framework Programme allows participation of more than 30 countries). The drive for

internationalisation of science and technology is stronger than ever, due to a number of factors, among which:

- The pace of mergers and acquisitions and their size are growing. This is particularly marked in high tech sectors (e.g., telecom, biotechnology). International technology alliances involving European companies doubled in the 1980s and witnessed a slower growth in the 1990s. In the latter period, U.S. companies emerged as the clear preferred partner while, during the preceding decade, further to the Single Market objective, intra-European alliances were the trend:

International technology alliances	1980	1989	1995
EU-EU	186	412	178
EU-U.S.	221	439	457

- Information diffusion is increasingly rapid and global.
- Global issues are shaping the research agenda and call for tighter international cooperation: global warming, health or environmental protection, dependability of e-commerce, and such are areas in which although competition is fierce the need for international S&T cooperation is very strong, but in which S&T also runs the risk of becoming an instrument of political arguments. The exact balance between sharing information or competing for the best technical solution to assert one's leading position is neither obvious nor simple to strike.

In this context, what type of attitudes and partnerships should one have?

- The third challenge concerns policy adaptation to an increasingly fluid environment. In a world where complexity and velocity are the dominant features, how can one ensure the speed and appropriateness of policy responses (for example, the average life duration of an American company is today four years against 13 years only a few years ago). What changes does that entail for the training, culture and mobility of the political elite? How can one ascertain that science and technology support to policy making is both timely and efficient?

The first challenge is the only specifically European one. Europe shares the other two with other countries. Europe is willing to play its part, together with its partners, in building a more wealthy, safe and secure world. And although solutions may be country-specific to fit with the economic, social and cultural contexts, a lot can be gained from exchange of information and dissemination of good practice. It is the merit of the conference on which this volume is based to contribute to facilitate and structure this exchange of ideas and information, and I am glad to have contributed to it.

NOTES

1. The Commission's Green Paper on Innovation (1995) defines innovation as "the successful production, assimilation and exploitation of novelty". It continues, stating that "R&D and the use of technologies—in other words the technological factor—are key elements in innovation, but they are not the only ones" and that "strengthening the

capacity for innovation involves various policies: industrial, RTD, education & training, tax, competition, regional, SME support, environment, etc."

2. "In order to foster further growth and sustain our competitiveness, America must maintain a high rate of technological innovation" and "the United States could lose its preeminence in technology unless a new national innovation agenda is developed". Council of Competitiveness, The Innovation Index, 1999

3. Metcalfe's law states that the value of a communications system grows as the square of the number of users of the system. First formulated by Robert Metcalfe in regard to Ethernet, Metcalfe's law explains many of the network effects of communications technologies and networks such as the Internet and World Wide Web. Robert Metcalfe founded 3Com Corporation and designed the Ethernet protocol for computer networks. Metcalfe's Law states that *the usefulness, or utility, of a network equals the square of the number of users.*

4. Communication [COM(99)42 final].

5. They include the Alternative Investment Market in London, the federation of national stock exchanges called Euro-NM (Paris, Brussels, Amsterdam and Frankfort) and EASDAQ, a private initiative at the European level. The Neuer Markt in Frankfurt experienced the highest growth: created in March 1997 it listed its 100th company in mid-May 1999 and its index increased by +170% in 1998.

6. Birch, D. (1995). *Who's Creating Jobs?* Cambridge, MA: Cognetics, Inc.

Introductory Note 3

Current Situation of Venture Finance for University Spin-Off Companies in Japan

Akio Nishizawa

INTRODUCTION

Japan's "third venture boom," which started in 1993, has faced a crisis as a result of a "credit crunch" caused by a chain of bankruptcies of major securities houses, city and local banks, and their affiliated finance companies. And the Japanese economy is still in recession, while so many economic stimulus measures have been introduced, such as huge fiscal spending through conventional ways of public construction. All of these measures for economic recovery have not yet made any good results in Japan, as those in the late 1970s and early 1980s in the United States. In fact, unemployment rates have grown higher and higher every month. The real remedy for the recessed economy in Japan needs to change the structure of its corporations and industries by providing sufficient growth conditions for emerging new technology-based firms (NTBFs). Therefore, "the venture boom" cannot be finished even under the severe credit crunch without successful cases of NTBFs to rescue the Japanese economy from the current recession.

The Japanese government—in particular the Ministry of International Trade and Industry (MITI), in charge of taking the initiative in changing the corporate and industrial structure—has actively responded by introducing "venture supporting policies." MITI is attempting to create new high tech industries by supporting the growth of NTBFs from many start-up ventures based on innovative technologies. All of these policies can be classified into three fields: human resources, technology, and finance.

However, despite the assisting measures that have been strongly initiated and supported by the Japanese government, the traditional financial market for NTBFs has not worked well during this period of severe credit crunch. In addition, even alternative financial markets, which comprise venture capital funds (VCs) and business angels (BAs), and which emerged in the United States and United Kingdom in the early 1980s and 1990s, respectively, instead of conventional ways of corporate financing through banks, do not exist on any significant scale in Japan. These financial situations will hinder such new trials taken by the Japanese government from achieving good results in assisting NTBFs, especially university spin-off companies (USCs) which are strongly expected under the new relations among universities, industry and government.

The objectives of this chapter are threefold: (1) it describes the new three pillars of venture supporting policies; (2) it explains the new scheme of technology transfer from universities to industry; (3) it outlines the problems of scarce risk capital suppliers, such as VCs and BAs through private equity markets in the United States and partly in Europe.

NEW VENTURE SUPPORTING POLICIES

Japan's new venture supporting policies are composed of three pillars in terms of human resources, technology, and finance. To facilitate the recruitment of good talented people as follows:

- Introduction of stock option programs, and adjusting related tax measures
- Mobilization of human resources
  - Deregulation of labor-related laws and regulations
  - Realization of portable corporate pension systems
- Other measures
  - Matching service between retired executives and ventures
  - Seminars and internships to enhance students' entrepreneurship

To facilitate access to innovative technology by:

- Promotion of university-industry cooperation
- Legislation and new laws to promote university-industry technology transfer
- Reorientation of R&D assistance to start-up ventures
- Vitalization of the patent market (incl. reutilization of dormant patents)

To provide sufficient risk money to start-up ventures by:

- Diversification of financial resources and the change from debt to equity
- Legislation of limited partnership for venture capital in November 1998
- Deregulation to allow venture investment by pension through the new limited partnership
- Tax incentive to promote investment by angels

- Improvement of capital markets
- Activation of the japanese over-the-counter market (JASDAQ)
- Expanding public financial assistance such as low-interest loans, loan and investment guarantees by affiliated agencies of the central government and local governments

Among these policies, this chapter will focus on the new law of tech-transfer from the university and the prospect of USCs in Japan.

TECHNOLOGY TRANSFER FROM THE UNIVERSITY

According to the data from MITI, there are many researchers in Japanese universities (240,000 people; over one-third of 670,000 researchers in Japan), and they use a large amount of research funds in universities (over one-fifth of the whole of public and private R&D expenditure), and lucrative technologies have been transferred from universities to private companies. This may bring about new business creation and activation of the Japanese economy.

In Japan, a notice issued by the Ministry of Education, Science, Sports, and Culture (Monbusho), which takes care of national universities, sets forth the system according to which inventions made by professors and researchers of national universities are treated. Major research universities in Japan are national universities.

According to this notice, the national universities should establish Invention Committees and the Committee of each national university decides whether inventions should belong to the central government or inventors, such as professors or researchers. Usually, only inventions that have been funded directly or designedly by the government itself or its affiliated institutions are assigned to the government, but this is quite a rare case in Japan. Under this system at national universities, inventions are usually decided to belong to individual inventors, even during their working time at the university. And these inventions tend to be passed informally to big corporations, with which the professors and researchers happen to have personal contacts—often contacts reinforced by regular corporate scholarship donations.

Under these situations, technology transfers from the universities have been achieved without formal royalty contracts or written commitments to develop the inventions. In fact, these are rarely or never negotiated with any attempt by inventors for royalties or commercializing commitments. Usually transferees make patent filing decisions by themselves. In most cases, big corporations, which can easily access the patentable inventions from the universities informally, become the patent owners, because professors and researchers in universities do not have enough time and money to obtain patents by themselves.

These informal technology transfer processes from the national universities create problems in that there are no assurances whether the technologies should be transferred to the best companies to develop them, and also whether these companies will develop the technologies they receive informally.

As noted earlier, all inventions that are made with government project-specific funds and that have practical applications, are, at least theoretically, under the threat of being classified as "Inventions Belonging to the Nation" or "National Inventions." With certain exceptions, classification as a National Invention means that patenting and licensing is done under the name of the university by central government agencies. This process is highly bureaucratic and the licenses should be nonexclusive. The chance that any National Invention will be commercially developed is very small. Both university inventors and companies want to avoid the National Invention classification. Therefore, all parties concerned have an incentive to bypass formal reporting to university Invention Committees.

In summary, informal transfers of university inventions to industry are very common in Japan, but these inventions are usually undeveloped or underexploited by industry. This seems to be the fundamental problem of the Japanese technology transfer system between universities and industry.

To change this university technology transfer system in Japan, MITI, jointly with Monbusho, tried to introduce a new law, which is to encourage universities to establish Technology Licensing Organizations (TLOs). The Law for Promoting University-Industry Technology Transfer helps the establishment of TLOs in some major research universities in Japan which handle evaluating the inventions, obtaining patents, marketing, and licensing on behalf of university researchers. The law includes three main measures to assist the establishment and operation of TLOs:

1. Approved TLOs can receive public subsidies from the Industrial Structure Improvement Fund (ISIF), an affiliated institution of MITI, up to about $150,000 in the current fiscal year. ISIF also guarantees loans to them. Moreover, ISIF provides useful information about TLOs in order to contribute to smooth technology transfer.
2. The law also directs existing industrial development programs to give preferential treatment such as special investment to small and medium-sized enterprises trying to commercialize the fruits of university research transferred through approved TLOs.
3. Approved TLOs receiving patent rights from the central government do not have to pay annual and handling fees for them. But this provision has not yet worked due to severe regulations for the treatments of national assets.

TLOs must be approved jointly by MITI and Monbusho before getting these assisting measures. The requirements for approval of TLOs are as follows:

1. A TLO should be a legal entity to keep patent rights and realize active technology transfer to industry.
2. A TLO should obtain from researchers a continuous supply of patentable technical seeds with potential for industrialization.
3. When a TLO receives royalties from the licensee, a portion of the income should flow back to the university as a kind of research fund.
4. A TLO, whether open to the public generally or operating under a membership system, should provide equal treatment to the public, or each of its member companies, regardless of their nationality.

5. Membership TLOs are allowed to provide advance information to their members. A TLO should care for SMEs and not leave them at a disadvantageous position with respect to information about technology-transfer.

The law came into effect on August 1, 1998. On December 4, 1998, the following four TLOs were approved by MITI and Monbusho as the first group:

1. Center for Advanced Science and Technology Incubation, Ltd. (CASTI) established by professors from the University of Tokyo.
2. Kansai Technology Licensing Organization Co., Ltd. (Kansai TLO) established by professors in the Kansai district (in the western part of Japan), the University of Kyoto, and Ritsumeikan University, and corporations in the district.
3. Tohoku Techno Arch Co., Ltd. (T^2A) established by professors of national universities in the Tohoku area, especially Tohoku University.
4. Nihon University Business Incubation Center (Nubic) established inside of Nihon University, which is a major private university.

As of the end of October 1999, four TLOs—belonging to Tsukuba University, Tokyo Institute of technology, Keio University, and Waseda University—were added as approved TLOs. According to the survey conducted by Nihon Keizai Shinbun, Inc., *Japan Economic Journal*, one of the major economic newspapers in Japan, in October 1998, 51 universities are planning to establish TLOs. The organizational structure and operating policies might be different depending on policies of each university. Some universities are planning to establish TLOs jointly to cover a particular area.

But this kind of activity is quite new to every university in Japan, and there are few experienced people within the universities; therefore it may be quite difficult for Japanese TLOs to conclude whether they could bring out good results or not. In addition, the law is focusing only on establishment and operation of TLOs, and is also different from the U.S. Bayh-Dole Act, which places both the authority and the incentives for universities themselves to conduct effective technology transfer.

Japanese TLOs will confront the problem of how to give incentives for professors and researchers to assign their patentable inventions to TLOs, and also how to finance them to get and maintain patents both inside and outside of Japan. There is also the difficult procedure of how to match the seeds from universities and the needs of private companies, especially SMEs in each areas. And who can deal with these technology transfer businesses? Japanese TLOs need to adopt more strategic ways to create successful cases as soon as possible for professors and researchers to acknowledge the important roles of technology transfer through TLOs.

Though there are a lot of difficult problems to be solved for TLOs, some universities, especially major national and private universities, should pursue successful technology transfer from the universities to industry by using TLOs' schemes to survive as world-class research universities in Japan. In fact, these universities shifted their focus on postgraduate courses and the number of doctoral students will increase drastically. So these universities should take care of these postdoctoral students as do their U.S. counterparts. One of the promising ways to deal with these situations is encouraging postdoctoral students with innovative ideas of new technologies to start up their own businesses around the universities, as USCs, which can expect to be assisted by TLOs and their related universities.

While USC approaches seem to be an appropriate way to both technology transfer from universities and postdoctoral students, TLOs cannot create and assist USCs. There are other resources needed, such as entrepreneurs, good talented people, risk money, and other professional service providers. Especially in Japan, the financial problems will become severe when TLOs take these policies to assist USCs, due to the rack of risk money in Japan.

THE LACK OF RISK CAPITAL

There are several reasons why equity financing for start-up ventures has not emerged in Japan in conditions of a severe credit crunch. In the case of institutional VCs, there are two reasons. First, it is quite difficult for VCs to expand their investment activities because of the structure of Japanese venture capital industry, which comprises the affiliated companies of financial institutions and securities houses. VCs have sought to avoid accumulating bad debts because this might seriously damage the financial viability of their parent companies.

Second, stock prices on the OTC market have declined from the peak after "the bubble" burst. The OTC is the most important exit route for Japanese VCs to realize their investment gains. However, because of this price decline in the OTC market, most VCs are unable to realize capital gains following the successful floatation of their investees because of the negative spread between the previous high investment prices in the "bubble" days and their initial public offering (IPO) prices, which remain low in the present economic conditions. The number of disbursements by VCs has therefore declined. There are number of independent VCs, but they are too small in terms of the amounts of funds that they have available to invest to play a significant role. Moreover, these VCs are concerned that any businesses in which they invest might be pressured by financial institutions to use the money to repay any outstanding loans rather than to invest in growth-related projects.

Another important source of equity finance for start-up ventures in the United States and United Kingdom is business angels. However, in Japan, there are still too few BAs to have a significant impact on financially supporting start-up ventures. There are no BAs networks in Japan to introduce start-up ventures as potential investees to BAs. Japan does not have the Regulations of Private Placement Exemptions for Accredited Investors (as is the case in the United States). MITI plans to start a new research program to introduce BA networks in Japan and is proposing that the Securities Trading Act (1948) of Japan be revised to incorporate exemption rules for private placement to accredited investors, which is strongly opposed by the Ministry of Finance.

However, even if these new schemes and rules are introduced, there is still a fundamental problem: because of the corporate culture in Japan there are few BAs who are successful entrepreneurs, starting and growing their own businesses and becoming wealthy by selling the shares that they own in their company through an IPO. There is an implicit business rule in Japan that does not allow successful entrepreneurs to retire and sell the shares in their own ventures, even after an IPO. They are expected to continue to manage their ventures throughout their lives, and so it is quite difficult for them to invest in other start-up ventures as BAs because of possible conflicts of interest between their own companies and those in which they invest.

There is a further reason why equity finance for start-up ventures has not expanded in Japan. It is difficult for most Japanese entrepreneurs to raise finance by selling shares to outside investors because of a general unfamiliarity with equity finance. Since World War II, Japanese corporate finance has been provided by banks through secured loans. If management needs money for their business operations, they approach their "main" bank to borrow with collateral (mainly real estate).

If businesses attempt to raise equity finance, they need to prepare business plans to offer to potential investors. It is quite a new practice for entrepreneurs to write business plans, and they may not be able to prepare them well enough to persuade potential investors to invest. Moreover, most SMEs do not have financial statements that are audited by CPAs, and it has not been normal practice to provide a full public disclosure of their business operations.

In short, there is not a well-established infrastructure and culture of equity financing in Japan at the present time.

NEW APPROACHES AND THEIR PROSPECTS

In order to operate TLOs effectively, there will be a need to change these financial hindrances for assisting USCs. First, we need to provide practical education of management, marketing, and equity finance to students in postgraduate courses at engineering schools.

Second, we must cultivate an equity finance culture by assisting existing SMEs to go public, and showing the merits of equity financing and successful management as role models in each area. MITI should restructure many of the venture policies that were introduced from 1993 on, focusing on these cultural changes and look again at BAs' networks around the university and related policies including tax incentives, securities regulations, and the development of OTC markets.

In relation to the small-cap stock market, there is new competition arising in Japan after declaration of NASDAQ Japan and "Mothers" of Tokyo Stock Exchange in late 1999. This new competition among these two markets and JASDAQ with further reforming plans for better trading will be expected to enhance the possibilities of IPOs of SMEs and new ventures. But there are only speculative expectations for IT start-ups to be overestimated, which has pushed the JASDAQ Index up drastically, and the new type of "mini-bubble" it is concerned with these days. While markets' competition makes short-term effects on stock prices, there is no assurance for risk money providers to expand their investments in USCs.

Third, it is important for CPAs and attorneys to help these start-up USCs by way of an option payment system. This kind of payment system is also severely regulated by the Ministry of Finance, which makes it difficult for these small USCs to ask for some professional advice on accounting, disclosure, investment contracts, and related matters.

More time is needed to realize all of these structural and cultural changes to prepare a new infrastructure of equity financing for emerging USCs in Japan. Nevertheless, these conditions should be consolidated for USCs started on innovative research activities in universities to rejuvenate the Japanese economy. According to the experiences in the United States, an assisting network should also be created to exploit "social capital", such as human resources, money, and information in relation with starting NTBFs in each area based on university, industry, and governmental cooperation. Japanese TLOs must eagerly learn how to organize this kind of network for creating innovation clusters centering around the universities.

REFERENCES

Borton, J.W., 1992. *Venture Japan*. Cambridge, England: Woodhead-Faulkner.

Brett, A.M., Gibson, D.V., and Smilor, R.W., 1991. *University Spin-off Companies*. Lanham, MD: Rowman & Littlefield Publishers, Inc.

Harrison, R.T., and Mason, C. M., 1996. *Informal Venture Capital: Evaluating the Impact of Business Introduction Services*. Hemel Hempstead: Prentice Hall

Hashimoto, M., 1998. "Desirable Form of Academia-Industry Cooperation," *Journal of Japanese Trade & Industry*, Japan Economic Foundation, Vol. 17, No. 2.

Japan Securities Dealers Association. Annual Report of Japanese OTC 1998, and its Monthly reports, various issues in 1999.

Kneller, R., 1999. "Intellectual Property Rights and University-Industry Technology Transfer in Japan," *Science and Public Policy*, Vol. 26, No. 2.

SBA Office of Advocacy, 1998. *The New American Evolution: The Role and Impact of Small Firms*. Washington, DC: Small Business Administration.

Sohl, J. E., 1999. "The Early-stage Equity Market in the USA," *Venture Capital: An International Journal of Entrepreneurial Finance*, Vol. 1, No. 2.

Tashiro, Y., 1999. "Business angels in Japan," *Venture Capital: An International Journal of Entrepreneurial Finance*, Vol. 1, No. 3.

Walshok, M. L., 1994. "Rethinking the Role of Research Universities in Economic Development," *Industry & Higher Education*, March.

PART II:
REGIONAL ECONOMIC DEVELOPMENT, LEARNING NETWORKS, AND SYSTEMS OF INNOVATION

2

Learning Regions in Europe: Theory, Policy, and Practice Through the RIS Experience

Mikel Landabaso, Christine Oughton, and Kevin Morgan

INTRODUCTION: INNOVATION AND REGIONAL POLICY

One of the priorities for the new generation of regional development programmes in the European Union for the period 2000-2006 is the promotion of innovation. This is clearly stated in the official Commission Guidelines adopted in June 1999 as the basis for the negotiation of the new generation of regional programmes which should channel to the European regions, less favoured in particular[1], most of the €213 billion of the Structural Funds for this period. These Guidelines[2], entitled "Economic and social cohesion: growth and competitiveness for employment" are based on two broad principles: (1) identification of integrated strategies for development and conversion, and (2) the creation of a decentralised, effective and broad partnership. They state that "Structural assistance should therefore give an increasing priority to promoting RTD and innovation capacities in an integrated manner in all fields of intervention of the Funds" though actions such as: (1) promoting innovation: new forms of financing (e.g., venture capital) to encourage start-ups, spin-outs/spin-offs, specialised business services, technology transfer; (2) encouraging interactions between firms and higher education/research institutes;

(3) encouraging small firms to carry out RTD for the first-time; (4) networking and industrial cooperation; (5) developing human capabilities.

The reason for setting this priority within the 2000-2006 Guidelines might lie in the recent evolution of European regional policy due to a new understanding of regional competitiveness[3] and the corresponding matching role of public policy, to which we now turn.

As stated in the Treaty of the European Union, regional policy is mainly about the reduction of disparities among regions in Europe.[4] Thus, European regional policy aims at the creation of the right economic and institutional conditions in a given region for a sustained and a sustainable economic development process, which creates economic opportunity and jobs that might increase regional income.

Over and above an appropriate level of physical infrastructures and workforce skills, which have been the traditional target of regional policies, these conditions also involve the existence of regional strengths and opportunities to be further exploited such as the capacity of regional firms to innovate, the quality of management, a business culture which promotes entrepreneurship, an institutional framework which encourages interfirm and public-private cooperation, a dynamic tertiary sector providing business services and the transfer of technology, a minimum level of R&D capabilities, the availability of appropriate interfaces between the demand for and supply of innovation inputs, particularly by/for small firms, the existence of adequate financial instruments conducive to innovation, and so on. These conditions are closely related, at the microeconomic level, with "intangibles" and "real business services" concepts as opposed to traditional horizontal aid schemes and "automatic" business subsidies.

At the "mesoeconomic level" they are related to "institutional thickness" and "social capital" concepts. The latter has been defined (Henderson & Morgan, 1999) as a relational infrastructure for collective action which requires trust, voice, reciprocity and a disposition to collaborate for mutually beneficial ends. In short, the idea being not simply to alleviate costs to an individual entrepreneur but to change corporate strategies and business culture as well as improving the "productive environment" or "milieu" in which these firms work. This approach can be exemplified in Bellini's words: "the provision of real services transfers to user firms new knowledge and triggers processes within them, thereby modifying in a structural, nontransitory way their organisation of production and their relation with the market" (Bellini, 1998).

The legitimacy of public policy for the improvement of these conditions is critically dependent on the assumption that the competitiveness of firms relies not only on its own forces but, in no less extent, on the quality of its environment, sometimes referred to as "structural competitiveness" (Chabbal 1994). The assumption here is that businesses, and SMEs in less favoured regions in particular (mainly because they are working in imperfect markets with limited information and "know-how"[5] access) may need assistance in tapping into the necessary resources (related to knowledge, in the form of technology or qualified human capital in particular), to face up to the new forms of competition developing in the global economy. In short they may need more than simply less taxes and lower interest rates to fully exploit their competitive position and thus maximise their contribution to the regional economy in the form of more jobs and higher wealth, which ultimately justifies public financial support for a policy aimed at improving competitiveness.

This assumption might particularly hold true in the case of small and medium-sized firms, whose key economic difficulties are related not just to size but also to isolation. And this is ever more true in the case of SMEs working in less favoured regions which are often small size, family-owned, working in traditional sectors for local markets and ill-prepared for new competitive pressures induced by the globalisation process to which they are increasingly exposed. Moreover, this assumption is particularly important for regional policy, since small and medium-sized firms constitute the basis of the productive fabric of the regions whose development is lagging behind (see Figure 2.1).

Figure 2.1
The Networked Economy

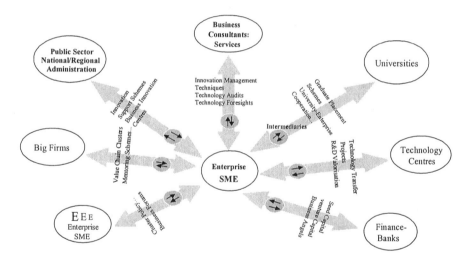

Linked to the above, a generally accepted assumption is that the high road to competitiveness for these regions whose firms are progressively exposed to international competition runs through innovation, which enables them to adapt at the right time to increased competition and the fast pace of technological change. Innovation must apply to all aspects of the activity of a small firm (new markets; new, different or better products, processes and services). In this sense, the concept of innovation embraces research and development, technology, training, marketing and commercial activity, design and quality policy, finance, logistics and the business management required for these various functions to mesh together efficiently.

Since small and medium-sized firms, particularly in less favoured regions, do not usually have either the necessary strategic information or the skills and staff specialising in all the functions listed, some of the latter will have to be carried out by outside contractors. This means that the competitiveness of a small firm depends in part on the quality of the links with and the efficiency/availability of its geographical neighbours (research and technology transfer centres, training centres, business services companies and so on) and it is largely dependent on the quality of the institutional system providing support for innovation (regional authorities responsible for industrial/regional policy in particular). In this sense, innovation is more accessible to small and medium-sized firms when they are working within rich and dynamic regional innovation systems.

Regional innovation systems have been defined (Autio, 1998) as a distinct concept from national innovation systems (Lundvall, 1992), as "essentially social systems, composed of interacting sub-systems; the knowledge application and exploitation subsystem and the knowledge generation and diffusion sub-system. The interactions within and between organisations and sub-systems generate the knowledge flows that drive the evolution of the regional innovation systems". Now, while the core regions of the world economy are well endowed with robust interactive networks, less favoured regions have underdeveloped, fragmented and much less efficient regional innovation systems, as we shall see in the next section.

In short, the creation of the right economic and institutional conditions in a given region for a sustained and sustainable economic development process implies the triggering of learning processes in the regional economy which allows regional firms to become more innovative, anticipative and adaptable to rapidly evolving markets and technoeconomic conditions. This is why European regional policy has set innovation promotion as one of the priorities for action in the period 2000-2006, starting from an exploration of new paths by bolstering intangibles[6], social capital and regional "learning" capacities.

REGIONAL INNOVATION SYSTEMS AND LEARNING REGIONS

Regional Innovation Systems in Less Favoured Regions

Today, in Europe, advanced regions spend more public money and in a more strategic way on the promotion of innovation for their firms than less favoured regions (LFRs).[7] In 1996, for example, while countries such as Denmark, Finland and France spent over €200 of public aid to R&D per person employed in manufacturing, and Austria, Belgium, Germany and the Netherlands were around the €100 rate, Greece and Portugal spent €10 or less, and Spain did not reach €50 (CEC, 1998b). This is increasing the interregional innovation gap across Europe, which has a direct relation to the cohesion gap. If regional policy is to be effective in reducing the cohesion gap, it has to address this problem by increasing the innovation capacities in less favoured regions. This, in turn, is dependent on the establishment of an efficient regional innovation system in these regions, as a precondition for an increase of public and private investment in the field of innovation.

Otherwise, if policies are solely concerned with increasing the amount of public aid for innovation, "absorption" problems will soon appear and the efficiency of these investments will be undermined, as has already happened in a number of regions with previous policy experiments (e.g., European Programme for Science and Technology for Regional Innovation and Development [STRIDE]). The reasons for this lie in what we will call the "regional innovation paradox."

The regional innovation paradox refers to the apparent contradiction between the comparatively greater need to spend on innovation in less favoured regions and their relatively lower capacity to absorb public funds earmarked for the promotion of innovation, compared to more advanced regions. That is, the more innovation is needed in less favoured regions to maintain and increase the competitive position of their firms in a progressively global economy, the more difficult it is to invest effectively and therefore "absorb" public funds for the promotion of innovation in these regions. In other words, one might have expected that once the need is acknowledged/identified (the innovation gap) and the possibility exists, through public means, to respond to it, these regions would have a bigger capability to absorb the resources destined to meet this need, since they start from a very low level ("everything is still to be done"). Instead, these regions face considerable difficulties in absorbing this money. Such is the nature of the regional innovation paradox.

The main cause that explains this apparent paradox is not primarily the availability of public money in the less favoured regions. Its explanation lies elsewhere. It lies in the nature of the regional innovation system and institutional settings to be found in these regions. The regional innovation system in less favoured regions is characterised by its underdevelopment and fragmented nature. The institutional setting in less favoured regions is characterised by the absence of the right institutional framework and policy delivery systems, public-sector inefficiency and lack of understanding by policy makers of the regional innovation process in particular. The two combined explain the regional innovation paradox (see Figure 2.2).

The underdeveloped size of the regional innovation system in less favoured regions and lack of articulation/coherence of its different subsystems and innovation players is illustrated by some of the following characteristics in less favoured regions: money earmarked for innovation is sometimes utilised exclusively for the creation of R&D physical infrastructures and equipment for which no real demand has been expressed by the regional firms. Funding might fall in the hands of those responsible for research/science or technology policies which do not have an economic development perspective; innovation being primarily about economic competitiveness and the exploitation of new, better or different markets, products and services. Moreover, the regional government's departments responsible for research and education, industry and economic planning may seldom meet to discuss and agree an integrated policy for the promotion of innovation. That is, there is often no multidisciplinary approach in the planning of funding, which is critically important for a successful innovation policy.

Figure 2.2
A Fragmented Regional Innovation System: Less Favoured Regions

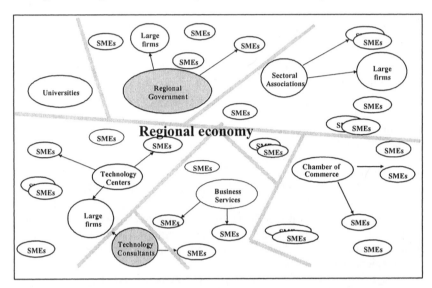

University departments from relatively new universities, for example, which do not have a long tradition of university-industry collaboration, use new funding to strengthen research activities which do not always reflect the needs of the regional firms.

On top of that, regional innovation systems in less favoured regions suffer from isolation from the RTD networks of "excellence" internationally. Thus, SMEs find it hard to access the technology sources and partners, including informal personal contacts, which are necessary for the continuous feeding of the innovation system in order to keep abreast of technological change in the global economy.

The regional firms, often small, family-owned and competing among themselves in relatively closed markets, do not have a tradition of cooperation and trust either among themselves or with the regional RTD infrastructure, particularly universities, as illustrated for example by the Spanish case in which "80% of firms in Spain with fewer than 200 workers undertook no R&D in 1994, whether internally or through outside contractors" (Fundacion COTEC, 1997). Cooperation for innovation is particularly critical in their case due to their limited internal human resources and "know-how" required for the innovation effort. Firms do not express an innovation demand and the regional RTD infrastructures are not embedded in the regional economy, and therefore are unable to identify the innovation needs and capabilities existing in the regional economy. Thus, there is a lack of integration between regional supply and demand for innovation (see Table 2.1).

Table 2.1
Ten Structural Factors Affecting the Regional Innovation Systems in LFRs

1. Shortcomings relating to the capacity of firms in the regions to identify their needs for innovation (and the technical knowledge required to assess them) and lack of structured expression of the latent demand for innovation together with lower quality and quantity of scientific and technological infrastructure.
2. Scarcity or lack of technological intermediaries capable of identifying and "federating" local business demand for innovation (and RTD) and channelling it towards regional/national/international sources of innovation (and RTD) which may give response to these demands.
3. Poorly developed financial systems (traditional banking practices) with few funds available for risk or seed capital (and poorly adapted to the terms and risks of the process of innovation in firms) to finance innovation, defined as "long-term intangible industrial investments with an associated high financial risk" (Muldur, 1992).
4. Lack of a dynamic business services sector offering services to firms to promote the dissemination of technology in areas where firms have, as a rule, only weak internal resources for the independent development of technological innovation (Capellin, 1992).
5. Weak cooperation links between the public and private sectors, and the lack of an entrepreneurial culture prone to interfirm cooperation (absence of economies of scale and business critical masses which may make profitable certain local innovation efforts).
6. Sectoral specialisation in traditional industries with little inclination for innovation and predominance of small family firms with weak links to the international market.
7. Small and relatively closed markets with unsophisticated demand, which do not encourage innovation.
8. Little participation in international research, technological development and innovation (R&TDI) networks, scarcely developed communications networks, difficulties in attracting skilled labour and accessing external know-how.
9. Few large (multinationals) firms undertaking R&D with poor links with the local economy.
10. Low levels of public assistance for innovation and aid schemes poorly adapted to local SMEs innovation needs

Source: see Landabaso (1997).

In short, the regional innovation system in these regions does not have either the necessary interfaces and cooperation mechanisms for the supply-demand matching to happen, or the appropriate conditions for the exploitation of synergies and cooperation among the scarce regional RTD actors which could eventually fill gaps and avoid duplications. In this situation, investing more money in the creation of new technology centres, for example, without previously coordinating and adapting the work of existing ones, risks further distorting the system. At the same time it also risks imposing a new budgetary burden on public budgets through the running costs of these institutions, which are unlikely to reach a satisfactory level of self-financing in a reasonable time period due to the mismatch referred before. The same goes for a number of technology park initiatives in less favoured regions, which end up becoming property development operations dependent on external capital attraction, poorly linked to the regional industry and playing a very limited role in the economically strategic function of technology transfer regionally.

Moreover, advanced business services and networking agents/interfaces such as those existing in developed regions are few and not necessarily specialised in the innovation domain. This hinders the innovation opportunities of firms through proper technology auditing and accessing strategically important services such as innovation management, technology forecasting, training, and so on. These initiatives, particularly private ones, get trapped in the vicious circle of little demand and poor supply which is rarely spontaneously broken from within the system. When they do respond, due to firms' defensive and adaptive reactions (rather than proactive ones) to market pressures, it is often as late technology followers and innovation opportunities are lost to local industry. Something similar can be said about financial instruments and institutions in less favoured regions, which on top of usually imposing higher than (European) average interest rates offer little attention to long-term, higher risk and intangible investments which are characteristic of innovation projects.

Finally, the quality of the institutional setting in these regions is often the main obstacle for the creation of an efficient regional innovation system. Over and above the different degree of regional autonomy in the conduct of regional/industrial policy, several regional governance structures in less favoured regions suffer heavily from lack of credibility, political instability and absence of professional competence (and awareness) in the field of innovation. These three factors are characteristic of underdevelopment.

The lack of credibility of these governance structures, notably vis-à-vis the private sector, is reflected in their limited capacity for consensus building and partnership arrangements with private firms and other institutional actors, be it universities or national RTD correspondents. Political instability and short-term political consideration (linked to the political cycle) undermine any serious effort in the implementation of an innovation policy which by its own nature is medium- to long-term. Moreover, it makes the necessary regional leadership for the development of a regional innovation system even more difficult and more prone to fall in the hands of consolidated lobbies and parochial interests which hinder innovation. Lack of professional competence is reflected in the fact that these administrations tend to favour "traditional" and "easy to manage" regional instruments rather than more sophisticated and complex policies such as innovation policy. In some instances even where the political commitment has been clearly expressed to support such a policy, governance structures are often inadequate and it may be difficult to find the necessary management resources to implement it efficiently.

All the above explains to a certain extent the conclusions reached recently by the R&TDI evaluation of Structural Funds for the period 1994-1999 in less favoured regions (Higgings et al., 1999, p. 9) in which the major policy issues identified were:

- Lack of coordination between the bodies in charge of public research and those in charge of private research.
- Gap between universities and enterprises.
- In many regions there seems to be a lack of coordination of the science and technology policy between departments of industry and departments of education.
- In some regions there is overlap and inadequate coordination between national and regional measures.
- There is little involvement of the regional R&TDI actors, private sector in particular, in policy planning.

Learning Regions

The innovative capacity of the regional firm is directly related to the learning ability of a region (see Figure 2.3). That is, innovative capacity and the regional learning ability associated with it are directly related to the density and quality of networking within the regional productive environment. Interfirm and public-private cooperation and the institutional framework within which these relationships take place are the key sources of regional innovation. Innovation being the end-product, and the regional learning dependent on the quality and density of the above relationships being the process[8].

Asheim (1998, p. 3) defines a learning region as "representing the territorial and institutional embeddednesss of learning organisations and interactive learning" and goes on to argue that in the promotion of such innovation-supportive regions the interlinking of cooperative partnerships ranging from work organisations inside firms to different sectors of society, understood as "regional development coalitions," will be of strategic importance.

A learning region is not a parochial region, which ignores the importance of the national and international dimensions, particularly in the fields of science, research and technology over and above a narrowly defined concept of innovation as such. The regional dimension is important but not exclusive. In this sense it is crucial to acknowledge the need for firms to be close to open gates to the national and international (see Glover, 1996) dimensions regionally, in particular for SMEs. Recently, some authors (Koschatzky, 1998, p. 403) have emphasised that even though "space clearly matters in innovation, this takes place more on a perceptive rather than on a politically defined territorial basis" because "it is not a specific region which matters in innovation but an environment fuelled by actors from different regions which, in its complex (inter-regional) structure, has to exceed a critical minimum to be regarded as supportive factor in each region. This environment originates only in part from each single region, but its impact is regionally specific, depending on the structural characteristics of the regional firms". This leads them to conclude that "cross-regional activities would increase the impact of regionally oriented measures, and therefore, provide stronger support for innovation management and the competitiveness of both local and regional firms."

Learning as an economic process can be subject to virtuous circles and increasing returns to scale. The more a region (or a company) is in a position to learn (identify, understand and exploit knowledge, in the form of technological expertise for example, to their own economic benefit) the more capable, and possibly willing, it becomes to build on and increase its demand and capacity to use further new knowledge. But learning depends critically on two key factors: a certain degree of (business-economic) intelligence, which would trigger the demand for new knowledge, and access to/availability of knowledge.[9]

Figure 2.3
A Learning Region: An Efficient Regional Innovation System

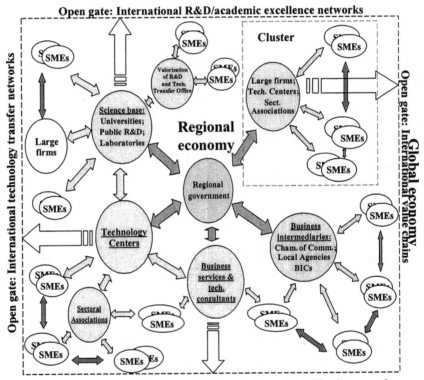

At the mesoeconomic level we also need an "intelligent cell" to trigger a learning process in a regional economy. The regional government (and its development-related agencies) can play a major role in articulating and dynamising a regional innovation system, understood as the process of generating, diffusing and exploiting knowledge in a given territory with the objective of fostering regional development. In this dynamic and systemic sense, the regional innovation system is in itself the process of learning which learning regions are aiming for. The regional innovation system is what determines the effectiveness and the efficiency of regional knowledge building/transfer among the different integrating parts of the system, including individual firms, sectoral/value-chain clusters, business consultants, technology centres, R&D centres, university departments, laboratories, technology transfer and utilisation of R&D centres, development agencies, and such. The regional innovation system is what makes the whole bigger than the sum of the individual parts.

Thus, the regional government can play the role of the "collective intelligence" necessary for a region to spark the process to become a learning region. It is best placed in terms of political legitimacy and economic powers, including its ability to eventually use the carrot (with, for example, financial backing: not least as a key decision maker in the process of Structural Funds allocation) and the stick (for example, through its regulatory powers and public procurement policies among others), to facilitate the articulation of the regional innovation system regarding two key aspects in particular. Articulating means linking (regional actors: firms, technology centres, universities, business service providers, etc.) and matching (innovation needs with knowledge supply) in search of synergies and complementarities among the different actors, policies and subsystems which integrate a regional innovation system. Links, synergies and complementarities are precisely the learning vehicles which may allow a region to effectively learn and increase its innovative potential, due to the nature of the innovation process at the regional level.[10]

The first way is by matching innovation (the capacity to use knowledge) demand by firms with existing R&TDI regional supply (the availability of knowledge centres) and eventually finding open gates to external innovation sources and partners capable of addressing the innovation needs of the regional economy. This includes the initial important task of identifying and helping to express innovation demand and needs, be they latent or not, from regional organisations, most notably SMEs. And the second way is by facilitating cooperation and coherence between the different agents and policies (science policy, research policy, industrial policy, regional policy, human resources policy, competition policy, etc.) which are integral parts of the regional innovation system.

In this sense, the regional government, as evidenced by the regional innovation strategy (RIS) experience explained in the next section, can and should play an important role as a catalyst, a facilitator and a broker in the articulation of the regional innovation system. This is particularly important for less favoured regions where the regional innovation system is more fragmented and its subsystems and integral parts are more underdeveloped or, at times, simply completely absent. It is above all a necessary "agent for change" which stimulates and develops networking among the different actors of the regional innovation system in the region. In this "enabling" capacity it can dynamise the regional endogenous potential in terms of entrepreneurship and technical expertise and know-how within the existing business culture and distinctive economic characteristics of the region. Notably it does this by building its own distinctive path to an efficient regional innovation system, since there is not and can not be a unique model of a regional innovation system exportable to all regions. Regional diversity is precisely an asset for regional innovation to build upon.

For the regional government to be able to play the progressive role outlined above regarding the articulation of the regional innovation system, a major cultural and organisational change has to occur in regional governance structures in most regions, and particularly in less favoured regions. This change should go along the lines of more flexible, less bureaucratic structures capable of much tighter partnerships with the private sector (and a higher degree of professional competence in strategic planning capabilities in particular). This also means an increased disposition to consensus building and inclusiveness in the policy process, including the policy delivery system, away from stop-and-go policy decisions dictated by short-term political instability and parochial interests. It is only then that the necessary social capital and institutional thickness will be reached in order for the public sector, regional government in particular, to lead the process of articulation and dynamisation of the regional innovation system. That is, the process of learning conducive to the actual realisation of a learning region in practice.

Finally, it is important to note that regional collective learning takes place in a context of coopetition (cooperation and competition happening at the same time among the same actors). In this sense, some authors (SRI, 1997, p. 7) argue that "Competition in the future may be less between individual firms and more between the value networks (these will include suppliers to the business and other trading partners, even traditional competitors) in which they participate. There will still be competition, but increasingly the participants in the network will also coordinate, cooperate, and co-create new opportunities." Trust is at the heart of this horizontal integration process (Sweeney, 1999, p.19).

This is important from the policy-making point of view since it adds a novel role to public action: that of a broker/mediator and facilitator among economic agents in order to create the right conditions for collective learning to happen. In the right context, entrepreneurs could then, through enlightened self-interest, maximise their contribution to this collective learning task, thus providing further impetus to the broader regional development goals. This has been so far the experience of a number of RIS, as explained in the following section.

RIS: TOWARDS COLLECTIVE LEARNING IN LESS FAVOURED REGIONS

The main objective of innovative actions under the European Regional Development Fund (ERDF) is to influence and improve European regional policy in order to make it more efficient in terms of its content and policy action. These innovative actions rely on "the principle of helping regions to help themselves through initiatives designed to mobilise local knowledge in a process of collective social learning" (Henderson and Morgan, 1999).

Regional Innovation Strategies are part of these ERDF innovative actions. These strategies cost on average half a million € cofinanced at 50% between the EU Commission and the region, and last for two years. They are not studies or diagnosis of the R&TDI infrastructure of a region in light of the identified needs of firms. Although they do use these studies and diagnoses, they are fundamentally about establishing a socioeconomic dynamic (social and institutional engineering) based on a bottom-up open discussion and consensus among the key innovation actors in a region about policy options and new ideas/projects in the field of innovation. In this sense, RIS are also about interinstitutional coordination and establishing linkages and collaboration networks among the different elements and players of the regional innovation system. A short definition of RISs might be "an instrument to translate 'knowledge' into regional GDP". RIS are a tool to strengthen Regional Innovation Systems (territorial systems that efficiently create, diffuse and exploit knowledge that enhances regional competitiveness) in less favoured regions.

Within the RIS operation, the Commission also provides regions undertaking an RIS with a network secretariat which facilitates interregional cooperation in the form of joint seminars, publications, and the like which promotes cross-fertilisation and the exchange of good practices among participating regions. Furthermore, the Commission also develops a number of accompanying measures to enhance the learning capacity of participating regions. One of these actions is Rinno, which is intended as a tool for policy makers to cooperate and learn from each other and avoid reinventing the wheel.

Rinno (which will take the form of a Website, CD-Rom and Printed Publication of a Database) has as a key objective the creation and maintenance of an "intelligent" directory of regional public support measures for the promotion of innovation and the identification and diffusion of good practices among regional policy makers. The areas covered by the database are (1) stimulation and detection of innovation needs in SMEs, (2) support for the development and implementation of innovation projects in SMEs, (3) stimulation and coordination of innovation and technology transfer-related business services, and (4) linkage mechanisms between the knowledge base and regional SMEs.

RIS Methodology: A Regional and Demand-led, Bottom-up Approach

RISs have six key methodological principles:

- RIS should be based on public-private partnership and consensus (the private sector and the key regional R&TDI players should be closely associated in the development of the strategy and its implementation). Regional administrations should be fully involved, in partnership with the relevant key regional innovation actors, in the design, implementation, monitoring and follow-up of the exercise.

- RIS should be integrated and multidisciplinary: an effort should be made to link efforts and actions from the public sector (EU, national, regional, local) and the private sector towards a common goal. Innovation within RIS includes not only technology considerations but also issues regarding human capital, research and education, training, management, finance, marketing, as well as policy co-ordination among regional policy, technology policy, industrial policy, R&D and education policy and competition policy.
- RIS should be demand-led (focusing on a firm's innovation needs, SMEs in particular) and bottom-up (with a broad involvement of R&TDI regional actors) in their elaboration.
- RIS should be action-oriented and should include an action plan for implementation with clearly identified projects (at the end of the process new innovation projects in firms and/or new innovation policy schemes and interfirm networks should appear);
- Regions participating in RIS should exploit the European dimension through interregional cooperation and benchmarking of policies and methods.
- RIS should be incremental and cyclical: the exercise is dynamic in the form of a strategy and plan for action that has to be reviewed in light of previous experience and on-going evaluation.

These principles reflect an approach opposite to one that is top-down, *dirigiste*, based on existing institution/power structures and driven by a fiscal transfer/financial distribution rationale, which is characteristic of some of the traditional regional policy stands in a number of less favoured regions. This is in line with the argument that "innovation policy is rather (and increasingly) a matter of networking between heterogeneous (organised) actors instead of top-down decision making and implementation" and it follows that "'successful' policymaking normally means compromising through alignment and 're-framing' of stakeholders' perspectives" (Kuhlmann et al., 1999, p. 12).

Moreover, the Commission does not try to promote one standard methodology to be applied religiously in all the regions partaking in RIS projects. In view of the sheer diversity of regional productive environments and their different institutional frameworks, and on the basis of the principle of subsidiarity, the Commission proposes broad guidelines and a flexible methodological approach to regions participating in RIS, which includes:

1. Raising awareness about innovation and building a regional consensus among key regional actors;
2. Analysis of the regional innovation system, including technology and market trends assessment, technology foresight and benchmarking with other regions;
3. Analysis of the strengths and weaknesses of regional firms: assessment of regional demand for innovation services, including technology audits (in SMEs in particular) and surveys regarding firms needs and capacities, including management, finance, technology, training, marketing, etc.;
4. Assessment of the regional innovation support infrastructures and policy schemes;
5. Definition of a strategic framework—including a detailed action plan and the establishment of a monitoring and evaluation system. The action plan may involve pilot actions and feasibility studies as well as concrete projects that might be financed under existing structural funds operational programmes.

It is expected that a broad spectrum of local political, economic and academic actors will be involved in this process by actively participating in the Steering Committee responsible for RIS as well as through working groups, seminars, interviews, audits and surveys. In this sense, the suggested institutional setting for carrying forward the RIS is considered to be as important, if not more so, than the proposed methodological stages outlined above. That is, a Steering Group with broad and active participation of key regional actors and a management unit with the necessary skills (i.e., economic planning capabilities, business understanding and RTD competence) together with Working Groups (regional stakeholders which critically review RIS findings and act as a source of innovation projects and new policy approaches) and eventually a process consultant plus regional or international consultants. This institutional setting is essential in order to create the institutional dynamism and social engineering that are at the heart of a successful RIS, as we will see in the next section.

Both the principles and the methodology suggested to the regions, which are supposed to be sufficiently compulsory and flexible at the same time so as to provide a clear reference framework while respecting regional diversity of needs and stages of development, are based on a "systemic"[11] vision of the innovation process at regional level.

RIS Objectives: Helping Regions to Help Themselves

RIS have four key objectives:

1. Place the promotion of innovation as a key priority for the policy agenda of regional governments and develop an innovation culture within regions, particularly less favoured regions.
2. Increase the number of innovation projects in firms, particularly SMEs.
3. Promote public/private and interfirm cooperation and networks, which facilitate the connection of R&TDI supply with business needs, and the flow of knowledge needed for innovation.
4. Increase the amount and, more important the quality, of public spending on innovation through innovation projects, structural funds assistance in particular, and thus promote a more efficient use of scarce public and private resources for the promotion of innovation.

In short, the main objective is to set foundations of an efficient regional innovation system (a learning regional economy) by improving existing regional innovation capacities as well as by exploiting the possibilities for new areas of development. RIS focuses on SMEs but is not limited to high-tech sectors and touches upon traditional sectors as well as the service sector (e.g., tourism) which tend to be important in less favoured regions (see Table 2.2).

Table 2.2
Member States and Their Regions Involved in the RIS Action

Member State	Region and Objective region eligibility
Austria	Niederösterreich (2&5b)
Belgium	Limburg (2), Wallonie (1&2)
Spain	Aragon (2&5b), Castilla La Mancha (1), Extremadura (1), Galicia (1), Pais Vasco (2&5b), Cantabria (1), Castilla y Leon (1)
Finland & Sweden	Luleå & Oulu (2, 5b, 6)
Greece	Dytiki Makedonia (1), Sterea Ellada (1), Thessaly (1), Epirus (1), Central Makedonia (1)
Germany	Weser-Ems (2&5b), Leipzig-Halle-Dessau (1), Altmark-Harz-Magdeburg (1)
France	Auvergne (2&5b), Lorraine (2)
Ireland	Mid-West, Shannon (1)
Italy	Abruzzo (non-objective), Calabria (1), Puglia (1)
United Kingdom	Strathclyde (2), West Midlands (2&5b), Yorkshire & Humber (2&5b), Wales (2)
The Netherlands	Limburg (2)
Portugal	Norte (1), Algarve-Huelva (1)

Note: The numbers in parentheses refer to type of objective regions in the European regional Development Fund regulation covering the 1994-1999 period.

In short, RIS is a "social engineering" action at the regional level whose main aim is to stimulate and manage cooperation links among firms and between firms and the regional R&TDI actors, which may contribute to their competitive position through innovation, notably by facilitating access to "knowledge" sources and partners. In this sense, RIS social engineering means creating the right environmental conditions, institutional in particular, for increasing the innovative capacity of the regional economy.

THE IMPACT OF RIS PROJECTS

In the last five years, more than 600 leading figures in the public and private sectors participated directly in the steering committees of the 32 RIS. The chairmen of most of these steering committees are leading businesspeople (e.g., Director, Philips International in Limburg (Belgium), Managing Director of Tellabs in Shannon (Ireland), Chairman of Surgical Innovations in Yorkshire and the Humber, Managing Director of Wolff Steel Ltd. in Wales, Managing Director NTLCableTel in Strathclyde, etc.) or political figures (e.g., the presidents of the region in Calabria, Puglia, and Weser-Ems; the regional ministers of industry in Niederosterreich, Castilla La Mancha, Castilla y León, Galicia, Magdeburg, etc.; the Secretary General of the Region in Sterea, Thessaly, Central Macedonia, etc.).

More than 5,000 SMEs have been reviewed through technology audits and/or interviews (e.g., 350 firms audited in Wales; a regional innovation survey of 6,000 firms with a 10% response rate in West Midlands; 1,500 innovation questionnaires sent to regional firms in Thessaly; a survey of 760 companies in Castilla La Mancha, with a 18% response rate and 50 technology audits; a questionnaire survey of 4,000 firms with a 15% response rate in Niederösterreich, followed by 30 in-depth firm interviews and 250 companies participating in five workshops, etc.).

Several hundred R&TDI organisations consulted in the process of drawing up the strategies and in the implementation of action plans based on the RIS (e.g., over 150 businesspeople working in 11 innovation boards in Yorkshire and Humberside; over 200 businesspeople participating in 12 sectoral boards in Castilla y León; 39 experienced innovators from the private sector and 40 academics involved in 17 discussion groups in Shannon; 80 innovation support organisations have worked in RIS Strathclyde; over 150 key regional actors participated in thematic working groups in Calabria, etc.).

What then has been the outcomes of RIS so far?

1. Identification of new innovation projects in firms:

"In Limburg (Netherlands) 400 companies are taking part in almost 60 projects to date involving the preservation and/or creation of 1,500 to 2,000 jobs. Participation will be intensified from 1999 (aiming at 500 companies per year). Moreover 22 million ECU from the Structural Funds have been earmarked for Regional Technology Plans (RTP) projects from the ERDF Objective 2 resources for 1997-1999 and project volume is expected to come to approximately 30 Mecus per annum from 1998 until 2001."

Most common RIS generated action:

1. Creation/strengthening/animation of sectoral business networks, clusters (supply chain or cross-sectoral) and business forums around innovation issues.
2. Establishment of new interfaces between business and the knowledge base, including technology centres, universities, public labs, specialised consultants, etc.
3. Integration and coordination of R&TDI services and agencies, including diffusion of their activities vis-à-vis the SME base through guides, inventories, one-stop shops, etc., and support to access national/international R&TDI schemes
4. Development of new financial instruments for the financing of innovation (seed corn fund for high tech. start-ups, risk capital, business angels, guarantee funds, etc.) including brokerage services between innovators and the banking sector.
5. Ensuring improvement of market intelligence for forecasting SME technology needs and future leading-edge skills needs
6. Identification of innovation projects in firms, SMEs in particular, through the combined efforts of university trainees and R&D labs from universities and/or other firms
7. Promotion and extension of technology audits in SMEs and innovation management training for businessmen
8. Facilitation of university/big firms spin-outs and technology-based start-ups

"The Welsh RIS Action Plan, launched by the Secretary of State for Wales in June 1996, includes 66 projects to be led by over 30 different organisations working together in partnership. Of these, over 60 are in progress."

2. Placement of the promotion of innovation as a priority for the regional policy agenda and increasing the amount and, more important the quality of innovation public spending through innovation projects, structural funds assistance in particular:

"In Castilla La Mancha, following the RIS, they have increased fivefold the regional budget for innovation promotion from 2.000 million pts for the period 1994-99 up to 15.000 million for the period 2000-2006."

"RIS has clearly become the most important transregional cooperation project in central Germany and this impacts extremely positively on its practical implementation, firmly establishing the RIS as one of the main priorities in the regional development programmes" (RTP Leipzig-Halle-Dessau).

"The Welsh RIS has been incorporated into the rationale and project scoring criteria of the Innovation priority of the Industrial South Wales Objective 2 Structural fund programme for 1997-1999, which offers the potential to draw down 18% of the total programme value of €630 million to support RTP priorities in South Wales."

3. Creation of new regional partnerships for economic development and promotion of interfirm and public-private cooperation:

"In Central Macedonia RIS lasted for two years (April 1995-March 1997) and about 200 scientists, public officials and businessmen participated directly in the working groups for the preparation of 39 reports necessary for the Action Plan. Furthermore, 2,000 businesses and 277 laboratories for applied research participated indirectly during the process of audits, technology demand and supply analyses, and consultation for the selection of projects."

"In the RIS Yorkshire and Humberside 11 Sector Innovation Boards have been established. Each Sector Innovation Board comprises representatives from both large and small sector businesses plus representatives from the main Business Support agencies in the region, TEC (Technology) & Business Links, Universities and Further Education Colleges, Local Authorities and Trade Associations."

"With 41 funding partners involved in the project to date, over 100 organisations from the support network and more than 150 private companies have participated in the project" (RIS Strathclyde).

"In Castilla y León nearly 800 companies were involved in the RIS process through a dozen sectoral strategic discussion meetings. A total of 447 million ECU has been pledged for the first four years of implementation (1997-2000), with the objective of increasing the regional "technological effort" (R&D expenditure over GDP at factor costs) to reach 1% in the year 2000, from a current 0.8%."

In 1997 an external evaluation was carried out by Technopolis (Netherlands/U.K.) and the University of Athens (Greece). The overall conclusion reached by the evaluation team was that "the Regional Technology Plans have had an important impact on the policy formation process, i.e. they created a policy planning culture where innovation and RTD are well embedded in the overall regional development strategies." More specifically the evaluation team pointed to a number of positive results and formulated recommendations for future policy actions in the field of innovation: the strategic nature of the policy approach, which entailed the involvement and cooperation of a broad spectrum of actors in the regional political economy in a detailed planning process, facilitated the development of an endogenous learning environment. It also resulted in a growing awareness of the innovative needs of the regions' firms and therefore instigated a reappraisal of the Structural Fund priorities and spending. Another interesting point to make concerns the flexibility of the RTP and RIS approach. The RTP evaluation demonstrated that despite being applied in many different ways in many different contexts RTPs still had a considerable effect on the regional innovation systems; the model is applicable in dissimilar environments.

Note: all quotes in this section refer to the RIS and RTP final and intermediary reports provided by the regional authorities responsible for these programmes.

RIS WEST MIDLANDS CASE STUDY

In this section we explore how the theoretical concepts of social capital,[12] the learning region[13] and external economies of scale[14] have been both utilised and enriched by the development and implementation of a regional innovation strategy in the West Midlands, England. The methodology and process of the West Midlands Regional Innovation Strategy project followed the broad structure outlined in Figure 2.4. However, there are important features of the West Midlands experience that offer valuable insights into the ways in which this overall framework can be adapted in different regions to maximise the use and development of social capital, learning and external economies of scale.

The West Midlands Regional Innovation Strategy project commenced in September 1996. Phase 1 was completed by December 1996 and phases 2 to 5 (see Figure 2.4) were completed by early 1999, but the process side of the project continues through the perpetuation of the Steering and Operational Groups. The strategy has been adopted and endorsed by the newly established Regional Development Agency (RDA) and is being implemented by the RDA in partnership with all the key players in the region.

Three fundamental and interrelated concepts underpinned the approach adopted in the West Midlands region: social capital, learning and external economies of scale, particularly *collective* external economies (Oughton and Whittam, 1997). The combination of these three elements is crucial in any regional innovation system, particularly from the perspective of small and medium-sized enterprises. Yet, paradoxically, SMEs are usually less likely to exploit these factors. This implies there is a need not only to raise awareness but also to find ways of making these concepts operational for SMEs. In the discussion that follows we illustrate how these concepts relate to the standard RIS approach and outline the contribution of the West Midlands RIS to: (1) providing new insight into what these terms actually mean, and (2) illustrating how theses concepts can be operationalised within a regional economy.

Figure 2.4
Schematic Presentation of RIS Work Programme and Methodology

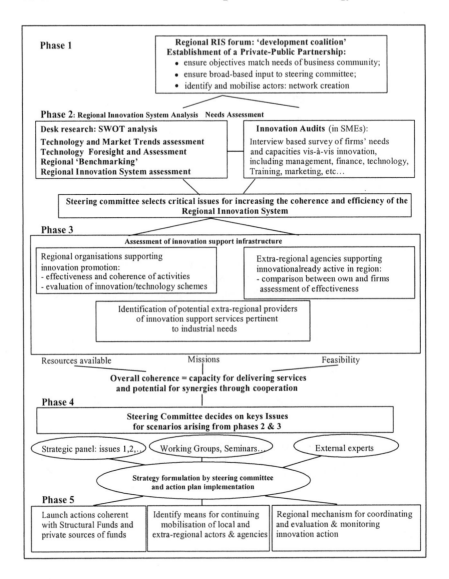

Social Capital

Phase 1 of the West Midlands RIS saw the formation of two fora that brought together key players within the region: the Operational and Steering groups. The creation of these two distinct, yet related groups (see Figure 2.5) is an important feature of the West Midlands RIS and one that serves to build social capital.[15] Both groups are of similar size with members from the *same* organisations represented at both senior (Operational Group) and executive (Steering Group) levels. The Operational Group consists of over 20 senior representatives from a range of public and private organisations including the business sector, the science base, local government, regional government and policy intermediaries, such as innovation centres, training and economic development agencies. The Operational Group met on a monthly basis and was involved in a hands-on way in the development of the strategy. Representatives on the Steering Group were drawn from roughly the same set of organisations but at the executive level. The team that conducted the research that informed phases 2-5 was also represented on these two groups and worked in an interactive way with the membership.

Figure 2.5
The Operational and Steering Groups—West Midlands RIS

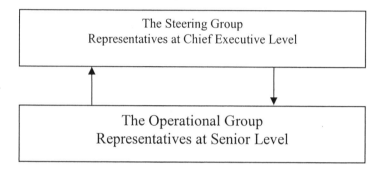

The advantages of this dual structure are threefold. First, each organisation had committed its senior personnel to participate in the Operational Group, to help with the development of the strategy and to provide constant feedback on the research. As a result of this involvement, each organisation had ownership over the strategy. Second, the existence of a dual structure whereby the Steering Group is a (higher level) mirror image of the Operational Group meant that members of the Steering Group (which met 3-4 times a year) were kept informed of the progress of the project through their own staff as well as through the project manager. At the same time members of the Operational Group knew that they and their fellow members had backing at the executive level to design and implement the strategy. This feature of the dual structure, therefore, increased the level of credibility and commitment within the Operational and Steering Groups. Finally, the existence of participation at both executive and senior levels facilitated trust and cooperation—the temptation of any individual member to follow a noncooperative strategy in, say, the Operational Group was reduced by the knowledge that cooperation was likely to occur at a higher level. Moreover, the strategy was agreed at both Operational and Steering Group levels, thus minimising the chances of it falling down either due to lack of executive commitment or because of difficulties in implementation. In short, the dual structure enhanced the formation of social capital in the region by encouraging participation, trust and civic cooperation.

In terms of Coleman's (1988) three forms of social capital: (1) the level of trust, (2) information channels, and (3) norms and sanctions that encourage or constrain actors to work for the common good, it can be seen that the dual structure adopted in the West Midlands embodied and promoted each of these three forms. The level of trust was enhanced by cooperation at both senior practitioner and executive levels. Information channels were opened up both horizontally between organisations and vertically within organisations. And finally, norms were established at two levels with the possibility of sanctions for noncooperative behaviour at any one level.

The institutional structure of the West Midlands RIS also consisted of five subregional groups to develop subregional strategies reflecting the particular sectoral mix and priorities of the subregions. Each subregional group had at least one (often more) representative on the Operational and Steering Groups and involved local economic actors and agencies. This approach helped foster institutional thickening and embeddedness based on a bottom-up approach.

Finally, it is important to consider the functional membership of the Operational and Steering Groups, which was based on bringing together representatives from industry, SMEs, the science base, technology transfer and research centres, training organisations, the finance sector and policy intermediaries. This multifunctional membership enabled networking and trust to be developed across a range of organisations to build multidisciplinary networks and was an important prerequisite to both the design and implementation of policy actions (discussed below) that require cooperation across organisations.

The organisational or process side of the West Midlands RIS described above was crucial to all of the subsequent phases. Phases 2 and 3 were conducted by the research team in conjunction with members of the Operational and Steering Groups. The establishment of an effective institutional process laid the foundation for the successful completion of subsequent phases of the West Midlands RIS.

The Learning Region

Learning is widely regarded as a necessary prerequisite for innovation. Few people would disagree with the suggestion that individuals learn,[16] but the idea that organisations or regions learn is less well understood or accepted. What is it that regions and organisations learn and how? In many ways phases 2-5 of the RIS methodology are about learning. Any region has an innovation system, learning about that system is a necessary prerequisite to improving it, and given that competitiveness depends, at least in part, on innovation, improving the innovation system is a necessary prerequisite to improving competitiveness and attaining real convergence. Phases 2 and 3 of the RIS provide concrete examples of how a region (or rather the regional actors represented on the Operational and Steering Groups) may learn, apply and implement knowledge in a strategic way to promote innovation. Phases 4 and 5 of the RIS programme are very much about stimulating learning, between firms, between firms and other actors, such as scientists, financiers and policy intermediaries so that learning becomes an integral and ongoing feature of the system.

Phases 2 and 3 of the West Midlands RIS

Phases 2 and 3 of the West Midlands RIS consisted of:

1. an extensive review of regional economic performance (including firm and sector performance) and the regional innovation system which was later summarised into a SWOT (strengths, weaknesses, opportunities, and threats) table;
2. a large-scale survey of firms' needs (with over 450 usable responses) and the piloting of an innovation audit;
3. an assessment of the regional innovation support infrastructure based on comparative analysis of key regional data (on productivity, investment in R&D, education and training and fixed capital) and a series of semistructured interviews with supply side agencies and policy intermediaries.

As is customary in a RIS project, the analysis of firms' needs (in terms of innovation inputs) is matched against the supply-side picture of innovation support infrastructure to identify areas where there are gaps in the regional innovation system and areas where there may be duplication of service provision. However, it is important to note that both the analysis of firms' needs and the assessment of the region's innovation infrastructure were conducted in relation to an external standard, or best practice. In the case of firms' needs the objective is to discover their *latent* needs for innovation inputs, and one way of doing this is to look at the extent to which firms in the region were underinvesting in knowledge, training and fixed capital equipment relative to the to leading firms in the region, leading firms in the United Kingdom and leading international firms. In the case of the supply side, the West Midlands innovation system was compared with best practice regions, such as Emilia Romagna and Baden Württemberg.

The comparison of firms' actual demand for innovation inputs with their latent (or best practice demand) was used to identify targets for improvements in innovation performance. The comparison of firms' needs with the supply of innovation inputs, and the further comparison of the West Midlands regional innovation infrastructure with that of best practice regions, was used to develop the framework for the regional innovation strategy. Hence, phases 2 and 3 were very much based on interfirm, interorganisational and interregional learning.

In the West Midlands region the main findings under phases 2 and 3 were as follows:

1. Productivity in the West Midlands region was only 90% of the U.K. average and only approximately 67% that of leading European regions, such as Emilia Romagna and Baden Württemberg.

2. The aggregate productivity gap of West Midlands manufacturing firms vis-à-vis their U.K. counterparts reflected both a long tail of underperforming firms *and* lower productivity among the region's leading firms. This finding was significant because it meant that closing the productivity gap would mean that typically *both* lagging and leading West Midlands firms were underperforming and would benefit from adopting international, or even U.K. best practices, i.e., there is a need for interregional learning as well as intraregional between firms.

3. West Midlands firms underinvest in broad capital—fixed capital, R&D and training—vis-à-vis their U.K. and international counterparts. Compared to the U.K. average, the West Midlands R&D figures are skewed by the fact that the region has a very small pharmaceutical sector which has very high R&D spending. Analysis of sectoral data revealed that West Midlands investment in R&D in the transport and engineering sectors was high by U.K. standards but still low compared to leading engineering regions, such as Baden Württemberg.

4. Public investment in R&D is more on less in line with the U.K. average but low by international standards. The Defence Evaluation Research Agency (DERA) at Great Malvern in the West Midlands accounts for a significant part of this investment, but DERA is not closely embedded in the region and its resource is underutilised in the West Midlands.

5. There is a lack of appropriate technology transfer institutions to link industry and the science base. The West Midlands (and U.K.) innovation system has an institutional gap between basic/applied research in the science base and commercial research.

6. Firms stated that they found the innovation support system complex and confusing; there are too many agencies and too many schemes with areas of overlap and gaps. Moreover, in order to innovate firms' need packages (e.g., technology, marketing advice, finance, training) of support there is a lack of coordination between agencies providing different services. There is a need for greater networking between supply-side organisations as service provision is predominately on a bilateral basis—i.e., there is a need for interorganisation learning and coordination. Moreover, there is a conflict incentive mechanism operating as a result of the dual objectives of *Business Link*[17] to signpost firms to other service agencies and to generate fee income.

7. The West Midlands (and U.K.) system of business and innovation support is generic rather than sector-specific and there is a need to create more sector-specific support infrastructure mechanisms that provide packages of support rather than individual services.

8. There is a lack of innovation culture among firms: our survey revealed that almost 40% of firms had not introduced a new product between 1994 and 1996, and 30% of firms had not introduced a new, *or improved* product; 33% of firms had no plans to innovate over the coming year; nearly 80% of respondents spent less than 5% of turnover on R&D.

9. The finance system suffers from short-termism—most firms finance innovation activity by bank overdraft. There is little use of long-term funds and the venture capital market is underdeveloped. The survey of firms' needs also revealed that the finance problem is multidimensional and includes problems in validating

technology, market forecasting, inadequate collateral and weaknesses in management's capability to present good business plans.

10. There are some examples of networking that realise external economies of scale—e.g., the Rubber and Plastics Research Association and networking in the automotive sector—but unlike highly successful regions, such as Baden Württemberg and Emilia Romagna, the system of networks is patchy across sectors and the multidimensional service provision is not fully integrated into networks.

The analysis carried out in phases 2 and 3 of the West Midlands RIS provided the basis for the development of the strategy in phases 4 and 5. The strategy was based on increasing opportunities for learning and realising collective external economies of scale through the catalysation of sector-based interfirm and interorganisational networks.

Networking, Collective External Economies and Learning

Successful innovation requires the correct combination (or package) of innovation inputs—knowledge, technical expertise, design, finance, managerial expertise, marketing expertise, trained labour and capital equipment. Unlike large multidivisional firms, small firms often lack the scale and resources to conduct research, development, design and training in-house. As a result they are unable to reap the internal economies that large firms enjoy; instead SMEs are forced to use the market. This is problematic when the market for specialised business services is fragmented and incomplete—that is, when there are missing markets. Cooperation within networks offers SMEs the possibility to reap collective external economies and enables them to compete on equal terms with larger firms. Examples of such networks are commonplace—for example, CITER and Centro Ceramico in Emilia Romagna. Collective external economies of scale have four distinguishing features. (1) They are realised within a network of participating firms; hence they are external to the firm but internal to the network. (2) They require the active rather than passive involvement of participating firms (i.e., firms need to make joint investments either in financial terms or in terms of human resources). In this regard collective external economies are different from agglomeration economies realised in clusters where the source of the economy is purely locational—that is, firms benefit simply from locating next to each other. (3) They depend crucially on the maintenance of effective cooperation between firms. (4) While they depend on cooperation they are pro-competitive in that, provided entry to the network is not restricted, they reduce barriers to entry (Oughton and Whittam, 1997, p. 9).

Results from the West Midlands Survey of firms showed that firms that engaged in joint innovation activity were up to six times more likely to innovate than firms that acted in isolation. Moreover, the stronger the degree of cooperation in terms of resources (for example, joint investment as opposed to cooperation in kind/time) the greater the impact on innovation.

Phases 2 and 3 of the RIS identified numerous interfirm and interorganisational networks in the West Midlands and showed that they had an appreciable effect on innovation performance both because they provide scope for interfirm and interorganisational learning and because they offer firms the possibility to reap collective external economies scale. Social capital or trust is crucial to the success of networks; but it should also be noted that cooperation can evolve even among selfish firms, provided there is a sufficiently long time horizon and a small proportion of firms who are willing to initiate a cooperative network. It can be seen that the approach in the West Midlands RIS was to jointly promote social capital building, learning and collective external economies of scale. The following subsection outlines how these were to be promoted through policy actions.

The Strategy and Action Plan

The findings from phases 2 and 3 of the West Midlands RIS fed into a strategic framework that formed the basis of a consultation document launched in July 1998 at a regional conference. The document was widely circulated to over 2,000 parties. Twelve working parties (led mainly by members of the Operational Group) were set up to develop different policy actions, from productivity to training.[18] The action plan was developed by the Operational and Steering Groups in light of the research findings from phases 2 and 3, the feedback from consultation and the reports of the 12 working parties.

The first step in strategy design was to engage firms and regional actors by adopting a definition of innovation that had operational meaning and to set targets that were ambitious, realistic and measurable. Hence, innovation was defined under the heading of "profitable change" and results from the survey of firms were used to show that the average rates of growth of profits and sales for innovating firms were double those of noninnovators.[19] Four targets were set out:

- To increase the proportion of innovating firms from 60% to 90% by 2004
- To increase investment in R&D, fixed capital equipment and training to, at least, the U.K. average by 2004
- To increase the proportion of firms who engage in joint innovation activity from 50 to 90% and the proportion who make joint investments from 22 to 50% by 2004
- To spread best practice and close the productivity gap so that productivity in the West Midlands is in line with the U.K. average by 2004

The strategy is based on four interrelated cornerstones illustrated in Figure 2.6. Policy actions sit within this framework and are being implemented by the RDA in conjunction with all partners. While there is not the space here to outline all of the policy actions (see Oughton et al., 1999) several key actions deserve consideration.

The first priority action was to ensure mechanisms are established to implement the strategy and action plan and champion RIS for the future; that is, there is a clear commitment to continue to build social capital. This is being done through the RDA endorsing the strategy and perpetuation of the

Operational and Steering Groups. Second, a team of network brokers is being established to build on existing sector-based interfirm and interorganisational networks and catalyse new ones. These networks are designed to encourage interfirm, interorganisational and interregional learning and promote joint innovation activity and the realisation of collective external economies of scale. Third, three technology centres will be developed to serve three-four sectorally based networks to act as a focal point of technological expertise and a bridge between the science base and industry. Fourth, a sector-network-based system of designing and vetting business plans and loan applications will be established that closes the information gap regarding validation of technology and market assessment and increases the chances of attaining finance. In addition a seed corn fund is being set up for high-tech firm start-ups and a regional brokering scheme is being developed to match venture capitalists (business angels) with innovators and entrepreneurs.

The above list is not exhaustive but it is indicative of a set of policy actions designed to stimulate social capital, learning (interfirm, interorganisational and interregional) and collective external economies in order to promote innovation. The West Midlands case study shows not only how these terms may be operationalised but also adds greater theoretical precision and meaning to these concepts and the mechanisms by which they impact on regional economic performance.

Figure 2.6
The Cornerstones of the Strategy: West Midlands RIS

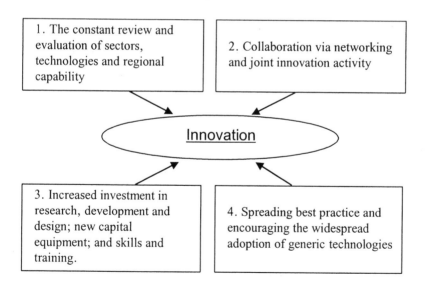

CONCLUSIONS

A new kind of regional policy is emerging in the European Union in which the accent is on collective learning and institutional innovation rather than basic infrastructure provision. Thus emphasis is being put on social capital (i.e., a relational infrastructure for collective action based on trust, reciprocity and the disposition to collaborate to achieve mutually beneficial ends) rather than on physical capital building.

In our opinion, in these small regional experiments we can begin to discern a new and more innovative form of economic governance, the hallmarks of which are interactive, strongly based on public-private partnership and network based, rather than hierarchical on solely market-driven, the respective governance modes of *dirigisme* and neoliberalism. In this sense these actions are concerned not with the scale of state intervention but its mode, not the boundary between state and market but the framework of effective interaction (Henderson and Morgan, 1999). In RIS, governance is based on public-private partnership and consensus, with the public sector playing a role mainly as an animator, a catalyst and a dynamic force for networking among all the relevant regional agents. Thus making scarce regional efforts and energies converge towards innovation promotion with a regional development objective.

Although regional experiments like RIS have triggered some encouraging institutional innovations, the key question is how to evaluate success in this context. It is clear that these new regional policies, which aim to raise regional innovation capacity, and the establishment of an efficient regional innovation system, cannot be judged by the standards of the old regional policies (short-term job creation). In order to overcome this problem, we need a new set of indicators that allow us to assess longer term changes in regional innovation capacity, away from "linear" indicators such as standard R&D input and output indicators. That is, we need interactive indicators which aim to measure "soft" processes like institutional linkages and network formation in order to capture the important changes in a region's institutional architecture which are beyond the grasp of more conventional linear indicators (Nauwelaers and Reid, 1995).

Notwithstanding this lack of appropriate indicators, the external evaluation of the first 7 RIS experiences, as well as the on-going evaluation carried out for the new generation of 20 RIS, clearly point out that RIS have been a novel approach in each of the regions involved—an approach that has significantly contributed to establishing a strategic planning culture based on consensus and partnership by which innovation promotion has been put high in the regional development agenda. Moreover, most regions which have undertaken an RIS have managed to increase considerably the quantity of public funds targeted for innovation, which is expected to trigger a parallel increase from private funds.

In conclusion, we believe that RIS may help prepare the ground so that those responsible for innovation promotion at regional levels can better respond to the need of increasing the regional innovation potential and addressing the problem of absorption related to the regional innovation paradox mentioned before. This can be done specifically through work on basic strategic planning involving key regional actors which will result in new innovation projects consistent with regional policy objectives. Social capital, learning (interfirm, interorganisational and inter-regional) and networking to promote collective external economies of scale are crucial to this process. Thus, RIS seems to be a fertile ground for further experimentation and learning in the quest for efficient regional innovation systems that can consolidate sustained and sustainable economic development processes in those regions where these are most needed.

NOTES

1. Over two-thirds of this amount is earmarked for regions whose income per capita is less than 75% of the European average. Nearly 20% of people in the EU still live in regions with output per head 25% or more below the EU average. By comparison, just 2% of the people in the United States are in a similar position, and average disparities between states are less than half those between equivalent regions in the EU (CEC, 1998a).

2. CEC (1999; 1998a, p. 12).

3. P. Cooke (1998, pp. 15-27). This paper summarises the findings of research conducted in the "Regional Innovation Systems: Designing for the future" (REGIS). This research was funded by the European Commission DG 12 under the Fourth Framework—Targeted Socio-Economic Research Programme.

4. The Treaty of the European Union has "economic and social cohesion" as one of its main pillars, as established in the following articles: Article 130a: In order to promote its overall harmonious development, the Community shall develop and pursue its actions leading to the strengthening of its economic and social cohesion. In particular, the Community shall aim at reducing disparities between the levels of development of the various regions and the backwardness of the least favoured regions, including rural areas. Article 130c: The European Regional Development Fund is intended to help to redress the main regional imbalances in the Community through participation in the development and structural adjustment of regions whose development is lagging behind and in the conversion of declining industrial regions.

5. We will use Von Hippel's (1988) definition of know-how as "the accumulated practical skill or expertise that allows one to do something smoothly and efficiently (e.g., the know-how of engineers who develop a firm's products and develop and operate its processes). Firms often consider a large part of this know-how proprietary and protect it as a trade secret".

6. This perspective is in line with the institutional perspective which insists that these intangible resources merit as much attention as tangible resources (Cooke and Morgan, 1998). The so-called institutional perspective "echews the bloodless categories of 'state' and 'market' in favour of a more historically-attuned theoretical approach in which the key issues are the quality of the institutional networks which mediate information exchange and knowledge-creation, the capacity for collective action, the potential for interactive learning and the efficacy of voice mechanisms" (Sabel, 1994; Amin and Thrift, 1995; Storper, 1997; Morgan, 1997; Cooke and Morgan, 1998; Maskell et al., 1998; Amin, 1999).

7. A more detailed explanation of this section can be found in Landabaso (2000).

8. An excellent insight on this learning ability can be found in Lundvall, and Borras (1997). Chapter 7, in particular, regarding the creation of networks and stimulating interactive learning, is most enlightening.

9. Similarly, someone who starts reading for the first time, once he or she enjoys a book, looks for more while increasing his or her capacity to understand it better, read faster and combine the new knowledge with previously recorded knowledge from other books, thus extending its learning capabilities in a sort of virtuous circle.

10. For a further tentative explanation of the characteristics and nature of the innovation process at the regional level, see Landabaso (1997).

11. The limitations of the linear model of the innovation process have been clearly exposed in the work of Soete and Arundel (1993) by contrasting this model with their systemic model of the innovation process. These limitations relate, in particular, to the lack of interrelation between the different stages and retroactive nature of the innovation process within the linear model, which is fundamentally a science and technology-push model. It is only by focusing on the demand of firms and the economic nature of the innovation process that policy approaches can deal successfully with the promotion of innovation. Thus, recognizing the importance of the economic-pull factors (demand by firms) in the innovation process is critically important in the design of policy.

12. Coleman (1988), Putnam (1996), Knack and Keefer (1997), Temple and Johnson (1998) and Schuller and Field (1998).

13. Glover (1996), Cook (1997), Cooke, Uranga and Etxebarria (1997), Morgan (1997), Hassink (1997), Glasmeier (1999) and Hudson (1999).

14. Oughton and Whittam (1996 and 1997).

15. Putnam (1996) has defined social capital as "the features of social life—networks, norms and trust—that enable participants to act together more effectively to pursue shared objectives."

16. Although, of course, there is strong debate about how and what people learn, the relative worth of applied and abstract knowledge and the ways in which knowledge is utilised.

17. Business Links were set up by the government as local one-stop shops to provide SMEs with business services. They are briefed to sign-post firms to appropriate service providers, but they also have to generate fee income themselves, hence they face a contractual incentive to keep customers rather than to signpost.

18. See page 30 of Oughton et al. (1999).

19. See Table 1.1, page 3 of Oughton et al. (1999).

REFERENCES

Asheim, B. T. (1998) *Learning regions as development coalitions: partnership as governance in European workfare states?* Paper presented at the second European Urban and Regional Studies Conference on "Culture, place and space in contemporary Europe," University of Durham, U.K., 17–20 September 1998.

Autio, E. (1998) *Evaluation of R&TD in Regional Systems of Innovation*, European Planning Studies, 6, 2.

Bellini, N. (1998) *Services to Industry in the Framework of Regional and Local Industrial Policy.* Draft paper OECD Modena Conference (28-29 May 1998) on "Up-grading knowledge and diffusing technology to small firms: building competitive regional environments."

Capellin, R. (1992) "Technological Change and spatial networks in economic lagging regions". Paper presented at the IV World Congress of the Regional Science Association, Palma de Mallorca, Spain, 26-29th May.

CEC (1998a) *Sixth Periodic Report on the Social and Economic Situation and Development of the Regions of the European Union*, Brussels.

CEC (1998b) *Seventh Survey on State Aid in the European Union in the manufacturing and certain other sectors,* Brussels.

CEC (1999) The Structural Funds and their Co-ordination with the cohesion fund: guidance for programmes in the period 2000-2006 tabled by Mrs. Wulf-Mathies in agreement with Mr. Flynn, Mr. Fischler and Ms Bonino, Brussels. (www.inforegio.cec.eu.int/wbdoc/docoffic/coordfon/coord_en.htm).

Chabbal, R. (1994) *OECD Programme on Technology and Economy,* Paris.

Coleman J. S. (1988) "Social capital in the creation of human capital", *American Journal of Sociology,* 94.

Cooke, P. (1998) The role of Innovation in Regional Competitiveness, in Jan Cobbenhagen (ed.), Conference Proceedings, Maastricht, The Netherlands, 28-29 May 1998, Cohesion, Competitiveness and RTDI: their impact on regions.

Cooke, P. and Morgan, K. (1998) *The Associational Economy: Firms, Regions and Innovation.* Oxford: Oxford University Press.

Cooke, P., Uranga, M. G. and Etxebarria, G. (1997) Regional innovation systems: institutional and organisational dimensions, *Research Policy,* 26, 4-5, 475-491.

Fundacion COTEC (1997) *Tecnología e Innovación en España,* report, Madrid.

Glasmeier, A. K. (1999) Territory-based regional development policy and planning in a learning economy: the case of "real service centres," *European Urban and Regional Studies,* 6, 1, 73-84.

Glover, R. W. (1996) The German apprenticeship system: lessons for Austin, Texas, *Annals of the American Academy of Political and Social Science,* 544, 83-94.

Henderson, D. and Morgan, K. (1999) Regions as laboratories: the rise of regional experimentalism in Europe, in *Innovation and Social Learning,* D. Wolfe and M. Gertler (eds.). New York: Macmillan and St. Martin's Press.

Higgings, T. et al. (1999) *R&TDI Thematic Evaluation of the Structural Funds 1994-1999—Spain country report.* Brussels.

Hudson, R. (1999) The learning economy, the learning firm and the learning region, a sympathetic critique to the limits to learning, *European Urban and Regional Studies,* 6, 1, 59-72.

Knack, S. and Keefer, P. (1997) Does social capital have an economic payoff? *Quarterly Journal of Economics,* November, 1251-1287.

Koschatzky, K. (1998) Firm innovation and region: the role of space in innovation processes, *International Journal of Innovation Management,* 2, 4, pp. 383-408.

Kuhlmann, S. et al. (1999) *Improving Distributed Intelligence in Complex Innovation Systems,* Final report of the Advanced Science & Technology Policy Planning Network, Karlsruhe, June.

Landabaso, M. (1997) The promotion of Innovation in regional policy: proposals for a regional innovation strategy, *Entrepreneurship & Regional Development,* 9, 1-24.

Landabaso, M. (2000) EU Policy on innovation and regional development, in *Knowledge, Innovation and Economic Growth,* Silvia Bakkers, Frans Boekema, Kevin Morgan and Roel Rutten (eds.). Cheltenham: Edward Elgar.

Lundvall, B.A. (ed.) (1992) *National Systems of Innovation: towards a theory of innovation and interactive learning.* London: Pinter Publishers.

Lundvall, B.A. & Borras, S. (1997) *The globalising learning economy: implications for technology policy.* Final Report under the TSER Programme, EU Commission, December.

Morgan, K. (1997) The learning region: institutions, innovation and regional renewal, *Regional Studies,* 31, 5, 491-503.

Muldur, U. (1992) "Le financement de la R&D au croisement des logiques industrielle, financière et politique". Fast-Monitor Programme, Brussels.

Nauwelaers, C. and Reid, A. (1995) *Innovative Regions*. Brussels: European Commission.

Oughton, C. and Whittam, G. (1997) Competition and Cooperation in the Small Firm Sector, *Scottish Journal of Political Economy*, 44, 1, 1-30.

Oughton, C. et al. (1999) *West Midlands Regional Innovation Strategy and Action Plan: Shaping Our Future*, May, Report Number 25.

Putnam, D. (1996). Who Killed Civic America? *Prospect*, March, pp. 66-72.

Soete, L. and Arundel, A. (eds.) (1993) *An integrated approach to European Innovation and Technology Diffusion Policy: A Maastrich Memorandum*. CEC Ed., Brussels.

SRI Consulting (1997) *A new formula for competitiveness: trust*, August.

Sweeney, G. (1999) Local and regional innovation: governance issues in technological, economic and social change, Report of the Six Countries Program conference in Ireland 1997.

Temple, J. and Johnson, P. (1998) Social capability and economic growth, *Quarterly Journal of Economics*, 113, 3, pp. 965-990.

Von Hippel, E. (1988) *The sources of innovation*. New York: Oxford University Press.

3

The Role of Innovation in Regional Economic Development: Some Lessons and Experiences for Policy Making

Claudia P. Salas, Gabriela Susunaga, and Ismael Aguilar-Barajas

INTRODUCTION

Knowledge and Development

The role of knowledge in the development process remains as one of the issues governing the agenda at the turn of the 21st century. It is very illustrative that the *World Development Report 1998/99* (World Bank, 1999), examines this role with great concern. The *Report* begins by recognizing that economies develop not simply by accumulating physical capital and human skills, but "on a foundation of information, learning and adaptation" (p. 14). The *Report* also stresses the importance of sharing what is learned, but acknowledges that there is much to be known about the complex relationship between knowledge and development.[1] In the *Human Development Report 1999*, published by the United Nations Development Program (UNDP, 1999), one of its major parts is dedicated to new technologies and the global race for knowledge. In studying the access to the network society, this *Report* relates directly the new rules of globalization with its impacts on people, and ends by stressing the need to reshape the path of technology. As found in a recent study of the Organization for Economic Cooperation and Development (OECD, 1999:7), "innovation is not an activity of a single firm; it increasingly requires an active search involving several firms to tap new sources of knowledge and technology and apply these in products and production processes. The system of innovation approach demonstrates that the competitiveness of companies is becoming more dependent on complementary knowledge acquired from other firms and institutions." It is highly significant that this report ends with a hopeful thought: The finer understanding of the process of innovation leading to some innovation of innovation policy making itself. This concern with *knowledge for development* frames the discussion presented below regarding the role of innovation in regional economic development.

The Role of Innovation in Regional Growth and Development

For many years people have tried to understand the complex relationships between innovation and regional economic development. This interest increases significantly. Although this topic has been addressed at least since the 1960s and 1970s, it is in the 1980s and 1990s that its discussion has intensified, partly due to the new avenues given by the informational economy. A new technological revolution mainly based on information, and diffused through the global economy, is influencing the spatial distribution of economic activities. This new paradigm has received several names, such as postfordism,[2] postindustrial or tertiary economy,[3] and informational economy.[4]

According to Castells and Hall (1994:3), this new form of production and management "is characterized by the fact that productivity and competitiveness are increasingly based on the generation of new knowledge". The latter is regarded as the major factor of production, essential for organizing and using information. Thus an innovation process is generated. Innovation was defined by Norman (1993:5) as the creation or implementation of a new alternative that achieves a better performance in some selected objective, measured by the respective criteria. Innovation is not limited to manufacturing or high technology; it also includes processes and ways of organization within a company or industry.[5] There are various elements that interact to generate innovation well beyond research and formal development to create new inventions, and their outputs are not necessarily new products. However, these questions were taken into account until the emergence of postfordism or the informational economy.

The relationships between innovation and regional development are extremely complex. Vertova (1997)[6] pointed out that the concrete processes, in which innovative activities happen, differ even across countries that face the same technological and economic levels. According to OECD (1998:63), this is due to the particularities that arise from different mixes of endogenous processes, such as "investment in fixed capital, R&D and education, building on and extending advantages in the mastering of specific technologies, economies of scale, resource endowments, and a variety of institutional factors which vary across countries".

The previous statement applies not only for nations, but for regions too. The industrial geography diversifies, resulting in a regional differentiation based on the particular vocation of places relating those parameters. In this sense, Hilpert (1991a) distinguished: (1) recent postfordist industrialized regions; (2) regions specializing on fordist production (on decline); and (3) peripheral regions.

In fact, Hilpert (1991a) found that the innovative industries of the new technological revolution do not show a generalized spatial dispersion. On the contrary, they are located in regions where requirements to innovate are found. Mills (1992)[7] indicates this is the way industrial complexes or clusters are formed, taking advantage of regional agglomeration economies. On the other hand, regions benefit from productivity and competitiveness gains, which fordist production was unable to create. So there are greater economic growth and lesser dependency with respect to the spatial distribution of national economic development. CEC (1991) argues that regional economic development in an increasingly competitive world depends upon time, and on the progressive introduction of process and product innovations, to accomplish competitiveness in the regional economic base.

These regional differentiation patterns have deep effects on the economic performance of regions. Variables such as employment, productivity and investment follow various dynamics that lead to different rates of economic growth and unequal quality of life. According to Polèse (1998), the largest part of long-term increases in *per capita* income depend on increases in productivity per worker—which in turn rely on the region's ability to continually renew its supply of production factors such as human capital, knowledge stock, physical capital, among others—and on the "progress of knowledge".

In this sense, the generation of innovation *per se* is not a guarantee for regional development. OECD (1998) recognized harmful effects of rigidities in the markets for goods, labor and finance. In addition, a scarce knowledge about the nature and mechanisms of innovation still persists, so the state-of-the-art does not seem promising to policy makers seeking an infallible formula for regional development through innovation.

However, the euphoria with innovation (and its extension to regional development) should not overlook the fact that some of the current findings already have been referred in the past. For instance, at the end of the 1980s Harris (1988) made use of the Science Policy Research Unit (SPRU) survey of significant innovations—which covered the period 1945-83 for the United Kingdom—to highlight the effect of industrial structure on innovation. He found more innovations were developed in plants that were externally owned, and showed an overwhelming dominance of the South of England. Furthermore, his research underlined some of the major determinants of innovation: the nature of the industry, along with R&D commitments; the size of plants and industry concentration; the type of manufacturing system employed; and access to knowledge, information and skilled resources to develop and implement innovations (pp. 361-362).

At the beginning of the 1980s, and again in the British context, Goddard (1983) had argued the case for improved telecommunications and information access, as a key component of an innovation-oriented regional policy, particularly in the case of small independent firms in lagging regions. Therefore, the policy aim should be to integrate these firms into the *diffusion* process at an early point in time, an explicit observation made by Ewers and Wettmann as early as 1980. For them, an innovation-oriented regional policy should realize that small and large firms required different institutional frameworks. Moreover, these authors argued that this policy needed to be more responsive to the demand capacity of small and medium-sized firms, rather than be only supply-oriented. Still in the policy side, Gibbs (1984) had found that while investment incentives formed a useful tool of regional policy regarding process innovation, new types of policy were necessary to encourage product innovation. Another interesting finding concerns the ability to protect innovation programs from political influences, as has been the case of the Thomas Edison Program in the United States (Weinberg and Mazey, 1988). However, this means the explicit incorporation of political criteria into the drafting of programs, as well as substantive expertise in innovation programs.

The current concern with both external benefits and agglomeration costs has also been addressed before. As expressed by Dorfman (1983), as the size of a spatial cluster grows, congestion-induced negative externalities may begin to overtake the positive benefits. The author goes on to point out evidence that high land and housing costs in Silicon Valley (Santa Clara County) have in the relocation of some establishments. However, in more recent times it has been found that Santa Clara County continues to enjoy such an attraction that it is common to find homes at half a million dollars; in a place where housing prices could easily go up $1,000 a week, with no end in sight, "who can afford not to buy a house now?" This statement is considered to be a pretty good assessment of Silicon Valley overall. Under the rapid rate at which it is evolving, "can you afford not to get in?" (Bronson, 1999:248).

Notwithstanding the previous consideration about former research, an urgent task for researchers and development planners is, of course, to investigate further the role of innovation. Considering technology as an independent variable in growth models, Erickson (1994) has concluded that frequently this variable takes credit for what is not understood about growth. Thus there's not advance towards a greater understanding, rather innovation takes the proportions of a genuine "black box" permanently uncharted, and whose prospects for state and local governments and firms appear to be very limited.

Focus and Major Concern of the Chapter

This work is focused on the study of innovation strategies for regional development, with the main objective of *finding the fundamentals for the existence of a model*. In order to achieve this, the conditional factors for innovation strategies' performance will be analyzed, considering several international experiences. Theory—review of models and methods, and empirical evidence—and a practical focus to regional policy formulation will be complemented to reach the proposed objective.

Even though innovation can be developed endogenously[8]—as in the cases of Silicon Valley and Route 128[9]—for the purpose of this work, regional innovation strategies matter as policy instruments. That is, the ability to influence the *status quo* and make regions benefit from industrial specialization and cluster formation. Therefore, a wide concept of innovation will be used,[10] to include from high technology products and industries—semiconductors, electronics, computing—to any industry in which a region can specialize, products, processes, and other kinds of social innovation through links of various actors—companies, government, universities, among others.[11]

On principle, the policy rationale must be specified. OECD (1998) found, (1) market failures, including asymmetric information, economies of scale, indivisibilities,[12] external effects, imperfect appropriation of returns and uncertainty; (2) government failures, with respect to wrong incentives that worsen the market situation, due to information lags; delays in implementation; administrative costs and lobbing; (3) systemic failures, which are mismatches on the innovation system's conditional factors of performance, since innovation relies not only on individual performance of the specific actors, but on their interaction. In this sense, OECD (1998) recommends including aspects like the timing and duration of each measure, to avoid weakening initially effective instruments.

It has to be considered that opportunities to re-create the *Silicon Valley effect* are limited.[13] The timing and the particular characteristics of each experience must be considered, to avoid indiscriminate transplants of strategies in different contexts. Besides knowing how to develop successful innovation strategies, policy makers must also know the effects of a regional specialization of this kind to assure that objectives being pursued are feasible through the means employed, being also aware of the costs involved.[14]

Main Conclusions

Innovation for regional development has been a theme of growing interest in economic literature within the frame of the transition towards an informational society. Particularly, the interrelationship of actors and resources which intervene on the innovative process will determine the performance of regions in generating innovations. A review of theory and international experiences suggests that economic structures, universities, local governments, labor markets, entrepreneurs, communities, infrastructure and financial funding are the basic elements of interaction within local environments.

The major finding about innovation strategies for regional development drives attention to the complexity of their practical applicability. On principle, regional policy has a limited influence on innovation processes since those depend on the recombination of several factors, including a lot of exogenous mechanisms following a dynamic evolution. An important lesson is that there's not a formula to make a region optimize benefits from innovation. However, regional policy has instruments to foster performance of regions by providing strong advantages through the linkage between relevant elements.

The international nature of innovations outlines several questions to be explored in new research. Despite innovation and specialization being global trends, they still locate in delimited geographical space.[15] Furthermore, political structures—central or federal—capabilities of national and local governments, and specific ideologies—conservative, social democracy or liberal—have various implications for regional innovation policy that must be considered. In this context, regional innovation poses questions about the relationship between economics and politics, and about the role of the state in the new economic trends.[16]

Considering the complex nature of innovations, a broader approach becomes essential. For example, the study of cooperative networks has a double dimension, (1) formal strategical alliances requiring research over incentives arising from the regulatory and legal framework; and (2) informal social networks relevant to sociology.[17] Therefore, a fertile vein for future research will have to combine multidisciplinary analysis.

INNOVATION STRATEGIES FOR REGIONAL DEVELOPMENT

Starting in the 1980s, the interest on regional development based on high technology has been increasing. The technological revolution has been proven to be an informational revolution, with major advances arising from the automation of information processing.[18] Informational technology has facilitated the distribution of production and has led to formation of innovative centers, technopoles, technological parks—among others—that will be explained in the first section of this chapter. However, not all regions are interested in applying those strategies. As a result of a region's inner limitations, high technology strategies could be inadequate. Otherwise, regional problems could ask for different objectives, such as the case of regions requiring employment creation. Therefore an alternative strategy is proposed, the local innovation system. The latter's objective is to generate innovation through the interrelationship of various elements present in a region. Finally, a functional distinction between sources of innovation will be outlined. Thus a strategy for innovation in a specific sector context will be made operative, mainly on the basis of the particular characteristics of regional economic structure and its potential for the generation of innovation.

Local Innovation Policy

Local governments have recognized the importance of the diffusion of technological development, so several innovation policies have been designed to foster that process. Support strategies for innovation must be considered to examine existing models of innovation and regional development. Those strategies have the objective of diffusing technological development; a documentation of them is presented in Table 3.1. For instance, incubators have been undertaken with governmental support, while scientific and research parks have developed due to linkages between universities and industrial communities.

Regarding technological parks, those have arisen due to benefits of business based on technology.

Table 3.1
Support Strategies for Innovation

Innovation Centers	Their main task is to provide consultance on trading of ideas or inventions, and also to help entrepreneurs to start their business, usually through the networking between the innovation center and the existing companies.
Incubators	These support environment for creative entrepreneurs in the initial phase of the company, supply them low-price land, shared facilities and expert support on techniques and management.
Research Parks	These link the best academic research and the industry's R&D, creating the opportunity to locate the R&D activities of industry as close as possible to a research institute.
Scientific Parks	These are agreements that link the university research and the commercial operations. They are known because of the central role of university, government and society support, and the strict controls over land uses.
Technological Parks	Their objective is to introduce industrial growth in terms of production and employment, attracting manufacturing companies of high technology to an advantageous space.
Corporative Parks	Shared facilities are limited to installations and conference equipment.
Enterprise Zones	These are districts or areas within a city with a special designation by zones and provide special funds concessions or also attract a specific business to the region.
Scientific Cities	Scientific research complexes without a territorial link to manufacturing, to take advantage of the innovation environment's synergy to create scientific excellence.
Technopoles	These are the creation of a whole new city, designed to provide a total technology industrial environment. They are used as instruments for regional development and industrial decentralisation.

Adapted by the authors, based on: Kumm & Nimmervoll (1988) cited in Bailey (1991:83); Preer (1992:13-19, 75-81) and Castells & Hall (1994:10-11).

Scientific parks are the result of collaborative efforts between universities and local governments. Therefore linkages between universities are considered to be very important for the parks' success, due to the stream of labor and ideas among two types of institutions: universities and companies. The target of scientific parks is to transform every idea developed in universities into commercial products. However there are scientific parks not linked to university, such as Sophia-Antipolis in France, which is the largest scientific park in Europe.[19]

The concept of a technopolis or city with a completely technological industrial environment arose in Japan[20] as a private and public strategy designed to foster regional development through the commercialization of new technologies. Since their creation, technopoles have become a global phenomenon.[21] In most cases, technopoles have deviated from their original concept, to participate in a broader policy including programs to promote regional equity, international competitiveness and national defense.[22]

Until now the functioning of several support strategies for innovation has been explained; however a local innovation system goes beyond them.[23] Moori-Koening and Yoguel (1998) define a local innovation system as a collection of various institutions that individually and jointly contribute to technology development and diffusion. Therefore, an attempt to create an innovation strategy with a single determinant would be like making an airplane fly with a single motor.

Preer (1992:29) cites John Friedman (1966), who said that planners who intervene on regional development must understand the process for generating it. That points out the importance of understanding the factors determining performance of a local innovation system, which will be presented in the following section.

Determinants of Performance of the Local Innovation Policies

The reproduction of experiences with innovation policies has become a panacea to local authorities all over the world.[24] However it is clear that the contexts where these policies have been successfully implemented contain specific factors that constitute opportunity areas for action, and lessons have not been isolated out of context. Gomes, Hoche-Mong et al. (1991) mentioned that it is possible to have a genuine internationalization of the technopole phenomenon, even to make it replicable and franchising.[25]

Table 3.2 shows a review of the determinants for local innovation models' performance. These references were selected in an attempt to exhibit different contexts to elaborate on a broader frame. Breheny and McQuaid (1988b) justified the study of cases on innovation strategies, for academic and practical reasons.[26] Thus, the authors referred to in Table 3.2 focused their studies on Norway, Argentina, European Union, United States, Singapore and other sites all over the world, besides to a theoretical review surveyed by Fach and Grande (1991).

Table 3.2
Review of Local Innovation Systems

Context	Determinants of the Model	Author
Theoretical Review	*Entrepreneurs*, who have the vision and the opportunity to innovate. Their success depends on three factors—virtue, faith and fate—to be the agents of the "creative destruction" through millions of small companies.	Fach & Grande (1991:44-52)[a]
	The Innovative State, which leads innovation strategies to increment the economy's competitiveness and in the long run citizens' life standards, focusing its efforts on high-value niches and industries based on advanced technology.	
	The Innovative Community, which offers an alternative to the state-market dichotomy, providing an appropriate environment for business, creating cooperative links that reduce competition risks to small companies in the global economy.	
Successful Experiences all over the World	*The Economic Structure*, contrasting the state vs. the market model, with implications on the companies' location, the financial funding and the links between elements.	Castells & Hall (1994:224-235)
	The State Intervention, either as client or strategic coordinator, that arranges the economy at different levels and with different styles.	
	Other elements like universities and financial institutions, besides the social organization, that derives in the creation of synergy between all these elements.	
Argentina	Incubator companies, an attractive, close potential market, universities with strong links to firms, R&D projects, and governmental support to innovation.	Moori-Koening & Yoguel (1998:245-246)
	Companies, entrepreneurs and the society that creates a favorable social environment for innovation.	
	The institutional milieu, the existence of a public-private management center, in addition to the mobility of information which is a fundamental element for the development of the innovative ability.	
Bradford and Massachusetts	Manufacturing facilities, the availability of financial funding, and excellent communication and transportation networking.	Jowitt (1991:224-235)
	The proximity to highly qualified educational institutions, and the availability of highly qualified and low cost labor force.	

Context	Determinants of the Model	Author
Table 3.2 (Cont.)		
European Union	The complementarity on technological quality and the networking between participants and institutions. The commercialization on a grand scale and the investment in R&D are very important for the generation of innovations, in addition to the interaction between users and producers of new technology.	Gambardella & García (1996:19-24)
Norway	Economic activity and innovation, inter-intra regional links, labor force abilities, education and training demand. Technological infrastructure, including links to support organizations, and the public sector's role as support supplier. Strong commercial links and the presence of a large number of companies, particularly in the three main industrial sectors, which imply the creation of clusters. Companies' and other institutions' cooperation to obtain product and process innovation, in addition to the labor force training, cooperation on services and joint technological expectations.	Wiig & Wood (1995:23)
Singapore	Innovation policies, strategic alliances for the cooperation between firms and countries, financial funds, and infrastructure for technological support. Skilled labor force in continuous training, the entrepreneur mind, the importance of the social cohesion and political stability.	Yip (1991:87-101)
United States	Knowledge has a major role, and in this sense the universities and research institutes play a determinant role in the generation of innovations. Innovative environments, and within them are the nature of local relationships, markets, labor force, infrastructure for knowledge, agglomeration economies and support services.	Preer (1992:57-64)

[a] *Gilder (1981) on the entrepreneurs, and Reich (1983) on the Innovative State, are cited by Fach and Grande (1991:44-52).*

Starting from the contrast of references in Table 3.2, we propose the following determinant factors for the innovation policies' spatial impact.

Regional Economic Structure. Huallacháin (1992) argues that the sector specialization of regions and the spatial association between sectors influence the incidence of growth induction, resulting from the introduction of an innovation strategy. This also includes the differences in location economies,[27] and the vertical—forward and backward[28]—and horizontal[29] links of firms within the productive chain. At the firm level, successful innovation is becoming more and more dependent on the capacity of the firm to foster cooperation within the firm (between different levels of organization), and outside the firm (with suppliers and clients, other firms and institutions at the local, regional or national level) (Cooke & Morgan, 1998).

Universities. Implicitly throughout this chapter we have pointed out the importance of universities as determinants for the good functioning of regional innovation strategies. According to Gibson and Smilor (1991), universities function like development poles, because they create, develop and keep new technology for emergent industries.[30] They are an essential element for education and training of the required labor force, in addition to the necessary professions for the economic development through technology.[31]

Local Government. Schmandt (1991) considers that local or state governments are gathering importance with respect to federal government, because of three reasons: the trend towards policies' decentralization; the states wish to take their own policy decisions over important matters; and the states look for opportunities to intervene in markets without assuming great financial and managerial obligations. So local governments operate like catalysts and facilitators, because they can work in close cooperation with universities and the private sector, and this is the reason why they are desirable promoters of innovation strategies.[32]

Entrepreneurs. Bailey (1991) explains that the importance of entrepreneurs emerges from the fact that finally no strategy or governmental effort to foster innovation will have value without them. Therefore, to understand them is necessary to influence their decisions.[33] Smilor (1991) documented their main motivations in starting a new firm based on innovation: self-fulfillment, independence and to find a market niche.

Labor Market. A spatial division of labor exists in different regional scales,[34] which have implications for location. Breheny and McQuaid (1988a) acknowledge three determinant factors for the region's labor advantages: (1) the importance of local availability of various kinds of labor force;[35] (2) the region's ability to attract workers; and (3) the labor cost.

Community. According to Fach and Grande (1991), the community management of innovation combines the benefits and avoids the costs of the other alternative approximations—the "entrepreneur" and the "state"—by balancing competence with cooperation and because it doesn't have excessive bureaucracy and abstract plans. The community links—ethnic, political or religious—set the basis for social cohesion and for the local capacity to connect different actors and create the synergy referred to by Castells and Hall (1994).

Infrastructure. The innovation activities require an advanced infrastructure, particularly in telecommunications and transports. Gillespie, Howells et al. (1987) stress the importance of *Just in Time*, or the acceleration of delivery time, essential for companies' competitiveness and for a quick response to the market. Besides, Gomes, Hoche-Mong et al. (1991) argue that innovation requires a continuous exchange of information and personal interaction in a global level using digital nets, optical fiber and satellite communication.

Financial Funding. Thompson (1991) recognizes that a successful commercial development of innovations finally depends on the availability of funds in all phases of the process. Jensen (1991) typifies the next financial alternatives: friends and family; individual and informal investors, clients and suppliers; professional venture capital;[36] governmental contracts and concessions;[37] mergers; and the initial public offer.

Innovative Environment. Aydalot and Keeble (1988), cited by Preer (1992:59), suggest that local environments are really important as incubators of innovation activities. These environments are like a prism that innovations must cross over, like an interaction net that guides innovation in particular areas, combining the aforementioned determinants,[38] so that the firm is not an isolated innovation phenomenon, but an element supporting industrial development. Within the innovative environment, there are the following elements:

1. *The nature of local relationships.* Refers to the relationship between the main agents within a region, whose interaction leads to a rich information environment.[39]
2. *Markets.* The presence of markets is an important element to innovation developments. However not all innovations emerge pushed by a market, for example in both *Silicon Valley* and *Boston Route 128*, the existence of a market was not an initial condition.[40]
3. *Agglomeration economies.* According to Beeson (1992), they are the result of externalities associated with the agglomeration of activities. Citing Kaldor, this author stresses that their advantages include more productivity and economic growth, through the development of skills and *know-how*; opportunities for the communication of ideas and experience; and opportunities to increase the differentiation of processes and the specialization of human activities. Despite these great advantages, agglomeration economies also have major disadvantages such as environmental degradation, and saturation of labor markets and housing.
4. *Quality of life.* Includes cultural activities, entertainment, amenities, cost of living, environment quality, public security, housing availability, social relations and others.[41]
5. *Legal, regulatory and institutional environment.* Gomes, Hoche-Mong et al. (1991) stress the importance of assuring the free flow in all dimensions: people, products, information and investment, to facilitate innovation process. In addition, intellectual copyright protection is essential to foster innovation.[42]
6. *Temporary dimension.* Castells and Hall (1994) emphasize the importance of long-term planning for innovation strategies, because the benefits will be harvested after a long time, so that keeping consistency in the program is crucial. On the other hand, since these recommendations come from a review of different experiences, the temporary context—a period's particular characteristics—in which an innovation strategy is to be applied must be taken into account.

The central idea behind the determinants is that their presence is not enough. The relevant links between them must exist, so that the innovation strategies could have opportunities for success. As mentioned above, links could be formal mechanisms of cooperation, or interaction of informal social nets.

Cooke and Morgan (1998) distinguish a dual sense in what they call "the institutional milieu", consisting of "both 'hard' institutions (the ensemble of organizations, like government agencies, banks, universities, training industries, trade associations, etc., which have bearing on economic development) and 'soft' institutions (the social norms, habits, and conventions which influence the ways in which people and organizations interact)".

National and global economies are linked to the local innovation system, either with their particular determinants or the whole system. Some examples of these links are the research agreements between universities located in different states or countries, investment flows, interregional and international labor migration and the search for new markets. In general, the success of a local innovation strategy depends greatly on creativity and imagination, which are important requirements to innovate.[43]

Figure 3.1 contains a summary of the major determinants of success for local innovation systems, stressing the dynamic nature of the process in which, as Cooke and Morgan (1998) argue, "the key question is how agents learn in a world of uncertainty". Coupled with uncertainty there is the issue of plausibility of events, so that the development of Silicon Valley and other high tech places could not have emerged in the absence of personal and fortuitous factors.

Figure 3.1
Determinants of Success for Local Innovation Systems

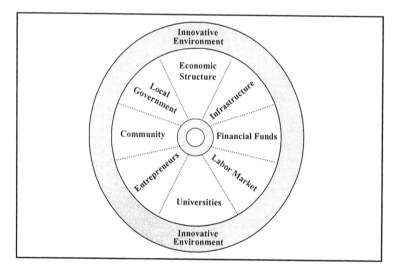

Functional Distinctions of Innovation Sources

After the theoretical review about different models and determinants of local innovation systems, it is necessary to identify the location of knowledge sources. Hippel (1988)[44] examines the functional distinction between the manufacturers', providers' and users' contributions to the innovation process. Furthermore, Pavitt (1984) creates a sector taxonomy that identifies different innovation sources. More specifically, he distinguishes four company types: Supplier-Dominated, Scale Intensive, Specialized Suppliers and Based on Science, whose links are represented in Figure 3.2.

Figure 3.2
Main Technological Links according to Pavitt's Taxonomy

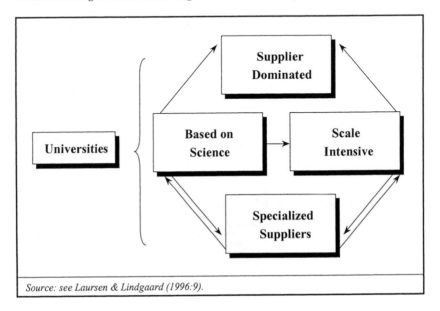

Source: see Laursen & Lindgaard (1996:9).

Supplier Dominated. These kinds of companies are found in traditional sectors like manufacturing, agriculture, construction, financial services, commerce, domestic and professional services. They are small companies and their R&D investment is insignificant. Most of their technology comes from their suppliers.

Scale Intensive. These are heavy materials and assembly companies, which have internal technology sources like R&D and engineering departments. They also present external sources, mainly interactive learning with Specialized Suppliers, and inputs from Based on Science Companies.

Specialized Suppliers. These are small enterprises that produce equipment and control instruments. Their technology sources are design and development, while their external sources come from Based on Science and Scale Intensive Firms.

Based on Science. Generally these are enterprises from the electric/ electronic and chemistry sectors. In both sectors the main technology source is R&D activity, supported by universities. Another technology internal source from these types of companies is their engineering department. Patent protection is used in the chemistry industry. The learning dynamic economies are a hard entrance barrier in these sectors. In this type of enterprise there is a mix between product and process innovation.

As Figure 3.2 shows, there are technological links—acquisition and transfer of technology—between the enterprises that form Pavitt's Taxonomy. These links include information flows. To Laursen and Lindgaard (1996:9), the relative importance of product innovation is large in the cases of Based on Science Enterprises and Specialized Suppliers, while the Scale Intensives and Supplier Dominated take importance in their process improvement. Thus, for the creation of a local innovation system, in addition to the last-cited determinants, it is necessary to concentrate economic activities in the region that, according to Pavitt's Taxonomy, are Based on Science and Specialized Suppliers Firms.

It is now important to focus on formal and informal innovation systems networks (Wiig & Wood, 1995). In this regard, useful data refer to informational sources used by companies, innovation barriers, technological cooperation patterns, support measurements, among others. Machado (1998:614) further classifies innovation technologies of firms (Figure 3.3).

Figure 3.3
Typology of Technological Innovation Patterns of Firms

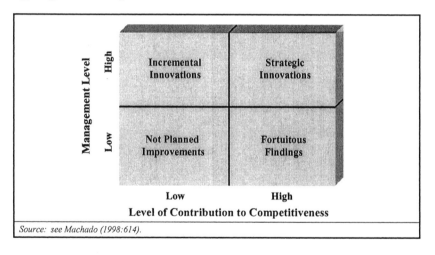

Source: see Machado (1998:614).

The *not planned improvements* emerge from workers' creativity, clients' complaints and others. These improvements require a management-limited technological capacity so that their effects on an enterprise's competitiveness appear to be limited. The *fortuitous findings* are not planned innovations, but they have a great effect in the company, most of them in the short run. These improvements emerge by accident and do not require a high-skilled technological management capacity. *Incremental innovations* constitute the recipe to competitiveness, but not in a sustainable way. *Strategic innovations* are continuous processes in which the firm synthesizes technological and industrial prosperity with a deep knowledge about markets. These types of strategies require technology and market intelligence, willingness to take risks, wide vision and integral strategies.

Accordingly, it is possible to create innovation strategies, not only in high technology specialized regions but in those that Pavitt's Taxonomy considers more attractive to innovation. In this way, innovation does not necessarily equate with high technology. Of course, there still remains creative improvements and fortuitous findings. These results are relevant to design an innovation-based regional development policy, because they emphasize the region's particular conditions, among other things.

CONCLUSION

The transition towards informational economy sets several complex challenges to regions. First, it increases the importance of knowledge and intelligence as basic factors of the system. These elements are key for the access and appropriation of information, which nourishes the dynamics of innovation by allowing technological transformations and modernization of the economic sectors.

Second, it involves a growing interrelationship between several actors and resources. Among them are firms which shape the economic structure of the region, universities, local governments, labor markets, communities, entrepreneurs, infrastructure and financial sources. These elements interact on a local environment, determining the performance of a region as to the generation of innovation. The latter is in turn the motor of growth and productivity of regions.

Third, it increases the integration between regional and global networks. The paradox of the 20th century is that facing the emergence of a global economy, regions and cities are becoming more and more important even though they are less powerful than national governments. Regions have great advantages to compete on a global level, arising from a larger flexibility to adapt to changing conditions that at the national level can only be addressed with lags and very hard efforts.

Starting from the successful experiences of Silicon Valley and Route 128 among others based on high tech industries, a boom of attempts to imitate them began. Despite the fact that these experiences arose endogenously, policy makers saw a possibility to intervene on regional dynamics through the fostering of innovation strategies based on the concentration of research and development for technological change. Sometimes these policies came to be a myth or panacea to solve local problems of all nature,[45] from short-term low growth and unemployment to the depression of an economy based on declining resources.

However, later on two facts were discovered. First, that strategies based on high technology are not viable to all regions. And second, that increasing innovation in regional firms does not necessarily require constructing a research complex such as technopoles or scientific parks.[46] These findings opened new avenues for regional policy conducive to the development of local innovation systems.

In this chapter innovation strategies for regional growth and development have been approached from the perspective of the above findings. So we have intended to characterize the determinants of success of a local innovation system in order to find the basis of the existence of a model. We have not forgotten the lesson of preventing the creation of a formula that does not take account of temporary and spatial contexts. On the contrary, we pretend to foster two critical and complementary conditions for knowledge and innovation: imagination and creativity, and analytical ability.[47]

The main findings of this chapter have to do with recognizing the complexity of applying innovation strategies in regions. Even though the determinants of success of innovation were in fact present in the region, just their presence does not imply a certain success. Recombination, linkage of elements, is crucial for success, not from a static perspective, but providing a dynamic relationship between innovation and the processes that generate it and the need of adaptation to exogenous changes in conditions.[48] Who may predict the exact outcome of a starting enterprise?

That is how we have to recognize that innovation policies—but not because of their objective—are limited *a priori* by the chancy nature of reality. Nevertheless, if a role for regional innovation policy has to be justified, this will be based on the fact that the new technological revolution and economic globalization have brought up the need to reposition regional comparative advantages, expecting to guarantee a long-term competitiveness under the new rules of the informational era.[49] In this sense, regional policy has a limited chance to induce innovation process where some favorable initial conditions are left, but it can create situations which provide strong advantages to regions as the linkage of pertinent elements.[50]

Thus, the understanding of the starting conditions prevailing in a region must be the first task on the agenda of regions that want to implement strategies of innovation. As Wiig and Wood (1995) point out, this effort not only has to be focused on successful experiences, but also to apply the model in other regions wanting to develop.

There are some practical recommendations of great relevance for decision makers suggested by Castells and Hall (1994), and Tatsuno (1991). (1) Constructing a clear strategy, which is compatible to the stage of development of the region. (2) Using study missions to get new ideas. (3) Having a long-term horizon and consistency in the program. (4) Creating synergy or linkage for the long term. (5) Identifying the sources of innovation. (6) Having selectivity on strategies. (7) Providing continuous revision of results.

Some pending questions deal with the role of national government. The political structure—central or federal—and the specific ideologies—conservative, social-democratic or liberal—have different implications for the strategies of innovation that require to be taken into account.[51] Innovation policies, to be effective, need to be framed within countries' development strategies.[52] In addition, further research is required on the relationship between economics and politics, and on the role of the state in the new economic trends.

On the other hand, it has been mentioned that a local innovation system can be developed in several different sectors. This sets new directions for research with respect to the outcomes of sectorally different experiences. For example, to know more about what can be expected of a strategy applied on a traditional economic base, or even on an economy based on declining resources like Silicon Valley.[53]

Finally, the complex nature of innovation makes it unavoidable to approach the matter combining various fields. A focus on theory together with the formulation of regional policy and multidisciplinary analysis are required. This new perspective may advance to contribute the construction of a stronger theoretical framework, necessary not only for the growth of regions but beyond, for a more integral development of human societies.

NOTES

1. From the Foreword by the World Bank's president.

2. According to Moulaert and Swyngedouw (1991), the last paradigm was fordism, or mass production, which came to an end due to some inner contradictions. From a "regulatory" point of view, some of the effects of the fordist crisis are massive unemployment and social disintegration in declining industrial regions; fiscal crisis in cities; ecological crisis and changeable patterns in regional development. Postfordism instead is characterized by flexible production systems that combine flexibility and high productivity.

3. This term was created by Daniel Bell in 1973, meaning that the growth of employment in services has been produced at the expense of employment in goods production. For a detailed review of empirical evidence and theory about this topic, see Hall (1990).

4. Brotchie, Hall and Newton (1987:444) characterized the effects of transition toward an informational society on industrial and tertiary sectors, with respect to employment, production, productivity, costs, market participation and uses of information technologies.

5. Arthur D. Little—cited by Boksjo and Delin (1991)—indicates that innovation is a way of living related to products, technologies, processes, marketing, distribution methods, financing, management and the structure that shapes industrial competition and segmentation. Fach and Grande (1991) mention that innovation arises at various levels, (1) intrafirm, in the productive process; (2) interfirm, through production networks and subcontracting relations; (3) on union structures; (4) at political and legal levels; and (5) in social institutions such as family, in the relation between work and private life.

6. Cited by OECD (1998:63).

7. An analysis of the sources and effects of agglomeration economies on regional income and productivity, is presented in Beeson (1992).

8. See Hilpert (1991a:9-12) for a discussion on endogenous factors for regional growth.

9. A documentation elaborated by Castells and Hall (1994) about these two experiences points out that chancy events had a major incidence on their success. Both of them were fostered initially by the efforts of researchers who shaped the link between university and entrepreneurs; and by the great demand of technology of the United States

Department of Defense. However, they emerged in regions with very different previous economic structures (Santa Clara was basically rural, while Boston was already industrialized), and both developed very distinct organizational styles (horizontal, cooperative and with highly mobile labor in Silicon Valley; vertical and focused on "loyalty" in Route 128). Dorfman (1983) also discusses the genesis of these two developments and underlines the personal involvement of Frederick Terman and his idea to develop a research park on the Stanford University campus in 1954. The influence of Kenneth Olsen in shaping the Route 128 effect is also stressed. Though these personal reasons could not necessarily be seen as accidents, Dorfman also considers that had these people, and those around them, not settled where they did, perhaps these developments could not have taken place. Something that seems clearer is that their efforts changed the face of these regions.

10. Given the complexity of the concept and the difficulty to make it operative, Erickson (1994) recommends that researchers clarify what they mean by the term and in what context they use it, since alternative definitions may lead to several scenarios of economic performance.

11. Fach and Grande (1991). The technological or engineering bias in the definition of innovation must be avoided.

12. Polèse (1998:95) defines indivisibilities as objects that can not be divided into smaller elements.

13. Jowitt (1991:129) notices there are not enough commercial ideas, scientists, entrepreneurs and venture capital. Furthermore, Hilpert (1991a), Castells and Hall (1994) and Smilor (1991) stress the importance of certain "initial conditions" for regional development through innovation, that would hardly be created artificially by government. Erickson (1994) also recognizes a limited role for government, particularly at local and regional levels; besides, he questions if companies really have the capacity to envisage the potential for the formation of urban agglomerations based on technology, like Silicon Valley and Route 128.

14. Preston (1988), Macdonald (1988) and Schmandt (1991) draw the consequences on employment and economic structure; while Goldstein and Luger (1991) indicate advantages and disadvantages of economic development through innovation. Norman (1993) pays attention to the impacts upon lifestyle and social structure of communities. Encel (1990) explores the effects on wealth distribution; while Pym (1990) and Ironmonger (1990) focus on repercussions over informal economy and domestic economy.

15. Erickson (1994) suggests the need to integrate innovation as a crucial element in production geography and regional economic change, emphasizing the global nature of companies' strategic decisions with respect to innovation.

16. Zysman (1987) documented three technical and political approaches for achieving growth: state-oriented, market-oriented and negotiations-oriented; discussion focuses on the ability of governments to intervene selectively and accomplish industrial policy objectives. On the other hand, Hilpert (1991a), Hilpert & Ruffieux (1991), Jowitt (1991) and Hilpert (1991b) conclude that innovation could become a myth or panacea in the mind of policy makers to solve economic troubles and guarantee regional growth, leading to wrong decisions based on mistaken perceptions and expectations.

17. An example is provided by Granovetter (1985), who tries to discover to which extent economic action is determined by the structure of social relationships in modern industrial societies.

18. Brotchie, Hall and Newton (1987)—cited by Preer (1992:4)—argue that the second phase of technological transformation will be a knowledge revolution, in which

human reason and knowledge will be automated. Thus a further development of artificial intelligence and its applications must be required.

19.   Laffitte (1988), cited by Preer (1992:14).

20.   Tatsuno (1986), cited by Bailey (1991:82). For a comprehensive review of innovation strategies in Japan, see Tatsuno (1991).

21.   Preer (1992:32) points that technopoles as a development policy have appeared in the United States as a result of the World War II; Silicon Valley being the first modern technopolis.

22.   Preer (1992:55) defines technopole as a region that propulsively and sustainably generates economic activity through the creation and commercialization of new knowledge.

23.   Moori-Koening and Yoguel (1998:642). Technopoles are just a single element of a regional strategy for innovation, based on interfirm cooperation; the linkages among entrepreneurs and institutions; and public-private complementation—all of them generating productivity and competitiveness.

24.   See footnote no. 13.

25.   Gomes, Hoche-Mong, et al. (1991) defined the Multifunctional Polis Model. They identified a core applicable everywhere that grasps an intelligent complex of regional factors linked to a global system.

26.   The understanding of the innovation process, from local to global scale, could be benefited from learning just if different experiences (empirical evidence) are taken into account so that the practical lessons could be more effective.

27.   Goldstein and Luger (1991) suggest that great urban agglomerations and small metropolitan areas are the two kinds of local economies which can be successful for the innovation system's location.

28.   Hilpert and Ruffieux (1991) notice that these links between the firm and the productive chain depend also on the staff that founds the firm, resulting in different relations with the established industrial structure and the universities.

29.   Horizontal links can arise from informal nets or by formal cooperation agreements between companies. On formal cooperation through strategic alliances, see Duysters (1996).

30.   Kozmetsky (1991) warns that the innovation process is chaotic and dispersed, because many things could be made at the same time and in different places; this complicates attempts to lead innovations into trading. In this context, Botkin (1991) stresses that the university role is one of first order.

31.   Bozzo, Gibson, Sabatelli and Smilor (1991:71).

32.   Berra and Gastaldo (1991) argue that local innovation strategies contribute to regional development, making more attractive the region for location. On the other hand, Goldstein and Luger (1991) document some kinds of governmental support to innovative companies through subsidies that diminish the business costs, such as land, buildings, infrastructure, taxes, education and training programs and temporary assistance programs.

33.   Botkin (1991) explains that the nature of entrepreneurs is changing, while their image in the policy makers' minds is remaining static, so they receive incentives that do not satisfy them. To get a better understanding of who is an entrepreneur, Bailey (1991:76-80) offers a characterization of his profile.

34.   See Morgan and Sayer (1988) and Henderson and Scott (1988) who examine some sector patterns of the spatial division of labor, starting from the international empirical evidence.

35.   Managers; professional and scientific staff; office staff; qualified labor and supervisors; semi- and not-qualified labor (Breheny & McQuaid, 1988a:334).

36.   For a venture capital historic and regional perspective in the United States, see Florida and Smith (1992).

37.   In Silicon Valley and Boston Route 128, the contracts of the Defense Department had a major role. Markusen and Yudken (1992) present research on the difficulties for the Pentagon's supplier industries in facing the transition toward peaceful times at the Cold War's end.

38.   Saxenian (1994) points out that the agglomeration of elements is a self-reinforcing, accumulative process. Nevertheless, just the presence of some elements is not what promotes these dynamics, but the links between them.

39.   Aydalot and Keeble (1988:9) cited by Preer (1992:59) sketch the distinctive relationships between big firms and subcontractors, manufacturing and service companies, the government and the academy, business and community groups, among others. These relationships can be formal or informal.

40.   Preer (1992:60) suggests that lately, markets are required to maintain the technopolis' growth, and that the stability of markets could determine the prosperity of high tech regions.

41.   Preer (1992:61) shows that quality of life does not create a successful innovation strategy, but interacts with other factors for its development, participating in the innovative environment and the entrepreneur firms. The perspectives on quality of life for society framed in the new technological revolution are speculated by Meier (1987) and Gappert (1987).

42.   Norman (1993) explains that the promotion of innovation is required to solve the conflict between the free flow of ideas and the economic incentives to invest on innovation.

43.   Botskjo and Delin (1991:235) find that a major part of innovation is "to break the rules" and to dare to go beyond the conventional knowledge.

44.   Cited by Laursen and Lindgaard (1996:8).

45.   We can also use the term "ideological addiction", referred by Fuentes (1997), to designate "the perversion of logic" and "the blind faith" for the sake of defending a model.

46.   See Goldstein and Luger (1991:149-151).

47.   See Sanchez (1995:72-75).

48.   This linkage between innovation, regions and firms is what Cooke and Morgan (1998) call the *Associational Economy.*

49.   This is how the challenge of transformation has been understood in Japan. See Tatsuno (1991).

50.   Hilpert (1991a:28-32) reviewed the subject of regional industrial modernization and the limits for regional policies, highlighting some implications for regional disparities. This matter of the initial conditions is not very well developed by the author—say what they are—but it could be understood as a concern about the context or starting point of each particular experience.

51.   Alburquerque (1997) argues that for the Latin American experience, local innovation policies as part of a broader policy scheme are yet to be dealt with in the frame of the process of social and institutional change now under way, given the centralist sector and aggregate profile of the predominant macroeconomic approaches.

52.   This conclusion is drawn from the Latin American context (Alburquerque, 1997) and from the international experience (OECD, 1998).

53.   Castells and Hall (1994) referred that Santa Clara County, where Silicon Valley is located, was until the decade of 1950 basically a rural area.

REFERENCES

Alburquerque, F. 1997, Desarrollo Económico Local y Distribución del Progreso Técnico: Una respuesta a las exigencias del ajuste estructural, *Cuadernos del ILPES*, no. 43, Comisión Económica para América Latina y el Caribe, Santiago de Chile.

Aydabt, P. & Keeble, D. 1988, High Technology Industry and Innovative Environments in Europe: An Overview, in *High Technology Industry and Innovative Environments: The European Experience*, eds. P. Aydabt & D. Keeble, pp. 1-21. London: Routledge.

Bailey, J.E. 1991, The Entrepreneurial Spirit and Technology Diffusion: An Australian Perspective, in *Technology Companies and Global Markets: Programs, Policies, and Strategies to Accelerate Innovation and Entrepreneurship*, ed. D.V. Gibson, pp. 75-86. Savage, MD: Rowman & Littlefield.

Beeson, P.E. 1992, Agglomeration Economies and Productivity Growth, in *Sources of Metropolitan Growth*, eds. Edwin S. Mills & John F. MacDonald, pp. 19-35. New Brunswick: Rutgers.

Berra, M. & Gastaldo, P. 1991, Science Parks and Local Innovation Policies in Italy, in *Regional Innovation and Descentralization: High Tech Industry and Government Policy*, ed. U. Hilpert, pp. 89-111. London: Routledge.

Boksjo, L. & Delin, G. 1991, Fostering Innovation and Corporate Entrepreneurs: Implications for Organizational Policy and Action, in *Technology Companies and Global Markets: Programs, Policies, and Strategies to Accelerate Innovation and Entrepreneurship*, ed. D.V. Gibson, pp. 235-244. Savage, MD: Rowman & Littlefield.

Botkin, J.W. 1991, Innovation and Entrepreneurship: Future Developments in the U.S. and World Economy, in *Technology Companies and Global Markets: Programs, Policies, and Strategies to Accelerate Innovation and Entrepreneurship*, ed. D.V. Gibson, pp. 147-156. Savage, MD: Rowman & Littlefield.

Bozzo, U., Gibson, D., Sabatelli, R. & Smilor, R.W. 1991, Socioeconomic Development Though Technology Transfer: Technopolis Novus Ortus, in *University Spin-Off-Companies*, eds. A.M. Brett, D.V. Gibson and R. W. Smilor, pp. 71-82. Savage, MD: Rowman & Littlefield.

Breheny, M.J. & McQuaid, R. 1988a, H.T.U.K.: The Development of the United Kingdom's Major Centre of High Technology Industry, in *The Development of High Technology Industries: An International Survey*, eds. M.J. Breheny and R. McQuaid, pp. 297-354. London: Routledge.

Breheny, M.J. & McQuaid, R. 1988b, Introduction, in *The Development of High Technology Industries: An International Survey*, eds. M.J. Breheny & R. McQuaid, pp. 1-9. London: Routledge.

Bronson, P. 1999, *The Nudist on the Late Shift and Other True Tales of Silicon Valley*. New York: Random House.

Brotchie, H., Hall, P. & Newton, P.W. 1987, The Transition to an Information Society, in *The Spatial Impact of Technological Change*, eds. J.F. Brotchie, P. Hall & P.W. Newton, pp. 435-451. New York: Croom Helm.

Castells, M. & Hall, P. 1994, *Technopoles of the World: The Making of Twenty-First-Century Industrial Complexes*. London: Routledge.

CEC. 1991, Four Motors for Europe. An analysis of cross-regional cooperation, *Fast Occasional Paper*, no. 241, vol. 17.

Cooke, P. & Morgan, K. 1998, *The Associational Economy: Firms, Regions, and Innovations*. Oxford/New York: Oxford University Press.

Duysters, G. 1996, *The Dynamics of Technical Innovation: The Evolution and Development of Information Technology*. Cheltenham/Brookfield: Edward Elgar.

Dorfman, N.S. 1983, Route 128: The development of a regional high technology economy, *Research Policy*, vol. 12, pp. 299-316.

Encel, S. 1990, Perspectives on Post-Industrial Society: An Australian Viewpoint, in *The Spatial Impact of Technological Change*, eds. J.F. Brotchie, P. Hall & P.W. Newton, pp. 18-35. London: Routledge.

Erickson, R.A. 1994, Technology, Industrial Restructuring and Regional Development, *Growth and Change*, vol. 25, pp. 353-379.

Fach, W. & Grande, E. 1991, Space and Modernity: On the Regionalization of Innovation Management, in *Regional Innovation and Descentralization: High Tech Industry and Government Policy*, ed. U. Hilpert, pp. 35-58. London: Routledge.

Florida, R. & Smith, D.F. Jr. 1992, Venture Capital's Role in Economic Development: An Empirical Analysis, in *Sources of Metropolitan Growth*, eds. Edwin S. Mills & John F. MacDonald, pp. 183-209. New Brunswick: Rutgers.

Friedman, J. 1966, *Regional Development Policy: A Case Study of Venezuela*. Cambridge, MA: MIT Press.

Fuentes, C. 1997, *Por un Progreso Incluyente*. Mexico City: Instituto de Estudios Educativos y Sindicales de América.

Gambardella, A. & García, W. 1996, European Research Funding and Regional Technological Capabilities, *Network Composition Analysis*. June.

Gappert, G. 1987, Urban Issues in an Advanced Industrial Society, in *The Spatial Impact of Technological Change*, eds. J.F. Brotchie, P. Hall & P.W. Newton, pp. 424-434. New York: Croom Helm.

Gibbs, D.C. 1984, The Influence of Investment Incentives on Technological Change, *Area*, vol. 16, pp. 115-120.

Gibson, D. & Smilor, R.W. 1991, The Role of the Research University in Creating and Sustaining the U.S. Technopolis, in *University Spin-off Companies*, eds. A. M. Brett, D.V. Gibson & R. W. Smilor, pp. 31-70. Savage, MD: Rowman & Littlefield.

Gilder, G. 1981, *Wealth and Poverty*. New York: Basic Books.

Gillespie, A., Howells, J., Williams, H. & Thwaites, A. 1987, Competition, Internationalisation and the Regions: The Example of the Information Technology Production Industries in Europe, in *The Development of High Technology Industries: An International Survey*, eds. M.J. Breheny & R. McQuaid, pp. 113-142. London: Routledge.

Godddard, J.B. 1983, Industrial Innovation and Regional Economic Development in Great Britain, in Spatial Analysis, *Industry and the Industrial Environment, Vol. 3 Regional Economies and Industrial Systems*, eds. F.E.I. Hamilton and G.J.R. Linge, pp. 255-277. Chichester: John Wiley & Sons.

Goldstein, H.A. & Luger, M.I. 1991, Science/Technology Parks and Regional Development: Prospects for the United States, in *Regional Innovation and Descentralization: High Tech Industry and Government Policy*, ed. U. Hilpert, pp. 133-153. London: Routledge.

Gomes, S.L., Hoche-Mong, E., Hoche-Mong, R., Ivanek I. & Wakelin, M. 1991, Global Factors in the Successful Implementation of Technology-Driven Development Strategies, in *Technology Companies and Global Markets: Programs, Policies, and Strategies to Accelerate Innovation and Entrepreneurship*, ed. D.V. Gibson, pp. 273-289. Savage, MD: Rowman & Littlefield.

Granovetter, M. 1985, Economic Action and Social Structure: The Problem of Embeddedness, *American Journal of Sociology*, vol. 91, no. 3, pp. 481-510.

Hall, P. 1990, The Geography of the Post-Industrial Economy, in *The Spatial Impact of Technological Change*, eds. J.F. Brotchie, P. Hall & P.W. Newton, pp. 3-17. London: Routledge.

Harris, R.I.D. 1988, Technological Change and Regional Development in the U.K.: Evidence from the SPRU Database on Innovations, *Regional Studies*, vol. 22, pp. 361-374.

Henderson, J. & Scott, A.J. 1988, The Growth and Internationalisation of the American Semiconductor Industry: Labour Processes and the Changing Spatial Organization of Production, in *The Development of High Technology Industries: An International Survey*, eds. M.J. Breheny & R. McQuaid, pp. 37-79. London: Routledge.

Hilpert, U. 1991a, Regional Policy in the Process of Industrial Modernization: The Descentralization of Innovation by Regionalization of High Tech?, in *Regional Innovation and Descentralization: High Tech Industry and Government Policy*, ed. U. Hilpert, pp. 3-34. London: Routledge.

Hilpert, U. 1991b, The Optimization of Political Approaches to Innovation: Some Comparative Conclusions on Trends for Regionalization, in *Regional Innovation and Descentralization: High Tech Industry and Government Policy*, ed. U. Hilpert, pp. 291-302. London: Routledge.

Hilpert, U. & Ruffieux, B. 1991, Innovation, Politics and Regional Development: Technology Parks and Regional Participation in High Tech in France and West Germany, in *Regional Innovation and Descentralization: High Tech Industry and Government Policy*, ed. U. Hilpert, pp. 61-87. London: Routledge.

Huallacháin, B.Ó. 1992, Economic Structure and Growth of Metropolitan Areas, in *Sources of Metropolitan Growth*, eds. Edwin S. Mills & John F. McDonald, pp. 51-85. New Brunswick: Rutgers.

Hippel, E. 1988, *The Sources of Innovation*. New York: Oxford University Press.

Ironmonger, D. 1990, The Impact of Technology on the Household Economy, in *The Spatial Impact of Technological Change*, eds. J.F. Brotchie, P. Hall & P.W. Newton, pp. 50-60. London: Routledge.

Jensen, J.U. 1991, Venture Capital Needs and Sources, in *Technology Companies and Global Markets: Programs, Policies, and Strategies to Accelerate Innovation and Entrepreneurship*, ed. D.V. Gibson, pp. 177-188. Savage, MD: Rowman & Littlefield.

Jowitt, A. 1991, Science Parks, Academic Research and Economic Regeneration: Bradford and Massachusetts in Comparison, in *Regional Innovation and Descentralization: High Tech Industry and Government Policy*, ed. U. Hilpert, pp. 113-131. London: Routledge.

Kozmetsky, G. 1991, The Challenge of Technology Innovation: The New Globally Competitive Era, in *Technology Companies and Global Markets: Programs, Policies, and Strategies to Accelerate Innovation and Entrepreneurship*, ed. D.V. Gibson, pp. 3-15. Savage, MD: Rowman & Littlefield.

Kumn, J. & Nimmervoll, N. 1988, *Technology Parks and other Real-Estate Based Support Strategies for Business*, Paper presented at Small Enterprise Association of Australia and New Zealand Annual Conference, June 23-25.

Laffitte, P. 1988, Sophia-Antipolis and the Movement South in Europe, in *Creating the Technopolis: Linking Technology Commercialization and Economic Development*, eds. R.W. Smilor, G. Kozmetsky & D. Gibson, pp. 91-95. Cambridge, MA: Ballinger.

Laursen, K. & Lindgaard, J. 1996, *The Creation, Distribution and Use of Knowledge—A Pilot Study of Danish Innovation System*. Copenhagen: Danish Agency for Trade and Industry.

Macdonald, S. 1988, High Technology Industry in Australia: A Matter of Policy, in *The Development of High Technology Industries: An International Survey*, eds. M.J. Breheny & R. McQuaid, pp. 223-261. London: Routledge.

Machado, F. 1998, Administracion eficiente de la innovación tecnológica en los países en desarrollo, *Comercio Exterior*, vol. 48, no. 48, pp. 607-616.

Markusen, A. & Yudken, J. 1992, *Dismantling the Cold War Economy*. New York: Basic Books.

Meier, R.L. 1987, Thinking Beyond Post-Industrial: The Social Perspectives, in *The Spatial Impact of Technological Change*, eds. J.F. Brotchie, P. Hall & P.W. Newton, pp. 407-423. London: Routledge.

Moori-Koening & Yoguel, G. 1998, Capacidades innovadoras en un medio de escaso desarrollo del sistema local de innovación, *Comercio Exterior*, vol. 48, no. 48, pp. 642-662.

Morgan, K. & Sayer, A. 1988, High Technology Industry and the International Division of Labour: The Case of Electronics, in *The Development of High Technology Industries: An International Survey*, eds. M.J. Breheny & R. McQuaid, pp. 10-36. London: Routledge.

Moulaert, F. & Swyngedouw, E. 1991, Regional Development and the Geography of the Flexible Production System: Theoretical Arguments and Empirical Evidence, in *Regional Innovation and Descentralization: High Tech Industry and Government Policy*, ed. U. Hilpert, pp. 239-265. London: Routledge.

Norman, A.L. 1993, *Informational Society: An Economic Theory of Discovery, Invention and Innovation*. Boston/Dordrecht/London: Kluwer.

OECD. 1998, *Technology, Productivity and Job Creation: Best Policy Practices*. Paris: Organization for Economic Cooperation and Development.

OECD. 1999, Boosting Innovation—The Cluster Approach, *OECD Proceedings*. Paris: Organization for Economic Cooperation and Development.

Pavitt, K. 1984, Sectoral Patterns of Technical Change: towards a Taxonomy and a Theory, *Research Policy*, no. 6.

Polèse, M. 1998, *Economía Urbana y Regional: Introducción a la Relación entre Territorio y Desarrollo*. Cartago: Libro Universitario Regional/BUAP/GIM.

Preer, R. 1992, *The Emergence of Technopolis: Knowledge-Intensive Technologies and Regional Development*. Westport, CT: Praeger.

Preston, P. 1988, Technology Waves and the Future Sources of Employment and Wealth Creation in Britain, in *The Development of High Technology Industries: An International Survey*, eds. M.J. Breheny & R. McQuaid, pp. 80-112. London: Routledge.

Pym, D. 1990, The Informal Sector: On the Prospects of Doing Things Together, in *The Spatial Impact of Technological Change*, eds. J.F. Brotchie, P. Hall & P.W. Newton, pp. 36-49. London: Routledge.

Reich, R.B. 1983, *The Next American Frontier*. New York: Times Books.

Sánchez P., R. 1995, *Enseñar a Investigar: Una Didáctica Nueva de la Investigación en Ciencias Sociales y Humanidades*. Coyoacán: UNAM/ANUIES.

Saxenian, A. 1994, Lessons from Silicon Valley, *Technology Review*, July, pp. 42-51.

Schmandt, J. 1991, Regional Technology Policy: A New Role for the American States, in *Regional Innovation and Descentralization: High Tech Industry and Government Policy*, ed. U. Hilpert, pp. 157-176. London: Routledge.

Smilor, R.W. 1991, The Chaos of the Entrepreneurial Process: Patterns and Policy Implications, in *Technology Companies and Global Markets: Programs, Policies, and Strategies to Accelerate Innovation and Entrepreneurship*, ed. D.V. Gibson, pp. 105-122. Savage, MD: Rowman & Littlefield.

Tatsuno, S. 1986, *The Technopolis Strategy*. Reading, MA: Addison-Wesley.

Tatsuno, S. 1991, Building the Japanese Techno-State: The Regionalization of Japanese High Tech Industrial Policies, in *Regional Innovation and Descentralization: High Tech Industry and Government Policy*, ed. U. Hilpert, pp. 219-235. London: Routledge.

Thompson, W.D. 1991, Combining the Venture Capitalists and Technical Innovator, in *Technology Companies and Global Markets: Programs, Policies, and Strategies to Accelerate Innovation and Entrepreneurship*, ed. D.V. Gibson, pp. 207-218. Savage, MD: Rowman & Littlefield.

UNDP. 1999. *Human Development Report 1999*. New York: Oxford University Press for the United Nations Development Program.

Weinberg, M.L. and M.E. Mazey. 1988, Government-University-Industry Partnerships in Technology Development: a case study, *Technovation*, vol. 7, pp. 131-142.

Wiig, H. & Wood, M. 1995, *What Comprises a Regional Innovation System? An Empirical Study*. Oslo: Studies in Technology, Innovation and Economic Policy.

World Bank. 1999, *World Development Report 1998/99*. New York: Oxford University Press for the World Bank.

Yip, V.F.S. 1991, The Asian Challenge: A Singapore Perspective, in *Technology Companies and Global Markets: Programs, Policies, and Strategies to Accelerate Innovation and Entrepreneurship*, ed. D.V. Gibson, pp. 87-101. Savage, MD: Rowman & Littlefield.

Zysman, J. 1987, *Governments, Markets and Growth: Financial Systems and the Politics of Industrial Change*. Ithaca/London: Cornell University Press.

4

Characteristics of Innovation in a Non-Metropolitan Area: The Okanagan Valley of British Columbia

J. Adam Holbrook and Lindsay P. Hughes

INTRODUCTION

Governments in most jurisdictions support, in one way or another, S&T programs in the firm belief that investments in S&T have a positive, if indefinable, effect on economic growth. The first theoretical constructs of the benefits of S&T knowledge focused on the "linear" model of innovation, where an investment in R&D would eventually lead to wealth creation or a social benefit. There were intervening steps where the technologies resulting from R&D were developed and commercialized, but the model suggested that resources expended on R&D would inevitably result in some good at the end of the chain, and that incremental resources would result in incremental benefits.

Current theories take a much wider view of the innovative process, and recognize that R&D is only one of several inputs to wealth generation and social development. In a developing economy, the actual level of R&D activities may be quite low, but the level of investment in related science activities may be substantial. The United Nations Educational, Scientific and Cultural Organization (UNESCO) in its definition of S&T includes not only R&D but also national investments in S&T support services (such as libraries and statistical agencies) as well as investments in scientific and technical education.

Similarly statistics on industrial investment in R&D often miss other innovative activities particularly in those industries that are not R&D intensive. Firms profit from the larger pool of external knowledge by absorbing and adopting some of it to their own needs; the source can be a competitor, another industry, government, universities or another country. Just as it is important to measure physical capital stocks, it is important to measure and follow the stocks of knowledge and technological capital.

These issues have been addressed by the Organization for Economic Cooperation and Development in a recent report (OECD, 1996b), which concluded that investments in technology embedded in capital equipment, whether imported or produced domestically, were equally important as investments in R&D and should be included in assessments of the knowledge intensity of nations. In addition, the authors noted that measuring these investments in technology (as opposed to investments in domestic R&D programs) was particularly important in small industrialized nations and in developing nations.

THE POLICY IMPLICATIONS OF ANALYSES OF NATIONAL SYSTEMS OF INNOVATION

It is convenient, when analyzing the stocks and flows of knowledge in an economy, to describe the process of innovation in an economy as a system. Chris Freeman (1968) has noted:

> The rate of technological change in any country and the effectiveness of companies in world competition in international trade in goods and services, does not depend simply on the scale of their R&D...It depends on the way in which the available resources are managed and organized, both at the enterprise and national level. The national system of innovation may enable a country with limited resources...to make progress through appropriate combination of imported technology and local adaptation and improvement.

A national system of innovation (NSI) can be characterized as follows:

- Firms are part of a network of public- and private-sector institutions whose activities and interactions initiate, import, modify and diffuse new technologies.
- An NSI consists of linkages (both formal and informal) between institutions.
- An NSI includes flows of intellectual resources between institutions.
- Analysis of NSIs emphasizes learning as a key economic resource and that geography and location still matter.

The emphasis on institutions is the cornerstone of NSI analysis. Charles Edquist (1997), in the introduction to his recent book on innovation, analyzes the literature on NSI, and notes that all of the NSI approaches emphasize the role of institutions: "Institutions are of crucial importance for the innovative process....It is therefore a great strength of the systems of innovation approach that 'institutions' are central in all versions of it."

Thus, in analyzing NSIs, it is necessary to be able to measure the stocks and flows of knowledge among institutions, both public and private, and if necessary to develop indicators appropriate to this task. Innovation does not necessarily occur only in the private sector, but there is, as yet, no agreement on procedures for the assessment and quantification of innovation in the public sector.

The OECD (1997) has concluded that the study of NSI offers new rationales for government technology policies. Government policies in the past have focussed on *market failures*; studies of NSI make it possible to study *systemic* failures. The analysis of NSIs enables policy makers to identify successes and failures, choke points and areas of overcapacity.

The Government of Canada (1997) in a speech from the throne set the following as a policy objective: "The Government will explore innovative policies and measures that give particular attention to increasing opportunity for Canadians in rural communities. It will adapt its programs to reflect the social and economic realities of rural Canada. Further the Government will redouble its efforts to ensue that rural communities and all regions of Canada share in the economic benefits of the global knowledge-based economy."

This statement sets out the need to understand how innovation works in non-metropolitan areas and how government policies can overcome the reduced levels of knowledge-based infrastructure in areas outside large cities. It is the opposite of the analysis of "poles" of innovation: what happens in those vast spaces between the poles? In comparing case studies of regional systems of innovation in Canada and Europe, Acs et al. (1996) have noted that there has been a lag in the recognition of the bottom-up dynamics of innovation in Canada compared to what may be observed in Europe. They found:

- The way in which relationships develop between private concerns and both the community and the public actors, and the way in which "enabling agencies" foster collaboration.
- The importance of leadership—what enables the complex interinstitutional and intersectoral partnerships to develop and become operational—it appears the ability of communities to shape their future depends more on social than on technological processes (see Davis, 1991).
- The great fragility of many local systems of innovation because they are "weakly institutionalized."

Current systems of S&T and innovation indicators have been developed primarily by and for large complex national economies. Although smaller economies may not have extensive systems of innovation, they too use S&T directly in support of their specific economic and social objectives. In analyzing national systems of innovation, it may be easier to aggregate upward from a series of regional systems of innovation to the national level than to try to develop an understanding of a complex national system from the top-down.

There have been many studies of regional industrial clusters (or "poles") and comparisons of regional, or subnational, innovative performance. A recent review of these concepts, in the Canadian context, has been presented in "Local and Regional Systems of Innovation" (de la Mothe, 1998). In Canada, regional systems of innovation are the building blocks of the national system; a national network, the Innovation Systems Research Network (ISRN), has been set up to study this[1]. The network is itself composed of five regional research networks which correspond to the economic and social regions of the country.

A PILOT STUDY ON INNOVATION IN SMALL ECONOMIES

British Columbia is an ideal laboratory for experiments in the measurement of innovation. The economy is simple, with one large metropolitan area, where most of the innovative firms are located, supported by a hinterland whose primary outputs are in the natural resources sector. BC is a relatively separate economic and geographic region, so that external influences in the acquisition and adoption of technology are readily noticeable. Thus (in theory) economic measurements in BC should be relatively well-behaved and predictable.

Within BC, the Okanagan Valley forms a distinct economic subregion. With a population of about 140,000 centered on the city of Kelowna, the region consists of a long, narrow, fertile valley surrounded by the Rocky Mountains. Its main economic activities are agricultural (fruit and wine), wood products and tourism. The region is about 400 km. from Vancouver (about one hour by air). According to BC Stats (1997) the region has 307 high tech-based establishments, approximately 6% of the provincial total. Of these, 238 are service based and 69 are manufacturers.

According to survey work carried out by de Wit and Lipsett in 1994, while Okanagan companies were on average as likely to be innovative as other firms in BC (which is of course heavily biased by the concentration of high tech firms in the Greater Vancouver/Lower Mainland area), they were substantially less likely to have accessed the Scientific Research and Experimental Development (SRED) tax credit program. Only 21% of Okanagan firms had used the program compared to 35% of firms in the two metropolitan areas of BC (Vancouver and Victoria) (de Wit and Lipsett, 1995).

The first element in this study was to carry out a survey of technological innovation in the area. A short questionnaire for use with BC enterprises had been prepared for the project. The results from a survey using this questionnaire in the Lower Mainland area have been reported by Holbrook and Hughes (1998). The questionnaire was not intended to cover all aspects of technological innovation identified in the OECD "Oslo Manual" (OECD, 1996a) but it had to conform to the main points in the OECD standard. To ensure a reasonable response rate, the questionnaire had to be short (no more than one page, printed on both sides) so that it would be user friendly, take little managerial time to complete, be comprehensible to a small technology-based entrepreneur located in BC and be faxable to expedite its return.

THE OKANAGAN SURVEY

Sample

As in the Lower Mainland study, the sample was drawn from two industrial sectoral groups, "high technology" and "policy" sectors. For the "high tech" sectors, the sample was drawn from a list of firms provided by the Science Council of British Columbia. This list was compiled in the fall of 1996, and was a comprehensive listing of firms falling into the category of "high technology" as defined by BC Stats. All firms from this list of more than ten employees were included in the sample. The sample for the "policy" sector was drawn from the following: "agricultural products and food processing" (which included wines and spirits), "forest and related products" and "construction" from the 1997 BC Manufacturer's Directory database provided by BC Stats. Standard 1990 SICs were used.

Conducting the Survey

The survey of the Okanagan was conducted in June and July 1997. As in the Lower Mainland study, firms were first contacted by telephone, to solicit their participation and to identify the target recipient in the firm, again the CFO. Unless the recipient requested otherwise, the survey package was faxed to the firm, along with two covering letters, one from the Centre for Policy Research on Science and Technology (CPROST) and one from the Central Okanagan Regional Development office. Firms from whom no package had been received within two weeks were recontacted by telephone. These follow-up calls acted as reminders to the respondents, but also gave the researcher an opportunity to get feedback on the actual survey. Respondents' comments regarding the survey included:

- the questions were good
- the survey was short and they did not mind filling it out
- they had to use their own interpretation on some of the questions
- the survey was "painless" to complete
- a very nonintrusive questionnaire

FINDINGS

In all, 204 surveys were sent to firms in the Okanagan. Of these, 111 were completed and returned, giving an overall response rate of 54%. Firms ranged in size from 10 to 500 employees, with the majority, 82%, having fewer than 50 employees. The firms also tended to be regional in focus, with 61% of those responding reporting less than 40% of their sales to be outside the province.

Innovativeness

A majority of the firms in the Okanagan believed that they were innovative; 86% (n = 95) of firms reported having introduced a new product in the past five years, with 65% (n = 62) of these firms reporting that their product was unique. By the "New & Unique" filter, therefore, 56% of the firms responding to the survey were innovative.

The differences between high technology firms and those in the Okanagan were much more pronounced than in the Lower Mainland. In the policy sectors, 50% of firms were innovative, while 74% of high tech firms reported that their new products were unique in their market.

Firms that had introduced new products and/or processes (unique or not) reported similar impacts as firms in the Lower Mainland. The new products/processes had positive effects on profitability (87%), cash flow (70%), market share (75%) and competitiveness (85%). Impacts were less clear with respect to productivity (48% no effect, 45% positive), and quality of service (46% no effect, 52% positive), while respondents strongly stated that innovation had no effect on labour relations (81%).

Figure 4.1
Sources of Innovation, by Sector and Innovativeness

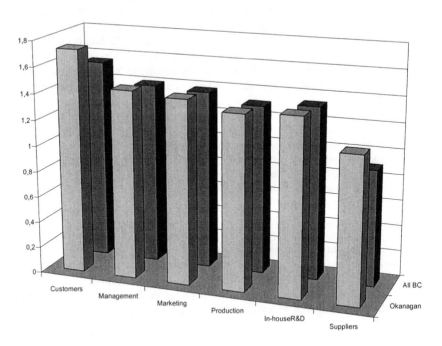

Sources of Innovation

A value index of innovation was developed for the Lower Mainland results. It is simply the arithmetic mean of responses to the questions in the survey, where a negative response ("hinder") = 0, a null responses ("no effect") = 1, and a positive response ("help") = 2. Okanagan firms ranked customers (1.73), management (1.45), sales and marketing (1.42), production (1.35) and in-house R&D (1.34) as valuable to their innovation processes (see Figure 4.1).

Suppliers were seen as significantly more valuable in the Okanagan (1.13) than in the Lower Mainland (0.90). This is likely a result of the isolation of the Okanagan—for the most part, suppliers are providing technology from outside the region. Another element is that the suppliers are physically located outside the region, usually in the Lower Mainland, so their participation is taken less for granted.

As in the Lower Mainland, out-sourced R&D and production are more important to innovating firms in the policy sectors than in the sample as a whole, indicating process rather than product innovation.

Factors Affecting Innovation

Responses from Okanagan firms to this section agreed quite well with Lower Mainland responses. Firms identified customers (87%), competition (65%) and the risks/rewards of innovation (64%) as the main external factors to "help" innovation in their firms. Firms in the Okanagan identified government policies (42%), the availability of financing (24%) and the availability of personnel (13%) as the main factors hindering innovation. The case of financing is ambiguous, although it is often a factor hindering innovation, 46% of all firms and 50% of innovative firms identified it as a factor helping innovation.

Okanagan firms were much harder on the government than their Lower Mainland counterparts, who were mostly indifferent. Only 14% of firms in the Okanagan responded that government policies "help" innovation, while 43% responded that it had no effect.

As in the Lower Mainland, there is more agreement in the responses to this section among innovative firms, regardless of sector, than there is among firms within each sector. However, the converse is not the case. Non-innovative firms in the high tech sectors identify a different set of challenges than do firms in the policy sectors. In particular, high tech non-innovating firms identify development and production costs, government policies and the availability of financing and personnel as their major obstacles. High tech firms that were innovative, however, only identified government as a major obstacle, although 35% of them did identify cost as hindering their innovative process.

Other Findings

Investment in Capital Equipment. Purchases of capital equipment were reported by 89% of firms in the Okanagan responding to the survey. Of these,

70% confirmed that this equipment contained significant technological advances. These results were reflected by sector; however, 95% of innovative firms reported having purchased new equipment, 80% of these purchases containing significantly new technologies.

Resources for Product/Process Development. Two in three (69%) Okanagan firms reported that they had applied some kind of resources—money, time and/or effort—to the development of new products/processes. By sector, this breaks down to 60% of respondents from the policy sectors, and 81% of high tech firms. Of firms classified as innovative, 88% reported applying resources to product/process development; only 42% of firms listed as non-innovative reported the same.

Use of Government Incentive Programs. Only 35% of firms in the Okanagan reported having used government incentive programs such as the Scientific Research and Experimental Development (SR&ED) or Industrial Research Assistance Program (IRAP) (these two were specifically listed in the survey). This broke down to 28% of firms in the policy sectors, and 52% of high tech firms. Only 48% of innovative firms in both sectors reported having used these programs.

An interesting result is obtained by comparing the use of government incentives to the perception of government's effect on innovation. Unlike in the Lower Mainland, there is little difference between those who had and had not used incentive programs in the perception of government as an obstacle to innovation. Firms in the Okanagan, if they care, do not like the government.

Human Resources. Okanagan firms reported that training existing personnel was the preferred method for obtaining needed skills—89% of firms responded this way; 69% reported that they would hire a new employee to obtain needed skills, while only 45% said they would engage a consultant or contractor. These results were consistent by innovativeness and by sector; however, 55% of innovative firms said they would engage a contractor to obtain needed skills.

Some 73% of firms reported formal or informal training programs. Policy sector firms were slightly higher than this average, high tech firms somewhat lower. Innovative firms were more likely to have training programs than non-innovative firms.

Exports. Firms in the Okanagan, both innovative and non-innovative, tend to be regional in focus. A third of innovative firms (34%) reported 60% or more of total sales outside BC, compared to one in five (22%) non-innovative firms. However, only 16% of firms in both segments report more than 60% of total sales outside Canada.

AN OVERVIEW OF THE RESULTS

The results of this survey can be used to give some indication of the strength (or weakness) of the linkages in the BC system of innovation. Two-thirds (66%) of respondents in the Okanagan district reported having introduced a new product or process in the past five years. However there is more to innovation than product or process development. Inherent in the concept of innovation is the idea of uniqueness. For a development to be innovative it must be unique in that firm's competitive market. Thus the questionnaire also asked if the new product or process was unique to the industry. A product or process unique in the industry (to the knowledge of the respondent) would likely be unique in the firm's market, thus innovative. By this measure only 56% of respondents were considered innovative.

In terms of sources of innovation, there were few apparent differences between the regions in BC (except "networks"). Indeed, both regions showed clustering around two specific "actor-networks," with in-house R&D units, sales, production management and customers forming a tight network, and out-sourced R&D, competitors and suppliers forming a second tier. Networks formed a significantly higher source of innovative ideas in the Okanagan, possibly reflecting the relative isolation of the region.

Regional differences, however, played a much more significant role in factors affecting innovation. The Okanagan firms appear to be much more dependent upon the innovativeness of their personnel, with management attitudes and personnel being much more important than in the Lower Mainland. Understandably, lower costs were a factor in the Okanagan, and the stronger response around raw materials probably reflects the stronger agri-food and forest products sectors in the Okanagan economy.

Of interest to governments should be the stronger negative view of the role of government in innovation in the Okanagan. The results do suggest that all levels of government (primarily the federal government) need to improve linkages between their laboratories and local industry. While some of this response may be attributed to the more individualistic nature of entrepreneurs in the area, it probably also reflects the greater distance from government services and a feeling that these services are not assisting innovation in the district. Thus successful technology transfer is not just a matter of having appropriate technologies available, but also having an appropriate marketing strategy.

Government technology transfers to firms, particularly in regions where the local system of innovation contains less than a critical mass of technology, often follow a linear process:

1. Technology services (e.g., equipment calibrations)
2. Technology assistance (e.g., improvements to production equipment)
3. Research and development (on problems of immediate benefit to the local firms)

Technology services provide opportunities for government technology infrastructure services to "acquire a customer". Through learning about a firm's needs by providing services, government agencies can identify areas for technical assistance and possibly areas where R&D might be useful. The role of technology outreach advisors in this process is crucial.

Included in the analysis was an effort to develop index of innovativeness, based on responses to questions about firms' management of technology. Seven questions were used to build up a raw score of innovativeness. As has been reported by Hughes and Holbrook (1998) there was a high correlation between above-average scores from this index and the responses to the question on having developed a product or process that was new to the market which the firm served (Figure 4.2). This "knowledge management index" may provide a shortcut to assessing the innovative potential of a single firm or group of firms within a specific industrial sector.

A similar index could be developed using human resource-related questions from the survey. There was a high response to the question "Does your company have employee training and education programs?" Both high tech firms and policy sector firms reported having such programs. The significance of the responses to this question will require further analysis.

Anecdotal comments regarding why the Okanagan Valley, and especially the city of Kelowna, were perceived as conducive to innovation:

Figure 4.2
Knowledge Management Quotient

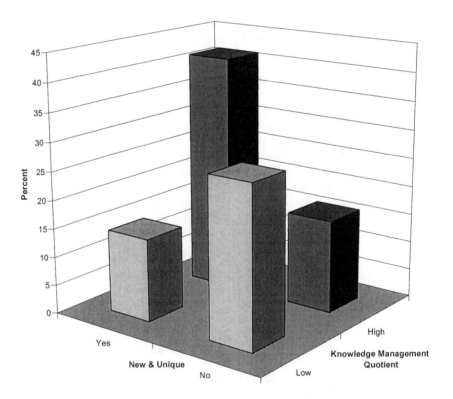

One respondent referred to Kelowna as a "hotbed of activity". The respondent believes that this is due primarily to the lifestyle the area offers. She referred to it as a "playground", one that has the amenities of a big city while maintaining a small-town atmosphere, with endless outdoor activities. The participant also mentioned Kelowna's proximity to Vancouver, while not actually being part of a large metropolitan area, as being one of the benefits of living there. She stressed that a key reason why innovative firms were doing business in the area were lower costs, particularly for housing, compared to those of Vancouver.

Another respondent observed there are roughly 50 high tech service firms in Kelowna. He noted there is a seven-year cycle to business endeavors in the area. He felt that high tech firms with creativity and vision will survive and prosper; and felt that Kelowna could represent a microcosmic view of future communities—a self-contained, medium-sized city that offers residents a lifestyle alternative and the opportunity to run a successful enterprise. He did not feel that a service business such as a restaurant could enjoy the same level of success as a high tech/knowledge-based enterprise. The primary reason for this is that high tech firms can enjoy lower costs associated with a smaller community, while being able to do business on a global scale, for example via Internet. This respondent felt Kelowna could house many more global high-tech businesses.

TOURISM

Tourism and tourist-related activities are an important element of the Okanagan economy. As well as there being many conventional tourist activities based on the surrounding environment, many of the advanced agri-foods businesses include tourist activities in their business activities. The researchers were asked by the regional economic development authorities to apply their survey to the tourist sector, and determine to what extent the tourism sector was an innovative one. The initial results suggest that tourism enterprises can be, and are, innovative, just as the other firms in non-high tech sectors. In compiling the tourism sector data, data from 12 agri-businesses which had tourist facilities (such as vineyards that offered wine tasting and a retail product outlet) were included; they are also included in the main resource/manufacturing/service sample.

CONCLUSIONS

The problem is simple: policy makers need information on the state of investment in knowledge and how that investment flows through the NSI and, by extension, through regional systems of innovation. The data, although crude, identify specific issues: external factors are less important than internal ones in influencing innovation. In particular the direct role of governments is relatively unimportant. What is important is the internal environment within the firm and feedback from their customers. For a corporate manager, the results clearly indicate the need to ensure that the firm is sensitive to signals from the marketplace. For government policy analysts the results might suggest the need to move away from direct support programs to less visible programs designed to support the competitive environment.

There are, however, some extensions to these direct results, which stem from systems of innovation analyses. In non-metropolitan areas it is important to have a seamless technology delivery system. A "single window" through which public agencies deliver services might improve their standing in the view of their clients. Non-metropolitan areas require more efforts by governments simply because regional institutions are weakly institutionalised—they lack the richness of the networks and connections usually found in technical poles. Government agencies in these regions can and should assume a greater role as knowledge suppliers. The need for personal networking and contacts is paramount; the technology advisor's "little black book" may be the most important source of initial ideas for development and subsequent innovation by firms.

An area requiring further analysis is the level of transfers of knowledge from formal studies to employment. Given the high cost of postsecondary education, we need to know more about how the resulting talents are used, and how over time technical knowledge is either augmented or depreciated. Studies of the stocks and flows of human capital lead directly to the study of the actors and networks that make up an NSI. This is a field which is only just beginning to be being examined, but which is probably important in smaller economies than in larger ones, where the sheer number of networks and individual actors means that individual actor-network complexes have less individual influence on the system.

With the current emphasis on job creation as a policy goal in itself, the analysis of non-high tech sectors becomes more important. Natural-resource-based industries and consumer-service-based industries can all be innovative within their markets. In BC these industries tend to predominate outside metropolitan areas, so it is important to be able to situate them in any policy framework devoted to enhancing the innovativeness of firms as a whole.

While this project is only at the beginning of the analysis of regional results in BC, the effects of geographical separation do appear to influence the responses. More detailed analysis of the data may suggest specific policy initiatives and improvements. The simple fact that government programs are much more negatively regarded in the hinterland suggests an immediate need to improve existing program delivery and a need to develop new programs specifically designed to benefit firms that do not have adequate access to the complete knowledge economy infrastructure available in metropolitan areas.

ACKNOWLEDGMENTS

The authors would like to acknowledge the encouragement and support from the Social Sciences and Humanities Research Council of Canada, Statistics Canada, the Science Council of BC and the Central Okanagan Regional Economic Development Commission.

NOTE

1. See the ISRN Website at www.toronto.ca/isrn/

REFERENCES

Acs, Z., de la Mothe, J., and Paquet, G., 1996, "Local Systems of Innovation: In Search of an Enabling Strategy", in *The Implications of Knowledge-Based Growth for Micro-Economic Policies*, ed. P. Howitt. Calgary: University of Calgary Press.

BC Stats, 1997, *The British Columbia High Technology Sector, 1988-1995*. Victoria: British Columbia Ministry of Finance and Corporate Relations.

Davis, C., 1991, *Local Initiatives to Promote Technological Innovation in Canada: Eight Case Studies*. Ottawa: Science Council of Canada.

de la Mothe, J., 1998, ed., *Local and Regional Systems of Innovation*. Amsterdam: Kluwer Academic Publishers.

de Wit, R., and Lipsett, M., 1995, "British Columbia's Industrial Landscape: Technology and Innovation Outside the Metropolitan Areas", CPROST Report 95-03-28. Vancouver: Simon Fraser University.

Edquist, C., 1997, *Systems of Innovation: Technology, Institutions and Organizations*. London: Pinter.

Freeman, C., 1968, "Science and Economy at the National Level," in *Problems of Science Policy*. Paris: OECD.

Government of Canada, 1997, *Speech from the Throne*. Ottawa: Parliament of Canada.

Holbrook, J.A.D., and Hughes, L.P., 1998, "Innovation in Enterprises in British Columbia," in J. de la Mothe, ed., *Local and Regional Systems of Innovation*. Amsterdam: Kluwer Academic Publishers.

Hughes, L.P., and Holbrook, J.A.D., 1998, "Measuring Knowledge Management: a new indicator of innovation in enterprises", *CPROST Report 98-02*. Vancouver: Simon Fraser University.

OECD, 1996a, *Oslo Manual*, 2nd edition, DSTI. Paris: OECD.

OECD, 1996b, *Technology and Industrial Performance*. DST. Paris: OECD.

OECD, 1997, *National Systems of Innovation*, document DST/STP/TIP(97)2, DST. Paris: OECD.

5

Incubating and Sustaining Learning and Innovation Poles in Latin America and the Caribbean

David V. Gibson, Pedro Conceição, and Julie Nordskog

Technology continues to shrink the world. There is no choice other than to participate in the global community. Science and technology is too precious a resource to be restricted from drawing the world together. That is what the 21st Century is all about.

Dr. George Kozmetsky
Chairman of the Board
IC² Institute
The University of Texas at Austin

It appears that well-developed capabilities to learn—the abilities to put knowledge to work—are responsible for rapid catch-up....The basic elements [to develop these learning abilities] appear to be skilled people, knowledge institutions, knowledge networks, and information and communications infrastructure.

The World Bank
World Bank Development Report 1998: Knowledge for Development

INTRODUCTION

This chapter presents the conceptual framework of an initial action plan to accelerate technology-based economic development in Latin America and the Caribbean (LAC). The fundamental premise is the possibility of leveraging codified knowledge and tacit know-how through Web-based networks and face-to-face training programs. The suggested action plan will bring together business entrepreneurs, academia, and regional government in targeted LAC regions where a select number of small and mid-sized enterprises (SMEs) will be designated Learning & Innovation Poles (LIPs). Each LIP will be viewed as an "experiential learning laboratory" where lessons learned will be used in world-class research, education, and training programs.

The activities described in this chapter are designed to function as an integrated program that, over time, will contribute to and leverage local and global initiatives for knowledge transfer, accumulation, use, and diffusion to accelerate sustained economic growth and shared prosperity in the Southern Hemisphere.[1]

The organization of the chapter is as follows. The first section describes the lessons learned from more than forty years of experience with technopoleis[2] and uses the framework of the technopolis wheel to clarify understanding of the private and public sectors that support regional, technology-based economic growth. Next is presented the Learning & Innovation Pole model as a 21st-century-oriented evolutionary extension to the concept of technopoleis, one that is more attuned to the knowledge-based economy and the special characteristics of LAC. Then the conceptual background on knowledge transfer, adoption, accumulation, and diffusion is discussed. Finally, we present a modular framework for translating the principles of LIPs into concrete initiatives for sustainable economic growth and high quality job creation.

TECHNOPOLIS: LESSONS LEARNED

There are many labels applied to regional and national initiatives to foster technology-based economic development: technopolis; technopole; multi-function polis; science, research, university, and industry parks; economic development zones; high tech corridors; and industry clusters. There is also a range of views on how such labels should be defined as well as metrics for success. In this chapter we use the term technopolis.

Strategies for building and sustaining successful technopoleis (i.e., high technology regions) have been proposed and implemented world-wide ever since leaders from business, government, and academia began to take notice of the wealth and job creation potential of technology-spurred growth in such pioneering technopoleis as Silicon Valley, California and Route 128 in Boston, Massachusetts (Rogers and Larsen, 1984; Botkin, 1986). However, outside of a few select and important visionaries, these initial and perhaps most successful technopoleis were not planned, nor were they managed as strategic regions. They were primarily fostered by entrepreneurial behavior in local universities and businesses, which at times led to spin-out and fast-growth companies that were nurtured and supported by the region's "smart infrastructure" (i.e., finance, legal, and business know-how).

Despite massive funding and detailed plans, most "planned" or "managed" science cities or technopoleis—such mega-projects as Tsukba and Kansai Science Cities in Japan; Taedok Science Town in Korea; Pudong in China; Multi-Function Polis in Australia; and Multi-Media Corridor in Malaysia—have not brought forth the entrepreneurial fever, and wealth and job creation desired by the public and private sectors.[3] Indeed, many planned technopoleis are financial drains needing continuing public sector financial support.

Two important lessons have been learned since the mid-1900s beginning of the technopolis movement:

1. Technology commercialization is not an automatic process based on institutional excellence (i.e., building centers of research excellence is not sufficient).
2. Build a physically impressive science city, science park, or business incubator and wealth and jobs will NOT automatically follow.

While scholars and practitioners argue over the necessary and sufficient conditions to grow and sustain technopoleis, most would agree that, at least in the past, the following have been most important, if not crucial:

1. Universities and centers of research and educational excellence;
2. Technology-based industry clusters of start-up, mid-sized, and large firms;
3. A quality of life that facilitates recruitment, retention, and creativity of employees and firms;
4. Supportive government and policy regulations, (e.g., tax law, technology and transfer regulations, and intellectual property law);
5. Developed physical infrastructure (e.g., roads, airports, ISDN lines, etc.);
6. Developed "smart" infrastructure (e.g., finance, legal, management, etc.);
7. Sufficient amounts of venture capital;
8. An entrepreneurial culture; and
9. The training and retraining of a skilled workforce.

In view of the above findings, the IC² Institute conceptualized the framework of the Technopolis Wheel (Smilor, Kozmetsky and Gibson, 1988) to emphasize the importance of seven regionally based sectors in technopolis development: education; large companies; emergent companies; federal, state, and local government; and support groups.

While the *education* sector emphasizes the important role of the research university, it also stresses the importance of community colleges and vocational, primary, and secondary education. A quality education system is a central component of a region's quality of life.

Large companies are wealth generators by means of providing employee salaries and taxes and are often magnets for attracting subcontractors and service providers to a region. They also offer training to employees who at times become a source of skilled managers and technical talent for start-up firms in the region.

Emergent companies and entrepreneurs build new industries, foster job growth, and accelerate technology transfer through spin-outs and start-up companies. The most successful of the world's technopoleis foster thriving entrepreneurial and technology-venturing cultures.

In the United States many would argue that the role of *federal and state government* is to foster environments that support research, education, and business development as well as infrastructure improvements, while *local government* needs to focus on balancing regional economic development with a sustainable and affordable quality of life.

Finally *support groups* include such community-based organizations as chambers of commerce, business and entrepreneurial groups, professional associations, and the like. This sector also includes business "know-how" in the legal, managerial, advertising, and venture capital professions. This support sector might also include science parks and incubators to foster technology transfer and the accelerated growth of start-up companies.

However, as Gibson and Kozmetsky (1993) stress, excellence in any one or even a range of business, academic, or government sectors is not sufficient for technopolis development and growth. Many regions have excellent universities, successful large companies, and supportive governments, but they are not successful, growing technopoleis. The networking and cross-institutional collaboration that is fostered by champions and influencers is a critical ingredient. These visionaries and implementers cross all segments of the Technopolis Wheel. They are the ones who make things happen.[4]

A key result and advantage of the formation of technology-based regions is the fostering of a favorable environment for establishing technology-based start-up and spin-out fast growth companies. This favorable environment consists of regional networks of talent, technology, capital, and know-how that provide support essential to successfully commercializing innovations and new technology, as illustrated in Figure 5.1:

- *Entrepreneurial talent* results from the perception, drive, tenacity, dedication, and hard work of special types of individuals—people who make things happen. Where there is a pool of such talent, there is opportunity for economic growth, diversification, and new business development.
- When talent is linked with *technology*, when people facilitate the push and pull of viable ideas to commercialization, the entrepreneurial process is under way. Every dynamic process needs fuel, and here the fuel is capital.
- *Capital* is the catalyst in the technology-venturing chain reaction.
- *Know-how* is the ability to leverage business or scientific knowledge through the linking of talent, technology, and capital in emerging and expanding enterprises. This "smart infrastructure" finds and applies expertise in a variety of areas such as management, marketing, finance, accounting, production, manufacturing, sales and distribution, and law, often making the difference between venture success and failure.

Figure 5.1
Critical Success Factors for Technology Venturing

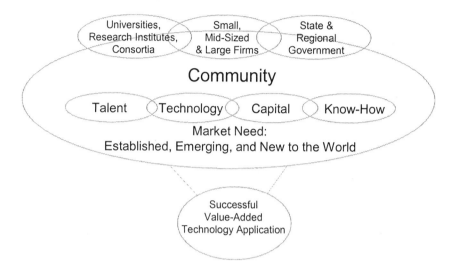

In summary, the most successful technopoleis in the United States have been built from the "ground-up" not the "top-down." In Silicon Valley, California, Hewlett Packard and Apple Computer were indeed started in garages and in Austin, Texas, Dell Computers was launched out of a college dorm room and the trunk of a car. The entrepreneurs who launched these pioneering ventures were successful, in large part, because of their ability to access and use needed knowledge—talent, technology, capital, and business know-how—to be competitive in the marketplace. And in large part, these entrepreneurs accessed needed resources within the regions where they started their businesses.

The accelerated success of these ventures and the quality of life within the regions where they were located facilitated the later recruitment of "brainpower" from other regions in the United States and abroad. Supplier and service companies located in these emerging technopoleis and start-up ventures were spun-out of the existing firms and universities within the regions. Over time, in a few regions a positive synergy is developed—based on the flow of talent, technology, capital, and know-how—between the regions' academic institutions and the regions' businesses.

MOVING FROM TECHNOPOLEIS TO LIPs

This section provides a framework for translating the lessons learned with technopolis development in developing country contexts. It presents the Learning & Innovation Pole as an evolutionary improvement to the concept of technopolis that is more attuned to the needs of developing countries. The fundamental importance of networks to successful technopolis development is stressed and the challenges and benefits of launching the LIP network presented. Finally, a selection of regionally focused success metrics for evaluating Learning & Innovation Poles is presented.

While tech cities have had varying levels of success in the developed world, the experience of developing countries has largely been restricted to a much smaller version, commonly referred to as "science parks." Science parks are property-based initiatives that create formal operational links between universities and other research institutes and technology-based businesses normally resident on-site (Massey et al., 1992). Sometimes, technopoleis evolve out of science parks. Silicon Valley in California can trace its origins to the Stanford Industrial Park established by Stanford University in the 1950s (Saxenian, 1994).

However, there are important differences in the approach to technopoleis in the developed industrial nations and developing countries. In the world's most developed technopoleis, their physical and smart infrastructure and their "knowledge networks" emerged over a relatively long time span—30 or 40 years—and some of these areas have yet to "take off" with entrepreneurial fever (Muller et al., 1997). For reasons of time and economy of resources, such a process is not suitable for developing countries. There are a variety of shortcomings in the available infrastructure in developing countries, which lack the full range of expertise required to form the networks that give birth to and sustain technopoleis. Furthermore, due to existing conditions, it cannot be assumed that innovation networking between the various different sources of innovation potential will spontaneously occur.

While traditional approaches to establishing technopoleis may not be the preferred path in the developing country context, there is instead considerable promise in creating globally competitive technology firms and "technopoleis without walls" using resources available in cyberspace and leveraging many of the support functions through Web-based relationships. Rapid advances in scientific and technical knowledge, and declining costs of producing, diffusing, and processing information (due to advances in information and communication technologies) are transforming the organization of social and economic activity worldwide, and thereby leading to the emergence of the so-called knowledge-based economies. A new opportunity for rapid catch-up is emerging in developing countries, in a context in which the stock of knowledge is increasing, more easily available, and more broadly disseminated than ever before.

An important objective of the International Development Research Center (IDRC) study is to benefit from the lessons of the world's challenged and successful strategies to accelerate technology-based regional growth in developing countries. This chapter supports the importance of a regional focus, but it also emphasizes the fostering and leveraging of national and global linkages through universities, large and small companies, local government, and support groups (see Figure 5.2). In the latter part of the 20th century, even for the more established worldwide technopoleis, wealth and job creation in a sustainable environment increasingly depend on globally linked public/private collaboration. A major challenge facing high tech regions and the firms that reside in these regions is how to effectively and efficiently acquire, transfer, and commercialize science and technology—technology that is developed nationally and globally. This is a challenging task as the source of key knowledge—technology and know-how—is increasingly distant, physically and culturally, from the organizations that seek to apply and commercialize these assets.

Figure 5.2
Globally Networking the Regionally-based Technopolis Framework

In many ways the ongoing "communications revolution" is making the tasks of globally linking public/private collaboration and knowledge acquisition and transfer easier. Indeed, there are two important advantages for today's tech firm that were not available to entrepreneurs in the mid- and late 1900s:

1. the distance-canceling power of Internet and Web-based communication; and consequently
2. the possibility of global access to talent, technology, capital, and know-how by leveraging increased trade and cultural interactions through modern information and communication technologies (ICT).

This "death of distance" as Frances Cairncross (1997) puts it, reduces the inherent economies of knowledge clusters and opens up the field to new entrants. These advances appear especially promising for the developing world, potentially enabling them to economically tap into informational and technical sources hitherto available only in the industrialized world.

To summarize, the proposal to create LIPs in Latin America and the Caribbean is based on the realities that:

1. few regions in the developing world can hope to match, at least in the short term, the physical and smart infrastructure of established technopoleis such as Silicon Valley, California and Austin, Texas, where there is an overwhelming agglomeration of technology, talent, capital, and know-how; and
2. regional, national, and global computer-based networks in the knowledge age allow for, if not encourage, the development of nongeographic bound or virtual technopoleis.

A key question for the proposed research project and for the 21st century, therefore, is how necessary and sufficient is the regional development of "smart" infrastructure in all its aspects (i.e., talent, technology, capital, and know-how) or physical infrastructure (i.e., science parks, incubators, and high tech corridors) in the emerging Internet-based economy where the movement of knowledge is increasingly through ICT? And it may be asked, which sectors or components of this infrastructure must be physically co-located or digitally networked at different stages of a firms becoming globally competitive?

As a starting point we focus on the importance of fostering entrepreneurship at the grassroots level. To do this we target, in each selected Latin American and Caribbean site, small and mid-sized technology-based companies that might be considered relatively successful at the local level but are in need of assistance (e.g., talent, technology, capital, and know-how) to achieve accelerated growth and global market penetration. At the moment that these virtual networks are created around the SME, it becomes a Learning & Innovation Pole.

A Learning & Innovation Pole is operationalized at the most basic level as an SME that is linked to other SMEs in an Internet and Web-supported global network and also has access to a range of support activities such as training programs, workshops, and mentoring activities. Rather than relying on a well-defined geographic area to provide all of the networks and services required for success in knowledge-based economic efforts, LIPs rely on regional and global cooperative and collaborative networks and training programs to provide service and assistance on a real-time, as-needed basis. LIPs can be thought of as virtual technopoleis that constantly shift and grow to take advantage of emerging opportunities and market needs.

LIP Value-Added Networks

The thrust of this chapter is that physical proximity is becoming less and less important to regionally based economic development because of the pervasiveness of advanced ICT. Successfully fostering the growth and global competitiveness of select SMEs in targeted LAC regions, however, will take more than computer-based networks and Web connections. There needs to be a sense of community and relationship building. There need to be local visionaries, champions, and implementers. In addition to meaningful regional and global partnerships and alliances that need to be formed and maintained, there needs to be a meaningful flow of know-how and resources among all members of the network.

The objective of this project is to foster the global linking of regional champions and enterprises in view of the realities and challenges of the international marketplace. The networks that we propose building via the LIP project are centered on identifying select SMEs and regional champions for long-term partnerships. These networks will be sustained by being task focused for short-term success as well as for longer-term vision. Figure 5.3 depicts how LIPs know-how networks will assist targeted companies in targeted regions cross the knowledge transfer and application gap to market applications, leading to firm diversification and expansion and new firm formation.

Figure 5.3
Crossing the Knowledge Transfer and Application Gap with Know-how

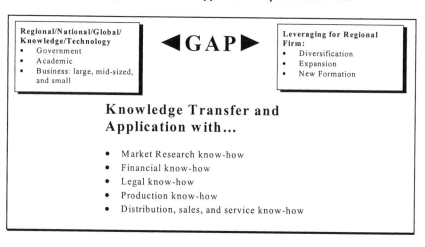

Learning & Innovation Poles will strive to shorten product development cycles by broadening entrepreneurs' global know-how in such areas as market research, finance, advertising, quality issues, management, sales, and service (see Figures 5.4 and 5.5).

Figure 5.4
Learning & Innovation Poles to Foster Venture Success and Accelerated Growth

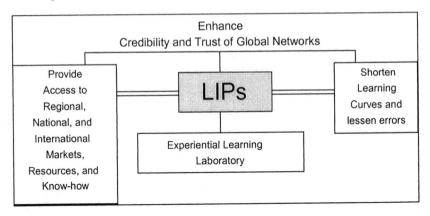

Figure 5.5
Ten Success Factors for a Learning & Innovation Pole (LIP) Development

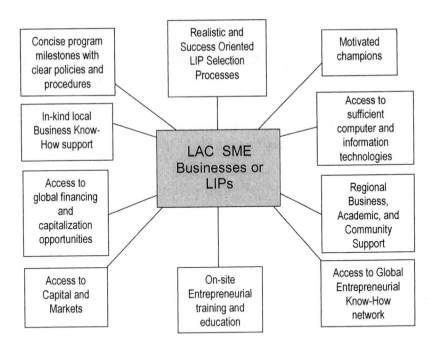

Initial Challenges to Successfully Launching the LIP Network

Common challenges to having the targeted LIP SMEs think and act globally are believed to be:

1. Success in home markets and a home-country bias.
2. Limited personnel.
3. Limited resources.
4. Limited time.
5. Limited tolerance for extra problems and challenges of going global (e.g., the fear of losing control of one's intellectual property).
6. Ignorance of critical success factors in foreign markets.
7. Legal, trade, and governmental constraints.

These challenges need to be balanced against the benefits of a SME being part of the LIP Program. These benefits include:

1. Access to needed and often-critical knowledge.
2. Global market access and niche market opportunities.
3. Access to needed talent, technology, capital, and know-how.
4. Minimizing mistakes and misspent resources.
5. Maximizing speed to the market and the commercial potential of a venture.
6. Being globally aware of a firm's strengths, weaknesses, opportunities, and threats.

Metrics for Success

Learning & Innovation Poles will focus on selected entrepreneurs and business enterprises in the targeted regions. These sites will be studied over time to provide data and case examples for research and publications as well as for job and skills training. It is important to involve a range of LAC regions with a variety of characteristics, challenges, and opportunities for wealth and job creation. Metrics for success will be regionally focused and will be identified and followed over time. In general these metrics will include:

Targeted to Specific LIPs/SMEs

- World-class technology and business assessment.
- Market assessment: regional and global, existing and emerging.
- Intellectual property creation.
- Capital access.
- Increased profit.
- Accelerated growth.
- Access to new technology and business processes.
- Shorter time to market.
- Management and employee development.

Government-Oriented

- Enhance competitiveness and accelerate growth of local firms.

- Job creation.
- Space utilization.
- Capital creation.
- Incremental revenues (i.e., taxes, services, etc.).
- Development of regional "smart infrastructure".
- Increased global awareness and competitiveness.

Academic Oriented

- Training of faculty and students.
- New curriculum development.
- Successful placement of students.
- Experiential, on-the-job learning.
- Enhanced favorable relations with community.
- Research and publications.
- Revenue generation (i.e., royalty, license fees, etc.).

CONCEPTUAL BACKGROUND

Traditionally wealth creation, in developed and developing nations, has emphasized physical assets. The capital stock of a nation was thought to be a measure of national prosperity, and the attraction of foreign direct investment became a prime strategy of less-developed regions. As the world moves into the 21st century, however, the emphasis is on knowledge transfer, accumulation, adoption, and diffusion as being critical to economic development. As the World Bank noted in its 1998 *World Development Report:* "It appears that well-developed capabilities to learn—the abilities to put knowledge to work—are responsible for rapid catch-up....The basic elements [to develop these learning abilities] appear to be skilled people, knowledge institutions, knowledge networks, and information and communications infrastructure."

This section provides a summary of the theory of knowledge transfer, accumulation, and use to create a better understanding of the process through which knowledge and learning can be leveraged for regional economic development in Latin America.

Knowledge Transfer, Adoption, Accumulation, and Diffusion: Key Drivers for Regional Economic Development

Knowledge transfer, adoption, accumulation, and diffusion are key to sustainable economic prosperity in the emerging global economy of the 21st century. As stated by Abramovitz and David in a 1996 OECD report, "The expansion of the knowledge base...[has] progressed to the stage of fundamentally altering the form and structure of economic growth." Rapid advances in information and communication technologies and declining costs of producing, processing and diffusing knowledge are transforming social and economic activities worldwide (World Bank, 1998).

While the current knowledge revolution is resulting in many positive outcomes, there is concern that it is accelerating the polarization of the "haves" and "have nots." Scientific and technical advances have increased the economic welfare, health, education, and general living standards of only a relatively small fraction of humankind to unmatched levels. The unevenness of such development among and within both developing and developed regions has increased significantly. Two hundred and fifty years ago, for example, the difference in income per capita between the richest and poorest countries in the world was 5 to 1. Today, the difference is approaching 400 to 1 (Landes, 1998). The underlying reasons for these inequalities are complex and, according to most analyses, are to be found in the outcomes of the social and economic revolutions that predate the current knowledge revolution. While the industrial revolution lowered the costs of manufacturing and distribution, over time this economic and social revolution also tended to divide the world into industrialized and nonindustrialized nations and fostered bimodal societies of wealthy and poor.

The current knowledge revolution is critically different from the past industrial revolution. It is based upon a shift of wealth-creating assets from physical things to intangible resources based on knowledge (Stevens, 1996). Knowledge-based economic regions tend to be located near leading universities and research centers in the most advanced regions of the world (Smilor et al., 1988; Quandt, 1998). Lucas (1988) argues that people with high levels of human capital tend to migrate to locations where there is an abundance of other people with high levels of human capital. Indeed, the importance of the physical proximity of talent, technology, capital, and know-how, or "smart infrastructure," has been argued to be crucial to fostering regional wealth and job creation (Rogers and Larsen, 1984; Gibson et al., 1992; Audretsch and Feldman, 1996; and Audretsch and Stephan, 1996).

Despite the strong arguments for the importance of physical proximity or agglomeration of "smart infrastructure," advances in telecommunications and information technologies are transforming our perceptions of geography (Cairncross, 1997). Advances in ICT are key to explaining the shift from the industrial age—coal, steel, and material things—to a global knowledge-based age—information, human capital, and ideas. While it is still difficult to realize what William Mitchell (1995) calls "cities of bits"—where the majority of the world's people are connected through telephones, televisions, faxes, and computers to a Worldwide Web—key influencers in business, academia, and government are increasingly realizing opportunities to use the special characteristics of knowledge and ICT to foster regional development through cooperation, collaboration and competition.

A better understanding of the process through which knowledge and learning can contribute to economic development in developing as well as developed regions is urgently required. In this regard, it is important to define knowledge and to realize how it differs from physical things (Dosi, 1996). Here we follow the analysis of Conceição et al. (1997), who build on Nelson and Romer's (1996) differentiation between ideas and skills, or *software* and *wetware*.

- *Software ("ideas")*: Knowledge that can be codified and stored outside the human brain, for example in books, CDs, records, and computer files. *Software* (as defined here) is referred to as the "structural capital" of private and public organizations and includes intellectual property that is codified (Edvinsson and Malone, 1997). When employees leave their place of work the *software* remains.
- *Wetware ("skills")*: Knowledge that cannot be dissociated from individuals is stored in each individual's brain, and includes convictions, abilities, talent, and know-how. *Wetware* is referred to as the "human capital" of private and public organizations and is the know-how or intangible resources that provide key added-value for enterprise development and accelerated growth (Edvinsson and Malone, 1997). When employees leave their place of work the *wetware* leaves with them.

These two kinds of knowledge differ (1) in the way they are produced, diffused, and used, and (2) in the level of codification. While ideas correspond to knowledge that can be articulated (in words, symbols, or other means of expression), skills correspond to knowledge that cannot be formalized or codified. This apparently simple difference has very important consequences in terms of the way knowledge is produced, diffused, and used (Gibson and Smilor, 1991).

The classification of knowledge in this manner is very significant in the context of this proposal, which aims to use Internet and Web-based links to accelerate growth and job creation in LAC. The transmission of software, or codified knowledge, is not much affected by geographic distance, especially in this age of high-bandwidth and near-zero transmission cost (Swann, Prevezer and Stout, 1998). However, the transmission of wetware, or tacit knowledge, cannot be easily accomplished without face-to-face contact.

Not only does this indicate the importance of including face-to-face contact in the proposed LIP Program, it also indicates the types of industries that will most benefit from an Internet and Web-based network. That is, from a technology transfer point of view, leading-edge technologies that are highly dependent on wetware skills are unlikely to benefit from only the access that LIP networks provide. But more standard technologies that are further along their life-cycle and therefore require more codified knowledge would benefit greatly from the financing and marketing links provided through the LIP network. This is because new technologies spur the development of skills required to use them. However, as these technologies become more sophisticated, the required skill levels tend to decrease and the ability to codify the required knowledge increases. As a result, selection of SMEs in the targeted LAC regions will not necessarily focus on advanced technology (e.g., new materials, semiconductors, biotechnology), but will emphasize the use of appropriate ICT and business processes in the regionally based enterprises. It is clear that modest technology and innovative management processes can produce substantial wealth and job creation for a region (Conceição and Heitor, 1998).[5] The business and networking focus of LIPs therefore will be based on the assessment of the technology and infrastructure strengths, weaknesses, opportunities, and threats (SWOT) of each selected LIP and targeted region.

Knowledge to Wealth for Shared Prosperity: The Principles

Today, the really substantial gains in wealth are to be found in the use and diffusion of knowledge. However, without skills, ideas may be irrelevant. Similarly without ideas, there may be no need for new and better skills. In short, it is important to stress that the accumulation of knowledge leads to the creation of wealth only if the knowledge is effectively transferred, adopted, and diffused.[6]

In the proposed LIP Program, personal networks and partnering programs (e.g., education and training, conferences, etc.) linked via ICT will be used to facilitate the collaboration of regionally based Learning & Innovation Poles as members of a global learning and innovation network. This global learning and innovation network will facilitate the transfer and use of existing knowledge and the creation of new knowledge for regional economic development. To foster equitable knowledge transfer, accumulation, diffusion, and use of both *software* and *wetware*, this project holds to three principles of operation.

Principle #1: When establishing Learning & Innovation Poles, we must deal with social as well as physical constructs that link participating people and institutions in networks of knowledge production, sharing, adoption, and diffusion that lead to self-reinforcing learning cycles (Figure 5.6).

Figure 5.6
Learning & Innovation Poles as Networks Among Regions

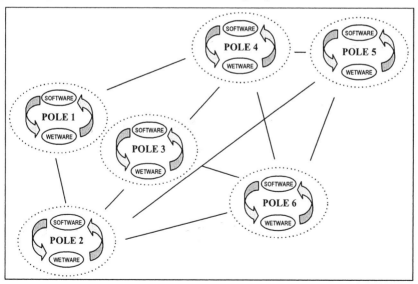

In competitive, marketplace economies, business or financial global networks often do not operate to the benefit of less-developed regions, indeed such networks often contribute to unequal development. A key question is whether such networks, linking the "haves" with the "have nots," go beyond awareness to the actual development of capabilities for knowledge accumulation and application in the less developed sites.

Principle #2 centers on fostering networks in which the interaction leads to increased learning capability in all network nodes, but in which the rate of learning is higher in the less developed nodes (Figure 5.7).

Figure 5.7
A Learning Network Based on Proportional Reciprocity

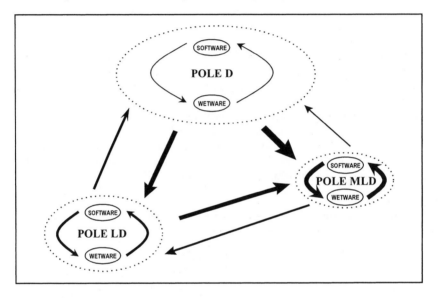

D = Developed Pole
LD = Less Developed Pole
MLD = Much Less Developed Pole
Arrow density implies the richness of knowledge transfer and application

This project also strives to encourage and facilitate local ownership of activities and results. To be truly sustainable, the processes of innovation must occur within and be "owned" by the champions in each node. Therefore, it is critical that regional champions or businessmen and women feel that they "own" LIPs.

These ideas lead to *Principle #3, which centers on fostering the regional "ownership" of the activities and the results or return on investment of the network.* A sense of ownership can be fostered by shared decision-making structures in which the ultimate choices and responsibilities lie with local figures rather than external facilitators.

ELEMENTS OF AN ACTION PLAN

The final section of this chapter provides some elements to consider for an Action Plan for incubating and developing Learning & Innovation Poles in select LAC regions. It begins with a listing of selected regions. The targeted LAC regions are not required and not expected to have in place the public and private resources often cited as central to technopolis success (e.g., a major research university doing state-of-the-art work in emerging technology areas; local and ample venture capital; and sophisticated business know-how or smart infrastructure). Nor are selected regions expected to have the resources or time to construct physically impressive technology parks or science cities. Indeed, even if the targeted regions were capable of such large construction or infrastructure building projects, present research and current regional initiatives suggest that this would not be the preferred strategy (*Wired*, June 1998, pp. 138-155).

Targeted Regions in Phase I and Phase II

IDRC has asked us, for illustrative purposes only, to target the following Latin American regions that could serve as Beta Sites or "experiential learning laboratories."

- Argentina: Buenos Aries.
- Brazil: Curitiba, Rio de Janeiro, and Recife.
- Chile: Santiago.
- Mexico: Monterrey.
- Uruguay: Montevideo.

These initial locales have demonstrated existing institutions and/or private-sector efforts, as well as some familiarity with technology that would facilitate their development as centers for learning and entrepreneurial activity. For example, Curitiba has made a name for itself as one of the most modern and technologically oriented cities of Brazil—a result of both local governmental policies and private-sector efforts. A concerted effort has been made to achieve diversity in the choice of Beta Sites, and this offers a range of challenges and opportunities. One rich advantage of networking, for example, lies in the linking of geographically distant, smaller local economies and distinct entrepreneurial cultures with larger, historically commercial locations.

Present initiatives for technology-based development in Latin America and the Caribbean have been relatively few. At the end of 1997, there were a total of 2,000 science parks and business incubators in the world. Of these, Europe accounted for 39 percent, North America 35 percent, Asia 17 percent, and the rest of the world 9 percent. Such activity in the LAC region has traditionally revolved around multinational enterprises rather than national science and technology-based development policies. Multinational manufacturers often build training facilities in order to provide themselves with skilled employees, a common practice in the automotive industry. Indeed past efforts of many Latin American countries, from the immediate post-World War II era to the present day, have been to attract foreign investment with incentive programs (i.e., tax exemptions, subsidies) while requiring multinationals to commit to technology transfer and obliging them to implement worker training programs. In terms of technology, Latin American countries have focused more upon acquisition than innovation.

Over the past decade however, Latin American policy makers have also begun to stress the need for greater investment in technology activities and research and development. There is a growing interest in both public- and private-sector mobilization for promoting technology and the SME sectors.

The 1994 Summit of the Americas Plan of Action called for multilateral action to develop information infrastructure and science and technology. One medium utilized to promote interconnectivity is the Hemisphere-Wide Inter-University Scientific and Technological Information Network (RedHUCyT) of the Organization of American States (OAS). The objective of RedHUCyT is to connect institutions of OAS member countries to the Internet, integrating an electronic network for the exchange of science and technology information. Governmental ministries are developing new programs and making greater efforts to provide information and services to SMEs, especially in Mexico (SECOFI) and Brazil (SEBRAE). SEBRAE has developed two branches, SEBRAEtec and Patme (Technology Consulting Services for SMEs), to provide technology consulting and solutions to problems specific to SMEs.

Multilateral aid and financial institutions such as the Inter-American Development Bank (IDB), the World Bank, and the United Nations Development Program have stressed the importance of the economic contribution of the SME sector to sustainable development. Such agencies have promoted both financing and technical consulting for country and regional SME and technology development programs. The Regional Management Training Project funded by the IDB provides an example of one in a handful of regional initiatives utilizing information technologies to support training institutions and SMEs in Argentina, Brazil, Mexico, Colombia and Uruguay. The IDB project incorporates a bilingual interactive website designed by the Latin American Network Information Center (LANIC), which is the leading organization for Latin American information on the Internet. The site connects the participating institutions, disseminating and facilitating the exchange of information on SME development in the Americas.

Nongovernmental organizations, such as FUNDES and the Latin American chapter of the World Business Council for Sustainable Development (WBCSD-LA) promote SME competitiveness with programs established throughout the region. These nongovernment organizations (NGOs) utilize information technologies such as the Internet to link their national programs. For example, Programa Bolivar, a nonprofit private institution, promotes national and international cooperation and alliance of Latin American companies. With over 100 offices worldwide, Programa Bolivar services emphasize networking/ matchmaking, finance, consulting, and technology transfer.

National Research and Development Background

The countries identified as Beta Sites for the LIP Program are members of major regional integration pacts. Argentina, Brazil, and Uruguay are members of Mercosul, with Chile as an associate. Mexico, of course, forms part of North American Free Trade Association (NAFTA). This section provides a brief overview of the countries' experience with science parks and regional S&T-based regional economic development initiatives.

In *Argentina* a "virtual business incubator" to support technology-based firms was sponsored by the Empretec foundation. Empretec began local activities in 1988 under the sponsorship of a United Nations entrepreneurship support program. Industrial associations and financial institutions also sponsor the foundation, with technological support from the National Institute for Industrial Technology. Argentine technology parks such as the Parque Tecnológico del Litoral and the Polo Tecnológico Constituyentes are closely linked to educational institutions.

Brazil is by far the frontrunner in terms of government support for S&T development, both in terms of economic investment and institutional experience. In absolute dollar terms, Brazil's total expenditures on S&T activities surpassed the total expenditures of all other Latin American countries combined from 1990 to 1995. In fact, technology promotion in Brazil began in the early 1980s. In 1982, Brazil created 13 "technological innovation nuclei" in selected universities and research centers throughout the country. This effort was followed by the creation of a Program for Implementation of Science Parks in 1984. These programs were designed to foster (1) technology transfer from university to industry, and (2) the creation of high technology parks and incubators. In 1987, after a study identified 18 potential regions for development, the national association of science parks (Anprotec) was created to disseminate information and support incubator development. Since 1993 an increasing number of public and private Brazilian entities have become involved in the promotion of incubators and science parks. There are currently about 15 regions nationwide classified as emerging high technology centers, 7 science parks with a few operating enterprises, and approximately 60 incubators housing nearly 500 firms. The most significant clusters are located in Campinas, São José dos Campos, and São Carlos (São Paulo State); Curitiba (Paraná); and Rio de Janeiro. As further testimony to the growing consciousness of the need for technology development, the Fifth World Conference of Science Parks, of the International Association of Science Parks (IASP), was held in Rio de Janeiro in 1996.

Mexico began building business incubators in 1990 and now has approximately 15 operating with eight more under development. Most of are supported by CONACYT (the National Council on Science and Technology) and AMIEPAT (the Association of Incubators and Technological Parks). Some of these efforts are led by public universities, such as the incubators in Guadalajara, Colima, Hidalgo, Nuevo León, Monterrey, and Mexico City. Others are led by R&D centers and government institutions, and at least two are private-sector initiatives: CIDET and IETEC in Cuernavaca. The Technology Institute of Superior Education of Monterrey, Mexico (ITESM) has been particularly active in distance learning, using a sophisticated satellite network to link its multiple campuses to one another and to the University of Texas for videoconference courses. The Programas de Simulación Empresarial of the Autonomous University of Mexico (UAM) and the Programa Desarrollo de Emprendedores of the Technology Institute of Mexico (ITEM) are further examples of successful university-based initiatives.

In Chile the Chilean Corporación de Fomento de la Producción (CORFO) oversees the Program for Technology Innovations which subsidizes research and development and technology institutions. Of particular interest is CORFO's Proyecto de Fomento (PROFO), an "associative business program". Groups of at least five companies with similar or complementary activities and geographical proximity form associations sponsored/cofinanced by PROFO in order to jointly resolve common problems, exchange experience and information, market products, invest, and, ultimately, enhance their competitiveness. Established in 1968, Chile's Corporación de Investigación Tecnológica (INTEC) is a nonprofit private corporation whose mission is to facilitate technological change in companies and public and private organizations. In collaboration with CORFO and the ICT University of Chile, INTEC has developed EmpreNet, a business incubator offering a number of internet-based services. Additional groups supporting small business in Chile are the Instituto de Promoción para la Capacidad Emprendedora, PRONUEVO and the Programa Permanente de Cultura Emprendedora.

Uruguay hosts the United Nations Development Program's TIPS network for Latin America. TIPS is a worldwide network for electronic commerce and business information. In 1997, 200,000 companies subscribed directly to the TIPS network in Latin America. The TIPS network will also be used for a computerized training system that provides "at-a-distance" learning and skill development. Furthermore, the International Development Research Center (IDRC) in Montevideo pursues a number of projects promoting small business development.

Other LAC Countries—Panama, Costa Rica, Venezuela: A few smaller economies in Latin America have also pursued the construction of technology parks, though on a less expansive scale. For example, to foster growth and to better attract innovative industries, Panama is building a "knowledge city" in the Canal Zone. This Ciudad del Saber will include education institutions as well as technology parks. In 1994 the Department of Business Administration of the Technology Institute of Costa Rica launched its Incubation Center, with the additional backing of the Grupo Zeta-Parque Industrial of Cartago, the Ministry of Science and Technology, and the Foundation for Popular Economics. Venezuela has registered two technology parks with the IASP, the Corporación

Parque Tecnológico Sartenejas and the Corporación Parque Tecnológico de Mérida. These locations have been identified for possible development of LIPs in subsequent phases of the LIP Program.

Modules for the Development of LIPs

A modular design is suggested for the framework of activities at Beta Sites. There are four advantages to a modular framework of this kind. First, modular frameworks give flexibility to the process, which permits different LIPs to define their own pace and emphasis on each module depending upon available information, resources, and interests. Second, modular frameworks make it easier to segue from one stage of the process to the other, whether they overlap, run concurrently, or follow sequentially. Third, modular frameworks can be designed as relatively freestanding and independent of each other, which makes it easier to change the order of implementation if so desired. Finally, responsibility for implementing, executing, and managing the modules can also be divided easily among different agencies and organizations, with or without overlap. By creating a modular design for the projects, we also encourage and facilitate local decision makers and influencers to "take ownership" and adopt procedures and objectives most appropriate to their region, according to their interests and judgement. This ability would go a long way in encouraging local "buy-in" and local responsibility for the project.

The focus of the LIP Program is on fostering and accelerating the development of SMEs in these regions and linking them to each other and to the more developed "mentoring regions" such as those of Austin, Texas, and others in the United States and Canada. We label the SMEs' Learning & Innovation Poles as we integrate them into an Internet and Web-based network. This network will link newly incorporated SMEs to other LIPs in the LAC, the IC²'s Austin Technology Incubator in Texas, and many others though the Internet, the Web, personal networks, and partnering programs. Subsequent phases could apply the lessons learned from Beta Sites and expand the targeted regions to Paraguay, Costa Rica, Panama, the Caribbean, Venezuela, and Colombia.

Module I: Building Awareness in the LIP

A series of meetings are suggested at each LAC site to initiate a project. These meetings will facilitate regional input at an early stage of the project on the aims of the LIP Program and the structure of the cooperative arrangements between the LIPs and IDRC. At these meetings the project proponents would present an overview of the project to the regional business, academic, and government leaders to initiate community support and "buy-in"; locate key institutional and individual champions; and encourage appropriate regionally based financial and in-kind support. While large grants will be sought from such organizations as the World Bank and foundations, project success and sustainability will require local and regional support and ownership.

One targeted outcome of these meetings will be the formation of local advisory committees at each LIP site; they would consist of key influencers from the business, academic, and government sectors. A global advisory committee will also be formed and will include experienced business, government, and academic leaders from the LIP regions as well as Austin, Texas, and a Canadian site.

Module II: Assessing the Technology and Innovation Potential in LIPs

The objective of the LIP Program is to foster the global linking of regional champions and enterprises with venture financing, managerial and marketing know-how, and supporting services. Each targeted LAC region (i.e., Buenos Aires, Curitiba, Monterrey, Montevideo, Recife, Rio de Janeiro, and Santiago) will be assessed for LIP candidate technology-based firms. Ideally, each region will be represented by three to six LIP firms, small and mid-sized.

Partnerships with local champions (e.g., business leaders, professors, and students from local universities/colleges, and influencers from the local chambers of commerce) will be formed. Existing institutional data will be used, as much as possible, to conduct a benchmark/scorecard of each targeted region. This benchmark will focus on identifying and leveraging existing capabilities:

1. for nurturing Learning & Innovation Poles in each target region, and
2. for networking these poles nationally and globally through the use of ICT and personal networks.

These regional assessments will focus on:

- R&D and technical expertise related to current and future businesses activities in the region—the talent and technology base for growing existing and new firms and industries.
- Core strengths and assets, competitive advantages in terms of regional, national, and global markets.
- Assessment of existing regional innovation systems.
- Scorecard (employment, founding date, spin-offs, growth, etc.) of existing small, mid-sized, and large firms in the region.
- Assessment of emerging clusters of activity, location of multinationals, branch plants, and headquarters.
- Interviews and surveys of key regional leaders (academic, business, and government) to facilitate regional understanding by the researchers and regional support and ownership by key local champions.

A number of data-collection activities are recommended to provide local advisory boards and stakeholders the information necessary for them to make informed decisions regarding the facilitation and challenges to technology-based economic development in selected LIPs. These aspects may include, but are not restricted to:

- Specific and measurable objectives for the regional LIP/SME.
- Formation of business partnerships.
- Location and size of specific components of the regional LIP.
- Technological profile; market and competitive orientation of LIP.
- Expansion stages, options for extension.
- Financing needs and sources.
- Time schedule.
- Networks strengths and needs.
- Supply of services and consulting.
- Structure of LIP oversight.

Figure 5.8 presents suggested matrix for performing a SWOT analysis of each Beta LIP region based on the proposed evaluations and assessments.

Module III: Building Networks

Using ICT, personal networks and partnering programs will link key regional institutions (e.g., incubators, science parks, universities, etc.) as important resources for sustaining each LIP. These networks will be centered on each Beta Site. Internet and other ICT links (e.g., video) will be established between each site and Austin and the Canadian sites with an emphasis on fostering collaboration among the LIPs. The proposed networks will attempt to identify regional champions for long-term partnerships. These networks will be sustained by being task focused for short-term success as well as longer-term vision.

While there is an appreciation for the national, institutional, and organizational contexts of each LIP, the focus is on the level of individual entrepreneurial organization of analysis and action (Figure 5.9). The initial objective is to have the selected LIPs immediately benefit from the codified knowledge and tacit know-how of the LIP network and training activities that focus on access to talent, technology, capital, know-how, and market access. The LIP network will strive to shorten product development cycles and time-to-market by broadening local firms' global knowledge in such areas as finance, market research, advertising, quality control, sales, and after-sales support and service.

Figure 5.8
Proposed Matrix for Targeting Specific Strengths, Weaknesses, Opportunities, and Threats (SWOT) to Regional-based Business growth of the Targeted LIPs

Global Location	Talent	Tech	Capital	Seed	VC	Estbl	Other	Know-How	Mrktg	Sales/Distr	Legal	Mgmt	Prod	Prototype	Mass
Brazil															
Curitiba															
Rio de Janeiro															
Recife															
Argentina															
Buenos Aires															
Uruguay															
Montevideo															
Chile															
Santiago															
Mexico															
Monterrey															

Figure 5.9
Individual Entrepreneurial Organization of Analysis and Action

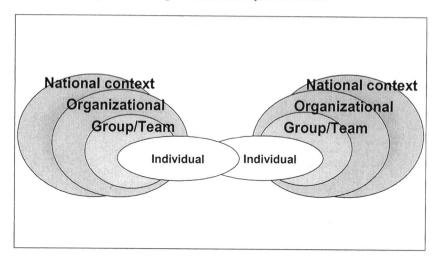

The LIP networks will focus on six functional objectives:

1. *Networking for Markets*: The identification of markets and successful execution of marketing strategies is a determining factor in the success and sustainability of small and medium technology-based firms. Direct links between customers in North America could be facilitated through the networks between the LIPs and North American sites. This would immediately and greatly expand the global market reach of firms resident in the LIPs.

2. *Networking for Capital*: Access to adequate financing is one of the most critical factors for the success of technology-based firms. Conceivably, broad public/private/NGO partnerships could be established to offer integrated access to services such as financial planning, support for obtaining grants, opportunities for access to venture, development, and seed capital.

3. *Networking for Interfirm Linkages*: A networked approach is ideal for maximizing the impact of programs and projects, such as partnerships, alliances, and linkages to outside suppliers. Most clusters in developing countries tend to rely heavily on the local supplier base, which may become insufficient for their rapidly growing needs. Careful coordination is required to ensure that the local suppliers are able to match increases in demand so that jobs may be retained and created and that other substitute supply streams can be brought online as required.

4. *Networking for Technological Support*: Electronic networks are extremely useful tools to diffuse the benefits of technological support, providing services such as technology assessment and forecasting, technology gateway (assistance on technological choices and on marketing assessment of innovative projects), and access to outside technical information. These services could also be concentrated in one or a few centers and could be provided by public agencies, private consultants, and business associations.

5. *Networking to Expand Access to Technology Transfer Opportunities*: The use of electronic networks for technology transfer is already being established in several

places to stimulate investment in S&T, R&D, technology transfer, development of commercial potential of R&D, and spin-offs. Networks are necessary tools to facilitate access to technology transfer opportunities worldwide.

6. *Networking for Talent and Know-How*: SMEs often do not have and cannot afford the entire range of technical and business talents and know-how required for success in local and global markets. The process of identifying and hiring such talent and know-how on a short-term as-needed basis is also difficult for smaller enterprises, especially in LAC locations. Networks of talent and know-how would be a great asset that would allow SMEs access to the experts at affordable rates and opportune moments.

Module IV: Selecting Demonstration Set of Target Firms

Selection criteria for the LIPs include:

*   Identification of champions within the LIP (SME) that will actively support and contribute to the LIP Program.
*   Having the LIPs submit a business plan for realistic assessment of the chances of early success by being a member of the LIP network.
*   Assurance that the LIPs' accelerated growth would be a positive catalyst for the targeted LAC region.

The selection of demonstration firms could be made by the global and local advisory committees based on business plans, market potential, or other criteria jointly determined by the advisory committees, IC^2 Institute, IDRC, and local partners and funders.

To achieve early successes, we will initially focus on the downstream needs of technology-based SMEs, rather than attempt to create new firms from existing research and business plans. It is expected that these existing firms will have established and marketable products. It is planned that with access to LIP networks and training these firms will become more regionally and globally competitive and will experience accelerated growth fostering regional job and wealth creation. The LIP network will assist these firms in finding, creating, and addressing markets and providing access to short-term business needs. The underlying strategy is the pursuit of short-term wins with a long-term vision.

The long-term vision will address issues of developing regionally based smart infrastructure, cutting-edge technology research, and training the local trainers and influencers. If the focus were initially on incubating start-up firms, it would take five to seven years for any noticeable market successes to be realized. Instead by focusing on established firms whose potential is not fully realized and providing them with crucial missing knowledge links—technology, talent, capital, or markets—we provide successful role models, energize the region, and in small but important ways create tangible wealth and jobs.

Module V: Plan and Initiate Supporting Infrastructure

While established SME firms will be the initial focus of the LIP Program, there is a critical need to develop the infrastructure and resources of the region to promote accelerated development of knowledge-based firms from the bottom-up as a longer term strategy. The basic need is to improve the process of knowledge transfer, acquisition, absorption, and diffusion. The issues involved include basic and higher education, physical infrastructure construction, and improved policy environments. For example, if knowledge acquisition—whether imported from abroad or created at home—is to lead to economic development, it must be absorbed and applied. This requires universal basic education and opportunities for lifelong learning (World Bank, 1998). The extent and economy of modern ICT greatly expand the potential for both acquisition and absorption of knowledge, but this can only happen after a basic level of telecommunications infrastructure is acquired.

The following are potential areas for action (Quandt, 1998):

- *Creating and Strengthening Local Technopolis Management Structures*: The first step is the creation of an organizational and functional structure for the local cluster, preferably leveraging existing groups and associations. This would involve both private- and public-sector participants. The establishment of linkages with other technopolis managers will enable a better understanding of stakeholder needs and markets and will improve organization methods. The creation of a permanent, dedicated business and technology information network would make communications more continuous and interactive, rather than sporadic exchanges that normally occur only at periodic meetings.

- *Determining Educational Needs and Offering Training*: Based on regional descriptive profiles and targeted interviews with local stakeholders, educational requirements for the LIPs and targeted companies can be ascertained. Courses could then be offered through local workshops as well as via the Internet to help improve the skills of local trainers. For example, the IC^2 Institute is currently working with several global partners to offer long-distance educational programs—degree and certificate—focusing on technology commercialization and forming virtual teams of "students" to evaluate the commercial potential of innovative technologies.

- *Fostering Personnel Exchanges*: Visits of key personnel among regions in the network would greatly facilitate knowledge, technology, and know-how transfer. For example, one of IC^2 Institute's global partners, the Instituto Superior Técnico in Lisbon, has established an IMPACT Program for leading Portuguese entrepreneurs to build markets in the United States. Exchanges of students, faculty, and entrepreneurs facilitate these processes.

- *Building Local Skills and Training IT Specialists*: In order to incubate a local cluster that will depend heavily on virtual linkages, a comprehensive adaptation to the IT paradigm is crucial. The development of new types of specialists will be needed, including Technology Brokers, Research Experts, Information and Technology Guides, and Animators. This type of program would benefit greatly from the experience and resources of North American universities and research institutes.

At a more general level, a skilled workforce is one of the most important localization factors for technology-based companies, and a major constraint to the development of technopoleis in many LAC nations. This characteristic is essentially place-based, yet virtual technologies may boost the development of human resources in more remote locations through training centers, distance education, career planning, virtual job markets, and also support business development through the establishment of virtual entrepreneur schools providing all kinds of training—technical, managerial, marketing, and so on.

- *Optimizing and Sharing Facilities*: For each region, the required facilities for a viable technopolis could be kept to a minimum, provided they are integrated into a shared system. The operational support infrastructure could be optimized and many facilities could be shared over the network, including incubators, prototype centers, pilot plants, online library, test laboratories, and online conferencing facilities.
- *Supporting Electronic Commerce*: Electronic commerce is quickly becoming an essential business tool in an increasingly integrated world economy. E-commerce capabilities are another kind of technopolis function that is much more feasible when implemented at a larger scale. It depends to a great extent on government policies and measures to support electronic commerce, addressing issues such as privacy, security, and consumer protection. Before it faces these obstacles, however, a successful cluster must build the skills and knowledge to enter the field. This is also an area in which LAC nations could benefit greatly from the experience and resources of North American universities and research institutes.

Module VI: Lessons from Early Successes

We expect to have concrete successes and lessons at about the one-year mark after the selection of demonstration firms. At this stage, a joint workshop involving all the LIPs would be extremely productive in analyzing and disseminating the experience with the demonstration firms and the concurrent research activities. The workshop would produce an analysis of the lessons learned, major success points, failures, and, if required, would redirect the program based on the analyses, evaluations and feedback.

Some of the metrics that would be useful in evaluating the performance of LIPs at this stage are:

- Creation of new and high quality jobs.
- Formation of regional innovative networks.
- Raising the technological sophistication of the region.
- Enhancing the image of the region.
- Combating "Brain Drain".
- Facilitating transfer of technology and skilled persons into the region.
- Enhancing the regional infrastructure.

Module VII: Move Upstream

At the initial stages of the project, we choose to select firms with market-ready products to develop within the network, and provide them with assistance in creating and entering markets. Access via the network is also provided to fill any gaps in talent, technology, capital, and know-how. Creating the technopolis, however, consists of two aspects: facilitating the success of established firms, and the upstream founding of new tech-based firms.

The ultimate objective of the program is to create a mechanism for more rapid technology-based job creation. This can be done even more effectively if the focus of the initiative eventually shifts upstream to facilitate and incubate the founding and relocation of new firms with innovative products and services. At the initial stages of the project this would not have been feasible because the infrastructure shortcomings are likely to be too severe to overcome merely through ICT associations. However, a concerted long-term approach to building basic required infrastructure should make bottom-up technology-firm incubation a possibility. In addition, the firms selected for the demonstration projects would serve as valuable showcases. As we learn from the experiences of the demonstration firms and in cooperation and consultation with them, we can slowly move to more initial stages of firm foundation.

CONCLUSIONS

Under the Mercosul trade regime, Latin American countries will open their economies to greater international competition, thereby accelerating a process that will further integrate them within the global economy. By mobilizing and focusing LAC talent, technology, capital, know-how, and institutional resources to stimulate entrepreneurial activity and strengthen the innovative processes in the region, the Learning & Innovation Pole Program will be an important catalyst for building the world-class, sustainable, regionally based, smart infrastructure necessary for technology-based wealth and job creation.

The feasibility of establishing meaningful and sustainable LIPs in the targeted LAC regions centers on the effective use of ICT as well as regional and global partnerships and partnering programs. While the role of business, academic, and government sectors in building regionally based technology centers (i.e., technopoleis) has been observed and experimented with for over 20 years, it is much less clear what are the key resources and conditions for accelerating the growth of virtual technopoleis and how these criteria might change depending on geographic location. The questions the LIP Program seeks to examine in detail are:

1. How does one accelerate entrepreneurial wealth and job creation in SMEs through Internet and Web-based access to talent, technology, capital, know-how, and markets?
2. What "smart" infrastructure must be physically co-located in SME sites and what can be virtually linked regionally, nationally, and globally?
3. What are the critical components of technopolis development in the emerging Internet and Web-based knowledge economy of the 21st century?
4. Can a developing region "leap-frog" the 20-40 years it has traditionally taken to build technopoleis without first building world-class research facilities and state-of-the-art science parks, and the agglomeration of "smart" infrastructure (i.e., finance, legal, marketing, manufacturing, sales and distribution, global expertise, etc.)?

The proposed research and action initiatives will explore these issues in real-life experiential learning laboratories—selected SMEs in targeted regions in Latin America and the Caribbean. World-class research will be based on these "experiments" and lessons learned will be used in on-going education, training and economic development programs in Latin American and Caribbean nations.

NOTES

1. The authors thank Dr. Scott Tiffin and others at The International Development Research Center (IDRC)/Centro Internacional de Investigaciones para el Desarrollo, Montevideo, Uruguay [www.idrc.ca/lacro] for their patient and valued support and advice on this research.

2. *Techno* reflects an emphasis on technology; *polis* is Greek for city-state and reflects a cooperative spirit between regional public and private sectors. The modern *technopolis* interactively links technology commercialization with the public and private sectors to spur economic development and promote technology diversification. The Greek plural of the word *polis* is *poleis*.

3. As a telling example, Japan was one of the first nations to engage in long-term planning for managed high tech growth with the 1983 passage of the technopolis law that fostered 20-year economic development plans. In May 1986 the Japanese government approved MITIs Regional Research Core Concept which called for the establishment of 28 research centers or technopoleis. The program passed by the Japanese Diet promoted four types of facilities (Tatsuno, 1986): (1) experimental research institutes for joint industry/academic/government research; (2) new research, training, and educational facilities; (3) the creation of conference and exhibition halls, and database systems for improved access to technical information; and (4) venture business incubators. Ample funding and meticulous, long-term plans led to the emergence of Tsukuba (about 70 miles north of Tokyo) and Kansai (outside of Osaka). Attractive buildings have been constructed and beautiful parks landscaped; however, the creation of wealth and high-value jobs has been lacking. A ten-year survey of Kansai revealed there have been few spin-out companies and return-on-investment for Kansai Science City.

4. First- and second-level influencers are identified in the communication literature as (1) cosmopolites (individuals who have a relatively high degree of communication with a system's external environments), (2) opinion leaders (individuals who are able to influence other individuals' attitudes or overt behavior), and (3) liaisons (individuals who connect otherwise separate communication networks). The personal communication networks of first-and second-level influencers tend to be outward looking and global, as opposed to closed and provincial.

5. For example, a Fortune 500 company, Dell Computers, was started out of a university dorm room in 1982 by one entrepreneurial student at the University of Texas at Austin. The entrepreneurial idea was to build customer-designed computers using off-the-shelf technology and direct marketing, initially over the phone and increasingly over the Internet. Based on this modest start-up, over 7,000 people are employed in the Austin area with additional manufacturing and sales operations in Asia, Europe, and Latin America.

6. History is full of examples where the producers of an innovative technology by not using and diffusing it were surpassed by others who did. Two examples serve as illustrations—one at the grand scale of the history of civilization; the other at the much smaller scale of contemporary corporate warfare. China developed what was, after the invention of writing, one of the most important ideas for the progress of humankind: the

movable-type printing press. This technology dramatically increased the possibilities of codifying knowledge. However, Imperial China restricted the use and diffusion of this technology to the affairs of the emperor and his court. As a result it was Europe that benefited most from this invention by promoting its widespread use and diffusion (Landes, 1998). A more contemporary example is provided by Xerox PARC, a state-of-the-art R&D facility located in Sunnyvale, California. In the 1970s, housing some of the world's most brilliant researchers, PARC-discovered many of the fundamental computer and software concepts and technologies that have become the basis of today's computer industry. Apple Computer, at the time a Silicon Valley start-up, used PARC developed knowledge and technologies in its innovative and successful Macintosh computer, generating considerable wealth and jobs. In the 1980s it was Seattle-based Microsoft that benefited from the software technologies developed years earlier at PARC.

REFERENCES

Abramovitz, M., and P. David (1996). "Technological Change and the Rise of Intangible Investments: The US Economy's Growth-path in the Twentieth Century", *Employment and Growth in the Knowledge-based Economy.* Paris: OECD.

Audretsch, D. B., and M. P. Feldman (1996). "R&D Spillovers and the Geography of Innovation and Production", *American Economic Review*, 86(3), 630-640.

Audretsch, D. B., and P. R. Stephan (1996). "Company-Scientist Locational Links: The Case of Biotechnology", *American Economic Review*, 86(3), 641-652.

Botkin, J. (1986). "Route 128: Its History and Destiny," in *Creating the Technopolis: Linking Technology Commercialization and Economic Development.* Cambridge, MA: Ballinger.

Cairncross, F. (1997). *The Death of Distance.* Boston: Harvard Business School Press.

Conceição, Pedro, D. Gibson, M. Heitor, and S. Shariq (1997). "Towards a Research Agenda for Knowledge Policies and Management," *Journal of Knowledge Management*, Volume 1, No. 2, December, pp. 129-141.

Conceição, P., and M. V. Heitor (1998). "A Knowledge-Centered Model of Economic Development: New Roles for Educational, Science, and Technology Policies", *Proceedings of the 2nd International Conference on Technology Policy and Innovation,* Lisbon, 3-5 August.

Dosi, G. (1996). "The Contribution of Economic Theory to the Understanding of a Knowledge-Based Economy", *Employment and Growth in the Knowledge-based Economy*, Paris: OCDE.

Edvinsson, L., and M.S. Malone (1997). *Intellectual Capital.* New York: *Harper Collins.*

Gibson D.V., and G. Kozmetsky (1993). "Networking the Technopolis: Cross-Institutional Alliances To Facilitate Regionally-Based Economic Development," *The Journal of Urban Technology*, Vol. 2, No. 1, pp. 21-39.

Gibson, D.V., G. Kozmetsky, and R.W. Smilor (1992). *The Technopolis Phenomenon: Smart Cities, Fast Systems, Global Networks.* Lanham, MD: Rowman & Littlefield Publishers, Inc.

Gibson, D.V., and R. Smilor (1991). "Key Variables in Technology Transfer: A Field-Study Based Empirical Analysis," *Journal of Engineering and Technology Management*, Vol. 8, pp. 287-312.

Landes, D. (1998). *The Wealth and Poverty of Nations: Why Some are so Rich and Some so Poor.* New York: W. W. Norton & Company.

Lucas, R. E. (1988). "On the Mechanics of Economic Development", *Journal of Monetary Economics*, 22, pp. 3-42.

Massey, D., P. Quintas, and D. Wield (1992). *High-Tech Fantasies: Science Parks in Society, Science and Space.* London: Routledge.

Mitchell, William J. (1995). *City of Bits: Space, Place, and the Infobahn.* Cambridge, MA: The MIT Press.

Muller, E., U. Gundrum, and K. Koschatzky (1997). "Methods for Ascertaining Firms' Needs for Innovation Services," in *Technology-Based Firms in the Innovation Process: Management, Financing and Regional Networks.* Heidelberg, Germany: Physica-Verlag.

Nelson, R. R., and P. Romer (1996). "Science, Economic Growth, and Public Policy," in B. L. R. Smith and C. E. Barfield (eds.), *Technology, R&D, and the Economy.* Washington, D.C.: Brookings.

Quandt, Carlos, (1998). "Developing Innovation Networks for Technology-Based Clusters: The Role of Information and Communication Technologies," paper prepared for the workshop on "Tech-regioes: Ciencia, tecnologia e desenvolvimento—passado, presente e futuro," Rio de Janeiro, December 6.

Rogers, E.M. and J.K. Larsen (1984). *Silicon Valley Fever: Growth of High-Tech Culture.* New York: Basic Books.

Saxenian. A. (1994). *Regional Advantage: Culture and Competition in Silicon Valley and Route 128.* Boston: Harvard Business School Press.

Smilor, R.W., G. Kozmetsky, and D.V. Gibson (1988). *Creating the Technopolis: Linking Technology Commercialization and Economic Development.* Cambridge, MA: Ballinger Publishing Company.

Stevens, C. (1996). "The Knowledge Driven Economy", *OECD Observer*, June/July.

Swann, G. M .P., M. J. Prevezer, and D. K. Stout (1998). *The Dynamics of Industrial Clustering.* London: Oxford University Press.

Tatsuno, S. (1986). *The Technopolis Strategy.* Englewood Cliffs: Prentice Hall.

World Bank (1998). *World Development Report 1998: Knowledge for Development.* Washington, DC: The World Bank.

6

Venture Capital in Latin America for New Technology-Based Firms

Scott Tiffin, Gabriela Couto, and Tomas Gabriel Bas

INTRODUCTION

While working at Canada's International Development Research Centre (IDRC), on programs to promote small enterprise development in Latin America and the Caribbean, one of the authors of this paper (Tiffin) gathered informal evidence which seemed to indicate there was very little knowledge about venture capital for new technology-based firms (NTBFs). He then commissioned a series of feasibility studies to explore the topic[1] and engaged the services of a research intern (Couto) to help undertake a preliminary survey of firms, practices and research in this area. This was followed up contracting the services of another researcher (Bas, a doctoral student), to review the literature in detail pertaining to NTBFs and venture capital in Latin America. Our exploratory work focussed on the situation in Buenos Aires (Argentina), Rio de Janeiro, Belo Horizonte and Porto Alegre (Brazil), Montevideo (Uruguay), Santiago (Chile) and San Jose (Costa Rica). Some information was gathered from other countries in the Latin American region.

We are pleased to note that some of the information presented in this chapter is by now out of date! The investigation reported here has led to the preparation of a major research support program by the IDRC. The individual projects being supported have already begun to make a significant impact on the state of research knowledge and professional awareness about venture capital for

NTBFs in Latin America. Public and private investors are beginning to move into the field in several countries.

Our chapter and the accompanying reports at this conference from papers on preliminary results of the IDRC-supported research in Argentina, Brazil, Chile and Uruguay, appear to be one of the first formal analyses of this topic oriented to university researchers, industry professionals and policy makers in Latin America. Being surpassed by the events it put into motion, our chapter now has value more as a historical benchmark to analyse a policy situation in Latin America at a time now gone by. It is hoped that the IDRC research program on venture capital will encourage others to follow and expand its work.

OBJECTIVES

The objectives of this chapter are to:

- Write a short review of why venture capital is important to Latin American development.
- Clarify to Latin American policy professionals how venture capital for NTBFs is distinct from standard private equity placements in mature firms.
- Present a state-of-the-art review of venture capital in Latin America as of the beginning of 1999, in terms of availability of finance for NTBFs, research activity in the field and professional and policy awareness of the importance of this topic, focussing on Southern Cone countries.
- Explain how this analysis led to the design and setting up of a major research program on the topic that attempts to put venture capital on the research, policy and professional agenda in the Southern Cone.

THE IMPORTANCE OF VENTURE CAPITAL

It is commonly accepted that knowledge, based on science and technology, is one of the most important, and certainly the most rapidly changing, factors in creating wealth and building industrial systems. This is widely recognized in developed countries. Despite the widespread appearance of the words "information economy and knowledge society" in Latin American media, there is relatively little awareness that the industrial base oriented (on the whole) to dependent local market manufacturing and resource exports is not structured in the most appropriate way to get there. Furthermore, there is very little awareness about the significant social and cultural factors that are required to sustain a knowledge-based society. There are a range of interrelated factors involved: innovation policies usually exist but are often only weakly implemented; research support institutions are abundant but on the whole their amounts of money oriented to R&D and innovation are very small; universities are abundant, but often isolated from the industrial and political structures, while the private ones have money but tend to focus only on teaching;[2] there are few local innovation systems and clusters, and cultural values do not typically emphasize entrepreneurship based on technology; equity finance for technology-based start-ups is usually not available. In the words of *America Economia* magazine, "Mejor busque afuera"—or, better look abroad! if you need venture capital to grow your technology-based business.[3]

The phrase venture capital in Latin America seems to be burdened with a less-than-desirable connotation. In Spanish it is called *capital de riesgo* and in Portuguese *capital de risco*. Both mean risk capital. Discussions in the IDRC workshop leading up to a definition of the program area, involving some 15 researchers and practitioners from North and South America, showed this might be a factor in creating an unfavourable impression of the subject. It took us almost a half-hour to come up with a more positive term. Many were in favour of simply using the English term to avoid the use of the word risk or, at least, to distinguish it from venture capital that was not applied to NTBFs[4]. In discussions after an earlier paper on this topic was presented,[5] Mexican intervenors from Monterrey stressed the risk-averse nature of society in their area, one of the most advanced technologically in the country, and agreed that the fear of business failure and the attendant social ostracization that often accompanied it were critical factors limiting the formation of NTBFs.

Given these interrelated problems, where is the most critical starting point for policy intervention based on research knowledge? From working in the field of promoting research on new enterprise formation in Latin America, it seemed to Tiffin that there was one area that was almost completely missing: equity funding for technology start-ups. Improvements in all the other interlinked areas mentioned above would stumble on the lack of equity investment funding, so this appeared critical to help resolve. Furthermore, given the installed research capacity, technically trained graduates and relatively sophisticated traditional capital markets in many Latin American countries, it seemed that research knowledge generated in this area could be relatively quickly turned into policy and professional practice, to make equity capital available to NTBFs. Therefore, a decision was made to undertake work in this field.

In the course of this work, however, it became increasingly apparent early in 1998, when feasibility studies began, that knowledge about venture capital on the part of academics, policy analysts and investors was extremely limited[6]. It still is. Therefore, it is important to begin with a short, clear summary for readers of what venture capital for NTBFs is and why it is important in a modern, knowledge-based economy. We start with the broader issue, why it is important, then in the next section make more precise definitions of what it is based on, and provide a clearer understanding of the need to focus on NTBFs and innovation systems.

Knowledge application for the creation of state-of-the-art technologies (biotechnology, electronics, compound materials, etc.) has been long considered as the key for the economic success of nations[7]. Innovation done through fine-tuning of these new technologies is the motor that must promote innovation strategies inside a knowledge-based company as well as the nation itself. On the other hand, supporting the creation of specific actions that favour industrial innovation also constitutes a strategy closely associated to the creation, growth and revenue of the NTBFs[8].

It should be noted that there is a great difference between the new companies that adopt high state-of-the-art technologies and those that do not. Among other aspects, this difference can be measured by the progress of those establishments through the financial demand they make. All during the 1990s, NTBFs have kept their role as drivers of new markets, offering better salaries and presenting superior productivity and profitabililty than those NTBFs that do not use a strategy associated with technological innovation. Launching of new products and new procedures founded in high technology is a fundamental element of success in a world where excellence of knowledge, innovation and state-of-the-art technology occupy a more important place for the wealth of the nation[9].

The great question that must be faced by the developing nations and their NTBFs, is what is the solution of financing such knowledge (highly qualified human resources, research and development of universities, public or private laboratories, etc.), that carries the production of the different state-of-the-art technologies. They have high cost and risk of elaboration. Through the literature[10] we can verify the existence of big gaps in the treatment of the financial question of these new scientific knowledge-based enterprises (biotechnology) and/or technology (information), where the active principal conformed by knowledge and human capital, has been proved[11]. This fact makes it more difficult for the financial institutions to agree on the economic value for these assets, which in turn makes it more complicated for the NTBFs to get adequate financing. Table 6.1 allows us to see more clearly the financial question that must be faced by the NTBFs, where we can observe the different success and risk factors confronted by them.

Knowledge-based firms based on communications, information technology, electronics, biotechnology and new materials are considered as money makers and are involved with every sector of such a modern economy where the use of knowledge becomes the main player in the production process. According to studies undertaken by the Canadian government[12], knowledge-based local economy represents 17% of the Canadian GDP. Growth shown by the knowledge industry has been extraordinary. Data show that from 1990 to 1994, the performance of this industry has been higher than the total average of the rest of the Canadian economy, as measured by its contribution to GDP in salaries and exports. Contribution of knowledge-based enterprises to GDP has grown five times faster than the rest of the national economy. Banking studies made in England explain the importance that knowledge-based small and medium firms (SMEs) have on the economic plan of a nation. This study shows that the most fruitful basis of a national economic plan is to promote NTBFs, since they have a competitive advantage and diffuse their products widely within the economic space, in addition to rapid growth[13].

Table 6.1
Typology of Different Success Factors and the Risks Confronted by the NTBFS

Type of Firm	Typical Sectors	Product Development Cycle	Critical Success Factors	Major Risks
Science-based	➤ Pharmaceutical ➤ Health biotech ➤ New materials	Long (5 to 10 years) ➤ Need for clinical trials, regulatory approvals, testing	Breakthrough scientific product or application, protected by patents	➤ Rival patents ➤ Undiversified patent portfolio
High-tech craft	➤ Software products ➤ Medical equipment ➤ Avionics	Long (5 years) ➤ Accumulation of knowledge and testing	State-of-the art product dominating a niche market	➤ Loss of innovation team ➤ Loss of market niche
Integrators	➤ Information technology services ➤ Telecom	Short (1 to 2 years) ➤ Rapid development of competing services	Superior delivery of complex products or services into a broad market	➤ Failure of project management/ overruns ➤ Changes in standards
Technology users	➤ Food processing ➤ Financial services	Short (1 to 2 years) ➤ Need for continual fine-tuning to market	Innovative distribution of new technology embedded in mature product or service	➤ Loss of tech suppliers ➤ Changes in standards

Source: Groupe Secor, *Le financement des petites enterprises axées sur le savoir.* Task Force on the Future of the Canadian Financial Services Sector, 1998.

These antecedents are important elements that show the influence and importance that supporting the creation of NTBFs, as well as collaborating with universities that work in industrial innovation, have for an economy of a developing nation. It is also fundamental to encourage, through the same channels, the *creation of venture capital networks and companies* to help finance the generation and maintenance of knowledge-based companies, inside an innovation system, in order to facilitate the impulse of a higher source of development of the national economies[14].

We know that innovation is a key element that stimulates the growth and competence of a nation[15]. The objective consists of supporting (within the industrial innovation system) the new knowledge-based enterprises to urge and favour production and growth, as well as knowledge distribution. In a national innovation system, the role of the state is related to a peripheral process designed to help external conditions to become favourable, as well as to favour the availability of the necessary technological resources. In innovation, leadership belongs to the private sector since it is inside the companies where innovation takes place. It is also necessary to clarify that cultural innovation in society tends to develop an interest in technology and an understanding of the role of innovation within the economy and the quality of life in a society[16].

The new knowledge-based enterprises do not innovate by themselves. They do it along with their associate or allied institutions (public and private organizations, universities and government, etc.) that are prepared to share the risks. In the knowledge industry, support from the state within a national innovation system must be available to assist the needs NTBFs have for the hiring of highly qualified personnel, as well as retention of outstanding researchers and innovators. The state must also assist the access to finance, especially in the field of venture capital, indispensable during the different steps of product innovation and firm growth that the NTBFs go through[17].

DEFINING VENTURE CAPITAL

Venture capital is clearly one of the keys to creating NTBFs and the dynamic industrial activity they generate. Furthermore, it seems that there is responsibility at a public-sector level to ensure an adequate supply of venture capital. However, there is considerable lack of precision about what the term venture capital means in Latin America, where there seems to be a significant difference in the meaning than in North America and Europe. It seems to be loosely used in Latin America to refer to any kind of enterprise financing, and furthermore, financing oriented to large infrastructure or industrial investments.

Venture capital as it is known in more industrially developed countries tends to have a different and more restricted meaning, as this chapter will show. Part of this difference obviously reflects the relative lack of importance of new technology-based firms up to now in the industrial development of Latin America. It is therefore important to give some broad definition of the basic concepts involved.

Investors Targeting Mature Firms

There are many different kinds of financing required over the life cycle of a typical private firm.[18] For the purpose of this chapter, one can divide the enterprise life cycle into two parts: first, the start-up and early growth stage, which may be from 5 to 10 years; and second, the mature stage, typically, but by no means always, when the firm is publicly owned (trading shares on the stock market). During the mature stage, finance for operation comes from profits, public share purchase, institutional investors, bank loans and public grants or subsidies. In Latin America there is a good deal of equity investment that targets mature firms. Many of them are called venture capitalists and Table 6.2 lists some of them. This list is by no means complete, but it certainly gives a good impression of the private capital sources available. In addition, there are numerous national public funds and behind many of them, international development banks like the Inter-American Development Bank (IDB) and the World Bank (WB) through their multilateral investment funds (Multilateral Investment Fund-MIF at IDB, Interamerican Investment Corporation-IIC at IDB and International Finance Corporation at WB).

Investments made by these funds focus overwhelmingly on projects that are large (several tens of millions) and in mature applications such as financing new or expanding manufacturing facilities, building public infrastructure (i.e., roads and airports), creating housing complexes, investing in retail firms and financial institutions and, in recent years, financing privatization of public assets. What they almost never do is invest in the early stages of firm growth when the firm is small, without assets, facing several years of going deeper into a loss situation as a new product is innovated and without an experienced management team. Yet this is where firms come from, especially those involved with new biotechnology, information technology and new materials. For the purposes of this chapter and the IDRC research program, this type of finance may be labelled venture finance, but it is completely excluded from our focus.

Table 6.2

Some Private Latin American Funds Currently Operating (US$ M)

Country, City	Fund Name	Fund Target
Argentina, Buenos Aires	*Exxel Capital Partners V. L. P.	$ 850
Argentina, Buenos Aires	*Galicia Advent, Socma Private Equity Ltd.	$ 50
Argentina, Buenos Aires	*Mercosur Equity Fund, L.P. (Perez Company Family Group)	$ 200
Argentina, Buenos Aires	TCR South America II	$ 250
Brazil, Rio de Janeiro	*Brazil Private Equity Fund, L.P.	$ 181
Brazil, Rio de Janeiro	*Patrimonio Private Equity Fund, L.P.	$ 62
Brazil, Rio de Janeiro	CVC-Opportunity Equity Partners, L..P.	$ 1000
Brazil, Rio de Janeiro	Icatu Equity Partners, L..P.	$ 200
Brazil, Sao Paulo	TMG Fund	$ 150
Brazil, Sao Paulo	Pactual Electra Capital Partners P.E. Fund	$ 200
Mexico, Mexico City	ZN Mexico	$ 100
Mexico, Mexico City	Baring Mexico Private Equity Fund, L.P.	$ 50
Puerto Rico, San Juan	Guayacon Private Equity Fund, L.P.	$ 50
USA, Arlington, Va.	Terra Capital Fund, L.P.	$ 50
USA, Arlington, Va.	EcoEnterprises Fund	$ 10
USA, Boston, Mass.	Schooner Latin America P.E. Fund, L..P.	$ 250
USA, Coconut Grove, Florida	*Latin American Enterprise Fund II	$ 164
USA, Dallas, Texas	*Hicks, Muse, Tate & Furst Latin America, L.P.	$ 1000
USA, Littleton, Mass.	Latin Healthcare Fund, L.P.	$ 50
USA, New York	South America Private Equity Growth Fund II, L..P.	$ 500
USA, New York	Deltec Overseas Investments, Ltd.	$ 100
USA, New York	Communications Equity Assoc., Inc.	$ 150
USA, San Diego, California	North American Environmental Fund, L.P.	$ 50
USA, Washington	Darby Overseas Investments, Ltd.	$ 800**
USA, Washington, DC	TCW/Latin American Mezzanine & Infrastructure Fund, L.P.	$ 1000
USA, Houston, Texas	Growth Fund of the Americas L.P.	$ 175
USA, Stamford,Conn.	FondElec Essential Services Growth Fund, L..P.	$ 200
Venezuela, Caracas	Venezuela Restaurant Sector Fund, Ltd.	$ 25

* Funds that held final closings in 1998

Source: Latin American Private Equity Analyst, July 1998.

Investors Targeting Early Stage Firms

The kind of venture capital this chapter is concerned with is financing that goes to new, technology-based firms, those that are in the start-up and early growth stage, as opposed to mature operations. To most people in highly industrialized countries working with the venture capital industry, this is the heart of the venture capital business. Unfortunately, there is no universally accepted definition for venture capital. The Venture Capital Association of Canada, for instance, is unable to define the term succinctly for its members and the clients of its members. Instead, it resorts to description running several pages of what venture capital firms commonly do. This involves working pools, sitting on the target company's board, seeking higher than usual returns, focussing on exit from the outset, adding management skills and accepting high risk. Their investment preferences are usually defined according to stages in the business development cycle:[19]

- Seed financing—proof of concept.
- Start-up—there is a business plan but usually the firm is less than a year old.
- First stage—firm has started to sell product, but is not into commercial production.
- Second—firm is making progress, but still has not moved into profits.
- Mezzanine—firm is moving to major growth potential and is breaking even.
- Leveraged buyouts—purchase of an existing firm.

In this progression, the amount of money required by the NTBF nearly always increases sharply from stage to stage as Figure 6.1 shows. In addition, the time for payoff can be long. According to the American Pharmaceutical Manufacturer's Association, the costs of development of a product for a new knowledge-based enterprise (biotechnology) are found approximately at around US$231 million, and 12 years are needed to take the pharmaceutical product from its initial state of investigation to its approval by the regulation organizations.

Figure 6.1
Needs for Finance

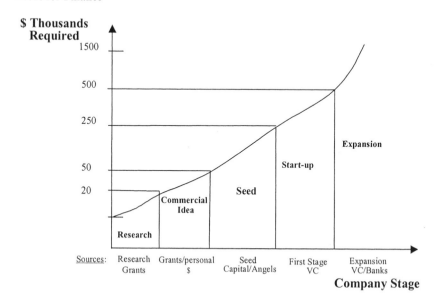

Source: see Groupe Secor, Le financement des petites enterprises axées sur le savoir. Task Force on the Future of the Canadian Financial Services Sector, 1998.

Note the common and strong characteristics for all activities to be dealing with firms, not public infrastructure. Note as well that five out of the six activities deal with firms that have been recently established and are not yet making a profit. This early-stage orientation is so prevalent that the Association specifically states that venture capital is not confined to start-ups, in order to ensure that its membership and users keep broader potentials in mind. Similarly, the Association specifically states that venture capital is not confined to technology investments. It is clear from this description that technology start-ups obviously constitute the main, although not exclusive, focus of this industry as it operates in practice.

The same vagueness of formal definition is found in other institutions and people that are strongly involved with this industry, but they all circle around the points made by the Canadian Association. The British Venture Capital Association uses much the same definition, but in more detail, especially concerning management buy-ins and buy-outs.[20] One technology transfer and commercialization expert interested in setting up venture funds in Latin America says "Venture capital is an equity investment in start-up business that is perceived to have excellent growth prospects but does not have access to capital markets."[21] The standard text by Gladstone uses a whole chapter to define the industry, beginning with "it is easier to begin the description of venture capital by explaining what venture capital is not"![22] For Doyle, the exclusive focus is on technology investments at early stages.[23] We will draw all these threads together in the next section, to create a working definition for this chapter.

A Working Description of Venture Capital for NTBFs

Following the guidance of the above discussion, we can come to some simple, explicit definitions of what we mean by venture capital that should guide further research and public policy that is concerned with the founding and growth of NTBFs in Latin America. The following description may emphasize some points differently than the international literature, in order to reflect the situation in Latin America.

First, we use the term venture capital to refer to privately owned firms, or publicly owned firms that are privately managed and operate according to market principles. While the public sector often has large investments in venture capital funds and public policy is essential to promote and regulate the industry, we are concerned only with firms that operate on market as opposed to political principles.

Second, while venture capital can be applied to any kind of business venture, our focus in this project is strictly on the subset of business ventures that involve new, technology-based enterprises. For our purposes, these enterprises are innovating new technology-based products—that is, taking science and technology, embodying it in a productive manner, building a product and bringing it to market.

Third, venture capital involves equity investments, not loans. While some of the financial instruments in a venture capital deal may have a loan-like flavour under limited conditions (e.g., convertible debentures are sometimes mixed in a deal), the essential condition is the purchase of shares by the investor, resulting in partial ownership of the company.

Fourth, the treatment of risk is different than in traditional banking. Venture capitalists accept significantly higher risk than lending banks and are prepared to lose money on most of their individual investments, as long as they continue to find a small percentage of their deals with extremely high payoff, enough to guarantee overall profitability to the investment fund.

Fifth, the payback time for venture capital investments is typically between three and seven years.

Sixth, in the context of our proposal, venture capital is taken to include the provision of management services as well. In fact, the importance of management services to the new and growing firm is about as important as the provision of capital. Technical entrepreneurs almost never have the full range of skills necessary to manage and grow a profitable firm. These skills are present only in a variety of experienced, senior professionals who cover a range of disciplines including design, marketing, finance, accounting, personnel management, sales, manufacturing, research, electronic commerce and so on. Many of these skills are tacit knowledge; that is, of the kind that is not formally delivered in courses, but only embodied in experienced professionals. Tacit knowledge includes such things as how to select the right board members, or when to freeze a design concept and go to market. The most successful venture capitalists are usually those with the greatest tacit knowledge and ability to impart it to senior management in their investments. Usually, they know the industry intimately and have prior experience growing small, high tech firms. All entrepreneurs, not just those in Latin America, need this support of management skills provided by venture capitalists[24].

Seventh, we need to realize that venture capital really refers to an entire industry group of firms of different sizes, strategies, locations and capabilities— not just one company. It is immediately obvious that more companies will increase the absolute amount of capital available. However, it is also important to note that the industry is made up of firms that specialize in different types of deals and that deals are usually syndicated in order to minimize management costs and risk. Some firms will consider deals in almost any sector and stage, but most specialize to varying degrees in sector and stage.

Typical Investment Dynamics

Given the relative novelty of this topic in Latin America, it is important to summarize how venture capital typically works with NTBFs. Some readers of this chapter will not come from specialized academic and professional fields already involved with the topic.

The dynamics of venture capital investment follow the growth patterns of innovating firms. The first stage of a technology-based firm is often a spin-off from a lab or university and is usually called a start-up. Start-up firms usually get their very first financing from their founding partners. After a few months or a year or so, this money runs out and the owners usually have to go to friends and family. This injection of capital is usually translated into an ownership position, diminishing the control of the founding partners over the enterprise, but on the whole, this first stage of financing is rather informal. It is often called "love" financing because of the close personal links involved.

All too quickly, this love money starts to run out as the innovation and research requirements keep growing and the managers need to seek other, bigger, sources of capital. Typically their search is local as they do not have resources to travel and the amounts of money needed are insufficient to interest investors living a long way away. This is the second general stage of venture capital investment, which we call start-up, as the firms need to formalize their structure and business plans to interest this new type of investor. Although these investments are made strictly on market principles, as opposed to the previous stage, second-stage investments are made by people who have strong community "development" objectives. Partly for this reason, they are called "angel investors" in the trade[25]. During technology innovation projects, the financing requirements greatly increase when the innovation process gets to a pilot or prototype manufacturing stage—or when test marketing begins.

At this point, much more capital is required, and here the companies need to approach professionally managed venture capital corporations. This stage, which will last several years and possibly involve multiple rounds of investment, is generally known as expansion. Although professionally managed venture capital firms may be involved in the earlier stages, in practice they tend to focus overwhelmingly on the expansion stages when there is a demonstrable product insight and manufacturing actually seems feasible.

It should be noted that up to this point, there typically has been no involvement in the financing packages by banks. Banks are always prohibited by regulation from making equity investments, and the risk profile involved with specialized technology innovation projects, often relatively small in the bank's eyes, are not attractive. Early-stage firms usually have no or insufficient collateral to guarantee loans.

In North America, however, one of the fastest growing areas of commercial banking is the development of more equity like loan instruments, which allow banks to move "upstream" into new technology-based business. This is seen as a major new market.[26] Banks, however, are still restricted in making direct equity investments, so often invest indirectly in venture capital funds. But once the firms begin to acquire a reasonable base of fixed assets, which can be used for collateral, banks will come in with venture capital firms on investment deals. All this process, which can take from five to ten years, is leading up to one single objective on the part of the formal investors—to get out of the deal by selling off the investment at the highest possible profit.

This is the exit stage, which is done in a variety of ways: the highest returns will be generated when the company goes public and the shares can be sold on the stock market; typically, however, a larger firm buys up the technology firm or the managers buy back the shares. Planning for exit at the outset of each investment is critical; if there is no viable exit strategy, there will never be an equity investment.

SURVEY OF VENTURE CAPITAL IN LATIN AMERICA

Based on the prior discussion, we will divide the venture capital industry into two parts, informal (earliest stages) and formal (early growth stages), in order to describe what seems to be known about it in Latin America. The former consists mostly of individual angel investors and the latter of professionally managed private corporations. For both areas, the formal academic literature that pertains to Latin America was extremely scarce as of the end of 1998. In fact, a literature search conducted by Couto using the IDRC library system[27] and Bas, based at University of Quebec at Montreal (UQAM) in Canada, encountered not a single reference on venture capital in academic journals for the previous four years relating to Latin America. The only literature discovered during this survey was in Uruguay two undergraduate theses[28] in progress and in Brazil an undergraduate thesis from the early 1980s,[29] a few reports made by consultants contracted by international development organizations[30] and a report by German consultants contracted by FUNDASOL in Uruguay in 1991.[31]

Since there was so little formal information available to guide a research program design, it was necessary for IDRC to contract several feasibility studies in Argentina, Brazil, Chile and Uruguay, as mentioned earlier. After this, Couto was hired as a research intern to investigate the topic further and host an electronic conference and manage a workshop on the topic. In the course of proposal preparation for IDRC financing, proponents created four more reports in which additional information on venture capital can be extracted.[32] Highlights are presented in the following sections according to the country.

Informal Venture Capital

In Couto's survey there was found no documentation on angel financiers in Latin America. The only explicit reference to angel financing was in Voulgaris' survey for Uruguay, where he concluded there were no angel networks such as in North America[33]. Tiffin's personal experience in preparing the financing mechanism for the research projects following up this survey work, is that the term angel financing is rarely understood in government, financial and industry quarters.

However, this is not to say that angel financing does not exist. Angel investors do not seek publicity, and in fact tend to shun it. Anecdotal evidence seems to indicate that loans from family, friends or relatives are quite common in starting up NTBFs. They are based on a trust relationship. In Latin America, in general, a trust relationship is necessary in order for business to take place at the start-up stage. It is interesting to note that we also found repeated anecdotal evidence that entrepreneurs tend to avoid noninstitutional financing that does not come from friends, family and relatives. Entrepreneurs described their perceptions that there is not sufficient legal protection to defend the firm from undue exploitation by an informal financier and the legal processes involved in making such investments are too lengthy.

Professionally Managed Venture Capital

Using the definitions developed earlier, one can see the results of a survey done by Couto of those companies that come reasonably close to being professionally managed venture capital firms, in Table 6.3. The fieldwork for this study concentrated in the Southern Cone; therefore these data show only Argentina, Brazil, Chile and Uruguay. This table presents summary information for quick comparative purposes. It can be seen that most do not, in fact, support NTBFs. Following this are described some of the characteristics of these firms in more detail and the environment for venture capital in each country, as well as the results of the preliminary data searches for the rest of Latin America.

Argentina

According to Marschoff[34] there is a marked difference in the existing knowledge and perception on venture capital among the main actors in Argentina. Entrepreneurs, executives and public functionaries (principally in economics and science and technology) have a good perception about the global, theoretical and operational characteristics of venture capital, while scientists and technological investigators lack enough means of knowledge. Marschoff also states that the main misinformation problem would be linked to the difficulty that Argentina has to establish new ventures targeting funds' attraction to the country's venture capital. On the other hand, most of the existing funds are provided by the state to finance innovation projects for private companies, combined projects (companies-state) or those presented by the state.

We were unable to find any formal venture capital activity under the definition that is being considered in this study. Of course, there is corporate or family capital available outside the NTBF restriction we impose. For example, Advent International, the largest global private equity firm, has had a subsidiary in Buenos Aires, Galicia Advent, since 1995, but has made placements mostly in relatively safe and traditional areas. However, this firm does not support investments in high-risk technology-based enterprises in early or development stages. Table 6.2 shows four funds summing a total of US$1,350 million dedicated to placements in Argentina. These funds generally invest in infrastructure, real estate and large industry, rarely in more risky businesses that involve technology-based products.

Table 6.3
Venture Capital Activity in Southern Cone Countries

Country	Name	Investors	Size of Fund ($ US M)	Administrators	Investment Conditions	Investments/Comments
Argentina	No initiatives under definition described in point 4.3					
Brazil	Companhia Riograndense de Participações					
	Fund 1. CRP	BADESUL, BRDE, private holding	6*	CRP	Diverse	Metallurgy, electronics, software, biotechnology
	Fund 2. CADERI	IFC, IIC, CRP, BNDESPAR, private inv.	15	CRP	Diverse	Metallurgy, software, auto-parts, paper, poultry, etc.
	Fund 3. FITESC	MIF, SEBRAE, BNDESPAR,	10	CRP	Technology-based	Under final negotiation
	Fund 4. FIETEC	MIF, SEBRAE, BNDESPAR, FINEP	10	CRP	Technology-based	Under final negotiation
	BNDESPAR	CONTEC-Program for Capitalization of Technology Based Enterprises. PROSOFT		BNDES or agents	Technology-based	Various. PROSOFT is only for software companies.
	Pernambuco S.A.	BNDESPAR, private holding	8	Same	Technology-based	3 electronic and software companies
Chile	ChileTec	Fundación Chile, Fundación EuroChile, CORFO, MIF	14	VENTANA Chile	Firms with US$ 1-3 M annual income	Evaluating projects to begin first investments.
	H&Q Moneda Chile Fund,L.P.	Hambrecht &Quist , local private investors	20	Moneda Asset Management	Diverse	3 telecommunications, software companies
	Gestión PYME	CORFO, MIF, Bank & Union Labor Life Insurance Co.	20	Estrella Americana	Small and medium firms	Under negotiation
Uruguay	CND (Corporación Nacional para el Desarrollo)	Public allocation and international credit	N/D	CND	Innovative exporting firms that generate employment	Various. Includes tourism projects.
	SAINDESUR	MIF, CND, SIDI, others	0.6	SAINDESUR	young entrepreneurs	Various. Some ready to exit
	FOFIP	IIC, CITIBANK	6	N/D	N/D	Currently changing structure.

*The CRP fund was initially set at US$ 6 M but declined to US$ 1.8 M due to devaluation and failure of some initial partners to disburse.

More closely related to venture capital in our definition is what the firm Endeavor was just setting up in 1998 in Buenos Aires. Endeavor is a nonprofit organization that promotes the development of entrepreneurial business leaders to help them prepare ventures for financing. Endeavor is a New York-based initiative, working with a US$900,000 loan from the Inter American Development Bank's Multilateral Investment Fund (MIF) program, as an intermediary between the entrepreneur and the investors to screen and prepare local entrepreneurs in search of venture financing. Endeavor grants a ten-week internship of an MBA student from selected American universities to assist Argentinean companies in the preparation of a business plan or related activities. Medium to large enterprises with annual sales of US$1 to 15 million are eligible, paying a US$5,000 fee. Five companies were to be selected in 1998 for presentation to a panel of U.S. investors in the year to come. As we understand it, Endeavour is an important facilitating mechanism in a local innovation system, but is not itself the venture capital firm.

Brazil

In Brazil there have been various attempts at venture capital financing since the beginning of the 1980s. Some were successful and most have not succeeded due to many reasons, mainly because of the lack of management skills. No analyses seem to exist, but our interviews indicated that half a dozen firms were established in this period with public and private investment. Some funds were cancelled without even investing and others turned into lending companies. We are not sure how many of these firms would really fit the established criteria.[35]

The only research found on venture capital, mentioned before, a MBA thesis by Leonardos in 1984, referred only to two previous documents relating to Brazil. One was a survey by Weiss at the International Finance Corporation (IFC)[36] and another a consulting study sponsored by the IFC as a feasibility/design input to the creation of the firm Companhia Riograndense de Participaçoes (CRP), described below.[37] In the Brazilian version of this thesis, there are extensive introductory remarks by Roberto da Costa, who confirms that despite the large and sophisticated financial markets, it is surprising to note that there is not venture capital available in Brazil and that the meaning of the term is widely unknown or misunderstood[38]—unfortunately almost the same impression we got from researching the subject 15 years later in Brazil. Leonardos does not mention venture capital for NTBFs except on page 56, to point out explicitly that the industry could start up more easily by involving itself with tech transfer applications or just mature technology-based business ventures.

Schlemm[39] shows that three firms seem to exist by the end of 1998. The first is Pernambuco S.A., a privately administered venture capital firm that promotes the development of small and medium enterprises in the northeast region of Brazil (comprising the states Alagoas, Paraiba, Pernambuco and Rio Grande do Norte). Pernambuco S.A. administers a US$8 million fund with investors from 81 private enterprises of the State of Pernambuco (60%) and BNDESPAR (see below). The maximum investment is US$600,000 and holds up to 49% of company shares with annual income of US$1 to 12 million. So far it has invested in three technology-based firms and has not yet exited from any.

The second group is BNDESPAR (BNDES Participações S.A.), the private equity branch of the national bank for economic and social development. High technology small and medium enterprises are supported through a program for capitalization of technology-based enterprises, CONTEC, for investments over US$ 4 million. Smaller investments are made only through financial agents such as the PROSOFT program aimed at promoting national software companies. The total size of the fund has been about US$600 million since 1995. As a quasigovernment development bank it comes close, but is not really the kind of firm that typifies a mature venture capital industry.

Only one truly private firm has been able to survive up to now and is the one we present in the next section as a case study, Companhia Riograndense de Participações. It now administers four separate funds. This is the only firm in all of the four countries studied by IDRC that corresponds to the venture capital definition, which focuses on technology-based early-stage businesses.

In contrast to this very small amount of NTBF-oriented venture capital, there are many private equity funds investing in large mature enterprises and infrastructure in Brazil, some of which are listed in Table 6.2. One such firm is Bozano Simonsen Securities Inc. which specializes in servicing institutional investors, pension funds, foreign investors and participants in privatization schemes. Bozano Simonsen has had a presence in New York since 1990 specializing in Brazil. Advent International (described in the Argentina section) also has participation in this fund.

Chile

Similar to the Brazilian experience, Chile began promoting venture capital financing in the beginning of the 1980s.[40] Through a World Bank credit line, CORFO[41] developed a publicly administered private equity fund (US$5 million) with the technical support of another state entity for project evaluation (SERCOTEC[42]) in 1986. A short technical assessment contract with the Spanish Society of Venture Capital (SEFFINOVA) concluded that Chile had adequate economic and social conditions for development of venture capital finance. The fund was established a year later and intended for small and medium enterprises with exporting capability. Unfortunately only two investments were made before CORFO decided to close the program after four years of operation. Lack of specialized training and the fact that the fund was administered by a public institution were the major problems, which limited the success of the program. No formal evaluation or any documentation showing the results of this program was found.

Ten years after this experience, however, CORFO again has begun to participate in promoting venture capital. This time it is applying quasi-equity financing to privately administered investment firms through a mechanism called Fondos de Inversión para el Desarrollo de Empresas (FIDEs). FIDEs are the only local option for domestic institutional investors looking to invest in privately held companies and Greenfield projects[43]. At present there are eight FIDEs (CMB-Prime, Estrella Americana, Las Americas, Monitor, Proa, Sabco, Santander Crucero and Toronto Capital Group) with a variety of investments such as a pizza delivery chain, a pharmacy chain, public transport and infrastructure. While none of the investments we found out about seem to be NTBFs, there is nothing stopping a FIDE from working with this type of firm. Despite this new activity, there are concerns about its effectiveness. Bitran[44] comments that the new regulation is still too restrictive, it has not been successful at stimulating private pension fund investments and lacks tributary incentives for both investors and investees.

At present CORFO, Fundación Chile, Fundación EuroChile and MIF have established a venture capital fund, ChileTec, administered by Ventana Chile, a subsidiary of a U.S. venture capital firm based in Long Beach, California[45]. Alvaro Alliende, the recently hired manager of ChileTec, considers this to be the only Chilean venture fund for medium- to high-technology-based companies. Even though there exists a critical mass of projects for evaluation, Alliende predicts that it will be difficult to attract local private investors due to lack of guarantees such as poor intellectual property protection. A crucial point to venture capital investments in new technology-based businesses will be the exporting capacity of the products produced by the NTBFs, since local Chilean markets are small. At present two groups connected to biotechnology development and promotion—CamBioTec and CEOs (formed by BiosChile, Biotecnia, and Bio Forest)—use venture funding for their initial growth[46].

In addition, Endeavor, the firm mentioned in the section on Argentina, began in Chile in 1997 and has made a preliminary selection of six companies for international investment by the end of 1998, although no investments had been made by August 1998.

Uruguay

The sources of financing in this country for small and medium-sized enterprises are offered by groups such as the Corporación Nacional para el Desarrollo (CND), the Corporación Interamericana de Inversiones (CII), SAINDESUR, and others.[47]

SAINDESUR initially intended to be a venture capital firm when established in 1991. It applied many of the recommendations resulting from the feasibility study contracted by FUNDASOL[48]. This study depicted some major weaknesses such as the limited market of the small country, the lack of confidence in basing economic development on the growth of the national industrial sector and the absence of a developed public stock market. Taking into account that exiting through the traditional means of an initial public offering of stock (IPO) would be highly unlikely, this study suggested a more modest style of venture capital firm in which placements would be evidently smaller (i.e., around US$100,000) and exiting would be made through third-party buy-out, through buy-back of the founder or by acquiring formal credit from a bank. Despite its limitations, Uruguay is comparable to other developing countries that have a sufficiently mature financial market to be eligible for venture capital projects supported by international development banks.

SAINDESUR developed a venture fund of US$600,000 with investments from IDB, CND and other European banks as well as private investors. Even though it did not focus on technology-intensive companies, it made several small investments with a program that encouraged young entrepreneurs backed by a local training institute of the Christian Association of Entrepreneurs, Instituto Superior de Educación de Dirigentes de Empresas (ISEDE). The destiny of SAINDESUR within its seven years of existence was, however, to turn into a lending agency, as it could not maintain its original equity investment objectives. The major problems encountered were the high costs of mentorship to the firms and scrutinizing their operations. There is no tradition of technological entrepreneurship in the country producing business-ready innovators.[49] In addition, small enterprise has a history of keeping a parallel set of books—one for the tax collectors and the real ones for internal management. Equity investment was simply too risky under these circumstances and social traditions, so loans secured by collateral was the only business seen as feasible. Another interesting point was finding that most researchers from the university did not feel capable of undertaking their own business and preferred being hired by an entrepreneur as assessors of the technology, while remaining in the university environment.

CND is a half public-half private institution for the economic development of Uruguay. It offers quasi-venture capital of up to 30% of the value of a company with management assistance for innovative companies that have exporting capability and generate employment. Many successful investments have been made in the range of US$300,000 to 900,000. A few years ago it was decided to broaden the eligibility of business to tourism, a traditional business with great potential. Notice that high technology-based companies have not been a target even though they would fall within the selection criteria. CND has recently been carrying out negotiations with MIF to open a venture fund for technology based companies, but this apparently fell through since they could not come to an agreement with the private investing counterpart. Currently, we hear that the national laboratory, LATU, is also negotiating with the MIF to set up a venture capital fund.

SAINDESUR will invest in biotechnology companies, but the amount is not more than US$30,000.[50]

FOFIP is currently undergoing a restructuring into venture capital activity. It is based on more than 80% funding from Citibank and the rest is complemented by IIC, totalling a fund of US$6 million. A new manager has been recently hired at FOFIP and the fund was intended to start activity mid-1999.

Other Countries

Costa Rica is an interesting case of a small country outside the traditional power centres that is rapidly moving ahead where there are two active firms.

Corporación Financiera Ambiental (CFA) (Environmental Financing Corporation)[51] was the first venture capital fund in Central America and remains the only one investing exclusively in small environmental companies. Equity investments are made in small and medium-sized enterprises that promote environmentally sustainable products or services in Central America. Shareholders are MIF (49%), Swiss Office of Foreign and Economic Affairs, Swedfund International AB, Stichting Hivos/Triodos Fondos, Environmental Enterprises Assistance Fund, Hivos/Triodos bank, Citizen Energy Corporation and a private investor. CFA invests in the following industry sectors: renewable energy, energy efficiency, recycling, sustainable agriculture-forestry and aquaculture, pollution abatement and nature tourism.

CFA total capitalization is US$10 million, investing on average US$330, 000. Eligible projects should demonstrate profitability, experienced management with its own money at risk, established entities or start-ups that are backed by previously successful principals, private-sector ownership and precommercial activities. Feasibility studies must be completed and company activities must have a positive environmental impact. CFA transactions are structured so that the entrepreneur retains the majority of shares and management control. If equity is sold, the entrepreneur always has the first option to recover full ownership of the business in the future. Some projects already funded include a hydroelectric facility, a tree plantation, water treatment, an erosion control company, a nature-tourism hotel, a private utility company and a sustainable-harvested project. In our definition, this is not really a venture capital firm working with NTBFs, in practice.

Central America Investment Managers Limited (CAIM)[52] is the first venture capital firm dedicated exclusively to the seven countries of *Central America* and the *Dominican Republic*, based in the British Virgin Islands. It administers a US$26 million fund, CAIF (Central America Investment Fund Limited), whose investors are CDC[53], Swedfund International AB[54], IIC and seven national and regional private banks[55]. CAIM invests in medium-sized companies with growing potential but without involvement in tobacco, liquor, armaments and casinos. Investments range from US$750,000 to US$5 million per company, corresponding to a maximum of 49% of the total shares. CAIM requires a member on the board of directors and expects to exit through public offering, sale to another financial institution, a third party or buy back from the other shareholders. The investment period usually goes from two to seven years. Up to now they have invested in seven companies out of which three are high tech (software and digital communications) and the others are manufacturing and agriculture-oriented.

In *Peru*, we gained limited information about the Fondo de Asistencia a la Pequeña Empresa (Small Enterprise Assistance Fund, FAPE)[56], Peru's first and only venture capital fund for the small enterprise sector. It backs small and medium-sized entrepreneurial firms with great export potential. It holds a US$7 million capital with an average investment of US$160,000. Shareholders are MIF (49%), Netherlands Development Finance Co., Andean Development Corporation and others.

In *Mexico*, there are half a dozen technology-oriented funds in the Mexico City area and in Monterrey. However, these fall into the category of general private equity funds, those that buy companies ranging from food chains to airport terminals, and only exceptionally consider new technology-based firms. SINCAs (Sociedades de Inversión de Capital, parallel to FIDEs in Chile and FEEs in Brazil) have developed in the last two years, totalling 50 SINCAs in Mexico with capital assets of about US$330 million. SINCAs are designed to invest in start-ups or small and medium-sized companies that do not have much access to the capital markets[57]. The Mexican state development bank, Nacional Financiera S.A. (Nafinsa) is partner in 30 out of the 50 SINCAs with seed capital. The comparative advantage of SINCAs is that they become appropriate instruments for foreign investors to bring venture capital to Mexico by offering knowledge of the local opportunities and governmental support, in the case of Nafinsa participation.

It was reported to us that *Columbia* and *Venezuela* have or have had venture capital firms but none were tracked down by our efforts in this study.

A great deal of effort would be required to cover the other countries of Latin America and to go into full detail on these histories, which apparently seem not to have been documented in any formal manner. Doing so would be a worthwhile exercise before investing in new funds for NTBFs, in order to learn the lessons from past experience.

CASE STUDY OF A SUCCESSFUL FIRM: COMPANHIA RIOGRANDENSE DE PARTICIPAÇOES (CRP)

One of the authors (Couto) undertook a study of what appears to be the only working firm in the Southern Cone that fits most of our definitions of venture capital. This firm is Companhia Riograndense de Participaçoes.[58] Throughout its 17 years of activity in Brazil it has not only been involved in numerous investments, but promotion of the industry as well through dissemination of publications and conferencing in many regions of Brazil and abroad. It has been capable of surviving extremely difficult economic and political situations in Brazil.

The philosophy of CRP is to foster the development of small enterprises in the state of Rio Grande do Sul, by betting on the capability of the entrepreneur. CRP believes that the entrepreneur is the single most important factor since he or she is the one who finds market niches and has the driving force to give rise to small enterprises. Investing in a company means investing in an entrepreneur with a good product. Nevertheless, the need to diversify its portfolio has meant investments in medium-sized firms as well. Since the local stock markets are suitable only for large companies to go public, CRP performed some investments in medium enterprises specifically to grow them up to an initial public offering.

This firm is an excellent example of how the North American[59] venture capital experience can be successfully adapted to local conditions and culture, considering the typical conservatism of entrepreneurs and the typical aversion of investors to technology-based risk. Certainly CRP has demonstrated that venture capital as a financing mechanism for technology-based companies is a necessary and useful tool not only through the injection of money, but especially by bringing along a wide range of tacit knowledge that assists an entrepreneur in the development of his or her company.

History of the Firm

In the region of Rio Grande do Sul (the southernmost state of Brazil), much of the population is of Italian and German origin, and there is a strong tradition of family business. Responding to the development of so many small and medium enterprises concentrated in this region, the Development Bank of Rio Grande do Sul (BADESUL, at present called BANRISUL) began to examine how to set up an investment company for private capital placement in the late seventies.

Consultants recommend by the International Finance Corporation[60] suggested that this investment company be managed as a venture capital firm due to the size of the fund and the type of local enterprises, mostly small and medium companies. Venture capital was quite unknown in the region at the time. Different variations of it were practiced by development banks in the region, but none were privately administered. A previous experience in the early 1970s, setting up an equity investment fund managed through public administration, ended up turning into a lending institution. This experience showed the upcoming investment company should be privately administered and the staff would need to have specific training in venture capital.

Federaçao das Industrias do Estado Rio Grande do Sul, FIERGS (Federation of Industry for the State of Rio Grande do Sul) backed the idea, offering the infrastructural support and network of contacts to begin a long period of promotion and diffusion of the venture capital concept throughout the industry to attract investors. The nearly one-year process of giving seminars and conferences and talking individually to industry entrepreneurs resulted in a holding of 156 investors throughout the state, which was named Participaçoes Riograndense (PARGS S.A.). Each investor put in a base amount close to US$100,000, allowing one vote for choosing the holding's representatives for the fund investment council.

Companhia Riograndense de Participaçoes was finally created in December 1981 through the leadership, among many, of Prof. Ary Burger, who at the time was financial director of Grupo Gerdau. Some of the most important industries of the state including Grupo Gerdau, Ipiranga, Petropar, Habitasul, Arbi and local banks invested in the holding (PARGS S.A., 58.6%). The fund was complemented with investments from BADESUL (20.7%) and BRDE (Regional Development Bank, 20.7%).

At the time there were no specific regulations that permitted state or federal banks to invest in private funds. Legal authorization from the Central Bank of Brazil was necessary and CRP had the justification since the development banks involved were essential for supplying a solid background of financing experience, clients and technical support of its staff for project evaluation and others.

Helped by a grant from the Canadian International Development Agency (CIDA), CRP had most of its managers trained in venture capital companies overseas, such as Advance in Boston, Patricof in New York, SB Capital Ltd. in Toronto and SEFFINOVA in Madrid. These managers are still working at CRP and comment that this training was fundamental to the success of this privately administered venture capital fund.

The period 1982-1986 was very successful for Brazil after the petroleum crisis, when Brazilian manufactured products were in widespread demand. This permitted a first round of dividends to be delivered in 1985 and 1986 to the funds' investors. Unfortunately, the following period yielded fewer investment opportunities due to the worsening political and economic situation. Half a dozen venture capital-type funds that had been developed at the time in Brazil went under and CRP was the only to survive at a cost of great personal sacrifice to all employees of the firm.

In 1990 CRP organized a second fund, CADERI (Capital de Risco S.A.), with private investors (25%), international development banks (IFC, IIC[61], 15% and 20% respectively) and the national development bank (BNDESPAR, 20%) as well as CRP (20%).

During the 1980s, CRP participated with the Comissao de Valores Mobiliários (CVM)[62] in the elaboration of regulations for venture capital partnerships. In 1994 the firm also helped create new legislation for regulating Fundos de Empresas Emergentes (FEE)[63] and established the structure for the Brazilian stock market for smaller firms.[64] Inspired by the North American venture capital experience, the new regulation permitted pension funds to place up to 5% of their investment portfolio in venture capital funds for SMEs and regulated the exit of investments.

By late 1998, CRP was closing negotiations for administering two more new funds: FITESC, a US$10 million fund supported by National SEBRAE[65], Santa Catarina pension funds, Multilateral Investment Fund (MIF-IDB) and BNDESPAR (National Bank for Economical and Social Development); and FIETEC, same size, supported by SEBRAE-RS (Rio Grande do Sul), FINEP, MIF and BNDESPAR. These two funds must invest in up to 30 enterprises in three years and will have a life of ten years. Negotiations are also being held with SEBRAE in which CRP would invest in early-stage enterprises that SEBRAE would assist during the start-up phase.

Administrative Structure and Operations

CRP relies on an Administration Council, which has five representatives from the private sector and four from the public sector to give support, advice and supply an informal network of contacts. The council meets to twice a year and is in charge of selecting the Board of Directors with four members. The Board together with CRP managers is responsible for investment decisions as well as important internal management decisions. At present CRP has ten salaried employees of which three are managers. All other services, such as auditing, accounting and legal, are supplied by contract. Revenues come from several sources: return on investment in the target firms; fees from administration of the CADERI fund; and from occasional consulting services, as indicated in the next paragraph. Expenses are mainly salaries, rent, utilities and local expenses, travel, hospitality and such. Three employees are responsible for most of the prospecting for companies as well as networking and conferencing.

Almost one-third of management's time is spent promoting the firm and the venture capital investment mechanism in events such as seminars, congresses, courses, business fairs, associations and federations. The managers are affiliated with many different social associations where they are constantly looking for prospects. An international network maintains close contact with venture capital companies abroad, monitoring the evolution of industry trends and scanning for possible partners.

CRP offers other services to its clients and financial consulting such as:

- identification of investment opportunities
- intermediary in fusion of companies, acquisitions and other types of associations
- company evaluations for negotiating a sale
- feasibility and assessment studies for capital investments or other financial projects.

These services do not represent more than one-third of the firm's income in order not to deviate from the venture capital focus. However, offering these services is evidently a significant source of income for the firm.

Main sources of income are the management fee (from 1.5 to 3.5% of the total value of each fund) and a success fee. The latter fee corresponds to the cases in which an investment has produced capital gains. CRP pays back the fund investors with a 6 to 10% annual interest rate, and the gains are divided 20% to CRP (corresponds to the success fee) and 80% for the investors.

Investment Patterns

Target companies for CRP investments are generally small and medium-sized firms in need of capital for expansion or market consolidation. Investments are usually not made in start-up companies, although there are exceptions when the entrepreneur seems exceptionally capable. Investments range from US$300,000 to 1,000,000 per company. Larger investment cases require leverage of funds, which CRP helps to negotiate with coinvestors either from investment banks, other venture capital-type funds or family groups that wish to diversify their investments.

Criteria for selecting companies is based on:

- the entrepreneur
- location
- size of the company
- production sector

- financial projection.

CRP bets on the entrepreneur's ability to survive conflicting situations through wise decision making. The entrepreneur is the only guarantee for CRP to make an investment decision in a company. A prospective company should not be farther than a 1,000-km radius from Porto Alegre, easily accessible by plane or car and within the three southern states of Brazil. The production sectors that CRP may invest in are established by the regulations of each fund that CRP operates. Generally speaking, investments in tourism, real estate or non-environment-friendly companies are not considered. However, the experience of CRP shows that the fund necessarily has to diversify its risks by investing in different industrial sectors.

Usually investments in a company are negotiated as shares, convertible shares and debentures or a combination of these. An advantage of using convertible debt is that it allows more time for developing a trust relationship with the entrepreneur and in cases when it is difficult to agree to the value of the company.

Partnering is desired for a minimum of two years and not more than five years as a minor partner, up to 40% of total company capital. CRP requires the following before making an investment:

- Company should be a corporation in which each shareholder is liable for his or her own assets (sociedad anónima, S.A.)
- CRP should have the right to one board member
- Can sign a shareholder's agreement
- Company should be audited.

Prospective entrepreneurs have a first meeting with CRP after which an answer indicating if there is further interest is given within 15 days. Cases that are considered attractive (minimum 25% return on investment) are presented to the Investment Committee. If there is further interest, CRP requests the entrepreneur to elaborate a business plan, and usually suggests where to get assistance. Most of the entrepreneurs are able to prepare a business plan with limited assistance from CRP. In some cases (usually very early-stage companies) they request SEBRAE services or hire consultants recommended by CRP. Interestingly, all the entrepreneurs with whom CRP has invested have a university degree. In CRP's experience technical entrepreneurs are more open to receive suggestions for improving the company performance. Family businesses without technical administrators find it more difficult to deal with an external partner.

Due diligence is undertaken over a period of 45 to 60 days in which the entrepreneur's background and the company profile are evaluated. CRP always meets first with the entrepreneur to get a feeling of his or her entrepreneurial capability to take forth the project, and if there is further interest they will require a business plan which they may guide in its elaboration or suggest consultants.

Once there is a suitable business plan and the company has been evaluated thoroughly, a summary is presented to the Investment Committee for which each member has to prepare for a meeting with the entrepreneur. If the proponent accomplishes this phase, the last period consists of negotiating the deal. Negotiating time is variable, ranging from two to twelve months. Usually the period from the first meeting with the entrepreneur to the signing of an investment contract will take from three to six months.

Formal visits are made to an invested business at least once a month. In some cases close management support is necessary to help the company gain strength, which may take up to one visit per week when necessary. In all cases CRP follows the enterprise by placing one of its managers on the Board of Directors of the company. Informal follow-up is done by occasional phone calls and by contacting the company with other customers. CRP tries to motivate the entrepreneur to help look for new opportunities to expand the company. Client database, senior managerial experience and contacts are some of the key benefits that a company acquires when CRP makes an investment.

Three entrepreneurs from companies in which CRP had invested were interviewed to give their point of view on their venture capitalist partner. In all cases the entrepreneurs were eager to say that the association with a venture capitalist improved the professional performance of the company, with a consequent increase of sales. Only one case dealt with a company that needed financial aid to complement the investment that had partially been made for diversification of its products. In this case, the company needed to recover from a financial problem as well as benefit from strategic financial orientation from CRP. This was a case of a family business typically hesitant about having external partners in the business. However, a nearby business had had CRP investment for many years and highly recommended the partnering experience. The company decided to deal with CRP, negotiated in record time, and after a few years of working together the entrepreneur remarked "it is a perfect marriage."

Some companies visited are now coming close to the point where CRP will exit. The entrepreneurs interviewed felt a moral commitment to collaborate in achieving a successful exit mechanism suitable for both sides. Similar to the way the entrepreneurs needed a positive reference about the venture capital company, now they want to be able to finish the deal in good terms to encourage others to follow in their path.

Exiting investments is the most difficult part of the venture capital experience in Latin America. CRP remarks that it does not consider an investment without foreseeing an exit mechanism. Still, exits usually turn out to be troublesome and sometimes even the clauses in a signed, legally binding shareholders' agreement do not help. CRP had to take legal action in one case where they saw the entrepreneur lost faith in the company, and although he had personal capital to invest in the company he did not do so. CRP must have the Investment Committee approve the exit of each investment.

Summary of the CRP Experience

CRP has been active for more than 15 years managing its own fund and administrating others. In all these years their experience has demonstrated that out of 10 companies that they invest in, two-three die, about three cut even and five are successful with varying returns. About 60 cases are analyzed per year. Almost half of these are not applicable, 36% are monitored for future reference and 15% are studied closely for potential investment.

Some of the sectors that CRP has invested in are manufacturing, electronics, pharmaceutics and chemicals. CRP has invested through its second fund, CADERI, in auto parts, software, paper, hydraulics, poultry and others.

Considering the two funds that CRP has operated upon, a total of 23 investments were made, almost one and a half investments a year. Out of these, 13 divestments have already been made, of which almost 50% had the entrepreneur buy back the venture capitalist; 30% were bought by a third party; 15% had the company sold to a larger company; and 5% went to an IPO. CRP invests in a company in which it expects to have an excellent return on investment (ROI). The average ROI in the last ten years has been around 26%.

The last word should be directly from CRP Director Ary Burger, who stressed the following experience gained from these years of operation:

Behavior Rules

- Mutual trust is absolutely necessary between the invested company and the venture capital firm.
- When visiting the companies it is essential to sense the relationship between the administrators and the personnel.
- Relationships should be based on a transparent behavior.
- Before investing it is necessary to have clear how to exit.

Administration and Teamwork

- "Investment managers should be trained by the venture capital firm. In the financial market where venture capital firms are nonexistent, there are no professionals with the mindset to operate this type of investment.
- Given that the entrepreneur is the cornerstone for the company's progress, the investment managers should be able to develop a good grip on the entrepreneur's ability and behavior.
- An investment manager should also have good negotiating power. And when this person reaches the negotiating level with the entrepreneur he or she should have been prepared as to the limits and orientation that can be worked with.
- The venture capital firm staff should have a strong team spirit, commenting on and discussing problems in an integrated manner.
- Weekly meetings for analyzing portfolio and pipeline issues.
- Twice a year it is recommendable to have general meetings with the team and administration discuss the strategy for the firm.

Market Structure

- This is essential for development of venture capital activity that there be an organized and functional secondary market where there is liquidity for investment.

Lessons from the Case Study

- It is obviously difficult, but not impossible, to operate successful, privately managed venture capital firms oriented to NTBFs in Latin America. One of the critical elements in an investment is the exit strategy, which is likely to involve buy-back by the successful entrepreneur. Venture capital firms need to be generalists, accepting deals from a variety of technical and industrial sectors, and supplementing their incomes with consulting fees to survive.
- There is probably still a critical gap of angel financing to be filled for early-stage or start-up NTBFs, as venture capital in Brazil behaves like venture capital elsewhere, avoiding this stage in favour of more market-ready firms.
- Venture capital firms can be an important engine for growing NTBFs.
- International development assistance can and seems to be essential in helping grow venture capital firms
- Public-private cooperation is essential to the establishment and operation of venture capital firms.
- A critical success factor in a venture capital company is management skill and commitment for the long term.
- It is essential that the firm be located in a region with good business infrastructure and a supporting social climate.
- The venture investment success depends equally on the management assistance given to the firm as well as the financing package.
- Personal contacts and relationships are very important, possibly more so than formal business documents, in establishing and maintaining deals.

CONCLUSIONS

The exploration and design activity reported on in this chaper represents some important preliminary research, which has laid the groundwork for future investigation. Although there remain many gaps in our knowledge at this early stage, there are some important conclusions that can be drawn about the situation in Latin America and the Caribbean in 1998.

Lack of Venture Capital

There is very little venture capital oriented to NTBFs in Argentina, Brazil, Chile and Uruguay, and probably throughout all the rest of Latin America. Furthermore, there are very few people with professional skills in fields closely related to venture capital finance and associated management of NTBFs in our four target countries.

Importance of the Lack of Venture Capital

Venture capital is a critical factor in the formation, profitability and growth of new, technology-based firms, as well as local innovation clusters and systems. The lack of it in the Southern Cone probably presents major limitations on the creation and growth of NTBFs in the region. More generally, this significantly inhibits the necessary transition from dependent, resource-exporting economies to knowledge-based societies.

Interest in the Topic

At the time of the conclusion of the IDRC feasibility studies, late 1998, there was very little formal knowledge about the problems, opportunities and dynamics of the venture capital industry in Latin America, although there has been a small and significant history of attempts to create such firms. Furthermore, there was very little research base to work with on this topic in local universities. Work now under way being supported by the IDRC research program in venture capital in Argentina, Brazil, Chile and Uruguay has begun to make a major change in this situation.

Dynamics of the Industry

Despite the frequency of statements about the importance of the different context in Latin America, the problems, opportunities and dynamics of venture capital in Latin America seem to be quite similar to those in developed regions, such as North America. Most firms that work in venture capital tend to deal with commercially ready firms, not early-stage companies. Few NTBFs are chosen for investment. Public agencies have to work to avoid being turned into lending institutions, given the costs of finding and nurturing potential investees. University researchers seem reluctant or unable to become entrepreneurs. This is a familiar list of problems to anyone who has studied venture capital in developed countries—outside of Silicon Valley! In Latin America there are greater barriers to overcome in terms of regulations, policies, stock markets and so on, but these are not different in kind to the situation in North America, only in degree. The only major difference seems to be that business culture in Latin America relies significantly more on personal involvement and family relationships; less on formal, arm's length relationships.

Drawbacks and Opportunities

There is a solid science and technology research base in the region and a good number of knowledge-intensive firms, at least in the biotechnology area, which was the only one investigated in this light. Therefore, it seems likely there is already a sufficient base of research, innovation and firms to support a venture capital industry. There have been significant failures in the past to establish profitable venture capital firms oriented to NTBFs, but better knowledge about how to operate these firms and better training would make a significant difference in their success rate. Development agencies have a critical role to play in promoting the creation of venture capital funds, training people and funding research, at least in the initial stages. The main difficulties in operating venture capital for NTBFs in the region (with significant national variations) seem to be:

- the necessity for small enterprises to work to some degree outside legal norms
- the lack of appropriate stock exchanges to facilitate exits via initial public offerings
- the untested and sometimes ambiguous protection of intellectual property.

RECOMMENDATIONS

It is essential that researchers follow up with more studies of venture capital and the closely related fields of financing and management support signalled here, in order to create knowledge that can better guide decision makers. With the knowledge currently available, we can make only very general recommendations. IDRC-sponsored research teams will make a significant improvement, but this knowledge will relate primarily to only four countries in the region.

Senior managers in public research and technology-oriented business support organizations, especially those responsible for technology transfer and business incubation, should learn more about venture capital and promote its establishment and use. However, they should be extremely wary of the temptation to step in where there is no apparent market interest, by creating and operating these venture funds themselves. These public-sector technology innovation organizations should promote early-stage funds managed by the private sector, in which they may be investors, but only taking on the active role of supplying technical support advice.

Public policy professionals in national governments should involve themselves more with creating favourable regulatory structures relating to intellectual property rights, business formation, tax incentives for creating venture capital pools and restrictions on bank and pension funds investing in venture capital. In addition, normal business regulations need to be applied and enforced in a fair, consistent and transparent manner.

Professionals in international and state development banks should be more active in supporting research and investment in venture capital, aimed at promoting the establishment of local, privately managed and owned funds.

It might be viable to start a Latin American Venture Capital Association, similar to the national organizations in developed countries. Certainly there is a need for such an information, facilitation and promotion agency like this. At the least, a university or business-based Website with information on venture capital for NTBFs in the region would be very useful.

Research on venture capital needs to explore the whole range from angel funding of start-ups through classic venture capital to knowledge-based bank lending and IPOs on the stock market.

Research is required to explore venture capital financing for other areas critical to development in Latin America, not just for NTBFs. For example, there is relatively little local venture capital for the large mining industries in the Southern Cone and no functioning stock exchange to facilitate such capital markets.[66] Locally generated and managed risk equity funding for community enterprises is also in extremely short supply, probably throughout most of Latin America.[67] It appears the whole field of venture funding is a major area needing research and policy intervention throughout the region.

NOTES

1. Chris Ostrovski, Technology Partners International. The Feasibility Study for Research on Venture Finance for Technology Firms in Argentina, Brazil, Chile and Uruguay. IDRC, March 31, 1998.
Country collaboration with: *Argentina*: Aspectos Relevantes para un Estudio de Factibilidad de un Fondo de Capital de Riesgo que Financie Proyectos de Biotecnologia en Argentina. IDRC/LACRO, March 1998. By Carlos M. Marschoff. *Brazil*: Perspectivas de Financiamento de Capital de Risco em Projetos de Biotecnologia no Brasil. IDRC/LACRO, March 1998. By Marcos Schlemm. *Chile*: The Interface Between "Hard" and "Soft" Technologies: Biotechnology, Venture Capital, and Management in Chile. IDRC/LACRO, March 1998. By Jorge Nef. *Uruguay*: Capital de riesgo en el Uruguay. IDRC/LACRO, March 1998. By Myriam Aldabalde. *Canada*: Venture Capital in Canada: Focus in Small and Medium Technology Enterprises. IDRC, August 1998. By Jay A. Lefton.
2. Mario Albornoz and Ernesto Polcuch, Principales Indicadores de Ciencia y Techología. RICYT, Universidad Nacional de Quilmes, Buenos Aires, 1999. It should not be forgotten that the research establishments in countries like Argentina have traditionally been strong enough to gain 3 Nobel prizes in science.
3. Romina Nicaretta, Mejor busque afuera. *America Economia*, pp. 46, 47, 1 July 1999.
4. In a bulletin from the Camera de Industrias of Uruguay, a feature article on venture capital uses the words venture capital in English to avoid distinguishing the target of NTBFs (Constantino Voulgaris, Proyecto CIU—Programa Bolivar: Introducción al Venture Capital. Cronicas, 30 December 1999).
5. Scott Tiffin, Planning and Financing Knowledge for Development. Third International Conference on Technology Policy and Innovation, Austin, Texas. August 30 to September 2, 1999.
6. It is interesting to note that venture capital as a separate field of research came fully of age only in 1999 when Colin Mason and Richard Harrison set up the new journal *Venture Capital* as the first and only academic publication devoted to this topic. Their innagural survey (Editorial, Venture Capital: Rationale, Aims and Scope. *Venture Capital*, Vol. 1, No. 1, pp. 1-46) indicates that there were no articles on venture capital in Latin America or pertaining to Latin America.
7. R. Price, Quand la technologie fait la différence. *L'expansion management review*. September 1996. J. Baldwin et al. Avantages et problèmes liés à l'adoption de la technologie dans le secteur de la fabrication au Canada. Enquête sur l'innovation et les technologies de pointe. *Statistique Canada*. 1996.
8. J. Baldwin et al. Stratégies de réussite: Profil des PME en croissance (PMEC) au Canada. *Statistique Canada*. 1994. B. Amable et al. Les systèmes d'innovation à l'ère de la globalisation. *Economica*. Paris. 1997.

9.   Baldwin et al. 1996, op. cit. Groupe SECOR. Le financement des petites entreprises axées sur le savoir. Task Force on the Future of the Canadian Financial Services Sector. September 1998.

10.   Baldwin et al. 1996, op. cit. SECOR, op. cit. R. Miller et al. International Joint Venture in Developing Countries. Vol. 29. International Finance Corporation. World Bank. 1994. S. Sagari and G. Guidoti, Venture Capital. Lessons from the Developed World for the Developing Markets. Vol. 13. International Finance Corporation. World Bank. 1992. R. Schwindt, Entrepreneurship, Small Business and Venture Capital. *Business Administration Reading Lists and Course Outlines*, vol. 13. Durham, N.C.: Eno River Press. 1990. A. Aylword, *Trends in Venture Capital Finance in Developing Countries*. World Bank. 1998.

11.   Baldwin et al. 1994, op. cit. SECOR, op. cit.

12.   F. Lee and H. Has, Évaluation quantitative des industries à forte concentration de savoir par rapport aux industries à faible concentration de savoir. La croissance fondé sur le savoir et son incidence sur les politiques micro-économiques. Approvisionnement et Services Canada. 1996.

13.   SECOR, op. cit.

14.   Conseil de la science et de la technologie du Québec (CST). Pour une politique québécoise de l'innovation. Rapport de cojoncture 1997. Quebec, Canada. 1998.

15.   H. Drouvot and G. Verna, *Les politiques de développement technologique. L'exemple brésilien.* (Paris: Ed. L'IHEAL, 1994). Amable et al., op. cit.

16.   Ch. Edquist, *Systems of Innovation. Technologies, Institutions and Organizations*. (London: Pinter, 1997). Conseil de la science et de la technologie du Québec, op. cit. Amable et al., op. cit.

17.   Conseil de la science et de la technologie du Québec, op. cit.

18.   A. Riding, Financing Entrepreneurial Firms: Legal and Regulatory Issues. Task Force on the Future of the Canadian Financial Services Sector. 1998.

19.   Canadian Venture Capital Association (CVCA). *Venture Capital in Canada, A Guide & Sources* (Toronto, 1992), pp. 6, 7.

20.   British Venture Capital Association. *Directory, 1998/9*, pp. ii, iii.

21.   Chris Ostrovski (Duke University, 1998).

22.   David Gladstone, *Venture Capital Handbook.* (Englewood Cliffs, NJ: Prentice Hall, 1988).

23.   D. J. Doyle, *Making Technology Happen.* Doyletech Corporation, 3rd Edition. 1992.

24.   Castillo's 1998 study on technical entrepreneurs in Chile showed that of 3 sample groups, totalling some 199 cases, only 2 had ever prepared business plans, the most basic kind of management document for any firm.

25.   Patrick Coveney and Karl Moore have made an excellent description of angel finance in *Business Angels: Securing Startup Finance.* (Chichester, England: Wiley, 1998).

26.   Ross Laver describes the new Royal Bank Growth Corp., a NTBF investment firm owned by the second largest commercial bank in Canada which has recently been formed and is capitalized at $205 million (CAD). Millionaires in the making, *Maclean's Magazine*, June 14, 1999, p. 51.

27.   This was not an exhaustive search and it is quite possible there may be articles turned up after a much more thorough investigation, especially in gray literature, but it is quite clear the formal literature is not treating this topic.

28.   Ana Maria Morales and Karina Azzinnari, Fondos de Capital de Riesgo: Una Alternativa de Financiamiento. Universidad de la República del Uruguay, work in

progress. Constantino Voulgaris, Venture Capital en el Uruguay. Faculty of Business Administration. Universidad Católica de Montevideo. Uruguay, 1998.

29. Ricardo Leonardos, Sociedades de Capital de Risco: Capitalização da Pequena e Média Empresa. (DOCIMEC, 1985).

30. Mentioned several confidential reports, which we were unable to see or even get explicit references.

31. G. Schor and E. Terberger, Reflexiones en torno a la Aplicabilidad del Capital de Riesgo como Tecnología Financiera para la Promoción de la Pequeña Industria en el Uruguay. FUNDASOL, Uruguay, April 1991.

32. Castillo, op. cit., claims that aside from her study on entrepreneurs and new technology, there appears to be no other formal academic study available that has looked at the venture capital experience in Chile to date.

33. Voulgaris, op. cit.

34. Marschoff, op. cit.

35. This information came from the extensive interviews with CRP. Clearly, it is very preliminary and approximate, but worth signalling that more research on past events would probably yield some useful lessons for future activities.

36. Charles Weiss, Promoting Venture Capital in the Developing World—the IFC Experience. Washington DC, International Finance Corporation, December 1983.

37. Tessler and Cloherty Inc., Pre-Appraisal Study of Companhia Riograndense de Participações. January 1982.

38. In Leonardos, op. cit., p. 5.

39. Schlemm, op. cit.

40. Couto conducted interviews at IDB in Chile, FONTEC at CORFO, SERCOTEC, Fundación Chile, Comité de Inversiones Extranjeras, Estrella Americana, Ventana Chile, Endeavor and First Group Chile.

41. CORFO: Corporación de Fomento de la Producción. A national agency for local business development.

42. SERCOTEC: Servicio de Cooperación Técnica. A governmental technological cooperation institution.

43. Latin American Private Equity Analyst, May 1998.

44. Eduardo Bitran was director of CORFO and a major driving force for the elaboration of the FIDE regulation. He is now director of Fundación Chile, a private nonprofit foundation for promotion of technology transfer and business development.

45. Ventana Global Limited of California jointly with Fundacion Chile and FOMIN/BID, Ostrovski, 1998, op. cit.

46. Nef, J., op. cit.

47. Ostrovski, 1998, op. cit.

48. Schor and Terberger, op. cit.

49. Happily, this is changing. A recent newspaper article describes the steps taken by Dr. Alberto Nieto, dean of the Chemistry Faculty of the Universidad de la Republica, to create a NTBF incubator on campus. El Pais, April 2, 2000, p. 4, Section 3.

50. Ostrovski, 1998, op. cit.

51. Information was obtained from Tiffin's visit to CFA in July 1998 and through the Instituto Tecnológico de Costa Rica.

52. Central America Investment Managers Limited, CAIM. See http://www.caim.com/

53. CDC: Commonwealth Development Corporation, a development bank of the Brittish government. See http://www.cdc.co.uk

54.   Swedfund International AB: a private venture capital branch of the Swedish government with private-sector participation. Its actual portfolio is comprised of 65 companies of which 7 are in Latin America. See http://www.swedfund.se

55.   Capital Finance International (CFI), Banco Mercantil, Céntrica, Banco del País, Corporación Banex S.A., Banco del Istmo (BDI) and Banco Centroamericano de Integración Económica (BCIE).

56.   Information made available through the IDB corporate journal, 1998.

57.   Latin American Private Equity Analyst, May 1998.

58.   The authors greatly appreciate CRP's transparency and hospitality to make this case study possible.

59.   North America in this paper refers to both the United States of America and Canada.

60.   International Finance Corporation is a World Bank multilateral finance institution with 30 Latin America and Caribbean country members. See http://www.ifc.org/depts/html/lac.htm.

61.   Inter-American Investment Corporation (IIC) is a multilateral investment corporation, which began in 1989 to promote the economic development of its Latin American and Caribbean member countries through financing of small and medium private enterprises.

62.   CVM: Liquid assets committee, the equivalent of the U.S. Securities and Exchange Commission (SEC).

63.   FEE: Investment funds for start-up enterprises. During 1998 Brazil had up to 4 FEEs adding a total of US$93 million.

64.   Comparable to the U.S. NASDAQ.

65.   SEBRAE: Serviço Brasileiro de Aprendizado Empresarial. A private nonprofit training and assessment entity for entrepreneurs. SEBRAE functions at a national level, with headquarters in Brasilia, as well as at the state level with independent administration. Services offered include technological consulting and assistance in negotiations, development of incubators, design and marketing tools, among others. It is funded through compulsory contributions from export tax revenues.

66.   Personal communication from Luke Danielson, director of Mining Policy Research Initiative at IDRC.

67.   Greg MacLeod, Report on Community Economic Development in Cape Breton and Mexico, IDRC Project 96-1550-01. Final Report, November 1999.

7

Mapping Knowledge Flows in Clusters and Networks: Case Studies of Technology-Based Firms in Brazil

Carlos Quandt

THE CHALLENGE OF A KNOWLEDGE-BASED ECONOMY FOR LATIN AMERICA AND THE CARIBBEAN

The emerging knowledge-based economy is bound to generate major impacts in nearly every industry, region and country in the world. It is associated with the rapid pace of technological change, the increasing importance of knowledge-intensive industries and occupations, and the globalization of production, markets, information and capital. It reinforces the widespread notion among academia, business and government that knowledge and advanced skills are the fundamental strategic resources of our age: "knowledge is now recognised as the driver of productivity and economic growth, leading to a new focus on the role of information, technology and learning in economic performance" (OECD, 1997). The divide between more developed and less developed areas is likely to be increasingly defined in terms of their relative ability to innovate, diffuse and apply knowledge rather than their stock of capital or other factor endowments. The knowledge-based world economy calls for the design of strategies, policies and institutions to support a new model of development—based on innovation, the promotion of knowledge diffusion and the development of advanced skills, world-class industries, technologies and products.

Technology-intensive firms in Latin America and the Caribbean (LAC) typically face great obstacles in their access to new technology and markets within and outside the region. The main problems are related to the relative isolation of individual firms with respect to external sources of knowledge and information, as well as deficiencies in the required institutions, skills and R&D that prevail even in some of LAC's more developed areas. Many strategies and policies to tackle these obstacles have typically focused on two related objectives: First, to foster the creation of technology-intensive clusters in the region and to strengthen existing ones, recognizing their role as catalysts of local innovation, development and commercialization of technology. Second, to develop wider networks to expand and complement the capabilities of local firms and clusters with knowledge and resources from other regions within and outside LAC. In the context of a knowledge-based, globalized economy, in which regional and national economies are increasingly based on the production, distribution and use of knowledge and information, the question that arises is: what would be the relative roles of these two types of strategies in promoting the development of competitive industries, technologies and products in the region?

There seems to be a growing consensus that innovative regions, regardless of their location, must become integrated into wider networks. This is due to several reasons, such as the rise of the network form of organization as a strategy for global competitiveness; the role of information and communication technologies (ICT) in the expansion of interfirm linkages worldwide; the nature of interactive learning processes and externalities among knowledge-intensive firms; and the need to expand and revitalize the technology base of existing clusters. Indeed, a recent comparative study of several clusters worldwide showed that the most important partners in alliances were usually located outside the cluster—and the most important competitors as well (Voyer, 1997). In the specific case of developing-country clusters, the insertion in wider networks obviously provides access to externalities and assets that are not available in the region. This trend often seems to lead to the conclusion that cluster-based interactions may take a secondary role and be replaced in many cases by supraterritorial networks; however, they should be seen as complementary and self-reinforcing, because they involve different types of flows of knowledge.

The research task of this chapter, which is still a work in progress, is to focus on the knowledge transfer aspects of each spatial level of interaction. The cluster-based linkages usually involve informal, person-to-person, mainly tacit knowledge flows, while the supraterritorial network usually involves more formalized, negotiated, codified types of knowledge flows. The understanding of each type of linkage is essential to determine how any given cluster may take advantage of wider networks by becoming part of a "virtual high-tech region," while preserving its identity and its local ability to foster a self-reinforcing process of innovation and growth. The strategy to accomplish the research task is to map external knowledge flows to each firm by source and importance to the innovation process, according to the perceptions of the individual firms themselves. This preliminary survey comprises small and medium firms in two emerging high-technology clusters in Southern Brazil, in the cities of Curitiba and Campinas.

MAPPING KNOWLEDGE FLOWS

The rationale for this project is, in the first place, the recognition that knowledge and information are the fundamental strategic resources of our age. At the same time, it is recognized that networks are emerging as significant tools of social change, and that access to global information resources has become an essential condition to maintain international competitiveness and develop a knowledge-based society. Yet, above all, it is recognized that, in addition to investments in R&D, education, training and new entrepreneurial skills, *knowledge diffusion* through formal and informal networks is just as essential to economic development as the creation of knowledge itself.

Lundvall and Borrás (1997) point out that the fast development of information and communication technologies gives a strong impetus to the process of codification by increasing the economic value of codified knowledge. Most knowledge, which can be codified and reduced to information, can now be transmitted over long distances at very limited cost. This in turn makes more attractive the allocation of resources to the process of codification, and knowledge production is accelerating along the lines of faster codification.

According to Foray and Lundvall (1996), codification is an important process for economic activity and development for four main reasons: codification reduces the costs of knowledge acquisition and technology dissemination; codification adds commodity-like properties to knowledge and facilitates market transactions by reducing the uncertainties and information asymmetries of knowledge exchanges; codification facilitates knowledge externalization and increases the amount of knowledge than can be acquired at a given cost; finally, codification helps to speed up knowledge creation, innovation and economic change.

The most important barrier to this codification trend is change. Complexity may increase the cost of codification but this might be overcome if the knowledge remains stable. This means that tacit knowledge is still a key element in the appropriation and effective use of knowledge, especially when the whole innovation process is accelerating. When the content of knowledge is changing rapidly, it is only those who take part in its creation who can get access to it. This explains the cluster phenomena as well as the formation of industrial networks and interfirm alliances aimed at technology development.

In sum, while knowledge is increasingly being codified and transmitted through communications networks, tacit knowledge is also required, including the skills to use and adapt codified knowledge, in a process of continuous learning by individuals and firms. Innovation in a knowledge-based economy is driven by the interaction of producers and users in the exchange of both codified and tacit knowledge. As access to information becomes easier and less expensive, the ability to select and use it efficiently is essential. In that sense, local agents and structures which support the use and expansion of knowledge in the economy and the linkages between them are crucial to the local ability to diffuse innovations; to absorb and maximize the application of technology to products and processes; and for developing a common cultural basis for the exchange of information.

Therefore, the development of high-tech regions or clusters is but one part of the answer to the challenge that LAC is facing. It is also apparent that a focus on the mobilization of local assets to build synergy and achieve regional competitive advantages must be matched by a broader focus, on the ability to join increasingly wider spatial networks and to develop alliances, partnerships and opportunities with outside firms and investors as well as science parks and incubators, universities and research institutes. Rather than being mutually exclusive, the two concepts (the cluster-based personal contact and the wide network linkage) are deeply linked and complementary.

Both the territorial network and a global network linking sets of local systems have the function of activating and adding value to knowledge produced locally. That is, the local system may interact with a wide range of other nodes or levels through the intermediation of actors which belong simultaneously to a supraterritorial network. Clustering is similar to the network model in the sense that both are technological learning systems that help to socialize innovation-related knowledge and reduce uncertainty in the environment in which innovative agents operate.

The diverse dimensions of the knowledge base—such as tacitness, diversity and complexity—help to understand how cooperative behavior affects the process of innovation and technical change. First, the more the knowledge is tacit, the higher the need for complex linkages between agents with complementary competencies to transfer it. Networks help to "codify" tacit knowledge, facilitating its transmission, verification, storage and reproduction. Second, different kinds of knowledge flow through different channels, involving social practices developed in specific communities; this creates the need for mechanisms to consolidate a diversified knowledge base. Third, the greater the complexity of the knowledge base, the higher will be the need for individual firms to develop mechanisms to integrate the various fragments of knowledge generated externally.

In order to map the distribution of knowledge flows, it is necessary to begin with a basic categorization of endogenous and exogenous knowledge inputs. Endogenous knowledge derives from the firm's internal efforts and experience, and its ability to learn systematically from research, observation and practical experimentation in order to build its internal capabilities. For the purposes of this research, it is appropriate to use two spatial levels to categorize exogenous knowledge flows: The first level refers to the acquisition of new information outside the firm, but within the cluster. The intensity of this type of knowledge acquisition relates to the extension and depth of the firm's involvement in linkages with other agents in the cluster as well as on the relevant stock of collective assets that the cluster is able to offer. The second level of knowledge acquisition refers to improvement of internal learning, innovation and production efficiency from sources of knowledge or skills that are new to the firm and to the cluster. This outer level is where cooperation networks and ICT play a major role, since they can improve the "collective efficiency" of existing clusters by expanding the scope of knowledge search and deepening the capability to generate and manage technical change, indeed creating a "spaceless" economic environment.

It is clear that the different types of knowledge flows require different channels and different types of learning processes. In the specific case of technology-intensive industries, the complex environment in which firms and clusters operate highlights the importance of access to a wide range of complementary assets and competencies. More than in any other case, knowledge and competence flows matter more than flows of ordinary goods and services. At the same time, flexibility and rapid responses in the linkages between firms and other institutions, as well as close user-producer relations, are crucial to support innovation in new and unstable technologies that involve a great deal of uncertainty.

Therefore, this study seeks to map knowledge flows on the basis of their assessment by the technology-based firms themselves. The basic dimension to be considered is whether such flows are endogenous or exogenous, and in the latter case, what is the extent of their spatial reach (within the cluster, outside the cluster but within the region or country, or outside the country). The second dimension relates to the channels through which these flows occur, and what the relevant interfaces are. The third dimension has to do with the magnitude of the flows, or their perceived importance to the innovation process. The fourth dimension is the impact of the knowledge flows on the firm's different types of capabilities, such as its strategic, internal and external capabilities. Finally, perceived gaps and bottlenecks related both to sources and channels of knowledge should be identified.

THE SURVEY OF TECHNOLOGY-BASED FIRMS

The sample of *technology-based firms* (TBFs) in the regions of Campinas and Curitiba was selected with the assistance of the local technology incubators, universities and research institutions. Due to the constraints of this study, the survey covered a small sample of 27 TBFs. In addition to the interviews with entrepreneurs, local government officials and specialists in institutions connected with technology development and transfer were also interviewed. The sample of TBFs comprises a total employment of approximately 2,500 workers, but the majority (70%) of the TBFs are small firms with fewer than 50 employees. The firms are distributed among seven fields of activity: telecommunications equipment, electrical machinery and equipment, computers and office equipment, scientific instruments, information, engineering and scientific services, and software.

Due to its small size, the sample cannot be interpreted as a statistically significant representation of all technology-based firms in the region. My previous study of clusters in Sao Paulo State (Quandt, 1993) and other sources suggest, for example, that Campinas presents a high concentration of telecommunications equipment producers, and a significant concentration of firms in the computer industry. The sample is not indicative of such concentration, and small firms are certainly overrepresented in it. Nearly all the Curitiba TBFs in the sample are software firms. The fact that the size distribution of the TBFs in the sample is skewed toward small firms is because more than half of the firms interviewed operate out of the technology incubators in each region.

Competitive Linkages

According to the survey, most firms (60% of the sample) rank domestic firms located in other regions of the country as their main competitors. Other domestic firms located within the firm's region are also regarded as important competitors. Surprisingly, global competition is not an important issue for the majority of the firms. This relates to their strategy of concentrating mainly in domestic market niches, and it is also reflected in the local scope of the dominant flows of knowledge, as shown below. Similarly, domestic firms (either in the region or outside it) are the main customers of the firms in the sample. External markets appear to have little importance for most firms. Domestic firms (either in the region or outside it) also appear as the main suppliers for the firms in the sample. Local firms tend to be ranked as the top suppliers, while external suppliers remain relatively unimportant for most TBFs.

As far as the competitive advantages of the location are concerned, the location factors that rank highest are availability of skilled people, proximity to markets, a diverse industrial base and overall quality of life. Other important factors are presence of science parks, presence of companies in the same industry and the importance of both the local university and the civilian research lab. The least important factor is the fiscal environment—which relates to the limited ability of local governments in Brazil to affect tax levels.

A key aspect of these clusters is the fact that most firms are far from being involved in global trade. Although foreign competition is important to many of them, these firms are not seeking foreign markets. As Brazil moves toward more open markets and less intervention of the government in the production system, reducing trade barriers and privatizing many state-controlled economic sectors, it is questionable whether these companies can remain competitive. This may affect the cluster's composition and dynamics. As an example, Campinas has been strongly affected by the end of market protection for computers, which has caused a drastic reduction in the local operations of manufacturers of microcomputers and peripherals. On the other hand, new TBFs have been created at an appreciable rate in recent years; they tend to be less dependent on government orders and market protection than many of the older, larger firms.

This territorial concentration of specialized knowledge has also propelled many small-scale efforts to exploit market niches, which rarely reach a global scale. Among other factors, the scarcity of capital has limited their possibilities for growth and diversification. This in turn constrains the opportunities for increased specialization and the collective flexibility allowed by the development of external economies of scale and scope, which would arise from an expanding cluster of specialized interdependent producers linked by dense transaction networks.

Sources of Knowledge

According to the firms surveyed, the most important factor perceived to affect the company's performance is access to a skilled labor pool, followed by ties to the local research base and access to qualified suppliers. The least important factor is government incentives, which probably reflects their limited availability. This item highlights the fact that a skilled workforce is one of the most important localization factors for technology-based companies, and a major constraint to the development of high-tech clusters in many LAC regions. For a cluster to be successful, it must ensure an adequate supply of skilled personnel, usually provided by technological training from universities, research institutes and other forms of scientific and technical training within public and private organizations. It is essential to have a "critical mass" of entrepreneurs, scientists, engineers, technicians, skilled labor, as well as ongoing education and training programs.

More generally, the development and growth of any industrial complex are interrelated with the development of a local labor force which embodies the necessary skills and characteristics demanded by industry. The spatial concentration of skilled workers is conducive to a series of agglomeration economies. For example, the vitality of Silicon Valley has been long connected with the pervasive intercompany diffusion of ideas, personnel mobility and informal networks that evolved from its close clustering of technically interrelated firms (Saxenian, 1985). However, labor force mobility has not been a major source of knowledge for the vast majority of firms in the sample for both clusters. On the other hand, a large number of TBFs mention local universities as the predominant source of new professional employees, with 60% of the total; local companies and other local organizations are not regarded as an important source of new professionals for the majority of the firms.

In any cluster, local competitors may serve as a source of knowledge to the innovation process, a role that may be more important than market-based linkages with other firms. This kind of input is more subtle than what is implied in conventional transactions: it involves the acquisition of information by monitoring competitors and sectoral trends through informal networks, trade journals and mutual suppliers and customers. This helps the firm to evaluate continually its position and to assess the viability of its responses to a rapidly changing technical environment. A significant number of TBFs indicated that informal conversations and social interactions are important means to absorb competitive information. Direct observation and analysis also appear as important ways in which companies gather new knowledge, benefitting from their closeness to other firms in the area.

Cooperative alliances are also very important means to acquire relevant knowledge: 65% of the firms cite alliances with other firms; 20% with universities. In the Campinas case, most firms regard partnerships with local universities as very important, followed by collaborations with other universities. Indeed, that cluster is characterized by strong linkages between research institutions and local firms, especially the smaller ones. Almost 66% of the TBFs in Campinas said that the dominant provider of their external research and technology needs is a local university or research institution; 50% of the companies also mentioned a local or outside firm and 10% mentioned other universities. The question allowed for multiple answers. My previous survey also showed that approximately half the entrepreneurs in small TBFs originated from local universities, and 30% of them were still linked to those institutions. In Curitiba, collaboration arrangements with universities are far less important. This is likely to be related to the much more limited scientific and technological capabilities of local universities, in comparison with the other region. In both cases, alliances with other firms, both locally and outside the region, are highly ranked as sources of knowledge.

The survey results show clearly that universities, research institutions and R&D labs may or may not play an important role as the sources of basic knowledge; what ultimately matters is the development of relationships that integrate the isolated technological capabilities of institutions, firms and individuals into a collective, territorial asset. The establishment of mechanisms to coordinate efficiently these relationships is essential to create a supportive environment for many forms of technical interchange, cross-fertilization, risk-sharing and collective learning that are essential to innovation and growth. During the course of the survey, several entrepreneurs pointed out that one of the major obstacles for university-industry collaborations is the competitive pressure brought by the pace of technological change and rapidly changing markets. They argue that the university is generally unable to respond with the flexibility and speed that would be necessary to develop a joint project and bring a product to the market before it becomes obsolete.

In addition, the evidence from this survey as well as from studies of other high technology complexes suggests that, in addition to pure market transactions, cooperative linkages among firms are also extremely important. This is because knowledge exchanges are vital for the survival of innovative firms. Therefore, the external economies of high technology complexes are quite different from those of previous forms of industrialization, because they are strongly rooted on a set of social relationships that facilitate a continuous flow of scientific and technological information between firms and individuals. In order to be effective, such relationships demand in turn a certain degree of trust and cooperation, which contributes to lower transaction costs. Thus spatial proximity may convert high transaction costs into low ones indirectly by facilitating the establishment of collective norms, shared understandings and mutual obligations, as well as the discussion of new ideas. These relationships are reflected in the significance of local suppliers and competitors, as well as in the large number of respondents that point out the importance of cooperative alliances as means to acquire competitive knowledge.

Other relevant sources of knowledge may include the local press and trade papers, and local events, such as trade fairs, meetings and seminars, but all of them appear as relatively unimportant for these firms. On the other hand, the importance of outside events (elsewhere in Brazil and abroad) was mentioned by 55% of the firms, 35% of them mentioned the Internet, 25% information from clients, 10% outside press, 5% benchmarking. However, most of these sources are regarded as useful for general information on the business environment, technological trends and markets, rather than as sources of competitive business intelligence. The exception in this group of sources is the crucial role of clients as suppliers of knowledge that is regarded as vital for product and process development, particularly by the firms in the Curitiba sample.

Flows of Knowledge

There is a strong correlation between the regional specialization in high technology industries and their interaction with top-level universities and other local organizations such as R&D centers, research institutes and industrial associations. The survey confirms the close connection between the TBFs and these sources of technology, skilled labor and infrastructure—much more so in the Campinas case. In terms of a basic categorization of endogenous and exogenous knowledge inputs, the importance of the universities is reflected in the creation of the first type of knowledge, or in the creation of the firms themselves. As noted, endogenous knowledge is built upon the firm's internal efforts and experience, and its ability to learn systematically from research, observation and practical experimentation in order to build its internal capabilities. The study shows that the local universities, research institutions and R&D labs have had a less important role as the sources of exogenous knowledge inputs.

The first spatial level of exogenous knowledge flows, which refers to the acquisition of new information outside the firm, but within the cluster, is predictably the most significant in this case. The importance of this kind of knowledge acquisition depends on the extension and depth of the firm's involvement in linkages with other agents in the cluster as well as on the stock of collective assets offered by the cluster. Inputs and feedback can occur as a result of interaction between firms, the flow of information through diverse channels and the movement of skilled labor.

It is observed that, although the geographical reach of most technology-based firms tends to expand rapidly, they remain dependent on regional capabilities in order to maintain and increase their competitiveness. Johnson and Lundvall (1992) point out that interactive learning involves a social process, and the more complex the learning, the more will be the required interactions to accomplish it. In addition, the deepening of interactions requires a continuous improvement of intercommunication codes. Therefore, the preexistence of cooperative links among agents with complementary competencies and skills become an important advantage. The interactive character of learning processes is also related to spatial proximity. Although ICT facilitate interactions over an ever expanding geographical space, interactive collaboration is bound to be less costly and more efficient over shorter distances.

In this case, there is an evident predominance of local transactions, cooperative linkages and, consequently, localized flows of knowledge. For most TBFs, their major competitors, customers and suppliers are located within the region or the country. Although in some cases a large share of the components is sourced from remote locations, specific knowledge for product development is rarely obtained abroad. Cooperative arrangements are also important for access to relevant knowledge: alliances with other firms—and to a lesser extent with universities—both locally and outside the region are highly ranked as sources of knowledge. Again, local partners play a dominant role. Finally, clients are also seen as crucial sources of knowledge for product and process development by a significant number of firms.

This predominance of territorially based interactions is a central characteristic of any cluster. In addition to the reasons already mentioned, the high degree of tacitnesss of much of the knowledge inputs for innovation implies that regular and direct face-to-face contact is extremely important, and so is spatial, social and cultural proximity, since the exchange of tacit knowledge is facilitated by a high degree of mutual trust and understanding. According to several of the TBFs interviewed, the acquisition of new technology, the solution for a production problem, or the search for new suppliers is often done with the help of familiar sources that have developed a close relationship with the firm. For example, a trusted supplier may act as a bridge to specific knowledge about a new component or a way to improve product or process development. This occurs in part due to the small firm's inability to conduct a comprehensive search of possible solutions. A broader, worldwide search is usually done only when the objective is to obtain more generic information about products and markets; then the sources are published materials and the Internet.

The second spatial level of exogenous knowledge acquisition refers to the improvement of internal learning, innovation and production efficiency that arises from sources of knowledge or skills that are new to the firm and to the cluster. Evidently, even though the process of knowledge creation, transfer and collective learning is essentially territorially rooted, it is also increasingly influenced by globalization pressures and inducements, in which ICT play a major role. Increasingly, product development, manufacturing and marketing will be managed through complex relationships and alliances between key suppliers, manufacturing subcontractors and the final assembler. Innovative regions may then become specialized hubs in global production networks, and intraregional transactions may become quantitatively and qualitatively less important than national and international linkages.

For the diverse agents in a cluster, opening up to wider cooperation networks implies differentiated benefits. Although the costs and risks can be high, small firms and start-ups tend to gain more, because they generally have limited access to technology networks and international events; in less developed regions, they tend to feel (and are) isolated, and many lack ICT capabilities. At the same time, supraterritorial networks require a complex integration of productive activities, competencies and knowledge.

Camagni (1993) argues that the local *milieu* and the external network might be seen as complementary and mutually reinforcing organizational forms. Both of them facilitate the search, decoding and use of information; reduce the degree of uncertainty for innovative firms; and bring an element of cooperation into economic behavior. Camagni adds that the evolution from the local to the wider network "parallels a natural process of all systems, moving towards increasing complexity, a process which in our specific context goes from proximity relationships to long distance ones, from the same local culture to the integration of different cultures, from casual to selected and intentional linkages, from mainly informal to formalized relationships, and from open and generic networks to closed and targeted networks."

This outer level is where cooperation networks and ICT play a major role, since they can improve the "collective efficiency" of existing clusters by expanding the scope of knowledge search and deepening the capability to generate and manage technical change. It is also particularly important for small and medium enterprises (SMEs), because they tend to have a limited ability to interface with the infrastructure due to their small size. As Arnold and Thuriaux (1997) point out, "while there are many actors emitting 'signals' about technology and about support opportunities, SMEs rarely have good 'receptors' for this information." They may also lack other key skills and resources—such as marketing or business capabilities, which is often the case for new technology-based firms.

It is clear that the wider level of knowledge flows requires different channels and different types of learning processes. This appears to be a significant shortcoming of many of the firms surveyed. In the specific case of technology-intensive industries, the complex environment in which firms and clusters operate highlights the importance of access to a wide range of complementary assets and competencies. Given their limited ability to take advantage of supraterritorial networks, an important function of the institution— the cluster's incubator or managing institution—would be to help screening, decodifying and channeling relevant information into the cluster. The technology incubators in Curitiba and Campinas have attempted to perform that function, yet the results are still quite limited.

CONCLUDING REMARKS AND POLICY IMPLICATIONS

For technology-based industries, more than in any other case, knowledge and competence flows increasingly matter more than flows of ordinary goods and services. At the same time, flexibility and rapid responses in the linkages between firms and other institutions, as well as close user-producer relations, are crucial to support innovation in new and unstable technologies that involve a great deal of uncertainty. This preliminary study has shown that, for the TBFs surveyed, the range of knowledge flows is still very limited, not only in terms of their spatial reach, but also with respect to the channels and interfaces through which these flows occur. This in turn constrains the relevance of such flows to the innovation process, since the firms face simultaneously a difficult access to a small number of sources.

Furthermore, this case also reveals the difficulty of developing high-technology agglomerations in other regions of LAC, where an appropriate knowledge base—such as a concentration of dynamic industries, high-level research programs and a substantial pool of scientists, engineers and technical workers—is much more scarce. In other words, the locational flexibility of high technology firms in developing countries is severely restricted. Very often, basic research, education, training and physical infrastructure in those countries are not only inadequate, but also concentrated in a few metropolitan regions.

The policy implications are connected particularly to the triple role of the scientific and technological infrastructure of any given region in the knowledge-based economy: It comprises the production of knowledge (research and development), its transmission (education and training) and its diffusion (or transfer) so that such knowledge may be applied by the productive sector to generate wealth and development. This implies, for example, that the focus of public support to innovation should include not only strategic science and technology projects, but also specific programs to enhance knowledge diffusion.

This includes efforts to stimulate university-industry-government cooperation, more efficient mechanisms of technology transfer, and the development of "smart" infrastructures. It also means that technology incubators should expand their outreach role, which is usually limited to the local community including universities, firms, and clients. Successful incubators need to be integrated into the local infrastructure but also to national and global sources of technologies and markets. For example, the German network of technology and innovation centers is the largest in Europe with links to 250 centers including those in Central and Eastern Europe (OECD, 1997).

All forms of networking should be fostered at diverse spatial levels. This may range from local venture forums/fairs to bring together potential investors and tenant firm owners to links with incubators in other regions or even in other countries as a way to broaden their sources of information, but also as a way to build markets for their tenant firms and diversify their client base.

The establishment of transterritorial networks enables firms in each cluster or incubator to expand their access to knowledge and resources from a broader range of sources, in addition to an expansion of the available resources to the incubators and clusters themselves (Gibson et al., 1999). A cluster/network-based system of innovation may have a strong impact in specific areas such as the following:

- Access to new markets and marketing strategies
- Access to capital: integrated access to services such as financial planning, support for obtaining grants, opportunities for access to venture, development, and seed capital.

- Expansion of interfirm linkages: a networked approach is ideal for maximizing the impact of programs and projects, such as partnerships, alliances and linkages to outside suppliers.
- Technological support: electronic networks may facilitate access to services such as technology assessment and forecasting, assistance on technological choices, marketing assessment of innovative projects and access to outside technical information.
- Technology transfer opportunities: networks may be used to stimulate investment in S&T, R&D, technology transfer and spin-offs.
- Access to talent and know-how: networks may help in the process of identifying and hiring talent and know-how on a short-term as-needed basis.
- Strengthening local cluster governance structures: the establishment of linkages with other clusters enables a better understanding of stakeholder needs and markets and improves organization methods. Networks may also be used to disseminate best practices in business incubation to improve the performance of firms in each cluster.
- Optimizing and sharing facilities: the operational support infrastructure may be optimized and many facilities could be shared over the network, including incubators, prototype centers, pilot plants, online library, test laboratories and online conferencing facilities.

Evidently, the discussion of knowledge diffusion also has policy implications in terms of human capital and the role of the government in promoting organizational changes to address issues such as flexibility, decentralization, networking and enhancing labor skills. A skilled workforce is one of the most important localization factors for technology-based companies, and a major constraint to the development of clusters in many LAC regions. The development of new types of specialists is also needed, including technology brokers, research experts, information and technology guides and animators. Labor markets are essentially place-based, yet virtual technologies may boost the development of human resources in more remote locations through training centers, distance education, career planning, virtual job markets and also support business development through the establishment of virtual entrepreneur schools providing all kinds of training—technical, managerial, marketing, and so on.

As a concluding comment, it should be stressed that the competitive potential of individual firms and regions, even technologically dynamic ones, is severely constrained when localities have scarce political and financial power. In the case of Brazil in particular, the need to coordinate industrial and technological policies with macroeconomic policies that create an environment of innovation and competition for local firms represents an urgent and challenging issue for the country. This includes the establishment of decentralized support mechanisms—such as adequate and accessible financing, education and training and technological services—that build on regional strengths to stimulate innovation activities; policies that address the demand for scientific and technological applications through the development of human resources; the provision of mechanisms to stimulate R&D activities by private firms; the facilitation of cooperative agreements, alliances and consortia involving public institutions, local firms and foreign organizations to encourage the pooling of resources; the constitution of technology information networks, technology transfer mechanisms and liaison agents to promote exchanges of knowledge among firms, research institutions and regions.

REFERENCES

Arnold, E. and B. Thuriaux, 1997, *Developing Firms' Technological Capabilities,* report to OECD, Brighton, Technopolis. www.technopolis-group.com.

Camagni, R. 1993, "Inter-firm industrial networks: the costs and benefits of cooperative behavior", *Journal of Industry Studies*, Vol. 1, No. 1, October.

Foray, D. and B.-Å. Lundvall, 1996, "The Knowledge-Based Economy: From the Economics of Knowledge to the Learning Economy", in D. Foray and B.-Å. Lundvall, (eds.), *Employment and Growth in the Knowledge-Based Economy*, OECD Documents. Paris: OECD.

Gibson, D., J. Burtner, P. Conceição, J. Nordskog, S. Tankha and C. Quandt (1999), "Incubating and Sustaining Learning and Innovation Poles in Latin America and the Caribbean," IC² Institute.

Johnson B. and B.-Å. Lundvall, 1992, Closing the institutional gap?, *Revue d'Economie Industrielle*, No. 59.

Lundvall, B.-Å. and S. Borrás, 1997, "The globalising learning economy: Implications for innovation policy", Report based on contributions from seven projects under the TSER programme DG XII. Brussels: Commission of the European Union.

OCDE, 1997, Technology Incubators: Nurturing Small Firms, OCDE/GD(97)202.

Quandt, C. 1993, Technological Learning, Competition and Regional Development: Emerging High-Technology Industrial Districts in São Paulo State, Brazil. Ph.D. Dissertation in Urban Planning, UCLA. Ann Arbor, MI: University Microfilms International.

Saxenian, A. 1985, "The genesis of Silicon Valley" in Peter Hall and Ann Markusen (eds.), *Silicon Landscapes.* London: Allen and Unwin.

Voyer, R. 1997, *Emerging High-Technology Industrial Clusters in Brazil, India, Malaysia and South Africa.* Paper prepared for IDRC.

8

Regional Innovation Systems in Korea

Sunyang Chung

INTRODUCTION

During the 1970s and 1980s, the main goal of technology policy was to improve national competitiveness. However, the goals have been extended to such areas as harmony with society and environment, especially in the 1990s (Majer, 1992; Chung, 1996b, 1999b). One direction of this goal extension is regional innovation policy that seeks to develop the regional and national economies under the jurisdiction of local governments. This policy uses various policy measures that have already been utilized in national innovation policies (Meyer-Krahmer, 1990; Süss et al., 1992). The background is that regional development policy in the past, which had focused on inducing as many enterprises in a region as possible, has resulted in an imbalance among regions from the aspect of wealth-creating capability, number of induced enterprises and employment, social infrastructures, and so on.

Based on this recognition, the newly emerging regional innovation policy tries to avoid the weaknesses of traditional regional policy, to extend the qualitative capability of regional development, and, using technological innovation, to focus on transforming regional industrial structures into future-oriented ones. This concept of regional innovation policy has been generated from a combination of technology policy and regional development policy (Meyer-Krahmer, 1990; Chung, 1995). The goals of this new policy are to remove the differences in technology and innovation capability between regions, to promote fair economic development among regions, and to pursue the modernization of national and regional economies efficiently.

In general, regional innovation policy has been widely discussed in relatively small European countries with decentralized local political systems. Since the middle of the 1980s, a new theory of a *national innovation system*[1] has become influential in efforts to improve national technological capability. The concept aims at efficient national development under turbulent technological and economic environments (Lundvall, 1992; Nelson, 1993; Patel & Pavitt, 1994; Chung, 1997; OECD, 1996a). However, the discussion on a national innovation system has been concentrated on a rather theoretical level (e.g., Lundvall, 1992) and superficially on the national level (e.g., Nelson, 1993). Therefore, a new approach will be needed to concretize the concept in policy practice. One good approach would be the concept of a *regional innovation system*. When we apply the concept of national innovation system to regional development, the concept of a regional innovation system can be identified as a subsystem of a national innovation system (Chung, 1996a, 1999b; Braczyk et al., 1998). This concept reflects well the increasing importance of regions in science and technology, business, and economic activities. The regional innovation system will be a good policy concept to generate, implement and appropriate efficient sectoral innovation systems in a region. Therefore, many regional governments have tried to formulate their own regional innovation system in terms of various policy instruments (e.g. Braczyk et al., 1998).

Recently, regional governments in South Korea (hereinafter Korea) have also been making a great effort to establish regional innovation systems, especially since the introduction of a regional government system in 1995. They have prepared an organization for S&T development, tried to increase their S&T budget, and established legal and institutional framework conditions. These efforts have been made around historically accumulated region-specific industrial sectors. These regional governments have also tried to keep a close relationship with the central government and to promote new key technologies very ambitiously.

This chapter analyzes Korean regional innovation systems as a whole and tries to draw some policy implications, which would be of interest for other countries. This chapter is based on a series of studies on Korean regional innovation policies by the author and others (e.g. Chung et al., 1997; Chung & Lee, 1998). We have visited all regions in Korea and interviewed relevant persons in regional governments, regional research institutes, and universities. In addition, we have held a series of meetings, in which at least two delegates from each region have participated, in order to hear the opinions of regions systematically. This chapter is composed of four sections. In the following section we discuss theoretical aspects of a regional innovation policy. Here, the historical development of a regional innovation policy, a national innovation system, and a regional innovation system are analyzed. Based on the theoretical discussion, in the next section we analyze Korean regional innovation systems as a whole. Special attention is given to major aspects of regional innovation systems—i.e., regional distribution of innovation actors and regional governments' S&T budgets, relevant organization in regional administration for S&T promotion, and major policy programs of the central government. Finally, in the last section we identify some policy implications for improving Korean regional innovation systems, which would be helpful for other countries that want to introduce the concept of a regional innovation system into their regional development.

THEORETICAL REVIEW OF A REGIONAL INNOVATION SYSTEM

Development of a Regional Innovation Policy

It was not until the late 1960s that the importance of technology was recognized in regional development. Many developed countries discussed the modernization of their national economies from traditional economic structures. They were experiencing the limits of economic growth that had been based on traditional approaches (Hauff & Scharpf, 1975). As one of the ways to modernize the national economy, regional development strategy was pursued and studies about innovation capabilities and business R&D activities in regions were begun. These studies showed that there were differences in the innovation capabilities between the enterprises located in metropolitan and rural areas. Researchers started to appreciate the innovation capabilities of small and medium-sized enterprises (SMEs), even though they acknowledged the relatively bigger innovation capabilities of large enterprises (Kamien & Schwartz, 1975; Oppenländer, 1975). The modernization policy was propelled by the central government, but it lacked the concrete consideration about regional factors in attaining these policy goals. It focused only on superficial and secondary factors—for example, number of stationed companies, natural resources, and so on. They dealt with the different impacts of the policy instruments of the central government among the regions.

At that time, governments neglected technological factors in regional development, but they had some interest in how research institutes were regionally distributed, how national R&D resources were spent in individual regions, and whether each region had demands of its own for technology policy. The central government played a role only in financing, but it did not make an effort to reinforce regional innovation capabilities such as the reinforcement of educational training services, preparation of information services, and establishment of R&D cooperation networks. However, the economic modernization policy of the central government lacked active consideration of technology, so that the central governments of many countries could not minimize regional differences in economic development, employment, and income distribution. As a result, economic modernization, which was guided by the central governments, did not attract much attention from regional governments.

Therefore, a strong demand for the decentralization of technology policy was raised (Hucke & Wollmann, 1989; Hilpert, 1991). Since the end of the 1970s, this decentralization demand was met with regional development policy that had become conscious of the importance of technology. As a result, regional innovation policy or innovation-oriented regional development policy has been conceived (Meyer-Krahmer, 1985, 1990; Süss et al., 1992). The policy was oriented to the development of one region by increasing its internal technological capabilities (Kreibich, 1989). It aimed at establishing innovation-friendly industrial structures under the leading role of regional governments. Various efforts were undertaken, including financial support, education and training, institutional setting, and so on, to increase regional innovation capabilities. Some developed countries introduced systems approaches, such as the establishment of technology parks, even though they were not comprehensive. In any case, technological factors began to be projected into regional development policy. In particular, policy measures in regional innovation policy were focused on increasing the number of researchers in quantitative and qualitative terms and cultivating the innovation potential of small and medium-sized enterprises as they are the most important actors in regional economic development. (Simon, 1992, 1996). Regulation-oriented policy measures were not welcomed, and the government depended heavily on institutional and indirect supporting measures.

In order to accomplish the objectives of regional innovation policy, however, a systems approach in broad terms, in which relevant innovation actors should be identified and utilized, is needed. Therefore, a new policy concept of a regional innovation system (RIS) has been introduced under the broad framework of a national innovation system. This concept can efficiently include region-specific characteristics, such as economic structure, technology infrastructure, and regional supporting systems. This regional point of view could be well integrated with the industrial and national levels of technological innovation by emphasizing close cooperation between central and regional governments.

National Innovation System

In order to understand a regional innovation system, we need to know a national innovation system first. The concept of "national innovation systems" has frequently been discussed in S&T policy research (e.g. Freeman, 1987; Nelson, 1993; Lundvall, 1992; Patel & Pavitt, 1994; Chung, 1996a, 1996b, 1997). Experts in this area emphasize an effective institutional setting and interactive learning between major actors within the setting, which can be classified into knowledge producers and users (Lundvall, 1988, Chung, 1996a), are very important for generating innovations and strengthening and maintaining national competitiveness. The main purpose of a national innovation system is to strengthen and maintain national competitiveness, especially in economic terms. As a relevant institutional framework for innovation, experts concentrate on the analysis at a national level.

The concept starts from the interrelationship between innovation and institution, and learning arises from that relationship (Johnson, 1992). It emphasizes that interactive learning of all actors in an institution is a source of innovation. Therefore, a systematic setting-up of actors and institutions, which activates learning effects, is especially emphasized in this concept for the effective generation of innovations. In a rapidly changing technological and economic environment, an institution tries to innovate itself and to produce as many innovations as possible in order to challenge and adjust effectively to the environment. It means that an institution should be changed in time to adapt itself and challenge a turbulent environment by producing diverse innovations.

The concept reflects this background and sees an institution as a complex of innovation actors on a national level. There are several definitions for a national innovation system (e.g. Freeman, 1987; Lundvall, 1988, 1992; Patel & Pavitt, 1994). They can be classified into broad and narrow definitions. The broad definition encompasses all interrelated institutional actors that generate, diffuse, and exploit innovations. The narrow definition includes organizations and institutions in searching and exploring technological innovations, such as R&D departments, universities, and public institutes. The narrow definition deals mainly with "technological" innovations. Whereas a broad definition has been preferred in theoretical analyses, a narrow one has been widely utilized in actual and empirical analyses.

In this chapter, the narrow definition is followed. We understand innovation to mean technological innovation and define a national innovation system as a complex of innovation actors and institutions that are directly related to the generation, diffusion, and appropriation of technological innovation and also the interrelationship between innovation actors. Here, the active relationship between users and producers of innovation is established (Lundvall, 1992). The major concern in this concept is how we can formulate an effective national setting of major innovation actors and how to motivate information flows among them in order to generate and appropriate innovation effectively.

A national innovation system consists of four comprehensive actor groups around innovations: industry, public research institutes, academia, and government. The first three categories are actual research producers who carry out R&D activities, while the government plays the role of coordinator between them in terms of its policy instruments, visions, and perspectives for the future. The most important actor in a national innovation system is industry or manufacturing companies, as national competitiveness depends heavily on industrial competitiveness (Nelson & Rosenberg, 1993). The role of government is strongly emphasized in the system, as it promotes the interactions between major innovation actors and prepares for innovation or learning-friendly environment. These four groups should not only generate innovations but also innovate themselves in order to survive and prosper in the rapidly changing environment.

Regional Innovation System

A national innovation system should be understood and analyzed as a complex of subsystems, which can be classified according to individual industry, region, or major technology. We argue that a national innovation system is composed of both regional and sectoral systems of innovation (see Table 8.1). As the user-producer relationship of innovation is established in almost every region and industrial sector, the concept of a national innovation system will be very helpful for the enhancement of regional and industrial competitiveness by activating interaction and flow of qualitative information among major innovation actors in a region and sector. Following the classification of industrial sector, many subsystems can be formulated; for example, a national innovation system of the capital goods industry, a national innovation system of agriculture (e.g. Senker, 1996; Breschi & Malerba, 1997)

Table 8.1
Regional Innovation System and National Innovation System

	Region A	Region B	Region C	. . . .	
Sector 1	O □ ◊ τ ■	O □ ◊ τ ■	O □ ◊ τ ■	. . . .	SIS-1
Sector 2	O □ ◊ τ ■	O □ ◊ τ ■	O □ ◊ τ ■	. . . .	SIS-2
Sector 3	O □ ◊ τ ■	O □ ◊ τ ■	O □ ◊ τ ■	. . . .	SIS-3
Sector 4	O □ ◊ τ ■	O □ ◊ τ ■	O □ ◊ τ ■	. . . .	SIS-4
. . .	. . .	. . .	. . .		. . .
.	RIS-A	RIS-B	RIS-C	. . . .	**NIS**

Note: O: university; □: public research institute, ◊: industry, τ: regional government; ■: central government
Source: Chung (1996b).

However, we emphasize that regional innovation systems are very helpful for attaining effective sectoral innovation systems (SIS) and also a competent national innovation system. As sectoral innovation systems target to increase sectoral competitiveness at a national level, and there are many sectoral innovation systems in a nation, a central government has difficulty in formulating and managing these sectoral innovation systems, especially due to many innovation actors in a nation and their complicated interactions. In contrast, the concept of a regional innovation system focuses on securing regional competitiveness. Therefore, it is easier to implement this policy concept than a sectoral innovation system. Regional innovation systems lead sectoral innovation systems in a nation. In this chapter, we define a regional innovation system as a complex of innovation actors and institutions in a region that are directly related with the generation, diffusion, and appropriation of technological innovation and with an interrelationship between these regional innovation actors. Through trust and close interaction among regional innovation actors, a regional innovation system can generate its own sectoral innovation system. Here, the consensus on the future direction of S&T development and the historically accumulated regional industrial structure play a very important role.

Nowadays, the concept of a regional innovation system has been gaining much attention from policy makers and researchers (e.g. Brazyck et al., 1998; De La Mothe & Paquet, 1998). More basically, Ohmae (1995) argues that the nation-state has been losing its importance in a globalized economy and that the region-state has become a focal point of economic activities. In support of this, he argues that regions are more dynamic and reflexive than states in R&D and economic activities. Breschi and Malerba (1997) argue that regional clusters of innovation activities are more advantageous, when the levels of technological opportunities, technological appropriability, and technological cumulativeness are high. They emphasize also that the regional cluster will result in an industrial cluster in innovation activities. The basic reason is that the region has a sufficient trust that can motivate interactive learning among innovation actors, generate and appropriate innovations. When a region doesn't have sufficient trust, the trust can be studied and accumulated. In this sense, there is a new concept arising, i.e., a *learning region* (Florida, 1995, 1998). Florida (1998) argues that a region should become a learning region by appreciating the importance of knowledge and that public policy should not only target short-term economic competitiveness but also the long-term sustainable advantage of regions.

We argue that a systems approach is needed for generating a learning region and also a *learning state*. Here, the regional innovation system is a good tool. As we illustrated above, regional innovation systems are closely related to sectoral innovation systems. Efficient regional innovation systems build up a competent national innovation system by generating competitive sectoral innovation systems in respective regions. Therefore, it would be very interesting to investigate how regional innovation systems are generated and implemented in a nation, and what kinds of strengths and weaknesses are in these regional innovation systems.

KOREAN REGIONAL INNOVATION SYSTEMS IN GENERAL

Korea in General

In 1995 Korea introduced a regional political system for the first time. Since then, Korean regional governments have made a great effort to extend innovation potential in their regions. As depicted in Figure 8.1, nowadays there are 16 regions in Korea: 7 metropolises and 9 provinces. Until 1997 there were only 15 regions, but Ulsan was separated from Kyongnam to become the 6th metropolis. As we took the survey from 1997 to 1998, we could not analyze Ulsan separately. Therefore, in this chapter, we will discuss 15 regions by including Ulsan in Kyongnam. The metropolitan areas have traditionally been industrialized areas, as the Korean government has tried to bring up regional clusters. Among provinces there are significant differences in the degree of economic development. Kyonggi province has been developed remarkably well based on its proximity to the capital, Seoul. The eastern regions of Korea, especially Kyongbuk and Kyongnam, have been much more developed than the western parts of Korea, for example, Chonnam and Chonbuk. Kangwon and Chungbuk have also been less developed, as they are not geographically suited for industrial activities (NSO, 1998).

Figure 8.1
Map of South Korea

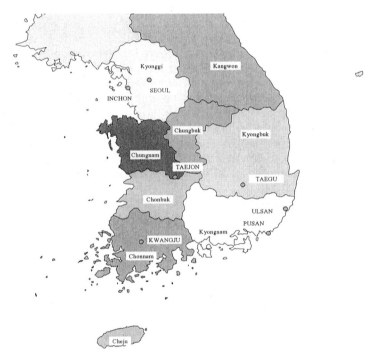

Nowadays, however, many regions have been making a great effort to develop their regional economies, especially based on S&T activities. They have prepared an organization in their regional administrations for regional S&T activities, increased regional S&T budgets, and tried to induce and establish research institutes in their regions. In this section we will analyze these activities from the point of view of a regional innovation system. We will investigate the regional distribution of innovation actors, who are the building stones of a regional innovation system. We will also investigate the S&T budgets in regions and compare them from different points of view. In addition, we will analyze whether and how many Korean regional governments established an organization for S&T promotion in their administrations. Finally, we will analyze the regional distribution of recipients of major S&T programs of the central government, as the central government has played and should play an important role in Korean regional innovation systems.

Regional Distribution of Innovation Actors

In general, a regional innovation system is composed of four main actors: governments, universities, industrial enterprises, and public research institutions. In the governmental sector, the role of regional governments must be emphasized. But the actual actors of innovation activities are public research institutes, private companies, and universities. Among public research institutes, government-sponsored research institutes (GRIs) and national laboratories (NLs) are important. As a proxy variable for private companies' innovation activities, we deal with private research institutes. As Korean universities are heavily focussing on education, university research institutes are included for measurement of innovation potential in the university sector. By this approach, we can approximately measure the innovation capability of Korean regional innovation systems as a whole. Table 8.2 shows the distribution of major innovation actors through the 15 regions. According to the table, innovation actors are unfairly distributed in Korea, as Korean industry itself has been unfairly developed from a regional perspective. We can identify some interesting characteristics as follows.

First, as of 1996, there were 3,452 innovation actors in Korea. It means that each local government has 230 research institutes on the average. The Seoul metropolis has the most innovation actors, with 1,082 research institutes. Kyonggi (844 institutes) and Inchon (187 institutes) follow Seoul in the number of research institutes. Therefore, these metropolitan areas have 2,133 innovation actors. This accounts for 61% of the total number of research institutes in Korea. However, Cheju, Kangwon, Chonbuk, Kwangju, Chungnam, and Chungbuk have a small number of research institutes.

Second, with regard to the public research sector, public research institutes are heavily located in Seoul, Kyonggi, Taejon, and Chungnam. In the case of government-sponsored research institutes, Taejon has 16 institutes, which is more than Seoul (10 institutes). The reason is that many government-sponsored research institutes are located in Daeduck Research Park in Taejon. But, in the case of national laboratories, there are 19 institutes in Seoul, followed by Kyonggi (17 institutes), and Chungnam (10 institutes). In particular, Kyonggi has many national research institutes, because Suwon in the Kyonggi province has traditionally had many national research institutes in agriculture, forestry, and fisheries. In total, Seoul (29 institutes), Kyonggi (19 institutes), Taejon (18 institutes), and Chungnam (13 institutes) have relatively many public research institutes.

Table 8.2
Regional Distribution of Innovation Actors in Korea (as of 1996)

(Unit: number)

Region	Public research sector			University sector		Industry sector		Total
	GRIs	NL	Subtotal (A)	Institutes* (B)	Faculty	Institutes (C)	Research personnel	(A+B+C)
Seoul	10	19	29	224	5,362	829	18,911	1,082
Pusan	1	4	5	71	1,979	77	1,021	153
Taegu	2	7	9	27	801	61	1,051	97
Inchon	3	3	6	13	447	168	4,274	187
Kwangju	1	2	3	24	949	21	767	48
Taejon	16	2	18	28	979	106	5,633	152
Kyonggi	2	17	19	66	1,791	759	29,245	844
Kangwon	1	4	5	31	1,193	21	291	57
Chungbuk	2	7	9	23	791	79	2,084	111
Chungnam	3	10	13	46	1,149	97	1,518	156
Chunbuk	2	2	4	44	1,264	35	1,284	83
Chunnam	-	-	-	19	463	24	521	43
Kyongbuk	-	-	-	64	1,371	113	3,284	177
Kyongnam	3	5	8	40	1,197	200	4,283	248
Cheju	-	4	4	7	168	3	25	14
Total	46	86	132	727	19,904	2,593	74,192	3,452

* Except for engineering research centers (ERCs) and regional research centers (RRCs)
Source: see Chung et al. (1997).

Third, examining the regional distribution of university institutes, we can see the absolute tendency of concentration in Seoul because it is related to the location of universities. Seoul has 30.8% of the total number of university institutes, Kyonggi 9.1%, Pusan 9.8%, and Kyongbuk 8.8%. Since the beginning of the 1990s, the number of university institutes has increased as the university sector has gained importance in the Korean national system of innovation. However, compared with their counterparts in developed countries, Korean universities are still in the beginning stage of extending their R&D activities (see OECD, 1996b; Chung & Lay, 1997). Actually, there are only a few university institutes that can perform systematic R&D activities at the international level. However, university institutes are relatively fairly distributed among regions, compared to institutes in other sectors. In particular, there are many university professors in each region. Therefore, universities can be focal points for regional innovation activities.

Finally, private research institutes are also concentrated in metropolitan areas. About 32% of total private research institutes are located in Seoul (829 institutes), which is followed by about 29.3% in Kyonggi (759 institutes). In particular, Kyonggi has almost the same number of private institutes as Seoul. The Seoul and Kyonggi areas have good R&D infrastructures and a relatively strong advantage in recruiting well-qualified research manpower. Therefore, Korean enterprises prefer these areas for the location of research institutes. Kyongnam, Taejon, Chungnam, Taegu, and Kyongbuk also have relatively many research institutes. Kyongnam province has 200 private institutes that represent about 7.7% of the total number of private research institutes. Inchon, Kyongbuk, and Taejon have also relatively many private research institutes. They are characterized as relatively industrialized areas in Korea. Compared with the distribution of other innovation sectors, the industry sector shows a relatively fair distribution of innovation actors. Therefore, Korean regional innovation systems have a relatively good starting base, as the internal demand of private firms for innovations is regionally distributed.

S&T Budget of Regional Governments

The S&T budget is vital for S&T development in a region. In this chapter, we consider the S&T budget to be all expenses to be used for S&T activities by regional governments. This budget can be divided into R&D-related and S&T-related budgets. The R&D-related budget includes all expenses to be used for the R&D activities of regional innovation actors, while the S&T-related budget is those expenses indirectly related to R&D activities—for example, experimentation, training, consulting, and innovation support. Therefore, we define the S&T-related budget as that for various S&T developments, excluding R&D activities. Table 8.3 shows the R&D-related and S&T-related budgets based on the regional governments' budget statements in 1997. In particular, we compare them with the S&T budget of the central government. As of 1997 the S&T-related budget of regional governments was 4,218 billion won (about US$4.43 billion), which represents about 1.27% of the total budget of Korea. It is very small, compared with the central government's S&T-related budget, which represents about 4.15% (40,841 billion won) of the total budget of the central government. The relative size of the S&T-related budget of local governments is about 10.33% that of the central government.

Table 8.3
S&T Budgets of Regional and Central Governments in Korea (1997)

(Unit: billion won)

Item	Regional governments	Central government	Regional/Central
Total budget (A)	33,174	98,330	33.74%
S&T-related budget (B)	4,22	40,84	10.33%
B/A	1.27%	4.15%	30.60%
R&D-related budget (C)	255	3,019	8.45%
C/A	0.77%	3.07%	25.08%
C/B	60.50%	73.93%	81.83%

Source: see Chung et al. (1997).

In addition, the R&D-related budget of local governments is 2,522 billion won, which represents about 0.77% of the regional governments' total budget. Compared to 3.07% for the central government, regional governments invest very little in R&D activities. The relative size of the R&D-related budget of regional governments is 8.45% of the central government. It is also relatively small, compared to the relative size of the S&T-related budget (10.33%). Therefore, we can say that regional governments have placed more emphasis on S&T-related activities than on actual R&D activities. Regional governments must increase their R&D-related budgets in order to generate, diffuse, and appropriate as many innovations in their region as possible. Fortunately, the Five-year Plan for S&T Innovation, which has been pursued according to the Special Act for S&T Innovation enacted in March 1997, sets a goal of expanding the R&D-related budget of regional governments to about 1% of their total budget by 2002 (STEPI, 1997). We expect that the R&D-related budget of regional governments will be expanded, because the central government has made a strong effort to induce regional governments to increase their R&D-related budgets, especially in terms of the matching fund system.

Table 8.4 shows the size of the S&T budget of each regional government in Korea. There are some interesting facts. First, the absolute amount of the R&D-related budget in provinces (average 21,337 million won) is about 2.0 times bigger than that in metropolises (average 10,533 million won). The average share of the R&D-related budget to total budget in provinces (1.46%) is about 5.0 times bigger than that in metropolises (0.32%). In addition, the absolute amount of the S&T-related budget in provinces (average 37,445 million won) is larger than that of metropolises (average 14,134 million won) by 2.6 times. The average share of the S&T-related budgets to the total budget of local governments is about 4.0 times bigger in provinces (2.58%) than in metropolises

(0.42%). Therefore, we can say that the S&T and R&D activities of metropolises are insufficient compared to those of provinces.

Table 8.4
Regional S&T Budgets in Korea (1997)

(Unit: million won)

Region		Total Budget (A)	Financial independence (%)	S&T-related Budget (B)	R&D-related budget (C)	B/A (%)	C/A (%)
Metropolitan city (average)		20,044,896 (3,340,816)	(81.4)	84,805 (14,134)	63,198 (10,533)	(0.42)	(0.32)
	Seoul	9,304,722	98.1	34,705	30,950	0.37	0.33
	Pusan	3,548,727	87.0	9,844	6,604	0.28	0.19
	Taegu	2,701,823	80.3	7,867	7,050	0.29	0.26
	Inchon	2,231,839	86.7	13,184	9,761	0.59	0.44
	Kwangju	1,231,962	68.0	10,668	4,045	0.87	0.33
	Taejon	1,025,823	68.4	8,537	4,788	0.83	0.47
Province (Do) (average)		13,030,189 (1,447,799)	(37.7)	337,006 (37,445)	192,031 (21,337)	(2.58)	(1.46)
	Kyonggi	2,864,291	78.7	76,438	26,342	2.67	0.92
	Kangwon	718,042	30.8	41,943	39,119	5.84	5.44
	Chungbuk	913,287	36.4	37,533	20,811	4.11	2.28
	Chungnam	1,517,317	28.2	35,351	23,239	2.33	1.53
	Chonbuk	1,473,714	23.4	26,172	16,786	1.78	1.13
	Chonnam	1,639,606	35.7	24,572	13,379	1.50	0.82
	Kyongbuk	1,616,021	30.4	40,177	22,143	2.49	1.37
	Kyongnam	1,822,432	45.2	38,116	21,853	2.09	1.20
	Cheju	465,479	30.1	16,704	8,359	3.59	1.80
Total		33,174,085		421,811	255,229	1.27	0.77

Source: see Chung et al. (1997).

Second, there is no relationship between the degree of financial independence and regional S&T investment. In general, provinces show more dependence on the central government than metropolitan areas. The average rate of financial independence of provinces is 37.7%, while that of metropolises is about 81.4%. However, as shown above, provinces show much stronger R&D intensity than metropolises. In particular, the level of S&T promotion of Kangwon and Cheju provinces, which have below-average financial independence, is very remarkable. In the case of the metropolises of Kwangju and Taejon, which have below-average financial independence for metropolises, they show relatively stronger R&D investment. This implies that the recognition by regional communities of S&T's importance in regional development is essential for extending S&T investment. In particular, the governor's interest in S&T activities is vital to the increase of the S&T budgets.

Third, regional governments in Korea compete strongly with each other in S&T promotion. Metropolitan regions like Kwangju, Taejon, and Inchon make a greater effort to promote S&T activities than Seoul, Pusan, and Taegu. As for provinces, developing regions like Kangwon and Chungbuk make more investments in R&D and S&T activities than traditionally developed areas, such as Kyonggi, Kyongnam, and Kyongbuk. In particular, Kangwon and Chungbuk deserve to be mentioned. Traditionally, both areas have been less developed compared to other provinces and metropolises in Korea. However, Kangwon shows the biggest S&T and R&D intensities, with 5.13% and 4.79% respectively. It is followed by Chungbuk. These areas are characterized by strong institutional supports by their respective regional governments. For example, both Kangwon and Chungbuk provinces established Industrial Technology Teams in their regional administrations.

Finally, relating the regional distribution of research institutes with the regional distribution of S&T budgets, we know that regions with relatively fewer institutes make more investments in S&T and R&D activities. Kangwon, Chungbuk, and Cheju provinces show a much bigger share of the S&T budgets to the total budget, even though they have relatively fewer R&D institutes: 57 institutes in Kangwon, 111 in Chungbuk, and 14 in Cheju. Among metropolises, Kwangju, Taejon, and Inchon show strong investments in S&T activities, even though they have fewer institutes than the metropolitan average.

Based on the evidence above, we argue that a recognition of regional governments for S&T's importance in regional development and the strong desire for investment in S&T are more important for extending regional innovation capabilities than historically accumulated industrial structures and the absolute number of research institutes. In particular, the governor's long-range vision for S&T development is a prerequisite. Based on his strong commitment, a regional government can effectively increase its S&T budget, prepare for institutional framework conditions, and induce S&T infrastructure from the central government. Such a strong commitment of regional government in S&T development will activate interactive learning and cooperation among innovation actors in a region.

S&T Promotion Organization in Regional Governments

In order to strengthen regional innovation systems, an organization that is directly concerned with S&T promotion should be established in a regional administration. Some advanced countries like Germany have very senior-level organizations for S&T promotion, such as Ministry for Science, Technology and Culture (Chung, 1997). In Korea, however, there has been no sufficient role for regional government in S&T promotion, especially until the middle of the 1990s. Fortunately, some regional governments have recently begun to recognize the importance of technology in the development of their regions and to establish organizations for S&T promotion in their administrations. The establishment of an organization for S&T promotion was based on Article 17 of the Technology Promotion Act, which forced the governors of regional governments to prepare an organization for S&T promotion in their respective regions. Chungbuk province is the first regional government that established a department of technology promotion in its administration.

According to our survey, as of April 1999, eight regional governments among a total of 16 regional governments have established a special organization for S&T promotion. Besides Chungbuk, Taejon and Kyongbuk have organizations at the department-level. Inchon, Kwangju, Kyongnam, Kangwon, and Chungnam have team-level organizations within a department of SME promotion or a department of industrial promotion and so on (Chung et al., 1997; Chung & Lee, 1999). In the case of regional governments that do not have such organizations, a department of SME promotion or industry promotion and so on is in charge of technology promotion in their regions. These organizations for S&T promotion collect data and information for comprehensive planning for technology promotion in their regions, report them to the governor, and help him in his policy making for S&T development.

In addition to S&T-related organizations, there are some regional governments that have specialists on regional S&T policy. In particular, Taegu, Inchon, Taejeon, and Chonbuk have such specialists. These specialists belong to such organizations as urban research team, policy-research team, and international cooperation office. They perform surveys, planning, policy formulation, and consultation in their regions. They function as think tanks to the governor, independently from organizations for S&T promotion. Their role has been growing because many regional governments have no official organizations for S&T promotion and, if any, the organization plays an insufficient role in regional S&T development.

Support of the Central Government

The central government plays an important role in regional development in Korea, as it is a traditionally centralized country. In particular, Korean regional governments have a short history of promoting S&T activities, and they are financially dependent on the central government to a large degree. Therefore, it is important to investigate how the central government has supported regions in their programs for enhancing innovation capabilities.

There are several ministries in the Korean central government that are engaging in S&T development, including the Ministry of Science and Technology (MOST) and Ministry of Commerce, Industry and Energy (MOCIE). Each ministry has its own promotion programs for S&T development. Even though such programs have not been obviously aimed at regional S&T development, they have had a very significant impact on regional S&T activities. There are four important programs for S&T development: the Basic Research Promotion Program (MOST), the National R&D Program (MOST), the Generic Industrial Technology Program (MOCIE), and the Technology Infrastructure Promotion Program (MOCIE). Table 8.5 shows the regional distribution of recipients of the central government's S&T programs.

First, with regard to the regional distribution of recipients of the *Basic Research Promotion Program*, over 40% of the projects and funds are concentrated in Seoul, where many competitive universities are located (KOSEF, 1995). This program has been implemented not according to regional distribution, but by the criteria of the research capabilities of universities. Therefore, the grants have been concentrated in Seoul and a few areas where good universities are located. With about 16% of the total amount of grants, Taejon follows Seoul by a significant margin, as it has the Korea Advanced Institute of Science and Technology (KAIST).

Table 8.5
Regional Participation in Major Programs of the Central Government

(Unit: number, million won, %)

Region	Basic Research Promotion Program		National R&D Program		Generic Industrial Technology Program	Technology Infrastructure Promotion Program	
	Number*	Amount	Number	Amounts	Number	Number	Amounts
Seoul	899 (44.0)	33,414 (41.0)	552 (39.7)	59,787 (23.4)5	803 (60.5)	17 (54.8)	18,250 (61.1)
Pusan	123 (6.0)	5,058 (6.2)	17 (1.2)	2,263 (0.9)	68 (5.1)	2 (6.5)	1,700 (5.7)
Taegu	137 (6.7)	4,300 (5.3)	12 (0.9)	1,186 (0.5)	17 (1.3)	3 (9.7)	3,500 (11.7)
Inchon	52 (2.5)	1,254 (1.5)	33 (2.4)	4,284 (1.7)	26 (2.0)	-	-
Kwangju	74 (3.6)	2,681 (3.3)	12 (0.9)	1,929 (0.8)	4 (0.3)	1 (3.2)	1,000 (3.4)
Taejon	208 (10.2)	12,896 (15.8)	480 (34.5)	139,059 (54.5)	56 (4.2)	2 (6.5)	1,300 (4.4)
Kyonggi	119 (5.8)	4,495 (5.5)	149 (10.7)	25,580 (10.0)	215 (16.2)	4 (12.9)	1,400 (4.7)
Kangwon	83 (4.1)	1,904 (2.3)	9 (0.6)	406 (0.2)	7 (0.5)	-	-
Chungbuk	54 (2.6)	1,189 (1.5)	7 (0.5)	1,059 (0.4)	19 (1.4)	-	-
Chungnam	47 (2.3)	1,275 (1.6)	14 (1.0)	2,920 (1.1)	16 (1.2)	2 (6.5)	2,700 (9.0)
Chonbuk	73 (3.6)	2,644 (3.2)	12 (0.9)	609 (0.2)	12 (0.9)	-	-
Chonnam	14 (0.7)	371 (0.5)	1 (0.1)	88 (0.0)	6 (0.5)	-	-
Kyongbuk	77 (3.7)	7,029 (8.6)	29 (2.1)	4,912 (1.9)	16 (1.2)	-	-
Kyongnam	76 (3.7)	2,481 (3.0)	63 (4.5)	10,834 (4.2)	63 (4.7)	-	-
Cheju	9 (0.4)	426 (0.5)	1 (0.1)	95 (0)	-	-	-
Total	2.045 (100.0)	81,417 (100.0)	1,391 (100.0)	255,011 (100.0)	1,328 (100.0)	31 (100.0)	29,850 (100.0)

*Number of projects.
Source: KOSEF's Statistics on Basic Research Promotions; STEPI's D/B on national R&D Program; ITEP's internal documents

The regional distribution of this program is also influenced by the regional distribution of excellent research centers (ExRC) and regional research centers (RRCs) that have been established in universities. ExRCs have been established since 1990 in order to bring up excellent basic research groups in universities. ExRCs consist of SRCs (science research centers), which aim at contributing basic scientific and technological capabilities, and ERCs (engineering research centers), which are aimed at developing industrial technological capabilities. Since 1995, RRCs have been established in order to raise regional S&T capabilities. As of June 1999, there are 20 SRCs, 28 ERCs, and 37 RRCs (KOSEF, 1999a, 1999b). Table 8.6 indicates the regional distribution of ERCs and RRCs. SRCs, which are to enhance basic research capabilities, are concentrated in Seoul National University in Seoul. The same number of ERCs as in Seoul are in the Korea Advanced Institute of Science and Technology in Taejon, as KAIST concentrates on developing engineering and technological capabilities. However, RRCs are relatively fairly distributed among regions, as they are targeted to increase regional research capabilities. According to our interviews with experts in the regions, RRCs have played an important role in enhancing regional innovation potential.

Table 8.6
Excellent Research Centers and Regional Research Centers in Korea (as of June 1999)

(Unit: number)

Region	ExRCs		RRCs	Total
	SRCs	ERCs		
Seoul	12	10	-	22
Pusan	1	2	2	5
Taegu	1	1	2	4
Inchon	-	-	3	3
Kwangju	-	1	2	3
Taejon	1	10	3	14
Kyonggi	1	-	3	4
Kangwon	-	-	3	3
Chungbuk	-	-	2	2
Chungnam	-	-	3	3
Chonbuk	1	-	3	4
Chonnam	1	-	3	4
Kyongbuk	1	4	3	8
Kyongnam	1	-	4	5
Cheju	-	-	1	1
Total	20	28	37	85

Source: KOSEF (1999a, 1999b).

Second, the *National R&D Program*, which was begun in 1982, has been the most important R&D promotion program in Korea. Innovation actors can participate in this program, especially jointly with other actors in different sectors. According to statistics in 1996, innovation actors participating in this program are concentrated heavily in Seoul (39.7%) and Taejon (34.5%). The reason is that Seoul has many good universities and Taejon has most of the government-sponsored research institutes. Therefore, the central government should motivate innovation actors in other regions to actively join in the program. In particular, regional innovation actors should initiate R&D projects that are closely related to region-specific industrial structures. For this purpose, regional governments should bring up specific research groups in their regional innovation systems.

Third, the *Generic Industrial Technology Program* aims at solving technological problems that are commonly faced by many industrial companies and also at extending technological capabilities that could not be easily increased by industry alone. A portion of the total project amount is financed by the central government as a grant. Recipients of this program are also concentrated on Seoul, as 60.5% of the total projects are carried out there. By a large margin, Kyonggi (16.2%) follows Seoul. This indicates that industrial technological capabilities are concentrated in Seoul and its outskirts. However, this program should also be targeted to increase regional technological capabilities, as it aims at developing generic technologies that are commonly faced by many enterprises, especially SMEs. Information about this program should be widely diffused among innovation actors in all regions.

Finally, the *Technology Infrastructure Promotion Program* was started in 1995 by the Ministry of Commerce, Industry and Energy in order to strengthen the technological infrastructure in Korea. In 1996 about 29.8 billion won was provided for 31 projects. Looking into the regional distribution of projects, more than half of the funds provided were invested in Seoul. About 55% of the total projects and 61% of the funds were concentrated in Seoul. It is interesting that a significant share of the funds are invested in Taegu and Chungnam. It indicates that some regions utilize this program actively. Taking the basic purpose of the program into account, this program should be targeted at less-developed regions, such as Kangwon, Chungbuk, Chonbuk, and Chonnam, instead of traditionally developed regions.

Based on the regional distribution of the recipients of major programs of the central government, we can conclude that the central government makes insufficient effort to strengthen regional innovation systems. Recipients are concentrated heavily in Seoul. Only RRC programs are effective for this purpose. The programs of the central government must be much more region-oriented. Here, universities in regions should become centers of excellence for enhancing regional innovation capabilities and improving regional economic performance. As discussed above, Korean universities are relatively fairly distributed among regions and the level of professors has almost been equalized. These advantages should be actively utilized in Korean regional innovation policy.

CONCLUSIONS

We reviewed the regional innovation systems of 15 regions in Korea. According to our study, Korean regional innovation systems are very weak, especially because of their short history. Innovation actors, especially public research institutes, are unfairly distributed among regions, regional governments make little investment in S&T activities, and there are weak interactions between innovation actors. In addition, the major programs of the central government are concentrated on specific regions, such as Seoul. This means that Korean regional innovation systems must be refined and strengthened. Here, we will discuss some policy implications that would be helpful for improving Korean regional innovation systems.

First, regional governments should increase their efforts to improve the potential of innovation actors and to activate interaction between them. In particular, metropolitan governments must increase R&D and S&T investment. Up to the present, the central government has played a main role in S&T investment. However, from now on, regional governments should increase their investment in S&T activities. As of 1997 the total R&D budget of Korean regional governments was only about 8.45% that of the central government. By contrast, in Germany, which has competent regional innovation systems, the total budget of regional governments (Länder) is almost equivalent with that of the federal government (Bund) (BMBF, 1996). However, it is encouraging that less-developed regions in Korea make greater efforts for enhancing innovation capabilities than traditionally developed regions.

Second, because Korean regional governments have a very low level of financial independence and little experience in regional innovation policies, regional governments have many difficulties in establishing their regional innovation systems. Therefore, active support by the central government is needed not only in financing, but also in formulation and implementation of regional innovation systems. As Korea has been a traditionally centralized country, it is not easy for Korean central and regional governments to decentralize S&T policy. The central government should accept regional governments as important partners in enhancing the national innovation system. The central government must recognize that regional innovation systems compose the national innovation system. It must promote regional innovation actors actively and coordinate regional S&T activities under the long-term vision of national development.

Third, regional economic development in terms of regional innovation systems must be based on regional industrial structures that have been accumulated historically. As discussed above, Korean regions differ from each other in industrial structure, S&T infrastructure, recognition of S&T's importance in regional development, and so on. Such differences should be considered in developing regional innovation systems. In addition, it should be kept in mind that, based on frequent fusion among modern, diverse S&T areas, traditional sectors could become advanced sectors by adopting new technologies. Such a relationship between regional innovation systems and industrial sectors could also lead to efficient utilization of scarce national R&D resources.

Fourth, Korean regional innovation systems should be established around universities in a region, because there is a relatively fair distribution of universities among regions. Actually, regional innovation systems of advanced nations have operated around technology-intensive universities (Süss et al., 1992). However, we should keep in mind that the university sector is the weakest sector in the Korean national innovation system, because most universities have been more focused on education than on R&D activities (OECD, 1996a; Chung, 1996b; Chung & Lay, 1997). Under the current situation, most Korean universities could not play an important role in their regional innovation systems. These days, many policy measures have been introduced in vain for extending university research capabilities. Therefore, some innovative policy measures—for example, recruitment of professors with practical experience, co-professorships of well-qualified researchers in public research institutes—should be introduced.

Fifth, Korean public research institutes should be diversified and distributed among regions. There are a small number of public research institutes in Korea. In particular, government-sponsored research institutes are very big and located in Seoul and Taejon. They should be increased, diversified, and distributed among regions. If it is not easy to increase and diversify them, branch offices or research groups should be separated and fairly located among regions according to their relevance to region-specific S&T and industrial structures. In addition, the research capabilities of national laboratories, which are relatively fairly distributed, should be strengthened, so that they can become important innovation actors in Korean regional innovation systems.

Sixth, regional development based on regional innovation systems should lead to the development of the national economy. As argued in this chapter, the summation of all regional innovation systems is the national innovation system. Implementing competent regional innovation systems is a prerequisite for a competent national innovation system. Therefore, reciprocal networks among research institutes beyond regions, close cooperation between the central government and regional governments, and interaction between regional governments are very important. It would be desirable to make a network among organizations for S&T promotion in regional governments under the strong support of the central government.

Finally, the experience of implementing regional innovation systems, including efficient division of labor between the central and regional governments, must be utilized for the unification of the South and North Korean innovation systems. In the knowledge-based society, the future of a unified Korea depends heavily on its S&T capabilities. In this sense, we have carried out a series of studies on S&T unification between South and North Korea (e.g. Chung, 1993, 1999a; Chung, Kim & Yim, 1996). The economic development as well as the S&T development in North Korea will need the active support not only of the central government, but also of the regional governments of a unified Korea. In particular, regional governments could diminish the central government's burden of modernization of North Korean S&T and economic infrastructure to a large degree. Therefore, the collaborative experience in South Korean regional innovation systems up to unification would be very helpful for the effective development of North Korean regional innovation systems and the national innovation system of a unified Korea.

NOTE

1. The terms national innovation system (NIS) and national system of innovation (NSI) often are used interchangeably. In this chapter the NIS form is used in coordination with regional innovation system (RIS).

REFERENCES

Braczyk, H. J., Cooke, P. & Heidenreich, M. eds. 1998, *Regional Innovation Systems*. London: UCL Press.

Breschi, S. & Malerba, F. 1997, Sectoral Innovation System: Technological Regimes, Schumpetarian Dynamics, and Spatial Boundaries, in *Systems of Innovation: Technology, Institutions and Organizations*, ed. Edquist, C., pp. 130-156. London: Pinter Publishers.

Bundesministerium für Bildung, Wissenschaft, Forschung und Technologie (BMBF) 1996, *Bundesbericht Forschung 1996*. Bonn: BMBF.

Chung, S. 1993, S&T Policy towards the Unification, pp. 60-73, *Science and Technology*, September, Korean Federation of Science and Technology Societies (KOFST), Seoul (in Korean).

Chung, S. 1995, Integrated Regional Innovation Policy?, *S&T Policy Trend*, May, pp. 38-53, Science and Technology Policy Institute (STEPI), (in Korean).

Chung, S. 1996a, Theoretical Review on National Innovation System: From the Aspects of Innovation User-Producer Relationship, *S&T Policy Trend*, October, pp. 46-59, Science and Technology Policy Institute (STEPI), (in Korean).

Chung, S. 1996b, *Technologiepolitik für neue Produktionstechnologien in Korea und Deutschland*. Heidelberg: Physica-Verlag.

Chung, S. 1997, Regional Innovation Policy in Germany, *Science and Technology Policy*, November, pp. 2-6, Science and Technology Policy Institute, Seoul (in Korean).

Chung, S. 1999a, *Unification of National Innovation Systems*. Seoul: STEPI.

Chung, S. 1999b, *Environmental Policy*. Seoul: Bak-Young Publishing Co. (in Korean).

Chung, S., Kim, B. & Yim, D. S. 1996, *Unification Strategy of South and North Korean S&T System*, Science and Technology Policy Institute (STEPI). (in Korean).

Chung, S. & Lay, G. 1997, Technology Policy between "Diversity" and "One Best Practice"—A Comparison of Korean and German Promotion Schemes for New Production Technologies, *Technovation*, vol. 17, pp. 675-693. Oxford: Elsevier Science Ltd.

Chung, S. & Lee, J. 1998, Regional Innovation Policy, in *National Innovation System in Korea*, ed., STEPI, pp. 169-190. Seoul: Science and Technology Policy Institute. (in Korean).

Chung, S. & Lee, J. 1999, *Five Year Plan for the S&T Development in Kwangju*, Science and Technology Policy Institute, Seoul (in Korean).

Chung, S., Lee, J., Song, J. et al. 1997, *Regional S&T Annual Report*. Seoul: STEPI/MOST. (in Korean).

De La Mothe, J. & Paquet, G. eds. 1998, *Local and Regional Systems of Innovation*. Dordrecht: Kluwer Academic Publishers.

Florida, R. 1995, Toward the Learning Region, *Futures*, Vol. 27, No. 5, pp. 527-536.

Florida, R. 1998, Calibrating the Learning Region, in *Local and Regional Systems of Innovation*, eds. De La Mothe, J. & Paquet, G., pp. 19-28. Dordrecht: Kluwer Academic Publishers.

Freeman, C. 1987, *Technology Policy and Economic Performance: Lessons from Japan*. London: Pinter Publishers.

Hauff, V. & Scharpf, F. W. 1975, *Modernisierung der Wirtschaft: Technologiepolitik als Strukturpolitik*. Frankfurt: Europäische Verlagsanstalt.

Hilpert, U. ed. 1991, *Regional Innovation and Decentralization: High Tech-Industry and Government Policy*. London: Routledge.

Hucke, J. & Wollmann, H. eds. 1989, *Dezentrale Technologiepolitik?: Technikförderung durch Bundesländer und Kommunen*, Basel: Birkhäuser.

Johnson, B. 1992, Institutional Learning, in *National Systems of Innovation: Towards a Theory of Innovation and Interactive Learning*, ed. Lundvall, B.-A., pp. 23-44. London: Pinter Publishers.

Kamien, M. I. & Schwartz, N. L. 1975, Market Structure and Innovation, *Journal of Economic Literature*, Vol. 3, pp. 1-38.

Korea Science and Engineering Foundation (KOSEF) 1995, *KOSEF Statistics*, Taejon (in Korean).

Korea Science and Engineering Foundation (KOSEF) 1999a, *Regional Research Centers*, http.kosef.re.kr, Taejon (in Korean).

Korea Science and Engineering Foundation (KOSEF) 1999b, *Centers of Excellence*, http.kosef.re.kr, Taejon.

Kreibich, R. 1989, Innovationsstrukturpolitik: Chancen, Probleme, Zukunftsoptionen, in *Technikgestaltung in der Stadt und Regionalentwicklung*, eds. Schuchard, W., Hack, L. & Naschold, F. Dortmund.

Lundvall, B.-A. 1988, Innovation as an interactive process: user-producer relations, in *Technical Change and Economic Theory*, eds. Dosi, G. et al., pp. 349-369. London: Pinter Publishers.

Lundvall, B.-A. ed. 1992, *National Systems of Innovation: Towards a Theory of Innovation and Interactive Learning*. London: Pinter Publishers.

Majer, H. 1992, *Wirtschaftswachstum: Paradigmenwechsel vom quantitativen zum qualitativen Wachstum*. Munich: Oldenbourg.

Meyer-Krahmer, F. 1985, Innovation Behavior and Regional Indigenous Potential, *Regional Studies* 12, pp. 523-524.

Meyer-Krahmer, F. 1990, Innovationsorientierte Regionalpolitik: Ansatz, Instrumente, Grenzen, in *Wissenschaft, Technik und Arbeit: Innovationen in Ost und West*, eds. Gramatzki, H. E. et al., pp. 343-359. Kassel: VWL-inform.

National Statistical Office (NSO) 1998, *Regional Statistics Yearbook*, Seoul (in Korean).

Nelson, R. R. ed. 1993, *National Innovation Systems: A Comparative Analysis*. Oxford: Oxford University Press.

Nelson, R. R. and Rosenberg, N. 1993, Technical Innovation and National Systems, in *National Innovation Systems: A Comparative Analysis*, ed. Nelson, R. R., pp. 3-21. Oxford: Oxford University Press.

OECD 1996a, *National Innovation Systems*. Paris.

OECD, 1996b, *Reviews of National Science and Technology Policy: Republic of Korea*. Paris.

Ohmae, K. 1995, *The End of the Nation-State: The Rise of Regional Economies*. New York: The Free Press.

Oppenländer, K. H. 1975, Das Verhalten kleiner und mittlerer Unternehmen im industriellen Innovationsproze, in *Die gesamtwirtschaftliche Funktion kleiner und mittlerer Unternehmen*, ed. Oppenländer, K. H. Munich: Ifo—Institute for Economic Research.

Patel, P. & Pavitt, K. 1994, The Nature and Economic Importance of National Innovations Systems, *STI Review,* pp. 9-32. Paris: OECD.

Science and Technology Policy Institute (STEPI) 1997, *5 Year Plan for S&T Innovations: Investment Enlargement and Efficiency*, Seoul (in Korean).

Senker, J. 1996, National System of Innovation, Organizational Learning and Industrial Biotechnology, *Technovation*, vol. 16, pp. 219-229.

Simon, H. 1992, Lessons from Germany's Midsize Giants, *Harvard Business Review* March-April, pp. 115-123.

Simon, H. 1996, *Hidden Champion: Lessons from 500 of the World's Best Unknown Companies*. Boston: Harvard Business School Press.

Süss, W., Marx, R., Langer, S. & Scholle, C. 1992, Regionale Innovationspolitik im Spannungsfeld von Europäischem Binnenmarkt und deutscher Integration, in *Politische Techniksteuerung*, eds. Grimmer, K., Häusler, K., Kuhlmann, S. & Simonis, G., pp. 154-181. Opladen: Leske und Budrich.

9

The Third Generation Technopoleis in Korea

Tae Kyung Sung

INTRODUCTION

Technology can contribute to the development of society, education, and economy of a nation through the discovery, transfer, diffusion, and application of new knowledge. Thus, technology development is closely associated with the competitive advantage of each nation under a fiercely competitive, mass customized, and rapidly changing global economy (Sung and Hyon, 1998). In this respect, technology-driven economic development has been the essence of central government policy of Korea for the last forty years. One of the more promising and attractive policies is to build concentrated industrial and/or research parks, better known as "technopoleis." Technopoleis are to foster close linkage among governments, universities, research institutes, and corporations to innovate new technology and products, to transfer and commercialize such technology and products, and to support ventures and incubate small businesses (ITEP, 1998).

In recent years there has been steadily growing interest in developing regional industries and economic poles for innovation-driven production (Oh and Masser, 1995). This idea of developing high tech industries through technopoleis and other initiatives by many countries of the world is firmly based upon the assumption that technological innovation leads to economic growth. Technopoleis, the new type of public and private alliance, are therefore gaining popularity, attracting attention in Korea from central and local governments to the private sector, universities, and research institutes (Sung, 1997).

Technopoleis development in Korea can be categorized into three distinctive generations. The first generation was in the 1970s and 1980s when Taedok Science Town (TST), the first technopolis, was being built. The second generation occurred in the late 1980s and early 1990s when the objective of technopoleis development was to vitalize the local economy (Oh, 1996). The third generation of technopoleis development started in the mid-1990s when the local governments began to get actively involved in the establishment of technopoleis to boost their regional economies in the national government supported era of local autonomy.

The purpose of this chapter is to review the characteristics as well as successes and failures of each generation of technopoleis development in Korea. The study addresses what comprises the third generation of technopoleis development and why it differs from the first two in strategy, configuration, participating sectors, operation, and funding. Also recent government policy on the third generation technopoleis is described along with the evaluation scheme of the central government on financial support. Out of thirteen finalists, six technopoleis received financial support from the central government. Finally, future directions for Korean technopoleis development are suggested.

TECHNOPOLEIS: CONCEPT AND GENERATIONS

The first archetypes of technopoleis can be traced back to the founding of research parks in the United States in the 1960s, followed by science parks established in England in the 1970s. Germany then tried, not too successfully, to establish technology innovation centers in the 1980s. More recently, technical cities or technopoleis have been established in Japan, and science-based industrial parks in Taiwan have also emerged as more functions were augmented to cope with more competition (MOST, 1989).

Recently, central and local governments, universities, research institutes, and corporations are beginning to realize the impossibility of counteracting a rapidly changing world economy and fierce international competition without integrating or networking research and development, technology innovation, commercialization of new technology, technology transfer, policy and financial support functions. Technopoleis, while based upon traditional industrial or research parks, are augmented by functions such as technology innovation, technology transfer and commercialization, as well as business incubation. There are several distinct types of technopoleis throughout the world, however, since each technopolis reflects its country's own economic, political, cultural, societal, and administrative factors (Gibson and Sung, 1995; Sung, 1997).

Whatever its unique environment, any technopolis is a special alliance defined as a cooperative relationship between two or more independent organizational entities, agreeing to work together to achieve specific, predefined objectives. The guiding principle is that participants in an alliance agreement should each specialize in performing individual tasks related to core competencies, thereby eliminating duplication where possible, as well as gaining operational synergy. Alliances typically extend over a considerable period of time, involving procedures to share benefits and risks and information exchange. By their very nature, technopolis alliances are complex and demand significant and coordinated commitment among partners (Gibson and Sung, 1995; Smilor, et al., 1988). Because of this, technopoleis development needs careful planning, management, and coordination, requiring that central governments historically play major roles as their primary planner, coordinator, initiator, operator, and financial provider.

Technopoleis are having far-reaching consequences on technology commercialization and economic growth. The modern technopolis links cutting-edge research with technology development and commercialization in order to spur economic development and to promote technology specialization and diversification (Gibson and Sung, 1995; Smilor et al., 1988). Under a fiercely competitive, mass customized, and rapidly changing international environment, every nation is desperately seeking to enhance its competitive advantage (Porter, 1990). One promising, attractive way to do this is to build concentrated industrial or research parks that aim at fostering close linkages among governments, universities, research institutes, and corporations so as to innovate new technology and products, transfer and commercialize such technology and products, leading to the start-up and incubation of small businesses (MOST, 1989).

According to Smilor, Kozmetsky, and Gibson (1988), the modern technopolis interactively links technology development with public and private sectors to spur economic development and promote technology diversification. In developing technopoleis, the following three factors are especially important because they provide a methodology framework to measure their performance:

1. the achievement of scientific pre-eminence,
2. the development and maintenance of new technologies for emerging industries,
3. the attraction of major technology companies and the creation of home-grown technology companies.

In Korea, technopoleis are defined as means "to effectively achieve technology innovation and high-tech development in a particular region, functions such as research and development, venture and incubation, education and training, assistance and services, and sample production are integrated into one site through close cooperative interaction among universities, research institutes, and corporations" (MOITI, 1997). Depending on the participating sectors, leading sector, objectives, scope, and formation, each technopolis provides a variety of functions. The comprehensive functions of technopoleis include (Gibson and Rogers, 1994; Gibson and Sung, 1995; Goto, 1993; Luger, 1993; Sedaitis, 1997; Smilor et al., 1988; Sung, 1997, MOITI, 1997; ITEP 1998):

1. research and development
2. education and training
3. technology innovation
4. technology transfer and commercialization
5. venture and incubation
6. production
7. providing high quality of life
8. promoting start-ups and spin-offs

The first generation technopolis in Korea, TST, was principally established based upon scientific considerations. Over the last twenty years, TST has structured many national and regional development efforts and policies (Oh and Park, 1992). While it was an orchestrated attempt by the central government to create a technopolis outside the capital region, TST was, nonetheless, an ad-hoc solution to three imminent and critical problems: (1) dispersing an overconcentrated population and industrial activities from the Seoul metropolitan area; (2) solving bottlenecks in the application and admission processes to first-class universities, most of which were located in Seoul; and (3) moving from labor-intensive to technology-intensive industries to compete with advanced nations in the world (MOST, 1989; Oh, 1990, Oh and Park, 1992).

The direction of the second development generation of technopoleis, however, was quite different in that it was intended to be a more technology-transfer, diffusion, and commercialization-driven program to promote regional economic development. Also the development experiences of American and Japanese technopoleis were intensively studied to replicate their successes and avoid their failures. In this generation, the objectives of technopoleis development were (1) to promote industrial development by upgrading the technological level of regional business and establishing high tech industries away from metropolitan areas, (2) to encourage R&D activities to sustain regional development, and (3) to create attractive local communities where people would wish to live and work (Oh, 1995).

Today, the central government has established a new policy on technopoleis development from the quite different perspective compared to the first two generations, extant to the early 1990s (Sung and Hyon, 1998). Traditionally, the central government had been not only the major initiating and operating sector for technopoleis, but also their largest funding entity.

But the situation changed in the mid-1990s as local governments were granted increased autonomy from the central government. Now, while the central government exerts influence over technopolis development through their establishment of policy and provision of basic financial support, local governments have increased their role in their development. In this schema, the central government supports the technopolis development efforts of local governments by funding a portion of the total investment, but only if the local government surpasses criteria set by central government policy. This structure thus comprises the third generation of technopoleis development. The key characteristics of each generation of technopoleis are summarized in Table 9.1.

Table 9.1
Key Features of Technopoleis Generations in Korea

Generations	Features	Examples
First (1973 – 1988)	- Science Cities - Basic Research Orientation - Central Government Initiative	Taedok Science Town
Second (1989 – 1996)	- Vitalize Local Economy - Research and Production foci - Central Government Initiative - Little Participation from Local Authorities	Kwangju Advanced Science and Industrial Complex
Third (1997 – Present)	- High-Tech Technopoleis - Mass Production by High-Tech Firms - Public and Private Sectors' Collaboration - Active Participation from Local Governments	Pohang, Songdo, Ansan, Taegu-Kyungbuk, Kwangju-Chunnam, Chungnam, Kyungsan

Source: Oh (1996).

FRAMEWORKS ON TECHNOPOLEIS

The central government has been developing its own impartial, valid and reliable, yet Korean-specific framework to effectively develop and support technopoleis in Korea. This move is motivated by several factors. In the first place, the main source for technopoleis funding remains the central government, notwithstanding increased local government responsibility. (Even though the level of funding is decreasing, the national government still contributes a significant amount of funding to start-up technopolis development.) Therefore, it is very important for local government (as well as participating sectors) to understand the policy framework of the central government concerning technopolis development. The most important three elements of the framework are initiating and operating sector, development strategy, and configuration (Sung, 1997).

Initiating and Operating Sector Policy

According to initiation and operating sector policy, technopoleis can be categorized into five types: central government initiated, local government initiated, university initiated, private-sector initiated, and third-sector initiated. In most cases, the initiating sector assumes operating authority and responsibility. Each type of technopolis is summarized in Table 9.2.

Table 9.2
Comparison Based upon Initiating and Operating Sectors

		Strengths	Weaknesses
Public	Central Government	- Strong planning, administrative, legal, political & financing capabilities - Stability - Credibility	- Insensitive to environment changes - Inflexibility - Budgetary constraints
	Local Government	- Fit to structure & characteristics of local environment	- Much dependence on local government - Budgetary constraints - Requires industry infrastructure
Private	University	- Low cost for technopolis site - Strong R&D resources - Utilization of existing facilities - Flexibility	- Too much dependence upon university - Possibility of university losing its identity
	Corporations	- Profitability - Flexibility - Sensitive to environment changes	- Unclear authority & responsibility - Possibility of easy structural breakdown
	The 3rd Sector	- Strong planning and flexibility - Division of initiating and operating sectors - Sensitive to environment changes	- Unclear about publicity vs. privacy needs - Manpower shortages - Restrictions on operations

Source: MOITI (1997).

Development Strategies

Development strategies of technopoleis can follow two paths, either in the establishment of new technopoleis, or the augmentation of existing functions in established industrialized areas. In establishing new technopoleis, strategies can be further categorized as either seeking globalization through technology or as seeking the specialization and invigoration of local economies. Depending on the kind of established industrialized areas to which the functions are augmented, three types of strategy can be utilized (see Table 9.3 for details).

Table 9.3
Comparison Based on Development Strategies

		Characteristics	
		Strengths	**Weaknesses**
Augmentation	Industrial Park	R&D, Venture/Incubation, Assistance/Services, Simulation University, Local government, The 3rd sector	
		Close linkage to production Easy management & control	Weak R & D resources Lack of leverage with universities due to geographical remoteness
	Research Park	Venture/Incubation, Assistance/Services, Technology transfer, Sample production University	
		Active R&D Venture & incubation Easy technology outsourcing	Difficulty in commercialisation
	Industrialized Area	Venture/Incubation, Assistance/Service, Technology transfer Local government, The 3rd sector	
		Synergy effects Integrating related industries	Hard to locate initiating sector Hard to locate proper sites
New	Globalization thru Technology Specialization	University (networked), Local government, The 3rd sector	
		Attracting corporations Technology specialization	Too much concentration on capital area Difficulty in implementation
	Vitalization of Local Economy	Local government, University (networked), The 3rd sector	
		Boosting local economy Vitalizing local industry	Hard to finance & commercialize Manpower shortages

Sources: MOITI (1997) & ITEP (1998).

Configurations

Depending upon location, objectives, and functions, configurations of technopoleis can be classified as centralized (park-type), distributed (network-type), and compromised (a configuration that centralizes or distributes certain functions or industries as needed). Various strengths and weaknesses exist, depending upon the different types of configuration and the characteristics of each type. These are summarized in Table 9.4.

Table 9.4
Comparison Based on Technopolis Configuration

	Strengths	Weaknesses
Centralized	Synergy effect Cost efficiency	Low participation from remote sector Too much standardization
Distributed	Meets the needs of each business Flexibility in site location	Difficulty in implementation Hard to provide one-stop services Low synergy effect Cost inefficiency
Compromised	Inherits both strengths and weaknesses of both types	

Source: MOITI (1997).

GOVERNMENT POLICY ON NEW TECHNOPOLEIS DEVELOPMENT

According to the national government's policy, the basic direction of technopolis development should be aimed toward creating competitive advantages of Korea on the world market by promoting excellence, not by seeking equal economic development of the nation's regions, nor even distribution of resources among them (MOITI, 1997; ITEP, 1998). Furthermore, any sound technopolis policy must promote business ventures and incubations, technology transfers from large corporations to SMEs, technology diffusion, and commercialization of innovations.

Principles of Technopoleis Development

The central government has thus established six strict criteria to govern technopolis development (ITEP, 1998). The first one requires clarity of roles of all participating sectors. Any technopolis development plan should clearly demonstrate proper roles of each participating sector, roles without duplication or omission. The principle states there will be no central government support of technopoleis, "without responsibility and contribution." The second requirement concerns the clarity of objectives. To maximize potential benefits of technopolis development, the objectives, contents, and implementation plan should be feasible and clearly documented.

Specialization is the third criterion. It is important to Korea that specific technologies are highly specialized to achieve competitive advantage of the nation as a whole, not only a region. Also, obtaining a productive balance of collaboration and competition among universities and research institutes is emphasized to overcome any lack of resources. The fourth requirement is openness. It is highly recommended for technopoleis to recruit excellent foreign research institutes (which own leading-edge technology) as partners to boost regional development. In short, technopoleis should be open to every opportunity that arises. The fifth requirement concerns creating synergistic connections among participants. Technopoleis should be well connected to the existing regional industry and business to maximize creative effects. Bluntly put, any technopolis effort that is not related to existing industries and resources is not worth trying. The last requirement is for a healthy state of competition to exist, where each partner in the technopolis development seeks to achieve what it can, thereby minimizing loads upon the central government, and maximizing capacities of local governments in the process.

Other Considerations

Even though not specified in the principles of technopolis development strategies by the central government, the following factors also ought to be taken into any planning consideration (ITEP 1998). The first one is the excellence of technology. Any technopolis development should be based on competitiveness of technology. Thus, the existence of excellent engineering colleges and institutions, as well as harmonious industry-academy collaborations are critical factors. Another important consideration should be the proximity of related industries. If related industries are physically located in one site, more chances for synergy effect, industry-academy collaboration, and venture and incubation are extant. An appropriate infrastructure is another vital factor for technopolis success. If infrastructure elements such as harbors, airports, transportation, utilities, and antipollution systems are well established, more opportunities to induce outstanding corporations, research institutes, and other related institutions (both in and out of Korea) follow. The most easily overlooked, but absolutely necessary, factor for technopolis success is the interest and support from local residents, for without enthusiastic support from local residents, any technopolis development plan, however ambitious, will become be a mere paper tiger destined for failure. Related to this community support, serious consideration should finally be given to the environment (including "quality of life" issues such as educational and cultural opportunities).

Critical Success Factors

In summary, to successfully develop technopoleis, the following Critical Success Factors (CSFs) should be taken into consideration (Gibson and Rogers, 1994; Gibson and Sung, 1995; Goto, 1993; Luger, 1993; Sedaitis, 1997; Smilor et al., 1988; Sung, 1997; ITEP 1998):

1. Strong leadership of the initiating sector
2. Balance of power and coordination among participating sectors
3. Information sharing among participating sectors
4. Financial assistance and taxation incentives
5. Low rental cost and utility
6. Existence of research institutes
7. Existence of good universities
8. Well-established industry infrastructure
9. Specialized and unique technology or industry
10. Systematic implementation of plan

11. Benchmarking results
12. Inducing highly skilled technicians and experts
13. Providing a high quality of life
14. Strong investment from participating sectors
15. Drawing interest and support from local residents
16. Attracting visible and prominent corporations
17. Providing one-stop administrative services

New Technopoleis Development

The central government evaluates the pros and cons of each development strategy very seriously, in that each technopolis inherits its own characteristics. The development strategies of technopoleis can be divided into two major types: new establishment or augmentation of functions to an established industrialized park. To establish new technopolis, strategy can be further categorized as globalization through technology specialization and vitalization of the local economy. Depending on what kind of established industrialized park to which the functions are augmented, three types of strategy can be utilized (Sung, 1997).

Table 9.5
Selection Criteria for Development Strategy

Items	Augmentation to Industrial Park	Augmentation to Research Park	Augmentation to Industrialized Area	Globalization thru Technology Specialization	Vitalizing Local Economy
Possibility of Developing into High-Tech Industries	Fair	Good	Good	Good	Fair
Specialization by Industry	Fair	Fair	Fair	Good	Fair
Local Industry Connection	Excellent	Poor	Excellent	Good	Poor
Vitalizing Local Economy	Excellent	Good	Poor	Poor	Good
Site Preparation	Good	Good	Fair	Good	Excellent
Firms' Inducement	Fair	Poor	Good	Good	Poor
Easiness of Implementation	Excellent	Excellent	Excellent	Excellent	Good
Cost/Benefit Analysis	Good	Poor	Excellent	Good	Poor
Away from Metropolitan	Good	Good	Poor	Poor	Good
Venture and Incubation	Excellent	Good	Excellent	Good	Good
Human Resources	Poor	Good	Good	Good	Fair

Sources: MOITI (1997) & ITEP (1998).

The following set of very specific criteria is developed by the central government (ITEP 1998). The set consists of (1) the possibility of developing high tech industries, (2) specialization by industry, (3) proposed connections to local industry, (4) plans to develop the local economy, (5) technopolis site preparation, (6) success in inducing firms to participate, (7) easiness of implementation, (8) cost/benefit analysis, (9) away from metropolitan areas, (10) venture and incubation possibilities, and (11) ability to acquire human resources. Table 9.5 summarizes the evaluation matrix and the set of criteria suggested by the central government.

In line with its declared policy of promoting local government autonomy and responsibility, the new Korean government policy on new technopoleis development clearly dictates that the financial support for the technopolis development of the local government will be made only if the local government surpasses set criteria. For the year 1998, the central government announced that any local government interested in establishing a technopolis should submit its proposal to receive any financial support.

To impartially evaluate submitted proposals for the technopolis development from local governments, the central government has devised the following judgment scheme. This scheme consists of five categories, twelve major items, and thirty-eight detailed items. The categories are (1) appropriateness of proposal, (2) initiating sector characteristics, (3) site conditions, (4) funding and investment options, and (5) success potential. Out of possible 1,000 total points, 300 are for appropriateness of proposal, 200 for initiating sector characteristics, 200 for site conditions, 250 for funding and investment options, and 50 for success potential. Total points will be determined by the sum of subtotal points of categories, in turn summed by points of individual items. The most weighted single item is local funding level (120), followed by private-sector funding level (80), local specialization strategy (60), site procurement (50), intent of initiating sector (50), and efficiency of investments (50). The weight is determined by the evaluation committee after a number of public hearings to avoid any controversy. The detailed evaluation matrix is presented in Table 9.6 (ITEP 1998).

Table 9.6
Evaluation Matrix for Technopoleis Development Proposal

Category	Major	Item	Points
Appropriate-ness of Proposal (300)	Appropriateness of Functional Plan (70)	Vision	20
		Human Resources Education & Training	10
		Information Management	10
		Technology Incubation	10
		R&D Support	10
		Pilot Production Support	5
		Open Laboratory	5
	Site Plan (80)	Site Procurement	50
		Site Utilization	30
	Appropriateness of Implementation Strategy (150)	Local Specialization Strategy	60
		Venture Business Inducement Strategy	20
		Timetable	10
		Project Team	10
		Feasibility of Plan	10
		Connectivity to Existing Industry	10
		Inducement Strategy for Int'l Firms	10
		International Cooperation Plan	10
		Academic-Industry Cooperation	10
Initiating Sector Characteristics (200)	Capability of Initiating Sector (100)	Intent of Initiating Sector	50
		Expert Inducement	20
		Support System	30
	Operation Plan (100)	Operating System	30
		Operating Strategy	30
		Development Strategy	40
Site Conditions (200)	Accessibility (40)	Geographical Accessibility	20
		Information Accessibility	20
	Economic Conditions (90)	Level of Social Infrastructure	30
		Size of Site	20
		Expandability	20
		Legal Constraints	20
	Sociocultural Conditions (70)	Social Conditions	30
		Amenities	15
		Environmental Conditions	25
Funding and Investment Options (250)	Funding (200)	Local Funding Level	120
		Private-Sector Funding Level	80
	Investments (50)	Efficiency of Investments	50
Success Potential (50)	Payoffs (20)	Chances of Success	20
	Expected Value (30)	Contribution to Local Economy	30
Total			1,000

Source: ITEP (1998).

THIRD GENERATION TECHNOPOLEIS

Financial Support Decision Process

Recent central government policy on new technopoleis development clearly dictates that the financial support for the technopolis development of the local government will be made only if the local or provincial government surpasses criteria set by the central government. For the year 1998, a total of thirteen technopoleis, representing each province, applied for central government financial support. Each technopolis passed the prescreening process from the provincial government prior to the evaluation of the central government. The profiles of the thirteen technopoleis are summarized in Table 9.7.

Table 9.7
Summary Profiles of Thirteen Technopoleis

Technopolis	Initiating Sector	Invest-ment (M$)	# of Participants				Specialized Industries
			Univ.	Insti-tute	Large Firms	SME	
* Taegu-Kyungbuk	Kyungbuk Univ.	241	6	0	5	77	Electric, Electronics, Info Mechanics, Materials, Bioengineering, Auto
* Kwangju-Chunnam	The 3rd Sector	65	6	1	3	242	Agriculture, Chemistry Mechanics, Art, Info Bioengineering
Wonju	Yonsei Univ.	80	2	0	0	60	Electronic Medical Equipment
Pusan	Pusan Univ.	517	10	0	4	146	Info, Environment Maritime, Mechanics Materials, Design, Ship
Taejon	Chungnam Univ.	80	3	5	0	83	Electronics , Software Mechanics, Materials
* Songdo	The 3rd Sector	201	2	1	5	95	Mechanics, Materials
* Chungnam	The 3rd Sector	70	18	1	10	437	Semiconductor, Autoparts Film, Bioengineering
Kyungnam	KMI	191	4	1	10	190	Mechanical Materials
* Ansan	The 3rd Sector	97	6	18	5	110	Venture, SME Training, Incubation
Chunbuk	The 3rd Sector	52	7	5	7	75	Mechanics, Environment Info, Bioengineering
* Kyungsan	Youngnam Univ.	216	4	0	9	123	Mechanics,Materials, Info Auto, Oriental Medicine
Seoul	Sogang Univ.	241	1	0	0	85	High-Tech Electronic Culture
Chungbuk	Chungju Univ.	32	6	0	0	72	Electronics

* Denotes the technopoleis that secured financial assistance by the central government.

To impartially evaluate the proposals for the technopolis development submitted by the provincial governments, the central government has put every effort into devising appropriate evaluation criteria and measurements. The central government evaluates each proposal based on the evaluation matrix for technopoleis development proposals (refer to Table 9.6). The final six nominated technopoleis that received financial support are Taegu-Kyungbuk, Kwangju-Chunnam, Songdo, Chungnam, Ansan, and Kyungsan.

Profiles of Six Selected Technopoleis

Taegu-Kyungbuk

With strong support from local governments as well as participating universities and private corporations, Taegu-Kyungbuk Technopark, located on the campus of Kyungbuk University, draws much attention from the central government. While cooperative atmosphere, positive attitude, and well-devised strategy promote the possibility of success, the evaluation committee expressed concerns over lack of taxational support and incentives for inducing prominent corporations, weak leadership of initiating sector, and not enough financial support. Table 9.8 summarizes the major characteristics of Taegu-Kyungbuk Technopark.

Table 9.8
Major Characteristics of Taegu-Kyungbuk Technopark

Initiating Sector	University-initiated (Kyungbuk University)
Development Period	9/1/1997 – 8/31/2004 (7 years)
Total Investment	241 M$
Site Size	77,235m^2
Site Cost	65.2 M$
Headquarters	On Campus of Kyungbuk University
Development Strategy	Vitalization of Local Economy
Configuration	Centralized
Specialized Industries	Electric, Electronics, Information and Communication, Mechanics, Bioengineering, Auto, Materials
Features	Campus Venture, Technoshop, Cyber Technopark

Kwangju-Chunnam

Located on the heart of Kwangju Science Complex, Kwangju-Chunnam Technopark is aimed at boosting the local economy in the areas of agriculture, chemistry, information and communication, mechanics, bioengineering, and traditional art. Kwangju-Chunnam has competitive advantage over other technopoleis in two elements. Kwangju already has a high technology and science complex which provides natural settings of venture businesses for high technology industries. Kwangju Institute of Science and Technology will be a major source for professionals and human resources (refer to Table 9.9). Strong leadership, local support, and site preparation were evaluated as excellent, the evaluation committee pointed out the need for further improvement in the areas of venture and incubation, role specialization among participants, and inducement of prominent corporations.

Table 9.9
Major Characteristics of Kwangju-Chunnam Technopark

Initiating Sector	The 3rd Sector
Development Period	9/1/1997 – 8/31/2002 (5 years)
Total Investment	65 M$
Site Size	66,000 m^2
Site Cost	5.8 M$
Headquarters	On the established Science Complex
Development Strategy	Vitalization of Local Economy
Configuration	Centralized
Specialized Industries	Agriculture, Chemistry, Information and Communication, Mechanics, Bioengineering, Traditional Art
Features	Kwangju Science Complex, Kwangju Institute of Science and Technology

Songdo

With connection to Songdo Media Valley, Songdo Technopark is located in the spacious industrial park of Songdo. The locational advantage of Songdo (only 45 minutes' drive from Seoul and 10 minutes from Incheon) together with the fact that 27.1% of industrial plants are located in the Songdo area make Songdo Technopark very attractive to a number of entrepreneurs. Strong support from local government, affluent venture capital, existence of SME support center, and active R&D are the strengths of Songdo; inducement of private R&D institutes, differentiation from Media Valley, and site preparation are the three areas of weaknesses pointed out by the evaluation committee. Table 9.10 summarizes the major characteristics of Songdo Technopark.

Table 9.10
Major Characteristics of Songdo Technopark

Initiating Sector	The 3rd Sector
Development Period	9/1/1997 – 8/31/2002 (5 years)
Total Investment	201 M$
Site Size	330,000 m^2
Site Cost	34.8 M$
Headquarters	Songdo Industrial Park
Development Strategy	Vitalization of Local Economy
Configuration	Centralized
Specialized Industries	Mechanics, Parts, Materials
Features	Great number of SMEs, Media Valley

Chungnam

The 3rd-sector-initiated Chungnam Technopark is located in the metropolitan area of Chunan City, which is known as a newly developed city with a high standard of living. With strong emphasis on venture and incubation, low rent, taxational support, affluent human resources, and well-established social infrastructure, Chungnam is expected to have a success in the near future. But the evaluation committee expressed concerns over the unclear role division among participating universities, lack of leadership, weak implementation strategy, and incomplete standard operating procedures. Chungnam is beginning to emerge as another technology town next to Taejon (Taedok) in middle part of Korea (refer to Table 9.11).

Table 9.11
Major Characteristics of Chungnam Technopark

Initiating Sector	The 3rd Sector
Development Period	9/1/1997 – 8/31/2004 (7 years)
Total Investment	70 M$
Site Size	120,282m^2
Site Cost	13.2 M$
Headquarters	Green Belt Area of Chunan City
Development Strategy	Vitalization of Local Economy
Configuration	Centralized
Specialized Industries	Semiconductor, Auto Parts, Film, Bioengineering, Media
Features	High standard of living

Ansan

Located in the southwest of Seoul, Ansan is putting every effort from local governments, universities, the private sector, and R&D institutes to revitalize the declining Ansan economy. Building a technopolis is the decision that the 3rd-sector-initiated local committee made in 1997. The Ansan technopolis preparation committee contacted Kyonggi Province for financial support and the City of Ansan for the site. The efforts paid off and six universities (Sungkyunkwan, Hanyang, Ajou, Kyunghee, Suwon, and Myungji) enthusiastically formed the consortium. Strong commitment from participating sectors, synergy effect with existing local companies, and strong R&D universities make Ansan very prominent; but the evaluation committee pointed out several weaknesses: weak incentives for venture businesses, unclear role division among participating universities, and unbalanced development plan. The major characteristics of Ansan Technopark are summarized in Table 9.12.

Table 9.12
Major Characteristics of Ansan Technopark

Initiating Sector	The 3rd Sector
Development Period	10/1/1997 – 12/31/2003 (6 years 3 months)
Total Investment	97 M$
Site Size	198,000m^2
Site Cost	13 M$
Headquarters	Industrialized Area of Ansan City
Development Strategy	Vitalization of Local Economy
Configuration	Centralized
Specialized Industries	Venture, SMEs, Education and Training, Incubation
Features	Local Support

Kyungsan

With strong support from local governments, participating universities (Kyungsan, Kyungil, Taegu, Taegu-Hyosung-Cathoic), and private corporations, Kyungsan Technopark, located on the campus of Youngnam University, is beginning to emerge as the technology-intensive region in the metropolitan area of Taegu. While cooperative atmosphere, positive attitude, specialized industry, and well-devised strategy promote possibility of success, the evaluation committee expressed concerns over too much burden on the private sector, weak incentives for inducing prominent corporations, and lack of venture and incubation efforts. Table 9.13 summarizes the major characteristics of Kyungsan Technopark.

Table 9.13
Major Characteristics of Kyungsan Technopark

Initiating Sector	University-initiated (Youngnam University)
Development Period	9/1/1997 – 8/31/2004 (7 years)
Total Investment	216 M$
Site Size	477,000 m^2
Site Cost	16 M$
Headquarters	On Campus of Youngnam University
Development Strategy	Vitalization of Local Economy
Configuration	Compromised
Specialized Industries	Mechanics, Materials, Auto, Information and Communication, Oriental Medicine, Mechatronics
Features	Developed Industrialized Park Strong Support from Local Government

SUMMARY AND CONCLUSIONS

The purpose of this chapter was to review the characteristics as well as successes and failures of each generation of technopoleis development in Korea, with the third generation being the focus of this study. The study addressed what comprises the third generation of technopoleis development and why it differs from the others in strategy, configuration, participating sectors, operation, funding, and so on. The new government policy on the third generation technopoleis was described and the evaluation scheme of the central government on financial support was explained. With this policy and scheme, six technopoleis that received financial support from the central government out of thirteen finalists are profiled.

Technopoleis development in Korea can be categorized into three distinctive generations: the 1970s and the 1980s, the late 1980s and early 1990s, and the mid-1990s.

The central government established six strict criteria to govern technopolis development (ITEP, 1998), and recommended five factors that also ought to be taken into any planning consideration (ITEP 1998). The current central government policy on new technopoleis development clearly dictates that the financial support for technopoleis development of local governments will be made only if the local or the provincial government surpasses criteria set by the central government. For the year 1998, thirteen technopoleis, representing each province, applied for central government financial support. Each technopolis passed the pre-screening process from the provincial government prior to the evaluation of the central government. To impartially evaluate submitted proposals for the technopolis development from local governments, the central government devised a judgment scheme consisting of five categories, twelve major items, and thirty-eight detailed items. The final six nominated technopoleis that received the financial support are Taegu-Kyungbuk, Kwangju-Chunnam, Songdo, Chungnam, Ansan, and Kyungsan.

It is expected that the future development policy of technopoleis in Korea will not be dramatically changed from that of current policy and will fine-tune the current policy as the socioeconomic environment dictates. Third generation technopoleis development policy is simple: "locally initiated with minimum intervention and support from the central government."

REFERENCES

Gibson, David V., and Rogers, Everett M., 1994, *R&D Collaboration on Trial: The Microelectronics and Computer Technology Corporation*. Boston: Harvard Business School Press.

Gibson, David V., and Sung, Tae K., 1995, "Technopolis: Cross-Institutional Alliances," *International Business Review*, Vol. 18, pp. 199-217.

Goto, Kunio, 1993, *Science, Technology, and Society: A Japanese Perspective*. Austin, TX: IC^2 Institute.

Institute of Industrial Technology Policy (ITEP), 1998, *Theory and Practices of Technoparks in Korea*, ITEP.

Luger, Michael, 1993, "Critical Success Factors for High Tech Development Policy: Science Parks/Innovation Centers in the U.S.," The International Workshop on Regional Science and Technology Research.

Ministry of International Trade and Industry (MOITI), 1997, *A Study on Establishing Legal and Systematic Infrastructure to Facilitate Techpark-type Research Complex*, MOITI.

Ministry of Science Town and Technology (MOST), 1989, *The Basic Plan of Technobelt in Korea*, MOST.

Oh, Deog-Seong, 1990, "Development of Taedok Science Town and the Linkage between its R&D and New High-Tech Industry," Proceedings of the Korea-UK Joint Seminar on High-Tech Center and Urban Development, pp. 113-125.

Oh, Deog-Seong, 1995, "High Technology and Regional Development Policy: An Evaluation of Korea's Technopolis Programme," *Habitat International*, Vol. 19, No. 3, pp. 253-268.

Oh, Deog-Seong, 1996, "Technopolis Development in Korea," Proceedings of the International Symposium on the Technopolis, Its Vision and Future, pp. 51-73.

Oh, Deog-Seong, and Masser, I., 1995, "High-Tech Centres and Regional Innovation: Some Case Studies in the U.K., Germany, Japan, and Korea," in C. S. Bertuglia et al. (eds.), *Technological Change, Economic Development and Space*. Berlin: Springer-Verlag, pp. 295-333.

Oh, Deog-Seong, and Park, M. S., 1992, *Development Strategies of Taedok*, Korea Science and Engineering Foundation (KOSEF).

Porter, Michael E., 1990, *The Competitive of Advantage of Nations*. New York: The Free Press.

Sedaitis, Judith B., 1997, *Commercializing High Technology: East and West*. Lanham, MD: Rowman & Littlefield.

Smilor, Raymond W., Kozmetsky, George, and Gibson, David V., 1988, *Creating the Technopolis: Linking Technology Commercialization and Economic Development*. Cambridge, MA: Ballinger.

Sung, Tae Kyung, 1997, "A Comparative Study on the Development Strategy of Technopoleis in Korea," Proceedings of the 1st International Conference on Technology Policy and Innovation, pp. 27.6.1-27.6.9.

Sung, Tae Kyung, and Hyon, Chong Min, 1998, "Government Policy on Technopoleis Development in Korea," Proceedings of the 31st Hawaii International Conference on Systems Sciences, pp. 252-261.

10

Weak and Strong Ties, Individualism-Collectivism, and the Diffusion of Technological Knowledge

Paul L. Robertson, Thomas Keil, and Erkko Autio

INTRODUCTION

Although local searches for technological capabilities are unquestionably important (Stuart and Podolny, 1996; Khanna, 1997), the ability of firms to gather new knowledge from their wider environments is now recognized as being as strategically important as their ability to generate new knowledge internally. Cohen and Levinthal (1989, 1990), for example, have emphasized the need for firms to develop absorptive capacity in order to make efficient use of external sources of knowledge, while Stinchcombe (1990), Chatterji (1996), Robertson (1998), and others have discussed the problems involved in distributing knowledge from those who have it to others (both individuals and firms) who need it. In recent years, much of this discussion has concentrated on building alliances or networks of firms that use strong relationships to generate and distribute knowledge among themselves in order to achieve economies of scale in problem solving beyond those available to individual firms. Networks and alliances, however, do not necessarily offer complete access to the knowledge that firms need and they may even block important channels. Moreover, for various reasons, many firms do not want to become closely involved in exchanging knowledge with other firms. As a result, they limit the depth of their contacts, but this does not in any way reduce their potential need for external knowledge.

Our concern here is to illuminate some of the types of contacts (or ties) that firms need in order to acquire new technological knowledge.[1] We argue that while the "strong ties" that exist among members of alliances and networks are often useful, emphasis needs to be placed as well on the building and maintenance of "weak ties" among firms that are not closely connected and may even be unknown to each other. In the discussion that follows, we pay particular attention to the needs of firms with individualistic cultures (Hofstede, 1980, 1991), because these firms are less willing than firms with more collectivist cultures to enter into explicit exchanges of information and knowledge. Therefore, they may shy away from government policies that encourage networks but may still benefit greatly from policies that permit them to tap external sources of knowledge without compromising their autonomy.

In the first two sections, we examine the problems associated with the gathering of new technological knowledge and the part that alliances, networks, and communities of firms can play in providing firms with broader sources of knowledge. The importance of Individualism-Collectivism (I-C) in determining the kind and degree of interaction that prevails among firms is discussed in the third section, where several propositions concerning the value of strong and weak ties are developed and discussed. A case study comparing the behavior of relatively individualistic firms in Australia with that of less individualistic firms in Finland is given in the fourth section to illustrate how firms in different cultures respond to various types of incentives to absorb new information. Specific recommendations for government policies to promote strong and weak ties among firms are followed by the conclusion.

THE DIFFUSION OF TECHNOLOGICAL KNOWLEDGE

The growth of technological knowledge is of importance to firms in both new and mature industries. In the former, companies must keep abreast of new developments in order to maintain competitiveness in rapidly changing environments. In mature industries, in which incremental change is the norm, the threat of renewed dynamism nevertheless presents both opportunities and threats (Lambe and Spekman, 1997). Firms that accomplish successful changes in product or process technologies can revolutionize long-standing competitive patterns to benefit themselves, while firms that are unprepared for changes by their competitors, including producers of substitutes, may suffer long-term damage.

To a degree, firms improve their internal knowledge capabilities through research and development activities. Through persistent activity in limited knowledge domains, firms extend existing knowledge and build new technological capabilities (Helfat, 1994; Nerkar, 1997). These technological capabilities tend to develop incrementally in the neighborhood of current knowledge (Dosi, 1982; Nelson and Winter, 1982) as firms search "locally" in the immediate vicinity of their existing domains of knowledge (Cyert and

March, 1992). However, access to externally generated knowledge is vital for this incremental technology development because few firms have the resources to be technologically self-sufficient. Furthermore, searches based on local knowledge often extend beyond the firm itself into a reference group of other firms with similar interests (Stuart and Podolny, 1996). In such cases, firms engage in "races" in which they benchmark their technological progress against developments occurring in a selection of competing firms with whom they identify (Khanna, 1995, 1997). Chatterji (1996) has suggested a number of reasons why external technological knowledge is becoming increasingly important to many firms. As product life cycles shorten, in part as a result of increased competition in globalized markets, firms can cut development times by drawing on knowledge generated elsewhere. At the same time, some firms have reduced their internal technological capabilities in order to contain costs, obliging them to outsource more of their research and development activities. In addition, it is possible to reduce risk by undertaking R&D cooperatively (Singh, 1997), and, finally, the reported success of some cooperative ventures has increased the willingness of firms to consider joint R&D projects.

There are several types of sources of external technological knowledge. Competitors, customers, suppliers, and firms or institutions from other fields may all have useful information. Von Hippel (1988) lists three types of exchanges of R&D information among competitors. They may engage in cooperative R&D programs, or they may have licensing or purchasing agreements for technological discoveries, or competitors may swap "know-how" informally. In the early stages of product or process development, cooperative R&D programs, or "learning alliances," are common (Gomes-Casseres, 1996; Leonard-Barton, 1995). Von Hippel (1988) contends that engineers from competing firms frequently engage in informal know-how trades. These swaps often occur in relatively unstructured environments such as technical and scientific meetings, and are undertaken without approval from supervisors. In general, information and knowledge are supplied only in the expectation that know-how of comparable value will be given in return. The possibility of exchanges among competitors is increased when firms in an industry are geographically concentrated (Robertson, Keil, and Autio, 1998), as in Marshallian "industrial districts" in which the "mysteries of the trade become no mysteries; but are as it were in the air, and children learn many of them unconsciously" (Marshall, 1961, IV.x.3, p. 271).

As the ultimate users of a firm's output, customers can also be invaluable sources of information. Although marketing experts sometimes claim that customers' assessments are unreliable and should be ignored (Schnaars, 1998), customers can provide technological information that firms could not easily obtain from other sources. As Von Hippel (1976, 1988) and Lundvall (1988) have noted, customers can themselves initiate product improvements that they let the original suppliers adopt at little or no cost. Furthermore, these product improvements may then lead to new demands for process equipment. The joint development of products by firms and their customers frequently occurs (Laage-Hellman, 1997), especially in the case of complex products and systems (CoPS) whose use is highly specialized (Hobday, 1998). Even when customers are not explicitly consulted, useful information can still be collected if customer support data are managed strategically (Davenport and Klahr, 1998).

Technological knowledge from suppliers is often useful. In Japan the use of "strategic sourcing" by firms to capitalize on the design skills of their suppliers is well-known (Nishiguchi, 1994). Similarly, design input for CoPS is often provided by subcontractors (Hobday, 1998). Suppliers can also provide information on the use of inputs that they have learned from other customers. Finally, suppliers can provide equipment and information for *complementary* goods to increase sales of their own products (Von Hippel, 1988).

Indirect links can also be important sources of important technological information and knowledge. Often knowledge is passed through several organizations so that the source and the ultimate receiver are not necessarily in direct contact. The literature on innovation networks describes the informational benefit of diverse networks of firms and government bodies for this purpose (Camagni, 1991; DeBresson and Amesse, 1991). Important technological knowledge can also be gathered from throughout a firm's environment, sometimes from formalized sources such as trade associations and journals, but also through more distant channels in other industries. In the case of a systemic innovation, which affects products and processes across a wide variety of fields, transmission may move indirectly and slowly from industry to industry but with far-reaching results (David, 1991). In general, the institutional structure for transmitting technological knowledge across fields is weak, but there are a few firms, as well as government bodies, that specialize as "knowledge brokers" who bring new knowledge to the attention of a range of possible users (Hargadon, 1998).

In practice, acquiring external technological knowledge poses a number of potential problems. First, many firms resist the spread of their proprietary knowledge for competitive reasons. Second, firms frequently do not know whom to contact even when it would be mutually beneficial for them to exchange information. In the absence of convenient channels of communications, this is as true for those who may wish to distribute technological knowledge as for those who wish to acquire it. Firms find random scanning of their broader environments to be highly inefficient since what they are looking for is not simply information, but rather the "news" (Stinchcombe, 1990). The "news" is knowledge and information of particular relevance to a firm's operations. Firms need, therefore, to devise some way of both locating the "news" and expediently separating it from other information that surrounds it. To achieve this, new institutions, or even new forms of institutions, may be needed to encourage the efficient spread of technological knowledge from "solution holders" to "problem holders" (Robertson, 1998). In the next section, we briefly describe some common classes of institutions that encourage knowledge flows and investigate the types of ties that bind them together.

INSTITUTIONS EMPLOYING STRONG AND WEAK TIES

In past two decades, popular and scholarly attention in English-speaking countries has turned to new forms of organization that seem to be able to overcome some of the drawbacks inherent in competitive individualism. Largely as a result of the success of Japanese firms (Miner and Haunschild, 1995; Gerlach, 1992a, 1992b; Fruin, 1992; Florida and Kenney, 1990), there have been numerous comparisons of the relative efficiency of Japanese networks and American atomism in industries such as electronics (Fruin, 1997; Saxenian, 1994; Browning, Beyer, and Shetler, 1995) and automobiles (Helper, 1990, 1991; Smitka, 1991). More recently, relationships in the biotechnology industry have received considerable attention (Powell, Koput, and Smith-Doerr, 1996; Powell, 1998; Walker, Kogut, and Shan, 1997; Liebeskind, Oliver, Zucker, and Brewer, 1996).

The literature on networks and other cooperative forms is vast and growing rapidly.[2] Virtually every issue of any management-related journal seems to contain at least one article on the topic. In Nohria's words (1992, p. 3), however, "Anyone reading through what purports to be network literature will readily perceive the analogy between it and a terminological jungle in which any newcomer may plant a tree." This holds as well for strategic alliances and other kinds of bonds between firms. For example, in popular usage networks range from tightly controlled organizations with well-defined operating rules that apply network-like organizational structures internally, to groups of dyads centering on a common firm, to any group of individuals who happen to interact with each other for any reason (i. e. "to network"). In the case of technological and other types of connections, particularly among start-up firms, relationships can assume several shapes and be of various levels of strength, spreading across a spectrum of overlapping forms from anonymous market ties through joint ventures and strategic alliances to common ownership and control (Chatterji, 1996; Roberts and Berry, 1985). All of these can play roles in technological diffusion since, as Chatterji (1996, 49) puts it, "It should be obvious that no single form of business relationship can address all the scenarios a company is likely to encounter in acquiring technology from external sources."

Frequently, technological information is exchanged between firms that are effectively subsets of larger groups. Whether, or how quickly, this information spreads beyond the subset depends on the rules under which the relationships have been established and conducted, and also on whether the rules are bent as a result of opportunistic behavior on the part of one of the participants. Figure 10.1 illustrates some important sets of relationships and their possible configurations relative to each other. On one interpretation, the network might comprise an industry of three firms and their respective suppliers and customers. While the principal firms, F1-F3, are all tied to each other, each firm's relationships with its suppliers and customers are dyadic. Supplier 1 and Customer 3, for example, transact business independently with each of the two firms with which they are connected. Thus, despite the presence of multiple suppliers and customers, direct network relationships in this diagram exist only between the representatives of the main industry. It is conceivable, although not certain, that there are no meaningful ties at all between suppliers and customers, or between the various customers, or between suppliers, or between any customer or supplier and any of the principal firms to which it is not connected dyadically.

Alternatively, F1-F3 may be thought of as subsets within an industry. For instance, they could represent the three "races" in the high-end computer industry as described by Khanna (1995, 1997), each of which had a different technology frontier over a 30-year period. In this case, the ties between firms within each of the collectivities, F1-F3, would be much stronger than the ties between the collectivities in the industry taken as a whole.

Figure 10.1
Dyads within a Network

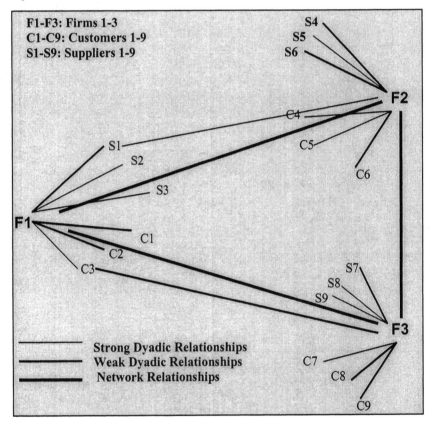

Figure 10.1 could also depict a strategic alliance, joint venture, or similar arrangement in which F1-F3, which may be from different industries, have banded together to promote a common goal, such as the development of a new

input or final product. Again, the various customer and supplier firms have only dyadic relationships with one, or on occasion two, of the principal firms. Moreover, it is possible that, even for related products, the relationships between the principal firms will also be dyadic. For example, as shown in Figure 10.2, in the 1970s and 1980s Nippon Steel carried out separate projects for developing coated steel with three auto manufacturers, Toyota, Nissan, and Mazda (Laage-Hellman, 1997). Although the projects overlapped chronologically, they were pursued using different coating technologies and Nippon kept the results of each research venture confidential from the other firms with which it was collaborating in order to avoid conflicts of interest.

Figure 10.2
Nippon Steel's Joint Projects with Automobile Producers for Developing Coated Steel

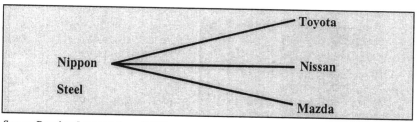

Source: Based on Laage-Hellman (1997).

The perspective can be extended to include a wider range of institutional contacts. Technology communities (Van de Ven and Garud, 1989, 1994; Garud and Van de Ven, 1989; Tushman and Rosenkopf, 1992; Rosenkopf and Tushman, 1994) concentrate on the emergence and consolidation of individual industries based on a particular class of technology. Innovation communities (Lynn, Aram, and Reddy, 1997), on the other hand, focus on the parties involved in the commercialization of a single innovation. Both look beyond the immediate membership of a network or alliance to include other stakeholders involved in promoting the interests of the industry or specific innovation. In building a picture similar in some respects to "national systems of innovation" (Nelson, 1993), for example, Rosenkopf and Tushman (1994) include governments and universities as well as groups of firms within the boundaries of a technological community. In an "era of ferment" in which there is rapid technological change, these institutions may remain largely unconnected, but subsequently, when incremental change has become common, a number of spanning organizations are able to coordinate the activities of the various parts, at least to a degree. Professional societies, standards bodies, and consortia are among the types of spanning organizations that they suggest.

The need to procure technological knowledge may even extend beyond the boundaries of technology or innovation communities, however, especially in periods of systemic change. Furthermore, it is necessary to take into account that the strength of ties between parts within a single configuration often vary. Here, we adopt the common classification of relationships based on *strong* and *weak* ties, but extend it to include situations in which there are no meaningful ties at all. In a market economy, almost all firms[3] are connected in some way with other firms since, except in rare cases of self-sufficiency, producers need suppliers and many firms also sell to other firms.

In this sense, nearly all firms are embedded (Granovetter, 1985; Grabher, 1993b; Uzzi, 1996, 1997), but the strength of embeddedness varies considerably from one relationship to another. Finding exact ways of defining the strength of ties and degrees of embeddedness in particular situations has proved elusive. Some ways of operationalizing ties are counting the number of contacts between different entities or asking participants in a relationship how strong they believe their ties to be (Mønsted, 1995), but these have clear limitations. For example, even though an organization may need specialist advice rarely, the relationship between the organization and its specialist supplier could be strong and important to both parties. Mønsted (1995) suggests that the strength of ties might instead be deduced from information on the characteristics of the participants, such as age and the degree of homogeneity of other factors, but this is again unsatisfactory since not all persons of a similar age or the same ethnic group have the same strength of relationships with each other, even if there are, on average, closer ties within the group than with outsiders.

Granovetter (1973) and Uzzi (1996, 1997) get closer to the heart of the matter by outlining some other characteristics of ties. According to Granovetter (1973, p. 1361), "the strength of a tie is a (probably linear) combination of the amount of time, the emotional intensity, the intimacy (mutual confiding), and the reciprocal services which characterize the tie", while Uzzi (1996) identifies levels of trust, fine-grained information transfer, and joint problem-solving arrangements as important criteria of the strength of ties between firms. But, in the end, as Granovetter (1973, p. 1361) contends, "It is sufficient ... if most of us can agree, on a rough intuitive basis, whether a given tie is strong, weak, or absent."

We believe, though, that the strength of ties is not necessarily a function of the form of a relationship and therefore that analyses (and policies) that concentrate on form may miss important dimensions of behavior. Even within a given network or alliance, there are likely to be ties of different strength (Figure 10.1). Relationships with some suppliers and customers are conducted through arm's-length market transactions, while other ties are stronger or more tightly embedded. This makes sense because, although Larson (1992) and Uzzi (1996, 1997) concentrate on the virtues of strong ties, organizations do not have the time or much incentive to establish close relationships with everyone with whom they deal. Some types of purchases or sales—particularly those involving homogeneous goods that are cheap or are traded infrequently—do not merit the resources that establishing strong ties with the supplier or customer would entail.

Moreover, what Granovetter (1973) calls "absent" ties and Burt (1992) calls "structural holes" can be highly significant when firms are in need of technological knowledge. According to Granovetter (1973, p. 1361 n. 4):

Included in "absent" are both the lack of any relationship and ties without substantial significance, such as a "nodding" relationship between people living on the same street, or the "tie" to the vendor from whom one customarily buys a morning newspaper. That two people "know" each other by name need not move their relationship out of this category if their interaction is negligible.

Figure 10.3 illustrates a situation in which there are weak, strong, and absent ties within Networks 1-3 as well as weak ties between those networks. Despite being part of the same environment, and therefore capable of being connected by weak or strong ties, however, Networks W and Y are not tied either to each other or to Networks 1-3. If there were no possibility of useful exchanges, absent ties and structural holes would be of no importance. But it is, in fact, probable that useful exchanges could occur in many cases.

Figure 10.3
Related and Unrelated Networks

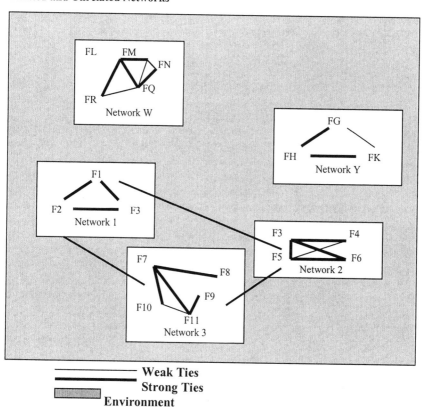

The need to build ties between networks is reinforced by elements of inertia that exist within relationships and networks. Relationships in networks have a tendency to reproduce each other. Aside from their economic benefits, all relationships also have a social dimension. Trust and social relationships that are built within an interfirm relationship make it difficult to abandon the relationship. This may lead to a path dependence effect in networks (Walker, Kogut, and Shan, 1997). In other words, even though a network may have expanded and even changed its scope, there is a tendency for firms to continue to look to other members of the network with whom they have dealt successfully in the past when they need new knowledge and other resources. In addition, not all valuable technological knowledge may be present within a network, especially when a competence-destroying (Tushman and Anderson, 1986) change has taken place. As a result, firms that restrict their searches to established relationships risk falling behind when important additions to technological knowledge occur outside their immediate networks (Rogers, 1995; Grabher, 1993a; Uzzi, 1996, 1997).

THE IMPORTANCE OF INDIVIDUALISM-COLLECTIVISM IN ESTABLISHING TIES

Firms and policy makers face two major problems in dealing with absent ties: (1) they need to identify as well as to fill the gaps that offer especially valuable possibilities for the exchange of knowledge; and (2) they must decide what kinds of ties are needed to fill particular gaps.

Burt (1992) suggests that structural holes offer good opportunities for entrepreneurial activity. Firms that spot gaps within networks can act as brokers that bring together solution holders and problem holders who would otherwise be unconnected. But in some cases, entrepreneurial activity may not be forthcoming or may be inadequate. Walker, Kogut, and Shan (1997) find the concept of brokers to be problematical because their effectiveness is likely to be limited by path dependency that encourages firms to continue to look towards preexisting contacts even after the possibility of using new ones has arisen. On the other hand, they concede that path dependency could also create opportunities for high returns to successful brokers.

A second reason why brokers may not act effectively is that the difficulty of identifying profitable opportunities *ex ante* may limit the range of opportunities that brokers are willing to tackle to those that are easiest (and cheapest) to spot. This would not necessarily mean, though, that the *social* returns to bridging gaps between distant networks might not be positive, even if high search costs reduced the *private* returns to brokers to inadequate levels. In a classic situation of market failure such as this, governments would be justified by any standard in themselves acting as brokers.

Still, the problem remains of deciding what kinds of ties need to be established. A great deal of recent government policy has been devoted to encouraging firms to build strong ties. In many cases, this has been aimed at establishing intraindustry networks that would allow firms to diffuse technological knowledge more widely than would occur if there were only weak ties, or indeed no ties at all. As Uzzi (1996, 1997) notes, strong (or embedded) ties offer great advantages for the spread of knowledge. They encourage joint problem-solving activities that combine diverse talents with scarce technological knowledge to broaden the range and improve the quality of R&D activities. Second, because of the possibility of achieving exchanges of knowledge and information that are more fine-grained, strong ties can overcome the problems associated with tacitness. Finally, strong ties are associated with higher levels of trust, which can make the parties more willing to exchange valuable knowledge than they would in arm's-length relationships. Nevertheless, this does not mean that the encouragement of strong ties and high degrees of embeddedness is the best policy in all cases. Our argument is that weak ties can also be of value to all firms and that the encouragement of weak ties in general may prove especially beneficial to firms whose management is individualistic rather than collectivist in its outlook.

Reliance on strong ties within networks is based on habit and past experience, but such heuristics can be misleading. Not only may firms, like individuals, judge wrongly in choosing the partners with whom they cooperate, but in a dynamic situation ties that were effective at one time may later become damagingly restrictive. In principle, useful knowledge can arise anywhere, but Rogers (1995) and Granovetter (1973) claim that novel technologies are more likely to come from outside mature industries than from within. Weak ties can therefore act as "bridges" (Granovetter, 1973) between networks that shorten the path from a given firm to sources of new knowledge, and new sources of knowledge, that are outside their own networks, providing them with a competitive advantage by potentially accelerating their ability to upgrade their technologies. Similarly, weak ties can benefit originators of new technological knowledge by bringing them into closer contact with a wider selection of possible users (Robertson, 1998).

Bridges can also be essential for firms in new industries that, for one reason or another, cannot become active members of the core networks in which most technological change is taking place. For example, firms in many parts of the world cannot by definition share the advantages that propinquity confers on competitors in districts such as Silicon Valley. This remoteness can be damaging even for firms in large and otherwise up-to-date economies such as those of the European Union as well as in more distant countries like Australia and New Zealand. While bridges with networks at the technological frontier are not a full substitute for having strong ties within those networks, they still provide an effective way for geographically remote firms to gain access to new ideas and also to commercialize new ideas generated on the periphery.

Another important consideration is the extent to which firms are willing to take advantage of ties. Shane (1992, 1993) contends that firms in relatively individualistic cultures are likely to be more innovative than are firms in more collectivist ones, but he does not discuss their sources of information. According to the Individualism-Collectivism literature, people and institutions in different cultures have varying degrees of willingness to engage in collective activities, that is, to form strong ties with each other (Earley, 1989; Cox, Lobel, and McLeod, 1991; Triandis, 1995; Tiessen 1997; Chen, Chen, and Meindl, 1998). Triandis (1995) proposes four factors that distinguish individualism from collectivism:

1. In individualism, the concept of the self is independent, but in collectivism it is interdependent. This affects behavior in areas such as the sharing of resources and conformance to group goals. In both cases, collectivists pay more attention to group needs and norms than individualists do.
2. Whereas personal and group goals are closely aligned in collectivism, they are not aligned at all in individualism.
3. In individualistic cultures, cognitions center on personal needs, rights, and attitudes and on contracts; in collectivist cultures, the focus is instead on norms, obligations and duties.
4. In collectivist cultures, relationships are emphasized even when they are disadvantageous, while in individualist cultures relationships are subjected to rational analyses of their advantages and disadvantages.

In practice, neither cultures nor the people who comprise them are likely to adopt purely individualist or collectivist attitudes and behaviors, but rather to employ a mix of the two types of conduct (Tiessen 1997, Uzzi, 1997). It is nevertheless possible to locate different clusters of conduct along a spectrum ranging from one extreme position to the other. These clusters can be expected to differ in their attitude to interfirm relationships and cooperation. Chen, Chen, and Meindl (1998) propose that in individualist cultures, cooperation will increase as long as it bolsters personal identities. In collectivist cultures, cooperation increases to the extent that the new group identity that results complements any existing group identities. Higher levels of cooperation are generated by face-to-face communication in a collectivist culture than in an individualist one, but mediated partial communication generates higher levels of cooperation in individualist cultures than in collectivist ones. Tiessen (1997) proposes that in individualist cultures, pragmatic relationships predominate. These are characterized by formal, highly structured contract-based agreements. In collectivist cultures, relationships are expected to be based on long-run commitments that are based more on mutual goodwill than on explicit formal structures. The Japanese *keiretsu* are examples of this form of relationship.

For our purposes, individualists can be defined as firms whose management is reluctant, or even unwilling, to cooperate actively with other firms in the exchange of technological knowledge, while collectivists are firms whose management feels comfortable in engaging in cooperative activities such as joint ventures, strategic alliances, and networks. We therefore propose the following propositions for technology policy based on the concepts that have been presented earlier:

• Proposition 1A: Firms in cultures with high degrees of individualism will, on balance, be reluctant to join in government-sponsored technology activities that require them to cooperate strongly with other firms, including competitors, suppliers, and customers.

- Proposition 1B: Firms in relatively collectivist cultures will, on balance, be more willing to join in government-sponsored technology activities that require them to cooperate strongly with other firms, including competitors, suppliers, and customers.

The four factors proposed by Triandis all suggest that individualistic cultures generate attitudes that would work against the sharing of information. Not only do firms from these cultures place their personal interests above those of larger groups, including their nations in an abstract sense, but they are apt to calculate closely the advantages and disadvantages that would ensue from cooperation. In addition, cooperative activities such as networks could create new group identities that would submerge rather than enhance the identities of the individual firms. As a consequence, firms operating in individualist cultures would harbor *a priori* suspicions of the efficacy of government-sponsored bodies and either be reluctant to join, or only pay lip-service to, cooperative ventures promoted by their governments. Firms in collectivist cultures, however, would be more likely to perceive benefits arising from government action that aligned their goals with those other firms and to exchange information in a government-sponsored framework.

- Proposition 2A: Firms in individualist cultures will not be eager to join in broad-based fine-grained activities that break down barriers created by tacitness but will prefer to exchange technological knowledge in coded form through channels that do not required them to become strongly tied to other parties.
- Proposition 2B: Firms in collectivist cultures will be willing to join in broad-based fine-grained activities that break down barriers created by tacitness.

In individualist cultures, managers are uncomfortable with strong ties that link them to a mass of other firms. This is especially true in the case of networks or other collective ventures that have been organized by outsiders and that include parties with whom the managers are not well acquainted. In part, this preference is based on a fear that their firms will give away information of more value than that which they receive in return. Government policy is therefore likely to be more effective if it encourages weak ties rather than strong ones in order to increase the knowledge that firms in individualist cultures have of technological developments in the wider world because an emphasis on weak ties will gain greater cooperation from firms that insist on maintaining their autonomy.

This, of course, does not mean that weak ties are in general more efficient than strong ties in transmitting knowledge. Tacit knowledge can be particularly valuable when a technology is new and not well understood. If firms are not willing to engage freely in cooperative activities, however, and are seriously concerned that they will lose by participation in such relationships, then the promotion of weak ties that are effective could ultimately lead to greater exchanges of valuable knowledge than ineffective strong ties would.

In collectivist cultures, however, strong ties are more likely to result, either through direct firm initiatives or through initiatives promoted by external bodies, which would allow firms to come to grips with tacit knowledge more quickly. Again, this would not obviate the need for other types of ties, as important information could still be gained through coded sources outside the range of strong ties of any given firm.

To promote effective strong ties, in individualist cultures incentive structures might be necessary that help to overcome the reluctance on the part of firms to associate closely with each other. In rare instances, a perceived common threat might be sufficient to overcome reluctance. The formation of SEMATECH might serve as an example for this argument (Browning, Beyer, and Shetler, 1995). When the U.S. semiconductor industry was faced with the increasing dependence on process technology suppliers from Japan, the otherwise highly competitive firms were able to cooperate and jointly repulse the threat of dependence. In many instances, however, an obvious threat might not be commonly perceived at all. To encourage cooperation between firms in both individualistic and collectivist cultures, incentive structures would need to match cultural predispositions. As we have discussed, in individualist cultures, the benefits accruing to the individual are valued more highly than benefits accruing to the group. Before joining government-sponsored programs, firms would need to perceive an individual benefit as opposed to only joint benefits. In collectivist cultures, firms would be more willing to accept indirect benefits as justification for joint efforts.

- Proposition 3A: Firms in individualist cultures will be more willing to join in government-sponsored technology activities if the benefits derived from these activities accrue directly to these firms.
- Proposition 3B: Firms in collectivist cultures will be willing to join in government-sponsored technology activities if they can see that there will be joint benefits to be derived from these activities as well as benefits that accrue directly to themselves.

A CASE STUDY: INDIVIDUALISM AMONG AUSTRALIAN AND FINNISH FIRMS

In this section we present empirical data from Australia and Finland to illustrate the relevance of our discussion. These data are not meant as a test of our propositions but rather as examples to underscore our arguments.

Australia is a geographically remote nation that is rich in natural resources, with high levels of education and literacy and per capita incomes that, in purchasing power parity terms, are approximately at the average of those in Western Europe. Finland also occupies a peripheral location, in this case on the edge of the European Union. Both countries are sparsely populated with the core of economic activity being concentrated in few cities. In Australia, the Sydney and Melbourne metropolitan areas alone contain around one-third of the total population. Although there is a history of strong state involvement in the economies of both countries, this has been stronger in Finland. Finally, both economies are becoming more open. In this respect, Finland is somewhat ahead of Australia as a result of its entry into the European Union in 1995.

There are similarities and differences between the innovation systems of the two countries. For example, Australia and Finland are among the top five countries in the world with respect to the amount of government and university funds devoted to R&D in relation to gross national product. In both countries, the share of private-sector research in their economies has grown substantially in recent years. However, with relatively few exceptions, Australian firms borrow their technologies from overseas sources instead of generating them locally. In part, this is a function of the small population, but it also derives from the low proportions of their resources that Australian firms devote to R&D activities by OECD standards. In contrast Finnish firms are more technology oriented than their Australian counterparts and devote significantly more funds to R&D activities, as Table 10.1 shows.

Table 10.1
Indicators of R&D Performance

	OECD Average (1992)	Australia (1992)	Finland (1992)
Gross domestic expenditure on R&D (GERD)/ GDP, %	1.91	1.56	2.18
Average annual % growth in GERD/GDP	2.22	4.04	5.50
Business enterprise expenditure on R&D (BERD)/GDP, %	1.18	1.24	0.69
Average annual % real growth in BERD	6.3	13.0	8.2

Source: Industry Commission (1995), Tables A3.1 and A3.2.

Australia and Finland differ significantly in regard to the proportions of individualism and collectivism present in their cultures. Both countries were part in the seminal study by Hofstede (1980). On the individualism scale that Hofstede devised, Australia was among the countries with the strongest tendency to individualism (Hofstede 1980, p. 222). Finland was considered an individualistic country but exhibited only moderate individualism compared to Australia.[4] This would lead us to expect firms from both countries to be reluctant to enter into network relationships. In interpreting the data presented here, one should keep in mind that we are considering small and medium-sized firms that are often managed by an entrepreneur. While differing in their cultural orientation towards individualism, one would expect the tendency of all these firms to be relatively individualistic (Tiessen, 1997). However, due to the cultural differences between Australia and Finland, we would also expect Australian firms to be more reluctant to collaborate than Finnish firms.

Table 10.2
Demographics of the Sample

Characteristic	Australia			Finland			ANOVA*
	Mean	Median	Standard Deviation	Mean	Median	Standard Deviation	
Age at the time of data collection (in years)	17.10	14.50	13.99	15.41	10.00	14,44	0.236 (1.411)
Total annual sales in 1996 (in million ECU)	1.86	0.65	4.37	1.89	0.58	4,56	0.943 (0.005)
Number of employees in 1996	19.05	8.00	34.03	16.11	7.00	27,46	0.357 (0.852)
Average yearly sales growth from 1990 to 1996 in percent	14.61	5.80	31.36	20.67	8.29	50,45	0.256 (0.256)

*In the ANOVA column, the upper value is the significance level. The value in parentheses is the F-value of the ANOVA test.

Table 10.3
Cross-Country Comparison of Alliances with Competitors

Variable	Australia		Finland		ANOVA	
	Mean	Standard Deviation	Mean	Standard Deviation	F	Significance
Total number of alliances with potential competitors	1.03	1.69	2.86	3.86	36.061	0.000
Information exchange with potential competitors	2.03	1.40	3.21	1.37	70.993	0.000
Joint consortia with potential competitors	1.91	1.38	3.32	1.52	93.591	0.000
Alliance contracts with potential competitors	1.75	1.34	2.46	1.67	21.891	0.000
Shared equipment or facilities with potential competitors	1.91	1.46	1.64	1.03	4.331	0.038
Joint ventures with potential competitors	1.88	1.44	1.63	1.17	3.415	0.065

Table 10.4
Cross-Country Comparison of Supplier Structure

Variable	Australia		Finland		ANOVA	
	Mean	Standard Deviation	Mean	Standard Deviation	F	Significance
Share of largest supplier (%)	34.74	24.91	34.11	26.52	0.052	0.820
Closeness of relationship with largest supplier*	3.05	1.67	3.73	1.72	14.793	0.000
Knowledge sharing with largest supplier	4.17	2.12	5.12	1.63	23.299	0.000
Joint product development with largest supplier	3.94	2.08	3.90	2.09	0.034	0.854

*The overall closeness of the relationship with the most important supplier was measured using the average of the replies to three Likert-type questions. The Cronbach Alpha score for this construct was 0.75.

Table 10.5
Cross-Country Comparison of Customer Structure

Variable	Australia		Finland		ANOVA	
	Mean	Standard Deviation	Mean	Standard Deviation	F	Significance
Share of largest customer (%)	35.52	24.84	37.21	24.77	0.421	0.517
Closeness of relationship with largest customer*	4.38	1.69	3.98	1.52	5.924	0.015
Knowledge sharing with largest customer	5.17	1.87	5.70	1.36	9.643	0.002
Joint product development with largest customer	5.63	1.76	4.93	1.87	14.620	0.000

*The overall closeness of the relationship with the largest customer was measured using the average of the replies to four Likert-type questions. The Cronbach Alpha score for this construct was 0.80.

The data that follow are based on a postal survey of approximately 2,600 small and medium-sized firms in the electrical engineering and electronics, mechanical engineering and machinery, and plastics industries. In Finland, about 1,200 firms were contacted that are located in the Helsinki and Turku region. In Australia, about 1,400 firms located in Sydney and Melbourne were contacted. We received 420 useable responses from firms with 250 or fewer employees. This translates into an overall response rate of 16.2 percent, which is not untypical for studies of firms of this size. The general demographics of the sample are presented in Table 10.2.

The degree of individualism of the firms surveyed is clear. On balance the respondents showed little enthusiasm for networking or for exchanging technological knowledge, particularly with competitors and suppliers. On average, the firms entered into only around two relationships with potential competitors. When looking at the two countries separately (Table 10.3), interesting differences emerge. For example, while the majority of Australian firms do not enter into any relationships with potential competitors, the majority of Finnish firms enter into at least one relationship of this type. Significant differences also exist for most other potential forms of collaboration with potential competitors.

Similarly, even though their largest suppliers accounted for about 34 percent of their total purchases of inputs, the degree of closeness of relationship with these suppliers was below the midpoint of the scale for both countries (Table 10.4). Finnish firms, however, were willing to enter into significantly closer relationships with their key suppliers. Finnish firms also exhibited a significantly higher extent of knowledge sharing with their key suppliers.

The results of the interaction with the key customer are less straightforward. In both the Australian and Finnish samples the largest customer accounted for about 36-37 percent of total sales. The Australian firms worked more closely with their key customers, particularly concerning new product development. However, the Finnish firms were significantly more willing to share confidential knowledge with their key customers (Table 10.5).

Our results, which are consistent with Propositions 1A and 1B, are similar to the findings of other studies. A survey by the Australian Bureau of Industry Economics (1995) found that only about one-third of the SMEs that responded exhibited any networking behavior. Of those that did, around 60 percent (or 20 percent of all firms) cooperated to a substantial degree with their customers, with slightly smaller proportions cooperating with suppliers and with other firms, including competitors. Dean et al. (1997) found a reluctance on the part of Australian SMEs to take part in *any* type of relationship with other firms; 75 percent of service-sector respondents and 50 percent of manufacturing respondents signified that they participated in "informal networks", which were defined as "loose informal arrangements between companies which facilitate the exchange of information", but "formal networks" ("formal arrangement[s] between three or more businesses to consolidate resources with a clear common business objective") attracted only 30 percent of service sector firms and 18 percent of manufacturing firms.

Moreover, of the respondents to the survey by Dean et al. only 22 percent of service and 10 percent of manufacturing SMEs believed that the term "business network" meant "exchanging ideas/resources". Only 19 percent of service-sector firms and 6 percent of those in manufacturing believed that it implied "contacts/interbusiness communication". Fifteen percent of firms in both categories saw "exchange of information" as a benefit of belonging to a network, but 71 percent of manufacturers and 63 percent of service firms cited "concern with information disclosure" as a major factor that discouraged involvement in networks.

DISCUSSION AND RECOMMENDATIONS

Altogether, the picture that emerges is of firms that persist in maintaining high degrees of autonomy. If firms require access to substantial pools of up-to-date technological knowledge in order to be competitive, then our findings raise concerns about the ability of Australian SMEs, in particular, to perform at anything close to world-class levels. This is also true by extension of firms in other individualist cultures that are not already operating at the technological frontiers of their respective industries. Because of their isolation, firms in both highly innovative and more mature sectors must suffer from an unhealthy scarcity of information on new product and process technologies. One way of attacking the problem that could be politically appealing in some circles would be through imposing trade barriers against goods produced overseas by firms with greater technological sophistication, but any reduction in incentives to improve the technological position of domestic firms is only likely in the long run to lead to a further deterioration in international competitiveness and, ultimately, in standards of living.

The problem is to find policies that induce firms to up-date their technological competences. In Propositions 3A and 3B, we contend that proper incentives need to be provided to reduce the reluctance of firms to form ties with each other. Encouraging firms to build strong ties through the formation of networks and alliances is one approach that has been favored by both the Australian and Finnish governments.

In Finland, where individualism is less prominent than in Australia, the response to government encouragement of strong ties has been relatively positive. The TEKES Technology Development Centre has been instrumental in encouraging interfirm collaboration. TEKES is the main financing organization for applied and industrial research and development in Finland. Financed through the state budget, in 1997 TEKES distributed grants of about €330 million to companies, private research institutes, and universities. This sum accounts for about 10 percent of the overall inputs into research and development. A large share of these funds is channeled through technology programs that aim at developing new technological expertise in important business areas.

TEKES sees itself as performing important functions in financing and coordinating international technological cooperation as well as in supporting technology transfer and exploitation in SMEs. To encourage collaboration and network formation, TEKES has included networking with other companies, joint ventures, and other forms of collaboration among the criteria that are considered beneficial in support of a grant application. In line with our Propositions 3A and 3B, TEKES supplies direct research and development funding to overcome the resistance of individualist firms. While quantitative measures of the success of this measure are difficult, international evaluations of the research programs have underlined repeatedly the high level of collaboration in the TEKES programs. These studies have found close cooperation between research institutes and industry, a widespread involvement of small and medium-sized companies, and a high level of international cooperation (Klipstein and McRae, 1996; Lepoutre, Lindström, and Page, 1997). For instance, in the injection molding business, Autio and Berger (1997) found that in 24 out of 29 cases participation in the TEKES technology program had a significant perceived impact on cooperation and communication between constituents of the industry value chain.

Encouragement of networks in Australia has led to less impressive results. In 1995 the Bureau of Industry Economics, which was then part of the Department of Industry, Science and Technology (DIST), published *Beyond the Firm: An Assessment of Business Linkages and Networks in Australia.* The study, which is nearly 350 pages in length, was sponsored by AusIndustry, another agency of DIST that houses the Business Networks Program (Bureau of Industry Economics, 1995, p. xiii). Perhaps understandably, the study praises the benefits that flow from network participation. Since then, AusIndustry has published a regular bulletin called *Network News*, which has featured articles with prominent headlines along the lines of "Networks Work!" (AusIndustry, 1998).

While this form of encouragement to build strong network ties is certainly important, our results illustrate that it might not be sufficient to induce individualist firms to overcome their reluctance to build interfirm relationships. We do not dispute that strong ties can be highly beneficial and should be promoted. Our concern is whether too much stress can be placed on building strong ties in an individualistic culture such as Australia's. Our survey and others all reveal reluctance on the part of Australian SMEs to form strong ties, apparently based on a belief that the firms have more to lose than to gain through sharing information. The encouragement of networking should continue, of course, on the premise that in time these feelings might be reversed and firms can learn to appreciate the virtues of cooperation. As Shane (1993, p. 59) argues, "Countries may not be able increase their rates of innovation simply by increasing the amount of money spent on research and development or industrial infrastructure. They also may need to change the values of their citizens to those that encourage innovative activity." Altering fundamental beliefs is generally a slow process, however, and additional initiatives are needed in the meantime to answer the immediate need of improving the technological knowledge of Australian firms.

On the basis of our Propositions 2A and 2B, we contend that an appropriate course would be to place much greater emphasis on the formation of weak ties, especially between Australian firms and those in other countries. There are several possible routes for accomplishing this through the use of Broking Institutions (Figure 10.4). Broking Institutions could either collect and disseminate technological knowledge themselves or they could assist other bodies to do so. While they would lack the fine-grained capabilities of institutions with stronger ties to the sources of their information, they would possess counterbalancing advantages. First, they could collect information more widely, which could be especially useful when the rate of technological change is high and new important new ideas are emerging from multiple sources. Furthermore, they would not be bound by considerations of confidentiality, as members of joint ventures or alliances might be.

Figure 10.4
The Role of Broking Institutions

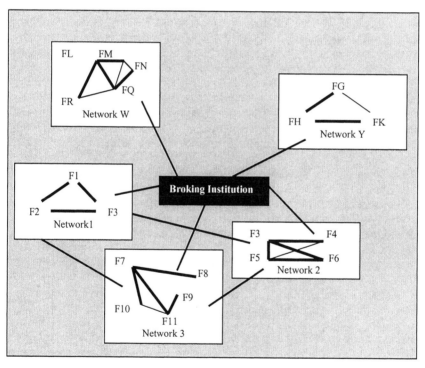

Broking Institutions could assume several forms. For example, governments could run their own agencies for gathering and distributing information. This would follow a long tradition that includes consular services that promote trade by, among other things, gathering "commercial intelligence". This type of agency would suffer from the problem, however, of not having clearly identified targets or customers. Agents would be hard-pressed to recognize what information constitutes "news" in Stinchcombe's (1990) sense. A large staff of industry specialists might be better qualified to gather information, but this would be expensive and run counter to the mores of an individualist culture that is suspicious of large bureaucracies.

Alternatively, industry-based boards could be used to collect and disseminate technological knowledge. These could be privately organized or government-sponsored. In the former case, firms would band together to further common goals. Historically, there have been numerous organizations of this type including industry associations. Professional associations, such as the various institutes of engineers, have also been very important in distributing technological knowledge both from local areas and internationally, as well as in providing venues for the informal exchanges of information described by Von Hippel (1988). Nevertheless, they have limitations in that they are influenced by the prevailing attitudes in individualist cultures and may be difficult for the managers of SMEs to penetrate either because of membership fees or because the level of discourse is too rarified for "practical" managers without much formal technical education.

A possible model for government-sponsored industry boards would be the organizations that have been developed in the "third Italy" (Best, 1990; Lazerson, 1988), in Tuscany, Emilia-Romagna, the Veneto, and other regions in north-central Italy. Firms in these areas protect their distinctive competences, which in areas like ceramics and textiles are often in design, but cooperate in the supply of business services like bookkeeping, the sponsorship of trade fairs and other marketing activities, and the provision of infrastructure. These ventures are government-sanctioned, as are official cooperatives that borrow from lending institutions and then distribute the funds to their members, guaranteeing the loans received (Brusco and Righi, 1987). Again, however, the boards reflect a traditional "communitarian" social structure (Paniccia, 1998) and might not thrive in individualist cultures.

Another, more promising, possibility would be to implement something along the lines of the self-organizing industry investment boards suggested by Romer (1993). The boards would be formed at the instigation of firms within an industry with the approval of the government. Firms that wanted to sponsor the establishment of an industry board would approach the appropriate government department with a proposal that would then be voted upon by all firms in the industry. If some agreed proportion, perhaps two-thirds, gave their support, then a board or boards would be set up and financed by a tax, backed by legislation, on the domestic sales of all firms in the industry. The specific research activities to be undertaken would be decided by member firms, who could direct how their own taxes were to be divided among a menu of projects suggested by members.

In some cases, these would be aimed at specific research goals, but they could also be concerned with the provision of technological infrastructure including educational programs and facilities that would be common property of the member firms. If a particular project lost support, or never had much, this would be reflected in low levels of funding voted by members in an annual ballot. All research findings would be freely available to all members and the boards would be regulated to prevent the misuse of funds.

There is precedent for boards of this type. In the United States, market orders for research and development and market promotion activities can be established under the Agricultural Marketing Agreement Act of 1937 (Romer, 1993). Growers of a particular commodity can petition the secretary of agriculture to establish a marketing order to meet a purpose that they support if it falls within the terms of the act. The secretary then holds a referendum of growers. If two-thirds approve according to a formula specified in the legislation, then the marketing order is issued. Subsequent referenda are held, usually at six-year intervals, to determine if support has been maintained. In Australia, Research and Development Corporations (RDCs) are also organized around particular agricultural commodities (Industry Commission, 1995). The RDCs do not conduct research themselves, but contract out research projects that are financed by statutory levies on producers matched by government grants. Priorities are set by boards that consult with producers, usually on an annual basis.

Strong political opposition could be expected to the establishment of industry research boards. In addition to suspicions concerning the effectiveness of government-sponsored activities, compulsory levies would be unpopular. This is especially true at the level proposed by Romer, which is around 2 percent of domestic sales (*not* profits). Lower taxes might be sufficient, however, to meet most important needs. In any case, the flexibility of industry research boards makes them attractive in several respects. First, they could be used to promote both strong and weak ties, although the Australian RDC practice of contracting out research would be most suitable for building weak ties. Second, firms would have total independence in how they used the results of the projects, which should be well suited to individualist tendencies and reduce suspicions concerning the need to cooperate with other firms in unwanted ways. Third, under Romer's proposal there is scope for competing projects and competing boards. If they wanted, members of an industry could endorse research into alternative ways of meeting the same goal as well as into alternative goals. This would increase the potential variety of outcomes and allow for greater choice by member firms. In addition, competitive research projects could increase both the range of weak ties with potential solution holders and the collective absorptive capacity of the industry. Fourth, firms would not themselves have to contribute knowledge to participate, which would help to allay their fears of being cheated. Finally, the money would not have to be spent on research directly, but could also be used to improve the technological infrastructure of an industry through, for instance, the establishment of information-gathering bureaus or the encouragement of better training and education programs.

CONCLUSION

Firms need to acquire technological knowledge from external as well as internal sources, but there are generally substantial barriers to collecting knowledge from outside a firm's immediate environment. In many cases, these are caused by the fact that knowledge is often generated in a decentralized and chaotic way, which makes it hard for firms to locate partners who can help them solve their problems. The choice of a policy to surmount these barriers is not straightforward since, as Shane (1993, p. 67) notes, "Societies in which people do not [have a proper mix of individualism and other values] may spend money on research and development and industrial infrastructure, but still fail to achieve the desired results in terms of rates of innovation because of the beliefs of their citizens." Proposals to establish strong ties between firms can offer a partial answer, but are unlikely to be highly effective when a high degree of individualism among managers makes them skeptical of the value of cooperation. Furthermore, if progress is to be made, at least some of the members of networks and other alliances must have knowledge at the technological frontier. Strong ties among organizations with low levels of expertise may be of less value in diffusing technological knowledge than weak ties between knowledgeable and less-knowledgeable firms would be.

To overcome these problems, we suggest that government action is desirable to help establish and maintain technological ties with the external environment. Particularly in countries with individualist cultures, however, governments need to promote weak ties and not concentrate principally on strong ties. This can be accomplished through the encouragement of Broking Institutions that, as far as is feasible, bring together problem holders and solution holders from throughout the worldwide environment. Industry research boards seem to be an especially promising way of doing this because they permit firms to tap broad sources of technological knowledge without seriously compromising their autonomy.

NOTES

1. By "new technological knowledge", we mean knowledge that is new to a given firm as well as knowledge that has only recently been discovered.

2. A definitely nonexhaustive list of some of the more important publications includes Nohria and Eccles (1992), Jarillo (1993), Buttery and Buttery (1994), Gomes-Casseres (1996), Dosi, Teece, and Chytry (1998), and Doz and Hamel (1998).

3. In our usage, a "firm" may also include an enterprise owned and run by a single person. While all suppliers would be firms on this definition, customers could be either other firms or final consumers.

4. Hofstede (1980) constructed his individualism score based on a factor analysis of work goals across countries. On this score Australia was the second most individualistic country (Score 90) after the US. Finland exhibited an individualism score of 63, which is relatively close to the demarcation point of 50 between countries exhibiting relatively high and low degrees of individualism.

REFERENCES

AusIndustry, Australian Commonwealth Government Department of Industry, Science and Tourism, 1998, Networks Work!, *Network News*, No. 9, January, 1.

Autio, E., and Berger, H., 1997, Partnership in Injection Moulding Business 1993-1997, Technology Programme Report 9/97, TEKES, Helsinki.

Best, M., 1990, *The New Competition: Institutions of Industrial Restructuring*. Cambridge, MA: Harvard University Press.

Browning, L. D., Beyer, J. M., and Shetler, J. C., 1995, Building cooperation in a competitive industry: SEMATECH and the semiconductor industry, *Academy of Management Journal* 38 (1), 113-151.

Brusco, S. and Righi, E., 1987, The Loan Guarantee Consortia, *Entrepreneurial Economy* 6 (1), 11-13.

Bureau of Industry Economics, 1995, *Beyond the Firm: An Assessment of Business Linkages and Networks in Australia*, Research Report 67. Canberra: Australian Government Publishing Service.

Burt, R. S., 1992, *Structural Holes*. Cambridge, MA: Harvard University Press.

Buttery, E. and Buttery, A., 1994, *Business Networks: Reaching New Markets with Low-Cost Strategies*. Melbourne: Longman Business and Professional.

Camagni, R. (Editor), 1991, *Innovation networks: Spatial perspectives*. London: Belhaven Press.

Chatterji, D., 1996, Accessing External Sources of Technology, *Research·Technology Management* 39 (2), 48-56.

Chen, C. C., Chen, X.-P., and Meindl, J. R., 1998, How Can Cooperation Be Fostered? The Cultural Effects of Individualism-Collectivism, *Academy of Management Review* 23 (2), 285-304.

Cohen, W. M. and Levinthal, D. A., 1989, Innovation and Learning: The Two Faces of R&D, *Economic Journal* 99, 569-596.

Cohen, W. M. and Levinthal, D. A., 1990, Absorptive Capacity: A New Perspective on Learning and Innovation, *Administrative Science Quarterly* 35, 128-152.

Cox, T. H., Lobel, S. A., and McLeod, P. L., 1991, Effects of Ethnic Group Cultural Differences on Cooperative and Competitive Behavior in a Group Task, *Academy of Management Journal* 34 (4), 827-847.

Cyert, R., and March, J. G., 1992, *A behavioral theory of the firm*. Englewood Cliffs, NJ: Prentice Hall.

Davenport, T. H. and Klahr, P., 1998, Managing Customer Support Knowledge, *California Management Review* 40 (3), 195-208.

David, P. A., 1991, Computer and Dynamo: The Modern Productivity Paradox in a Not-Too-Distant Mirror, in *Technology and Productivity: The Challenge for Economic Policy*. Paris: OECD.

Dean, J., Holmes, S., and Smith, S., 1997, Understanding Business Networks: Evidence from the Manufacturing and Service Sectors in Australia, *Journal of Small Business Management* 35, 78-84.

DeBresson, C., and Amesse, F., 1991, Networks of innovators: A review and introduction to the issue, *Research Policy* 20, 363 - 379.

Dosi, G., 1982,. Technological paradigms and technological trajectories, *Research Policy* 11, 147-162.

Dosi, G., Teece, D. J., and Chytry, J. (Editors), 1998, *Technology, Organization, and Competitiveness*. Oxford: Oxford University Press.

Doz, Y. and Hamel, G., 1998, *Alliance Advantage: The Art of Creating Value Through Partnering*. Boston: Harvard Business School Press.

Earley, P. C., 1989, Social Loafing and Collectivism: A Comparison of the United States and the Peoples Republic of China, *Administrative Science Quarterly* 34, 565-581.

Florida, R. and Kenney, M., 1990, *The Breakthrough Illusion: Corporate Americas Failure to Move from Innovation to Mass Production*. New York: Basic Books.

Fruin, W. M., 1992, *The Japanese Enterprise System: Competitive Strategies and Cooperative Structures*. Oxford: Clarendon Press.

Fruin, W. M., 1997, *Knowledge Works: Managing Intellectual Capital at Toshiba*. New York: Oxford University Press.

Garud, R. and Van de Ven, A. H., 1989, Technological Innovation and Industry Emergence: The Case of Cochlear Implants, in A. H. Van de Ven, H. L. Angle, and M. S. Poole (Editors), *Research on the Management of Innovation: The Minnesota Studies*. Grand Rapids, MI: Ballinger.

Gerlach, M. L., 1992a, The Japanese Corporate Network: A Blockmodel Analysis, *Administrative Science Quarterly* 37, 105-139.

Gerlach, M. L., 1992b, *Alliance Capitalism: The Social Organization of Japanese Business*. Berkeley: University of California Press.

Gomes-Cassseres, B., 1996, *The Alliance Revolution: The New Shape of Business Rivalry*. Cambridge, MA: Harvard University Press.

Grabher, G., 1993a, The Weakness of Strong Ties: The Lock-in of Regional Development in the Ruhr Area, in G. Grabher (Editor), *The Embedded Firm: On the Socioeconomics of Industrial Networks*. London: Routledge, pp. 255-277.

Grabher, G. (Editor), 1993b, *The Embedded Firm: On the Socioeconomics of Industrial Networks*. London: Routledge.

Granovetter, M., 1973, The Strength of Weak Ties, *American Journal of Sociology* 78, 1360-1380.

Granovetter, M., 1985, Economic Action and Social Structure: The Problem of Embeddedness, *American Journal of Sociology* 91, 481-510.

Hargadon, A. B., 1998, Firms as Knowledge Brokers: Lessons in Pursuing Continuous Innovation, *California Management Review* 40 (3), 209-227.

Helfat, C. E., 1994, Evolutionary trajectories in petroleum firm R&D, *Management Science* 40 (12), 1720-1747.

Helper, S. R., 1990, Comparative Supplier Relations in the U. S. and Japanese Auto Industries: An Exit/Voice Approach, *Business and Economic History* 19, 355-72.

Helper, S. R., 1991, An Exit-Voice Analysis of Supplier Relations, in R. M. Coughlin (Editor), *Morality, Rationality, and Efficiency: New Perspectives on Socio-Economics*. New York: M.E. Sharpe.

Hobday, M., 1998, Product Complexity, Innovation and Industrial Organisation, *Research Policy* 26, 689-710.

Hofstede, G., 1980, *Cultures Consequences, International Differences in Work-Related Values*. Beverly Hills, CA: Sage.

Hofstede, G., 1991, *Cultures and Organizations: Software of the Mind*. London: McGraw-Hill.

Industry Commission, 1995, *Research and Development, Report No. 44*, 3 vols. Canberra: Australian Government Publishing Service.

Jarillo, J. C., 1993, *Strategic Networks: Creating the Borderless Organization*. London: Butterworth-Heinemann.

Khanna, T., 1995, Racing Behavior: Technological Evolution in the High-End Computer Industry, *Research Policy* 24, 933-958.

Khanna, T., 1997, On Technological Evolution within and of Industry Boundaries, in R. A. Burgelman and R. S. Rosenbloom (Editors), *Research on Technological Innovation, Management and Policy* 6, pp. 55-88.

Klipstein, D. H., and McRae, G. J., 1996, *Evaluation Report of the Process Technology Programme*, Technology Programme Report 5/96, TEKES, Helsinki.

Laage-Hellman, J., 1997, *Business Networks in Japan: Supplier-Customer Interaction in Product Development*. London: Routledge.

Lambe, C. J. and Spekman, R. E., 1997, Alliances, External Technology Acquisition, and Discontinuous Technological Change, *Journal of Product Innovation Management* 14, 102-116.

Larson, A., 1992, Network Dyads in Entrepreneurial Settings: A Study of the Governance of Exchange Relationships, *Administrative Science Quarterly* 37, 76-104.

Lazerson, M. H., 1988, Organizational Growth of Small Firms: An Outcome of Markets and Hierarchies?, *American Sociological Review* 53, 330-42.

Leonard-Barton, D., 1995, *Wellsprings of Knowledge: Building and Sustaining the Sources of Innovation*. Boston: Harvard Business School Press.

Lepoutre, P., Lindström, T., and Page D., 1997 *New Generation Paper Technology Programme 1992-1996*. Technology Programme Report 6/97, TEKES, Helsinki

Liebeskind, J. P., Oliver, A. L., Zucker, L., and Brewer, M., 1996, Social Networks, Learning, and Flexibility: Sourcing Scientific Knowledge in New Biotechnology Firms, *Organization Science* 7 (4), 428-443.

Lundvall, B.-Å., 1988, Innovation as an Interactive Process: From User-Producer Interaction to the National System of Innovation, in G. Dosi, C. Freeman, R. Nelson, G. Silverberg and L. Soete (Editors), *Technical Change and Economic Theory*. London: Pinter, pp. 349-369.

Lynn, L. H., Aram, J. D., and Reddy, N. M., 1997, Technology Communities and Innovation Communities, *Journal of Engineering and Technology Management* 14, 129-145.

Marshall, A., 1961, *Principles of Economics*, 9th (variorum) ed. London: Macmillan.

Miner, A. S. and Haunschild, P. R., 1995, Population Level Learning, in L. L. Cummings and Barry M. Staw (Editors), *Research in Organizational Behavior* 17, pp. 115-166.

Mønsted, 1995, Processes and Structures of Networks: Reflections on Methodology, *Entrepreneurship and Regional Development* 7, 193-213.

Nelson, R. R (Editor), 1993, *National Innovation Systems: A Comparative Analysis*. New York: Oxford University Press.

Nelson, R. R., and Winter, S. G., 1982, *An evolutionary theory of economic change*. Cambridge: MA: The Belknap Press of Harvard University Press.

Nerkar, A. A., 1997, The development of technological competence within firms: An evolutionary perspective. Unpublished Dissertation. University of Pennsylvania.

Nishiguchi, T., 1994, *Strategic Industrial Sourcing: The Japanese Advantage*. New York: Oxford University Press.

Nohria, N., 1992, Introduction: Is a Network Perspective a Useful Way of Studying Organizations?, in N. Nohria and R. G. Eccles (Editors), *Networks and Organizations: Structure, Form, and Action*. Boston: Harvard Business School Press, pp. 1-22.

Nohria, N. and Eccles, R. G. (Editors), 1992, *Networks and Organizations: Structure, Form, and Action*. Boston: Harvard Business School Press.

Paniccia, I., 1998, One, a Hundred, Thousands of Industrial Districts. Organizational Variety in Local Networks of Small and Medium-sized Enterprises, *Organization Studies* 19 (4), 667-699.

Powell, W. W., 1998, Learning from Collaboration: Knowledge and Networks in the Biotechnical and Pharmaceutical Industries, *California Management Review* 40 (3), 228-240.

Powell, W. W., Koput, K. W., and Smith-Doerr, L., 1996, Interorganizational Collaboration and the Locus of Innovation: Network of Learning in Biotechnology, *Administrative Science Quarterly* 41, 116-145.

Roberts, E. B. and Berry, C. A., 1985, Entering New Business: Selecting Strategies for Success, *Sloan Management Review* 26 (3), 3-18.

Robertson, P. L., 1998, Information, Similar and Complementary Assets, and Innovation Policy, in N. J. Foss and B. J. Loasby (Editors), *Economic Organization, Capabilities and Co-ordination: Essays in Honour of G. B. Richardson*. London: Routledge.

Robertson, P. L., Keil, T., and Autio, E., 1998, Information, Regional Isolation and Technological Sourcing in Small- and Medium-Sized Manufacturing Firms: A Sectoral Approach, paper presented to the International Conference on Industrial Structure and Innovation Dynamics, Lisbon, October 16-17.

Rogers, E. M., 1995, *Diffusion of Innovations*, 4th edition. New York: Free Press.

Romer, P. M., 1993, Implementing a National Technology Strategy with Self-Organizing Industry Investment Boards, *Brookings Papers: Microeconomics* 2, 345-399.

Rosenkopf, L. and Tushman, M. L., 1994, The Coevolution of Technology and Organization, in J. A. C. Baum and J. V. Singh (Editors), *Evolutionary Dynamics of Organizations*. New York: Oxford University Press, pp. 403-424.

Saxenian, A., 1994, *Regional Advantage: Culture and Competition in Silicon Valley and Route 128*. Cambridge, MA: Harvard University Press.

Schnaars, S., 1998, *Marketing Strategy: Customers and Competition*. New York: Free Press.

Shane, S., 1992, Why Do Some Societies Invent More than Others?, *Journal of Business Venturing* 7, 29-46.

Shane, S., 1993, Cultural Influences of National Rates of Innovation, *Journal of Business Venturing* 8, 59-73.

Singh, K., 1997, The Impact of Technological Complexity and Interfirm Cooperation on Business Survival, *Academy of Management Journal* 40, 339-367.

Smitka, M. J., 1991, *Competitive Ties: Subcontracting in Japanese Manufacturing*. New York: Columbia University Press.

Stinchcombe, A. L., 1990, *Information and Organizations*. Berkeley: University of California Press.

Stuart, T. E. and Podolny, J. M., 1996, Local Search and the Evolution of Technological Capabilities, *Strategic Management Journal* 17, 21-38.

Tiessen, J. H., 1997, Individualism, collectivism, and entrepreneurship: A framework for international comparative research, *Journal of Business Venturing*, 12 (5), 367-384.

Triandis, H. C., 1995, *Individualism and Collectivism*. Boulder, CO: Westview.

Tushman, M. L. and Anderson, P., 1986, Technological Discontinuities and Organizational Environments, *Administrative Science Quarterly* 31, 439-465.

Tushman, M. L. and Rosenkopf, L., 1992, Organizational Determinants of Technological Change: Toward a Sociology of Technological Evolution, in B. M. Staw and L. L. Cummings (Editors), *Research in Organizational Behavior* 14, 311-347.

Uzzi, B., 1996, The Sources and Consequences of Embeddedness for the Economic Performance of Organizations: The Network Effect, *American Sociological Review* 61, 674-698.

Uzzi, B., 1997, Social Structure and Competition in Interfirm Networks: The Paradox of Embeddedness, *Administrative Science Quarterly* 42, 35-67.

Walker, G., Kogut, B., and Shan, W., 1997, Social Capital, Structural Holes and the Formation of an Industry Network, *Organization Science* 8 (2), 109-125.

Van de Ven, A. H. and Garud, R., 1989, A Framework for Understanding the Emergence of New Industries, in R. S. Rosenbloom and R. A. Burgelman, (Editors), *Research on Technological Innovation, Management and Policy* 4, 195-225.

Van de Ven, A. H. and Garud, R., 1994, The Coevolution of Technical and Institutional Events in the Development on an Innovation, in J. A. C. Baum and J. V. Singh (Editors), *Evolutionary Dynamics of Organizations*. New York: Oxford University Press, pp. 425-443.

Von Hippel, E., 1976, The Dominant Role of Users in the Scientific Instrument Innovation Process, *Research Policy* 5, 212-239.

Von Hippel, E., 1988, *The Sources of Innovation*. New York: Oxford University Press.

11

Enterprise Innovativeness and Farm Level Technical Change: A Case of the Floriculture Sector in India

Kavita Mehra

INTRODUCTION

Floriculture is a fast-growing sector worldwide, as it is the case for India where it has become a popular activity especially towards the turn of millennium. The world trade of flowers and ornamentals increased from US$2.5 billion during 1985 to US$6.0 billion during 1996, showing growth of up to 11% per annum in recent years (APEDA, 1999). The world trade data show that the share of developing countries amounts to more than 20%. The global market share of Columbia, Israel and Kenya remained 10%, 6% and 4% respectively during 1994 (Export-Import Bank, 1996). However the Indian contribution had never exceeded 0.5% of the world transactions. Realising the scope of India to earn more foreign exchange through this sector, the government of India declared floriculture as a high-thrust area and announced several policies in favour of the production of high-quality flowers. It led to large investments in this area and as a result by 1998, 186 projects with a production capacity of 1,833 million stems per annum were approved by the Indian government. Nearly 70 units have already commenced production (APEDA, 1999). These developments had an effect on cultivation of flowers in open field conditions and thus a significant growth in the floriculture sector took place. The Indian floriculture sector has by now experienced a change in terms of technology of production, packaging and storage; varieties and qualities of products; volumes of production; and marketing mechanism. This chapter refers to that visible change as the technical change in the floriculture sector in India. The entrepreneur (the farmer) has been found to play a crucial role in the innovative process so as to harness the benefits of the quantum jump seen in the domestic market. Thus the concept of capturing the market demand and exploiting the benefits by introducing innovations at the production to marketing levels based on the knowledge and skill of the entrepreneur has been a key factor of the farm level technical change noticed in the floriculture sector in India. It has in turn induced a new institutional arrangement.

LITERATURE REVIEW

The term "Innovation" has been defined in various ways in the literature, and there are several theories to explain the factors responsible for it. Innovation in the Schumpeterian trilogy means a particular stage in the technological change and, during that stage, the development of new ideas into marketable products and processes takes place. However, innovation is widely used to describe the whole process of technological change; it amounts to "doing something new" for a benefit. A firm is said to be innovative if it produces a new good or service or applies new methods or materials and thus bring about some technical change. Innovations are basically the outcome of innovative capability within each firm and within industry.

Innovative capability includes all kinds of activities ranging from radical new departures to incremental improvements of existing technology (Westphal et al., 1984). Lee (1998) refers to technical change as the ways in which problems are sorted out and inputs are transformed into outputs. There are number of studies on the factors that determine innovative activity.

Schmookler (1966) in his work has shown that the rate of innovation in a given industry is governed by the demand for innovation in that industry. His basic premise was that the more innovative activity would be directed towards larger (actual or potential) markets because apart from the rise in profitability of innovation with the market size, opportunities to innovate and demands for problem-solving activities are more frequent in such situations.

Vernon (1966) also considered the market size as an important factor for product innovation. However, demand-pull kinds of explanations for innovation processes have been refuted by many works (Mowery and Rosenberg, 1979; Lundvall, 1988). The other opinions are based on supply-side factors or on technology-push theories. They believe that the scientific and technical knowledge plays a significant role in the innovative process (Mowery and Rosenberg, 1979; Dosi, 1988). These supply-side studies emphasize the importance of supply of scientific knowledge to promote technological innovation.

In another approach, which is the synthesis of demand-pull and technology-push theories is called "coupling theory" by Lee (1998), the innovation process involves the recognition of potential markets for new products and processes on the one hand, and the exploitation of technological knowledge and capability, which is a result of research activity, on the other. Freeman (1982), similar to coupling theory, considered the role of an entrepreneur to be crucial in the linking of novel ideas and the market together. The market demand has induced entrepreneurs to bring about the technological change. Based on the same concept, the innovation process in the floriculture sector has been investigated.

In this chapter the role of entrepreneur has been found to be crucial in capturing the market demand. There are discussions on the issue of institutional change parallel to technical change. Ruttan and Hayami (1995) in their work on the 1960s made an empirical test of induced innovation against the history of agriculture and their analysis suggested the importance of extending induced innovation framework to the interpretation of the process of institutional change.

Binswanger, Ruttan et al. (1978) developed a theory of induced institutional innovation analogous to the theory of induced technical innovation. They argue that sources of demand for both technical and institutional changes are same, and they brought out a synthesis of the technical and institutional changes considering that these two changes are highly interdependent. Technical change has been considered a powerful source of demand for institutional change. Binswanger et al. have discussed the concept of induced innovation at the farm level in terms of factor of substitution, in case the price of any one of the input factors increases. A rise in the price of land in relation to the price of labour induces technical change designed to release the constraints on production that result from the inelastic supply of land. At the same time, it induces an institutional change that leads to greater precision in definition and allocation of property rights in land. In the same way, a rise in the price of labour relative to the price of land induces technical change designed to permit the substitution of labour, and it is accompanied by institutional change designed to enhance the productive capacity of the human agent and to increase the worker's control of the conditions of his own employment. This chapter also investigates the induced innovation process in the floriculture sector. A farm level technical change has demanded the setting up of new institutions to accommodate the technical change. The chapter illustrates the development process of technical and institutional changes, based on personal field level observations.

OBJECTIVE

The growth in the floriculture sector under open field conditions took place due to replacement of traditional crops such as wheat and sugarcane by flower crops marketed as cut flowers. The adoption of crop substitution and thereafter the changes brought in practices by farmers for better yields has been accepted as farm-level innovativeness. The objective of the case study is to reveal the process of technical and institutional changes in the floriculture sector in the Delhi region. The broad headings for that discussion are:

• Sources and signals for innovation

- Incentives for innovation
- Indicators of innovation
- "Learning by doing" as innovation
- Demand for a new institution to accommodate the technical change

METHODOLOGY

The process of innovation at the farm level in floriculture has been examined for Delhi and the region around it. The Delhi market gets the supply of flowers grown in greenhouses (under controlled conditions) as well as in open field conditions. Since the focus of the study was on the exploration of innovativeness in open field conditions, 30 farmers (who all adopted floriculture in the past 8-10 years) were interviewed based on a set of framed questions. Information or data were collected on sources of knowledge for adoption of floriculture, reasons to go for it, production volumes, marketing and gradual changes brought in the production process over time.

Estimations of market size and growth of the sector were done by comparing the recent data (1998-99) with primary data collected during two consecutive year-round surveys undertaken for the periods 1994-95 and 1995-96 (Mehra et al., 1996). The growth of the sector mainly took place in the 1990s and at that time no special mechanism existed from production to marketing of cut flowers. The development at the institutional level was initiated in the mid-1990s, when the surveys were being conducted and thus we could witness the efforts and processes involved in the emergence of a new institutional arrangement as a wholesale market mechanism for the bulk sale of cut flowers.

RESULTS

India has a long tradition of floriculture, but in the last 15-20 years it has assumed a commercial status. Flower production can be put under two categories—traditional flowers (loose flowers) and cut flowers (with stems). More than one-third of total area at the national level is devoted to cut flower cultivation. The area under cut flowers is gradually expanding and it has increased from 30,000 hectares to 36,000 hectares (Export-Import Bank, 1996). The area should have expanded further by this time. The promotion in the activity has been due to the replacement of other crops (e.g., sugarcane and wheat) by the farmers who were untrained for floriculture activity. The sector grew several times to the size it reached in the early 1990s. The significant contribution came through open field cultivation of gladiolus, tuberose, rose, carnation, and some other seasonal flowers. The growing affluence, people's interest in using flowers and favourable policies of the government towards floriculture has made it a lucrative business.

Moreover, government policies towards promoting floriculture, such as by declaring it as an extreme focus segment, led to the production of quality flowers under controlled as well as in open conditions. Increased production and consumption indicated the high demand in the domestic market. Capturing the market demand by untrained farmers on the basis of their farming experience was the innovativeness in the sector that is being discussed. The study of the floriculture sector in the Delhi region showed enormous changes in the market in the last half of the 1990s.

Sources for Innovation

It was found that more and more farmers were adopting flower cultivation. Following are the government policies which favoured innovativeness by the farmers:

- Floriculture was declared as an extreme focus segment for the development of exports.
- Financial support to government departments like the Agriculture and Processed Food Export Development Authority (Ministry of Commerce) and the National Horticulture Board (ministry of Agriculture) to implement various programmes to promote floriculture.
- Permission to import seeds and other planting material at zero duty for personal use and at 10% duty for trading.
- Import duty on seed development machinery for soil preparation and specified goods for greenhouses has been reduced to 25%.
- Floriculture to be considered as a 100% export-oriented unit, even when selling up to 50% of the produce in the domestic market.
- Loans available to purchase the cool vans.
- Exemption of taxes—profits gained from agricultural productivities are nontaxable.
- Subsidies by Indian airlines for point-to-point transportation of cut flowers.
- Sending and inviting trade delegations.
- Custom bonding requirement eased.
- Infrastructure at airports. For storage of export consignments awaiting cargo at the international airports, walk-in-type cold storage units have been set up.

The Ministry of Agriculture encourages floriculture by providing soft loans for floriculture projects through the National Horticulture Board. It is also implementing a commercial floriculture scheme under which model floriculture centers are to be set up in the nine states in the public sector for increased production of planting material and training farmers on production and postharvest activities. In addition eight centers are proposed for the private sector (APEDA, 1999). At present, nearly 200 hectares are under protected cultivation, which is expected to increase to over 500 hectares in the next two-three years (APEDA, 1999).

All these government initiatives as well as the recognition of the potential for low-cost production for export, in view of cheap land, labour and other resources, led to the setting up of a number of export-oriented floriculture units. These projects, located in clusters around Pune (Maharashtra) in the West; Bangalore (Karnataka) and Hyderabad (Andhra Pradesh) in the South; and Delhi in the north have been developed in technical collaboration with expertise mainly from Holland and Israel. These units produce flowers from imported planting material and know-how under greenhouse conditions. As the world market demand increases, the products of these units are of superior quality. At present there are 70 units under production and nearly 125 are in the pipelines. Common products under production are rose, gerbera, lilium, anthurium, gladiolus and carnations. Rose is the principal flower, grown all over the country. Though these products are mainly exported, the domestic market also receives a good amount and, in spite of higher costs, get very speedily consumed in the market.

Signals for Innovation

As the above developments were taking place in the country, supply and consumption of flowers in the domestic market also increased multifold. The consumption included the produce grown in greenhouses as well as in open fields. It was noticed that the number of small and medium farmers were motivated to flower production. Some of the following could have been reasons for expansion in open field cultivation:

- The superior quality of flowers produced in greenhouses were under high demand in the Delhi region market, which was an indication of demand for high-quality flowers and this factor was well understood by the farmers.
- The government policies to promote floriculture through loans and tax exemptions were becoming known and acted as initiatives to new entrepreneurs to venture in it.
- Due to the economic liberalised environment, a number of foreign companies, especially from the Netherlands and Israel, were selling their planting materials such as bulbs in the market. Thus the superior planting material of in-demand products became easily accessible to everyone.
- The Kissan (farmer) and Krishi (agriculture) melas (fairs), where the newly developed varieties are exhibited to the public, inspired the farmers to shift from sugarcane and other traditional crops to flower crops.
- The "seeing is believing" concept worked very well for Indian farmers. By observing fields of flower crops of farmers known to them or of neighbour farmers, more and more farmers developed faith in the crop substitution.
- Profits through floriculture were found to be much higher, which farmers were able to assess.
- No formal know-how required. Farmers were able to manage at least to the minimum level with the knowledge available to them.

Incentives for Innovation—Comparison of Economic Returns through Flower versus Wheat/Sugarcane Cultivation

Basically three interrelated factors were responsible for the induced innovation to take place:

1. Realisation of the market demand for good quality flowers by the farmers
2. Opportunity for more profitability through flower cultivation

3. Confidence among farmers to exploit market potential on the basis of available know-how and skills.

Better returns on investments through floriculture remained the main reason for the technical change. A broad comparison has been done between conventional crops such as wheat and sugarcane with flower crops for various types of input costs, net investments and returns per unit area (see Tables 11.1 and 11.2). Crop duration for two categories of gladioli flowers (local and multicolored) and wheat is five-six months, whereas sugarcane and tuberose are annual crops. The relative cost of various inputs for these crops reveals that in the case of floral crops, the cost of the planting material component is very high, which goes up to 87% of the total investment (Table 11.1). Because of this, the initial investment cost, in absolute terms, per unit area is much higher for raising flowers. For the same area, say one acre (1 acre = 1,048 square meters), total investment for raising a wheat crop is less than Rs.10,000/- compared to a multicolored gladiolus crop, where the investment goes beyond Rs.100,000/-. However farmers are able to minimise the investment cost by starting the flower cultivation at a much lower scale, perhaps to begin with one-quarter acre.

Table 11.1
Comparison of Input Costs in Wheat and Sugarcane versus Flower Crops

Factor	Wheat	Sugarcane	Tuberose	Gladiolus (L)	Gladiolus (M)
Seed Cost	9%	22%	25%	69%	87%
Fertilizer + Other Inputs	13%	17.5%	12%	3.5%	2%
Ploughing	39%	22%	3%	2%	1%
Irrigation	8%	7.5%	7%	1.5%	1%
Labour (All Types)	24%	27%	24%	10%	4%
Transportation	7%	4%	29%	14%	4%
Investment	100	100	100	100	100
Return	263	204	218-291		

In the second or third year, depending on the category of flower, apart from getting cut flowers as marketable products, growers get at least four times more to the bulbs (planting material) sown in the soil. Growers use these multiplied bulbs to expand their cultivation area, which could be up to four times without making any new investment in the sowing material. In subsequent years, growers can sell the surplus bulbs in the market, which adds to their income earned through cut flowers. The return on investment from the same unit area varies from 1.63 in case of conventional crops to more than 7.75 times with floral crops. The ratio keeps on increasing with time due to more and more multiplication of bulbs in the soil.

Comparison of the absolute investments and returns further explains flower cultivation as the better choice of farmers (see Table 11.2). In case of wheat and gladioli (six-month crops), growers get nearly Rs.8,000/- as an additional income by growing fodder or any such other crop in the same unit area in the second half of the year. The total profit earned amounts to Rs.20,400/- and Rs.17,700/- respectively for wheat and sugarcane compared to Rs.48,000/- in the first year and much more in case of local and multicolored gladiola in subsequent years. In flower cultivation the percentage of benefits keeps on increasing up to multifolds from the second year onwards due to earning made from the multiplied planting material. Thus in floriculture, by investing some more money in the beginning, percentage gains could be many times more than from other crops. This indicative economic analysis shows the reason why Indian farmers go for crop substitution. The minimum profit in the case of multicoloured gladioli could be Rs.50,000/- in the first year and in subsequent years, profit could be up to Rs.135,000 with a negligible investment on other inputs than sowing material.

Table 11.2
Comparison of Return on Investment Ratios in Wheat and Sugarcane versus Cut Flower Crops

Factor	Wheat	Sugarcane	Tuberose	Gladiolus (L)	Gladiolus (M)
1st Year	1.63	1.43	1.18-1.91	.62-.75	.37-.59
2nd Year	1.63	1.4	1.85-2.75(+)	4.0-5.5(+)	.37-.59
3rd Year	1.63	1.4	1.85-2.75(++)	4.0-5.5(++)	6.5-7.75(+)
4th Year	1.63	1.4	1.85-2.75(+++)	4.0-5.5(+++)	6.5-7.75(++)
Absolute amount invested along the factors mentioned in the 1st year	Rs.7,600	Rs.11,300	Rs.41,200	Rs.39,000	Rs.114,000
Absolute amount earned in the 1st year	Rs.20,000	Rs.29,000	Rs.90,000	Rs.60,000 -65,000	Rs.150,000 -175,000
1st Year earning	Rs.12,400 (Wheat)+ Rs.8,000 (Fodder)	Rs.17,700	Rs.48,000	Rs.22,000 approx. (gladiolus) + Rs.8,000 (fodder, etc.)	Rs.40,000 approx. (gladiolus) + Rs.8,000 (fodder)

(+), (++), Etc. indicate the degree of surplus amount earned.

Indicators of Innovation and Diffusion

Adoption of floriculture by farmers to meet the market demand for superior-quality flowers has been the premise of farm-level innovation in this chapter. The growth of the floriculture sector in recent years is thus a reflection of innovativeness of the farmers. Following are some of the indicators of induced innovativeness:

- Increase in market size. There has been 10-15% per annum average increases in the market size since 1990. A primary survey during 1995-96 (Mehra et al. 1996) estimated the size of the Delhi market with the turnover of Rs.300 million at the wholesale level and by 1998-99, business figures were more than Rs.400 million.
- Increase in the number of retail outlets. The number of such outlets increased from nearly 400 during 1994-95 to more than 1,500 by 1998-99.
- Increase in the number of farmers registered with associations for marketing their produce at the wholesale level: The number has increased from nearly 100 during 1995-96 to 350 in 1998-99 from the Delhi region. At the national level, more than 1,500 farmers are registered with Delhi-based societies/associations. Thus, there has been growth in adoption of floriculture activity.
- Increase in the quantum of exotic flowers. This is a category of expensive flowers such as gerberas, carnations, liliums, birds of paradise, tulips, orchids and such. At present exotic flower consumption is 20 to 25 times more than as compared to 1995-96. A few years earlier, these types of flowers were rarely seen at the wholesale level, whereas now they represent a significant portion (nearly 8-10% in terms of value) of the total wholesale business.
- Increase in the area devoted to floriculture. It is difficult to assess the total increase in area for floriculture. It has been observed that initially most of the farmers began with one-quarter acre and ultimately extended up to 50% of the land acquired by them (varies from 2-3 acres in most cases to 15 acres in a few cases).
- Substitution of products coming from outside Delhi to the market by the local production. Until the late 1980s Calcutta was fulfilling the bulk demand of the Delhi region for tuberoses. Now the scene has been totally changed and regions around Delhi produce so much surplus to the local requirement that products are being sent outside Delhi.

Innovation as Learning by Doing

Most of the new growers of flowers have an experience of three to seven years. They have not been formally educated or trained. However, evidence of learning by doing have been shown by them. Following are some of the improvements or gains of that phenomenon at the field level:

- The quality of product has been improved by manipulating the input supply (e.g., by supply of potash and certain other materials flowers become brighter). They also incorporated gypsum which otherwise is not used in other crops. Such manipulations have a scientific basis and are mentioned in the literature. However, the investigations undertaken reveal that farmers brought such changes on the basis of their farming experience or through trial and error experiments.

- The preservation of the planting material (bulbs) has been standarised. Bulbs of flowers are commonly kept in cold storage. Some farmers have developed alternative methods of preserving bulbs by burying them in sand and controlling the room temperature through ventilation, or in some cases bulbs are even been kept in open conditions and cold storage has not been essential.
- The flowering time has been manipulated to get the maximum flowering on the peak demand days such as on Christmas or New Year's Eve. To have flowers on the specified day, three-four days prior to that, fields are well irrigated.
- Manipulation of the sowing period times has increased the number of harvests during the year.
- Standardisation has been achieved for the depth of the pit for sowing the bulb, interbulb distance or when to dig out the bulb from the soil after harvest.
- Changes have been brought in the harvest time. Now harvesting is done in the evening and produce is kept under moist cover so as to maintain the moisture and freshness of the flowers.
- Changes have been brought in the packaging of different types of flowers. The purpose is to save the time and money and to maintain the freshness of flowers.

Induced Institutional Change

The technological change led to the production of bulk volumes of cut flowers in numerous varieties. This kind of change demanded some kind of arrangement for handling and marketing the perishable produce. Setting up a new institution—a wholesale market—was the specific need. The government agreed to it so as to accommodate the change and to promote the growth of the sector in the future.

The following account mentions the process involved in the institutionalisation of the marketing mechanism. In Delhi, no wholesale marketing structure existed until 1994-95, maybe because the volumes of the produce used to be very low in the market. The growers were either directly selling cut flowers to bulk users or big retailers. Some sale of produce used to take place at two places in Delhi: (1) at Chattarpur, outside a temple in the outskirts of south Delhi, and (2) at Connaught Place near Hanuman temple in the center of Delhi.

At Chattarpur sale of the produce from local farmhouses began in the late 1980s. Gardeners of the farmhouses were selling small quantities of local roses, tuberoses, gladioli and some multicolored gladiolus flowers.

At Connaught Place the amount of produce used to be slightly more. Since Connaught Place is a busy market for many consumer goods and household appliances and opens by 10 A.M., growers used to sell their products in the early morning before the regular market opened. With the growth of the business, the number of sellers also increased. Gradually with this change, wholesaler and commission agents also appeared on the market scene. By the mid-1990s Connaught Place became a full-fledged flower market in the morning hours. It led to the mismanagement of the area and the regular Connaught Place market in the following hours started to be affected. The flower business led to congestion in traffic and there used to be heaps of leftovers of the business as garbage which was not being immediately cleaned.

The Municipal Corporation of Delhi could not approve of the activity and people in the floriculture trade felt harassed and insecure. This was the time (1994-95), when our team was conducting the primary market survey and we were in close contact with the people of trade (growers, wholesalers and commission agents). At that time, there were no linkages among the people of the trade. We realised and they themselves also perhaps realised that there was a need for some unity and they were motivated to form an association or a society.

In these circumstances, the first association was formed in February 1995. The association named the place Birju Phool Mandi (after one of the leaders), and thus a forum for struggle was created with the primary demand from authorities to legitimise the existing place as the market for cut flowers, until an alternative permanent place with appropriate facilities to be provided. Our team also took interest in their problems and tried to help them. A few meetings for them were arranged with high-level government officials to pay attention to their problems. Through perseverance and hard work, they succeeded in seeking permission for the sale of flowers in Connaught Place until a place for a wholesale flower market is decided.

At Chattarpur also, with time, volumes of products increased along with problems of growers. The place was also inaccessible to the buyers. Growers of that area united together and registered themselves for a society. They managed to acquire a temporary place for marketing at Mehrauli, near the famous Qutab Minar. The place is better and more convenient for the buyers.

During 1997 a Pushp Samiti (Flower Committee) was constituted under the Agriculture Marketing Board to look into the welfare of the business as a whole. The primary objective of the committee is to organise the wholesale business of flowers and to provide a permanent place with appropriate infrastructure and facilities. In 1999 the decision was taken by the government on the location of an air-conditioned flower market to be built in an area of 35 acres. The flower market will be equipped with modern facilities and care has been taken to allot 20% space to local farmers and outlets shall be provided to bulk sellers. Thus, one could notice the growth of the sector and the creation of a new institutional mechanism to accommodate the change.

CONCLUSION

Entrepreneurs discussed above were engaged in agricultural activities and had no link with R&D or any kind of formal education. They intelligently linked the market demand of cut flowers with the basic know-how and skill and succeeded in the endeavour of floriculture business. Such an effort by entrepreneurs led to the farm-level technical change. As the technical and institutional changes have the same kinds of demands, the technical change resulted in the institutionalisation of the wholesale marketing mechanism. It resulted in a declaration of the government for setting up an air-conditioned, well-equipped market to accommodate the change. It is the market demand which has induced the technical and institutional change.

ACKNOWLEDGMENTS

The author is especially thankful to the growers and wholesalers and others of the flower business in the Delhi region and especially those from Connaught Place market for providing information from time to time. Thanks are also due to APEDA (Indian Ministry of Commerce) for providing the opportunity and the financial means to undertake the surveys during the mid-1990s, and to Sh. R. Kapoor and Sh. S. A. Nabi and Dr. S. K. Saxena who were part of the survey study team and whose surveys served as the basis for the formulation of this chapter.

REFERENCES

Agricultural and Processed Food Development Authority (APEDA), 1999. "Status of Floriculture—a report".

Binswanger, H.P., Ruttan, V.W., and others, 1978, *Induced Innovation: Technology, Institution and Development*. Baltimore: Johns Hopkins University Press.

Dosi, G., 1998, "Sources, procedures, and microeconomic effects of innovation", *Journal of Economic Literature*, 26, 1120-1171.

Export-Import Bank of India, 1996. *Floriculture: a sector study*. Occasional paper no. 50.

Freeman, C., 1982, *The Economics of Industrial Innovation*. London: Francis Pinter.

Lee, K.R., 1998, *The Sources of Capital Goods Innovation: The Role of User Firms in Japan and Korea*. Chur: Harwood Academic Publishers.

Lundvall, B.-Å., 1988, Innovation as an interactive process: from user-producer interaction to the national system of innovation, in *Technical Change and Economic Theory*, eds. Dosi, G. et al. London: Pinter Publishers.

Mehra, Kavita, Kapoor, R., and Nabi, S., 1996. "Floriculture Market Study—A case of wholesale market in Delhi. APEDA (Agricultural and Processed Food Development Authority)—sponsored study report.

Mowery, D., and Rosenberg, N., 1979, The influence of market demand upon innovation: a critical review of some empirical studies, *Research Policy*, 8, 102-153.

Ruttan V.W., and Hayami, Y., 1995, "Induced Innovation Theory and Agriculture Development: A Personal Account" in *Induced Innovation Theory and International Agriculture Development: A Reassessment*, ed. Koppel, B.M. Baltimore: Johns Hopkins University Press.

Schmookler, J., 1966, *Invention and Economic Growth*. Cambridge, MA: Harvard University Press.

Vernon, R., 1966, International Investment and International Trade in the Product Cycle, *Quarterly Journal of Economics*, 80, 190-207.

Westphal, L.E., Linsu, K., and Dahlman, C.J., 1984, *Reflections on Korea's Acquisition of Technological capability*. Washington, DC: World Bank.

PART III:
TRENDS AND OPPORTUNITIES FOR SCIENCE, TECHNOLOGY, AND INNOVATION POLICIES

12

Determinants of Successful S&T Policy in a National System of Innovation

Susanne Giesecke

INTRODUCTION

Since the end of the fordist era[1] several competing as well as supplementary theoretical approaches have been developed to explain why some national economies are falling behind while others are becoming the leaders of innovative activities on the global scale (Nelson and Winter, 1982; Porter, 1990; Naschold, 1997; Soskice, 1999). Recent contributions to the national system of innovation (NSI) literature have argued that these differences are anchored in the setup of national institutions (Freeman, 1987; Lundvall, 1992; Nelson, 1993; Edquist, 1997).

The NSI approach understands innovation as a process where factors from outside as well as inside a company are linked. Thus, this approach makes room for an institutionalist perspective on innovation as well as on the structure that integrates all relevant variables influencing innovation, thereby broadening the scope from descriptive and quantitative indicators to qualitative analysis. Some of these variables are defined to support innovative activities and to select and diffuse innovation. The variables are depending on the nation and technology analyzed in a particular case study.

For Lundvall, the central elements are the internal organization of firms, interfirm relationships, the role of the public sector, the institutional setup of the financial sector, R&D intensity and R&D organization (Lundvall 1992, 13). He gives a very broad definition of "system" that is open to integrating as many elements as necessary in order to explain national differences of innovative performance:

> The broad definition ... includes all parts and aspects of the economic structure and the institutional set-up affecting learning as well as searching and exploring—the production system, the marketing system and the system of finance present themselves as subsystems in which learning takes place...a definition of the system of innovation must be kept open and flexible regarding which subsystems should be included and which processes should be studied (Lundvall 1992, 12-13).

System in this context means a losely structured relationship of interdependent variables that influence innovative activity. This idea of a system stresses that innovation is the result of a dynamic process within a structured environment. It is neither an isolated act nor a linear one. This system comprises many elements of the innovation process. These elements are not isolated factors but interacting and changing through learning processes. Learning processes constitute feedbacks from the market and knowledge inputs from users, interacting with knowledge creation and entrepreneurial initiatives on the supply side. Thus, innovation is seen as a process of interactive learning and of accumulated knowledge. This definition implies that innovation reflects already existing knowledge, combined in new ways (Lundvall 1992, 8).

Even though the ideas of institutional learning and accumulated knowledge are central to the concept of a national system of innovation in order to explain why some nations are more innovative in some technologies than in others, there has been little theoretical account and empirical analysis on the issue whether nation-states can learn (from each other) as well. Coming from an evolutionary economics background, these authors avoid using labels such as "successful" and "unsuccessful" systems of innovation and thereby neglect the identification of those variables that determine successful S&T policies. A comparative analysis that identifies advantages or obstacles of one national system over another is avoided. To some authors national systems of innovation are not a question of success or failure because "the notion of optimality is absent from the systems of innovation approaches. Hence comparisons between an existing system are not possible" (Edquist 1997, 20). Accordingly, policy recommendations cannot be given as the authors do not deal with the issue whether or not the government is capable of controlling innovation activities.

This is why the predominant question to scholars of S&T policy still remains unanswered to a large degree: How can policy implications for the future be derived from the empirical evidence on successes and failures of national innovation systems? If institutional learning is a dynamic process most crucial to innovative activities, can nations learn from each other or, rather, can national systems of innovation learn from each other?

This chapter uses the case of pharmaceutical biotechnology in the United States and Germany to contrast two national innovation systems by means of their successes and failures. The analysis is set within the context of the national systems of innovation approach and thus focuses on the institutional determinants that account for the performance of a system of biotech innovation. Further, this analysis will consider what part S&T policy plays within a system of innovation and if policy actors are able to learn. In this context, the question whether a successful innovation system can be a role model to other nations will be discussed as a second major objective. One underlying hypothesis, however, is that institutional learning may have limits. Institutional arrangements have developed historically and are, therefore, path dependent. Accordingly, they cannot be changed easily. Institutional inertia and thickness (Amin & Thrift, 1994) block many efforts to modernize and adjust structures that would imitate the success model. Hollingsworth & Boyer (1997) have discussed the path dependency of national and regional institutional dependencies in modern capitalism in great detail. Scholars of national systems of innovation have argued similarly, concentrating on institutional arrangements that determine innovation processes (Lundvall, 1992).

Streeck (1991) has pointed out that some national styles differ in such a way that one national institutional arrangement supports "diversified quality production" (DQP) as in Germany, whereas another institutional arrangement may support industries that are characterized by more flexible organizational forms serving short-term, high-risk market-based economies as in the United States. This is not to say that other types of economic organization could not exist in a nation. Rather, the argument is that one type of institutional arrangement is dominant (Hollingsworth 1997) just as the metalworking, auto, engineering and chemical sectors have been dominant in Germany and the institutional arrangements to support these sectors still exist, even though information technology is overtaking these traditional sectors. The dominant structures, however, hamper the shift to a more flexible and volatile liberal market economy that would reward risk takers with high performance incentives up front and punish inertia. These latter market patterns are more supportive of emerging high technology industries as they develop in the United States. In comparison to the United States, the German system's high technologies such as biotechnology have been underperforming.

This chapter tries to explain why the United States outperforms all other countries on the pharmaceutical biotech sector—including Germany—despite the fact that German S&T policy targeted biotechnology earlier than any other national S&T policy.

The chapter first will present some empirical evidence on the contrasting performances of the U.S. and German systems of biotech innovation. The institutional setups which supported the U.S. performance will be mentioned briefly. Then German development, starting with the targeting of biotechnology as an objective of national S&T policy in the late 1960s until the beginning of the 1980s will be discussed. Subsequently, the turnaround and rethinking of national S&T policy on the biotech sector, and some catch-up strategies that account for institutional learning, will be presented. Blockages of institutional learning and the prospects of biotech development in Germany on the pharmaceutical sector are covered; and finally, the determinants of successful S&T policy will be summarized.

U.S. PERFORMANCE OF PHARMACEUTICAL BIOTECHNOLOGY

Before this section starts with the empirical evidence on the different national performances of biotech innovation in the United States and Germany, we have to ask, how can innovation be measured? Traditionally, performance indicators are used that measure input, throughput and output. On the input side, R&D expenditure, for example, is an indicator for investment in innovation. Patent statistics are one indicator for throughput. On the output side, revenues, loss, products on the market and market share are indicators for the performance of an industry or firm. These indicators are only indirectly linked to innovation, of course. One problem is, for example, that they do not measure process innovation. To give an overview on the competitiveness of national biotech industries for the two countries chosen, however, some of these indicators will be presented here.

Setting out from these artefacts, the NIS approach will then be applied to broaden the scope of measuring innovation by taking the quality and relevance of the organizational structure into account. Thereby organizational units such as strategic alliances, institutional learning, networks, academic education systems, and technology transfer will be considered.

Using figures from 1997, Table 12.1 shows that the United States outperforms all other countries in the biotech sector in terms of its number of companies and employees as well as in terms of sales and R&D expenditures. Table 12.2 shows that American biotech companies are dominating the world market for products sold. In 1993 and 1995 all top ten products were developed in the United States, and most of them were sold by U.S. companies. Foreign companies could not compete unless they bought licenses of products developed by U.S. biotech companies. The enormous growth rate of European figures indicates a catch-up strategy, wherein European countries are striving to make biotechnology a recognizable industry in their own countries as it is in the United States. The U.S. columns, on the other hand, show a consolidation of the national biotechnology industry. Net loss decreased and so did the number of companies. For the first time since the ups and downs the industry faced in 1993 and 1994, when a lot of new companies tried to enter the market and many established ones faced losses of capital and trust caused by negative testing results, the U.S. biotech industry appears to be stable once again. The fact that no comparative German figures for the prior year exist can be taken as an indicator of how little biotechnology is recognized as an industry in Germany and abroad.

The German biotech innovation system is hampered by the lack of innovative start-ups and by the dominance of big pharmaceutical companies

Table 12.1
Biotech Industries Compared

	Germany	Europe (incl. Germany)		USA	
	1997	1997	Percent change to prior year	1997	Percent change to prior year
Financial data (in mill. DM)					
Revenues	577	5.369	58%	31.498	19%
R&D expense	282	3.764	27%	16.292	14%
Net loss	69	3.980	81%	7.423	-9%
Industry data					
Number of companies	173	1.036	45%	1.274	-1%
Employees	4.013	39.045	42%	140.000	19%

Source: see Ernst & Young (1998).

with little innovative potential in modern biotechnology. Except for one medium-sized company, Boehringer Mannheim, which received approval for its genetically produced r-tpa factor Reteplase in 1996[2], the German pharmaceutical industry has no in-house biotech innovation on the market in therapeutics, vaccines or antibodies. Of the 31 genetically produced drugs admitted on the German pharmaceutical market, only nine were distributed, six produced and one developed by German pharmaceutical companies; 14 were developed entirely by or in cooperation with U.S. companies, mostly start-ups. The rest were developed by different European companies. In contrast, U.S. companies are dominating their own domestic market. As Table 12.3 shows, of the 41 genetically produced drugs admitted in the United States, 33 were developed, produced and distributed by U.S. companies, and only one by a German company (BIO, 1998; DECHEMA, 1998; Giesecke, 1998).

Another indicator reveals the interdependence of the decline of the German pharmaceutical industry and the lack of biotech innovation. Even though German companies were dominant on the world pharmaceutical market during the postwar period, they have lost their share on the market during the last 20 years due to the lack of innovation in the biotech sector. While German pharmaceutical companies made 17% of their turnover on the world pharmaceutical market in 1973, this share decreased to 8% in 1993 (BVK, 1997). The German chemical and pharmaceutical company Hoechst, ranked at the very top of the international scale in 1976, declined to number 10 in 1994. Hoechst could reclaim its position among the top three but only as a result of its merger with Marion Merrel Dow and Rhone Poulenc Rorer in 1996 (Sharp & Patel, 1996; *Handelsblatt*, June 24, 1997).

Table 12.2
Top Ten Selling Biotechnology Products, 1993 and 1995, Worldwide Sales

Product	developed by	produced by	Net revenues in mill. $ 1993	Net revenues in mill. $ 1995
Neupogen	Amgen (USA)	Amgen (USA)	719	829
Epogen	Amgen (USA)	Amgen (USA)	587	721
Intron A	Biogen (USA)	Schering-Plough (USA)	572	426
Humulin	Genentech (USA)	Eli Lilly (USA)	560	665
Procrit	Amgen (USA)	Ortho Biotech/ J&J (USA)	500	600
Engerix	Genentech (USA)	SmithKline Beecham (USA/GB)	480	582
RecombiNAK HB	Chiron (USA)	Merck (USA)	245	-
Activase	Genentech (USA)	Genentech (USA)	236	280
Protropin	Genentech (USA)	Genentech (USA)	219	225
Roferon	Genentech (USA)	Hoffmann-LaRoche (CH)	172	-
Humatrope	Eli Lilly (USA)/ Genentech (USA)/ Novo Nordisk (DEN)/ BioTechnology General (USA)/ Pharmacia AB (S)	Eli Lilly (USA)/Genentech (USA)	-	226
Ceredase/Cerezyme	Genzyme (USA)	Genzyme (USA)	-	215

Source: see Ernst & Young (1994, 1997).

Table 12.3
Genetically Produced Drugs Approved in Germany and the United States, June 1998

UNITED STATES		GERMANY
41	total	31
33	of U.S. origin	14
1	of German origin	1

Source: DECHEMA (1998), BIO (1998).

During the start-up phase of biotech industry development, U.S. biotech companies were more interested in forming strategic alliances with domestic pharmaceutical companies, because they wanted to conquer the U.S. market and needed strong partners with established distribution networks. Foreign companies became more of interest to U.S. start-ups during the expansion phase. Thus, some foreign companies such as Hoffmann-LaRoche of Switzerland or Kadi of Sweden were able to maintain their competitive position by aquiring licenses for biotechnology innovations (McKelvey, 1996). Both companies bought exclusive licensing rights for the European market for Genentech's first two innovations: human insulin and human growth hormone (Swanson, 1996). Genentech was the first economically successful biotech start-up with major innovations on the therapeutic market and served as a role model to other start-ups for nearly 20 years.

What were the crucial determinants for the U.S. success stories? The large basic research establishment in universities and government research institutes served as important incubators for the development of innovations in the biotech sector. Individual academics established small firms to commercialize their knowledge. The dense concentration of excellent research institutes and the high-level mobility within regional agglomerations of high technology firms have served both, as an important channel for technology diffusion and as a magnet for other firms to similar industries or firms downstream and upstream the innovation and product development process. This was made possible by a supportive financial infrastructure, the venture capital industry, that was at the same locations as the start-ups, namely in Silicon Valley and the Boston area, and by the NASDAQ, the equity market for high tech entrepreneurial firms (Kenney, 1986; Powell & Owen-Smith, 1997; Giesecke, 1998).

Public policy has played an indirect role within this system of biotech innovation. The National Institutes of Health (NIH) as a government agency that funds in-house and extramural research have played a crucial role in terms of knowledge and competence accumulation. Project funding by NIH has provided the best universities with the necessary monetary means to enhance basic and applied research in the field of biotechnology (Swain, 1962; Fredrickson, 1981; Schwartz & Friedman, 1992). A government program started by the Small Business Administration in 1958 created a U.S. venture capital industry that eventually gave rise to new high tech industries such as microelectronics, computer, biotech and multimedia (Green, 1991). In addition, the Bayh-Dole Act of 1980 has facilitated technology transfer from the lab to industry (Abramson et al., 1997). All these institutional arrangements summarized here have created a preferable opportunity structure for biotech innovations to develop. Today, these institutional arrangements that have developed in the United States over more than 50 years are discussed in Germany as a best-practice model. As will be shown, there have even been some attempt to imitate them. The German support for biotechnology, however, started under very different preconditions, which will be discussed in the next section.

BIOTECH DEVELOPMENT IN GERMANY: AN INTERVENTIONIST APPROACH

Government support for biotechnology development in Germany began in the late 1960s, when an OECD report identified this technology—among others—as one that was expected to play a key role in future economic development (OECD, 1968; Buchholz, 1979). Thus, biotechnology became one of the technologies to be supported by public funds. Historically, the government promoted future technologies because Germany was prosperous after the war, and it believed that the federal government was able to implement decisions for the achievement of intended outcomes that could continue this prosperity.

The so-called fordist crisis, starting in the early 1970s, however, put economic growth on hold. Political reaction to this crisis was an intensification of interventionist strategy. An active, direct and interventionist science and technology policy was regarded as a tool for developing a prosperous national economy (Hohn & Schimank, 1990; Hauff & Scharpf, 1975). For this purpose, a federal Ministry of Science and Technology was founded in 1972, taking over and expanding the tasks that up to this date had been the responsibility of the Ministry of Economy and the Ministry for Scientific Research (BMBW, 1972). Various research priorities were identified for biotechnology, believing that it had future scientific and economic potential. With the inclusion of biotechnology into its funding programs for new technologies, the federal government—mostly through its Ministry of Science and Technology—has initiated several working groups, advisory boards and funding programs for the advancement of biotech research. Figure 12.1 indicates the rise of government funding for biotechnology over the last 30 years. From 1974 to 1998 federal R&D expenditures for biomedical and biotechnology in Germany rose from DM 48 million to over DM 480 million (BMFT, 1993; BMBF, 1996b).

Even though the German federal government was the first to directly support biotech R&D and several tools were put into place to fund biotech research in academic and industrial research labs, the outcome has been quite different from what was intended. Despite the solid basic research that has been established over the years at the various universities and publicly funded research institutes, major innovations that can be transformed into marketable products have not emerged on the German pharmaceutical market. As in other cases of high technology (e.g., for information technology see Gebhardt, 1997), Germany has fallen behind some of its major international competitors.

Figure 12.1
German Federal Expenditure for Biomedical and Biotechnology Research, 1974-1995, in million DM

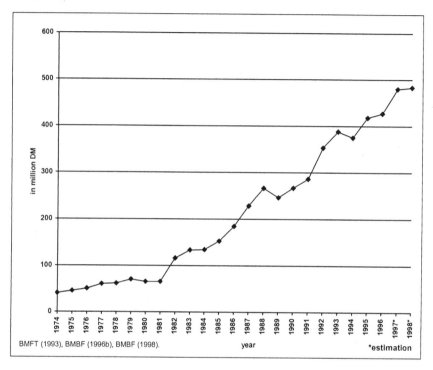

The federal government, which had almost no competencies in this technology, wanted to draft several programs that would support biotechnology in the sciences and industry. They asked an industry interest group, which ironically represented mainly those companies that had only little interest in biotechnology and a more profound background in synthetic chemistry, for help[3]. Several support programs were implemented but had no specific focus or any noticeable effect on either industry or academic research.

German S&T policy has two tools for pursuing its objectives in an interventionist policy style; both are monetary. The first is earmarked funds for research institutes and organizations; the second is extramural funding for projects.

1. Except for universities, which are financed through a different arrangement, all publicly funded research institutes are entitled by law to a fair share of national and state R&D expenditures every year (earmarked funding). In practice, they are not only guaranteed funding but receive an increase in funding every year.

2. In addition, there is a budget administered by the Science and Technology Ministry for extramural funding. Universities, publicly funded research institutes and industry may apply for a 50% coverage of their project's expenditures for a term of three to five years. The general research objectives have to match the priorities and guidelines of the national S&T programs.

Early public support for biotech in Germany funded research institutes as well as individual projects that focused on biotechnology (for total expenditure, again see Figure 12.1).

On the industrial R&D side, the chemical and pharmaceutical industry traditionally has been very strong in Germany, and some companies became global players during the postwar area. Their success was built on synthetic chemistry. Even though management and researchers were confronted several times about whether or not to pursue traditional biotechnology as an alternative innovation strategy, the decision almost always was in favor of synthetic chemistry over biotechnology until the 1970s (Marschall, 1997). Thus, most of the companies did not build up any capacities to deal with later scientific developments that were related to genetic engineering. Both industry and science experts, however, did not consider genetic engineering as a major source of product or process innovation in the early 1970s. Instead, they opted to continue research on traditional fields of biotechnology (Buchholz, 1979; Jasanoff, 1985; Marschall, 1997; BMFT, several years). The science and economic experts the government relied on were usually affiliated with those academic institutions and industrial companies that got extramural funds from the Ministry of Science and Industry. In this way, new incentives from outside the "inner circle" of government R&D funding were excluded. Instead, this structure perpetuated the same research directions that had been established over the years, resulting in lock-ins (Gebhardt & Giesecke, 1997; Giesecke, 1998).

We have discussed so far why the government could not find much support for its idea to expand biotech research in the pharmaceutical industry. In the sciences and academia, these programs did not inspire new lines of technology either. This has structural reasons: There is a division of labor between publicly funded research institutes and universities with their main focus on basic research, and industry R&D with its main focus on application and commercialization. The earmarked funding mentioned above supplies universities and research institutes with guaranteed autonomy on issues of research topics, money and personnel. Universities and federally funded research institutes show a high degree of resistance against attempts of intervention, whether on the part of the government or industry.

As with the pharmaceutical industry in Germany, most research institutes and universities did not change their priorities as a result of these new government programs. This in part explains why there was no noticeable perception of or even reaction to the Stanley Cohen and Herbert Boyer gene splicing event that occurred in California in 1973,[4] and to the subsequent scientific and economic developments started by this discovery.

In spite of the extraordinary engagement of the German federal government in biotech research, the gap between the United States and Germany is quite significant. In contrast, the U.S. biotech industry is the strongest but has not relied on direct government support. The question arises as to whether the federal government has any impact on the innovative performance of biotechnology or if the government's capacity, in fact, is limited. I will return to this question later on.

INSTITUTIONAL LEARNING AND EVOLUTIONARY CHANGE OF GERMAN BIOTECH POLICY

In 1981 the actors suddenly realized that the German biotech industry had fallen behind the U.S. development of modern biotechnology. One event in particular symbolized the beginning of a slight change in German biotech activities: The biggest German chemical and pharmaceutical company Hoechst signed a research contract with Massachusetts General Hospital for over $70 million (Culliton, 1982). This move to off-shore R&D in the United States was interpreted as going against the quality of German industrial and academic research in this field and is responsible for some—at least minor—reactions of government, academia and industry.

These actors discerned the U.S. strategy of technology transfer as a best-practice model and tried to imitate some of its features. The core of the American model is the biotech start-up—a symbiosis of academic knowledge and venture capital—that serves as a catalyst to bring both incremental and radical innovation from the research lab to the market. The start-up nurtures the new technology until big pharmaceutical corporations become interested in forming a strategic alliance and undertaking all subsequent steps of the product development process (Giesecke, 1998).

In order to catch up, the German Ministry of Science and Technology in the 1980s and 1990s initiated several programs as part of the extramural funding measure to support more applied research with the intention of yielding products that would be competitive on the national and international markets. The focus changed from basic to more applied biotech research (BMFT/BMBF, several years).

Industry at large remained apathetic to the genetic revolution that occurred overseas as well as to the government objectives until the 1980s. The largest pharmaceutical companies received the biggest share of the extramural industry funding from the Science and Technology Ministry. These companies were not used to trying out new directions of research. Only after the Hoechst shock did these major German pharmaceutical companies adjust their corporate strategies to challenges of international economic and scientific developments. The short-term strategy was to go off shore—to the United States—to engage in strategic alliances or mergers and acquisitions to catch up with the latest biotech development. Building in-house competences for modern biotechnology would be a long-term strategy.

Only a few entrepreneurs were willing to take the risk of setting up a start-up company of their own in Germany. At that time, there was only little support from government resources, and the financial market was not yet willing to fund such a risky and costly high-tech enterprise either. Big pharmaceutical companies neglected the emerging German start-ups because of their lack of quality.

Triggered by the Hoechst shock, a few changes occurred in academic research organizations as well. Centers of excellence, called gene centers, were introduced in four locations that had some tradition in medical, biomedical and genetic research: Heidelberg, Munich, Cologne and Berlin. These gene centers had two prevailing tasks: to consolidate all existing resources for biotechnology and to cooperate closely with industry in order to move from basic research to applied research. This program was supported by the national and the state (länder) governments as well as some big pharmaceutical and chemical corporations. At the gene centers as well as at the universities and other public research institutes, there were attempts to redefine research objectives to include more genetic engineering, that would generate marketable innovations. This strategy reminds us of the clusters of scientific competence at some U.S. campuses where academic knowledge was generated, diffused and finally transferred into innovations—for example, the human growth hormone developed in cooperation between Herbert Boyer, his lab at the University of California at San Francisco and his company Genentech.

Most of the researchers in publicly supported labs and at German universities, however, viewed themselves as dedicated to basic research and resisted all efforts by the Ministry of Science and Technology to turn to applied, industry-related research.

CATCH-UP STRATEGIES OF GERMAN BIOTECH POLICY

Thus, even though many actors and institutions were urged to reevaluate their traditional way of thinking and even though a few changes were started to move closer to the U.S. ideal type of biotech industry and research organization, it took more than a decade to see some early success and initiate some institutional learning on government, industry and academic levels. Further, a few institutional changes in the financial markets helped support a more preferable "economic ecology" for biotech development in Germany during the 1990s (Casper, 1998).

Project and Earmarked Funding

There is some evidence that the Science and Technology Ministry looked very carefully at the determinants for success in the United States and tried to imitate some of those by designing programs that were quite innovative for German policy standards. Traditional earmarked and project funding was continued. As a consequence, the federal budget for biotech and biomedical

R&D rose considerably since 1981 (see figure 12.1). Additionally, not only monetary instruments were designed to promote biotechnology. Under the Biotechnology 2000 program, all financial resources of extramural funding for biotechnology were orchestrated and new research directions defined in order to push academic and industry research toward more marketable products.

BioRegio-Contest and Business Plan Competitions

An additional program, that is still going on and already showing some effects, is the BioRegio-contest. It awarded the top three of 17 applicant regions with federal money of DM 50 million each over five years[5]. The winners were Munich, Heidelberg and the wider Cologne-Rhineland area. These funds are administered to each by a central coordination office. An independent board of advisors is in charge of approving the regional applications for these grants. This means that the funds are administered on the regional level instead of the federal or state level. Applicants usually are small biotech companies that are in a start-up or expansion phase. Similar to applying directly for project funds at the BMBF, applicants must provide for 50% of the sum themselves. The central coordination office provides help in finding additional sources, such as from banks or venture capital (VC) companies. They also assist in drawing up the applications and gathering information on patents.

It is striking that the selection criteria are similar to the characteristics of U.S. biotech innovation clusters as are found in Silicon Valley, San Diego or the Boston area. Among these were scientific expertise in biotechnology, existing services offered for database and patent research, existing small biotech companies as well as pharmaceutical companies, a network of banks, venture capitalists and other finance providers (Warmuth, 1996/97, 14 ff.).

All 17 regions applying for a BioRegio grant tried to orchestrate existing resources and to build a network that would support biotech research, innovation and the founding and expansion of start-ups in the area. Thus, even those 13 regions that did not receive any additional funding gained from this competition, because for the first time, all actors involved were integrated into a regional network. Today, almost all the networks still exist. The regional coordination offices provide help for (potential) entrepreneurs. Technology transfer and patent offices as well as venture capital pools are operating to promote biotech innovation. They are an important link between academic research at universities and public research institutes and the industry. All companies and research institutes may still apply for BMBF project funding through Biotechnology 2000, of course.

This initiative also changed the attitude of many academics who are traditionally very reluctant to think about entrepreneurship. Today, a lot of them are inspired by the business plan competitions that are carried out regularly in some of these regions and by the support of the new networks. These contests have also changed the attitude of investors and big corporations towards biotech entrepreneurship. Banks have become more open minded towards the needs and difficulties of young entrepreneurs who want to start a business in a science-based industry. This is not to say that they give credits more easily; however, German venture capitalists who try to be on the safe side and traditionally invest in low-risk technologies and services also want to get a piece of the biotech pie as well.

Patent Initiative

Additional programs were started by the government not only to help promote biotech innovation but high tech development and entrepreneurship in general. Academic researchers in Germany never had any significant incentives to file patents. According to German law, employees of public universities fully own their intellectual property. They do not have to share it with their employing institutions. This rule has turned out to be an obstacle to the overall innovative performance of German universities. Academics have to bear the cost of filing and sustaining patents all by themselves, and this can be very costly. In contrast, in the United States university technology transfer offices pay for the fees and in return get a share of the royalties. Technology transfer offices at German universities and at most public research institutes, however, are not run as for-profit enterprises.

Another disincentive for filing patents is the German and European patent law. Unlike the U.S. rule "first to invent", in Germany and at the European Patent Office the rule is "first to file". An invention that has already been published, say in a journal, cannot be patented afterward in Europe. For academics it is more important to publish than to patent. Subsequently the possibility to file a patent is missed.

The German government is aware of these problems, but it will still take some time to amend the laws. In the meantime, the Science and Technology Ministry has started a "patent initiative". This is a program that hopes to encourage public research institutes, universities, entrepreneurs and inventors to invent marketable products. It is a free information service; and it subsidizes a share of the cost for patenting if necessary (BMBF 1996c).

Exist-Contest

An additional BMBF initiative reflects the success of the U.S. model and the German imitation strategy. German policy makers realized that high tech start-ups are a crucial technology transfer mechanism that bring new results of academic research from the lab into the marketplace. Naturally this is an ideal scenario. Important, however, is the awareness of the entrepreneur's new role. The intention behind this thinking is to stimulate Germany's innovative performance and make its economy competitive on the global scale.

With the Exist-contest, the Science and Technology Ministry invited science- and technology-dominated regions organized as networks to encourage entrepreneurs and start-ups to participate in a competition for a total of DM 45 million federal subsidies for three years. More than 200 universities and 100 regions submitted proposals; five of those were selected winners. Of these five, three were networks in the western part of Germany (Wuppertal-Hagen, Karlsruhe, Stuttgart) and two in the east (Jena and Dresden). The funding is supposed to establish a "culture of entrepreneurship" by supporting and strengthening information services at the universities, hiring lecturers with industry experience, establishing a curriculum for entrepreneurship at the universities, establishing a virtual university on the Internet, providing contacts for investors, integrating international experience and raising public awareness for the prospects of entrepreneurship.

Similar to the BioRegio-contest, Exist was an incentive for many regions to consolidate existing resources and to integrate them into a network. Even though only five networks receive funding, many others have started operating on their own. They want to help academics market their research results and start their own businesses. One popular instrument for this is the business plan contest organized in several regions through a tightly cooperating network almost every semester.

State Governments: The Example of Bavaria

Paralleling science and technology policy efforts to support biotech development on the federal level, some *länder* in Germany have initiated support programs as well. A case in point is Bavaria which represents the most successful model to date.

It is not by chance that the greater Munich region in the heartland of Bavaria won one of the three BioRegio-contest prizes. Not only does this region have one gene center and three Max-Planck-Institutes operating in scientific fields that are relevant for modern biotechnology, but also the Bavarian government has been very supportive of emerging high technologies. By privatizing parts of its shares in power companies during the 1990s, it has created a pool of investment for subsidizing applied technology developments in Bavaria worth several billion DM (Focus, 1998; FAZ, June 17, 1998). Because of the optimism toward biotechnology as a future technology for Bavaria, permission for biotech production plants was issued with less delay and less obstacles than in most other federal states of Germany[6].

Most initiatives in Bavaria came from the Economics Ministry. It commissioned a study[7] to find out how biotechnology could best be promoted in Bavaria. The results are similar to the determinants of success of the "bio valleys" in the United States: venture capital as well as management support had to be provided for small start-ups and the transfer of research results from the academic lab to the market had to be facilitated (Koschatzky et al., 1995). Different from the United States, however, these objectives had to be part of an interventionist biotech policy. Accordingly, the Bavarian Economics Ministry financed an institute called Innovationszentrum Biotechnologie (IZB, innovation center for biotechnology) which has structures and objectives that are similar to incubator labs and technology parks. This office is located next to the Munich gene center and within reach of two of the Max-Planck-Institutes that focus on biotech research. At this location, which is on the outskirts of Munich, a lot of property is still available for companies that decide to leave the IZB so that they may expand without losing the close connection to the scientific infrastructure.

To solve the bottleneck of venture capital, the Economics Ministry set up a venture capital fund, Bayernkapital, with its office at the IZB. A triple multiplication effect is very attractive for start-up companies that choose to locate in Bavaria, especially in the Munich area: If a company can raise venture capital from a private source, such as a bank or a VC company, Bayernkapital will supply the same amount as well as will tbg, a federally owned investment bank that will be introduced in more detail in the next subsection.

Now that Munich receives additional funding through the BioRegio program, a coordinating office, BioM, is located at the IZB as well. BioM was set up as a corporation (*Aktiengesellschaft*) in order to make investments with its shareholder's money. Most of the shares are held by banks which did not only want to loan money but also earn high returns. Their motivation was also to learn more about biotechnology, its risks and prospects and to be part of a broader network that generates and exchanges crucial expertise on promising investments. BioM has become a company that is owned equally by three categories of stock holders: the state of Bavaria, banks and VC companies, pharmaceutical and chemical companies. BioM holds a central position over all biotech development in Bavaria: Not only does the company provide and generate venture capital, it also provides information services to investors, entrepreneurs, businesses and the like for free and is the nexus of the Munich biotech network. If additional expert advice is needed, say by lawyers, BioM makes contacts and provides subsidies. Thus BioM functions similar to for-profit technology transfer offices in the United States.

Finance

The German system of corporate finance is dominated by bank loans and existing company profits. Venture capital was almost nonexistent until the late 1980s and is still a rarity today. In the 1980s, the federal government realized that venture capital is necessary to finance entrepreneurs and *Mittelstand* (family-owned medium-sized firms), because venture capital was one of the most important mechanisms that gave birth to the U.S. biotech industry (Kenney, 1986). This realization, again, demonstrates the learning process that was going on within German state institutions. Under the auspices of the federal Economics Ministry, the Deutsche Ausgleichsbank (DtA), a state-owned investment bank, founded a subsidiary, the Technologiebeteiligungsgesellschaft (tbg), in 1989.

Tbg programs generally are based around equity participation in exchange for funding; however, due to the public status of the bank and, in particular, the provision of substantial loan guarantees by the German government[8], the tbg is able to provide highly favorable provisions to most clients. One of its main objectives is to provide loans that are underwritten by the German government (Economics Ministry, BMWi) in order to promote the foundation and expansion of new German technology programs[9]. These loans account for about 80% of all tbg lending.

In general, virtually all tbg funding is in the form of matching grants or "silent partnerships". The tbg charges a 5-6% interest rate for its investment which is granted up to ten years. The risk is substantially born by the government. Most loans are given for early phase financing of start-ups (usually after seed financing for business plan development, but before secondary financing or further expansion).

Thus, tbg's role is much broader than just providing for cheap loans. In general, the client firms also ask tbg to make contact with potential lead investors because tbg is part of a good network. The mandating of lead investors is crucial. By doing so, market judgments and risks are incorporated into every deal. Tbg leaves the selection of viable companies and technologies to the market, that is to say to the lead investors. Thus, the state withdraws from direct intervention, letting venture capitalists decide whom to fund. In general, DM 3 million is the maximum loaned to tbg projects for all normal start-up financing deals. Over its first eight years of operation, tbg has participated in 535 projects, lending a total of DM 426.9 million (tbg, 1998). It is still too early to assess the success of the funded projects because for most companies, the 10-year period is not yet over. Though state-backed, tbg's functions resemble those of venture capitalists.

Next to software (23%) which is a very broad category, biotech (17%) is the sector most invested in, while process technologies are underrepresented. In contrast, German venture capital investors from the privately financed market give only 2.6% of their investments to biotech companies but 60% to process technologies and 20% to services (BVK, 1997). Further, tbg focuses on early stage (seed and start-up) funding (67.7%), whereas the average VC investment in this phase is no more than 7% but for the expansion phase it is 65% (tbg, 1998; BVK, 1997). Interestingly, 36% of all tbg investments are in the Bavarian area; about 80% of those in Munich.

Other institutional changes in the German financial market during the last few years have facilitated biotech investments and expansion as well. Those were not necessarily pushed for by the government but by market forces. In 1997 a NASDAQ-modeled stock exchange for technology firms, the Neue Markt, was created. It has become a critical institution for technology firms, as it provides a legitimate exit strategy. As of April 1999 three out of 86 companies listed were biotech companies. One of them, Qiagen, a platform technology and utility company, has a second listing at the Neue Markt and is very successful; the others are Morphosys and Rhein Biotech, both started as platform technology companies but have the potential of becoming therapeutic companies. Morphosys was listed in March 1999 with moderate success; and Rhein Biotech's bid was very successful, but since they started selling stocks only in April 1999, it is too early for an assessment.

Thus the Neue Markt has not yet become a stock market for biotech shares but is successfully supporting equity listings of German and foreign firms in other technology sectors, such as software and information technology, and in other services. Finance experts in Germany think the Neue Markt rather than the Easdaq in Brussels could become the European NASDAQ because it is currently the most liquid high tech centered stock market in Europe. Neue Markt is popular with investors in retail trading and, thus, generates more volatility than Easdaq, which has more institutional investors. Investors have become hesitant to invest in London stock markets that used to hold the central position for European high tech investments until 1997. The scandal caused by negative testing results of British Biotech, a promising company that was listed there, has caused the loss of confidence of many investors in these stock markets. The Neue Markt could not absorb a high-cost failure like British Biotech. Thus, the quality of projects has to be evaluated very carefully.

Unlike the U.S. and U.K. corporate finance systems, where industrial expansion has been mostly financed through stock markets, the German system is bank-based (Zysman, 1983). The growing awareness that the stock market and venture capital represent an alternative to conservative bank loans has become very attractive for high tech enterprises, whose funding is dependent upon intangible rather than tangible assets.

In the United States, venture funds pool money from a variety of institutional and individual investors. The venture capitalists make profits as the value of their shares rise, assuming, of course, that the small company's products perform successfully on the market or that an IPO provides a profitable exit by selling shares on the public market. This money is invested into small start-ups which usually need a long period of time and several rounds of finance before becoming competitive on the market. So investors may not readily see profitable returns, which may vary of course. Kleiner-Perkins, the investors of Genentech, the first successful U.S. biotech company, earned 500 times their initial investments. The rate of companies that fail, however, is very high; estimates of successes range from 1 to 10 out of 100. Accordingly, venture capital companies are obliged to spread the risk. They don't put all of their money in one or two companies but invest in a wide range of firms. Further, they form investment syndicates with other VC companies, one of them being the lead investor overlooking how the small firm performs. Their task is not only to provide money but also to offer managerial advice to the start-up firms which usually have no experience in business planning, product management and so on. They are also part of an investment network, generating and providing information on prospects and promising investments, preparing IPOs and evaluating the due diligence and feasibility of the projects.

The number of VC companies with interest in German biotech, has risen from only two—Atlas Venture and Techno Venture Management—in the first half of the 1980s to more than 70 that are now engaged with biotechnology. Some of those are owned by banks; some are public or semipublic. Only recently have they discovered biotechnology as a profitable investment, after public participation programs stepped in to cover some of the financial risks involved in this high technology. As mentioned before, however, only a small portion of venture capital in Germany is invested in high technology. Of the total DM 6.6 billion venture capital in Germany in 1996, only DM 177 million was invested into biotechnology. Compare this to the United States: of the total DM 50 billion venture capital, DM 1.3 billion was invested into biotechnology (*Handelsblatt*, Feb. 10, 1998, 6).

Start-ups and Platform Technologies

Despite the dominance of big corporations in the German pharmaceutical sector, almost 200 biotech start-ups[10] have managed to set foot into the German market—with substantial federal and state support. The majority of them are indeed very small. They have an average turnover of only DM 100,000 and generally no profits. Only a few have a research staff of more than 15.

The latest boom has been started by the BioRegio-contest of 1995/96. Until then, only a few dozen firms existed in Germany. Today, all of them are trying very hard to find and defend their technological niches. Characteristic of German biotech start-ups today is their specialization in one of the so-called platform technologies, which are defined as instruments that have become crucial for further development of biotechnology. In Germany this specialization is more prevalent than in any other European country or in the United States as Figure 12.2 demonstrates. According to the Ernst & Young statistics, almost 33% of German biotech companies concentrate on this segment and only 15% on therapeutics. In contrast, therapeutics is the dominant sector for all other European countries, comprising some 40% of biotech companies, whereas platform technologies comprise roughly 20% (Ernst & Young, 1998).

Figure 12.2
Product Development Specialization in German and European Biotechnology, in %

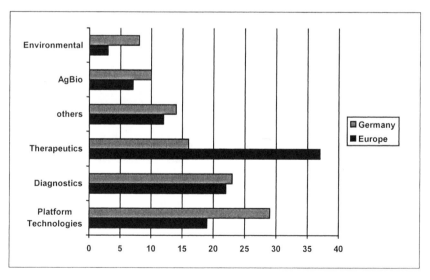

Source: Ernst & Young (1998).

Platform technologies include combinatorial chemistry and combinatorial biology as well as genomics and others. Specialization in one of the new platform technologies is the result of two specific features of biotechnology that only became visible along its path of development: First, the difficulties of the first generation of biotech companies in the United States to develop new drugs and to attain the capital, time and knowledge needed for innovative products caused a severe crises in the U.S. biotech industry in 1993 and 1994, which made clear the incapacity of most companies to become a diversified or integrated pharmaceutical company comprising the total process of developing a new drug. The need for capital, for know-how concerning clinical testing and upscaling, for distribution networks, and such, led to a disintegration of the development process. Instead, many companies started to specialize in certain technological or service units as part of the whole innovation and production process. Second, the diversity of biotechnology, the manifold possibilities of its integration with other technologies into new hybrid technologies and the standardization of some of the underlying processes (polymerase chain reaction, high throughput screening) for biotech research offered new market niches and, thus, possibilities for new specializations. The companies have learned from these developments. For German companies, a possible path to overcoming blockages in the national system of innovation and to containing technological and financial risks is to become a supplier of a technology or service component at the upstream or downstream end of the innovation and production process.

Thus some biotech companies in Germany have managed to conquer profitable niches despite the blockages. Success cannot be measured in terms of market innovations or sales. Rather, some German biotech companies have come up with promising business partners that invest in start-up developments and new ideas. Some of them were able to attract big German and international pharmaceutical companies. As these corporations are experiencing a lot of restructuring in order to be more competitive and innovative, small start-ups are becoming outsourcing partners, thus filling in niches that may give them a chance to survive in the long run.

LIMITS OF CATCH-UP STRATEGIES AND PROSPECTS OF THE GERMAN BIOTECH INDUSTRY

Since the early 1990s, the German biotech industry has been experiencing an evolutionary change. Actors and institutions involved have engaged in a process to mobilize and orchestrate resources. In doing so a lot of institutional learning was required. Some new strategies tried to imitate the U.S. success model (e.g., the government's BioRegio- and Exist-contests to create networks at promising locations; the financial market structure has moved in a similar direction by providing more venture capital and introducing the Neue Markt). However, all these new strategies are to a high degree rooted on the German institutional arrangements and cannot be interpreted as a sign of international convergence.

Though the federal government has been aware of biotechnology as a future strategy for German industry that needs to be supported early on, it has taken almost 30 years for a learning process that orchestrates all necessary resources and shows some positive results, to develop. This has often been a trial-and-error process.

This chapter has presented some evidence that despite the pattern of diversified quality production that is still dominating German industry, some institutional arrangements could be reconfigured to accommodate biotechnology as a future sector in this country. Due to limited space, some evidence had to be left out—for example, further technology transfer measures, new incubators, the role of scientific advisory boards at start-ups.

Before concluding, the new strategies pointed out in the last phase for German biotech development will be assessed. Finally, the question arises about what future prospects the German biotech industry might have. The government funding programs for start-up companies have borne a major part of the financial risk involved. As a consequence, venture capital companies have been more likely than usual to provide seed capital. More companies and projects have been started than will be able to survive in the long run or even remain financed through second and third rounds. Platform technologies cannot be a long-term strategy for German biotech companies. The international market is so competitive that only a few of them could survive on the single-product strategy. The others will have to use platform technologies to get started in this sector and then develop therapeutics on their own. This will be very cost-intensive. If only 50 of those almost 200 firms in Germany have a therapeutic product in their pipeline, between DM 12.5 to 350 billion will be required to develop marketable products[11]. Venture capitalists estimate, however, that the funds available can provide only DM 1 billion for further biotech development. The question arises as to whether the rest could be financed through stock markets and strategic alliances with pharmaceutical corporations. It is more likely, and we can learn this from the U.S. and U.K. restructuring phases in 1993/94 and 1997/98 respectively, that the German biotech industry sooner or later will experience a very painful consolidation process, either through mergers and acquisitions or through company close-outs. Analysts expect that in the long run only four to six German biotech companies may survive.

WHAT ARE THE DETERMINANTS OF SUCCESSFUL S&T POLICY?

This case study made clear that institutional learning capacities are a crucial determinant of successful S&T policy. This implies learning from the experiences of other nations as well learning processes within the innovation system. Learning from another country's experiences, however, is limited as the cases of biotechnology in the United States and in Germany demonstrate. The biotech industries in the U.S. and Great Britain have experienced a consolidation process including severe loss of capital and jobs. Even though it may be a bit speculative, similar developments are expected for the German biotech industry in the near future. It thus seems that certain restructuring processes cannot be avoided, even though negative effects are anticipated. Consolidation processes have a cathartic effect for the future survival and competitiveness of the industry and imply restructuring processes that help to accommodate biotechnology as a modern technology within the dominant DQP structure of the German industry. The institutional setups of national innovation systems are so unique that strategies from other countries cannot be copied in detail. The fine tuning has to be designed individually to each nation's innovation system. The directions of this fine tuning have to be found through trial-and-error processes over a long time period. In the case of German biotechnology, the NIS has to find a way to bridge the traditional DQP setup and the technological, economic, political and social challenges posed by the changes of the global market.

Of course, national role models do not exist in such a way that they can be copied easily. But learning from the successful strategies of other nations' experiences is possible if it implies openness for learning and accommodation of structures.

S&T policy has to be redefined as a crossover of a variety of policies stimulating innovation and industrial growth. The state cannot execute control directly on most actors, structures and processes involved in S&T policy. On the contrary, the state can gain control and be more successful if incentives to stimulate innovation are spread broadly and involve a variety of different leverages—for example, on the financial level supporting the growth of an independent venture capital industry instead of lending money to high tech companies directly. Thus, S&T policy gains most if learning processes are started, especially if the policy field, in this case a technology, is new.

Policy objectives, if they were ever formulated as such, are unlikely to be reached in the S&T policy field. It would thus be more reasonable to focus on the learning process of the entire innovation system and to reformulate policy objectives accordingly than to strictly focus on narrowly defined goals.

NOTES

1. See notes 2 & 3 in Chapter 3 of this volume for an explanation of fordism.

2. Boehringer Mannheim, however, could not maintain its independence on the market and was acquired by the Swiss corporation Hoffmann-LaRoche in 1997. Since Hoffmann-LaRoche owns most shares of the U.S. market for r-tpa through its 60% purchase of Genentech Boehringer Mannheim, for antitrust reasons and by order of the Federal Trade Commission, the company is not allowed to sell Reteplase in the United States (Ernst & Young, 1998).

3. This lobby group, called DECHEMA, represented the big corporations of the German pharmaceutical and chemical industry.

4. In 1973, Stanley Cohen and Herbert Boyer invented the technique of DNA cloning, which allowed genes to be transplanted between different biological species. Their discovery signaled the birth of genetic engineering. Herbert Boyer, of the University of California at San Francisco and Stanley Cohen, at Stanford University, reported the construction of functional organisms that combined and replicated genetic information from different species. Their experiments dramatically demonstrated the potential impact

of DNA recombinant engineering on medicine and pharmacology, industry and agriculture.

5. Plus an additional smaller grant for one of the East German regions, Jena.

6. Permission for biotech productions plants are issued by the länder administrations not by the federal administration.

7. From the Fraunhofer Institute for Innovation Research.

8. This program used to be supervised and financed by the Science and Technology Ministry (BMBF) until 1998. After the last elections all programs focusing on technology were transferred to the Economics Ministry (BMWi).

9. This program is called Beteiligungskapital für kleine Technologieunternehmen (BTU), venture capital for small technology enterprises.

10. Ernst & Young biotech report on Germany in 1998 counted 171. These figures are hard to assess, however, since they comprise so-called life science companies which are not necessarily the same as biotech companies and include a wide range of companies specialized in platform technologies. Some of those are not research-oriented companies. Thus, it is most likely that the actual number of companies is below 171.

11. These figures are calculated on the assumption that the development of one therapeutic product costs between DM 250 and 700 million (*Handelsblatt*, Sept. 19, 1999).

REFERENCES

Abramson, N. H., J. Encarnação, P. P. Reid and U. Schmoch, 1997, *Technologietransfer-Systeme in den USA und Deutschland*. Karlsruhe: Fraunhofer IRB Verlag.

Amin, A. and N. Thrift, 1994, "Living in the global", in A. Amin and N. Thrift (Editors), *Globalization, institutions, and regional development in Europe*. Oxford: Oxford University Press, pp. 1-20.

BIO, Biotechnology Industry Organization, 1998, Biotechnology Drug Products, http//:www.bio.org.library/3drugs.dgw, 17 pages, visited May 31, 1998.

BMBF, Bundesministerium für Bildung, Wissenschaft, Forschung und Technologie, 1996a, *BioRegio Wettbewerb*. Bonn: BMBF.

BMBF, Bundesministerium für Bildung, Wissenschaft, Forschung und Technologie, 1996b, *Bundesbericht Forschung*. Bonn: BMBF.

BMBF, Bundesministerium für Bildung, Wissenschaft, Forschung und Technologie, 1996c, *Patentwesen an Hochschulen. Eine Studie zum Stellenwert gewerblicher Schutzrechte im Technologietransfer Hochschule-Wirtschaft*. Bonn: BMBF.

BMBW, Bundesministerium für Bildung und Wissenschaft, 1972, *Biologie und Politik, Förderprogramm. Wissenschaft, Wirtschaft, Politik*. No. 47. Bonn: BMBW.

BMFT, Bundesministerium für Forschung und Technologie, several years, *Bundesbericht Forschung*. Bonn: BMFT.

BMWi, Bundesministerium für Wirtschaft, n.d., *Zukunftssicherung des Standortes Deutschland*. Bonn: BMWi.

Buchholz, K., 1979, Die gezielte Förderung und Entwicklung der Biotechnologie, in W. van den Daele (Editor), *Geplante Forschung*. Frankfurt/Main: Suhrkamp, pp. 64-116.

BVK, Bundesverband Deutscher Kapitalbeteiligungsgesellschaften, 1997, *Statistik 1996*. Berlin: BVK.

Casper, S., 1998, National institutional frameworks and high-technology innovation in Germany: the case of biotechnology, WZB Discussion Paper FD I 99-306. Berlin: Wissenschaftszentrum.

Culliton, B. J., 1982, The Hoechst Department at Mass General, *Science* 216, June 11, pp. 11-20.

DECHEMA, Deutsche Vereinigung für Chemisches Apparatewesen, 1998, http://www.dechema.de/deutsch/isb/wirkst.htm, 3 pages, visited May 31, 1998.

Edquist, C. (Editor), 1997, *Systems of Innovation. Technologies, Institutions and Organizations.* London: Pinter.

Ernst & Young, 1994, *Biotech 95. Reform. Restructure. Renewal* (The Ernst & Young Annual Report on the Biotechnology Industry, Palo Alto).

Ernst & Young, 1996, *Biotech 97, Alignment* (The Ernst & Young Annual Report on the Biotechnology Industry, Palo Alto).

Ernst & Young, 1997, *European Biotech 97: A New Economy* (The Ernst & Young Annual Report on the Biotechnology Industry, Palo Alto).

Ernst & Young, 1998, *Aufbruchstimmung 1998. Erster Deutscher Biotechnologie Report.* Stuttgart: Schitag Ernst & Young.

FAZ, *Frankfurter Allgemeine Zeitung*, June 17, 1998, "Initiative für eine neue Gründerkultur".

Focus 1998, "Das Würmtal als 'gene Valley'", June 15, 1998.

Fredrickson, D. S., 1981, Biomedical Research in the 1980s, *New England Journal of Medicine* 304, February 26, 509-517.

Freeman, C., 1987, *Technology and Economic Performance: Lessons from Japan.* London: Pinter.

Gebhardt, C., 1997, *Die Regionalisierung von Innovationsprozessen in der Informationstechnologie.* Wiesbaden: DVU.

Gebhardt, C. and S. Giesecke, 1997, Die Spezifität der Entwicklungspfade in der Biotechnologie und der Künstlichen Intelligenz, *Comparativ* 7 (3), pp. 76-97.

Giesecke, S., 1998, Die Triplehelix von Technologie, Markt und Staat. Innovationssysteme in der pharmazeutischen Biotechnologie. Inaugural dissertation, Free University of Berlin.

Green, M. B., 1991, Preferences for US venture capital investment 1970-1988, in M.B. Green (Editor), *Venture Capital. International Comparisons.* London: Routledge.

Handelsblatt, several issues.

Hauff, V. and W.F. Scharpf, 1975, *Modernisierung der Volkswirtschaft: Technologiepolitik als Strukturpolitik.* Cologne: EVA.

Hohn, H.-W. and U. Schimank, 1990, *Konflikte und Gleichgewichte im Forschungssystem: Akteurskonstellationen und Entwicklungspfade in der staatlich finanzierten außeruniversitären Forschung.* Frankfurt: Campus.

Hollingsworth, R., 1997, "Continuities and changes in social systems of production: The case of Japan, Germany and the United States", in R. Hollingsworth and R. Boyer (Editors), 1997, *Contemporary Capitalism. The Embeddedness of Institutions.* Cambridge: Cambridge University Press, pp. 265-310.

Hollingsworth, R. and R. Boyer, 1997, *Contemporary Capitalism. The Embeddedness of Institutions.* Cambridge: Cambridge University Press.

Jasanoff, S., 1985, "Technological Innovation in a corporatist state: The case of biotechnology in the Federal Republic of Germany", *Research Policy* 14, pp. 23-38.

Kenney, M., 1986, *Biotechnology: The University-Industrial Complex.* New Haven, CT: Yale University Press.

Koschatzky, K. et al., 1995, *Maßnahmen und Instrumente zur Förderung der Biotechnologie in Bayern: Endbericht an das Bayerische Staatsministerium für Wirtschaft und Verkehr.* Karlsruhe: ISI.

Lundvall, B.-Å., (Editor), 1992, *National Systems of Innovation: Towards a Theory of Innovation and Interactive Learning.* London: Pinter Publishers.

Marschall, L., 1997, Im Schatten der Synthesechemie: Industrielle Biotechnologie in Deutschland (1900-1970). Inaugural dissertation, Ludwig-Maximilian-Universität, Munich.

McKelvey, M., 1996, *Evolutionary Innovation. The Busisness of Biotechnology.* Oxford: Oxford University Press.

Naschold, F., 1997, "Ökonomische Leistungsfähigkeit und institutionelle Innovation - Das deutsche Produktions- und Politikregime im globalen Wettbewerb", in F. Naschold and D. Soskice (Editors), *Ökonomische Leistungsfähigkeit und institutionelle Innovation. WZB Jahrbuch.* Berlin: Edition Sigma.

Nelson, R. R. (Editor), 1993, *National Systems of Innovation.* New York: Oxford University Press.

Nelson, R. R. and S. G. Winter (1982), *An Evolutionary Theory of Economic Change.* Cambridge, MA: Harvard University Press.

OECD, 1968, *Fundamental Research and the Policies of Governments.* Paris: OECD.

Porter, M. E. 1990, *The Competitive Advantage of Nations.* New York: Free Press.

Powell, W. W. and J. Owen-Smith, 1997, Universities as creators and retailers of intellectual property: Life sciences research and economic development, in B. Weisbrod (Editor), *To Profit or Not to Profit.* Cambridge: Cambridge University Press.

Schwartz, S. M. and M. E. Friedman, 1992, *A Guide to NIH Grant Programs.* New York: Oxford University Press.

Sharp, M. and P. Patel, 1996, Europe's Pharmaceutical Industry: An Innovation Profile. Draft Report prepared for DG XIII - D4 (University of Sussex Brighton).

Soskice, D., 1999, Globalisierung und institutionelle Divergenz: Die USA und Deutschland im Verleich, *Geschichte und Gesellschaft* 25, pp. 201-225.

Streeck, W., 1991, "On the social and political conditions of diversified quality production", in E. Matzner and W. Streeck (Editors), *Beyond Keynesianism: the Socio-Economics of Production and Full Employment.* Aldershot: Edward Elgar, pp. 21-61.

Swain, D. C., 1962, The Rise of a Research Empire: NIH, 1930-1950, *Science* 138, December 14, 1233-1237.

Swanson, R., 1996, Speech at the Carolinas Chapter of the Association for Corporate Growth (unpublished manuscript).

Tbg, Technologiebeteiligungsgesellschaft, 1998, *Geschäftsbericht 1997,* Bonn.

Warmuth, E., 1996/97, "Zukunftschance Biotechnologie", *Chemie Heute.* Edition 1996/97, pp. 13-16.

Zysman, J., 1983, *Governments, Markets and Growth: Financial Systems and the Politics of Industrial Change.* Ithaca, NY: Cornell University Press.

13

Commercializing R&D in Small Businesses: The U.S. SBIR Fast Track Program

Reid Cramer, John Horrigan, Chuck Wessner, and
Robert H. Wilson

INTRODUCTION

The U.S. federal government assumed a leadership role in science and technology investment following World War II. Although a federal commitment to research investment and diffusion was a prominent feature of U.S. agricultural policy from the end of the 19th century, the federal government played a modest role until World War II and the decades to follow. Although research funding was heavily weighted toward national security concerns, in response to the Cold War, this period nevertheless established the federal government as an important actor in the country's system of knowledge production.

A positive relationship between R&D investment and economic growth was soon recognized. By the 1970s, increasing attention had been placed on the role of small business in the national economy, in general, and in technological innovation, in particular. In 1982 the U.S. Congress passed the Small Business Innovation Development Act in order to generate greater opportunities in federal research procurement systems to small businesses. The program's reauthorization in 1992 added an incentive for small firms involved in federal R&D to commercialize their projects.

In anticipation of the program's 2000 sunset review, the Department of Defense (DoD) asked the National Academy of Science to assess the performance of the small business commercialization element, the so-called Fast Track program, of the Small Business Innovation Research program (SBIR) in the Department of Defense. This chapter represents the initial results in this assessment. The chapter will trace the creation and evolution of the SBIR program. The justification for the recent concern with commercialization in a small business R&D program will be presented. Preliminary results of the current assessment effort, first in terms of broad patterns of performance and then in terms of impacts on individual firm's business strategies and access to capital, will be discussed.

ORIGINS AND GOALS OF SBIR

The impetus to direct a portion of federal research and development expenditures to small business started in the 1970s, when policy makers began to recognize that small businesses were a potentially rich source of innovation. As Roland Tibbetts, generally regarded as one of SBIR's founding fathers, recalls, federal commissions dating to the 1960s recommended directing R&D funds to small businesses, but such recommendations were not acted upon due to opposition from other recipients of federal R&D funding (Tibbetts, 1999). It was not until 1976 that any formal action was taken to channel federal R&D funds to small business. That year, prompted by Senator Edward Kennedy, the National Science Foundation increased the share of its funds going to small business from 7.5 percent to 10 percent. Small firms were enthused with this initiative, and proceeded to lobby other agencies to follow NSF's lead.

Finding little positive response from agencies, small businesses took their case to Congress and higher levels of the executive branch. One result was a White House Conference on Small Business held in January 1980 that explored specific ways to respond to small business concerns. From that conference came a recommendation for legislation that eventually became the Small Business Innovation Development Act of 1982—the bill that authorized the SBIR program. According to Archibald and Finifter (1999), the conference's recommendations received a sympathetic hearing because of mounting evidence of a declining share of federal R&D going to small businesses, as well as broader difficulties among small business in accessing capital. A number of studies (e.g., Birch, 1981) suggesting that small business were a fertile source of job creation further improved the climate for SBIR legislation.

The legislation authorizing SBIR had two broad goals from the outset. According to the report language accompanying the legislation (U.S. Senate, 1981): "The purpose of the bill is twofold: to more effectively meet R&D needs brought on by the utilization of small innovative firms (which have been consistently shown to be the most prolific sources of new technologies) and to attract private capital to commercialize the results of Federal Research."

More specifically, the 1982 act creating SBIR listed four program objectives (see Archibald and Finifter, 1999, for a detailed legislative history of SBIR):

1. To stimulate technological innovation.
2. To use small business to meet federal research and development needs.
3. To foster and encourage participation by minority and disadvantaged persons in technological innovation.
4. To increase private-sector commercialization of innovations derived from federal research and development.

To carry this out, the act required federal agencies with R&D budgets in excess of $100 million to set aside 0.2 percent of their funds for SBIR. This totaled $45 million in SBIR's first year, fiscal year 1983. Over its first six years of operation, the percentage set-aside increased to 1.25 percent. Modeled largely on the NSF's small business initiative, SBIR grants had three phases. Phase I, essentially a feasibility study, was a modest grant (in the neighborhood of $25,000 in 1983) to assess the technology's potential. Phase II, whose value was approximately seven times that of Phase I, was for more extensive development and prototype development. Phase III involved no federal funds, but was the hoped-for stage in which award recipients received private-sector financing for commercialization. Today, Phase I grants can be as high as $100,000 and Phase II grants are typically in the range of $750,000. Since the program's inception in 1983, SBIR has made over 45,000 awards, totaling $8.4 billion in 1998 dollars (Brown and Turner, 1999).[1]

When SBIR was reauthorized in 1992, Congress made two major changes to the program. First, the set-aside rate doubled to 2.5 percent. Second, Congress increased the emphasis on commercialization of federal R&D as a program goal (Archibald and Finifter, 1999). Whereas the original SBIR legislation specified that Phase I grants should demonstrate "scientific and technical merit," the 1992 reauthorization stated that Phase I should demonstrate "scientific and technical merit and feasibility of ideas that appear to have commercial potential."

With respect to Phase II, the 1992 SBIR legislation substantially increased the importance of commercial potential. In evaluating Phase II applications, agencies were directed to assess a technology's commercial potential as evidenced by:

1. the small business' record of commercializing SBIR or other research;
2. the existence of second phase funding commitments from private-sector or non-SBIR funding sources;
3. the existence of third phase, follow-on commitments for the subject of the research, and;
4. the presence of other indicators of the commercial potential of the idea (U.S. GAO, 1999).

Such explicit legislative language regarding commercialization was absent from SBIR's original authorizing legislation and reflected Congress' desire to encourage a higher commercialization rate for SBIR-funded technologies.

REAUTHORIZATION

The SBIR program is scheduled to sunset on October 1, 2000, and as of this writing in 1999, Congress is considering reauthorization of the program. Several hearings have been held to examine how the program might be improved. The program itself is broadly popular, and its existence is not likely to be challenged in the reauthorization process. However, views on the program vary, reflecting the different views of advocacy groups and of those charged with different aspects of agency missions. One general area of interest is commercialization of SBIR-funded technologies. Both advocates and critics of the program believe that SBIR's commercialization rates could be improved and that commercialization is an important criterion of program success.

As reauthorization of SBIR approaches, several issues are likely to generate discussion:

- frequent SBIR award winners
- geographic distribution of SBIR awards
- level of SBIR set-aside
- commercialization of SBIR technologies and measures designed to address this problem, such as DoD's Fast Track initiative.

Frequent Award Winners

An ongoing concern in the SBIR program has been multiple award winners (also know as "SBIR mills"), that is, firms that win a large number of SBIR awards, but tend not to commercialize SBIR-funded technologies. A recent study by the U.S. General Accounting Office (1999) found that the 25 most frequent winners of SBIR awards have accounted for approximately 11 percent of the program's awards from FY 1983 through FY 1997. Furthermore, roughly half of the program's awards have gone to one-tenth of the participants which, according to GAO, "bears out concerns about the concentration of awards." At the same time, GAO points out that from 1993 to 1997, SBIR attracted an average of 750 new firms per year. Multiple awards winners accompanied by low commercialization rates may not be a problem *per se* if these winners are producing good research and licensing it to others. However, some believe that a trade-off between research and commercialization exists. That is, a goal to produce quality research may conflict with creating technologies with commercial promise.[2]

Geographic Distribution of Awards

SBIR awards have been concentrated in a few states and this concentration has been a concern to some. Firms in California and Massachusetts have won a majority of SBIR awards, largely because they submit the most applications. The most basic reason for the large volume of SBIR applications from these states, according to a recent GAO report, is that they have vibrant venture capital industries and large public and private R&D investment (U.S. GAO, 1999). Whether the share of SBIR awards going to these states is excessive is difficult to say; according to GAO, in FY 1998 the SBIR proposals from states with historically lesser amounts of federal research funding won SBIR awards at the same rate as proposals from companies from other states. In general, there is no difference in SBIR award rates, as distinct from the number of applications, across different regions and states.

The Level of SBIR Set-Aside

The level of SBIR set-aside has risen historically, from 0.2 percent in 1983, to 1.25 percent by 1988, to 2.5 percent in 1992. As the set-aside grew, the perception that SBIR is a "tax" on federal R&D budgets for small business has taken hold in some quarters. Efforts to raise the set-aside above 2.5 percent encountered substantial opposition in 1998 and, at present, increasing the set-aside above 2.5 percent does not seem likely. The fact that the overall federal R&D budget is slated to increase in the coming years—thus increasing the amount of available SBIR funds—may reduce pressure from small business advocates to raise the set-aside. Based on statements from senior staff from both sides of the aisle at a recent SBIR meeting at the National Academies, a change in the 2.5 percent set-aside rate seems unlikely (National Research Council, 1999).

Commercialization

The 1992 reauthorization explicitly encouraged greater commercialization from SBIR grants, and directed agencies to assess commercial potential of SBIR proposals using the four criteria listed at the end of a previous section entitled "Origins and Goals of SBIR." A recent GAO study (1999) found that agencies have not adopted a uniform method for weighing commercial potential in SBIR applications. Moreover, operational definitions of commercialization appear to vary across and within agencies.

Because of the 1992 reauthorization's focus on commercialization, there have been a number of evaluations of commercialization of SBIR research. The GAO (1992) studied the commercialization track record of SBIR and concluded that "the program is showing success in phase III commercialization activity." For SBIR awards from 1984 through 1987, GAO found that $956 million in SBIR grants had generated $471 million in actual sales of new commercial products and $646 million in additional development funding as of July 1991.

These SBIR grants were expected to generate an additional $1.94 billion in sales by the end of 1993. DoD's SBIR program was seen quite favorably by GAO; DoD's 686 Phase II awards in this period resulted in a number of high-performance products of benefit to the both the military services and the private sector, and generated $410 million in additional sales and development funding through July 1991.

More recently, Josh Lerner (1999) attempted to measure the long-run impacts of SBIR awards on the firms receiving them. Lerner developed a database of SBIR firms and firms with similar characteristics that had not won SBIR awards. He concluded that "SBIR awards appear to have had a positive and substantial long-term impact on the firms [SBIR awardees] in regions with considerable venture activity. In particular, awardees appear to have grown substantially faster—whether measured by sales or employment—than a matching set of firms." Lerner also found that SBIR's positive impacts are most pronounced among firms in regions with supportive business infrastructure, such as major research universities and significant R&D activity.

Finally, an unpublished DoD internal study (cited in GAO, 1999), using the same methodology as GAO's 1992 report, found evidence of strong commercialization activity by DoD SBIR awardees. Over the 1983 to 1992 period, the average Phase II grant ($400,000) generated $760,000 in sales and attracted approximately $600,000 in non-SBIR developmental funding.

It is worth noting that while the average commercial performance of SBIR awards seems to be very good, the distribution of awards is another matter. According to DoD and Small Business Administration surveys of SBIR awards, 61 percent of SBIR projects resulted in no commercial sales at all. On the other hand, 4 percent of SBIR projects were responsible for 75 percent of all commercial sales. Because of this skewed distribution, evaluating the SBIR program can be very difficult, since a small number of successes account for a large share of positive commercial outcomes.[3] Partly because of this uneven distribution, the Defense Department implemented the Fast Track pilot to increase the rate of commercialization by SBIR award winners.

DOD'S FAST TRACK INITIATIVE

The Defense Department's Fast Track initiative can be seen as an important evolutionary step within DoD to further encourage the commercialization of SBIR research results. Across all federal agencies, the SBIR program funded approximately $1.2 billion in R&D grants to small businesses in FY 1998. As has historically been the case, the Defense Department is the government agency with the largest R&D budget, making its SBIR program the largest of all agencies. In FY 1998, DoD's SBIR program was approximately $550 million. Examining DoD's efforts to spur greater commercialization is therefore an important part of an overall assessment of SBIR. In addition to exploring overall SBIR program administration, examining the Fast Track Initiative is of general interest because it addresses the key question of whether the government's decision cycles can be shortened enough to meet the needs of fledgling high technology companies.

The Fast Track pilot program was instituted in October 1995 as a way to encourage greater commercialization of SBIR technologies. The principle way in which Fast Track seeks to improve commercialization is by closing the funding gap that can develop between Phase I and Phase II grants. A time lag between the conclusion of Phase I and the receipt of Phase II funds can create cash-flow problems for small firms. The Fast Track pilot addresses the gap by providing essentially continuous funding from Phase I to Phase II *as long as* applying firms demonstrate that they have obtained third-party financing for their technology. Third-party financing means that another firm or a government agency has agreed to purchase the SBIR firm's technology; it can also mean that a venture capitalist has committed to invest in the firm. Because outside funding validates the commercial promise of the technology, the expedited decision-making process for Phase II is seen as a justifiable acceleration of granting the SBIR award.

Two years into the Fast Track initiative, the undersecretary of Defense asked the Board on Science, Technology, and Economic Policy (STEP) at the National Research Council (NRC)[4] to assess Fast Track and related SBIR policy issues. In late 1998 the undersecretary asked the STEP Board to address three issues:

- whether Fast Track projects are achieving, or appear likely to achieve, greater success in SBIR than comparable non-Fast Track projects;
- whether Fast Track projects progress at different rates than non-Fast Track projects;
- what companies perceive as advantages and disadvantages of Fast Track participation.

Assessing an initiative that has been in place only for two years is inherently challenging. To meet that challenge, the STEP Board, under the rubric of its Government-Industry Partnerships for the Development of New Technologies project, undertook a multifaceted approach to the research.[5] Fast Track was examined from three different perspectives, two of which will be reported in this chapter:

1. Survey Research: STEP commissioned a large-scale survey of DoD SBIR firms, using a sample of firms that have participated in Fast Track, and those that have not. The almost 400 firms surveyed make up the largest survey to have focused on the Fast Track pilot. The response rate to the survey was high—64 percent.
2. Case Studies: STEP assembled a team of university researchers to conduct case study of SBIR awardees—both Fast Track and non-Fast Track participants. The case studies looked at firms in New England, California, North Carolina, Indiana, Texas, New Mexico, Colorado, and the Washington, DC metropolitan area. Approximately 50 case studies were conducted in total, and this chapter will present findings on the basis of the case studies in Colorado, New Mexico, and Texas.

COMMERCIALIZATION AND FUNDING: RESULTS FROM THE NATIONAL SURVEY OF SBIR FIRMS

In surveying SBIR firms, the NRC contracted with BRTRC, Inc. of Fairfax, Virginia, to conduct the survey.[6] BRTRC has extensive experience in survey research and with the SBIR program. In close collaboration with the NRC research team, BRTRC developed a survey instrument and administered the survey to 379 DoD SBIR award recipients in early 1999. The sample consisted of half Fast Track firms and half non-Fast Track firms. To increase the sample size, Fast Track was defined broadly to include the informal Fast Track program in effect at the Ballistic Missile Defense Organization (BMDO) since 1992. With DoD's department-wide Fast Track in effect for just two years, and with only one solicitation complete, the pool of department-wide Fast Track firms had reached 48, or about 6 percent of all DoD SBIR awards. Of the 48 Fast Track firms surveyed, 34 responded. Of the 379 surveys sent out, 232 were completed.

Characteristics of Firms Surveyed

In comparing characteristics of Fast Track and non-Fast Track firms among respondents, 61 percent of Fast Track winners had no prior Phase II awards, compared to 32 percent for other winners. This suggests, as intended, that the Fast Track program is attracting new firms to the SBIR program. On average, Fast Track firms are five years younger than non-Fast Track and the median founding year for Fast Track firms is 1994. Not surprisingly, given the relative youth of Fast Track firms, Fast Track companies have lower average annual revenue than non-Fast Track firms. Comparing 1996 Fast Track firms to a control group of non-Fast Track firms from the 1996 solicitation, only 21 percent of Fast Track firms reported revenue in excess of $5 million, compared to 43 percent for non-Fast Track. Fifty-one percent of Fast Track firms reported revenue less than $1 million, as opposed to 28 percent for non-Fast Track.

Commercialization

In general, Fast Track firms show much greater promise of and progress toward commercialization. Because Fast Track firms are new to the program, and because the first Fast Track solicitation was in 1996, Fast Track firms in general have not completed many Phase II projects relative to non-Fast Tracks (which includes BMDO firms). However, in comparing rates of completion of Phase II of 1996 Fast Track versus only 1996 non-Fast Tracks, 14 percent of Fast Tracks reported completing phase II versus 5 percent for non-Fast Tracks. This suggests that the Fast Track firms are actively seeking to move their technologies along toward the market, suggesting that Fast Track firms have a greater commercial orientation than non-Fast Track firms.

Turning to additional development funding, Fast Track projects have proven far better at attracting such funding than non-Fast Track. Strictly comparing

1996 Fast Tracks to the 1996 control group, Fast Track projects received an average of $1,193,000 in developmental funding, five times the amount of the control group. When the more mature BMDO projects were included, Fast Track firms received twice the amount of developmental funding than non-Fast Tracks. As for the source of additional developmental funding, Fast Track firms receive about three-quarters of that funding from the private sector, with the rest from federal government sources. The 1996 control group non-Fast Track firms, in contrast, receive only one-third (of a smaller level of developmental funding) from the private sector. Given Fast Tracks projects' greater rate of attracting private developmental funding, it is no surprise that Fast Track projects attract venture capital at a greater rate than non-Fast Track projects. Close to 20 percent of 1996 Fast Tracks report having attracted venture capital, while none of the 1996 control group had. For BMDO, 7.6 percent of Fast Track firms obtained venture financing, versus 2.5 percent for non-Fast Track BMDO.

In terms of actual sales, it is not surprising that few 1996 SBIR projects in the sample (Fast Track or not) have achieved any sales, because of the newness of the projects. Out of 34 Fast Track projects, only 11 report sales, and three of those projects account for two-thirds of the sales. Nonetheless, 1996 Fast Track project sales levels are about twice that of non-Fast Track projects. Looking at expected project sales, 1996 Fast Track firms reported that they expected their Fast Track projects to generate $8,950,000 in sales by 2001, six times the amount of expected sales of non-Fast Track projects from the 1996 control group. When BMDO Fast Track and non-Fast Track firms are included, the expected revenue from Fast Track firms is twice that of non-Fast Track.

Funding Gap

A key objective of the Fast Track initiative was to reduce the funding gap between Phase I and Phase II. As noted earlier, for new and very small firms, SBIR funds may be a substantial source of support, and a period of time without any funding may threaten the underlying research or continued commitment of such firms. According to the survey, Fast Track succeeded in narrowing this gap. Twenty of the 42 respondents from the 1996 Fast Track group reported no funding gap between Phase I and Phase II, and the average funding gap was 2.3 months. For the 1996 control group, nine respondents reported no gap, and the average funding gap was 4.7 months. Only four Fast Track projects (10 percent) from the 1996 group reported having to stop work because of the funding gap, whereas over half of the 1996 non-Fast Track projects reported that work ceased due to a funding gap.

FIRM-LEVEL IMPACTS OF FAST TRACK

With the priority placed on commercialization of SBIR-funded projects in the 1992 legislation and the pending reauthorization of the SBIR, several questions emerged that cannot be easily resolved through the national survey data. What types of firms tend to respond to the Fast-Track incentives? What specific effect does the incentive have on particular firms? For example, does the incentive change the firm's business strategy? What affect does external funding have on firms? Does the effect vary among firms? To explore these questions, a case study methodology was adopted. Firms from various regions of the United States were adopted, using a common interview protocol. In this chapter the results from firms in the Southwest and Mountain states are presented.

Methods

To examine these questions, case studies of 12 firms with SBIR contracts in the Southwestern and Mountain regions were conducted. Particular attention was given to potential differences in firms resulting from participation in the Fast Track program. Despite diversity in these firms' technological expertise, common experiences are apparent. This chapter will discuss some of the distinct patterns observed among the SBIR program firms.

Approximately 30 Phase II SBIR projects from the Southwestern and Mountain regions were included in a representative dataset developed by BRTRC for the National Research Council's evaluation. Individual firms could be represented on this list more than once if they had received multiple contracts. The four projects identified as participating in the Fast Track program were selected for case studies. Additionally, geography was taken into account as a selection criteria, and firms that were located in the Austin-San Antonio, Boulder-Denver, and Albuquerque metropolitan areas were contacted to learn about the firm's SBIR experience.

Interviews were designed to elicit information on the effects of the SBIR program on the firms, with a focus on a particular Phase II award. In this manner, information was gathered at firm and project levels. The findings are organized in several sections. First, a firm typology that emerged in the field is presented. This typology is then used to interpret differential impacts of the SBIR on firms. The costs and benefits of Fast Tack participation are considered. Finally, factors that inhibit participation in Fast Track are identified and related issues of SBIR administration are addressed.

Firm Categorization

The firms described in the SBIR case studies have diverse areas of expertise, but they are more fundamentally differentiated from each other by organizational characteristics. Primary among these are the firms' size, relationship to capital, and business development strategy. With the combination of these characteristics, firms can typically be classified in one of three categories of firm type (see Table 13.1).

Table 13.1

Typology of SBIR Firms by Organizational Characteristics

Firm Type	Primary Activity	Firm Size	Relationship to Capital	Strategy
Scientific	Basic Research	Small (0-15)	Distant	Pursue Research
Technologist	Applied Research	Small but growing (0-30)	Seeking Investors	Commercialize
Contractor	R&D Contracts	Large (30-350)	Partnerships and Contracts	Develop Expertise

The first category is comprised of firms that are committed to the business of research and development. Companies in this category can be called *contractor firms*. For this group, the SBIR program represents a source of contract revenue. The performance of research is a major business activity, and the SBIR program supports this work. The SBIR solicitation topics are interpreted as the articulated research needs of various government agencies. When a firm has the capabilities to respond to these topics through existing staff and resources, it will generally apply for an SBIR award. These firms are generally well-established and support larger staff than many SBIR participant firms. Typically, they have over 50 employees, and perhaps as many as 300-400 on their payroll. These firms are multiple recipients of SBIR awards and the SBIR program represents a significant portion of the firm's annual revenue. Other sources of revenue are pursued, such as marketing commercial products, signing licensing agreements, or forging partnerships with larger firms, building upon intellectual property rights, and research activities.

A second category is exemplified by firms focusing on the development of a specific product or promising enabling technology. These companies can be labeled as *technologist firms*. These firms may have applied for an SBIR award early in their history when the product or technology was at an early stage in the innovation cycle. For these firms, the SBIR program represented a means to develop technology and demonstrate its viability to the market. If the product is attractive to investors, either venture capitalist or angel investors, these firms can be transformed quite dramatically. The infusion of capital allows them to expand their staff, purchase capital equipment, and attract senior management. These firms are oriented toward the market and their growth decreases the relative importance of the SBIR program as an ongoing revenue source. The SBIR program represents an invaluable building block for these companies even as work on the SBIR contract loses importance relative to the goal of marketing a product.

A third category is represented by firms interested in pursuing basic research outside of a university setting, and thus may be labeled as *scientific firms*. These firms are generally small and were founded by scientists to explore whether or not a particular research area can generate ideas or products that might attract interest. The SBIR program enables these firms to work on specific projects, whose outcomes are unclear. They may have the chance to develop a commercial product, but they are not currently attracting interest from outside investors. For firms in this category, the SBIR contract represents a significant portion of revenue, and the size of a Phase II award provides enough resources to acquire equipment and man-hours to perform the work.

These three categories represent types of firms distinguished by their organizational characteristics (see Table 13.2). Firms develop these characteristics across time in response to evolving conditions. Inasmuch as these characteristics may change over time, a particular firm may need to be reclassified in this typology or may exhibit characteristics of more than one firm type. Still it is instructive to use this classification scheme to distinguish the firms in this case study analysis according to their own organizational characteristics (see Table 13.3).

Table 13.2
Characteristics of Case Study Firms

Firm	State	Found	Employees	Phase IIs	SBIR Project	Firm Type
AvPro	OK	1990	10	2	Fast Track	Technologist
Bolder Technologies	CO	1991	100	1	SBIR	Technologist
Chorum Technologies	TX	1996	60	2	Fast Track	Technologist
Coherent Technologies	CO	1984	90	27	SBIR	Contractor
Lipitek International	TX	1988	15	1	SBIR	Scientist
Mission Research Corp.	NM	1970	350	45	SBIR	Contractor
Picolight	CO	1995	26	5	Fast Track/ BMDO Co	Technologist
Radiant Research	TX	1994	12	8	BMDO Co	Scientist
SPEC	TX	1986	60	25+	BMDO Co	Contractor
TRAC	CO	1991	4	1	Fast Track	Scientist
TPL, Inc.	NM	1990	90	12	BMDO Co	Contractor

The SBIR program fills a different role for each type of firm. Furthermore, features of the Fast Track program make it more or less appealing for a firm depending upon their organizational characteristics. Additionally, where a firm is located in its own developmental cycle appears to be a major factor in how it will structure its participation in the SBIR program. Thus, a firm's relationship to the program will not be static. An SBIR grant can be invaluable to a young start-up company, but less essential after that same firm has attracted significant outside resources.

Table 13.3
Classification of Case Study Firms by Type

Scientist Firms	Technologist Firms	Contractor Firms
Lipitek International	AvPro	Coherent Technologies
Radiant Research	Bolder Technologies	Mission Research Corp.
TRAC	Chorum Technologies	SPEC
	Picolight	TPL, Inc.

Impact of the SBIR Program

Firms in all three categories are enthusiastic about the SBIR program and identify a range of positive impacts that the program has had on their work. The program provides resources to allow firms to conduct expensive research and development activities, and grow their firms through the acquisition of capital equipment, facility maintenance, and staff expansion. The SBIR program is valuable in that it provides an accessible revenue stream. It provides research support to move technology into core commercial directions.

From several perspectives, the SBIR program is lauded as providing numerous opportunities for young and less established firms. First, it offers a means to expand a firm's technical understanding of their research areas. Second, it encourages firms to develop commercially viable applications of their research. Third, it fills a funding gap difficult to bridge with conventional private investment. In several cases, the SBIR program provided the direct impetus for the founding of a company. There are a host of indirect but beneficial spillover effects related to the SBIR program. The SBIR experience creates relationships that continue to benefit participating firms. These include contacts with suppliers, manufacturers, and potential partners.

The SBIR program is used by many companies as a marketing tool. Receiving an award can illustrate a potential application for a technology, and provide the means to attract a partner. The SBIR award does not in and of itself certify the technology or the company on its own, but it gives the firm an advantage as it competes for the attraction of investors. Private investors are not attracted to the firm solely because of its SBIR award, but the SBIR award serves as an indication that the firm's technology may be promising after already being recognized by a government agency.

Firms in all three categories appeared to use their SBIR awards as marketing tools, but in distinct ways. For the scientific firms, such as Lipitek and Radiant Research, the presence of an SBIR award confirms the importance of their research agenda. For the contractor firms, such as TPL, Inc., Mission

Research Corp., and SPEC, their ongoing participation in the program demonstrates that they can deliver projects and maintain the in-house expertise sought after by government agencies. The technologist firms highlight their SBIR awards as indicative of innovation. Outside investors may still evaluate the technology of these firms on their own terms, but the award helps distinguish their work from others competing for the interest of investors and venture capitalists.

Many successful SBIR contracts do not result directly in a product, and thus appear to fail when judged according a narrow return-on-investment criteria. Yet the SBIR program can still lead to success in the long run by expanding a firm's understanding of its technology area, generating intellectual property rights, and supporting a young firm with promise. Often commercial success is realized when a product is developed after a succession of SBIR awards. This has been the case with several of the larger firms classified as contractor firms. In the case of TPL Inc., SPEC, and Coherent Technologies, commercial opportunities were identified after a series of contracts were executed.

These firms and others classified as contractor firms appear to be committed to innovative research and development work, and have come to rely on the SBIR program for a large portion of their revenue. These firms believe they are good at what they do and are using the SBIR program to respond to articulated government needs. These firms appear to be filling a niche market that consists of performing basic and applied research that responds to the need of sponsoring agencies. The basic research provides the building blocks for future product development, and is located earlier in the innovation and product cycle. The applied research often responds to the agenda of contracting agencies, and thus may be distinct from more commercial opportunities.

The range of work these firms undertake generates more opportunities for market-oriented endeavors. All of the four firms classified as contractor firms (Coherent Technologies, Mission Research Corporation, SPEC, and TPL, Inc.) have explored commercial opportunities, often in partnership with much larger and established firms. But in each of these cases, government research and development contracts continue to represent a higher significant portion of their annual revenues.

Some firms are relying even more heavily on the SBIR program for operating revenue. These are often small firms concentrating on basic research. In this set of cases, this describes two of the firms classified as scientific firms (Radiant Research and TRAC). Firms that appear interested in basic research are not as attractive to capital investors interested in a rate of return. Innovative research, by its nature, is the foundation upon which product development is based. Therefore, solid, innovative research is not readily commercializable. In this sense, the SBIR program's more recent focus on commercialization undermines one of the program's strengths: the SBIR program's ability to support the innovative work of small or young companies.

Participation in the Fast Track Program

As described above, the Fast Track program offers a valuable tool to firms looking to attract investors because they can offer prospective investors a means to leverage their investment. The Fast Track program generates advantages for firms with a higher potential for commercialization and an interest in producing for the market. Firms that are interested in commercialization prior to their application for an SBIR award appear most likely to succeed as Fast Track firms. These firms are more likely to have their sights set on pursing technological innovations that will attract market attention. Thus they will be closer to marketing their technology than a firm which is focusing on more conventional research and development activities.

Of the four Fast Track projects in this study, three were classified as technologist firms (see Table 13.4). Picolight, AvPro, and Chorum Technologies have articulated business plans that address how their work will respond to unmet market needs. Each of these firms have identified not only their innovation, but the clients and firm clusters that their products will serve. Two of these firms, Picolight and Chorum Technologies, have generated additional investment that has far exceeded the SBIR contract amount and the third-party Fast Track match. The fourth Fast Track firm, TRAC, has not had a successful Fast Track experience, and in fact lost its matching investment midway through the project. This case demonstrates how some of the organizational characteristics of scientific firms are related to difficulties in pursuing Fast Track projects. In TRAC's case, its small staff, limited administrative capacity, and undefined sense of its target market created difficulties after it received its Fast Track award.

Table 13.4
Fast Track and BMDO Co-Investment Projects by Firm Type

Firm	Project Status	Firm Type
AvPro	Fast Track	Technologist
Chorum Technologies	Fast Track	Technologist
Picolight	Fast Track	Technologist
TRAC	Fast Track	Scientist
TPL, Inc.	BMDO Co-Investment	Contractor
SPEC	BMDO Co-Investment	Contractor
Radiant Research	BMDO Co-Investment	Scientist

Depending on the technology area, the time between developing a product for market and the basic R&D stage varies, making Fast Track not as viable for some firms. For example, TPL, Inc. is primarily a materials company that projects a longer time horizon for product development than would a software or electronics firm. Even when it felt as though it had identified an important innovation, it recognized that it takes many years to develop a technology, streamline a manufacturing system, and market to other firms. While it may be competitive in its field, this extended timetable may not be attractive to investors requiring a quicker return.

The organizational characteristics of SBIR firms essentially determine whether or not a firm will be able to take advantage of the Fast Track program. These characteristics reveal those firms that are focusing on a later stage of the product cycle. Those firms that are committed to applied research and developing products or applications for an identified market have a greater likelihood of attracting investment. The later stage of the product cycle is represented by several other characteristics, such as whether a prototype already exists, products are being tested, or production facilities are in place. These are some of the conditions that appear to be prerequisites for firms to succeed in SBIR's Fast Track. This does not appear to be the case for participation in the BMDO co-investment program. In the cases included in this study, firms with a range of organizational characteristics took advantage of this program.

Fast Track Benefits and Costs

For firms participating in the Fast Track program, there is an advantage in making a quicker transition from Phase I to Phase II. This is especially important for young start-up or relatively small firms, which benefit from the short gap in awards and the arrival of matching funds. Fast Track investment addresses one of the major obstacles of small businesses, that of cash flow. The infusion of capital that comes with a Fast Track award can help alleviate many problems.

While addressing cash flow issues is important, the overwhelming benefit to the Fast Track program is the ability to use government funds to attract outside investment. Fast Track represents a means for research companies to offer third-party investors the opportunity to leverage their investment. This makes investing in a young start-up firm significantly more attractive. Picolight and Chorum Technologies specifically highlighted this phenomenon when discussing their participation in the Fast Track program.

Fast Track participation can also cause some peril. The shortened timetable for submitting a Fast Track application can propel a project prematurely, limiting administrative oversight. In the one Fast Track case study with a poor outcome (TRAC), the principal assumed responsibility for this lack of diligence in project administration, but felt seduced by the prospect of matching funds. In this case, the structure of the Fast Track program gave the investor undue influence on the course of the project.

There is some concern about the trade-offs which accompany attracting investors into a small firm. Primarily, firms are worried about losing control to outside forces. Still, most of the firms that have attracted substantial outside investment, either through Fast Track or other means, are pleased with the results. Venture capitalists do bring able valuable experience. In most cases, their presence on the board of directors is a vehicle for structuring input rather than taking over control. Picolight and the spin-off firm from SPEC both have appreciated the expertise that venture capitalists have brought to their firms, increasing the likelihood of market success.

Success with the SBIR program can lead to drastic choices. When a firm grows with support of the program, the firm must determine what kind of company it wants to be. It must decide whether or not it should pursue investors, should pursue acquisition, or take the company public. These are all drastic measures that change a company's profile significantly. For example, Chorum Technologies was adamant that it was not interested in being acquired by a larger company. As a result of this decision, it decided that it needed to develop the capabilities for large-volume manufacturing.

A company may be willing to consider drastic measures because of the difficulties associated with commercialization. Most firms recognize that there is a major gap between completing a Phase II contract and successfully marketing a product. Although access to capital is a major component of this gap, money is not the only solution. More than a money gap, many companies experience a maturity gap. They can develop a product prototype but much more is required to successfully produce and distribute a product in the market. Often what is missing is an understanding of the markets. This is an expertise that a third-party investor may possess, and thus the Fast Track program provides a vehicle for firms to collaborate, each bringing its own expertise to a particular project.

Factors that Inhibit SBIR Participation

The prime factor that inhibits a firm's participation in the Fast Track program is difficulty in attracting investors to meet the matching requirements of the program. This is because SBIR proposals which address issues of basic research represent work that occurs early on in the product cycle.

Many investors are more eager to support projects that have a potential return in the near future. Yet often the SBIR project is designed to pursue the development of an idea. The development of a prototype is a possible outcome of a Phase II contract, and this demonstration of a prototype's viability will likely increase investor's interest. At this point, it is too late to apply for a Fast Track award. Several firms that were multiple winners of SBIR awards, such as Mission Research Corp., Radiant Research, and TPL, Inc., noted that the higher matching requirements represented an obstacle to their participation in the Fast Track program. However, the Fast Track program addresses some issues which are not as essential for larger, more established firms. Contractor firms or those technologist firms that have attracted investment and expanded their activities do not have a financial needs for financing between Phase I and Phase II projects; these firms already have access to external capital. From DOD's perspective, some firms may already be focused on commercialization, and thus not need the Fast Track program to move them in this direction.

Program Administration

One central conclusion from this set of SBIR case studies is that the size of the firm affects the impact of the SBIR award. Larger firms with more staff resources have an easier time preparing applications, managing contracts, and performing the research. Firms with less staff cannot easily divide SBIR responsibilities. For example, the experience of being audited is particularly onerous for a small company with few staff resources. A small firm is also disadvantaged because administration of the contract takes time way from the people who would otherwise be "doing the science."

The firms interviewed identified two methods of contract execution. In a firm fixed-price model, deliverables are presented to the agency in exchange for incremental payments. In the cost-plus fixed-price model, a firm is reimbursed for eligible costs in additional to a contract price. This latter method creates a higher scrutiny for audit, and thus is less preferable for smaller firms. But the choice of how each contract is structured appears to depend on the DoD program officer, and is outside the influence of the executing firm. Regardless of the form of the contract, they are large documents that take much time and energy to monitor from the firm's perspective.

Small firms are particularly concerned when a cost plus fixed-fee system is employed in the disbursement of funds. Many firms, both small and large, spoke against this method of structuring SBIR contracts. Firms would rather be paid upon completion of work or the submission of results. Many costs that a firm might submit are ineligible as per government regulations, but the firm does not know what these costs are and feels as though a big staff would be required to successfully understand all of the government regulations and nuances of the SBIR program. There is the sense that contracts are written to make management easiest on the program officer rather than considering the needs of the recipient firm.

Technology companies also have a unique problem. Technological advances create products that do things that have never been done before, thus the firms must look for a home for the technology that is not readily apparent. This is the reverse of the process that most commercial companies pursue, where they know the market and compete with products that cost less or outperform existing products. Technology products can do new things, and markets are less defined. In this sense, the SBIR program's emphasis on commercialization may benefit from finding ways to support companies as they pursue commercialization and increase their understanding of markets where they can compete.

Many firms wished to see additional support for Phase III of the SBIR program, where commercialization is emphasized. The development of a marketable technology does not lead easily to commercialization; there are many additional steps that must be taken for a firm to succeed. If DoD wants firms to achieve commercialization, perhaps more thought should be given to firm needs during this phase of commercialization.

The requirement of matching funds for the Fast Track and BMDO co-investment program have motivated firms to explicitly explore commercial opportunities created by research and development activities. In one strategy, a spin-off company is created. This facilitates the investment of outside capital, which can target its investment to a specific project or product. While this might be viewed favorably by DoD, the creation of a new firm requires additional managerial and administrative tasks and services, including legal and accounting services. Second, once the companies were distinguished from each other, it has been difficult to get DoD to recognize the new firm and transfer the Phase II contracts accordingly. This was one of the main criticisms of the program from one of the spin-off firms. Even though the principals believed they were doing what DoD wanted, they did not believe that the administrative procedures are in place to facilitate meeting these objectives logistically. Also, the spin-off is treated as a multiple SBIR recipient and thus cannot take advantage of the most favorable matching requirements.

The Fast Track program is a good idea in that it ensures a positive cash flow and moves a project along a quicker timetable. In many technology areas, time is an important factor because long delays can have major market consequences. Accordingly, the speed with which programs are evaluated by DoD agencies is a major characteristic which sets them apart from one another. Those agencies with longer delays in evaluating proposals or transitioning a project from Phase I to Phase II are less desirable to work with for small companies. Additionally, DoD should recognize that developing commercial products takes different lengths of time depending upon the technology area in question.

CONCLUSIONS

Even though sufficient time has not transpired to assess rigorously the commericalization impact of the Fast Track program, a number of conclusions emerge from this NAS study. The national survey indicates that the program has attracted new firms to the Defense Department's SBIR program with greater expected commercialization prospects. The Fast Track firms are younger, more likely to have venture capital financing, and better able than non-Fast Track firms to attract additional development funding. Moreover, Fast Track has succeeded in closing the funding gap for Fast Track projects relative to non-Fast Track projects.

The case study firms revealed distinct patterns which may be more broadly representative of the program. SBIR award winners believe they benefit greatly from their participation in the program. These benefits are not necessarily expressed in commercial sales but also are related to expanding basic research, responding to government needs, and developing applications for technology.

The Fast Track program helps promote the commercial success of participating firms in several important respects. It helps firms move toward commercialization by offering a tool to attract outside investors and a means to bridge the financing gap that some firms experience between Phase I and Phase II of the SBIR program, a finding which also emerged in the national survey.

The Fast Track program appears to work best for firms fairly advanced in preparing a product or innovation for the market. Such firms in the latter phases of the product cycle are already well positioned to attract investment and the program brings benefits to investors whose capital is leveraged through SBIR support.

Even firms not able to take advantage of the Fast Track program nevertheless recognized DoD interest in commercialization and they frequently wanted to appear responsive to this SBIR objective. However, a concern emerged on the part of firms having difficulty in pursuing commercialization. An overemphasis on commercialization can detract from one of the SBIR program's most beneficial qualities, which is the provision of an accessible revenue stream for firms engaged in basic research and innovative development activities. Balancing the importance of support for these firms and the goals of commercialization is a policy question which needs to be explicitly addressed.

If commercialization does not become the sole objective of the SBIR program, DoD should continue to support non-Fast Track projects. Many SBIR projects focus on basic research and R&D activities that respond to the needs of contracting government agencies. These projects may be successful even if they do not lead to immediate commercial sales. The firm's relationship to the product cycle is relevant to its commercial potential. The appropriateness of Fast Track seems questionable for products or technologies that are distant from existing markets. The technology may need further development or the market may need time to understand and accept the product or innovation. The diverse objectives of the SBIR program appear to indicate that DOD should not exclusively pursue Fast Track projects since it might inhibit the involvement of several categories of firms that have successfully contributed to program and DoD objectives in the past.

In sum, in spite of some reservations and uncertainties, associated with its relative short life span, the DOD Fast Track initiative is promising. The results of this research project suggest that the Fast Track program is attracting the types of firms likely to achieve significant commercialization in the future and is providing an incentive for firms to resolve the funding gap through third-party investment. With greater expectation for commercial sales among Fast Track participants, in conjunction with the fact that Fast Track firms tend to be new to the program, the Fast Track initiative seems well-positioned to improve commercialization rates of SBIR technologies in the Defense Department.

NOTES

1. For a critical appraisal of SBIR, see the recent article by the late Representative George Brown, former chairman of the House Committee on Science, and James Turner (1999).

2. In Archibald and Finifter's (1999) survey of SBIR program technical points of contact (TPOCs), who are government officials responsible for monitoring SBIR grants, the TPOCs rated the research quality and commercial application of SBIR-funded technologies as virtually equal, suggesting no trade-off.

3. It is worth noting that the results of venture capital investments can also be highly skewed.

4. The NRC is the operating arm of the National Academy of Sciences, the National Academy of Engineering, and the Institute of Medicine.

5. An appendix to this chapter lists the members of the research team and provides background on the "Government-Industry Partnerships for the Development of New Technologies" project.

6. All results reported in this section draw from Cahill (1999). At this writing, the results are preliminary and do not constitute findings or recommendations of the National Research Council.

REFERENCES

Archibald, Robert B. and David H. Finifter (1999), "Evaluation of the DoD SBIR Program and the Fast Track Initiative: A Balanced Approach," in *The Small Business Innovation Research Program: Assessing the Fast Track Initiative.* Washington, DC: National Academy Press.

Birch, David (1981), "Who Creates Jobs?," *The Public Interest,* No. 65 (Fall), pp. 3-14.

Brown, George and James Turner (1999), "Reworking the Federal Role in Small Business Research," *Issues in Science and Technology.* Summer, pp. 51-58.

Cahill, Peter (1999), "Fast Track: Is It Speeding Commercialization of DoD SBIR?" in *The Small Business Innovation Research Program: Assessing the Fast Track Initiative.* Washington, DC: National Academy Press.

Lerner, Josh (1999), "The Government as Venture Capitalist: The Long-Run Impact of the SBIR Program," *Journal of Business,* Vol. 72, No. 3, pp. 285-318.

National Research Council (1999), *The Small Business Innovation Research Program: Assessing the Fast Track Initiative.* Washington, DC: National Academy Press.

Tibbets, Roland (1999), "The Small Business Innovation Research Program and NSF SBIR Commercialization Results" in *The Small Business Innovation Research Program: Challenges and Opportunities.* Washington, DC: National Academy Press.

U.S. General Accounting Office (1992), Federal Research: Observations on the Small Business Innovation Research Program (RCED-98-132).

U.S. General Accounting Office (1999), Federal Research: Evaluations of Small Business Innovation Research Can Be Strengthened (RCED-99-198).

U.S. Senate Committee on Small Business (1981), Senate Report 97-194, Small Business Research Act of 1981, September 25, 1981.

Wessner, Charles (Editor) (1999a), *The Small Business Innovation Research Program: Challenges and Opportunities Board.* Washington, DC: National Academy Press.

Wessner, Charles (Editor) (1999b), *New Vistas in Transatlantic Science and Technology Cooperation.* Washington, DC: National Academy Press.

Wessner, Charles (Editor) (2000), *The Small Business Innovation Research Program: An Assessment of the Department of Defense Fast Track Initiative.* Washington, DC: National Academy Press.

APPENDIX

The STEP Board's Government-Industry Partnerships for the Development of New Technologies project assembled the following research team to carry out assessment of the Fast Track initiative:

Charles Wessner, Program Director, National Research Council
Pete Cahill, BRTRC, Inc.
Robert Archibald, College of William and Mary
David Finifter, College of William and Mary
Reid Cramer, University of Texas at Austin
Robert Wilson, University of Texas at Austin
Maryann Feldman, Johns Hopkins University
David Audretsch, Indiana University
Albert Link, University of North Carolina at Greensboro
John Scott, Dartmouth College
John Horrigan, Research Associate, National Research Council

The Government-Industry Partnerships project is conducting analyses of partnership programs between government and industry, which have historically played an important role in U.S. technology development, but have been subject to relatively little objective analysis. The SBIR program is one such program the project is exploring, and two volumes on SBIR are available (Wessner, 1999a, 2000). Other work under way or envisaged include the Advanced Technology Program, SEMATECH, and partnerships in the biotechnology and computing industries. The Government-Industry Partnerships program has also examined international science and technology cooperation, having published *New Vistas in Transatlantic Science and Technology Cooperation* (Wessner, 1999b).

14

Lessons Learned About Technology Transfer

Everett M. Rogers, Shiro Takegami, and Jing Yin

INTRODUCTION

Many cities around the world look at technopoleis like Silicon Valley in Northern California; Austin, Texas; the Route 128 complex near Boston; Tsukuba Science City in Japan; Cambridge, England; and Bangalore and Hyderabad, India, and may seek to become more like them. The technology cities create jobs and wealth, and thus are a mechanism for economic development. For example, in Silicon Valley, undoubtedly the most widely known technopolis in the world, an average of 63 new millionaires were created each day during 1999 (Nieves, 2000). An analysis of the rate of economic growth by U.S. metropolitan areas during the 1990s found that two-thirds of the increase in this variable was due to high technology industry, fueled in turn by spin-off companies from research universities, federal R&D laboratories, and corporate labs (DeVol, 1999). So an important policy question has become how cities can harness such technology transfer for their economic development. The answer may lie in an improved understanding of the technology transfer process.

The purpose of this chapter is to summarize lessons learned about technology transfer in the past several years of research on (1) CRADAs (Cooperative R&D Agreements) linking Los Alamos National Laboratory (LANL) with private companies (Rogers et al., 1998); (2) spin-offs from LANL and Sandia National Laboratories (SNL) (Carayannis et al., 1998), and from research centers at the University of New Mexico (UNM) (Rogers et al., 1999); (3) the role of entrepreneurs' individualistic and collectivistic cultural values in high tech spin-offs in New Mexico and Singapore (Lopez et al., 1999); (4) the technology transfer effectiveness of 55 research centers at UNM (Rogers et al., 1999; Steffensen et al., 1999); and (5) the technology transfer effectiveness of 132 research universities in the United States as they move toward an era of "academic capitalism" (Slaughter and Leslie, 1997) in which the university becomes increasingly involved in the business aspects of transferring research-based technologies (Rogers, Yin, and Hoffman, 1999).

PROSPECTS FOR A NEW MEXICO TECHNOPOLIS

New Mexico is a large state in area (ranking fifth among the 50 states), small in population (only 1.5 million people, half of whom reside in the Albuquerque area), and poor (50th of the 50 states in per capita income). Albuquerque is remote from the metropolitan centers of capital and from consumer markets in the United States.

Despite these handicaps, state leaders and city officials in Albuquerque are strongly committed to creating a technopolis (technology city) in northern New Mexico. Technology transfer is regarded as a crucial factor for economic development in New Mexico. The state ranks fourth among the 50 states in federal and university R&D performance. The New Mexico Legislature created a variety of protechnology transfer policies in recent years, such as allowing venture capital firms to draw on the state's reserve funding (including that earned by a state severance tax) in order to provide up to half of the investment in new high-tech companies in New Mexico. LANL and SNL actively encourage high tech spin-offs and utilize other mechanisms of technology transfer. Numerous technology transfer institutions seek to facilitate the entrepreneurship process. Particularly important is the Technology Ventures Corporation (TVC), which is funded by Lockheed Martin, the aerospace company that manages SNL. UNM doubled its sponsored research funding over the past decade (to about $200 million annually), a faster rate of increase than any other U.S. research university in this time period (Rogers et al., 1999). Several of UNM's 55 research centers play an active role in technology transfer, including facilitating spin-offs. So technology transfer activity is increasingly under way in New Mexico, as Albuquerque moves toward becoming a future technology city.

Spin-offs can be a particularly effective means of technology transfer, leading to job and wealth creation. But the number of spin-offs occurring in a region is usually slow at first until a certain point (the critical mass) is reached, when the rate of spin-off activity begins to increase exponentially (Rogers, 1995). The availability of ample technology in a region is a necessary but insufficient factor in the development of a technopolis (much of the technology from federal weapons laboratories like SNL and LANL is defense-related and thus is particularly difficult to commercialize). Technology transfer facilitating organizations like TVC, several incubators and research parks, and the offices of technology commercialization at SNL and LANL can speed up the process of getting to critical mass in the growth of high tech spin-offs.

New Mexico provides a useful environment in which to understand the technology transfer process as a means of economic development, in part because, like many cities in the world, the Albuquerque area is at a fairly early state of high-tech development and faces important barriers to be overcome.

TECHNOLOGY TRANSFER

Technology is information that is put to use in order to accomplish some task (Eveland, 1986). *Transfer* is the movement of technology via some communication channel from one individual or organization to another. A *technological innovation* is an idea, practice, or object that is perceived as new by an individual or some other unit (Rogers, 1995). Therefore, *technology transfer* is the application of information (a technological innovation) into use (Gibson and Rogers, 1994). The technology transfer process usually involves moving a technological innovation from an R&D organization to a receptor organization (such as a private company). A technological innovation is fully transferred when it is commercialized into a product that is sold in the marketplace. So technology transfer is a special type of communication process.

Technological innovation-development is often described as a linear process, from basic research, to applied research, to development, to commercialization, to diffusion, and to the consequences of the innovation. A linear model of the innovation-development process may not fully take into account external environmental factors, such as market demand or regulatory changes, which may influence the technological innovation process. The technology transfer process spans the stages from R&D to commercialization and beyond, but with particular focus on the interface between R&D (often by a university research center, a corporate unit, or a government laboratory) and commercialization (often carried out by a private company).

Technology Transfer Mechanisms

Technology transfer occurs via various channels of communication.

1. A *spin-off* is a new company that is formed (1) by individuals who were former employees of a parent organization, and (2) with a core technology that is transferred from a parent organization (Rogers and Steffensen, 1999). Spin-offs thus represent the transfer of a technological innovation to a new entrepreneurial company that is formed around that technological innovation. Generally, a spin-off neighbors with its parent organization, especially as in Northern New Mexico, when they are located in an area with an attractive quality-of-life.[1] As more and more spin-offs occur, including spin-offs of spin-offs, an agglomeration of high tech companies is formed, eventually resulting in a technopolis.[2] A spectacular demonstration of this agglomeration process of high tech spin-offs occurred in Austin, Texas, in the 1980s and 1990s.

2. *Licensing* is the granting of permission or rights to make, use, and/or sell a certain product, design, or process or to perform certain other actions, by a party that has the right to give such permission (Licensing Executive Society, 1995). A licensing fee is usually paid in exchange for acquiring a technology license. Licensing royalties may earn considerable income for a research university or a national R&D laboratory. We believe that the increasing emphasis on technology licensing royalties by U.S. research universities may be transforming these institutions to "entrepreneurial universities" pursuing a path toward academic capitalism (Slaughter and Leslie, 1997). The University of New Mexico now has an active Office of Technology Licensing with a staff of four professionals who are organizationally part of the university's Science and Technology Corporation, a research foundation that also manages the university's real estate.

3. *Publications* can also be a means of technology transfer. Articles published in academic journals are the most frequently used means of technology transfer, as reported by university scholars. Unfortunately, journal articles are mainly written for fellow scientists, rather than for potential users of a research-based technology. Thus scholarly articles are not an effective means of technology transfer, although they are the most frequently cited technology transfer activity by university-based research centers (Rogers et al., 1999).

4. *Meetings* involve person-to-person interaction through which technical information is exchanged. In the late 1990s, three networks/associations were organized in New Mexico to facilitate information-exchange and entrepreneurial activity: (1) Biomedical Tuesday, (2) the New Mexico Optics Industry Society, and (3) the New Mexico Information and Software Association. Each association attracted from 50 to 75 entrepreneurs, venture capitalists, and others to their monthly meetings.

5. *Cooperative R&D agreements (CRADAs)* are intended to transfer technologies from federal R&D laboratories in the United States to private companies who collaborate in R&D with the federal laboratory (Rogers et al., 1998). CRADAs are comprehensive legal agreements for sharing research personnel, equipment, and intellectual property rights in joint government-industry research between federal R&D laboratories and private companies. Because federal R&D laboratories and private companies do not share a common organizational culture, they face certain difficulties in their collaboration in CRADAs (Rogers et al., 1998). Larger corporations are more likely to be involved in CRADAs with federal laboratories in New Mexico than are smaller companies, and CRADA partners tend to be out-of-state.

SPIN-OFFS

A spin-off is a technology transfer mechanism because it is usually formed in order to commercialize a technology that originated in a government R&D laboratory, a university research center, or a private R&D organization. A high rate of establishing spin-off companies is characteristic of technopoleis like Silicon Valley; Austin; Route 128; Tsukuba Science City (Dearing and Rogers, 1990); and Bangalore (Singhal and Rogers, 2000). In fact, spin-offs are the main mechanism for the rapid growth of each of these technopoleis.

We examined the high-technology spin-off process through which a new company is formed from a parent organization, in the case (1) of seven spin-off companies in New Mexico and Japan (Carayannis et al., 1998), and (2) of six spin-offs from the University of New Mexico (Steffensen et al., 1999). An investigation of 30 spin-offs, mainly from LANL and SNL, is now being conducted. Support from the parent organization, such as by providing venture funding, business management advice, building space, or other needed resources, is especially helpful to the spin-off company. In some cases, facilitating organizations support a new spin-off by providing resources and know-how.

Various support organizations have been established in New Mexico to assist high-tech entrepreneurs in the difficult process of formulating a business plan, obtaining venture capital, and getting their new business under way. For example, the Technology Ventures Corporation and the Business Technology Group (BTG), a collective of three Albuquerque-based incubators, play important roles in supporting spin-off companies. Small Business Innovation Research (SBIR) funding from federal research agencies is particularly important for high tech spin-offs in New Mexico. These companies received a total of $18 million in SBIR funding in 1998. We found that the SBIR funding, although typically in modest amounts per grant, often helped keep a spin-off alive until it could attract investment from a venture capitalist.

Our research on spin-offs began by identifying 70 new high-tech companies that had spun-off of the federal R&D laboratories or the University of New Mexico during the 1990s. This list, believed to be fairly exhaustive, was obtained through a snowball technique beginning with the technology transfer offices of the two Federal R&D labs and the various support organizations assisting new ventures in New Mexico, such as the Technology Ventures Corporation, business incubators, and the New Mexico Native American Business Development Center (NMNABDC).

The federal R&D laboratories in New Mexico have instituted entrepreneurial leave policies, which have increased the number of their spin-offs. We found that most parent organizations support their spin-offs, or at least do not try to destroy them. Several venture capital firms have moved to New Mexico in recent years. Spin-off facilitating organizations like TVC play an important role in assisting high-tech spin-offs.

We investigated three spin-off companies, one founded by a Native American, one by an Hispanic, and one by a Singaporean (in Singapore) in order to determine whether entrepreneurs with collectivistic cultures, in which the collectivity's goals are more important than the individual's (Rogers and Steinfatt, 1999), are disadvantaged in spinning off a new firm, compared to entrepreneurs with individualistic cultures, in which the individual's goals are more important than the collectivity's (Lopez et al., 1999). The ethnic make-up of New Mexico's population is 51 percent European-American Anglos, 39 percent Hispanics, and 9 percent Native Americans. People with more collectivistic cultures (for example, many Hispanics and Native Americans) make up a considerable share of the state's population. Is collectivism a barrier to individual entrepreneurship?

One example of a spin-off company from a federal R&D laboratory is Beta Corporation International, a minority-owned environmental, engineering, and management consulting company founded by Dr. Evaristo J. Bonano. He was born in Puerto Rico, earned his Bachelor of Science degree in chemical engineering from the University of Puerto Rico in 1975, and completed his Master's and Ph.D. degrees from Clark University in 1980. After employment for several years at Xerox Corporation, Bonano moved to New Mexico to work for Sandia National Laboratories. At SNL he conducted R&D on nuclear waste clean-up and other environmental problems. This research experience provided Bonano with the technology and business contacts to start his own company in 1992. Beta's original market niche was environmental risk assessment, with an emphasis on radioactive waste disposal. Bonano's ethnic background is a special advantage in that Spanish is his native tongue, and his bilingual fluency is beneficial in Beta's business projects in Latin America and Spain. Computer software for environmental engineering gradually became Betas's core technology. By mid-1999 Beta had 50 employees, and was operating in a dozen countries.

We conclude that collectivistic cultural values do not seem to be a strong deterrent to launching a high technology spin-off, and may provide certain advantages, such as when the collectivity (such as family members) provides capital.

TECHNOLOGY TRANSFER FROM UNIVERSITY-BASED RESEARCH CENTERS

A *research center* is a university-based organization whose purpose is to conduct scholarly investigations of an interdisciplinary nature, usually with financial support from private companies and other organizations outside the university (Rogers et al., 1999). So a university-based research center is a *boundary-spanner*, defined as a unit that exchanges information between an organization and its environment. Most research centers conduct multidisciplinary research drawing on scientific expertise from two or more academic disciplines.

In recent years the University of New Mexico has risen through the ranks of U.S. research universities in terms of its total amount of external research funding. Some 85 percent of this research (as measured by funding) is conducted by the 55 research centers at the university (the reminder is conducted by principal investigators in their academic departments). UNM pursued an aggressive policy of launching multidisciplinary research centers, especially in the early 1990s, in order to expand its functioning as a research university.

One example of UNM's many research centers is the Center for High-Technology Materials (CHTM), which was initiated by the State of New Mexico in 1983 as one of five centers of technical excellence. The original mission of CHTM was to conduct research on optoelectronics, specifically photonic-type applications and diode laser fabrications. After CHTM became a SEMATECH Center of Excellence in 1988, it devoted increasing research attention to semiconductor materials. CHTM is one of the largest research centers at UNM, with 91 employees including faculty, undergraduate and graduate students, and staff. CHTM's annual budget is about $6.5 million. CHTM funds half of the total number of research assistantships in the Department of Electrical Engineering and Computer Engineering at UNM, as well as several research assistantships in the UNM Department of Physics. This research center is located in its new building on the UNM Science and Technology Campus. Six start-ups have spun out of CHTM (Steffensen et al., 1999).

Our study of UNM's 55 research centers showed that (1) the director's role is particularly important in a university-based research center, (2) most research centers recognize technology transfer as one part of their mission, and (3) the main means of technology transfer reported by research centers are scientific journal articles, but such publications are not very effective in conveying research findings to nonscientist audiences (Rogers et al., 1999). We identified 19 spin-off companies from 6 of the 55 research centers (Rogers et al., 1999). Five or six of the 55 research centers, characterized by large budgets and conducting multidisciplinary research in engineering or the life sciences, were most active in invention disclosures, patents, and technology licensing.

TECHNOLOGY TRANSFER FROM RESEARCH UNIVERSITIES

A *research university* is one whose main purpose is (1) to conduct research, and (2) to train graduate students in how to conduct research. The first research universities were developed in Germany, like Gottingen (in 1737) and the University of Berlin (in 1810). The idea of the research university spread to the United States, first to Johns Hopkins University (in 1876) and to Clark University (in 1890), and then to Stanford University (in 1891), and the University of Chicago (in 1892). Today, several hundred U.S. universities are considered research universities.

Research universities in the United States play an increasingly important role in technology transfer, and are generally considered to be relatively more effective in transferring technology than are federal R&D laboratories. The Bayh-Dole Act of 1980 delegated the responsibility for the transfer of technology resulting from federally funded research at universities from the federal government to the universities. University offices of technology licensing were created and became important gatekeepers and boundary-spanners in the technology transfer process. Today, almost all U.S. research universities have an office of technology licensing, which typically earns technology licensing royalties for the university. However, at most of the 131 research universities responding to the annual survey conducted by the Association of University Technology Managers (AUTM), the office of technology licensing is relatively small, with only two or three professional staff members (Massing, 1998).

The rapid spread of offices of technology licensing in the 1980s and 1990s was encouraged by (1) the Bayh-Dole Act, which gave the intellectual property rights for technologies from federally funded research to universities, (2) the growing importance of life science research (especially in biotechnology) in creating patentable technologies, and (3) the attraction of having a "big winner" technology that will earn millions of dollars. Examples of such big winners are the $160 million that Michigan State University has earned from two cancer-related inventions, cisplatin and carboplatin (Blumenstyk, 1999), the $37 million that the University of Florida has earned from the sports drink Gatorade, the $27 million that Iowa State University has been paid for the fax algorithm, and the $143 million earned by Stanford University for the recombinant DNA gene-splicing patent (Odza, 1996). A "big winner" can dominate the total technology royalties at a research university; for example, $18 million of Michigan State University's $18.3 technology royalties in fiscal year 1998 came from the two cancer-related drugs (Urbisch, 1999). Pursuit of a "big winner" technology provided one motivation for the rapid diffusion of university offices of technology licensing, and, more generally, for the movement of U.S. universities toward academic capitalism,[3] which is also indicated by a university having a research foundation, a technology incubator for start-ups, a venture capital fund, a research park, and for taking an equity position in its start-ups.

The nature of technology transfer from research universities in the United States is a process through which (1) research expenditures, (2) lead to research activities, (3) that lead to invention disclosures, (4) that lead to patents applied for and granted, (6) that lead to active technology licenses, (7) which lead to technology licenses capable of generating income, (8) which lead to technology royalties and to start-ups, and (9) thus to jobs and wealth creation (Figure 14.1).

Figure 14.1
The Process of Technology Transfer from a Research University

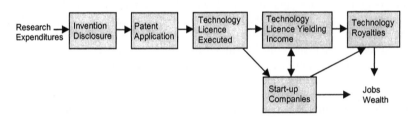

During FY1997, technology licensing offices at 132 U.S. research universities were issued 2,239 patents, executed 2,707 new technology licenses, had 258 start-up companies, and earned a total gross income of $483 million (Massing, 1998). AUTM estimated that $28.7 billion of U.S. economic activity, supporting 245,930 jobs, could be attributed to academic licensing activity in FY 1997 (Massing, 1998). University offices of technology licensing are important gatekeepers and boundary-spanners in the technology transfer process through which university research, funded at $19.9 billion in FY1997, is communicated to potential users, mainly private companies. From FY1996 to FY1997, most of the above indicators of technology transfer from U.S. research universities increased by 15 to 30 percent.

The Stanford University Office of Technology Licensing (OTL) earned an income of $52 million from technology licensing in 1997, which represented 13 percent of the university's total research funding. The OTL staff of 25 professionals handled 248 invention disclosures, filed 185 patents, and managed 272 licensed technologies yielding income in 1997, and over 1,044 active technology licenses (Massing, 1998; Sandelin, 1994). The mission of OTL "is to promote the transfer of Stanford technology for society's use and benefit while generating unrestricted income to support research and education."

MIT's office of technology licensing, with a staff of 27, had 360 invention disclosures, filed 200 new patents, was issued 134 patents, had 17 start-up companies, and earned $21.2 million in technology license income (Massing, 1998). MIT's 205 active patent licenses as of 1993 were associated with almost $1 billion of investment and created 2,000 jobs (Pressman et al., 1995). Spin-off companies from MIT accounted for only 35 percent of technology licenses, yet created 77 percent of the induced investment and 70 percent of the employment. Again, we see the importance of spin-offs as a mechanism of technology transfer.

In previous research, scholars used a number of different indicators to measure different aspects of technology transfer effectiveness (for example, Bozeman, 1994; Geisler and Clements, 1995; Muir, 1993; O'Keefe, 1982; Sandelin, 1994; Spann, Adams, and Souder, 1993, 1995; Tornatzky et al., 1995; Trune, 1996). We constructed a composite measure of technology transfer effectiveness for U.S. research universities based on the six steps in the technology transfer process (see Figure 14.1). This measure equally weights six indicators of technology transfer effectiveness: (1) the number of invention disclosures, (2) the number of U.S. patent applications filed, (3) the number of technology licenses and options executed, (4) the number of technology licenses and options yielding income, (5) the number of start-up companies spun-out of the university (based on a technology licensed by the university's office of technology licensing), and (6) the total amount of technology licensing royalties earned per year.

According to their technology transfer effectiveness scores, the University of California System, Stanford University, and MIT are among the 131 U.S. research universities with the highest technology transfer effectiveness scores. Another research university, with a technology licensing office staff of only one half-time person, might have only a dozen invention disclosures, a couple of patents and technology licenses, no spin-offs, and earn licensing royalties of $20,000 in FY1997. Why are some research universities much more effective in technology transfer activities than are others? Research universities that are relatively more effective in technology transfer are characterized by (1) more research resources, such as the number of faculty, student enrollment, and R&D expenditures, and (2) a stronger commitment to technology transfer, indicated by the support of university administrators, the number of staff members in the office of technology licensing, etc. (Rogers et al., 1999).

Many research universities are becoming growth engines for regional economic development through the technology transfer process (DeVol, 1999).

The University of New Mexico ranks 88th among the 131 research universities in the United States in technology transfer effectiveness. In the mid-1990s the university established a Science and Technology Corporation (1) to manage real estate and technology transfer activities connected with the Technology Park, and (2) to oversee the university's office of technology licensing, which became energized in the late 1990s. The university is thus involved in facilitating technology transfer such as through incubators, the research park, and so on. One role in this technology transfer process is provided by the university's office of technology licensing.

ENCOURAGING TECHNOLOGY TRANSFER IN NEW MEXICO

Although New Mexico is located in a relatively remote part of the United States and does not have adequate natural resources, population, or good per capita income to attract certain large businesses, the state ranks first in per capita funding received from the federal government. On the other hand, two large national R&D laboratories, the University of New Mexico, and numerous spin-offs create a technology-rich environment in northern New Mexico. The state is also an entrepreneur-friendly system. The Business Technology Group coordinates several incubators in Albuquerque, including the Albuquerque Technology Incubator and the Lovelace Research Institute's Incubator. The Technology Ventures Corporation, five venture capital companies, and other support organizations also help entrepreneurs in the daunting process of starting a new business and in attracting venture capital.

Technology transfer is an important mission of all 700 federal R&D laboratories in the United States in the post-Cold War era. Both Sandia National Laboratories and Los Alamos National Laboratory carry out technology transfer through their offices of technology commercialization. Both have an Entrepreneurship Program that encourages researchers to start up a new business while on leave from their laboratory position for two or three years (without pay), and with the option to return to employment at their laboratory.

The Technology Ventures Corporation was founded as a nonprofit organization in 1993 by the Martin Marietta Corporation, as part of its contract to manage Sandia National Laboratories (this aerospace company later merged with Lockheed). Lockheed Martin at present funds TVC at about $1 million per year. The mission of TVC is to identify technologies with commercial potential (especially from SNL), develop business capabilities, and seek venture capital for starting-up high tech companies. TVC is a nonprofit organization that takes no fees or joint ownership in the new companies that it helps start.

The typical annual process conducted by TVC for assisting spin-off companies is (1) to accept applications, including a business plan, from candidate spin-off companies in November of each year, (2) to select about a dozen spin-offs by mid-January, (3) to form an advisory group for each spin-off company, consisting of a management specialist, a venture capitalist, a marketing expert, and a TVC employee who assist the spin-off's entrepreneurs in sharpening their business plan, and (4) to conduct the New Mexico Equity

Symposium in mid-May in Albuquerque, attended by a number of venture capitalists. Each year, about 20 to 30 percent of the dozen new spin-off companies are successful in obtaining venture funding through TVC's activities.

After five years of operation, TVC estimated that it brought $134 million in investment to the state of New Mexico, and created 32 spin-offs and over 1,270 jobs (TVC, 1998). TVC is one reason for the increasing rate of technology transfer through spin-offs in New Mexico.

An example of a successful spin-off that was facilitated in the start-up process by TVC is EMCOREwest. This company is located in the newly established Sandia Science and Technology Park in Albuquerque, and was launched in 1998 by Dr. Tom Brennan, general manager and vice president of EMCOREwest. Its core business is to manufacture more efficient solar cells for use in satellites and in other applications. Brennan has an MS degree in solid-state physics from the Stevens Institute of Technology. After working as a researcher at AT&T Bell Laboratories from 1980 to 1984, and at Bell Communication Research for two years (1984-86), Brennan moved to Sandia National Laboratories, where he worked from 1986 to 1996.

Brennan requested a work assignment in the Small Business Development Office at Sandia National Laboratories for one year in order to gain relevant experience. He started MODE (*Mi*cro *O*ptical *De*vices), a laser company, in 1995, now a division of EMCORE Corporation (in New Jersey). The venture capital for MODE was provided by Arch Venture Corporation, which obtained part of its funding from the New Mexico Investment Corporation. Brennan used the same crystal material (that he had utilized at MODE) for photovoltaic cells of greater efficiency in converting sunlight to electricity. Brennan sold his ownership of MODE to the EMCORE Corporation for $19 million, and started EMCOREwest in 1996. EMCOREwest has 40 employees and is projected to expand to 400 employees in its second year. Brennan insisted in his negotiations with the EMCORE Corporation that EMCOREwest should remain in Albuquerque, in order to neighbor with Sandia National Laboratory.

A vision of creating a technopolis in New Mexico has gradually emerged in the late 1990s, and appropriate organizations and programs have arisen to facilitate technology transfer. Numerous high technology spin-offs from SNL and LANL and the University of New Mexico occur in Northern New Mexico, about 20 to 30 annually in recent years. Eventually, one of these high-tech spin-offs may become a "home run" and its entrepreneur will serve as a role-model for business success, perhaps similar to the role of Michael Dell in Austin, Texas.

CONCLUSIONS

We conclude with the following lessons learned about technology transfer, drawn from research in New Mexico:

1. *Scientific journal articles are a relatively ineffective mechanism for technology transfer, although articles are one of the main technology transfer activities of scientists.*
2. *Spin-offs are a particularly effective means of technology transfer, leading to job and wealth creation.* The rate of such start-ups in a region is relatively slow at first, but then, after a critical mass is reached, becomes self-sustaining and increases exponentially. This critical mass has not yet happened in New Mexico, but may lie in the decade ahead.
3. *The availability of ample technology in a region is a necessary but insufficient factor in the development of a technopolis.* Much of the technology from federal weapons laboratories like SNL and LANL is defense-related and thus is difficult to commercialize.
4. *Technology-transfer-facilitating organizations, and the favorable entrepreneurial leave policies of federal R&D laboratories like SNL and LANL are speeding up the process of getting to critical mass in the growth of high tech spin-offs.* Existence of spin-off facilitating organizations, such as the Albuquerque Technology Incubator, located in the university's Technology Park, the Lovelace Research Institute Incubator, the Business Technology Group, and TVC, help provide important assistance to entrepreneurs in launching spin-offs.

The early beginnings of a technopolis are getting under way in Northern New Mexico, but another decade may be required to reach the take-off point in this process. Meanwhile, New Mexico provides a useful laboratory in which to gain understandings of the technology transfer process.

ACKNOWLEDGMENTS

The authors express their thanks to the Mitsubishi International Corporation, San Francisco, for supporting the research on technology transfer. The chapter was originally presented at the International Conference on Technology Policy and Innovation, August 30-September 2, 1999, in Austin, Texas.

NOTES

1. Another reason for the agglomeration of spin-offs is that venture capital does not travel far, due to the need for the venture capitalist to remain in almost daily contact with the spin-offs in which the venture capitalist has invested.
2. Many of the high tech spin-offs of this study, while headquartered in Albuquerque, had "virtual employees" located at a great distance but who remain in contact with their co-workers and supervisors in Albuquerque by means of e-mail and other interactive communication technologies. For example, ATIP (Asia Technology Information Program) has nine employees at its Albuquerque headquarters, 20 or so in Tokyo, and a dozen more at scattered locations in Asia and Europe, all connected by e-mail. Permacharge, headquartered in Rio Rancho, a suburb of Albuquerque, recently hired a vice-president for marketing who lives in Milwaukee, in order to be closer to Permacharge's market; he stays in daily contact with the president of Permacharge by e-mail, telephone, and fax. MUSE Technologies, a spin-off from Sandia National

Laboratories in 1995, with 50 employees in Albuquerque, also has virtual employees in two other cities, in order to be closer to MUSE's customers.

3. *Academic capitalism* is defined as the degree to which a research university becomes involved in the transfer of university-conducted research into commercialized products and services.

REFERENCES

Blumenstyk, G., 1999. How one university pursued profit from science—and won. *Chronicle of Higher Education*, February 12.

Bozeman, B., 1994. Evaluating government technology transfer: Early impacts of the cooperative technology paradigm, *Political Studies Journal* 22(2), 322-337.

Carayannis, E.G., Rogers, E.M., Kurihara, K., and Allbritton, M.M., 1998. High-technology spin-offs from government R&D laboratories and research universities. *Technovation* 18(1), 1-11.

Dearing, J.W., and Rogers, E.M., 1990. Japan: Tsukuba Science City. In F. Williams and D.V. Gibson (eds.), *Technology Transfer*. Newbury Park, CA: Sage.

DeVol, R.C., 1999. *America's High-Tech Economy: Growth, Development, and Risk for Metropolitan Areas*. Santa Monica, CA: Miliken Institute. Report.

Eveland, J.D., 1986. Diffusion, technology transfer, and implementation. *Knowledge* 8(2), 303-322.

Geisler, E., and Clements, C., 1995. Commercialization of technology from federal laboratories: The effects of barriers, incentives, and the role of internal entrepreneurship. Whitewater: University of Wisconsin at Whitewater, Report to the National Science Foundation.

Gibson, D.V., and Rogers, E.M., 1994. *R&D Collaboration on Trial: The Microelectronics and Computer Technology Consortium*. Boston: Harvard Business School Press.

Licensing Executive Society of U.S.A. and Canada, 1995. *The basics of licensing*. Alexandria, VA.

Lopez, A.A., Pedro, R.F., and Rogers, E.M., 1999. When tradition meets technology: Collectivistic versus individualistic cultures and high-tech spin-off companies. Paper presented at the Sixteenth Annual Intercultural Communication Conference. University of Miami, Coral Gables, FL.

Massing, D.E., 1998. *AUTM Licensing Survey: Fiscal Year 1997*. Norwalk, CT: Association of University Technology Managers.

Muir, A.E., 1993. Technology transfer office performance index. *Journal of the Association of University Technology Managers* 5, 61-74.

Nieves, E., 2000. Many in Silicon Valley cannot afford housing, earn $50,000 a year. *New York Times*, February 20, p. 16.

Odza, M., 1996. Big winners in university tech transfer: And the winners are.... *Technology Access Report* 9(4), 1-4.

O'Keefe, T.G., 1982. Evaluating technology transfer: Some problems and solutions. *Journal of Technology Transfer* 6(2).

Pressman, L., Guterman, S.K., Geist, D.E., and Nelsen, L.L., 1995. Re-production investment and jobs induced by MIT exclusive patent licenses: A preliminary model to measure the economic impact of university licensing. *Journal of the Association of University Technology Managers* 7, 49-82.

Rogers, E.M., 1995. *Diffusion of Innovations*, Fourth Edition. New York: Free Press.

Rogers, E.M., Carayannis, E.G., Kurihara, K., and Allbritton, M.M., 1998. Cooperative Research and Development Agreements (CRADAs) as technology transfer mechanisms. *R&D Management* 28(2), 1-10.

Rogers, E.M., Hall, B.J, Hashimoto, M., Steffensen, M., Speakman, K.L., and Timko, M.K. 1999. Technology transfer from university-based research centers: The University of New Mexico experience. *Journal of Higher Education* 70(6), 687-705.

Rogers, E.M., and Steffensen, M., 1999. Spin-offs. In R.C. Dorf (ed.), *Handbook of Technology Management*. Boca Raton, FL: CRC Press and IEEE Press, pp. I-45-I-49.

Rogers, E.M., and Steinfatt, T.M., 1999. *Intercultural Communication*. Prospect Heights, IL: Waveland Press.

Rogers, E.M., Yin, J., and Hoffman, J., 1999. Technology transfer from U.S. research universities. Unpublished paper. Albuquerque: University of New Mexico, Department of Communication and Journalism.

Sandelin, J., 1994. Knowledge transfers through patenting and licensing. Stanford, CA: Stanford University, Office of Technology Licensing, Unpublished paper.

Singhal, A., and Rogers, E.M., 2000. *India's communication revolution: From bullock carts to cyber marts*. New Delhi: Sage/India.

Slaughter, S., and Leslie, L.L., 1997. *Academic capitalism: Politics, policies and the entrepreneurial university*. Baltimore: Johns Hopkins University Press.

Spann, M.S., Adams, M., and Souder, W.E., 1993. Improving Federal technology commercialization: Some recommendations from a field study. *Technology Transfer* 17, 63-74.

Spann, M.S., Adams, M., and Souder, W.E., 1995. Measures of technology transfer effectiveness: Key dimensions and differences in their use by sponsors, developers, and adopters. *IEEE Transactions on Engineering Management* 42, 19-29.

Steffensen, M., Rogers, E.M., and Speakman, K., 1999. Spin-offs from research centers at a research university. *Journal of Business Venturing* 15, 93-111.

Technology Ventures Corporation (TVC), 1998. *Report*. New Mexico Equity Capital Symposium. Albuquerque.

Tornatzky, L.G., Wagaman, P.G., and Casson, L., 1995. Benchmarking university-industry technology transfer in the South: 1993-1994 data. Research Triangle, NC, Southern Technology Council, Report to the National Science Foundation.

Trune, D.R., 1996. Comparative measures of university licensing activities. *Journal of the Association of University Technology Managers* 8, 63-106.

Urbisch, F., 1999. Personal interview. East Lansing: Michigan State University, Office of Intellectual Property, February 8.

15

The Global Regime for Intellectual Property Rights

Duane Windsor

INTRODUCTION

The present global regime for the protection of intellectual property rights was largely established by and is largely enforced by the advanced industrial economies. Certain aspects of intellectual property rights protection can arguably retard increases in global economic welfare, and certain aspects of protection arguably involve relatively high social costs for relatively infeasible enforcement efforts. These issues are most important in matters of information and knowledge as distinct from artistic performance and economic production. Because much of the market value of intellectual property is embedded into physical products or human services, it is difficult to disentangle rights and consequences. New forms of compensation for certain kinds of innovation—or their uses—may need to be considered. It is one thing to prevent direct competition through imitation (as in selling pirated software code); it is another thing to prevent someone else from making effective use of knowledge, even though that use involves what one may label partial piracy leading to indirect competition. An individual should not purchase a videotape and then charge admission fees for viewing a copy. But efforts to prevent individuals from making personal copies from broadcasts would seem relatively costly compared to any likely consequences of such personal copying (unless technology can be "locked" against copying). Then how is posting pirated software code on the World Wide Web different?

There is in place a collaborative global policy regime for registration and protection of intellectual property rights of various types that, at a minimum, provides strong moral authority (see Frederick, 1991) to the view that such rights should be fully protected and fully exploited by their owners. Protection is, however, a matter of national laws and enforcement. National governments must both adhere to the international regime and enforce that regime domestically. National adhesion to this collaborative global policy regime is accomplished partly through moral suasion and partly through the implicit threat of economic retaliation. The key issue is whether national exceptions are warranted and if so on what rationales.

The global policy regime is defined in principle by the formally coordinated efforts of two international organizations headquartered at Geneva, Switzerland: the World Intellectual Property Organization (WIPO), a UN agency established in 1967; and the World Trade Organization (WTO), the broadening (effective January 1, 1995) of the 1947 General Agreement on Tariffs and Trade (GATT) trade liberalization process to include in addition to physical goods both services of all types and intellectual properties of all types. As of July 1998, WTO had 132 members and WIPO had 171 members (Joint WTO-WIPO Press Release, July 21, 1998). The two intergovernmental organizations concluded an agreement on cooperation in force on January 1, 1996 (TRIPS-VI, "Agreement Between the World Intellectual Property Organization and the World Trade Organization"). WIPO is the institutional secretariat for the Paris Convention (1883, 1967) governing industrial patents; the Berne Convention (1886, 1971) for copyright and artistic performance (added 1961) and later computer programs and data bases; the Hague Agreement (1925) for industrial designs; and the Madrid System (1891) for marks. An integrated circuits agreement was added in 1989. WIPO established an Arbitration and Mediation Center in 1994.

Although the WIPO-WTO system is well established, there remain substantive questions about whether this system is the most appropriate global policy regime for intellectual property rights (Gadbaw and Richards, 1988; Howell, 1990; Jussawalla, 1992). The basic conception is one of a system ideally encompassing all economically significant forms of intellectual property rights, although certain kinds of exceptions, whether global or by member countries, can be identified. The essential issue most commonly articulated against this global protection system involves its effects on the developing areas of the world. The heart of the matter is, nevertheless, how future innovation will work.

The WIPO-WTO system expects in principle that all countries will protect all intellectual property rights. At least some developing nations adhere to the view that certain kinds of property rights should be less strictly enforced (or not enforced) where identifiably a means of accelerating economic development. Computer software and industrial designs are practical examples. (It is important to distinguish carefully among various types of intellectual property. Marks are not as readily subject to this criticism, since copying a mark would generally be both pure business imitation and falsification of information presented to consumers.) Such relaxation in enforcement is a form of concession, granted on twin bases that (1) faster economic development of developing areas will reward the advanced industrial countries, and (2) the advanced industrial countries have moral obligations to the developing areas, in any case. In this view, intellectual property (that is, knowledge of practical worth) developed in the advanced and rich countries comprising the Organization for Economic Cooperation and Development (OECD)—for practical purposes, the European Union (EU) and the North American Free Trade Area (NAFTA) with the addition of Australia, Japan, and New Zealand—should be shared with the developing countries at less than what the owners could hypothetically charge. On this view, knowledge is a common resource of humanity, and "high" prices for such knowledge arguably deter economic development.

This issue is arguably of broader concern, since it would also be applicable—in lesser degree—within the OECD countries themselves. (Some OECD countries are less advanced and wealthy than others.) A suggested solution (Jussawalla, 1992) is what amounts to a fixed licensing payment, with the marginal cost to specific users being essentially zero (i.e., free). This solution corresponds roughly to the present practice of site licenses for software (so long as the site license amounts to a lower price per user, so that volume discounts are granted).

In 1986 the United States may have lost some $23.8 billion in intellectual property values through deficiencies in protection, amounting to some 2.5% of worldwide sales of intellectual property (Jussawalla, 1992: 4). The figure approximated 15% of the U.S. trade deficit (Richards, 1988: 93). Some 2% of U.S. employment and 5% of U.S. gross national product (GNP) may be tied to international trade in intellectual property (Jussawalla, 1992: 4). While this specific information is now dated and precedes the WTO, one may presume that the nominal values rise with increases in world trade and investment flows. In any case, enforcement effort costing half of the reliably captured value would be a breakeven strategy—with no social value gained. The "profitability" of the enforcement effort must be reasonably dramatic, in the sense that enforcement should be a relatively low proportion of the value captured.

The remainder of this chapter proceeds in three main sections. The first section explains the concept of an international policy regime and the theory of how such regimes develop or evolve. The nature of intellectual property rights and why such rights should be defended are also examined. The second section details the global policy regime for intellectual property rights defined by the WIPO-WTO system. The third section discusses substantive issues about the WIPO-WTO system and proposals for its modification. A brief concluding section summarizes the findings and their implications.

THE CONCEPT OF AN INTERNATIONAL POLICY REGIME

The stated policy objective of the World Trade Organization is promotion of freer trade in the world economy (Ruggiero, 1997a). Ruggiero (until recently the WTO director-general) characterized the postwar development of the world economy as occurring in three sequential phases: (1) an "international economy" phase (1945-75) of "interlinked but still predominantly national economies"; (2) a "globalized economy" phase (1970s on) marked by rapid increases in information technologies and communications and systematic reductions in trade barriers resulting in foreign direct investment (FDI) flows greatly exceeding growing trade; and subsequently (3) a more truly "borderless economy" now detectable (1990s), at least for key sectors, in digital technologies and communications networks. This borderless economy, or "virtual" world market, is that built so far around information flows through the Internet, computerized financial markets, E-mail, telephone banking, and electronic data interchange. A transatlantic telephone call costs (i.e., "price") 1.5% of the cost (price) 60 years ago. The cost (price) of computing power has fallen by 100% since 1960. (Cost and price are not the same.) An important implication of the change is that international "trade" in services can occur without physical movement of people.

In addition to describing the breakdown of differences due to geography, time, and borders and the rise of information to be a critical resource and a main driver of world economic integration, Ruggiero emphasizes "the borderless economy's potential to equalize relations between countries and regions" through affording greater equality of opportunity (that is, to knowledge investors) as well as improvement of markets toward greater perfection (i.e., information efficiency) characterized by Bill Gates of Microsoft as "friction free capitalism." Ruggiero predicts "a significant shift in economic power towards the South and the East." Trade liberalization and technological progress are linked together in this scenario. Hence, there should be a free trade zone on the Internet (a proposal made by President Clinton), as well as free trade in computer products (Ruggiero, 1997b) and financial services (Ruggiero, 1997c).

Professor John Jackson (University of Michigan) has characterized various international arrangements as comprising a form of "constitution" for an integrated global economy (cited by Ruggiero, 1998). This "constitution"—if such it be—is comprised of a number of reinforcing (and sometimes overlapping) international policy regimes (Preston and Windsor, 1997). Whether characterization as a "constitution" is reasonably appropriate or not, there is good reason to suppose that institutions and rules strongly affect the efficiency and growth of economics (see North, 1990; Sherwood, 1990). Shoven (1988: 51) argues that "the U.S. legal system is particularly antiinnovation which accounts for part of the difficulty that we have in being competitive in today's worldwide marketplace." It is thus possible to think of an economic rather than a political constitution at work (Windsor, 1987). One may reasonably proceed from the premise that the goal or purpose of protection policy is, as posited at a 1987 conference on Intellectual Property Rights and Capital Formation in the Next Decade sponsored by the American Council for Capital Formation and other participating U.S. organizations, to be "in the long-term best interests of the United States and its trading partners" (Walker and Bloomfield, 1988: xii). This premise posits a win-win result in the long term arising from collaboration.

Linkages in the increasingly interdependent global economy occur through three key channels: trade and investment activities, multinational enterprises (embedding here the notion of information flows, which occur through organizational channels of some type), and international policy regimes (Preston and Windsor, 1997: 7). Panic (1988: 283) argues that international relationships depend on either formal agreement concerning or tacit acceptance of "a mutually satisfactory code of behavior" involving "the acceptance of certain obligations and rules of behavior."

One way of conceptualizing a policy regime is that it is whatever escape from "prisoner's dilemma" (a lose-lose outcome for any two or more parties) actually obtains. (And no escape may come into existence, even temporarily.) Where such escape evolves, "A regime is composed of sets of explicit or implicit principles, norms, rules and decision-making procedures around which actor expectations converge in a given area of international relations" (Krasner, 1983: 2). Such regimes may come into effect in various ways for various reasons, so that reciprocity (while desirable) is not necessarily the driving consideration in all regimes. (British dominance of international trade was an important consideration in the gold standard.) A regime can be either structural (i.e., institutionalized) or purely functional (i.e., in existence of practical necessity).

Structure may not lead on to function (the International Labour Organization at Geneva does not constitute a functioning global labor regime); function may not require structure (the gold standard of the 19th century operated without formal international agreement). But to some extent in today's complex global economy, much of the functioning is being addressed through formal international institutions. "It is important to emphasize that a regime consists primarily of functional and behavioral relationships and that formal organizations and agreements are subsidiary or, occasionally, entirely absent" (Preston and Windsor, 1997: 16). Although reciprocity may not always be present, it is important to retain a sense of the moral (i.e., the normative) underpinnings of economic interactions: "Markets are probably the social arrangements most dependent on normative underpinnings" (Kratochwil, 1989: 12).

Regimes often reflect collaborative arrangements (see Gray, 1989; Wood and Gray, 1991). However, relatively little is known about how collaboration efforts function. One view is that international policy regimes are like public (or club) goods provided without formal international government (Kindleberger, 1986). A public good is one that, once supplied, can be consumed by everyone without paying a fee. As a result, government must collect taxes by threat of force (although the citizens may see the desirability of public goods and good conduct); and a club must design some method for exclusion of nonpayers. Velasquez (1992) takes the view that an international enforcement agency is typically needed. There is likely a broader range of regimes without enforcement of this type, where such regimes reflect clear joint interests. Nevertheless, in patent and copyright protection, reciprocity is reinforced by the threat of economic retaliation.

Intellectual property rights are broadly definable classes of ideas, information, and knowledge possessing present or potential market values. Economic values are embedded in goods and services sold or rented to customers. For example, copyright is protection of a particular written work. Patent is protection of a particular process or product. Trade secrets are private knowledge (i.e., capabilities and information) secured against theft like any other private property. (By contrast, trademark is protection of brand equity, the assurance of product or service quality.) Information can be copyrighted or withheld. Knowledge is essentially a modern version of the traditional trade secret. It has never been possible to copyright, patent, or trademark an idea, as distinct from a specific product or process or brand equity. The purpose in protecting intellectual property from appropriation through competition is presumably to afford incentives promoting discovery and innovation that will in turn promote global economic welfare over time. Where such incentives do not exist, then presumably discovery and innovation, and hence global economic welfare, would be adversely affected. Lack of protection would result in more rapid imitation through counterfeiting and piracy. Protection of intellectual property rights, however, affords opportunities for appropriating economic rents above ordinary (i.e., competitive) profits.

International trade in an increasingly integrated global economy involves two distinct multilateral issues. One issue concerns reduction of various types of barriers to freer mobility of goods, services, capital, and people. (Labor mobility is a different matter outside regional arrangements like the European Union or the North American Free Trade Area, because it amounts to immigration.) The classical presumption is that freer mobility of resources tends to promote global economic welfare relative to some managed trade alternative. The other issue concerns protection of various property rights. There are two general types of property rights for present purposes. One type is inherited economic position (i.e., economic position carrying forward in time due to barriers to competition). Freer trade in agricultural goods is particularly difficult because of the political influence of farmers in various countries in resisting increased competition. The presumption for managed trade, however, must be that managed trade promotes global as well as local welfare under certain conditions. The other type of property right is a socially approved incentive to discovery and innovation. Enterprises must safeguard trade secrets as private information, and individuals must safeguard the value of efforts and unique attributes. A key consideration in modern business is that the source of economic rent is shifting from financial capital to human knowledge.

THE WIPO-WTO GLOBAL REGIME FOR INTELLECTUAL PROPERTY RIGHTS

The World Trade Organization arrangements reflect the tension between the two dimensions of the world economy: freer trade (and competition), and property rights protection (and monopoly power returns). WTO incorporated the eighth (Uruguay) GATT round on reduction of barriers to trade in manufactures and agricultural goods together with two new agreements concerning services and intellectual property. The General Agreement on Trade in Services (GATS) essentially extended barrier-reduction efforts to services, which of necessity require international movement of people and information. The Agreement on Trade-Related Aspects of Intellectual Property (TRIPS) was quite different, in that it ratified international collaboration through WIPO for the protection of intellectual property rights. An effort to reach an agreement on Trade-Related Investment Measures (TRIMS) was not successful in 1994 and had to be delayed to subsequent efforts, but this effort does not directly address investment in intellectual property.

The basic principles of the WTO trading system are: (1) nondiscrimination through granting "most-favored-nation" (MFN) status to all member countries, (2) continuous liberalization, (3) predictability, (4) reduction of unfair competition, and (5) more beneficial for less developed countries through more time to adjust, greater flexibility, and special privileges. "The WTO is sometimes described as a 'free trade' institution, but that is not entirely accurate. The system does allow tariffs and, in limited circumstances, other forms of protection. More accurately, it is a system of rules dedicated to open, fair and undistorted competition" (WTO, "About the WTO," <www.wto.org>).

TRIPS includes three main features: (1) minimum standards of protection to be provided by each member-country for areas of intellectual property covered by the agreement; (2) enforcement defined in terms of domestic procedures and remedies, so that right holders can effectively enforce rights; (3) dispute settlement procedures for handling disagreements between member countries. The basic agreements covered are the Paris Convention for the Protection of Industrial Property (1883, 1967), the Berne Convention for the Protection of Literary and Artistic Works (1886, 1971), the International (Rome) Convention for the Protection of Performers, Producers of Phonograms and Broadcasting Organizations (1961), and the 1989 Treaty on Intellectual Property in Respect of Integrated Circuits (IPIC Treaty).

TRIPS covers copyright and related rights, trademarks, geographical indications (appellations of origin), industrial designs, patents, integrated circuit layout-designs, and undisclosed information (trade secrets or know-how), while permitting governments to control anticompetitive practices in contractual licenses. Enforcement procedures address both domestic enforcement and border (i.e., import) measures. Copyright protection extends to expressions and not to ideas, procedures, methods of operation, or mathematical concepts per se. Computer programs, in either source or object code, are protected under copyright. Such protection extends for 50 years or more. Databases and other compilations of data or other material are likewise protected under copyright where selection or arrangement of contents constitutes intellectual creations, regardless of form. (Such protection does not extend to the data or material itself.) Performance and phonogram protection likewise extend at least 50 years, compared to 20 years for broadcasting organizations.

Geographical indications (appellations of origin) have essentially the character of trademarks, the object in both instances being to prevent misleading of the public as a form of unfair competition. Intellectual property protection is sometimes for the seller and sometimes for the buyer, but the underlying rationale is always that in the long term the consumers benefit. Diagnostic, therapeutic, and surgical methods for the treatment of humans or animals may be excluded from patentability. Similar exclusions for plants and animals and biological production processes other than micro-organisms and microbiological production processes must be replaced by some other system of protection.

"Members may provide limited exceptions to the exclusive rights conferred by a patent [minimally 20 years from filing date], provided that such exceptions do not unreasonably conflict with a normal exploitation of the patent and do not unreasonably prejudice the legitimate interests of the patent owner, taking account of the legitimate interests of third parties" (Article 30). The injunction considering third parties opens the door to exceptions on various grounds. "Compulsory licensing and government use without the authorization of the right holder are allowed, but are made subject to conditions aimed at protecting the legitimate interests of the right holder" (Article 31). Again, the door is opened to exceptions on various grounds. As will be discussed further below, the language in Articles 30 and 31 is consistent with a stakeholder reasoning framework for considering intellectual property rights.

TRIPS (effective January 1, 1995) incorporated the essential features of the existing World Intellectual Property Organization, a UN agency headquartered in Geneva, established by a 1967 convention (amended in 1979), which in turn incorporated the essential features of the preexisting Paris Convention (1883) for industrial property (inventions, trademarks, industrial designs, appellations of origin) and the Berne Convention (1886) for copyright (literary, musical, artistic, photographic, audiovisual property), including data bases and performance rights. The Patent Protection Treaty includes the Madrid System (1891) for trademarks and the Hague System (1925) for industrial designs. These conventions and treaties are incorporated in TRIPS as WTO minimum standards for national conduct. TRIPS includes integrated circuit layouts and "undisclosed information" (trade secrets and test data). TRIPS also specifies procedures for domestic enforcement and an international dispute resolution process.

In 1995 about 710,000 patents (i.e., registrations of inventions) were granted worldwide, with some 3.7 million in force at the end of the year (WIPO, "International Protection of Industrial Property," <www.wipo.int>). About 1 million marks (both registrations and renewals) were effected (not including some 22,660 international marks under the Madrid Agreement corresponding to 226,000 national registrations), and over 8 million were in force (not including 300,000 under the Madrid Agreement corresponding to 3 million national registrations). There were about 235,000 industrial designs effected (not including 5,613 under the Hague Agreement), with some 1.35 million registrations in force. Copyright covers literary works, musical works, choreographic works, artistic works, maps and technical drawings, photographic works, and audiovisual works—together with derivative works (translations, adaptations, collections, or compilations including databases), computer programs, and sometimes sound recordings, broadcasts, and typographical arrangements. Perhaps some 1 million books or titles, 5,000 films, and more than 3,000 million copies of phonograms are produced annually (WIPO, "International Protection of Copyright and Neighboring Rights," <www.wipo.int>).

GATS (for which there is a WTO Council for Trade in Services) provides legally enforceable rights to trade in all services, with periodic multilateral negotiations leading to continuous trade liberalization. By extension, GATS includes investment, since it covers all possible means of supplying a service including establishing a commercial presence in an export market. The three basic principles underlying GATS are: (1) all services are included except those involving exercise of governmental authority; (2) nondiscrimination with respect to national and foreign providers; and (3) the most-favored-nation principle must apply to all member countries. While no protection mechanisms may be applied to services, there are some exceptions afforded in GATS permitting government intervention. GATS covers international payments, financial services, telecommunication services, professional services, movement of natural persons (for temporary service provisions), and air and maritime transport services. Countries need to provide national treatment for foreigners only by specific commitment with exemptions allowed—unlike the general principle adopted in trade (GATT) and intellectual property (TRIPS). In 1997, WTO completed a global pact on telecommunications and financial services (Ruggiero, 1997c). There is a related effort within the International Organization for Standardization (ISO) to address harmonization of standards in services. The key sectors involved are tourism, banking, financial accounting, engineering consultancy, and education.

In March 1997, 40 countries agreed to implement the WTO Ministerial Declaration on Trade in Information Technology (ITA)—adopted December 1996—eliminating all customs duties on computer (hardware, software, semiconductors) and telecommunications products, scientific instruments, semiconductor manufacturing equipment, and related products (e.g., word processors, calculators, cash registers, ATM machines, and so on) but specifically excluding consumer electronic goods between July 1, 1997, and January 1, 2000. The 44 countries involved in the ITA II negotiations in 1998 accounted for 93% of world trade in information technology products (WTO, 1998b). It is important to note that "This accord, which covers nearly $600 billion in world trade, means lower prices for consumers and fewer barriers to the spread of technology that is so critical to the development of all our [WTO] members" (Ruggiero, 1997b). Electronic commerce ("E-commerce") may amount to $300 billion value in the year 2000, drawing on estimates that Internet users will increase from 5 million in 1991 to more than 300 million in the year 2000 (WTO, 1998c; Ruggiero, 1997a, places the estimate at 550 million users). A WTO study (WTO, 1998a) identified as key issues the legal and regulatory framework for Internet operation and the access of developing countries to both infrastructure and user skills. It is now necessary to reserve a unique Internet domain name by paying a registration fee.

SUBSTANTIVE ISSUES IN THE WIPO-WTO REGIME

When should exceptions exist for protection of intellectual property rights? One exception (and perhaps a pseudo-exception at that) is easy: an enterprise or individual sees a strategic advantage (i.e., a greater future economic opportunity) in reducing price on a property right. A second exception is more difficult, because it argues that the poverty of the consumer places a special moral obligation on the enterprise or individual to reduce price. A third exception concerns the possibility that reduction of price to certain types of consumers or even other producers will enhance global welfare through stimulation of other efforts. (The distinction from the second exception is that knowledge and information serve as intermediate rather than final goods.) A fourth exception concerns government as a purchaser (whether of intermediate or final goods). It is not clear that government should necessarily pay monopoly power prices as distinct from simple cost recovery. A fifth exception concerns social costs of enforcement. If enforcement costs fall on society at large, but benefits accrue largely to enterprises and individuals, there is a problem in justifying protection. The general case for enforcement is that the benefits accrue to society.

One example of these problems is that some of the existing copyright protections arguably stand in the way of university education (as distinct from research, although copyright protections sometimes happen in the latter as well). Education is the cultivation of the human intellect. There have been a number of lawsuits brought against abuse of copyright for teaching purposes (and no doubt there has been commercial abuse). Duplication companies might neglect copyright fees and permissions for the purpose of maximizing their own revenues. On the other hand, strict copyright protection compels professors to plan well in advance of classes and figure out how to obtain reimbursement for fees (typically from students in some manner). But are late-breaking news reports really the same issue? Must every student purchase a daily newspaper for educational purposes? How do any rules and procedures established in the advanced countries apply to universities and students in developing countries? Is there overall an insidious effect in reducing the free flow of ideas, information, and knowledge in the educational process. One issue bearing on such policy questions is that of the slippery slope: if X is allowed an exception, who else will adhere to the copyright protection? Nevertheless, some flexibility for the broader goals of intellectual capital development would seem perfectly reasonable. The social justification is the supply of a broader base of skilled people. Social welfare reflects a combination of private activities and social infrastructure.

The objective of domestic and international policy concerning intellectual property rights protection is not defense of owners' "rights" to profits per se, but rather the promotion of social and global welfare. "Protection of industrial property is not an end in itself: it is a means to encourage creative activity, industrialization, investment and honest trade. All this is designed to contribute to more safety and comfort, less poverty and more beauty, in the lives of men" (WIPO, "International Protection of Industrial Property," <www.wipo.int>).

This objective is then a strictly utilitarian one (i.e., one defined within a consequentialism framework), so that economic property rights (as distinct from human rights) are instruments rather than ends (as would be the case in a strictly teleological framework). The heart of the matter is neither law nor ethics, but rather choice of rational policy (Wilson, 1989: 60-61, distinguishes among the three approaches). There is a distinction between economic rights and moral rights. The former are rights to compensation. The latter are rights to recognition (of creative authorship) and protection of the creative form of the original work itself. (For example, neither books nor films should be mutilated.)

One should be careful to note that intellectual property rights involve both enterprises and individuals. There should be greater concern for the creative efforts of the latter than for the former, although these efforts may substantially overlap. In social cost-benefit analysis, there is a difficulty concerning the relationship between the majority (i.e., gainers) and the minority (i.e., losers). Strictly speaking, society overall gains where a majority gains even at the expense of a minority. The principle of eminent domain in the U.S. Constitution permits the majority to take private property for public use, where there is fair (i.e., market value) compensation. A property owner may prefer not to sell, or may prefer to receive a premium over market value, but these considerations are judged irrelevant under the principle (so that some loss may actually be imposed). There is a view that such "hypothetical compensation" (i.e., the majority can afford to compensate the minority but does not do so) is morally suspect (see Mishan, 1976: 390-393). However, even this view leaves open the possibility of defining market value. Markets may embed monopoly elements (the very essence of intellectual property protection), but social cost-benefit analysis theoretically proceeds on the basis of competitive market conditions (so that price approximates marginal cost).

A general approach to the problem would be to reduce price as income declines. Sellers (or renters) of products and services typically set one price designed to recover average cost and generate economic rent (price being dependent on fixed cost and predicted volume). The marginal cost of additional users is really very low. The problem, in this approach, arises when the additional users turn into competitors and begin selling similar products and services. But the nature of this problem is that it involves strategic restriction of the spread of knowledge in order to preserve trade secrets as the basis of economic rent generation. There is a social (and by extension global) trade-off between encouraging innovation and discouraging narrowing of the market. And a converse case can arise in which an innovation arises in the emerging or developing countries which then naturally want to sell such innovation, or its product and service consequences, to the advanced countries at the highest possible price.

Jussawalla argues two points concerning information technology. First, "a global marketplace of ideas" (1992: 1) will yield strong benefits; copyright monopolies tend to stifle competition and technical progress. Second, information technology makes it nearly "impossible to monitor and restrict the flow of information. ... particularly true of computer software" (114).

Jussawalla suggests replacing usage fees enforced by civil suits with lump-sum payments through licensing or government. The author grounds this argument in the short product life cycle of intellectual product. Copyright protection is based on mechanical printing press technology (42-43). Property rights protection in an information technology world will require encryption, which may or may not prove compatible with widespread market distribution and low-cost access.

Rational policy toward intellectual property rights protection turns on how one views the relationship between "static efficiency" (Mansfield, 1988: 12) and the sources of dynamic growth: "long-term economic growth ... has been due largely to technological change" (5-6). The social rate of return to innovation is very high. The chief characteristic of all types of "knowledge goods" is that they are "free collective goods" potentially benefiting all members of society. "New technological knowledge differs from most other goods in an important way: It cannot be used up. A person or firm can use an idea repeatedly without wearing it out; and the same idea can serve many users at the same time" (12). In general, a knowledge good involves very low marginal cost and should therefore be readily available. Pricing above this very low marginal cost will retard diffusion and use (12). "A view sometimes expressed in developing countries is that knowledge should be made available at minimal cost to everyone since it is a common property of all. Also, it is argued that, because the development of the relatively impoverished countries of the world is a goal that benefits everyone, the technology needed by these countries should be given to them at a low cost" (21). By the same token, such pricing will arguably tend to retard innovation due to inability to recover investment costs. Inability to appropriate returns from innovation means that the private rate of return is much lower than the social rate of return (8, 23). Innovation is good for society, but costly to innovators.

Mansfield (8-10) summarized information on speed of imitation through leakage. He concluded that trade secrets seem to persist longest in chemical processes and pharmaceuticals. By comparison, protection may be less effective and therefore important in other industries. Legal protection of innovation permits inventors to appropriate more returns than would otherwise occur. The key issue is whether lack of such protection would depress investment in innovation, and hence capital formation over the longer run. The answer turns on the incentive system expected to govern the behavior of inventors and innovators.

There is a widespread recognition that the developing countries may constitute a special case. Under TRIPS, together with other WTO agreements, developed countries were to be in conformance by January 1, 1996. Developing countries have a January 1, 2000, deadline for conformance. (Least developed, that is very poor, countries have until January 1, 2006.) In July 1998, WTO and WIPO agreed on a joint initiative to provide technical assistance in helping developing countries meet this deadline (Joint WTO-WIPO Press Release, July 21, 1998). The WTO High-Level Meeting for Least Developed Countries (October 1997) endorsed a trade assistance program and preferential market access measures by 19 developed and developing countries—burdening especially the European Union and the United States (WTO, 1997).

A key issue in intellectual property rights concerns the likelihood that innovations will occur in the advanced industrial economies and could be of value to the developing economies, which cannot afford to pay the market prices that would be commanded in the advanced economies. Under these specific conditions, some intellectual property rights may retard the global development process. A major barrier to world development and integration may be lack of low-cost access. At the 1988 Montreal GATT meetings, the developing countries argued against protection of intellectual property (Jussawalla, 1992: 57). Low-cost access to information should improve global economic welfare. Within WTO, developing countries have a longer period to phase in with special delays for countries not already providing patent protection for pharmaceuticals; and new plants and animals represent a particularly difficult problem. Medical methods are typically exempt from patent and copyright protection.

It has been argued that developing countries are net importers of technology and creative works, as was the United States in its early history (Costa, 1988: 61). The basic position of the developing countries has been expressed as follows: (1) "As we see it, a patent is not given with the sole object of protecting an invention. Instead, it is granted to establish an equitable legal basis between the inventor and the society at large, through which both sides exchange interests and responsibilities" (Costa, 1988: 60); (2) "In an unequal world, any attempt to make intellectual property norms uniform would lead, in practice, to perpetuating the world's uneven division of knowledge and information resources" (61). These views are bound up with a defense of national diversity (i.e., sovereignty) in grappling with how to balance these considerations. (Brazil was one of the 11 countries that created the 1882 Paris Convention for the Protection of Industrial Property [61]). A People's Republic of China view was expressed in GuiRu (1988).

One approach involves enterprises (and by extension, individuals) voluntarily giving away (or providing at very low cost) at least products embedding intellectual property rights, if not such rights themselves. It is increasingly common for software and Internet vendors to provide services for free. For example, Adobe provides free reader software by downloading (because it sells conversion software, and free reader software increases demand for its conversion product). Other software and Website companies can behave similarly. The objective is to bind the consumer to the company. (Similarly airlines provide points and upgrades, for example, to the same purpose.) Dell Computer has been offering free access (not including local telephone charges) to its dellnet.com service in several European companies. There are similar instances to be found in other industries (see Lincoln Electric, 1998; Merck, 1991).

CONCLUSIONS AND RECOMMENDATIONS

The criticisms of the WIPO-WTO regime covered above can be viewed as a variant of what is commonly labeled stakeholder management theory or stakeholder reasoning. The stakeholder framework evolved as an explicit critique or at least broadening of strict stockholder (or shareowner) value maximization doctrine (see Freeman, 1984). That doctrine holds that not only should the owner of an economically valuable property right exploit that right as fully as possible (within moral and legal constraints) in his or her self-interest, but further that such exploitation will advance social welfare. Just as capital should seek maximize returns, so should innovation (in its various forms). Stakeholder reasoning argues on a number of bases—Donaldson and Preston (1995) distinguish among descriptive, instrumental, and normative dimensions—that strict stockholder doctrine is inadequate for guidance of the firm and maximization of social welfare. Descriptively, the firm is comprised of various stakeholder constituencies, each of which is essential to success; instrumentally, the firm (i.e., its owners and managers) will prosper more by treating the other stakeholder constituencies as if they held "ownership" shares; normatively, the contributions of the various stakeholder constituencies constitute moral entitlements to such shares (in some manner). The essence of the stakeholder approach is that multiple types of stakeholders make different contributions to the success of the firm, and these contributions should be rewarded accordingly. Two of these stakeholder types are the national society and the local communities in which the firm is domiciled. Donaldson and Preston (1995) argue that the core of stakeholder reasoning is normative: moral entitlements to property rights based on contributions to the firm. A concrete illustration of the stakeholder approach is found in the recent calls by Drucker (1999) and Blair (1995) for the issuance of ownership rights to knowledge employees. The basic argument, which is outlined in Drucker and detailed in Blair, is that the key resource of the firm is shifting to knowledge employees (i.e., mental workers). If stakeholders are not properly rewarded, they will underinvest in the firm. (Blair adopts a broad conception of "investors-at-risk" such that all contributions to the firm constitute investments.) As a result, the firm's operations do not maximize social welfare.

This set of arguments has echoes in the debates over how to handle compensation for intellectual property rights. In a sense, knowledge can be viewed as a common set of resources on which all should be able to draw; and such broader drawing should in turn increase the common set of resources even more rapidly. The key difference is that, whereas in the stakeholder framework the stakeholders make contributions that cause the firm's success, in the intellectual property rights debate the matter concerns future success of mankind. The balancing act is between sufficient incentive to induce socially valuable innovation and the diffusion of such innovation leading on to additional innovations elsewhere. The line between the two is a delicate one. If Mansfield is correct, and social returns to innovation are very high, then interfering with economic incentives for innovation is risky. Even so, there appears to be a case for considering changes in pricing of access to at least certain kinds of knowledge. The key change would be from charge per use (as in buying or renting a product or service) to more of a licensing arrangement in certain cases. This chapter does not argue a general case for such a change in pricing. Rather, it points to the possibility that special exceptions (which already exist in intellectual property rights protection) may have wider ambit. It is clear that the standard or criterion for how to address the special cases is that of social welfare enhancement: the objective in intellectual property rights protection is less one of "rights" (with the exception that the "right" to reputational rewards for innovation should be strictly preserved—either Columbus made it to the New World first, or he did not) than of incentivization. Intellectual property rights— that is, rights to the economic rewards of the fruits of innovation—are instruments to social welfare, which is the goal.

REFERENCES

Blair, M. M. 1995, *Ownership and Control: Rethinking Corporate Governance for the Twenty-first Century.* Washington, DC: Brookings Institution.

Costa, M. E. C. 1988, A View From Brazil, in C.E. Walker and M.A. Bloomfield (eds.), *Intellectual Property Rights and Capital Formation in the Next Decade.* Lanham, MD: University Press of America, pp. 57-63.

Donaldson, T. & Preston, L. E. 1995, The Stakeholder Theory of the Corporation, *Academy of Management Review*, vol. 20, pp. 65-91.

Drucker, P. F. 1999, *Management Challenges for the 21st Century.* New York: HarperBusiness.

Frederick, W. C. 1991, The Moral Authority of Transnational Corporate Codes, *Journal of Business Ethics*, vol. 10, pp. 165-177.

Freeman, R. E. 1984, *Strategic Management: A Stakeholder Perspective.* Boston: Pitman.

Gadbaw, R. M. & Richards, T. J. 1988, *Intellectual Property Rights: Global Consensus, Global Conflict?* Boulder, CO: Westview Press.

Gray, B. 1989, *Collaborating: Finding Common Ground for Multi-Party Problems.* San Francisco: Jossey-Bass.

GuiRu, Q. 1988, A View From a Commercial Official of the People's Republic of China, in C.E. Walker and M.A. Bloomfield (eds.), *Intellectual Property Rights and Capital Formation in the Next Decade.* Lanham, MD: University Press of America, pp. 83-91.

Howell, D. J. 1990, *Intellectual Properties and the Protection of Fictional Characters: Copyright, Trademark, or Unfair Competition?* Westport, CT: Quorum Books.

Jussawalla, M. 1992, *The Economics of Intellectual Property in a World without Frontiers: A Study of Computer Software.* Westport, CT: Greenwood Press.

Kindleberger, C. P. 1986, International Public Goods without International Government, *American Economic Review*, vol. 76, pp. 1-13.

Krasner, S. D., ed. 1983, *International Regimes.* Ithaca, NY: Cornell University Press.

Kratochwil, F. V. 1989, *Rules, Norms and Decisions: On the Conditions of Practical and Legal Reasoning in International Relations and Domestic Affairs.* New York: Cambridge University Press.

Lincoln Electric: Venturing Abroad. 1998, prepared by J. O'Connell under supervision of C. A. Bartlett, Harvard Business School, case 9-398-095 (revised April 22, 1998), Boston.

Mansfield, E. 1988, Intellectual Property Rights, Technological Change, and Economic Growth, in C.E. Walker and M.A. Bloomfield (eds.), *Intellectual Property Rights and Capital Formation in the Next Decade.* Lanham, MD: University Press of America, pp. 3-26.

Merck & Co., Inc. 1991, prepared by D. Bollier and adapted by S. Weiss under supervision of K. O. Hanson, Harvard Business School cases 9-991-021/022/023/024 (A-D), Boston.

Mishan, E. J. 1976, *Cost-Benefit Analysis*, 2nd ed. New York: Praeger.

North, D. C. 1990, *Institutions, Institutional Change and Economic Performance*. Cambridge: Cambridge University Press.

Panic, M. 1988, *National Management of the International Economy*. New York: St. Martin's Press.

Preston, L. E. & Windsor, D. 1997, *The Rules of the Game in the Global Economy: Policy Regimes for International Business*, 2nd ed. Dordrecht, The Netherlands: Kluwer Academic Publishers.

Richards, T. J. 1988, Intellectual Property Rights: Reconciling Divergent Views, in C.E. Walker and M.A. Bloomfield (eds.), *Intellectual Property Rights and Capital Formation in the Next Decade*. Lanham, MD: University Press of America, pp. 93-98.

Ruggiero, R. 1997a, Charting the Trade Routes of the Future: Towards a Borderless Economy, address to the International Industrial Conference (IIC) in San Francisco (September 29). Geneva: WTO.

Ruggiero, R. 1997b, Launching of Free Trade in Computer Products to Benefit Everyday Life of Consumers and Companies, says Ruggiero, WTO Press Release (March 27), Geneva.

Ruggiero, R. 1997c, Statement by WTO Director-General Renato Ruggiero on the Agreement on Financial Services, (December 12), Geneva: WTO.

Ruggiero, R. 1998, WTO Denies Claims by Special Interests Linking Ruggiero to MAI [Multilateral Agreement on Investment], WTO Press Release (February 17) summarizing speech (January 16) at Chatham House, London. Geneva: WTO.

Sherwood, R. M. 1990, *Intellectual Property and Economic Development*. Boulder, CO: Westview Press.

Shoven, J. B. 1988, Intellectual Property Rights and Economic Growth, in C.E. Walker and M.A. Bloomfield (eds.), *Intellectual Property Rights and Capital Formation in the Next Decade*. Lanham, MD: University Press of America, pp. 46-52.

Velasquez, M. 1992, International Business, Morality, and the Common Good, *Business Ethics Quarterly*, vol. 2, pp. 27-40.

Walker, C. E. & Bloomfield, M. A., eds. 1988, *Intellectual Property Rights and Capital Formation in the Next Decade*. Lanham, MD: University Press of America.

Wilson, J. Q. 1989, Adam Smith on Business Ethics, *California Management Review*, vol. 32, pp. 59-72.

Windsor, D. 1987, Economic Constitutionalism: Madison, Marx, Buchanan, paper presented at the annual meeting of the American Political Science Association, Chicago.

Wood, D, J. & Gray, B. 1991, Toward a Comprehensive Theory of Collaboration, *Journal of Applied Behavioral Science*, vol. 27, pp. 139-162.

World Trade Organization. 1997, The High-Level Meeting for Least Developed Countries, WTO, 27-28 October 1997, WTO *Focus* (November).

World Trade Organization. 1998a, *Electronic Commerce and the Role of the WTO*. Geneva: WTO Publications.

World Trade Organization. 1998b, Participants Agree to Give Final Push to ITA II Talks. Geneva.

World Trade Organization. 1998c, Study from WTO Secretariat Highlights Potential Trade Gains from Electronic Commerce, WTO Press Release (March 13), Geneva.

16

Restructuring and Financing R&D: New Partnerships

Annamária Inzelt

INTRODUCTION

Recent developments in world economy have made knowledge generation, diffusion and use a global phenomenon, but his process creates many new opportunities and threats for less developed economies. All of us are responsible to strengthen opportunities and try to minimise threats. There are plenty of avenues for knowledge and technology flows. The use of knowledge is influenced by many factors and actors—the macroeconomic situation and regulatory context, education and training systems, firms' capabilities and networks, science system supporting institutions. Research and development activities are important not only for producing knowledge but also for acquiring knowledge. Former command economies and developing countries had weak economies and problems in the distribution of their own accumulated scientific knowledge. Isolation of the actors cannot help to overcome underdevelopment and catch up to world technology.

Leading scholars in the history of innovation argue that science interacts with technological progress in the innovation process. The national innovation system (NIS) "is a set of knowledge institutions whose interactions determine the innovative performance of national firms" (Nelson, 1993). In this complex system, innovations are frequently undertaken in a collaborative mode and almost always involve external interactions with customers, suppliers, regulators and providers of knowledge (Edquist, 1992; David and Foray, 1994; Freeman, 1982, 1991; OECD, 1997, 1998; Guinet and Polt, 1998; Bryant and Wells, 1998).

This chapter studies in detail only the emerging partnership between university and industry and takes into account its international dimension. Attention is paid to (1) the transformation of the governmental role from mission-oriented S&T policy making toward facilitating, and (2) the influence of a new financing mode on partnerships and performances. This study investigates how the transformation of business as performer and financier of R&D and redeployment of universities are influencing their linkages and ability to interact.

The chapter investigates the transformation of linkages as reflected by R&D financing sources. It uses financial data and indicators as measures of linkages to capture the changes in interactions. These provide some insights into the formation of relationships but they cannot describe either the complexity of interactions or their characters.

In Hungary there are two databanks for measuring university-industry relationships: official statistical data collection offers an overview, and a new administrative database (developed by the Ministry of Education) allows some insights into government-business-university interactions.[1] By employing these data we can try to highlight the tendencies of university-industry linkages while still in the embryonic stage. However, this also means we take the risk of misinterpreting tendencies instead of waiting and observing.

Before going into the details of financing and interactions, the first section briefly summarises the recent trends in R&D efforts to put the country into an international context. The second section makes a closer examination of government as facilitator of R&D and innovations. The third section highlights briefly the effects of restructuring by firms of their own R&D initiator and receptive capabilities. The fourth section concentrates on universities that need a double transformation to escape from the trap of mass education factory-type organisation, created by the Soviet model, toward becoming 21st-century research universities. Restructuring the business and role of government may encourage or hamper the self-transformation of universities. So on the one hand the new role of universities is shaped by interactions, and on the other hand this new role is a precondition for intensive R&D interactions. The fifth section presents a plan for new partnerships between businesses, universities and governments. The final section provides some concluding remarks.

RECENT TRENDS IN R&D EFFORTS

Some indicators may illustrate the recent overall impact of transformation on Hungarian R&D activities[2]. The sources, amounts and modes of financing R&D have enormous impacts on R&D performance in each type of organisation, and on their linkages.

By international comparison Hungary spends a smaller fraction of its GDP on R&D than many other small OECD economies. Figure 16.1 shows Hungary ranked among small OECD countries by gross domestic expenditure on R&D to

GDP. Hungary sits at the lower end of the scale. Only the less advanced OECD countries like Greece and Portugal devoted a smaller proportion than Hungary and the Czech Republic. Since the late 1980s, a sharp decline can be observed in Hungary. This tendency runs counter to that observed in other small European economies, but similar to other Central and Eastern European countries.

Figure 16.1
Gross Domestic Expenditure on R&D (GERD) as a Percentage of GDP in European Small Economies

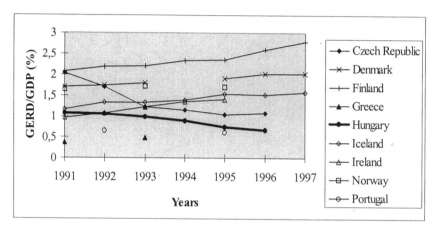

Source: OECD (1998).

R&D is funded from various sources. OECD uses four funding sector categories: government, business, nonprofit organisations and foreign. All sources have their own functions in funding R&D and encourage and facilitate interactions for R&D and innovations.

The *government sector* is the leading financier of R&D. In those countries where industry has not yet developed to a sufficient level and/or has been weakened by transformation, the role of other spheres is salient. In laggard economies governments have to devote more resources to facilitate/encourage greater business involvement than other parts of the world. It may be observed that the funding role of the government sector has increased since 1990, although expenditure decreased in real terms (see Figure 16.2). The next section discusses the character and role of government funding.

Business R&D expenditure declined faster than governmental expenditure[3]. An international comparison of business participation as financier and performer of R&D highlights the correlation between them and economic development. If we rank the latecomer OECD member countries in subgroups of EU members and nonmembers by GDP per capita, we can observe a strong correlation between this former indicator and R&D financed/performed by business enterprises (see Table 16.1). The less-advanced countries are not only way behind as financiers but as performers of R&D too. Ranked correlation between economic performance (measured by GDP/capita) and business financed/performed R&D was 0.8 for peripheral EU member countries (Ireland, Spain, Portugal and Greece) and the same indicator was 0.9 for new OECD member countries (Czech Republic, Hungary, Turkey, Poland and Mexico).

Figure 16.2
Proportion of R&D Expenditure by Funding Sector in Hungary

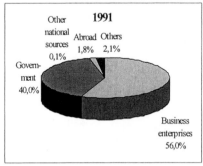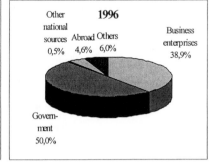

Source: OECD (1998).
Note: sector institutes belonged to different sectors (governmental and business) and during this period some of them moved from one sector to another; thus we cannot characterise their changing role by expenditure.

Table 16.1
Relation Between Business R&D Expenditure and GDP Per Capita

| Countries | BERD/GERD (%) | | GDP per capita in 1996 (USD) |
| | financ. | perform. | |
	in 1995		
Ireland	67.4	70.5	14566.9
Spain	44.5	48.2	11861.6
Portugal	18.9	19.8	9649.5
Greece	20.2*	26.8*	9187.0
Czech Republic	63.1	65.1	8234.8
Hungary	38.4	43.4	5198.7
Turkey	30.8	23.6	5151.9
Poland	31.5	39.0	4898.3
Mexico	17.6	20.8	4688.3

Notes:* in 1993
Sources: OECD (1998), EC (1997).

In both groups the proportion of business enterprises as financiers/performers of R&D is increasingly parallel with GDP per capita

(Table 16.1). So the level of development has a strong influence on business R&D expenditure, and vice versa. Among less-developed countries, the relative advantage of Hungary is its higher proportion of business R&D expenditure (BERD) to gross domestic expenditure on R&D (GERD).[4] The Hungarian proportion in 1995 is roughly double that of Portugal (18.9 %), Greece (20.2 %) or Mexico (17.6%), and higher than Turkey (30.8%).

The *nonprofit sector* is almost negligible as a financier. Foreign experiences also suggest that funds and associations—except for some enterprise-based or giant private funds—rarely engage in R&D financing. Naturally there have been funds in Hungary which were created to support R&D activity. According to a 1996 survey by the Hungarian Statistical Office (HSO), domestic nonprofit organisations (foundations and associations) spent 2.5% of their total expenditures on R&D activities.

In funding, *foreign* (including foreign state support) sources are small but have increased very quickly since 1990 (see Figure 16.3).

Figure 16.3
Percentage of GERD Financed by Abroad

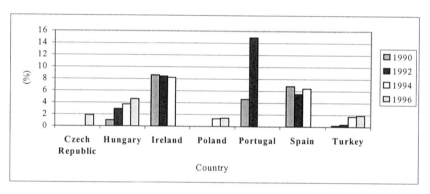

Source: OECD (1997, 1998).

Many factors influence the R&D effort of a country. One of them is the country's economic performance. After a couple of years of transition, Hungarian economic growth declined. This trend caused decreasing absorption of S&T. Further opportunities and significant advances in S&T and innovation depend on expected economic prosperity and how the country can minimise losses in S&T. Key R&D input indicators (R&D capacities in terms of personnel and in expenditure) have fallen.

Recent R&D results are backed up by the accumulated knowledge in the country. The exact value of *knowledge assets* left behind after the Cold War era is not known, but the minimisation of losses in these knowledge capabilities is crucial. The legacy of socialism in the field of R&D activities includes not only research findings (e.g., new disciplines, patents, prototype development) but also accumulated individual and institutional skills and capabilities. The crucial role for government is to encourage investment in the exploitation of accumulated country-specific knowledge.

CHANGING ROLE OF GOVERNMENT

All over the world policy focus is gradually moving from picking winners towards encouraging winners. Policy programmes tend to call for collaboration and integration. Governments are offering incentives and encouraging universities to go beyond performing their traditional functions, to cooperate with industry and thus to contribute directly to economic development.

The collapse of socialism coincided with this new wave in policy making all over the world. Government involvement in the innovation process of the knowledge-based market economy is completely different from its previous position, where the omnipotent state tried to pursue an extremist mission-oriented top-down S&T policy. Midway towards democratisation and the building of a market economy, the question of how to solve the shrinking of the public sphere, to develop new governmental roles and to manage such governmental interventions that replace—albeit temporarily—other players without jeopardising their future role is extremely sensitive. Practical implementation of this new recognition of policy formulation is—for several reasons—more difficult for former socialist countries. They have to redefine the government role as ruler and regulator, and to create a new environment. New legislation, new policy making, a renewed governmental structure and new ways of thinking are crucial in finding the government a new role as facilitator.

The governments of transition economies have to withdraw themselves from their former positions as science and technology policy makers and guides of the innovation process, and build up their new sphere of action as night-watch-type states. There still remain plenty of tasks to shift in governance from omnipotent decision maker toward facilitator in the S&T sphere.

The transformation of governmental roles—which may influence the relationships among the three players (government-industry-university)—is summarised here. It takes into account the setting of priorities, highlighting the breakdown of public funding by objectives, financing instruments and beneficiary organisations. The international dimension of state intervention is also pointed out.

Priority setting is a delicate question in a transition economy. The country is starting to learn how to draw a distinction between priority setting and the socialist-type mission-oriented policy. The first years of the transition period can be characterised as an adjustment process in S&T policy. The socialist system allocated a high priority to science as a tool of national and economic development.

The recent Hungarian government has some general views on S&T policy formulation and its relation to economic policy. However, it still does not have a comprehensive S&T policy. It has some initiatives (Modernisation Programme, National Programme for Information Technology, etc.). So the real transformation of S&T policy making is clearly observable as reflected by R&D

funding. The share of government funding devoted to R&D, and initiatives to encourage R&D and innovations, reflect current government priorities. These priorities are expressed in the breakdown of funds by objective—for example, oriented and nonoriented R&D programmes, advancement of research and estimated R&D content of block grants (including general university fund [GUF]) to universities.

The *breakdown of objectives* describes policy priorities. In recent years the main declared priority has been to stimulate business demand for R&D, to encourage technology transfer, to promote new technology-devoted SMEs and to preserve and strengthen R&D capabilities.

The distribution of public funding for R&D and innovations has been changing *by channels of financing instruments.* In Hungary it is reflected in new economic and institutional environments. Many new channels of public funding have appeared, but it is still difficult to get reliable data on their proportion.[5] Because of the lack of a scientific budget it is not possible to give a precise picture. A detailed and reliable overview would be important because the system of financing is a strong influencing factor of national R&D and innovation activities.

Irrespective of how many new support framework programmes and instruments are enacted, few of them have reached critical mass in financing terms to be effective. The proportion of direct public support remains vital. R&D contracts, reimbursable grants and R&D procurement have had a remarkable role in the redeployment of the public funding structure. These measures influence the interactions among different institutional players for innovations and R&D.

The government, either as contractor of R&D or customer of public procurement, can encourage the setting up of government-business-university or business-university consortia. An important incentive in setting up R&D consortia is public procurement. However, this still represents a minuscule proportion of total governmental R&D expenditure. Almost all programmes of the Hungarian Central Technology Development Fund (KMÜFA) encourage the establishment of R&D and innovation consortia between university-industry and among large and small firms. Few programme schemes support single applicants.

Another important dimension of government policy is the *beneficiary organisation.* Public support for R&D and innovation is offered to all domestic firms including nonnational firms operating in Hungary. There is no legal exclusion, but some programmes focus mainly on national firms because the players are usually nationals (small and microfirms). Some other programmes target mainly multinationals because only they can afford to fulfil such projects. Incentives such as state grants up to 25% of the investment to foreign firms which set up R&D laboratories with 30 researchers and invest HUF 500 million are important. Potentially they can create more knowledge-intensive jobs, and contribute to the double transformation of universities. The new initiative with a similar aim is being launched: government has offered a grandiose grant for three years to set up a cooperative research centre.

State intervention in R&D has *international dimensions*: intergovernmental and international cooperation in R&D activities. Intergovernmental state responsibilities started with megascience programmes after World War II in a bipolar world system (e.g., CERN, ESA). Since the late 1960s, international R&D cooperation goes beyond megascience to reinforce the scientific and technological basis of industry and support its international competitiveness (EU Framework Programmes, EUREKA, COST). This shift in public intervention may be observed in Hungary too. The new research policy aims are to join the international R&D cooperation programmes of advanced economies. This is one of the well-defined and real priorities of Hungarian S&T and innovation policy. Hungarian business, university and academy participation in bilateral or international programmes is strongly encouraged and supported. Policy pays attention to foreign direct investment (FDI) in R&D too, concentrating on multinationals.

EFFECTS OF RESTRUCTURING FIRMS

The transformation of enterprises into firms and the subsequent impacts on R&D, innovative capabilities and networks of these entities are highlighted in this section. Since the main burdening factor of the former Hungarian innovation system was the separation of actors and weak or missing receptive and networking business capabilities, it is worth briefly investigating the transformation of business organisations.[6] Here we will just sketch out this complex procedure to explain changes in business funding and R&D as well as changes in short- and long-term R&D demand. There were three main ways of transforming and privatising state-owned dwarf-giants: (1) privatised as a whole, and remained independent; (2) acquired or taken over in its entirety by a true giant; (3) downsized and/or split up and privatised by different owners. The results of these processes, the legal form, ownership, and size of state-owned enterprises changed completely. Transformation and privatisation strongly influenced the survival rate of business R&D departments and central laboratories.

This unique mass transformation of economic players in a relatively short period has caused rapid changes in their substance, organisational structure, capitalisation and the size structure of industry. Beside the transformation of established enterprises, new players, foreign companies and multinationals have rapidly penetrated Hungary. In a different way from market economies, during the 1990s many potential business players prepared to carry out and to outsource R&D in Hungary. The transition period not only created a new environment for the existence of firms, but it also pushed their own transformation and the redeployment of their linkages. All of these changes strongly influenced their capabilities and linkages. On the one hand the losses experienced in business R&D act against the exploitation of social capital, while on the other hand restructuring in business R&D activities has supported this exploitation with the creation of new demand for social capital. Apart from the many contradictory elements of transformation, lateral ties in business are getting better. However business R&D demand is still very low.

DOUBLE TRANSFORMATION OF UNIVERSITIES AND RESEARCH FUNDING

The transformation of Hungarian universities has been an on-going process since the late 1980s. "Broken-winged" universities have been regaining their research functions. The new mission of universities is now being formulated. The law on higher education (enacted in 1993) defined the tasks of a *double transformation of universities:* to return research to the universities and to transform traditional, old European-style universities into research ones.[7] The 1996 amendment of the Higher Education Act introduced a normative higher education research support system. The higher education budget separates a sum directly supporting R&D. This new law and new measures are encouraging higher education organisations to modify the role of research and their R&D interactions with other performing and innovator sectors (see Figure 16.4).

Figure 16.4
Proportion of R&D Expenditures by Performing Sectors

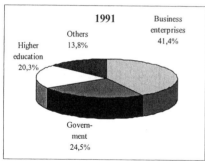
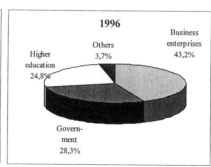

Source: OECD (1998).
Note: branch institutes belonged to different sectors (governmental and business) and during this period some of them moved from one sector to another; thus we cannot characterise their changing role by expenditure.

As the figures show, the role of Hungarian higher education expanded among R&D performing sectors. The proportion of R&D expenditure increased more than 10 points between 1991 and 1996. Higher education provides one-quarter of R&D activities. Beside encouraging university research, as potential contractors they were better placed in the S&T arena. The main reason for the fast-growing proportion of universities among all performers is the collapse of other R&D-performing organisations (branch R&D institutes, downsizing of academy institutes).

This increasing importance of university research has created much more demand for research funding. Earlier, the funding of research projects was virtually totally dependent upon government. Other sources such as philanthropic grants and tuition incomes played a limited role. The universities used to run predominantly publicly funded research by both models.

Governments are now pushing the universities to try to finance their R&D activities from nonpublic sources. This is motivated by different reasons:

- To develop linkages between the science base and the economy.
- According to the experiences of some advanced countries, if most or all research at universities is publicly funded, it is quite difficult to establish working relationships between the "science base" and industry and industrial research, even despite persistent measures aimed at linking them.
- To cut budget spending.

All motivations are present in all countries. The predominance of public-funded research is decreasing and other sources are emerging. The impact of reshaping the financial structure on a particular university's research performance depends on the size of the budget cut and the receptive/contracting capabilities of the university's potential partners.

Universities (as part of their own national innovation systems) in advanced and less-developed countries find themselves in very different situations establishing working relationships with government labs and industry. In less-developed countries, the research conditions in many fields are not only very far from the critical mass, but even from a minimum level. The most important "incentive" to encourage reshaping is the financial pressure on the universities in less-advanced countries, including transition economies.[8]

The changing pattern of R&D financing redeploys government-university-industry relationships.[9] New financing patterns may strengthen the knowledge-creation capabilities of universities and can support the development of the knowledge distribution and diffusion power of these economies, or can threaten them.

Budget cuts do not necessarily indicate decline, since the system is in transition.[10] The proportion of public funding for total university incomes is much more than a question of financing. The role of the university research society is heavily influenced by size and resources.

The government has to some extent pressured universities to collaborate more with industry. The two different government measures run in opposite directions: direct measures are decreasing (basic funding of research), while indirect incentives (earmarking research funding at universities and firms) are increasing. Table 16.2 takes into consideration the type of university income in advanced market economies and illustrates how they have penetrated into Hungary.

Table 16.2
Penetration of Different Funding Sources to Universities

Funding source	Type of Incomes	Before 1990s	After 1990s
🏛	government grants	+++	++
🏛	government granting programmes (OTKA, OMFB, FEFA1/2)	+	++
🏛	public procurement	-	-
	church foundations	-	+
👤	philanthropic grants	-	-
👥	tuition income	-	-
🏭	earning from technology transfers	+	+
🏛 🏭	contract research with enterprises/firms	+	+
🏛 🏭	consultancy	+	++
🏛	foreign government granting programmes	-	+
🏛	international granting programmes (FEFA1/2, ACE, Tempus, Inco-Copernicus, EU V. R&D Framework Programmes)	-	++
🏭	Contract research with foreign business	-	+

Notes: Some types of incomes have existed at universities (e.g. tuition income after 1990, international granting programmes before 1990) but they have not supported research activities.
OMFB is National Committee for Technological Development
OTKA is National Scientific Research Fund
FEFA is Foundation for Development of Higher Education

🏛 = Government sector   🏭 = Business sector   👥 = Individuals

Table 16.2 illustrates important changes in the university research funding structure. Parallel with declining *public funding* there is a slight shift in Hungary among channels of public sources. The government is shifting from general grants toward granting programmes by tender (introducing evaluation, peer reviews). Still, government has not created demand for universities even if a procurement system were to be introduced in Hungary. The public funding situation at universities worsened between 1990 and 1996; since that time some improvements may be observed[11].

Business-related sources remain important, but business players and their demands have changed completely. The changing economic potential of companies is influencing their cooperative efforts. The next section deals with this problem.

As Table 16.2 shows among the new financiers there are different groups of foreigners. Foreign government grant programmes may be seen as supplements to national government funding. International grant programmes are important not only as financial sources but as linkage mechanisms to advanced scientific communities and sophisticated competitive environments. Both of them help to get in the existing networks. Contract research with foreign business is a very complicated issue. They may just skim off the cream of public research, they may involve universities in the process of globalisation or they may just link Hungarian S&T to their short-term economic growth. In whatever manner, university collaboration with geographically distant companies is speeding up: cooperating with sophisticated industry and adjusting themselves to such partnerships.

Philanthropic grants and *nonprofit organisations* play a minor part in R&D financing. Foreign experiences also suggest that funds and associations—except for some enterprise-based or giant private funds—rarely engage themselves in R&D financing. Naturally there have been funds in Hungary which were created to support R&D activity. According to a 1996 survey by HSO, domestic nonprofit organisations (foundations and associations) spent 2.5% of their total expenditure on R&D activities.[12] Foreign foundations as financiers deserve special attention. Globally, these organisations usually play only a marginal role in financing R&D. However, during the period of transition their role has been relatively significant in Hungary.

The double transformation of Hungarian universities is taking place in a publicly underfinanced situation. The enormous pressure on universities created by an ever-tightening governmental budget has become the most important factor in their seeking other opportunities to survive.

NEW PARTNERSHIPS

For knowledge-based economies the key of the whole process is the partnership between universities, the business sector and governments. (Raymond, 1996) Broadening university-industry linkages is the key survival strategy not only for the university as a whole but for the faculty members too. New modes of government-business-university relationships are crucial for the universities and for the effectiveness of the economy.

The Impact of Funding Schemes on Relationships

There is very little empirical evidence allowing the study of the changes in government-business-university relationships. Our empirical data can afford limited analysis as to how arm's length players are moving toward the horizontal triple helix.[13] This section outlines how patterns of collaboration have emerged in Hungary and shows how national and international innovation systems are combined in a dimension.

Detailed information is available to us about research projects above HUF 5 million (US$ 21,365). However, on an international comparison this limit does not even reach the entry level in several disciplines for the basic research phase. The financing limit in the case of applied research and trial developments is about ten times that of basic research (this rough estimate heavily depends on fields and disciplines but is appropriate to illustrate the difference in magnitude). In the present situation in Hungary, HUF 5 million may be seen as a demarcation line where scientific services and consultancy may be separated from research work. The development in the number of contracts and their cumulated value is shown in Table 16.3.

Table 16.3
Characteristics of the R&D Contracts in Higher Education (above HUF 5 million)

	Financier	Number of contracts by sources		Sum of contracts (Million HUF)	
		1995	1996	1995	1996
Domestic	Government all	116	106	1083.4	1061.4
	OMFB-KMÜFA	*35*	*35*	*369.6*	*322.0*
	OTKA	*48*	*40*	*333.5*	*252.5*
	Ministries	*22*	*13*	*219.1*	*157.0*
	Others	*11*	*18*	*161.2*	*329.9*
	Business	16	26	227.9	327.5
	Non profit organis.	2	5	66.3	166.8
	All	134	*137*	*1377.6*	*1555.7*
Mixed	Government	7	16	60.5	212.8
	Business	1	-	9.3	-
	Non profit org.	*6*	9	38.5	61.2
	All	14	*25*	*108.3*	*274.0*
Foreign	Government	34	44	495.5	773.7
	Business	11	16	120.7	230.9
	Non profit org.	*5*	10	96.1	280.5
	Others	3	2	31.4	32.0
	All	*53*	*72*	*743.7*	*1317.1*
TOTAL		**201**	**234**	**2229.6**	**3146.8**

Source: indicators accomplished by the Innovation Research Center (IKU) of Budapest University of Economic Sciences and Policy Administration, based on the MKM databank.
Notes: OMFB-KMÜFA is National Committee for Technological Development—Central Fund for Technological Development
OTKA is National Scientific Research Fund
Sum of contracts includes the total sum of the contract in the period of the project

The number of research projects as compared to the number of universities, or research centres at higher education institutes, is rather low. This suggests that at many university departments (or groups of departments) reported as research centres there has been little or no research activity. The number of the research contracts above HUF 5 million was 201 in 1995 and 234 in 1996[14]. Cumulated R&D contract stock was HUF 2,229.6 million in 1995 and HUF 3,146.8 million in 1996. If we compare the total sum of these contracts to figures reported by Hungarian Statistical Office, we find it is one-third of the latter. This means that two-thirds of university R&D expenditure was below the (HUF 5 million) cut-off point. Apart from difficulties with the reliability of both data collections, it can be stated that a substantial part of R&D financing resources won at competitive tenders was consumed by daily operating costs (heating, lighting, social insurance contributions, "13th month" bonus salaries) instead of going directly to the project. These revenues were used to fill the gap created by a shortfall in the general university fund. The message is unambiguous: it is not possible to enforce modernisation in the financing of R&D merely by cutting the budget. Shrinking subventions in higher education have had additional negative consequences: a drop in the full-time teacher-research staff, and a reduction in the time teachers can give to research.

Distribution of Resources

When analysing R&D financiers by sector, the most important was the government sphere in the domestic, mixed and foreign group. Most payments (one-third) came from the domestic government sphere, mostly for research projects won at government-funded tenders. The direct budget financing was 22% in 1995 and 13% in 1996. The R&D financing coming from foreign governments—which represented an important proportion of the whole—played a great role not only as an additional source of income in the period of transition but also as a means of inspiring trust. It may be assumed that the latter-mentioned source contributed to foreign business involvement in R&D financing. This reached 52% of domestic business payments in 1995, and 45% in 1996. Table 16.4 summarises the rank order by discipline of the three most important income sources.

In all fields of science the main source of financing was, quite naturally, the domestic government. The foreign governmental sector—placed second—is not so straightforward. This place deserves attention because—according to HSO and other data sources (PHARE national aid programmes) —the role of foreign financing in R&D financing as a whole remains marginal, even if it has increased dynamically. This suggests that foreign R&D subventions have been concentrated in higher education research. Hungarian higher education has proved itself fully capable of attracting foreign (EU) resources.

Mixed government funding (where the Hungarian government is obliged to cofinance the project to get foreign support) turned out to be the third most important resource in one field of science (natural sciences), because in this sphere nongovernmental financing usually plays only a marginal role.[15]

International trends show that foreign funds generally do not behave as important contractors in social sciences. Foreign funds rank second as financiers in social sciences. That is perhaps due on the one hand to underfinancing from other resources, and on the other hand to international efforts to help Hungary in adapting itself to the world economy, democratisation, strengthening the market economy and to promote familiarity with this region.

Table 16.4
The Three Most Important Income Sources by Fields of Science

Fields of science	Government			Business			Nonprofit organisation		
	domestic	mixed	foreign	domestic	mixed	foreign	domestic	mixed	foreign
Total	1	-	2	3	-	-	-	-	-
Natural sciences	1	3	2	-	-	-	-	-	-
Engineering and technology	1	-	2	3	-	-	-	-	-
Agricultural sciences	1	-	2	3	-	-	-	-	-
Social sciences	1	-	-	3	-	-	-	-	2
Medical sciences	1	-	-	-	-	2	-	-	3

Source: indicators accomplished by IKU based on the MKM database.

The following sections analyse in detail two financier groups (government and business). In both cases comments will be made about particular characteristics of the domestic and foreign resources.

The Governmental Sphere

One may evaluate the government funding structure as more sophisticated, if the research communities get a relatively minor part of their resources from direct budget allocations and win the majority at tenders and in public procurement orders—that is, in competition among research projects and communities on the basis of performance evaluation. In advanced market economies an important part of government financing derives from public procurements.

The legal framework for cooperation between government and the universities has already been laid down in the area of R&D commissions. Since the enactment of the act on public procurement, public procurement orders may appear in the financing of R&D.

In the structure of governmental financing, the following rough picture can be drawn based on data reported by R&D players. The most important R&D resource was KMÜFA in 1995. In 1996 its percentage diminished by 10 points and the so-called other budget allocations became the key financier. The role of the OTKA (National Scientific Research Fund) and direct budget allocations diminished at a similar rate. Thus the period of economic austerity caused some sort of retrograde movement in the financing structure at the expense of competitive tenders. The pattern of financing by domestic governmental sector may be seen in Table 16.5.

Table 16.5
R&D Financed by Domestic Governmental Sector

Financiers	Sum of contracts (%)		Incomes of universities(%)	
	1995	1996	1995	1996
OMFB-KMÜFA	34.1	30.3	30.9	22.0
OTKA	30.8	23.8	18.9	14.9
Ministries	20.2	14.8	29.1	23.7
Others	14.9	31.1	21.2	39.4
Government all	**100.0**	**100.0**	**100.1**	**100.0**

Source: indicators accomplished by IKU based on the MKM database.

When considering financing resources in the sphere of contracts above HUF 5 million, it is worth noting that

- In the case of medical sciences, aggregated domestic governmental financing diminished by 13 percentage points, in a structure similar to the former disciplines.

- In the case of agricultural research the proportion of governmental financing dropped by 16 percentage points.
- KMÜFA disappeared as financier of the social sciences in 1996. Direct budget income sources shrank to one-fourth their original amount. However, income from other governmental sources increased significantly.
- In the case of natural sciences there was a similarly significant decrease (10%) in governmental financing. In this field the percentage of revenues from the Funds (KMÜFA, OTKA) diminished even further.

In summary, it may be stated that the government sector continues to be the most important financier, but its role in university R&D funding has been diminished. This clearly suggests that the government wishes to take only a relatively minor part in the costs of transition, and seeks to shift these costs to the shoulders of the universities.

The Business Sector

In countries where relationships between the economy and university have a long tradition, increasing numbers of studies analyse the advantages and disadvantages of this cooperation, its risks and dangers[16]. Interaction between business and the universities always depends on the characteristics of the innovation system. A competitive and innovative economy is continuously open to new scientific achievements; moreover it not only uses them passively but inspires and finances them. Industry-university cooperation will be born and developed if industry is interested in it. There are a number of reasons why firms outsourcing their R&D needs to other organisations (e.g., access to expertise not available in-house, access to extra R&D staff, etc.) (Faulkner and Senker, 1994a and b, 1995; Goldman, 1991; Hull, 1990; Webster, 1994). Over the past decade contracted R&D has provided both reduced costs and access to new technologies. If industry is looking for partners in R&D, the university is a very natural choice. On the other side, universities themselves are open-minded to new problems emerging from the praxis. In such circumstances the innovation process functions as a feedback loop in which industry and university are mutually cooperating partners.

In the transition period university and industry relationships are being reshaped. The level of cooperation was very low in former socialist countries, with a few exceptions. The number of R&D contracts above HUF 5 million was 28 in 1995 and 42 in 1996. Business enterprises entered most contracts (18) in engineering, with medical research (14) second. Businesses operating in Hungary were financiers of 15.0% of university R&D expenditures above HUF 5 million in 1996. This proportion differs from one field of science to another: the highest in the field of engineering (22.2%), and the lowest in social sciences (7.3%). Among corporate contracts the number signed with domestic companies was 16, 26 in the years investigated. The difference clearly demonstrates that foreign enterprises are important customers (11 in 1995, 16 in 1996) in the category of R&D activities of (relatively) significant value.

The cumulated sum of the contract value from business sources (domestic and foreign together) increased by 56% (in the case of incomes by 46%) from one year to the other. This signals intensive networking activity. Most revenue was attracted by technological institutes in both years. When analysing incomes from business by country of origin, the engineering universities take first place in the case of domestic financing, while medical universities obtain the greater part of financing from foreign enterprises (more than 70% in both years, see Table 16.6). This latter source is important for preserving research capabilities, improving technical facilities and increasing the incomes of universities. This cooperation as a first step in building linkages could lead to deeper, more valuable R&D cooperation, but it also has the potential to lead to the erosion of R&D culture and could be accompanied by ethical, legal and other problems. The question of impacts is still open. But its relatively large proportion draws our attention to changes in the research patterns of universities: the proportion of basic and applied research is diminishing and clinical pharmacological testing is increasing in their research portfolios.

Table 16.6
Distribution of the Business-Financed Incomes from R&D Contracts by Fields of Science (%)

Financier	Domestic		Mixed		Foreign		Business all	
	1995	1996	1995	1996	1995	1996	1995	1996
Natural sciences	9.7	12.1	-	-	5.0	6.8	7.7	10.4
Engineering and technology	61.4	50.0	100.0	-	23.5	18.0	51.1	40.0
Medical sciences	19.5	22.9	-	-	71.4	75.3	35.4	39.1
Agricultural sciences	9.4	11.3	-	-	-	-	5.9	7.8
All	100	100	100	-	100	100	100	100

Source: indicators accomplished by IKU based on the MKM database.

Few research contracts may be considered as stable and reliable sources of income for universities. Strategic partnerships are rare not only because of ownership disputes over the new scientific/technological results, but also due to the transformation of firms and unsettled business structure. There are still only a few business organisations in Hungary that are able to involve themselves in interdepartmental or even interuniversity collaborations. The multinationals established in Hungary are the forerunners in strategic partnership building. Several support schemes encourage these activities.[17]

The attraction of business resources which has been signalled by data in our tables has some particular characteristics both by discipline and by university. An accumulated knowledge base is only one of the latter. Besides the capacity of the university for networking, it is important to know whether firms can rely on the university as sources of information and partners in experimental development in their innovative endeavours. Another essential question is how cooperation between industry and university (its duration, depth, effectiveness) can be measured.

While no global evaluation can be undertaken, some conclusions may be drawn from the magnitude of contracts. In any international context the limit of HUF 5 million represents an incredibly low value in the case of R&D financed and (presumably) applied by the business world. If we accept HUF 5 million as a limit for basic research, then the limit for applied research activities must be drawn somewhere around HUF 50 million, but there were only three such contracts in 1995 and six in 1996.

The relatively low value of business-oriented R&D contracts gives some food for reasoning. There is no doubt that one of the causes might be found in changes of economic potential of economic organisations in their need to explore new situations. Assuming the stabilisation of the economy and successful execution of the present university R&D contracts, rapid growth in the present value of R&D contracts may be expected. Ever more companies seem to view university researchers as important players in the innovation process. Both large and small companies may be clients or cooperation partners of universities. Their interactive capabilities depend on how they fulfil their own (changing) tasks and on the process of mutual adjustment. The needs of life-long learning make companies more receptive to the external knowledge that is available from universities on both individual and organisational levels. Different groups of private firms are initiating different varieties of collaboration. We can deduce from the low income per project that the universities are ready to do anything to earn income. Short-term, market-oriented research conducted in a systematic linkage between universities and companies has become a dominant feature of academic life. Hungarian higher education places more emphasis on the knowledge transfer role of the institutions, rather than trying to strengthen the positions of the originality and the basic nature of the research (Patkós, 1998). In this period of transition, demand for quality certification, testing to standards and seminars on technical matters is increasing. Hungarian medium-sized firms need these to become competitive. It is a relatively new demand in Hungary to use universities for information, for library services or to make use of their software. Thus among the reasons for the limited value of cooperative R&D we can look not only at the weaknesses of the business sector, but the failures of universities as well.

Several universities are good enough for strategic university-industry partnerships in leading scientific fields and technologies. The average sum per contract of universities by fields of science can serve as a very rough measure of the attractiveness of universities. Looking at this indicator, we can observe remarkable differences among the universities in the same scientific fields. This indicator can characterise four different components of attractiveness: (1) knowledge base, (2) linking and knowledge-dissemination capabilities[18], (3) status of transformation from a "grey zone" toward a transparent economic institution, (4) capability for teamwork and research training.

It is not too risky to state that weaknesses in the third and fourth factors are the main causes of the low ratings. Many small-scale projects are signs of still-existing grey zones since the grey economy in academic R&D activity is still alive.

Behind the limited number of contracts lies a particular phenomenon: where legal and financial conditions of knowledge and technology transfer are unclear, universities will earn less. In such circumstances leading researchers in the universities enter into contracts on behalf of their own businesses, and only to a limited extent for the university (to legitimate the use of the university's facilities). In advanced economies, small enterprises around the universities are important players in effective knowledge and technology transfer, thus they are usually ranked among progressive organisational forms. But in Hungary some of these organisations have taken forms which have at least as many negative as positive characteristics.

There are deep-seated reasons why these small organisations continue to survive, why they remain "inner-outer" firms, why the parent universities themselves do not spin off. To mention just a few reasons for these outdated forms of socialism: the low salaries of university professors (their salaries are not sufficient to maintain a decent living standard), problems in the basic financing of universities (the general university fund was cut from the budget) these organisations are sponging on professors, unclear rules for sharing intellectual property, uncertainty of the share of revenues from R&D results, inadequate legal regulation and poor implementation of the existing rules, unresolved problems in rewarding personal achievement.

These circumstances are disadvantageous not only for teaching and research work at universities, the proliferation and flourishing of high-tech small enterprises and the revenues of the universities, but they are also unfavourable for the strengthening of industry-university relations. Some leaders of business R&D departments cooperating with universities have expressed the opinion that important research projects are hindered by these private realms in universities, because some universities are incapable of mobilising the critical mass of research capacities. If we accept these allegations as true, then this situation represents a loss not only for universities but researchers themselves too. Thus some strategies which seek to secure survival in the difficult transition period can actually undermine future opportunities in a stabilising economy.[19] All these factors contribute to the fact that today there are few contracts with the business sector above the HUF 5 million limit.

CONCLUDING REMARKS

One of the biggest "systemic failures" of Central and Eastern European countries was the mismatch between the different components of innovation systems. System failures were coded into the institutional structure and factors of economic environment. To overcome this systemic failure, Hungary is recoding each institution, and trying to create the proper economic environment for commercialisation and innovation. The collapse of socialism coincided with the new wave in policy making all over the world. Governments are shifting their relationships to academic and economic institutions. The programmes tend to call for universities to go beyond performing their traditional functions, to cooperate with industry and thus to contribute directly to economic development.

Path dependency in governance, confused ideas on market economy and ideas of institutional imitation of successful, advanced economies and budget pressures are burdening factors to facilitate the changes in relevant institutions and their relationships. New legislation, policy making, a renewed governmental structure and new ways of thinking are crucial in finding the government a new role as facilitator. If the main elements of policy in an institutional system remain intact, the imitation of institutions by best practice of other countries without taking into account different circumstances can lead to institutional disaster. Instead of channelling flows of existing knowledge they are blocking them. Hungary has avoided this trap more or less; however, some institutional elements (lateral ties) were fit to local circumstances without adaptation. Many new support framework programmes and instruments were enacted, but only few of them have reached critical mass in financing terms to be effective. Public procurement for R&D still represents a minuscule proportion of total governmental R&D expenditure.

A very common feature of backward countries is the lack of *effective demand* from the production system for local scientific and technological capabilities. During the transition period *government may replace temporary business* as financier of R&D to overcome the weak potential of domestic industry. Government may encourage and help the adjustment of universities to the challenges of our time. Substitutes for domestic industry may be found in the government budget, international research funding or foreign businesses. All can help to overcome short-term bottlenecks, but they have different impacts on the scope of research, cooperation and feedback loops in the innovation process. There is a fragile borderline between encouragement and replacement. But government has to perform its own role in R&D financing and does not imitate the role of business. Bankruptcies or the almost collapsed situations of many R&D institutes that we can observe from Hungary to Brazil originated when states replaced (imitated) the roles of business. So a temporary state role is crucial to avoid huge losses in knowledge capabilities but it is also crucial to encourage transformation, to create more incentives for R&D and innovations. Policy makers have to do more to improve legal conditions and enforce a new legal system and build up trust in the enforcement of the laws.

The *transformation of business enterprises* modifies firms' innovativeness, their involvement in intramural and extramural R&D, penetration of new players and networks of these entities. The transition period not only created a new environment for the existence of firms, but it pushed them toward their own transformation and the redeployment of their linkages.

One of the crucial lateral ties of firms for university-industry cooperation is the business R&D laboratory. These organisations were strongly influenced by transformation and privatisation. In the turbulent years of transition, the transformation of central laboratories coincided with the redeployment of enterprises into firms. The significant decline in R&D laboratories and departments caused decline in demand for academic R&D. During this adjustment procedure, several factors which used to burden R&D cooperation in promoting innovation have disappeared. Enterprises have been becoming firms and overcoming surviving troubles. They are able to involve into capitalisation of knowledge, and some of them may attempt to participate in producing knowledge in networks. The future of the business-university cooperation rests on development in industry.

In the transition period some business players have been able to develop links to universities. The future of the double helix rests on development in industry. The crucial task of policy makers is to create an environment in which industry is increasingly active in R&D cooperation. It is also important to create more incentives for R&D and innovations. Policy makers have to do more to improve legal conditions and enforce a new legal system and build up trust in the enforcement of the laws.

The price of universities' transformation from the traditional model toward the research one is higher for a laggard country if it cannot afford to increase budget support during this period. The process of *double transformation of broken-winged Hungarian universities* is taking place in a publicly underfinanced situation. The enormous pressure on universities created by an ever-tightening governmental budget has become the most important factor in their seeking other opportunities to survive. The research conditions in many fields are not only very far from the critical mass, but even from a minimum level. The universities' professors have to devote themselves too heavily to R&D services and prototype development to eliminate budget constraints on education, and basic conditions of research. The influence of reshaping structure could shrink knowledge-creation capabilities and the science base, if the funding level of universities remains unchanged. In a world more and more open to free movement of people and ideas, professors, researchers and students vote with their feet about universities, research conditions or levels of teaching. If universities in a region do not reach the quality needed to retain the research workers and attract guest researchers, if their share in the market of teaching is shrinking, then not only the knowledge-generating capacity but the knowledge-hosting ability will decrease.

Transformation takes its toll all over the world. This is higher in transition economies because the changes are more radical. The real threat for them is that the individual steps will not end up in a model change but the universities become stuck in some intermediate stage: organisational innovations and developments needed for competitiveness will not occur.

Hungarian universities have to develop their exploration and exploitation capabilities in parallel. Besides developing their knowledge-creating capabilities they have to strengthen their knowledge and technology distribution and diffusion power to become at least world second-class research universities. The institutionalisation of the economic functions of universities and their efficiency are crucial in this process.

The period of struggling for survival of universities is unfavourable to research and to build up external relationships, but the fact that the resource-attracting capacity of the universities had been strengthened from one year to another may be seen as a sign of vitality.

Different groups of private firms are initiating different varieties of collaboration. The majority of business contracts bring in low income per project. The relatively low value of business-oriented R&D contracts means that a high proportion of short-term, market-oriented research is a dominant feature of academic life. Strategic partnerships are rare not only because of ownership disputes over the new scientific/technological results, but also due to the transformation of firms and unsettled business structure. There are still only a few business organisations in Hungary that are able to involve themselves in interdepartmental or even interuniversity collaborations. The multinationals established in Hungary are the forerunners in strategic partnership building. Several support schemes encourage these activities further.

Contract research with foreign business is a very complicated issue. All types of foreign business contracting out may be observed in Hungary. In whatever manner, university collaboration with geographically distant companies is speeding up: cooperating with sophisticated industry and adjusting themselves to such partnerships. Looking at the indicator of the average sum per contract of universities by fields of science, we can observe remarkable differences among the universities in the same scientific fields. This indicator can characterise four different components of attractiveness: (1) knowledge base, (2) linking and knowledge-dissemination capabilities, (3) status of transformation from a "grey zone" toward a transparent economic institution, (4) capability for teamwork and research training.

The future success or failures of former socialist economies greatly depends on how their knowledge-creating institutions can get their regional industry and foreign industry to work in tandem. They need to form domestic and international research partnerships, pooling their expertise to develop and commercialise new products and discover new and better ways of doing things.

One of the main advantages of the realised transition is that the whole economic environment is encouraging business to be innovative and to work by the chain-link model. However in this model universities may have a very limited role depending on the innovative capabilities of business and their own knowledge and knowledge transfer capabilities.

NOTES

1. The Ministry of Economic Affairs made another administrative attempt to measure university-industry relationships. The results of that examination were not available for this chapter.

2. Without going into details it has to be mentioned that the S&T information system of transition economies is one of the most important burdening factors of any analytical work. Apart from revision of the statistical measurement system—adopting the standards of OECD Frascati Manual (1993)—many basic data are still missing and the reliability of indicators is still doubtful.

3. The OECD revision of Hungarian figures shows that BERD (business R&D expenditure) was overestimated (56% in 1991). Recent figures (39% in 1996) are closer to reality. We cannot solve the problem of overestimation of figures before 1992, although we can state that the proportion of business-funded R&D declined during the years of transition.

4. Because of the limited reliability of Hungarian and Czech figures, I do not analyse these data further.

5. The complete budget model is also under revision. Reform of the accounting procedures for the state budget has been going on for a long while. Some steps have been taken. There are many reasons why this reform is so slow. One important factor is that government departments are reluctant to improve the transparency of the budget: they are afraid of losing their positions.

6. Enterprises operating in the socialist system were not firms in economic terms. The creation of new enterprises resulted in loss of function, and there were tremendous horizontal mergers of many small and medium-sized firms to reach the desired economies of scale. Vertical mergers were also common, uniting former contractors and subcontractors in single organisations. Such organisational changes very rapidly increased the number of large enterprises (in terms of employees) and decreased the number of small and medium-sized firms. Hungarian enterprises were typically dwarf-giants in size. In international terms they were medium or lower-medium sized ones, but on the domestic market they were able to maintain a monopolistic position (Inzelt, 1988).

7. Briefly, the milestones of Hungarian transformation are the following: introduction of Master's degree and PhD curricula, new evaluation and grant system for professors if they conduct quality research, grant fresh-graduate PhD students, accreditation of universities, higher education research bidding system, participation in EU-funded cooperative research programmes (see OECD, 1998). Universities are becoming autonomous organisations, but authorities are enforcing mergers of higher education organisations. Professional organisations are emerging, such as Rectors' Conference, trade unions of scientific personnel.

8. This is a very different story from the ideal of research universities. In the postwar period, American universities were powerfully reshaped by a huge influx of federal financial funds. Not only the scale of this financial support but procurements were also important factors.

9. It has to be mentioned that university records do not offer much information for analyses.

10. For example, world first-class universities can earn income from technology transfer and are able to partially self-fund research projects. Selling R&D results off the shelf makes the universities self-funding institutions and contributes to industrial technologies and economic growth. Beside vendors and buyers of knowledge there are possibilities for cooperation (e.g., participating in producing knowledge) that are also modifying the funding structures of universities.

11. Data are available to 1996.

12. Donations from enterprise-created foundations to universities are concealed R&D orders, where the only role for the foundation consists of awarding contracts and making payments. This peculiarity of the emerging Hungarian system deserves attention because enterprise foundation financing—which is usually of a charitable type—acts in Hungary

as utilitarian in nature, at least in the world of science. If we look at the real processes, this type of financing should be classified into the category of business-like corporations, instead of the nonprofit oriented group. Naturally it may be assumed that this is a transitional phenomenon in which some currently absent forms of R&D stimulation are imaginatively replaced by other forms. A positive effect of this R&D order disguised in the form of a foundation is that some additional resources become available for R&D activities while the appropriate institutional forms will be slowly built up. But there are some negative aspects: it makes direct cooperation more difficult, because it involves some players who are not needed in market economies. At the same time this does not help the creation of enterprise-based charitable foundations as supporters of R&D.

It is impossible to differentiate between charitable and utilitarian financing by enterprise-based foundations. A distinction will be made only by a tax policy stimulating R&D activities, not by improving the statistical measurement system.

13.   A new administrative database (developed by the Ministry of Education) offers a two-year snapshot of the changing government-university-industry relationships. It allows some insights into this process. Data (for normative financing) was gathered. This databank contains information for two years (1995 and 1996) about the number of R&D contracts, the sum of contracts and incomes from the contracts. All types of contractors and science fields are covered. All statistical tables were prepared by the Innovation Research Center (IKU) of Budapest University of Economic Sciences and Policy Administration with the assistance of Noémi Gál.

14.   It must be noted that because of the HUF 5 million limit, some higher education institutes with research contracts have been left out of this sample. Apparently this indicates a problem with the limit value, which in turn focuses attention on several grave problems of the transition threatening future cooperation between the economy and universities. For in the financing of university R&D there are many contracts below HUF 5 million. This indicates partly that the business world wants scientific services from universities, but at the same time it shows that some research communities which have been less successful in attracting research funding undertake almost anything in order to secure their survival. In the stage of network building, minor research contracts have an extraordinary importance because they ensure references and a possibility to carry out research work.

15.   Financing of medical R&D is different from the general picture: here foreign enterprises occupy second place. Clearly this represents an important contribution to maintaining research capacity, increasing income, improving equipment and so on. It indicates, however, that a change has occurred in the pattern of R&D activity: the proportion of clinical pharmacological tests (i.e., services) has increased at the expense of basic and applied research. This cooperation as a first step towards partnership may lead to higher-level R&D cooperation, but it may also pose a risk of some degradation of the research culture, not to speak about other (legal, ethical) problems.

16.   An important body of literature discusses the research activities of universities, related organisational changes, and the economy-university relations. The literature (Crow et al. [1998]; Etzkovitz and Leydesdorff [1997]; Geisler and Rubenstein [1989]; Link and Tassey [1989]) treats the phenomenon of the "triple helix" (industry-university-government relationship, which can induce development) on the basis of the American experience and model changes in other countries. For in the period after World War II, industry-university cooperation may be characterised by a contribution of the government through public procurements and often governmental research laboratories.

In the transitional Hungarian economy, public procurement has so far been absent from the "triple helix". As far as cooperation between institutes is concerned, some research units financed by the Hungarian Academy of Sciences (HAS) or other organisations (e.g., Bay Foundation) take part in the industry-university relation. These tripartite partnerships are very important but bear only a very distant resemblance to their Western counterparts. Thus this study only analyses the "double helix" (i.e., industry-university cooperation).

17.   A new phenomenon is the appearance of international players, for instance R&D units of multinational firms and university researchers (e.g., Ericsson-Budapest Technical University), forming important local networks for developing new technology. The technology is developed locally, while the markets and science of the firms are international. In these scattered cases university-industry relationships are developing—through students employed in the firm, through joint studies or research and through personal consulting by faculty (and through which they gain significant incremental income). In other words, the university is becoming an important node in the social capital of the country. This group may be characterized by the cooperative attitude of leading professors and the input of PhD holders and PhD students around the world. If teamwork capabilities are weak at universities, firms hunting for R&D results will not invest in partnership building.

18.   Knowledge and technology transfer organisations are in their infant phase; this means that these years are a time for investment and not to reap benefits. But the difference is whether the infants have been born at all.

19.   It is probably only a minor loss that these scientific "backyard farms" use the assets of universities and make no effort to reimburse them. Very often these "passionate" researchers also make their own assets available to the universities. However, this friendly cooperation may be more useful in rural house building than in the university. Unclear legal relations between universities and professorial partnerships and small enterprises stuck in the universities can lead to losses. Professorial undertakings are not capable of accomplishing important tasks if only because they hinder cooperation among several departments and the creation of the critical mass. (See Laki [1992] on the causes of the survival of the "grey economy" in Hungary, and Vajda and Farkas [1988] on the system of reciprocal favours as a factor in the economy.)

REFERENCES

Bryant, Kevin and Wells, Alison (eds.) 1998, "A New Economic Paradigm? Innovation-based Evolutionary Systems", *Competitive Australia*, Canberra, Australia.

Crow, M., Gelijns, M., Nelson, R. R. and Bhaven, N. S. 1998, "Recent Changes in University–Industry Research Interactions, Preliminary Analysis of Causes and Effects", manuscript, Columbia University, New York.

David, Paul and Foray, Dominique 1994, "Accessing and expanding the science and technology knowledge base. A conceptual framework for comparing national profiles in systems of learning and innovation". OECD, DSTI/STP/TIP(94)4.

Edquist, C. 1992, *Technological and Organizational Innovations, Productivity and Employment, World Employment Programme Working Paper no. 33*. Geneva: Technology and Employment Programme, International Labour Office.

Etzkovitz, H. and Leydesdorff, L. (eds.) 1997, *Universities and the Global Knowledge Economy. A Triple Helix of University-Industry-Government Relations*. London: Pinter.

European Commission 1997, "The Second European Report on Science and Technology Indicators 1997", EUR 17639 EN, Brussels: EC.

Faulkner, W. and Senker, J. 1994a, *Knowledge Frontiers: Public Sector Research and Industrial Innovation in Biotechnology, Engineering Ceramics, and Parallel Computing*. Oxford: Clarendon Press.

Faulkner, W. and Senker, J. 1994b, "Making sense of diversity: public-private sector research linkage in three technologies," *Research Policy* Vol. 23, pp. 673-695.

Freeman, C. 1982, *The Economics of Industrial Innovation* (2nd ed.). London: Pinter.

Freeman, C. 1991, "Networks of Innovators: a synthesis of research issues," *Research Policy* 20, pp. 499-514.

Geisler, Eliezer and Rubenstein, Albert H. 1989, "University-Industry Relations: A Review of Major Issues" in Albert N. Link and Gregory Tassey (eds.), *Co-operative Research and Development: The Industry-University-Government Relationship*. Dordrecht, The Netherlands: Kluwer Academic Publishers, pp. 43-64.

Goldman, M. 1991, "Technology Institutions: When Are They Useful?" Washington, DC: World Bank (mimeo).

Guinet, J. and Polt, W. (eds.) 1998, "New Rationale and Approaches in Technology and Innovation Policy, " *STI Review* No. 22 (special issue). Paris: OECD.

Hull, C. J. 1990, "Technology Transfer between Higher Education and Industry in Europe," TII series. Luxembourg: European Union.

Inzelt, Annamária 1988, Rendellenességek az ipar szervezetében (Abnormalities in the structure of industry). Budapest: Közgazdasági és Jogi Könyvkiadó.

Inzelt, Annamária 1998a, "Institutional transfer in a post-socialist country: the case of the Bay Zoltán Foundation for Applied Research and its institutes" ATAS XI (New Approaches to Science and Technology Co-operation and Capacity Building).New York: UNCTAD, United Nations.

Inzelt, Annamária 1998b, "Are transition countries insiders or outsiders of the knowledge-based economies?" in A. Inzelt and J. Hilton (eds.), *Technology Transfer: from Invention to Innovation*. Dordrecht, The Netherlands: Kluwer Academic Publishers.

Inzelt, Annamária 1999, "Transformation Role of Foreign Direct Investment in R&D; Analysis Based on a Databank", in S. Radosevic, D. Dyker and L. Gokhberg (eds.), *Quantitative Studies for S&T Policy in Economies in Transition*. Dordrecht, The Netherlands: Kluwer Academic Publishers.

Laki, Mihály 1992, A vállalati magatartás változása és a vállalati válság. *Közgazdasági Szemle*, No. 6.

Link, A. N. and Tassey G. (eds.) 1989, *Co-operative Research and Development: The Industry-University-Government Relationship*. Dordrecht, The Netherlands: Kluwer Academic Publishers.

Nelson, R. 1993, *National Innovation Systems, a Comparative Analysis*. Oxford: Oxford University Press.

OECD 1993, *Frascati Manual*. Paris: OECD.

OECD 1997, 1998, *Main Science and Technology Indicators*. Paris: OECD.

Patkós, András 1998, "Excellence and Social Relevance in Hungarian Higher Education" in A. Inzelt and J. Hilton (eds.), *Technology Transfer: from Invention to Innovation*. Dordrecht, The Netherlands: Kluwer Academic Publishers.

Raymond, Susan U. 1996, "Listening to the Critics: Enlarging the Discussion of Policy for Science-Based Development" in S. Raymond (ed.), *Science-Based Economic Development: Case Studies around the World*, Annals of the New York Academy of Sciences, Vol. 798. New York: New York Academy of Sciences.

Vajda, Á. and Farkas, J. 1988, "Magánerő a lakásépítésben" (Private efforts in House construction), *Tervgazdasági Fórum*, No. 4.

Webster, Andrew 1994, "Bridging institutions: the role of contract research organisations in technology transfer," *Science and Public Policy*, Vol. 21. No. 2, pp. 89-07.

17

Challenges and Barriers of Technology Commercialization in Russia

Nikolay Rogalev

Macroeconomic tendencies observed in Russia from 1985 to the present might be divided into two main stages. The first one, from 1985 to 1989-1990, was characterized by increasing deteriorating tendencies in economics that mainly showed evolutionary development—that is, the rates of production increase were falling, the investment situation was unfavorable, and many projected parameters of the five-year plan were showing failure. The second stage, from 1991 to the late 1990s, has been notable for changes in the government's policy that have affected all spheres of life including politics, economics, and, among other things, the sphere of manufacturing.

Figure 17.1 shows at trend towards production recession over several years.

Tendencies observed in the majority of branches of the economy are indicative of a profound crisis which is characterized either by lasting recession or stagnation in manufacturing, deterioration of the industrial sector with increasing raw materials and resource-consuming branches, export of predominantly raw products, colonial export-import orientation, increasing number of unprofitable enterprises, and the unsolved problem of nonpayments.

Figure 17.1
Manufacturing Revenue over Time

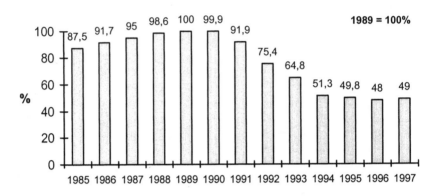

A radical reorganization of the economic system started in 1992 and its grave consequences have unfavorably affected the sphere of science and the higher education system. Among the main causes for the crisis in science and technology are the following:

1. The rates of cuts in the federal budgeting and the rates of recession in the demand for new developments on the part of the domestic industrial sector are significantly outstripping the rates of structural reorganization of the scientific and technological sectors. The result is loss of control and other losses.
2. Federal budgeting for R&D has dropped below the critical level. Among 25 members of the Organization for Economic Cooperation and Development, Russia is higher only than Turkey in terms of the ratio of allocations for scientific research to gross domestic product.
3. The altered structure of expenditures on R&D does not allow full-scale studies. Available funds are spent on electric power expenses and wages.
4. The existing system of taxation and tariffs as well as the rates of bank loans insufficiently stimulate scientific, engineering, and innovation activity and the influx of funds to that sphere from business enterprises.
5. The current system of administration in the sphere of science and technology fails to effectively pursue a common scientific and technological policy in full measure. Lack of proper coordination in the actions of the ministries and departments actually results in structural conservation and dissipation of resources which makes their full concentration on priorities of national importance impossible.

Figure 17.2 shows the data on the federal budget for research work and scientific developments for the years 1991-1997. As one can see, the estimate obtained by the deflator of gross domestic product reveals five-times decrease in the real financing as compared with the year 1991 (some experts estimate the reduction to be as high as ten-, twenty-, or thirtyfold).

Figure 17.2
R&D Financing from the Federal Budget

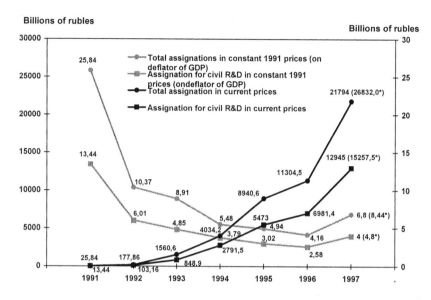

The number of employees in scientific establishments has decreased by nearly one-half since 1990, the majority being released from the establishments of industrial science (over 83%). The decrease in the number of the most highly qualified category of specialists engaged in science is considerable for doctors of philosophy but remains almost at the same level for doctors of science. The data on variations in the number of highly qualified scientific workers of high level qualification are presented in Figure 17.3.

Figure 17.3
Number of Research Fellows with Scientific Degrees

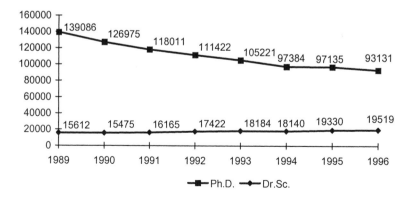

Not having accepted small business as one of the strategic priorities of economic development and having neglected the formation of the middle class, which makes up a stabilizing social base, the state bureaucracy (the government and bodies) has created a number of barriers aggravating the position of the most active part of society. These barriers have actually spread to all spheres of small business activity, including private security.

The major barriers include administrative, high taxes, access to start-up capital, and protection against organized crime and corruption. The administrative barriers are particularly unfavorable for small business activity:

- registration of business is very complicated and expensive;
- weak system of business activity licensing;
- redundancy in a number of control bodies with duplicate functions; and
- actions of the numerous government bodies which restrain the development of entrepreneurship.

For a long time in Russia, a well-known effect of "Laffer's curve" has been working. This consists of the following: whenever the tax rates exceed 45-50%, budget receipts from taxation stop growing and begin to decrease sharply. Business owners then stop paying taxes, which finally leads to reduction of the tax base.

Small business in Russia possesses some special features which make it different from the majority of other countries. The most significant features are the following:

- combination of several types of activity within the framework of one small business, and the impossibility in most cases to orient itself to the monoproduct model of development;
- striving for the greatest possible independence—in other countries, a significant part of small businesses work through subcontracts, franchising, etc.;
- high educational level (mostly engineering) of small business personnel due to the inflow of such specialists from the state sector of economics;
- low-level management skill, the lack of knowledge, experience, and culture in market relations;
- high adaptability to the complicated economic situation aggravated by the disorganization of the state administration system and the rampant criminal activity in society;
- insufficient development of the self-organization system and the infrastructure for small business support; and
- full and reliable information on the market is not readily available, and the system of informational, consulting, and training services is insufficiently developed.

However, the challenge of science and technology commercialization, and the problem with technology-based support infrastructure in former the USSR were first recognized in 1989 by the State Committee of Education. Because the initiators of science and technology parks were higher education institutions, most technoparks emerged at universities. The creation of technoparks is a priority of the Ministry of Education, and since 1992 there has been established an R&D program to study this problem in the Russian Federation. This program plays a catalyst role, encouraging and supporting universities in the set up and development of technoparks.

The plan-based economic transformation and movement into a market-driven economy in Russia required the establishment of legal foundations with respect to entrepreneurship and property, including intellectual property issues. A lack of suitable laws in the fields of patents, copyrights, trade secrets, and foreign investments, combined with a lack of small business support infrastructures—especially for technology-based industries—have forced universities to form their own policies to promote technology innovations through the establishment of companies and the creation of an environment for their successful development.

Technology regions which have had impressive success in countries with market-based economies—such as Silicon Valley, California, and Austin, Texas in the United States, a Japanese program for 19 technopoleis—have combined with the new possibilities for small company ownership to give rise to spontaneous entrepreneurial interest in various layers of Soviet and post-Soviet societies. Many researchers and engineers have a deep desire to build up technology-based products or services by making use of the results of their research and engineering activities in state-owned offices and to promote these products or services in the marketplace.

The Moscow Power Engineering Institute (MPEI) is one of the examples of technology innovation activity in Russia. Technology transfer in Russia has been a large problem, since most of the technologies were state-owned (or, as in the case of MPEI, university-owned). In its attempts to deal with the establishment and protection of spin-off companies as well as intellectual property issues, the university has tried to create a policy which satisfies both company founders and the university within existing legal restrictions. For these purposes, MPEI's research division set up a commission on new spin-off companies. This commission considers potential ideas, products, services, contributions, and the engineering and economic aspects of starting a company. The university considers innovation activity as a part of MPEI's teaching, research, industrial complex which unites business, academia (the research and engineering community), and governmental efforts in high technology development. MPEI's innovative structure is shown in Figure 17.4. The infrastructure's core consists of institute faculties and departments, the experimental steam plant, a special design bureau, and an experimental manufacturing plant. The most important elements of the university innovation system are human resources—the know-how of providing services—which are characterized by:

- high skill and qualification of human resources;
- wide range of research interests and knowledge areas at MPEI and easy access to networks of experts;

- developing university networks; and
- developing the university business school.

This core is the knowledge generation and basic innovation cycle, the educational know-how element, the design and industrial facilities for a product being manufactured within the university. This infrastructure's outside ring includes MPEI's spin-off companies and international joint ventures, as well as innovation process support elements for both the university and small companies; the MPEI Business Association, the University Commercial Bank, the Grants Competition Center, an insurance company, and the Science Park Izmaylovo are all part of this layer.

Figure 17.4
Innovative Infrastructure of the Moscow Power Engineering Institute

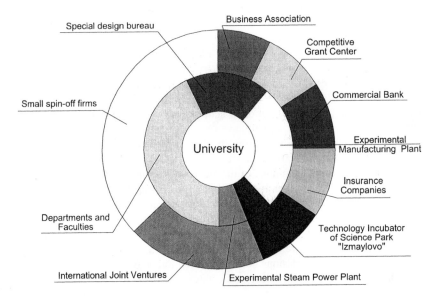

A special survey of university technology-based companies was conducted in order to determine the basic factors impacting the establishment and build-up of technology-based business. An approach used in the research of technology-based spin-off companies at The University of Texas at Austin was chosen as a model.

A list of MPEI spin-off companies was compiled according to University Business Association data and information obtained from reliable business sources. The list initially contained 59 entities. For the research, 21 companies were chosen from the list; companies whose activities were not connected with new technology-based products or with rendering technology services were excluded.

Information was compiled in the following areas:

- branch of industry in which the company works;
- reasons for establishment the company;
- role of other organizations in the establishment of the company;
- role of the university in the establishment of the company;
- role of the university in company development;
- major difficulties for the company; and
- major difficulties for the company's entrance into international markets.

The Lickert scale was used to evaluate the data in each category. Preliminary interviews were conducted with spin-off business owners, the staff of some departments, as well as administration employees in the office of the vice rector on R&D.

The research study was announced at a Business Association monthly meeting. Chosen companies were asked to take part in the research; two respondents refused, but the remaining 19 expressed their willingness to participate in the study.

All 19 of these companies were established by faculty researchers or university administrators. Among the founders there were 11 with Ph.D. degrees, three with Doctor of Science degrees, and five with Master's degrees. Most of them gained management experience through leading or administrative positions at the university.

While at the university, the founders of these companies were connected with engineering departments. The companies specialized in technologies, including services for high tech industries, software, hardware, electronics and electrotechnology, medical equipment, and others (see Figure 17.5). The other category includes R&D in energy and environmental control, and cryogenic technologies.

Figure 17.5
MPEI Spin-off Companies by Type

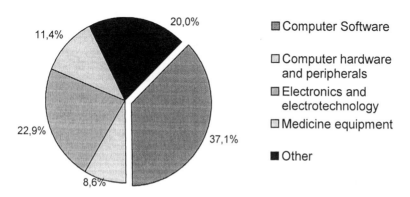

The comparison of spin-off company establishment between MPEI (Russia) and The University of Texas at Austin (U.S.) uses a research procedure which includes some approaches that have also been used by The University of Texas at Austin (UT) in a study of 23 technology-based spin-off companies.

The basis for comparison was the uniformity of the companies as well as of their products and services. UT companies were therefore divided according to type:

- 43.5 % are software companies (37.1 % at MPEI)
- 8.7 % are hardware companies (8.7 % at MPEI)
- 17.4 % are electronics companies, including electrotechnology (22.9 % at MPEI)
- 8.7 % are pharmaceutics companies (11.4 % at MPEI in medical equipment)
- 21.7 % are in other fields companies (20.0 % at MPEI)

Comparative analysis demonstrated a diametrical contrast in the numbers of employees at the time of start up. At UT, in contrast with the MPEI, individuality is predominant at the beginning of the company (Figure 17.6). There were no MPEI companies with a staff of only one person at start-up, while at UT this category exceeds 25%.

Figure 17.6
Number of Employees at Start-Up: MPEI vs. UT, Austin

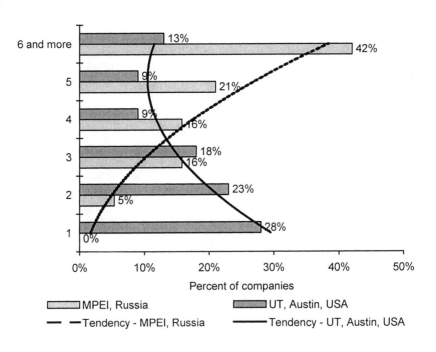

On the other hand, there is a high rate of correlation between Russian and American staff size some years after the company's establishment (Figure 17.7).

Analysis of initial capital sources (Table 17.1) reflects a trend in the self-financing of these ventures, but numerous differences in other sources of capital. The percentage of entrepreneurs drawing their own finances is very similar in both countries (68.4% at MPEI and 73.9% at UT) while the percentage of companies using private investments, venture capital and bank loans (36.8% at MPEI and 43.4% at UT) as starting capital vary considerably. Another major difference is that MPEI itself is an active investor into start-up companies, while this is not the case at UT (36.8% at the MPEI and zero at UT).

Figure 17.7
Number of Employees at Time of Study: MPEI vs. UT, Austin

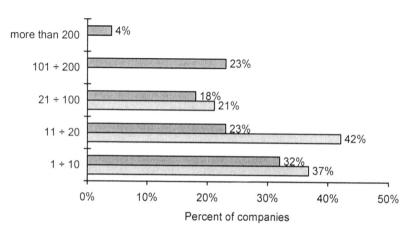

Table 17.1
Sources of Start-Up Capital.

	%%, MPEI, Russia	%%, UT, Austin USA	NN, MPEI, Russia	NN, UT, Austin
Self	68.4	73.9	13	17
University	36.8	0	7	0
Venture capital	15.8	4.3	3	1
Private investor	10.5	21.7	2	5
Bank	10.5	17.4	2	4
Research Grants	0	13	0	3
Family	0	26.1	0	6

An analysis of the university push factors for spin-off companies revealed similar importance placed on a number of factors—need more money, bureaucracy, rejections of ideas, and low career excitement (Figure 17.8). Aside from these, the most important factors for Americans were frustration, forced retirement, and dislike of their research; for Russian entrepreneurs, the dominating factor was concern for their future.

Figure 17.8
University Push Factors for Spin-off Companies: MPEI vs. UT, Austin

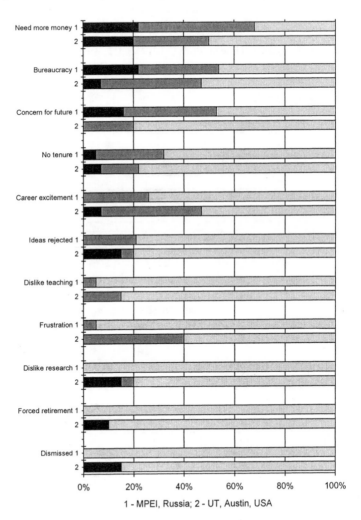

1 - MPEI, Russia; 2 - UT, Austin, USA

■ Very important ▨ Important □ Very unimportant

The pull factors affecting Russian and American university spin-off companies are less similar than the push factors (Figure 17.9). Despite relatively high correlation of the importance of some factors (the desire for individual independence, the possibility to implement theory and research into practice, gaining support for research, trying something new, desire to have their own company, and recognition of market opportunity), a separation of the "important" from the "very important" provides a different picture. For example, the recognition of market opportunity is "important" for 57% of Russian companies and for 7% of American ones; however, it is "very important" for 85% of UT companies, but only 10% of MPEI companies. A comparative analysis of such factors as the desire to have one's own company, fun with the venture, desire for wealth, and trying something new all revealed a common trend—a rather restrained evaluation of their own possibilities by Russian entrepreneurs, and a high level of self-motivation by Americans.

Figure 17.10 illustrates the role of universities (MPEI and UT) in company establishment. The main roles of the Russian university are to act as a source of personnel, ideas, intellectual property, to provide access to equipment, and an equity share in the company. The main participation of UT in the spin-off companies is in its provision of staff, ideas, and intellectual property, help with licensing technologies, and ideas from administration and faculty.

Figure 17.11 shows the universities' roles in company development. This includes such factors as being a source for personnel and ideas, research and consulting services, and technology transfer. In these roles, the American university's interactions with spin-off companies are more diversified and active.

The most serious problems met by the companies provide insight into the technology-based business peculiarities in Russia (Figure 17.12). While difficulty in the procurement of start-up capital was common for spin-off companies in both countries, looking at such factors as the search for suppliers or sources of financing reveals a lack of developed infrastructure in Russia that would aid in these business needs.

Most spin-off companies set up in 1989-1991 are located on the MPEI's campus and maintain close ties with the university, its administrative auxiliary services, and its research labs. In this way, they have secured access to university facilities. The companies used in this research study are shown in Figures 17.13 and 17.14. Looking at these companies, one could consider the university to be a dispersed incubator or an incubator without walls. Adoption of the incubator-without-walls concept enables us to trace companies' growth and determine the efficiency of the of spin-off incubation after their secession from the university.

The analysis shows that of the 11 Russian companies with three to four years' experience in the marketplace, only three met the criteria for successful incubation. This is only 27%; at successful technoparks and incubators worldwide, this number exceeds 80%. Successful companies have their own production lines, operating products distribution system, and skilled managers with occupational experience.

Figure 17.9
Pull Factors for Spin-Off Companies: MPEI vs. UT Austin

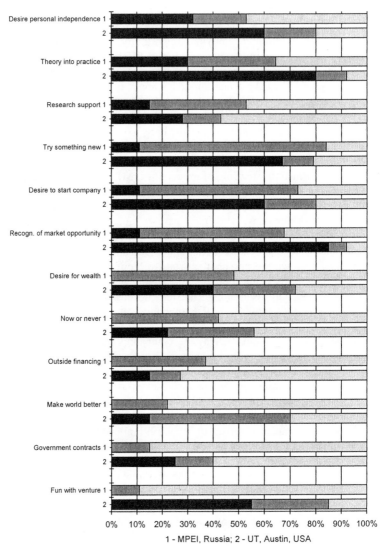

1 - MPEI, Russia; 2 - UT, Austin, USA

■ Very important   ▨ Important   □ Very unimportant

Figure 17.10
Role of the University in Company Formation: MPEI vs. UT, Austin

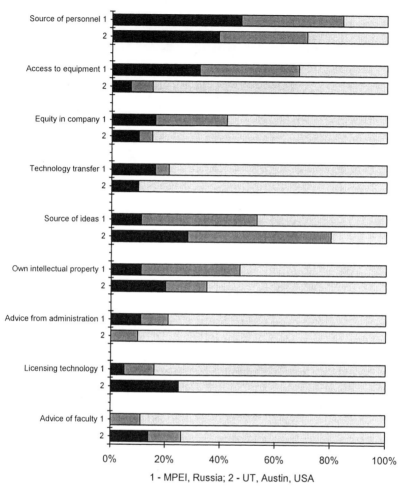

1 - MPEI, Russia; 2 - UT, Austin, USA

■ Very important ▨ Important □ Very unimportant

Figure 17.11
Role University in Company Development: MPEI vs. UT, Austin

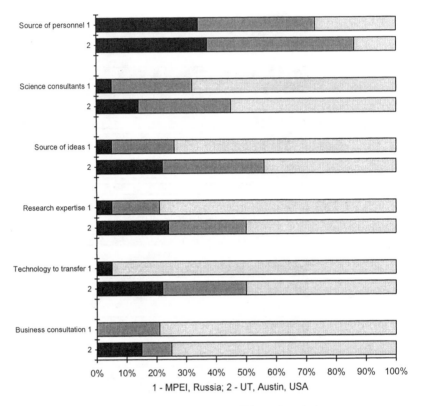

1 - MPEI, Russia; 2 - UT, Austin, USA

■ Very important ▨ Important □ Very unimportant

At 19 companies, 320 jobs were created for former or acting university staff. Analysis of the companies which did not survive shows that four companies ceased operation due to their failure to finalize their product and occupy their niche in the marketplace; four companies broke down due their weak management and departure of their leading experts. Five companies which were established with the university as a shareholder lost their ties with the university as a consequence of conflict between stockholders and managers. This is especially characteristic of international joint-venture companies.

Figure 17.12
Major Difficulties Facing Company: MPEI vs. UT, Austin

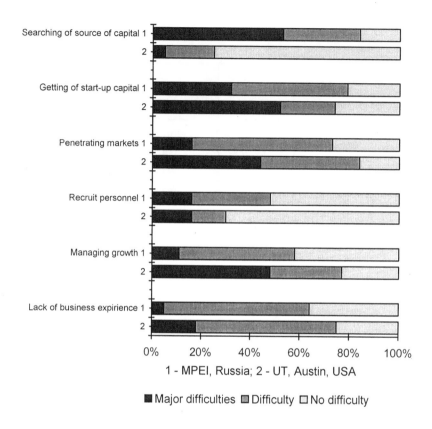

The dynamics of companies established with the participation of the research division and member companies of MPEI's Business Association confirmed the trend seen in the research of 19 technology-based companies. From 1988 an increase of spin-off companies establishment is observed, with a peak in 1991. In 1992 a number of newly established companies decreased more than two times, and in 1993 new company establishment, especially with MPEI's participation as a founder or consultant, virtually ceased—only one company was set up in 1993 and one in 1995. Graphic representation of these data is shown in Figure 17.13.

Figure 17.13
Establishment of University Spin-off Companies within MPEI

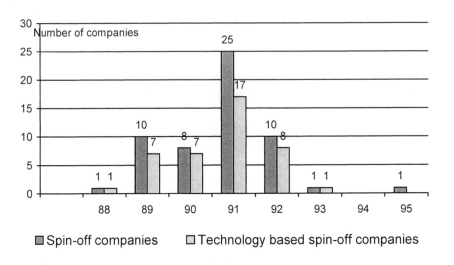

■ Spin-off companies   □ Technology based spin-off companies

Figure 17.14
Survival of University Spin-off Companies

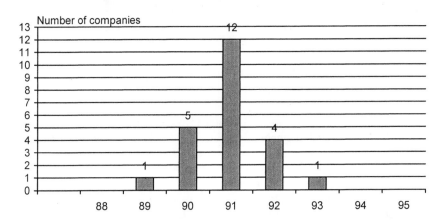

In analyzing company survival in 1989-1993, the first three years of their independent activities, three approaches were used to estimate company survival:

- estimation (a): ratio of companies still in operation to total number of university spin-off companies.

- estimation (b): there was no data available on several of the spin-off companies, since their connections with the main founders of the university have been lost. In this case these companies were excluded from the total being considered. This decreases the total and thus results in slightly increased survival value.
- estimation (c): ratio of technology-based companies still in operation to total number of technology-based companies that were spun out of the university.

Figure 17.14 and Table 17.2 provide data on the companies' survival estimation. As it is evident, the survival rate is 40-55% for companies located on the campus and having unlimited access, often preferential or free, to the university infrastructure, research labs, telecommunications, and so on (i.e., existing in environment close to that of Western science and technology parks and business incubator-without-walls concept).

Table 17.2
Spin-off Companies' Survival Estimation (July 1996)

Year	Number of companies	Estimation (a) %	Estimation (b) %	Estimation (c) %
1988	0	0	0	0
1989	1	10	14	14
1990	5	62	71	71
1991	12	48	55	65
1992	4	40	50	50
1993	1	100	100	100
Average	23	42	49	54

Worldwide statistics show that only 20-30% of companies survive past the first three years of their existence. The companies in this study have shown survival rates up to two times this rate. Nevertheless, these numbers are considerably lower than average efficiency of successfully operating science parks and business incubators around the world. In July 1996, of 19 companies being considered, only three university spin-off companies had more than 30 employees. Two of these companies have since reduced their staff to 14-17 employees, leaving only one company with a staff of over 30 employees.

The data illustrate the difficult environment for small business growth as a whole, and in particular for technology-based business. It is characterized by low company survival and ineffective incubation; the actual success rate for these companies is only 5% (one company with a staff over 30 employees).

This analysis of university companies would be incomplete without a comparison to trends being observed in Russia as a whole. Compared with the companies from the national branch of Science and Scientific Service, MPEI companies were set up considerably earlier. The formation peak at the MPEI was in 1991, while in the country as a whole it was in 1993—65,000 companies began in 1993, while only 10,000 began in 1991. This difference reflects the university's active policy towards innovations and the greater sensitivity of higher education to high tech business. Another factor affecting the effective companies' incubation in Russia is the larger staffs of university spin-off companies. The average staff size of a small company in Science and Scientific Service continuously decreased from 11 employees in 1991 to 3.5 employees in 1997, while MPEI company staff did not have a similar decrease. In early 1995, 63.2% of the MPEI companies had staffs of greater than 10 employees.

Looking at the formation of the infrastructure for support of small technology-based entrepreneurship and technology innovation reveals some peculiarities in a Russian university's innovation policy as compared to a Western university dealing with similar problems. This is related to the weak government policy at the federal and regional levels with respect to both R&D and innovative financing.

Financing in Russia is mainly provided by the ministries responsible for education and science, whereas in Western countries, university participation in technology commercialization is considered to be an important factor of regional economic development. Government-universities-industry cooperation is traced to a greater or lesser extent in all cases of high tech industry development. Such cooperation is by no means uniform across nations due to many factors: national traditions, university position and role, government priorities, and economic conditions in a region and/or country. However there are basic participants and roles. They are universities, large corporations, newly established companies, federal, regional, and local governments, and support groups. The federal government is responsible for research financing and defense spending; regional government is responsible for educational support and specialized engineering and entrepreneurship support programs; and local government is responsible for infrastructure, competitive tax policies, and standard of living. Support groups are involved in chambers of commerce, local communities, and the business community. Large companies are the major employers and provide R&D contracts. As for the university, it is responsible for training in engineering, sciences, and business, and for research centers.

In the case of MPEI, many of the above functions are performed by the University. The university acts as a large company by making direct investments and involving federal and state R&D budget spending for technology innovation financing.

Another peculiarity of MPEI is virtually absence of patents and licenses. During the period since the beginning of perestroika (1985-1997) and the beginning of spin-off company establishment at the university (1988-1996), not one case of technology licensing for transfer into companies who would pay the corresponding royalty has been registered.

The third peculiarity is the location of an overwhelming majority of the new companies on the university campus; in most cases they are located in departments, laboratories, and research centers. Rentable space became available following financial and research slowdowns, student cutbacks, and personnel reduction at MPEI. This is characterized as a "use" strategy; in countries such as Germany and Great Britain, the "construction" strategy prevails—where buildings are constructed specifically for innovation centers, business incubators, and science and technology parks. The Russian use strategy is based on economics: lack of financing, high cost of capital construction, and extremely low investments. While this strategy has numerous advantages, there are also considerable disadvantages. One of the greatest disadvantages for the university is the coexistence of the company and the academic department in the same space. This leads to the joint use of lab equipment, computing machines, mechanical workshops, and general university services. Many employees combine their work in a small company with their university work. This coexistence is good for a small company but requires that the university bear all costs related to running and upgrading equipment, as well as costs associated with maintenance of the building. However, the university is compelled to keep the companies on site to survive, as many of the university's faculty are also founders of these businesses, and 80% of the faculty members indicated that they would be unable to survive on only their university salary. If the university was to force the businesses off the premises, the faculty members would likely leave as well—something that the university cannot afford to have happen.

The results of the Russian universities' activities for generation of innovations and technology commercialization highlight the efficiency of the undertaken efforts. The major question now is which way Russia will choose to go. If the move is towards a raw materials export-import orientation, then all of these efforts and achievements will remain in embryo. If Russia tries to move towards the intellectualization of the economy, today's accomplishments can be a powerful driver for the fast growth and development of a market economy.

REFERENCE

Rogalev N. 1998, *Technology Commercialization in Russia: Challenges and Barriers.* Austin: IC^2 Institute, The University of Texas at Austin.

18

Policy Paradigm Shift in Japan from Science and Technology Policy to Innovation Policy

Schumpeter Tamada, Robin E. Sowden,
Manabu Eto, and Kenzo Fujisue

NEW POLICY PARADIGM FOR JAPAN IN THE NEW AGE

Increasing Importance of Product Innovation

A new era has come. People are consuming more and more intellectual or knowledge-intensive products, like movies and computer games, while continuing to consume traditional industrial products such as processed foods and automobiles at a steady rate. In addition, among those traditional industrial products, the proportion of the cost of intellectual inputs like programming and design is increasing. For example, the cost of avionics within the total cost of manufacturing an aircraft has increased rapidly of late and is now said to be more than 30%. Another example is the telephone: until quite recently, the telephone contained neither microprocessor nor program, but now, as Baker et al. (1997) pointed out, a cellular phone requires more than 300,000 lines of computer code. Similarly, the sales volume of a personal computer is determined nowadays not so much by performance as by the sophistication of the design.

These facts indicate that the importance of product differentiation or product innovation resulting from intellectual activity is increasing and the importance of capital-intensive mass production or process innovation is diminishing.

Japan has demonstrated technological prowess by continuously improving products and manufacturing processes, but has introduced relatively few epoch-making product innovations of its own. For example, Gover (1995) has shown that of 38 epoch-making products, none were invented in Japan, and only two of them were first commercialized in Japan (Tables 18.1 and 18.2).

Table 18.1
Invention, Commercialization, and Market Leadership (38 Items in total)

Innovations	USA	Europe	Japan
Invention	29	11	0
First Commercialization	30	6	2
Market Leadership	17	3	24

Table 18.2
Items Surveyed (38 Items)

Advanced composite materials	Consumer electronics
Advanced electric car batteries	Copiers
Anti-skid brakes for autos	Desk-top computers
Automatic focus cameras	Digital watches
Automobiles	DRAM memory
Biotechnology	Drugs and pharmaceuticals
Commercial jet aircraft	Facsimile machines
Communications electronics	Fiber optics
Compact disk players	Flat panel displays
Computer-aided design	[a]Fuzzy logic

Hand-held calculators	Numerical control machine tools
[b]High-temperature superconductors	Rocket propulsion technology
Integrated circuit manufacturing equipment	Robotics
Integrated circuit test equipment	Semiconducting lasers
Jet engines	Software
Medical imaging technology	Supercomputers
Microprocessors	Television sets
Military radars	Total Quality Management
Notebook computers	VCRs

[a, b] The two new products first commercialized in Japan.

Japan's strength in process innovation was highly effective in an earlier machine age, when quality and price mattered greatly, but the Japanese innovation system quickly showed its weakness in the new information age, when product differentiation and product innovation became more important. According to a questionnaire sent to 1,812 Japanese firms (response rate 26.5%

from 480 firms), which enquired into the level of creativity in their patents compared with those of U.S. companies, many respondents conceded that the patents filed by their own companies were less innovative than those filed by U.S. firms (Figure 18.1).

Figure 18.1
Japanese and U.S. Executives' Assessments of Level of Creativity in Patents

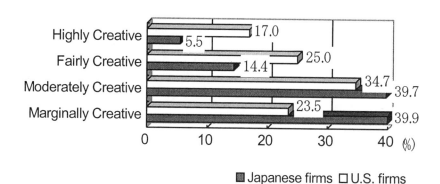

Source: Nomura Research Institute.

The new information age is an era of fierce global competition. The operational effectiveness that Japanese companies have enjoyed to date is necessary but not sufficient for Japan to maintain its present position in the world economy. What is required is not just the pursuit of lower prices merely by improving current products, but the introduction of strategies of differentiation that will also enable Japan to compete on the basis of added qualitative, nonprice values.

The Policy Paradigm Shift has Just Begun in Japan

Despite these dramatic socioeconomic changes, the science and technology policy of the Japanese government had mainly remained focused until recently on questions like "How can a nation best support basic scientific activities?" and "Which is the best way to initiate a joint research and development project between national laboratories and private firms?"

To justify government support for science-based activities, the static microeconomic theory of public goods was invoked: scientific knowledge has the characteristics of a public good and will therefore always be in short supply in the marketplace. At the same time, the positive economic impact of technology spillover was used to justify the use of government resources to encourage the creation of joint research and development consortia involving both public and private organizations.

However, that approach to the problems of science and technology policy is not the best way of securing sustainable economic growth through dynamic innovation in the private sector in a knowledge-based economy. For example, a joint research project established by several companies within the same industry might well reduce the costs and risks of R&D, yet actually hinder product innovation because all of the participants share the same key technologies in the same area. This shared knowledge can lead to the development of many similar products, so that the net outcome is an endless round of futile price competition without sufficient product differentiation.

Japanese industries are thereby losing competitiveness in this new information era. The Japanese government has therefore commenced transforming its science and technology policy paradigm into an innovation policy paradigm and, at the same time, restructuring governmental agencies and improving all the relevant policy tools. It is important that every organ of government and every tool of policy be examined and restructured or refocused as necessary from this standpoint, with a view to maximizing the speed of private innovation. The dynamics of national innovation systems should be enhanced if we wish to speed up the rate of innovation.

Innovation-Oriented Policy Paradigm

To maximize the rate of creation of innovative products, the Japanese government must understand better the workings of the national innovation system and concentrate on accelerating the innovative activities of private firms.

That is why, when working in the Technology Policy Division of the Ministry of International Trade and Industry (MITI), Eto and Tamada formed the Innovation Round Table and studied the Japanese national innovation system as to what was lacking in the system and what should be done to accelerate the pace of innovation. The major outcome of that work was the MITI Innovation Process Model (modified by the authors, Figure 18.2). Subsequently, the Council on Competitiveness was established under the chairmanship of the prime minister in order to devise a new economic policy to stimulate both the short-run and long-run economic well-being of Japan.

The MITI Innovation Process Model brings together three main components: the Industrial Activities (Producer), the Society (Consumer) and the Basis (Infrastructure). The relationships between the three components of the model are nonlinear. Industrial Activities are considered to be a driving force for innovation while the acceptance by Society of the goods and services thus produced drives further innovation. To maximize the rate of innovation, the needs of Society must feed back immediately to Industrial Activities. The Basis, which includes the human base, the knowledge base, and the social/physical infrastructure, supports Industrial Activities and has many of the characteristics of public goods. The spillover of the research activities of industry accumulates and thereby enriches the Basis (especially the knowledge base). There is also simultaneous feedback from the Basis to Society, for example in the form of education.

Based on this Innovation Model, government can enhance the speed of innovation in two ways:

- Build and strengthen the Basis
- Enhance the fit and reduce friction between the three main components of the model

Figure 18.2
MITI Innovation Process Model (modified)

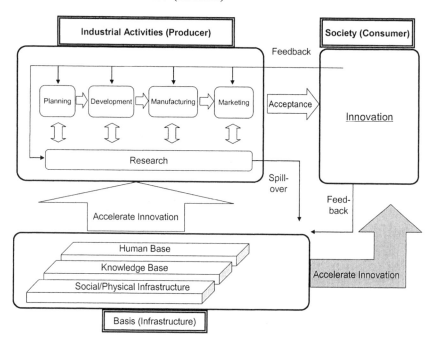

To realize an innovation-prolific economy requires the establishment and maintenance of all three elements of the innovation Basis in support of creative activities. The Basis includes the Social/Physical Infrastructure, comprising the physical infrastructure such as roads and telecommunication networks, and the social infrastructure such as universities, government laboratories and a legal system for the protection of intellectual property. The Human Base consists of those individuals and groups who create, maintain, and supply the knowledge required for innovation. The Knowledge Base includes industrial standards and all the other accumulated information/ knowledge that is necessary—for example, for the support of creative activities in industry and for consumer protection. Naturally, the three elements of the Basis are deeply interrelated. Taking the Human Base as an example, enrichment of the Human Base leads directly, according to the model, to the strengthening of the Knowledge Base.

NEW POLICY FOR THE NEW AGE

The role of government in Japan in this new era is to establish a socioeconomic environment that will facilitate and foster innovative enterprise. In the opinion of the authors, the best way for government to accelerate innovation is to strengthen the Basis (Infrastructure) and improve the three interfaces of the Innovation Model, which really means giving more autonomy to industry. In this section, a recent example of the planning and process of the implementation of Innovation Policy in Japan will be examined—that is to say, the policy-making process and the implementation of the experiment and research tax credits scheme, the results of a bibliographical search, an empirical study, and a statistical analysis of the results derived from a corporate questionnaire on the effectiveness of R&D tax credits as a means of promoting innovation.

R&D activities in firms are generally considered to be the major source of improvement in productivity. This is especially the case in Japan, where labor is relatively scarce because of the aging population and the capital growth rate is savings-limited. Technology spillover from private R&D activities enhances the national innovation Knowledge Base, which is one of the three elements of the Basis in the MITI Innovation Model. It should be noted that OECD (1998) has reported that tax concessions represent a market-friendlier form of government spending (as foregone revenues) to promote technological development and innovation than more direct means, such as subsidies or support for joint R&D projects. From the standpoint of private firms, taxation is an external condition that affects the costs of, and returns on, their investments: taxation modifies the external fiscal environment and so influences corporate decisions and executive behavior while maintaining their autonomy to decide in which technological areas to invest, how much, and when, without any government-specified directions.

Background of this Policy-Making Process

R&D Trends in the Private Sector

In Japan, private R&D expenditure rose by 14.6% per annum on average throughout the 1970s, and by 9.8% in the 1980s. Then, on entering the 1990s, the growth rate of total R&D expenditure in Japan begun to flag, falling to a mere 1.1% per annum on average. Prior to that, R&D expenditure had risen regularly until 1990 in almost every Japanese industry but, since 1991, the R&D expenditures have generally decreased, especially in heavy industries. In fact, in 1993, Japan's R&D activity was at its most sluggish since World War II, with R&D expenditure plunging for two consecutive years, despite significant annual increases in government R&D expenditure.

Status Quo of R&D Tax Incentives

New technologies resulting from R&D have a public goods-like property. Not only do they benefit the firm that carried out the R&D, but they also have a spillover effect that benefits other firms. In other words, technology is somewhat nonexcludable and spillover enhances a nation's knowledge base. If left to market forces alone, which work according to investment decisions made by individual firms, R&D investment will be below the optimal level for society. To make up for this shortfall, the majority of OECD members, including Japan, have introduced tax incentives for private R&D activities. In Japan, Articles 10 and 42(4) of the Special Taxation Measures Law provide "special credits for corporation tax in the case of increase in experiment and research expense and other similar cases".

Among Japan's R&D tax incentives, the tax credits applicable to incremental R&D expenditure (hereinafter referred to as incremental R&D tax credits) have been maintained unchanged since their introduction in 1967, aside from some minor modifications. The incremental R&D tax credits described below are the core of Japanese tax incentives for private R&D.

Incremental R&D tax credits, designed to encourage corporate R&D activity, provide tax credits when a firm expends more on R&D than the "benchmark R&D expenditure: the amount of R&D expenditure that the firm would use regardless of tax incentives". A firm satisfying this criterion is allowed to deduct a prescribed ratio of its incremental R&D expenditure from the corporate tax bill.

In more specific terms, if the amount of current-period R&D expenditure outstrips the amount of benchmark R&D expenditure, an amount equivalent to 20% of the incremental portion can be deducted from corporation tax. From a corporate perspective, this system has the same effect as awarding a 20% subsidy to extra R&D outlay in excess of the benchmark expenditure. The system is cost-effective because the incentive is offered not for market-mechanism-based R&D efforts made spontaneously by a firm, but for marginal R&D efforts beyond the benchmark figure.

Problem of the Japanese Incremental R&D Tax Credits System

The principal problem of Japan's incremental R&D tax credits system lies in the current rule for calculating the benchmark R&D expenditure. The rule has therefore been carefully reviewed in order to decide whether or not it is still appropriate in economic terms.

The benchmark R&D expenditure employed in the current Japanese system is "the highest R&D expenditure since 1965". Therefore, the more a company has spent on R&D expenditure, the higher the benchmark R&D expenditure. In other words, the system depends upon a historical all-time company high, since the benchmark R&D expenditure is renewed only if and when the previous highest R&D expenditure has been exceeded. This provides a ratchet effect.

Table 18.3 lists the countries having incremental tax credit systems and summarizes the differences between their systems. It is noteworthy that Japan alone has a low-incentive system with a strong ratchet effect, whereby the benchmark R&D expenditure is raised with every new application for an R&D tax credit.

Table 18.3
R&D Tax Credits in OECD Member Countries

Country	USA	France	Spain	South Korea	Japan
Tax credit rate	20% of incremental R&D expenditure	50% of incremental R&D expenditure	40% of incremental R&D expenditure + 20% of R&D expenditure	25% of incremental R&D expenditure + 5% of R&D expenditure	20% of incremental R&D expenditure
Benchmark	(R&D expenditure divided by sales from 1984- 88) x (Average sales in most recent 4 years)	Average R&D expenditure in the preceding 2 years	Average R&D expenditure in the preceding 2 years	Average R&D expenditure in the preceding 2 years	Highest previous R&D expenditure since 1967

The problem inherent in the Japanese system was not apparent in the days when firms could afford to undertake R&D unilaterally and both the size of corporations and their R&D budgets were rising continuously. However, with many a firm being forced by mounting pressures to change its corporate system by flexible restructuring of the company, this system, dependent as it is upon a high R&D expenditure benchmark, was thought to be no longer effective in providing an incentive to undertake R&D.

In fact, the total amount of R&D tax credits granted by the Ministry of Finance (Table 18.4) has fallen from ¥114.0 billion in 1992 to a low ¥53.0 million in 1997, with a negative growth rate registered consistently since 1993.

Since the Japanese incremental R&D tax credits system appeared to have become relatively ineffective in promoting innovation and the total amount of annual tax credits claimed was decreasing, a survey of Japanese companies was conducted in order to clarify the situation. The questionnaire therefore covered, among other things, the state of utilization of incremental R&D tax credits, their historical effectiveness as tax incentives, and the likely effects of changing the R&D tax credits regime.

Table 18.4
Trends of Total Amounts of Tax Credits

Fiscal year	Tax credits (¥100 ml)	Increase over previous years (%)
1988	930	3.3
1989	950	2.2
1990	980	3.2
1991	1 100	12.2
1992	1 140	3.6
1993	1 050	-7.9
1994	890	-15.2
1995	700	-21.3
1996	570	-18.6
1997	530	-7.0

Survey Method

The survey was conducted by sending a questionnaire in May 1998 to 1,753 randomly selected large Japanese firms capitalized at ¥100 million or more. The reason for sending the questionnaire to large firms only, which was adequate for the evaluation of the effectiveness of the Japanese incremental R&D tax credits system, was two-fold. First, the objective of the survey was to consider how to improve the incremental R&D tax credit system by understanding how the system was actually utilized and what were the effects. The majority of the users of the system were thought to be the larger firms capitalized at ¥100 million or more because small- and medium-sized firms (firms capitalized below ¥100 million or with fewer than 300 employees) have access to more advantageous alternative tax incentives, the so-called "tax credits to help small- and medium-sized firms bolster their technological base". This system allows small- and medium-sized firms to deduct unconditionally 10% of their R&D expenditure from their corporation tax bills. Since the small- and medium-sized firms can choose to make use of either this alternative system or the incremental R&D tax credits system, one would naturally expect the majority of eligible firms to prefer the former system.

Second, given that 95.4% of Japan's R&D expenditure (1996) was spent by firms capitalized at ¥100 million or more, the trends among the large firms surveyed give us a handle on behavior patterns in the Japanese private sector in respect of their mainstream R&D expenditure. The contents of the questionnaire are given below in detail, along with the results obtained.

Statistical Testing

The number of effective responses was 952, which put the net response rate at about 54%. The combined R&D expenditure of the respondents was ¥6,153.9 billion. This represented 82.3% of the ¥9,870.8 billion spent in 1996 on in-house R&D by private firms.

To obtain a 95% confidence level with a standard deviation of 5% would require 384 samples, while a 99% confidence level with a standard deviation of 5% would require 666 samples. The response rate of 952 firms exceeded both cases so, assuming that sampling was random, the results of the survey have a 99% confidence level with a standard deviation of less than 5%.

Results and Consideration

How Frequently Were Incremental R&D Tax Credits Used?

As shown in Table 18.5, 186 firms answered that they were "currently using" incremental R&D tax credits. This accounted for 20.1% of the effective respondents, which means that the system was being utilized by only 20% of private firms.

On the other hand, 400 firms, or 43.2%, said they had "used the current system (tax credits) in the past" but no longer did so because their R&D expenditure was below the benchmark. The number of firms which said they had "never used the system" was 340, or 36.7%.

Table 18.5
Use of Incremental R&D Tax Credits

Utilization	No. of firms	Proportion of respondents (%)
Currently using	186	20
Used in the past	400	43
Never used	340	37
No reply	26	
Total	952	100

The respondents who indicated that they had "used the current system in the past but no longer did so because their R&D expenditure remained below the benchmark" were asked when they had last used the system. Table 18.6 shows the years in which their R&D expenditure had been at its highest. There were responses from 384 firms and, of those, 62 firms stated that it was in 1996 and 51 firms said 1992. Indeed, as many as 81%, or 311 firms including the aforesaid two groups, replied that their R&D expenditure had reached its highest level in the 1990s.

The results of the questionnaire result show clearly that the majority of Japanese firms were no longer using incremental R&D tax credits because they had become ineligible earlier in the 1990s. In other words, this suggests that total annual corporate R&D expenditure had been set to plunge after entering the 1990s and, as we have seen, the amount of incremental R&D tax credits has indeed been in constant decline since 1993.

Table 18.6
Last Fiscal Year in Which Incremental R&D Tax Credits Were Used

Fiscal year	No. of firms	Fiscal year	No. of firms
1966	1	1987	6
1967	1	1988	13
1972	1	1989	13
1974	1	1990	31
1975	1	1991	61
1976	2	1992	51
1978	2	1993	34
1980	2	1994	33
1982	1	1995	39
1983	2	1996	62
1984	5	1997	3
1985	8	Before 1989 (Showa Era)	3
1986	8	Total	384

Effect of Incremental R&D Tax Credits

The respondents were questioned as to the extent to which the provision of incremental R&D tax credits influenced their R&D investment decisions. The results are summarized in Table 18.7. Of the respondents in the "currently using" group, 1.1% said the system provided the "principal motive" for increasing their R&D expenditure and 26.8% cited the system as "one of the motives" for doing so. The remaining firms, about 70% of respondents, said that they did not explicitly take the availability of incremental R&D tax credits into account when they decided their R&D budgets.

The weak incentives that the Japanese incremental R&D tax credits system provides to devote private resources to R&D expenditure is probably attributable to the aforementioned ratchet-effect.

Table 18.7
Motivation of Firms to Increase R&D Expenditure

	Principal motive		One of the motives		Not taken explicitly into account	
	No. of firms	%	No. of firms	%	No. of firms	%
Currently using	2	1.1	49	26.8	132	72.1
Used in the past	0		47	12.0	346	88.0
Never used	0		9	2.9	301	97.1
No reply	0				7	
Total	2	0.2	105	11.8	786	88.0

Spill-over Effect of Tax Credits

The respondents who reported that the availability of R&D tax credits motivated them to increase their R&D expenditure were asked by how much they intended to increase this because of the tax credits they were then eligible to receive.

Some 17.6% of those firms answered that they would increase their R&D expenditure by more than the amount of the tax credits. Combined with 40.8% of firms which had answered that they would transfer all the funds accruing from tax credits into R&D expenditure, about 60% of respondents stated that they would reinvest the funds from proceeds of tax credits in R&D. Their answers thus confirmed that the tax credits system has a spillover effect.

Expected Effects of a Revised Benchmark

The firms which answered that they could not apply for incremental R&D tax credits were questioned about the circumstances in which they would be able to use the system again if the benchmark R&D expenditure were to be revised in one of the three ways listed in Table 18.8. The replies, also tabulated in Table 18.8, clearly show that the greatest number of firms would be able to use the tax credits system if their R&D expenditure in the immediately preceding year were taken as the benchmark; what is more, there would then be no ratchet effect.

However, if R&D expenditure in the previous fiscal year alone were to be taken as the benchmark, a firm could receive tax credits without making any change in its net R&D expenditure by arbitrarily manipulating the timing of its R&D expenditure. For example, the firm could reduce the effectiveness of the tax credits system by carrying forward part of one year's R&D funds to the next year. A system that prevents such behavior would be preferable.

The average R&D expenditure of a firm in the two preceding years, if taken as the benchmark, would reduce this possibility by comparison with the above benchmark based on the firm's R&D expenditure in the previous year only, but there would still be some ratchet effect. The greater the number of years over which the benchmark is based, the less would be the risk of the abovementioned behavior but the more marked would be the ratchet effect.

Table 18.8
Expected Effects of a Revised Benchmark

Proposed benchmark	Would use	Proportion of firms	Would not use	Proportion of firms	Total no. of firms
Post-1994 highest R&D expenditure	125	33.1%	253	66.9%	378
Average R&D expenditure of immediately preceding two fiscal years	229	60.7%	148	39.3%	377
R&D expenditure in previous fiscal year	260	67.5%	125	32.5%	385

CONCLUSIONS

We have seen that in the 1990s Japan found itself in a new socioeconomic environment where the previous Japanese policy paradigm did not work well. Japan has therefore begun to shift from the policy paradigm of a science and technology policy to an innovation policy. Now, as before, tax incentives present unique advantages as a policy tool for stimulating R&D.

A properly designed system of tax incentives can stimulate innovative activities in a wide variety of firms, including those that may be shrinking in corporate size by, say, restructuring or the division of companies. An effective system should also be compatible with maintaining or increasing the autonomy of private firms in the context of their R&D activity.

It has been confirmed by the empirical research reported herein that the current incremental R&D tax credits system in Japan is no longer effective in providing an incentive for private firms to undertake R&D activities. In order to improve the motivation of firms to invest in more innovative R&D activities, it is therefore necessary to revise the Japanese tax credits system.

The Japanese incremental R&D tax credit system was originally designed to provide incentives to increase private R&D efforts by focusing on the incremental annual growth of corporate R&D expenditure and OECD has reported that this system is cost-effective. The authors endorse the view that the basically sound framework of the Japanese incremental R&D tax credits system should be retained. It should, however be made more widely accessible and enriched if it is to meet the expected demands of the new information era.

To that end, two options are available.

- Raise the tax credit rate on the incremental portion of R&D expenditure from the present rate of 20%.
- Change the benchmark R&D expenditure from the existing highest historical level of R&D expenditure to a less arbitrary benchmark.

Even if the tax credit rate is increased under the first of the above two options, the effect on total private R&D expenditure by Japanese firms is likely to be severely restricted because only about 20% of firms can take advantage of the tax credits system right now.

The second option, that of revising the benchmark, however, is entirely feasible, albeit with certain reservations. For example, among the possible variations of the second option is that of basing the benchmark for each firm on a fixed historical period, as in the United States. The U.S. approach, though, does not take fully into account the risk that there might be a significant change in the nature of a particular firm. The long-term cumulative risk to the tax credits system as a whole is therefore best avoided in the case of Japan.

Instead, it would be better to fix the benchmark for a firm on the basis of an average of its corporate R&D expenditure over the past few years. To fix the benchmark in this way would decrease the ratchet-effect of the current system, whereby the incremental tax credit system benefits the firm if, and only if, there has been an incremental increase in R&D expenditure. In other words, the current Japanese incremental tax credit system cannot adequately accommodate lengthy periods in which there is a downward trend incremental R&D expenditure.

On the other hand, employing a new benchmark based on the average R&D expenditure of each firm over the previous few years would enable even a newly restructured company to qualify for tax credits as an incentive to undertake more R&D activity.

The government of Japan therefore decided in January 1999, largely on the basis of the research reported in this study, to revise the incremental R&D tax credits system and the cabinet drafted a fiscal law, Special Taxation Measures Law, which was passed by the Diet in March 1999.

The new law has introduced a revised benchmark on tax credits payable in the forthcoming fiscal year. The revised incremental R&D tax credits benchmark for every eligible firm will be based on the average of the three highest annual R&D expenditures in the previous five years.

The changed fiscal regime is expected by the authors to improve significantly the incremental tax credits incentive for private firms to invest in creative and innovative R&D activities in the new millennium.

The next step in this research will be to investigate ways of refining the details of the new incremental R&D tax credits system in order to increase further the rate of innovation of firms operating in the Japanese fiscal environment. If, for example, governmental support for R&D activities between universities and industry has a greater net spillover effect than governmental support for R&D activities conducted by consortia of firms, then the introduction of a new university-industry liaison R&D tax credit could prove to be an effective new innovation policy tool. Similarly, if a certain multidisciplinary research area has the potential to deliver an unusually high net output-to-input economic ratio, then a new strategic technology area acceleration tax credits scheme might be worthy of consideration.

We have just set sail on the sea of innovation policy in a new information era.

ACKNOWLEDGMENTS

The authors thank all the participants of the Innovation Round Table. Tamada would also like to thank Professor Hitoshi Kikumoto for his warm-hearted perseverance; and the study would never have been completed without the sterling efforts of Ms. Yoko Nemoto and Mr. Tsuyoshi Takasu.

REFERENCES

Baker, S., McWilliams, G. and Kripalani, M. 1997, Forget the Huddled Masses: Send Nerds, *Business Week*, July 21.
Buch, Vannervar. 1945, *Science—the Endless Frontier* (A Report to the President on a Program for Postwar Scientific Research).

Gomi, Yuji. 1994, *Japan Corporation Tax Law*. Tokyo: Sozei Shiryo-kan.

Gover, J. 1995, *Research Technology Management*, March-April.

Kline, Stephen J. 1985, Innovation is not a Linear Process, *Research Management*, 28(4).

OECD, 1998, *Technology, Productivity and Job Creation—Best Policy Practices*, p. 165. Paris: OECD.

PART IV:
CORPORATE STRATEGIES FOR
THE KNOWLEDGE-BASED ECONOMY

19

The Cognocratic Organization: Toward a Knowledge Theory of the Firm

Filipe M. Santos and Manuel V. Heitor

INTRODUCTION

> In this society, knowledge is *the* primary resource for individuals and for the economy overall. Land, labor, capital—the economists's traditional factors of production—do not disappear, but they become sencondary. They can be obtained, and obtained easily, provided there is specialized knowledge. At the same time, however, specialized knowledge by itself produces nothing. It can be productive only when it is integrated into a task. And that is why the knowledge society is also a society of organizations: the purpose and function of every organization, business and non-business alike, is the integration of specialized knowledges into a common task.
>
> (Drucker, 1992)

The last twenty years have witnessed the development of a new paradigm in the areas of economics, management and organization theory, emphasizing the role of knowledge and contesting the orthodox understanding of the firm and the economy.

The neoclassical economic perspective views firms as rational entities, choosing among a set of feasible alternatives, in order to maximize utility given internal and external constrains (Nelson and Winter, 1982). This vision of the firm is static in the sense that the distribution of knowledge is given and the model does not explain how knowledge is created and changes over time (Nonaka and Takeuchi, 1995). In short, orthodox economic theory views firms as homogeneous input-output black boxes. This perspective has influenced organizational theory in viewing the firm as essentially an information-processing machine (Fransman, 1998), and strategy as a game of positioning and competition (Teece, Pisano et al., 1997).

The emerging knowledge perspective is concerned with the role of technological change and firm behavior in economic growth. The foundations of this approach can be found in the work of Joseph Schumpeter (1942), but its main development and application was done by Nelson and Winter (1982) in their seminal work on evolutionary economics. In their approach, the firm is understood essentially as a repository of knowledge, which is translated into routines that guide organizational action. Building on these perspectives and on earlier work in organizational theory that emphasized the mechanisms for the growth of firms (Penrose, 1959), a knowledge-based vision of the firm has been under development in the last decade, offering new insights for strategy and management theory (Teece, Pisano et al., 1997).

The aim of this chapter is to frame this new knowledge perspective in the area of organizational theory and show its usefulness for achieving a deeper understanding of organizations. We start by exploring the foundations of this new perspective, and proceed by discussing some of the key characteristics of the knowledge of the firm and presenting some dimensions in which knowledge can be classified. We then argue that the "language" of knowledge is extremely powerful to explain organizations. In fact, we propose that knowledge has always been one of the most important drivers of the functioning and structuring of organizations. We try to demonstrate this proposition by revisiting, using a knowledge lens, some of the most important organizational theories. Afterward, we discuss the contemporary approach to the knowledge-based firm and draw some implications for the field of organizational theory.

FOUNDATIONS OF THE KNOWLEDGE-BASED VIEW OF THE FIRM

The early foundations of a knowledge-based vision of the firm can be found in the work of Joseph Schumpeter and Edith Penrose, who developed alternative perspectives to the existing neoclassic economic theory. The orthodox economic theory, as discussed in the first section, views firms as machines operating according to a set of decision rules that determine what they do as a function of external and internal conditions (Nelson and Winter, 1982).

In contrast, the Schumpeterian approach is more concerned with understanding the dynamics of economic change and competition, and his work gave birth to a new school of economic thought. He conceptualizes capitalism as an evolutionary process in which changes in markets create the opportunity for entrepreneurs to generate new knowledge or new combinations of existing knowledge, in order to innovate and reap monopoly profits (Schumpeter, 1942). Schumpeter emphasizes the role of the entrepreneur as the agent of change, inducing firms to engage in a process of *creative destruction* through innovation. Nevertheless, being more concerned with the processes of economic growth in aggregate, Schumpeter did not develop a systematic theory of the firm.

In Penrose's seminal work (1959), a new theory of the growth of the firm is specifically addressed, giving birth to what was later called the resource-based view of the firm. Penrose sees the firm as a collection of productive resources (material and human) developed and accumulated over time. Thus each firm is unique and its history is important to understand its position and future opportunities. These resources can be combined in different ways by the administrative agents of the firm in order to produce services. The growth of the firm is dictated by the productive opportunities that arise, which are defined by the interaction between the firms' inherited resource situation and environmental opportunities. The managers of the firm, through the development of images of the environment, identify these opportunities and apply their managerial knowledge to enhance the firm's growth.

In the preface to the third edition of her book, Penrose (1995) states the relation between her growth theory and the knowledge vision of the firm: "growth is thus essentially an evolutionary process, based on the collective growth of accumulated knowledge in the context of a purposive firm."

These evolutionary processes of economic change were the focus of attention of Richard Nelson and Sidney Winter in their seminal work on evolutionary economics (1982). Nelson and Winter were concerned essentially with explaining the role of technical change in economic growth in a Schumpeterian tradition, but they went much further than Schumpeter in developing an underlying theory of the firm. They see individuals in organizations as responding to information complexity and uncertainty problems through individual skills and organizational routine behavior, in line with the behaviorist tradition of Herbert Simon (Fransman, 1998). Organizational routines are a metaphor for a collective notion of skills, and represent building blocks for understanding organizational capabilities and behavior (Tell, 1997).

For Nelson and Winter, routines represent repositories of productive knowledge. They state that *organizations know how to do things* through simple rules and procedures (routines) which represent the knowledge memory of the organization. Even firms in the same industry differ in the sense that they accumulate and develop idiosyncratic routines, which form the basis of the firms' distinctive capabilities. Fundamental to the idea of skills and routines is that they are constituted essentially by tacit knowledge (Polanyi, 1966) and are thus not easily replicated. Replication of routines is thus possible only as a costly, time-consuming process of copying an existing pattern of productive activity. Imitation of other firms' routines is thus a difficult process due to a lack of necessary knowledge.

The dynamics in the theory is brought about by the processes of searching for new routines and creating variety and mutations among firms, which are then subject to selection processes. The combined interaction of search and selection processes form the basis of the evolutionary approach and relate Nelson and Winter's approach to the theories of organizational learning and population ecology respectively. The routines are thus seen as the knowledge genes of the organization, being transformed by organizational learning and innovation.

Although Nelson and Winter's work provided a conceptual foundation for a knowledge-based view of the firm, an essential development was a deeper understanding of what constitutes the knowledge of the firm.

ON KNOWLEDGE

> Economists have of, of course, always recognized the dominant role that increasingly knowledge plays in economic processes but have, for the most part, found the whole subject of knowledge too slippery to handle.

(Penrose, 1959)

The purpose of this section is to clarify the concept of knowledge in order to facilitate a discussion of the relevance of a knowledge perspective for a deeper understanding of organizations.

Western epistemology has generally associated knowledge with the notion of "justified true belief"[1]. One can only know what is true, one has to believe that it is true and be able to justify the conviction. Frederik Tell (1997) defends a more pluralistic perspective on knowledge, based on the notion of justification. Knowledge should thus be viewed as *justified belief*. *Justification* means that one must be able to provide consistent arguments about the truth of knowledge, and *belief* means that knowledge is intrinsically a subjective creation. In other words, and without lengthening the epistemological discussion[2], *knowledge is a dynamic human process of justifying personal belief towards the truth* (Nonaka and Takeuchi, 1995). Using this definition of knowledge we turn next to a description of the central knowledge development process, clarifying the relation between knowledge and action and emphasizing the loose coupling between information and knowledge. This model will be fundamental to frame the discussion in the remainder of the chapter.

A Dynamic View of Knowledge

We start by considering the existence of a closed set of data about the world and defining information as "data relating to states of the world and the state-contingent consequences that follow from events in the world that are either naturally or socially constructed" (Fransman, 1998). We include in this definition of information the disseminated codified knowledge, which is external to the agent. The information set is thus continuously changing because new data are being created (as the world changes) and new knowledge is being made available. Nevertheless, in each moment in time, information can be considered as a closed and defined set (see Figure 19.1). The agent focuses its attention on the information set and tries to "process" it to obtain knowledge. This processing can happen both through cognition and sensing[3]. One key element is the attention process because it defines the pieces of information that the agent will focus and thus the enacted reality that he will construct (Pfeffer and Salancik, 1978).

Figure 19.1
The Process of Knowledge Development and Use

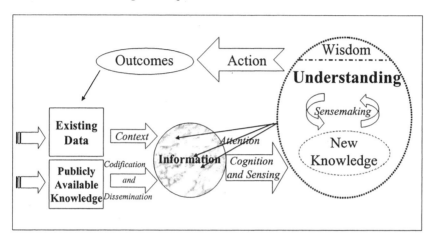

The creation of new knowledge is done by identifying patterns in the information and extracting meaning, placing it in the framework of what is already known and of one's identity. It should be noted that this process of sensemaking is essentially an ongoing social endeavor (Weick, 1995) of comparing new knowledge with the existing repository of shared knowledge. The end result of this process may be an evolution of the understanding of the world, the discarding the new knowledge because it opposes what is already known, or, if this opposition is too radical, a collapse of sensemaking. In this last situation the understanding of the situation disappears, leading to actions based on primary instincts (Weick, 1993).

The result of the sensemaking process, associated with the wisdom of the agent (which reflects its values and goals), leads to decisions and actions, oriented to the attainment of desired goals. These actions will have a certain outcome in the world (intended or not) and the outcome will lead to the creation of new data, which will then be contextualized into information, which the agent can focus again to create new knowledge and improve its understanding of the world.

This process of knowledge development and use, which is depicted in Figure 19.1, is very complex and ambiguous, and the proposed conceptualization deserves some remarks:

First, sometimes action is not derived from knowledge but, on the contrary, the process of attention and sensemaking will be the result of an attempt to justify retrospectively actions taken by random and ambiguous processes

(Weick, 1995), like the garbage-can model of decision-making (Cohen, March et al. 1972). In this way, action precedes sensemaking and the enacted environment will be an attempt to give meaning and coherence to behavior. Nevertheless, sensemaking is an ongoing process, and the retrospective sensemaking of past events will be important for the definition of new actions. We thus contend that a strong connection between knowledge and action still holds, and that the existing knowledge mediates between information and action.

Second, this conceptualization of the knowledge development process relaxes the long-held assumption of a tight coupling between knowledge and information. Knowledge is traditionally seen as a result of information cognitively processed and information can be a result of codified knowledge. Nevertheless the coupling of knowledge and information is far more complex (Fransman, 1998). Knowledge can be created with no new information as a result of improved cognitive processes. In addition there is always a degree of interpretive ambiguity, which means that created knowledge is subjective, contextual and open-ended. This interpretive ambiguity happens because information may be incomplete (due to uncertainty), leading to a weaker and sometimes conflicting understanding of the world. Even in a world of complete information, agents, constrained by bounded rationality and faced with abundant information, will focus attention selectively and might generate different pieces of knowledge[4]. Even when focusing attention in the same way in the same set of complete information, the process of sensemaking is dependent on the existing shared understanding of the world and on the cognitive capacities of the individuals, and thus will be subject and context dependent. The agents will enact reality according to their beliefs and will act based on the knowledge of their enacted reality. This means that a loose coupling best describes the relation between information and knowledge, and these two concepts should not be used interchangeably.

The previous discussion identifies knowledge development and use as a subjective, open-ended and context-specific process and highlights the cumulative nature of knowledge, the tight coupling between knowledge and action and the loose coupling between information and knowledge. The use of the term knowledge in the remainder of this discussion will mean the accumulated knowledge of an individual or organization, which is constructed into an understanding of reality and translated into routines of coherent behavior. The framework outlined above will be used as the basis for discussing some of the different dimensions in which knowledge can be classified.

Relevant Dimensions of Knowledge

The complexity of the construct of knowledge can be disentangled through an analysis of different dimensions of the concept. These dimensions will have important consequences for the discussion in the rest of this chapter.

Tacit versus Codified

When knowledge is created it appears in a purely tacit form in the sense that is context-specific and idiosyncratically linked to an individual or group (Cowan and Foray, 1997). Michael Polanyi (1966) first identified this dimension of knowledge by stating "we can know more than we can tell" and giving commonplace examples as riding a bicycle or recognizing faces. The most important aspect of tacit knowledge is that it is very difficult to transmit. Only through observation and doing is it possible to learn this type of knowledge. All the arts and craft activities are based on tacit knowledge, and a long-term relation between master and apprentice is required to transmit the knowledge of the profession, sometimes with a low chance of successful learning[5].

On the other hand, as knowledge is explored, used and better understood, some part of it may be codified (made explicit), being converted into messages which can then be processed as information. This process of codification requires the creation of mental models, reflecting the understanding of that piece of knowledge, and requires the existence of a language in which knowledge can be articulated. As codification entails a transformation in the organization of knowledge, it is always a creative process (Cowan and Foray, 1997) and does not replace entirely the tacit knowledge in which it was based. Furthermore, the use of codified knowledge always requires a certain degree of tacit knowledge, which is deeply rooted in action, commitment and involvement in a specific context (Nonaka, 1994).

The codification of knowledge into information allows an easy dissemination at a low cost, which leads to a cumulative expansion of the codified knowledge base of the society. The economic and social impact of this expansion is tremendous and may change the organization of economic activities and the structure of economic growth (OECD, 1996)[6]. Knowledge, once codified, becomes more like a commodity, which facilitates the creation of a market for knowledge assets (Cowan and Foray, 1997). On the other hand, the tacit dimension of knowledge will usually be governed within organizations, through flexible labor markets of independent professionals or through network structures (Powell, 1990).

In the context of this discussion, the concept of *technology* is related to the most visible and applied side of knowledge and it represents the embodiment of codified knowledge in order to enable its application. It can be defined as the tools, devices and systems that mediate between inputs and outputs, being used to create new products or services. The development and use of technology always involves a social dimension and an interrelation of tacit and codified knowledge within occupations, which is a point sometimes forgotten by researchers. One exception is Barley (1986) who studied the introduction of a new technology in two similar radiology departments and showed that it led to somewhat different structural outcomes in terms of the degree of centralization. The different outcome is explained by different institutional contexts and by the interactions of actors following scripts, which, on one hand, are constrained by existing structure but, on the other hand, enable a reconstruction of the social structure. What I think is surprising in Barley's study is the way in which the knowledge requirements directed the scripts followed by actors. The introduction of the new technology created a scarcity of knowledge, which upset the traditional status quo between the two professions involved in the study (radiologists and technologists). It is not surprising to observe that the profession that possessed more tacit knowledge about the daily use of the technology gained, comparatively, more decision autonomy[7].

Naturally it is simplistic to assume that knowledge can be classified in a broad measure of tacitness, ranging from purely tacit to codified knowledge. Some authors have proposed or implemented in their studies more elaborate constructs of knowledge. For example, Zander and Kogut (1995) have analyzed manufacturing capabilities based on the taxonomy of: *codifiability, teachability, complexity, system dependence and product observability* (Winter, 1987). This taxonomy, or variations of it, has been extensively used in empirical research.

Individual versus Organizational

According to Nonaka (1994), organizational knowledge should be understood as the processes that amplifies the knowledge created by individuals and crystallizes it as a part of the knowledge network of the organization. This process starts by the socialization of new knowledge (which can span the organizational boundaries), then advances to externalization (in which it is articulated in metaphors and analogies), then goes through a process of combination (in which is crystallized in new products and services) and finally is internalized by members in the operational routines of the organization. This *knowledge spiral* is highly iterative and occurs mainly through informal networks of relations in the organization.

As discussed before, Karl Weick (1995) presents this process in a different light, by considering that sensemaking is grounded in social activity and is thus a collective endeavor, through which shared meanings and systems of belief emerge, and new knowledge is created and legitimated.

Thus it seems that organizational knowledge should be seen as more than the mere aggregation of individual knowledge. Organizational knowledge includes not only the store of codified knowledge of the organization—the view of knowledge as a resource—but also the routines and processes through which the tacit knowledge of individuals and the existing codified knowledge are gathered, combined and used. These routines and processes help in shaping new knowledge and enable its integration into products and services. This dynamic perspective of the knowledge of the firm is more likely to serve as a foundation of a knowledge-based view of the firm (Spender, 1996). Later in the chapter we will explore this argument.

After this brief voyage through the realm of knowledge, we will now proceed by framing the emerging knowledge-based view in the traditions of organizational theory.

THE ROLE OF KNOWLEDGE IN ORGANIZATIONAL THEORY

In this section we propose to revisit, using a knowledge perspective, some of the most relevant theories of organization. The hypothesis that we advance is that the concepts related to knowledge have always been important to the field of organizational theory, especially in rational systems approaches (Scott, 1998), but have been implicit in conceptions or definitions, instead of being explicitly discussed, resulting in poorer constructs on knowledge. We will try to unravel the role of knowledge in organizational theory by placing it in its proper light in the context of scientific management and information processing approaches to the firm.

The Role of Knowledge in Scientific Management Theory

The scientific management movement represented the first systematic attempt to apply knowledge to the organization of work. Before the industrial revolution, economic activity was based on craftsmanship, which depended basically on tacit knowledge, embedded in individuals and disseminated through personal relations of master/apprentice[8]. The emergence of the large industrial firm and the introduction of mechanization and division of labor made necessary a standardization of the work practices. Frederick W. Taylor and his followers implemented this standardization by scientifically analyzing the tasks performed by individual workers in order to discover the procedures that would produce maximum efficiency (Scott, 1998). In other words, they wanted to codify the best practices through a scientific observation of the tacit knowledge of workers. For example, Frank Gilbreth, a disciple of Taylor, divided working activities in their most elementary movements (he identified seventeen basic movements which he called *therbligs*) and every type of work was codified as a sequence of therbligs (Cowan and Foray, 1997). In other words, movements were codified in a new language in order to facilitate the dissemination of best practices and their translation into organizational routines.

Taylor's approach to management involved concentrating all the knowledge in the hands of the managers of the firm, who would be in charge of designing the activity in the most efficient way, finding the best workers and planning the implementation and coordination of all tasks. He also proposed the creation of functional supervisors, knowledgeable about each specific area of the firm (maintenance, transportation, operation, etc.) cutting across the traditional unity of command[9]. For Taylor, the legitimization of authority and leadership would be derived from a deeper knowledge about work practices, and the behavior of managers should be more guided by knowledge and science than by individual discretion.

One of the drawbacks of scientific management, when analyzed in the perspective of a knowledge theory, is that Taylor and his followers didn't realize that every type of activity, even if codified to an extreme, involves the use of tacit knowledge by the individual worker. When they tried to codify work and afterward ignored entirely the tacit knowledge of the individual worker, they transformed workers into just mechanical appendixes of the machines and tools that they used, and in a sense, voided them of their intelligence and humanity. This approach of codification and concentration of knowledge could only be effective in firms using simple and routine tasks and operating in a stable environment.

On the other hand, the positive impact of scientific management in work productivity cannot be denied, and was essential to the accumulation of capital and purchasing power that occurred after World War I, and that led to a high rate of economic growth. Probably more than any other theory, scientific management was grounded on managing knowledge in organizations.

The Role of Knowledge in the Information-Processing Views of the Firm

Herbert Simon laid the foundations for the information-processing views of the firm by establishing the concept of bounded rationality of man. Simon focused on the cognitive capacity of agents to make decisions and solve problems. He recognized that, while agents intend to be rational and achieve their goals, their limited cognitive capacity does not allow them to process all the available information needed for making highly rational choices in a complex and uncertain environment. They are thus forced to operate in an environment of *givens*—premises accepted by the subject as a basis for his choices (Simon, 1976). Organizations supply these *givens,* through the definition of subgoals[10], the creation of stable expectations, the supply of information-processing infrastructures and the establishment of stable routines and procedures (Scott, 1998). Thus, organizational rules and routines support rational behavior within organizations (March and Simon, 1958).

Using this behaviorist concept of man as an information-processing organism with limited capacity, Jay Galbraith (1974) developed a contingent vision of the organization as essentially an information-processing machine, and considered information capacity as the critical bottleneck of the organization. The attempts to solve this bottleneck explain different strategies and organizational forms. Galbraith grounded his theory in the proposition that a greater uncertainty of the task environment leads to the need to process larger volumes of information, especially when associated with complexity and interdependence, because it's difficult to program and schedule the execution of uncertain tasks. Thus, during the actual execution of work, more knowledge and information needs to be acquired, leading to changes in resource allocation, schedules and priorities.

The information-processing view of organizations emphasizes the role of programs and routines in helping to deal with the complexity of the work and the environment. This interpretation is very close to the concept of routines as embedded organizational knowledge (Nelson and Winter, 1982). The focus of behaviorists on the uncertainty of the environment introduces the concept of change and adaptation, which is essential in a knowledge vision of the firm.

Nelson and Winter (1982, pp. 35-36) acknowledge the proximity of this perspective to an evolutionary view of the economy and the firm.

Nevertheless, when contrasted to a knowledge-based view of the firm, this approach entails some relevant differences. The information-processing view of the firm implies a tight coupling between information and knowledge, while, as discussed in a previous section of this chapter, the knowledge-based view of the firm should assume a more loose coupling (Fransman, 1998). This means that the vision of man as an information-processing organism overemphasizes the role of logical reasoning and organizational decision-making and neglects the role of nonlinguistic mental processes and tacit knowledge (Nonaka and Takeuchi, 1995). The proactive nature of man as a knowledge creator is thus neglected in an information-processing view of man and organization. It is illustrative to contrast this behaviorist approach to the vision of other authors who see the organizational man as an *image creator* (Barnard, 1938; Penrose, 1959).

Furthermore, recent developments in information technologies have increased the ability *to record, store, analyze and transmit information in ways that permit flexibility, timeliness, geographic independence, volume and complexity* (Zuboff, 1985)[11]. These developments mean that some activities within information processing are becoming increasingly easy to manage due to the tremendous advances of information and communication technologies. We contend that the activities of information transmission, analysis and communication are becoming commodities in the sense that it is very easy and cheap to buy resources to facilitate these activities. On the other hand, due to the accumulation of knowledge and overload of information, some other aspects within the broad definition of information processing have become critical, namely the capacity to scan the environment or the sensemaking capacity[12]. As we saw in a previous section this process requires intellective skills, a deep understanding of how things work and a focused attention. In summary, it requires previous knowledge, and thus knowledge development has become the critical bottleneck of organizations, the true scarce resource that is likely to be actively managed and explain different strategies and organizational forms.

RECENT APPROACHES TO THE KNOWLEDGE-BASED FIRM

Evidence has shown that the most successful organizations are those able to demonstrate timely responsiveness and rapid and flexible product innovation, along with the management capability to effectively coordinate and redeploy internal and external competencies (Teece, Pisano et al., 1997). This evidence led to the development of new theories of organization and strategy in the 1990s, with a more internal focus and dynamic perspective than previous decades. Although the proposed theories had similarities in approach and content, a diversity and confusion of definitions and concepts emerged (Tell, 1997), as capabilities, core competencies, resources and dynamic capabilities. This diversity suggests a scientific area in a preparadigmatic phase of development

(Kuhn, 1962). Nevertheless, some authors started to propose an integrated knowledge-based approach to the firm.

Kogut and Zander (1992) were among the first to lay out an organizational foundation for a knowledge theory of the firm. They emphasized knowledge and its strategic value as a source of advantage. They posited that what firms do better than the market is the sharing and transfer of knowledge within the organization. Knowledge, in their view, is held by individuals (know-what and know-how) but is also embedded in the organizing principles by which people voluntarily cooperate in an organizational context. Firms deter imitation by competitors through continuous innovation, which is achieved by a recombination of existing knowledge (Kogut and Zander, 1992).

Grant (1996) further articulated the theoretical foundations for a knowledge-based view of the firm. In his view, tacit knowledge is the most strategic resource of firms because it is idiosyncratic and nontransferable. As production activities usually require the combination of a wide array of specialized knowledge, which resides in individuals, the essence of organizational capabilities is the integration of individual specialized knowledge. The key integration mechanisms are direction and routines, and the main organizational problem is one of coordination.

Spender (1996) offered an alternative perspective of the knowledge-based firm, viewing organizations as dynamic, evolving, quasi-autonomous systems of knowledge production and application. He argued that researchers should move beyond the concept of knowledge as a resource of the firm and focus on the processes through which knowledge is developed and used in organizational contexts.

The contemporary knowledge-based view of the firm assumes that firms operate in dynamic environments, where markets and technology are changing fast and in unpredictable ways. It also assumes a highly competitive setting, with firms operating within ecologies of learning, interacting and adapting to the environment. In this framework, organizational capabilities or competencies are understood as clusters of knowledge sets and routines that are translated into distinctive activities. Dynamic capabilities are those that enable a firm to build, integrate and reconfigure internal and external competencies. The knowledge that is embedded in capabilities is a complex and dynamic combination of tacit and explicit knowledge. Individuals operate within organizational contexts in order to be able to share and use their specialized knowledge. In a nutshell, *the firm is a locus for knowledge creation and application.*

The concept of routine is central to the discussion of a knowledge theory of the firm, because it represents the basic unit of the knowledge memory of the organization (Levitt and March, 1988), and is the locus of embedded tacit and codified knowledge. A research seminar held at the Santa Fe Institute in 1995 revisited the initial definition of routine (Nelson and Winter, 1982), in light of recent research and uses of the concept. The discussants concluded that "a routine is an executable capability for repeated performance in some context that has been learned by an organization in response to selective pressures" (Cohen, Burkhart et al., 1996).

The careful choice of words in this definition helps to understand some of the core concepts of a knowledge theory of the firm. A capability is characterized as the capacity to generate action, to guide or direct an unfolding action sequence that has been stored in some localized or distributed form. Execution was perceived as repeatedly possible only in a given and well-known context, within which action accomplishes some transformation. A routine is learned in the sense that implies tacitness and automaticity, but also the possibility of search and selection in response to external or internal pressures.

The proposed definition of routines emphasizes their relation to learning[13] (Cohen, Burkhart et al., 1996), and is consistent with the proposition of James March (1991) that an appropriate balance between the exploration of new possibilities (associated with notions such as search and innovation) and the exploitation of the existing knowledge and routines (associated with notions such as refinement and execution) is a primary factor for the survival and prosperity of a system. This balance is difficult to achieve given the self-reinforcing characteristics of both exploration and exploitation, which can lead to learning traps. A firm needs to engage in sufficient exploitation to ensure its current viability and, at the same time, devote enough energy to exploration to ensure its future viability. The optimal mix of exploration and exploitation is thus hard to specify (Levinthal and March, 1993).

A determinant of the effectiveness of exploration and exploitation activities is the level of absorptive capacity (Cohen and Levinthal, 1990), which is defined as the ability of a firm to recognize the value of new external information, assimilate it and apply it to commercial ends. According to the authors, the absorptive capacity is largely a function of the level of the firm's prior knowledge (which emphasizes the cumulative nature of knowledge) and is also history or path dependent (which emphasizes the importance of earlier decisions). The level of absorptive capacity is heavily dependent on the level of absorptive capacity of each individual in the organization, but is different from the sum of the parts. It not only depends on the interface with the environment but also involves the internal transfer and communication of knowledge. This concept calls attention to the internal channels of communication, to the distribution of knowledge in the firm and to the pattern of R&D investment decisions.

Nonaka and Takeuchi (1995), as a result of their conceptualization of the organizational knowledge creation process, which was already discussed in a previous section, have also called attention to some organizational characteristics. Specifically they propose the institutionalization of a *creative chaos* and a reflection-in-action attitude. They also propose the creation of information redundancy and parallel processing modes in order to foster the knowledge-creation process, and they see middle management as having a crucial role in this process.

As we can see, the knowledge vision of the firm is starting to be clear enough to enable the inference of management, strategy and organizational design implications. This perspective has fostered the development of an extensive number of empirical works in recent years, aimed at testing and refining the proposed concepts and theories. It is not the aim of this chapter to review such literature[14], but to frame this new perspective in the tradition and future of organizational theory. This will be the theme of the final section.

IMPLICATIONS FOR THE FIELD OF ORGANIZATIONAL THEORY

The knowledge vision of the firm is grounded on the rational-open systems tradition of organizational theory, as described by W. Richard Scott (1998). It can be characterized as a rational perspective because it views the behavior in organizations as actions performed by purposeful and coordinated agents, while accounting for the existing cognitive limitations and organizational constrains. It can be characterized as an open systems perspective because it acknowledges the complexity of organizations, viewing them as a coupling of autonomous and interdependent parts in constant relation with their environment.

Nevertheless, the knowledge-based theory of the firm does not neglect the natural systems tradition of organizational theory, in the sense that it recognizes the ambiguity of the knowledge-creation process and the importance of the informal organization for the creation and sharing of organizational knowledge. It's also an institutional approach, both in the economic meaning of the word, since the organization of the firm truly matters, and in the sociological meaning of the word, because it recognizes the importance of the institutional environment and accounts for the dependence on historical trajectories.

Finally, it has perspective with a truly global origin because it has been developed jointly and in parallel ways by researchers and practitioners in the United States, Europe and Asia[15]. It thus is less American biased than the mainstream organizational theory, and probably reflects a broader context and applicability.

Due to all the reasons described above, we will contend that a knowledge theory of the firm will offer to the area of organizational theory a truly integrative approach. First, as it's a new approach, it was able to incorporate recent findings from other fields, namely economics, epistemology, psychology, sociology, biology and strategic management, thus reinforcing the multidisciplinary character of organizational theory. Second, it is capable of reconciling long-opposing perspectives, as the rational versus natural approaches to organizations, or the Western versus Eastern perspectives on knowledge and management. Finally, it will be able to provide a deeper understanding of organizations and the economy, in a society where the impact of knowledge accumulation is increasing and the rhythm of technology change is accelerating.

One question which arises from the discussion in this chapter is what can a knowledge theory of the firm explain which is not already explained by existing theories? We believe that a knowledge theory of the firm, using a focus on the knowledge processes of the firm, can unveil the sources of competitive advantage in an increasingly competitive, complex and dynamic environment. The knowledge-based view of the firm will allow researchers to go beyond general and abstract concepts, such as absorptive capacity or organizational knowledge creation, and explore the more specific and observable knowledge processes of the firm. They can explore how organizations access and acquire new knowledge, and how this knowledge is organized, integrated and applied into new products and services. They can also explore how knowledge evolves in organizations and explain how organizations are able to routinely innovate.

In conclusion, and in contrast to the general tone of this chapter, we offer a word of caution. We think that a knowledge theory of the firm does not yet exist. What exists now and was described here is a knowledge *vision* of the firm, the basic framework for the development of a more complete theory. The empirical research and management practices being implemented, or starting in the near future, will be essential to establish the validity and relevance of this approach to the field of organizational theory, and will make the difference between a marginal contribution and a mainstream theory. We have confidence that a knowledge theory of the firm will in fact emerge as a mainstream school of thought, and we believe that, when that happens, the crucial question asked by Ronald Coase in 1937, *Why does the firm exist?*, will have a new answer. An answer that will account not only for the prevalence of organizations in modern society, but one that will also account for the increasing importance of networks (Powell, 1990) as a third governance structure.

NOTES

1. For an interesting discussion on the contrast between Western and Eastern epistemology, see Nonaka and Takeuchi (1995, pp. 20-32).

2. For a thorough epistemological discussion of the most relevant concept of knowledge on which to build a knowledge theory of the firm, see chapter 3 of Tell (1997).

3. We thus adopt an empiricist view of knowledge in that knowledge can be gained both through reflection and sensation, leading to a broader definition of knowledge, encompassing the more cognitive mental constructs and the more intuitive skills and abilities.

4. This aspect calls attention to the importance of the information systems of the organization because these systems focus the attention of members of the organization in selected aspects of the environment and thus influence the enactment process (Pfeffer and Salancik, 1978).

5. Are the disciples of Picasso near as good as the master? Additionally, it is interesting to notice how much of the education of a PhD student incorporates tacit knowledge and requires a long-term relationship with the supervisor.

6. For a thorough discussion of the economics of codification and diffusion of knowledge see Cowan and Foray (1997).

7. Barley recognizes the importance but not the causality of this knowledge shift for the different outcomes observed, which means that knowledge should not be seen as a determinant of structure but as the key variable that constrains agency and helps to understand social events.

8. In this respect the medieval guild can be seen as an elaborate structure to nurture and protect the value of scarce knowledge assets embedded in individuals (Stewart, 1997).

9. This is a structure that resembles a matrix organization but which was not widely adopted at the time.

10.   Organizational goals are seen as being organized in a hierarchy of goals linking the several levels of organization through mean-ends chains (Simon, 1976).

11.   Zuboff's main point is that information technologies have the capacity to inform work, translating the physical reality into an informational reality based on real time data and analysis. Thus, information technologies replace physical and sensual activities that require embodied skills, by mental and analytic activities that require intellective skills.

12.   It's interesting to note that information systems have been developed at a higher rate and level of effectiveness than knowledge or expert systems.

13.   For an extensive review of organizational learning and its relation to routines and organizational knowledge see Levitt and March (1988).

14.   That will be our next research goal.

15.   The initial evidence of the importance of the knowledge-creation process came from the success of Japanese companies and some of the best ideas and practices have originated in Europe.

REFERENCES

Barley, S. R. (1986). "Technology as an Occasion for Structuring: Evidence from Observations of CT Scanners and the Social Order of Radiology Department". *Administrative Science Quarterly* 31(1): 78-108.

Barnard, C. I. (1938). *The Functions of the Executive.* Cambridge: MA, Harvard University Press.

Coase, R. (1937). "The Nature of the Firm." *Economica* 4: 386-405.

Cohen, M. D., R. Burkhart, et al. (1996). "Routines and Other Recurring Action Patterns of Organizations: Contemporary Research Issues." *Industrial and Corporate Change* 5: 653-698.

Cohen, M. D., J. March, et al. (1972). "A Garbage Can Model of Organizational Choice". *Administrative Science Quarterly* 17(1): 1-25.

Cohen, W. M. and D. A. Levinthal (1990). "Absorptive Capacity: A New Perspective on Learning and Innovation." *Administrative Science Quarterly* 35(1): 128-152.

Cowan, R. and D. Foray (1997). "The Economics of Codification and the Diffusion of Knowledge." *Industrial and Corporate Change* 6(3): 595-622.

Drucker, P. (1992). "The New Society of Organizations." *Harvard Business Review* (September-October): 95-104.

Fransman, M. (1998). Information, Knowledge, Vision and Theories of the Firm. In *Technology, Organization and Competitiveness*, G. Dosi, D. J. Teece and J. Chytry (eds.). New York: Oxford University Press.

Galbraith, J. (1974). "Organization Design: An Information Processing View." *Interfaces* 4: 28-36.

Grant, R. M. (1996). "Toward a Knowledge-Based Theory of the Firm." *Strategic Management Journal* 17 (Winter Special Issue): 109-122.

Kogut, B. and U. Zander (1992). "Knowledge of the Firm, Combinative Capabilities, and the Replication of Technology." *Organization Science* 3(3): 383-397.

Kuhn, T. (1962). *The Structure of Scientific Revolutions.* Chicago: University of Chicago Press.

Levinthal, D. A. and J. G. March (1993). "The Myopia of Learning." *Strategic Management Journal* 14: 95-112.

Levitt, B. and J. G. March (1988). "Organizational Learning." *American Review of Sociology* 14: 319-340.

March, J. and H. Simon (1958). *Organizations.* New York: Wiley.

March, J. G. (1991). "Exploration and Exploitation in Organizational Learning." *Organization Science* 2(1): 71-87.

Nelson, R. R. and S. G. Winter (1982). *An Evolutionary Theory of Economic Change.* Cambridge, MA: Belknap-Harvard University Press.

Nonaka, I. (1994). "Dynamic Theory of Organizational Knowledge Creation." *Organization Science* 5(1): 14-37.

Nonaka, I. and H. Takeuchi (1995). *The Knowledge-Creating Company.* New York: Oxford University Press.

OECD (1996). Technology, Productivity and Job Creation: Analytical Report, OECD.

Penrose, E. (1959). *The Theory of the Growth of the Firm.* Oxford: Basil Blackwell.

Penrose, E. (1995). *The Theory of the Growth of the Firm* (3rd edition). Oxford: Oxford University Press.

Pfeffer, J. and G. Salancik (1978). *The External Control of Organizations.* New York: Harper & Row Publishers.

Polanyi, M. (1966). *The Tacit Dimension.* London: Routledge & Kegan Paul.

Powell, W. W. (1990). Neither Market or Hierarchy: Network Forms of Organization. *Research in Organizational Behavior*, vol. 12, B. M. Staw and L. L. Cummings (eds.). Greenwich, CT: JAI Press, pp. 295-336.

Schumpeter, J. (1942). *Capitalism, Socialism and Democracy.* New York: Harper.

Scott, W. R. (1998). *Organizations: Rational, Natural and Open Systems.* Upper Saddle River, NJ: Prentice Hall.

Simon, H. (1976). *Administrative Behavior.* New York: MacMillan.

Spender, J.-C. (1996). "Making Knowledge the Basis of a Dynamic Theory of the Firm." *Strategic Management Journal* 17 (Winter Special Issue): 45-62.

Stewart, T. A. (1997). *Intellectual Capital—The New Wealth of Organizations.* New York: Doubleday.

Teece, D. J., G. Pisano, et al. (1997). "Dynamic Capabilities and Strategic Management." *Strategic Management Journal* 18(7): 509-533.

Tell, F. (1997). *Knowledge and Justification—Exploring the Knowledge Based Firm.* Linkoping, Sweden, Linkoping University.

Weick, K. (1993). "The Collapse of Sensemaking in Organizations: The Mann Gulch Disaster." *Administrative Science Quarterly* 38: 628-652.

Weick, K. (1995). *Sensemaking in Organizations.* London: Sage Publications.

Winter, S. (1987). "Knowledge and Competence as Strategic Assets." *The Competitive Challenge—Strategies for Industrial Innovation and Renewal*, D. Teece (ed.). Cambridge, MA: Ballinger.

Zander, U. and Kogut, B. (1995). "Knowledge and the Speed of Transfer and Imitation of Organizational Capabilities: An Empirical Test." *Organization Science, 6*(1), January-February: 76-92.

Zuboff, S. (1985). *In the Age of the Smart Machine.* New York: Basic Books.

20

Restructuring to Build Knowledge-Integration Capabilities for Innovation

Simon Collinson

INTRODUCTION

This chapter is concerned with how, and how well, different firms organise and manage specialist knowledge and expertise for innovation. Specialisation is a central feature both in knowledge-based approaches to understanding firm behaviour and in frameworks that explain corporate competitive advantage. Firms consist of combinations of individuals with specialist knowledge and of departments and divisions with specialist functions and capabilities. Specialisation in particular technologies, products and markets provides the primary corporate advantage.

All of these dimensions of specialisation together *differentiate* firms. Evolutionary approaches to understanding firm behaviour stress that maintaining particular kinds of differentiation and maintaining this distinctiveness ensures sustained competitive advantage. Innovative companies create new knowledge and (far more frequently) recombine existing knowledge and expertise to create new technologies, products, processes, services and to access new markets. But all firms, even the most innovative, copy the outputs and *behaviour* of other firms that prove to be the source of competitive advantage. So the ease or difficulty of replicating these sources of competitive advantage, of reducing or removing distinctiveness, is of significant interest for both management theory and practice.

This chapter supports the emerging view that in addition to the specialist knowledge and expertise developed in companies, the management practices, routines and structures by which they organise this knowledge underpins their distinctiveness (Leonard-Barton, 1995; Teece, 1998). These are dynamic capabilities since there is a need to continuously acquire, develop, integrate and leverage knowledge to fulfil evolving corporate objectives. Here we argue that the increasing importance of knowledge and intellectual capital in many competitive environments places a significant premium on knowledge management capabilities as sources of competitive advantage.

The following sections outline some of the theoretical background and evidence underlying the above assertions. The next section summarises some of the relevant theoretical approaches, and this is followed by a brief review of some of the changes in the competitive environment that are placing a premium on knowledge management and particularly knowledge-integration capabilities of firms. The chapter then describes a comparative study of eight large Japanese and British manufacturing firms (including ICI, British Steel, British Aerospace [BAE], British Telecom, Nippon Steel Corporation and NTT) which focused on the organisation forms and management practices they used for managing R&D, process and product innovation.[1]

The study reveals a range of cross-sector and cross-national differences between these firms in terms of their knowledge management practices and in some cases links these differences directly to their process and product development performance. This chapter addresses how the British firms have restructured in recent years in response to the new competitive pressures. The final sections briefly describe the study, summarise some of the main problems faced by senior managers in managing innovation and look at the new forms of organisation introduced by the U.K. firms in response to the above changes. These include a top-down coordination structure for directing R&D priorities at ICI; an Intranet for linking specialists across various departments at ICI; a cross-functional technology management role at BAE; a team-based structure for managing continuous improvement at British Steel Strip Products mill sites; and a customer-oriented product development unit at British Steel.

Given the focus on sustained distinctiveness, the restructuring processes in the case study firms are examined in terms of how easy or difficult various changes proved to be to implement. This highlights (particularly in the steel sector study) how "best practice" management or "ideal types" of organisation observed in competitors may or may not be replicated. At the same time, in looking at company efforts to improve knowledge management capabilities, the study identifies a number of factors which give rise to inertia or path-dependency within firms.

The study shows that while firms were usually able to put new practices in place, these often did not have a significant impact on knowledge management or innovative performance because broader organisation change was required to facilitate integrative capabilities. These observations led to the conclusion that some knowledge management capabilities are strongly embedded in the broader context of organisations. This means they represent *sustained differences*, often conveying competitive advantage, because they are difficult to emulate or transfer to different organisation contexts. This also means they may be difficult to change when new conditions demand a change in strategy and a revised set of capabilities. Some of the implications, for firms that are now looking to improve knowledge management capabilities and for Japanese firms currently faced with a range of new competitive challenges, are discussed.

KNOWLEDGE MANAGEMENT CAPABILITIES WITHIN AN EVOLUTIONARY PERSPECTIVE

Despite its recent resurgence the issue of how firms manage knowledge has long been of concern to economists, before it was taken up by management theorists. Adam Smith, Alfred Marshall and Frederick Hayek were all concerned with the valuation (pricing) and utilisation (management) of knowledge which was fragmented around organisations in specialist departments and skilled individuals (Fransman, 1999). The importance of knowledge management and learning in companies was emphasised by Edith Penrose (1959) among others, and strengthened by Cyert and March's (1963) "behavioural approach" and Arrow's later work on learning (1974).

Out of the huge range of recent studies looking at knowledge management this chapter draws mainly from those that adopt the dynamic capabilities approach associated with David Teece. A subset of this literature takes an evolutionary perspective, emphasising the significance of capabilities that are difficult to replicate and therefore convey distinctiveness which may (or may not) underpin competitive advantage (as described above). Through her book *Wellsprings of Knowledge* Dorothy Leonard-Barton (1995) is a leading exponent of this approach. Her concept of core capabilities follows the above description closely and is comprised of "employee knowledge or skill", "physical or technological systems", "managerial systems" and "values", with the latter dimensions representing knowledge-control or channelling mechanisms and the former representing "stocks" of knowledge and competence that need to be continually replenished. Organisational mechanisms that support learning activities and knowledge integration in firms are at the centre of Leonard-Barton's analysis. She also describes how core capabilities can act as "core rigidities", as the source of inertia and resistance to change in the organisation, again echoing other writers who take an evolutionary (or Shumpeterian) perspective.

Along similar lines but with a stronger link with evolutionary economics approaches and the innovation studies school, Metcalfe and Coombs' writing has emphasised dynamic capabilities and the importance of learning in the context of the adaptive firm-environment relationship. This draws on the much-cited work by Nelson and Winter (1982), and Winter (1987) which laid the conceptual foundations for analyses of routines, learning, organisational memory and path-dependency (Metcalfe and De Liso, 1998; Metcalfe and

James, 1998). The emphasis in this chapter on distinctiveness and the difficulty of replicating dynamic capabilities is drawn from these approaches. Innovation processes provide the focus because process, product and organisational innovation are *the* sources of differentiation in firms.

Preceding Leonard-Barton's work described above, Metcalfe and Gibbons (1989) proposed that the "knowledge base" of the firm is comprised of (1) individual human resources and (2) mechanisms of interaction. The latter encompass the routines and practices which support the communication and integration of knowledge around the firm, as part of its application or "leveraging" within particular businesses processes. Coombs and Hull (1997) similarly see path-dependency as "located" in the knowledge base of the firm, together with "technology-as-hardware", which jointly confine the strategic opportunities open to the firm and therefore place boundaries on its evolutionary path.

Teece (1998) is also aligned with this view in seeing competitive advantage as stemming "fundamentally from difficult to replicate knowledge assets." Following the dynamic capabilities approach it is necessary to interpret knowledge "assets" as being not just comprised of "stocks" or "reservoirs" of knowledge, but of organisation structures and management practices which underpin the ability of the firm to acquire, develop, update, focus, integrate and apply or "leverage" knowledge from a variety of sources to fulfil core corporate objectives.

Other studies that are relevant in this context come from Dodgson (1991) on learning and innovation; Cohen and Levinthal (1990) on absorptive capacity; Iansiti (1995) and Henderson (1994), among others, on integrative capabilities. O'Dell and Grayson (1998), within a very good collection of writings on knowledge in organisations, look at internal benchmarking for knowledge-sharing practices. The overall research project described here was also concerned with comparing the management of innovation and the development of knowledge management capabilities in British and Japanese companies. This builds on work, for example, by Nonaka (see Kusunoki et al., 1998; Nonaka and Takeuchi, 1995; Lam, 1997; Fransman, 1994; and Miyasaki, 1994).

This study aims to complement the above literature by adding a set of detailed, comparative case studies which illustrate the specific routines with which firms manage and coordinate knowledge for innovation. Innovation is of interest not least because it entails a change of knowledge and/or a change in the way knowledge is organised and leveraged by firms. Here we focus on various kinds of organisational innovation aimed at improving the management of product and process innovation in the face of a changing competitive environment.

A CHANGING COMPETITIVE ENVIRONMENT

Managers are faced with an increasingly complex, rapidly-changing business environment. A wide variety of sources attest to this, beyond exaggerated media headlines. Some of the most relevant trends for the purposes of this study, associated with the management of technology and innovation, include:

1. The increasing number of technological fields in which firms must maintain in-house capabilities and the increasingly specialist division of labour, not just science, engineering and technology as inputs into product and process-improvement activities but also in other functions such as marketing, finance and law.
2. The growing need to combine different technologies (including across industry sectors) to create new products [in Kodama's (1995) terminology: 'technology fusion'].
3. The emphasis on customisation, tailoring products to customer requirements, related to increased product differentiation and market segmentation.
4. The emphasis on supplier-linkages, with firms working more and more closely with suppliers to improve quality and to develop specific technologies (and joint capabilities) for new products and processes.

There are many drivers underlying these trends including globalisation and increasingly pervasive information and communication technologies (ICTs), both of which are having a deep impact on the forms of organisation adopted by companies. In general the "rise" of the "network form" (N-form) of organisation (Castells, 1996) and the growing scale and scope of strategic alliances managed by companies are responses to these new threats and opportunities (Ghoshal and Bartlett, 1998).

Another good indicator of some of these trends is the high level of M&A (mergers and acquisitions) activity across several key industry sectors.[2] The most recent and relevant in the context of the case study companies discussed later in this chapter is the engineering sector. Globalisation works together with the need for large firms to pool R&D resources and exploit opportunities across a wide range of technologies.[3]

Other studies, using aggregated data on the technological activities of large firms, also illustrate some of the changes in the competitive environment and general patterns of organisational responses. The work by Pavitt (1998) and Patel and Pavitt (1998) uses U.S. patent data to show how the technology portfolios of large firms are widening. In particular they note that technological diversity is rising faster than product diversity, again emphasising some of the above trends. (A more detailed description of these drivers and how companies are restructuring in response to them is given later in the chapter.)

Coombs and Metcalfe (1998), in stressing the increasing importance of "distributed capabilities" for firms, propose three "stylised facts" to describe some of the main drivers of change for the management of innovation:

1. Technological diversity: wherein processes, products and services embody an increasingly wide range of technologies and innovations in any of these require the integration of knowledge and expertise from an increasingly wide range of knowledge bases.
2. Systemic complexity: the growing need for products and services to be designed and developed in ways that are compatible with other related products and services. This is very evident in growing, R&D-based industries such as software and ICT

products where technology platforms and standards are very influential drivers underlying patterns of development, adoption and diffusion.

3. Connectedness: the growing interconnectedness of science and technology in terms of the way in which different scientific disciplines are applied in combination to develop new technologies. Biotechnology, biochemistry, nanotechnology or new materials, for example, all harness different areas of science in a diverse range of applications.

These evolving competitive pressures on firms place increasing importance on their integrative capabilities. Managers need to integrate knowledge and expertise from various business units (BUs) and functional divisions internally, and from outside sources, including suppliers, customers, collaborators and competitors, to implement product and process development. The organisational problems associated with these changes were highlighted by senior managers in the U.K. firms who were interviewed in the early stages of the research project reported here. Before describing the restructuring "challenges" and management of innovation problems they emphasised, the following section will provide a brief overview of the overall project.

A COMPARATIVE U.K.-JAPAN STUDY

As described above this study focused on a detailed comparative analysis of eight leading U.K. and Japanese manufacturing firms in telecoms, chemicals, steel and aerospace. In the initial phase of the study discussions were held with the most senior representatives in the British firms (including ICI, BAE, British Steel and British Telecom), to jointly identify specific questions relating to the management of innovation. This ensured that our study would be of practical relevance (as well as having theoretical relevance) to the participating companies and to other firms. The main issues that were identified are outlined below.

Detailed interviews were held with managers, engineers, scientists and technical staff in the participating companies and were supported by secondary information and data. The analysis focused on particular innovation activities, product development projects and process-improvement initiatives, and examined how company structures, human resource management, budgeting procedures and other management practices were being restructured to improve these activities. By comparing matched companies in the United Kingdom and Japan we were able to identify some of the specific problems relating to knowledge organisation affecting the management of innovation in different firms and the various solutions that firms have developed to cope with these.

During the study the above methodology was supplemented with a questionnaire completed by senior R&D managers in each firm. This added a range of comparable, quantitative details about R&D activities and mechanisms used to coordinate and manage R&D.

ORGANISATIONAL PROBLEMS IN MANAGING KNOWLEDGE FOR INNOVATION

The following areas for analysis were identified with the aid of senior managers in the U.K. firms and described as problems or management challenges. These were of interest in their own right as indicators of knowledge management concerns of senior managers in some leading manufacturing firms. Figure 20.1 gives a simple schematic of some of the problem areas and is used again later to map out the management mechanisms identified in the case studies.

Figure 20.1
The Management of Innovation: Related Units of Organisation

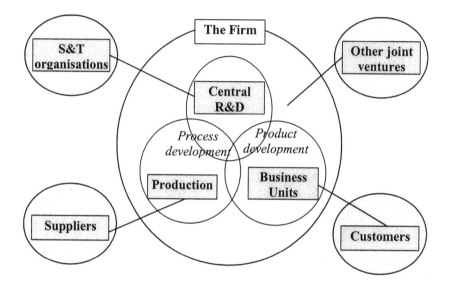

Central R&D (R+D)

1. Formulating an R&D strategy that optimises CR&D's ("value-added") contribution to the firm (how do central R&D laboratories determine their strategic priorities?).

This includes forecasting future markets, products, technologies and, in response to envisaged patterns of change, developing a strategic R&D focus over both the long and the short term; prioritising project selection accordingly; and assessing what competencies to keep or build internally and what to outsource. Given that knowledge (or "beliefs") relating to future trends is held in different parts of the firm and beyond the firm's boundaries, strategy-formulation can be considered a knowledge-integration process.

2.   Linking CR&D R&D objectives with those of BUs.

Related to point 1 since strategy must be developed and evolve in line with the BUs' current and future requirements. But also necessary (and problematic) for the immediate identification and selection of shared objectives and projects; the initiation of joint-R&D (bottom-up and top-down, identifying opportunities, promoting entrepreneurialism); and efficient technology and knowledge transfer for the implementation of projects.

Structure and routines need to be in place to "optimise knowledge development and exploitation"; this includes appropriate mechanisms to motivate, direct and enable scientists and engineers to fulfil corporate objectives. Budgeting procedures and internal markets for valuing the knowledge and expertise of CR&D personnel (e.g., through contracting mechanisms) were seen to be particularly important and difficult to get right by interviewees, with a direct impact on the balance between flexibility ("slack", or Nonaka's "redundancy") for creativity and long-term research versus accountability for control and to promote obvious applicability.

One manager combined these issues (1 and 2) into one phrase: *are we doing the right R&D and are we doing it right?*)

New Product Development

3.   Promoting cross-divisional/functional interaction for innovation (knowledge integration).

Developing new products requires technical expertise and knowledge from different divisions (including different scientific departments within CR&D) and different functions (particularly R&D, production and marketing) to be combined in the design and commercialisation process. Overcoming the departmental and cultural barriers that separate such divisions is a major problem for companies (Collinson and Molina, 1998).

4.   How to build-in customer requirements ("learning with the customer").

The product development process must also incorporate the knowledge, expertise and requirements of customers. Many firms that supply components to other manufacturers have to develop increasingly long-term alliances to establish new product requirements many years in advance of anticipated launch dates. In other cases firms are under pressure to diversify into new markets and meet the needs of new customers. Each strategic situation presents different problems for product developers in terms of building appropriate channels for knowledge integration.

Process Development

5.   Bringing CR&D expertise to bear on product quality and production control.

In addition to the problems faced by CR&D managers developing and applying their knowledge and expertise to BU objectives (problem area number

2 above), they must also play a part in continually improving production processes at manufacturing sites. This usually takes place through a three-way interaction between R&D, business units and production sites. Again departmental and cultural barriers create problems for managers.

Clearly these problem areas all refer to knowledge management capabilities and cross-functional integration at a number of levels. There is a need to continually recombine specialist knowledge from different sources to:

1. cope with product-related and process-related problems as they appear (troubleshooting),
2. improve products and processes incrementally (continuous improvement),
3. conduct R&D to create new technologies, and
4. integrate foresight or beliefs about future technologies, markets and competitive forces to aid strategic development over the long-term of knowledge and capabilities for future success or survival.

Firms that have mechanisms in place that help develop, deploy and leverage appropriate knowledge and expertise to most efficiently and effectively fill knowledge gaps and exploit innovation opportunities as they arise have a competitive advantage.

KNOWLEDGE MANAGEMENT SOLUTIONS?

Before looking at some more detailed structures developed by the case study companies to manage knowledge for innovation, it is worth summarising some of general restructuring trends emphasised by this set of companies and by other firms.

General Restructuring Patterns

In this study, which spanned leading firms in the telecom, aerospace, steel and chemical industries in Japan and the United Kingdom, there were large differences in the kinds of restructuring being undertaken, reflecting the different technological environments and business contexts in which the firms were operating. Despite this there were also some surprising similarities across a number of dimensions of organisational change.

Some of the main, shared patterns of reorganisation, demonstrated by the sample firms in response to new threats and opportunities, were:

*   *Large-scale restructuring and reorganisation.* Firms are particularly developing new business relationships between HQ, CR&D facilities and BUs. In most cases (though not in the case of BAE) this tends to be a decentralisation of R&D and of control and responsibility for fulfilling corporate strategy and creating complementary local strategies. In some companies (such as ICI) this change was associated with the development of stronger internal markets, like cross-functional contracting arrangements (rather than centrally allocated R&D funding) to promote market-led resource allocation for R&D (including the "valuing" and sharing of

knowledge). In cases where decentralisation was less apparent there was seen to be a need to reemphasise basic R&D or promote technology-led diversification, rather than allowing short-term requirements of BUs to dominate resource allocation.

- *Diversification* and/or significant shifts in product and/or market-focus, particularly arising from the need to exploit in-house technological competencies (or "technology platforms") in new markets. In some companies, again ICI was the most extreme example, this meant a shift away from basic and long-term research towards short-term, more applied R&D.
- *Outsourcing of noncore activities.* A general pattern of increased outsourcing was reflected in the outsourcing of specific aspects of R&D, to specialist firms or to universities. As is evident in the management literature alliances, and joint ventures were also growing noticeably. This study focused on the growth of technical alliances, which in some cases involved moving beyond the usual sector boundaries to combine diverse technologies in new ways. This required significant changes in knowledge-mapping and management practices. Alongside these more novel partnerships, alliances with existing suppliers and customers were seen to be more important sources of innovation than in the past.
- *New internal forms of organisation and human resource practices.* The British firms in particular in this study showed a marked shift towards team-based activities and cross-functional project structures as standard organisation mechanisms for supporting innovation. In many cases this meant establishing new cross-departmental managers, "network nodes" and versions of what used to be called "product champions" and in some firms are now seen as "knowledge brokers" (a specific example from BAE is described below). These also operated at the interorganisation level, building alliances and relationships to establish better quality control systems with suppliers, or ways of "learning with customers" for product customisation. Various ways of creating an innovative environment and motivating internal entrepreneurship ("intrapreneurs") was also high on most firms' agendas.
- *Growing use of IT networks.* Information and communication technologies (ICTs) are increasingly pervasive across all organisations in the private and public sectors. Even this limited survey showed a wide variety of structures and processes for using ICTs to link and coordinate intra- and interfirm activities. Some firms are now truly reorganising to exploit the opportunities offered by new interactive technologies and some firms are simply attaching network systems to existing structures.

Clearly our study covered only a sample of eight firms and the value from the research lies more in the in-depth case studies compiled, discussed below. Other, broader surveys do however confirm many of the above reorganisation patterns (for an overview of trends, see for example the CBI Innovation Survey, 1999).

One of the most recent and comprehensive surveys showing general patterns of restructuring in large U.S., European and Japanese companies has begun to yield insights into the main dimensions of reorganisation in large corporations. The INNFORM project has been conducted at Warwick University and divides indicators of change into three main categories:[4]

1. *Structural* change is characterised by decentralisation, delayering and an increase in project forms of organising.

2. *Process* change has involved particularly in investment in IT and in horizontal and vertical communications, together with a range of new human resource practices.
3. *Boundary* changes (changes in the external boundaries of the firm) have been emphasised by the growth in "down-scoping", outsourcing and strategic alliances.

Alongside the removal of layers of organisation (particularly prevalent in U.K. firms), decentralisation and growth of project-based activities there is an move in the majority of firms to strengthen both vertical lines of communication (coordinate strategy and increase accountability) and horizontal lines of communication (for better cross-firm knowledge integration).

One key finding from this large-scale survey was the rise of the project form of organising: "project-based organisation increased by 175 percent between 1992 and 1996" (Pettigrew, 1999). This can be seen as a "generic" organisational mechanism for coping with the changing conditions described earlier. Multifunction or multidivisional projects are one of the main mechanisms by which companies select and implement strategic initiatives for innovation, both product and process development and restructuring (organisational innovation). The rise of the project form is a clear indication of the growing need to integrate knowledge and capabilities across departmental boundaries (intrafirm) and corporate boundaries (interfirm) to innovate. The findings from our study demonstrate how the integrative capabilities required for effective project structures are dependent on a range of broader company characteristics.

Specific Restructuring Examples: Improving Knowledge Management for Innovation

A range of outputs from this research project focus on different aspects of the cross-sector and U.K.-Japan case study comparisons (some references are given below). Here we will focus on a number of organisational mechanisms or knowledge management practices recently implemented in three of the British firms surveyed (ICI, BAE and British Steel) in their attempts to address the problems described above. Figure 20.2 maps these onto the previous overview of the main units of organisation, given the project primarily looked at ways firms were attempting to improve knowledge-integration between these units.

ICI: Top-Down and Bottom-Up Integrative Mechanisms

ICI's Steering Groups and Business Technology Managers. In terms of top-level strategy-setting, all of the firms featured in the study had some form of senior, cross-division forum for deciding R&D strategy at the corporate level. The traditional structure is a committee consisting of BU heads and the head of R&D, chaired by or reporting to a member of the board. As part of a wide-ranging restructuring of R&D in the mid-1990s ICI attempted to improve on this model by implementing the structure featured in Figure 20.3. The aim in particular was to support cross-departmental interaction and coordination following a significant decentralisation of R&D and other core business activities. The Steering Groups were jointly chaired by the heads of individual businesses and the head of a particular central unit. These linked the remaining central capabilities with the BUs, "interpreting" scientific and technological knowledge in terms of the commercial objectives of the firm as a whole, and providing strategic direction to the three centres according to the plans put forward by the businesses.

Figure 20.2
Some Company Examples

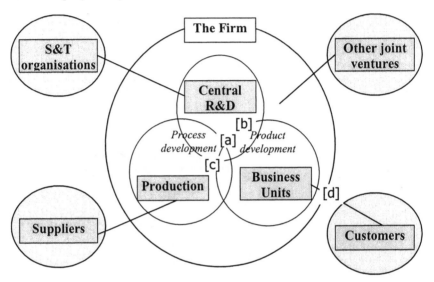

In addition to this, also at the most senior level, ten Business Technology Managers across ICI (four based abroad) represented the BUs and led each of the S&T Teams (specialist groups which operate across central and BU divisions), linking these to the Central Management Group. The Technology Board was comprised of the Business Technology Managers, plus representatives from the major market territories and the Heads of the three Technology Centres. It was chaired by the Director of Technology who had a direct link with the ICI Board.

The above changes were put in place in the mid-1990s, well after the spin-off of Zeneca in 1993. Further radical restructuring of the company, starting in 1997 with the acquisition of Unilever's speciality chemicals and cumulating in 1999 with the sale of titanium dioxide, polyurethane and other bulk chemicals to Huntsman of the United States effectively mean ICI is an entirely different company (Jackson, 1999).

In the years that the Steering Group structure was operational it did appear to benefit the organisation in a number of ways. In particular it proved to be effective for the creation and top-down dissemination of innovation strategy to both BUs and central functions. Moreover the Steering Groups helped in formulating strategies that "translated" scientific and technical capabilities in central departments into applied technologies and products in the context of the portfolios being developed by the BUs. Similarly BUs could together identify mutual R&T interests and achieve economies of scale by jointly funding central functions to carry out research, design or development work.

At the strategic level and to coordinate broad divisional R&T requirements and as a top-down steering mechanism, the structure appeared to have some strengths. A major weakness remained at ICI, partly stemming from the radical restructuring that had taken place in the early 1990s, creating gaps in the intrafirm networks for coordination and knowledge-sharing at lower levels.

Figure 20.3
Interdivisional Structures for R&D at ICI

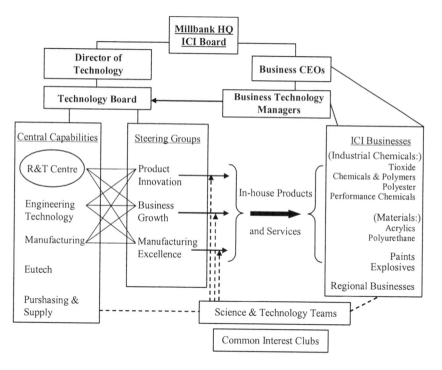

IT Networks to Supplement R&D Knowledge-Sharing at ICI. Alongside the above top-down strategic coordination of R&D, ICI tried to develop strong interdepartment IT networks to support knowledge-sharing further down the management hierarchies. For all R&D managers interviewed for the study, the increased use of Intranets, as well as the use of the Internet and other interorganisation networks, for communication and information searching, were important areas of development.

ICI based its network around Lotus Notes software to link scientists and engineers distributed around the company. The system enables knowledge-searching and knowledge-sharing among experts in any division and function of the firm, allowing groups to identify opportunities for applying specialist knowledge for problem-solving or commercial purposes. Some of the features of the system include: bulletin boards for announcing conferences, in-house seminars, journal articles and project progress reports; discussion groups based around specific scientific disciplines or specialist technical issues; document-sharing allowing multiple authoring; and access to a variety of databases and information on different corporate departments.

While the system was (and is) increasingly well-used at ICI, it evolved to serve mainly the R&D and technical personnel around the firm in their interactions with each other, rather than linking them with other functions. This adoption pattern can partly be explained by the recent history of restructuring (in the early 1990s) at ICI. Significant reorganisation, cost-cutting and downsizing of corporate R&D in the company left formal and informal networks between scientists and technologists around the firm highly fragmented. For example there are 23 S&T Clubs around the company, which are specialist discipline-based science groups (like the Physics Club) through which meetings and interaction to promote in-depth, basic scientific expertise are arranged. Many members have left and many have been moved, along with the redistribution of expertise to the businesses, and this has significantly weakened the operation of these clubs, and the interaction between scientists. Knowledge of the kinds of specialist expertise available in-house and of where this expertise is located has also been weakened. The Lotus Notes system is beginning to develop these networks once again, in particular allowing newcomers from any part of the firm to demonstrate their specialist expertise through on-line discussion and interaction.

As a management solution to a particular problem we can see that the IT network described helps ICI with some of the above problems but not with one of their main difficulties which is to effectively link CR&D and the BUs. Networking between commercial divisions, the business tubes, at ICI and R&D personnel, whether they are based at the R&T Centre or elsewhere in the firm, is markedly weak and the implementation of the IT network has yet to have a major impact on this.

ICI Mechanisms Compared. In a more detailed study (Collinson, 1997) the ICI mechanisms for improving knowledge integration are compared with those of its Japanese counterpart. This concludes that the Japanese firm, despite being relatively weak in the promotion of science-led product and process development and having a number of problems with its diversification strategy, has relatively good integrative capabilities for incremental innovation. Some of the organisational mechanisms that underpin integrative capabilities in the

Japanese firm include (many of these echo findings of other comparative international studies which are summarised in Collinson, 1997):

- *Career paths and job rotation.* Looking at the 1998 intake of new recruits in the Japanese firm, approximately 80 percent of those with a technical background *started work in R&D*, with the rest assigned to departments such as manufacturing and information systems. Of those new recruits, up to 20 percent will move to departments other than R&D within 10 years. By comparison, a quote from one manager at ICI stated that "less than 5 percent of R&D staff in the company work in more than one function" during their time with the firm. There is movement across R&D departments, but very few permanent transfers between R&D and the business units. Cross-functional movement of personnel, particularly from R&D to other divisions, promotes more understanding of other functions at the Japanese firm and an individual impetus to apply science and technology to the commercial needs of product divisions. It also underpins strong cross-functional networks (knowledge of where knowledge and expertise is located around the firm) to enable the bottom-up development of multifunctional projects teams. Training and rewards systems emphasise general company knowledge and cross-divisional experience and life-time employment practices promote longer-term career paths with an emphasis on an individual's overall contribution to the firm, rather than the development of specialist skills.
- *Financial and organisational flexibility.* Across all the research laboratories outside the BUs in the Japanese firm about 40 percent of funding came from central HQ and the rest from BUs, normally via joint selection committees. In ICI *all* the funding for the Wilton Research and Technology (R&T) Centre, ICI's central R&D facility, comes direct from contracts with the business units. Flexible funding allows the Japanese firms to promote bottom-up development projects by giving researchers time and money for self-initiated, underground research.
- *Multidisciplinary teams and external collaboration.* As has been observed in other comparative studies of Japanese firms (particularly in the auto sector) close relations with buyers and suppliers helps direct R&D activities.

By comparison with ICI, including an analysis of some aspects of innovation performance, the study concluded that the Japanese firm has better integrative capabilities which support its ability to commercialise knowledge and expertise developed in central R&D. This is discussed further below.

BAE's Technology Programme Managers Inside the CR&D Facility

The background at BAE was somewhat different from most of the other companies in this study and from reorganisation patterns identified in the broader surveys summarised above, in that there was a shift towards a more centralised R&D structure with the main R&D facility the Sowerby Research Centre taking a more central role in formulating R&D strategy for the whole firm. Alongside this there was a strategic shift to tie CR&D expertise to the needs of BUs and improve the commercialisation of new technology (to "moderate the ivory tower tendencies" of CR&D). To facilitate this the company introduced Technology Programme Managers (TPMs) at Sowerby. Although the roles were introduced in 1992 they began to be used effectively only in the mid-1990s as other aspects of strategy-setting, funding and project management were reorganised.

The TPMs work within a matrix structure across the more traditional line responsibilities of Heads of Research Departments who lead six specialist technology divisions including Aerodynamics and Vulnerability, Human Factors, Materials Sciences and Computational Engineering. The four TPMs, based in Sowerby, are responsible for 15 Strategic Technology Programmes which match combinations of scientific and technical expertise from each of these divisions to the particular needs of BUs. The TPMs are also responsible for identifying opportunities outside these top-down programmes for exploiting central R&D know-how, including initiatives that come from researchers. As budget-holders and senior managers in the central R&D division they have the power and responsibility (and experience, as they are ex-researchers) to help direct central R&D strategy, while representing the interests of BU managers who have a strong input into the selection of Strategic Technology Programmes.

As a knowledge-sharing mechanism the TPMs appear to work very well at BAE. In particular they combine with a high level of central funding of R&D (relative to the U.K. firms), contrasting the contract-funding system at ICI. They also work in an organisational context where cross-functional project teams are the norm, within an R&D-intensive sector dominated by large-scale, complex development projects and interfirm alliances.

There were some remaining integrative weaknesses, however, associated with the overall low density of networking connections and interactions between CR&D and BUs. The TPM role provided a number of advantages, as outlined above, but there seemed to be an overreliance on this connection for a range of interactions with BUs ("gatekeepers" can become "bottlenecks"). A related cause of the lack of linkages for knowledge-sharing and the initiation of innovative projects also seemed to be the cultural gap between CR&D and the BUs.

There are indications that these two weaknesses result in:

- some difficulties prioritising R&D projects and maintaining a fit with overall corporate strategy, which has a strong input from BUs and needs to take into account commercial opportunities as they arise, many of which emerge from the bottom-up in BUs;
- implementation problems; some R&D progresses without user/BU needs sufficiently taken into account, leading to glitches and redesigns at the commercialisation stage;
- a shortage of proactive CR&D-led initiatives (intrapreneurialism) in partnership with BU teams which requires close knowledge of BU needs and technology strategies.

Again, a number of the integrative capabilities of the Japanese firms in this study (again particularly job rotation) helped support this kind of interaction and coordination.

Process Enhancement Groups at British Steel Strip Products (BSSP)

One of the matched studies in the project compared Nippon Steel Corporation to British Steel in terms of their organisation of innovation, focusing on the management of quality control and incremental product development at strip-steel mill sites. The comparison benefited greatly from a technical alliance involving both firms in which managers were themselves examining differences and identifying good practice in the Japanese firm as an input into restructuring efforts in the British firm. This shows how the Japanese firm has developed a number of integrative capabilities, particularly based around interdepartmental networks and project-management practices, which underpin its superior productivity, product quality and customer-oriented product development.[5]

The study shows how over time the British firm has managed to adopt some of these practices and some of the integrative capabilities shown in the Japanese firm to be the source of competitive advantage. The capability gap has narrowed and the British firm has improved mill-level productivity and quality levels significantly over the period (illustrated by data on defect reduction and increased mill yield). Other capabilities have proved to be far more difficult to adopt and highlight aspects of both embeddedness and inertia discussed earlier in this chapter.

As part of a broader restructuring at British Steel its Strip Products division (BSSP), representing 25 percent of the company overall, established a Focused Problem Solving agreement with Nippon Steel Corporation in the early 1990s to improve mill-site production, quality control, and install better process-control and process-development management practices. The main changes made at BSSP mill-sites reflect the better management practices learnt through the alliance with the Japanese firm, which is the largest steel producer in the world and is acknowledged as having the highest productivity and quality levels of any steel maker.

One of the main changes was the establishment of cross-functional teams or Process Enhancement Groups (PEGs), with team members from the mill-site, technical support functions and R&D. These were introduced to provide (1) a mechanism to achieve daily, continuous improvement at the operations level (identifying defects and poor yields, tracing cause and effect, and problem-solving); and (2) capabilities for forecasting future problems and incorporating likely future customer needs into on-going process development plans (an ability to prepare for the future technological requirements of the customer).

Following the Nippon Steel model the aim was for these groups to be pro-active, rather than responsive, to increase the "predictability" of production subsystems and reduce the occurrence of unforeseen breakdowns while also improving quality. At the broader, organisational level this required bringing specialist technical personnel closer to mill operations and more in tune with operational priorities. This required changing, for example, the link between the Technical Centres (in Wales and Teesside) and the central R&D and technical facility at Swinden House in Sheffield.

The Welsh Technology Centre (WTC) had provided good technical support to the businesses into the 1990s but was restructured to work even more closely with the mill-sites. About 20 percent of its approximately 250 personnel joined PEG teams during the first five years of the alliance. Personnel from Sheffield and Teesside also joined PEGs and the role of the former also changed as the responsibility for primary process support was decentralised to the mill-sites.

Another objective of the PEGs was to standardise practices across different mill-sites that had traditionally competed against each other and developed very different ways of working (and their own sets of preferred customers). Again this followed Nippon Steel's example of sharing best practice across mill-sites.

Associated with these changes was a move towards greater team-working for groups of specialists to jointly tackle process problems; better cross-functional communication; and a customer-focus to emphasise the highest-priority improvements. This had significant implications for on-site personnel, particularly in terms of the required combinations of specialist versus generalist knowledge and expertise. The generalist role of plant operatives had to merge with the specialist role of inspectors (a long-term transition that continues today). Operators were taught to inspect and develop an understanding of the different measures of quality that were important to different customers and how defects were created by different process conditions. The inspector-operator divide in terms of status and responsibility was (and is still being) reduced.

The successful implementation (and longer term maintenance) of the PEG teams required a number of organisational changes which have been *partially* achieved, but are proving difficult at the British firm, including:

- increased involvement, a "volunteer attitude" among mill-site personnel, as part of a broader devolution of responsibility for making improvements to production systems (the Nippon Steel Corporation calls this kind of high involvement teamwork *jishu kanri*, meaning literally "self-management");
- a narrower cultural gap and more power-sharing between white-collar and blue-collar workers, as part of a broader shift towards team-based problem-solving and innovation;
- broader, cross-functional knowledge and experience among personnel (reduced dependence on key experts and network nodes);
- more process-focused expertise and production-led continuous improvement, rather than S&T-initiated change.

Differences in the knowledge, enthusiasm and decision-making power of technical personnel and plant-level operators in the two companies continue to be significant factors underlying the differences in performance between the Japanese and British strip steel mills. Plant-level personnel in the Japanese firm still play a much stronger role in directing technical change and continuous improvement, drawing on outside specialists when required. The British Steel structure remains more top-down with R&D and specialist technical divisions still not as closely connected to the production sites as they could be.

A Customer-Focused R&D and Engineering Centre at British Steel

At a different level to the process-oriented innovation activities described above, British Steel has established a customer-focused engineering centre to improve collaborative R&D with steel buyers in the car industry. The example contrasts the three described above in that it appears to have been almost wholly successful in its objectives. Its success stems mainly from the fact that existing structures were by-passed to break the organisational inertia that seemed to be limiting the supplier-buyer relationship and putting British Steel behind its competitors in this respect.

The Automotive Engineering Group (AEG) consists of 35 R&D personnel including a number of engineers and managers from car companies (the head of Product Development, for example, is from Lotus). The emphasis was on longer term R&D and a central objective was to develop a good in-house understanding of the long-term development plans of the main auto manufacturers and the implications of these plans for steel R&D. The new structure has substantially helped British Steel extend its involvement in new car-model design and development project teams, now measured in years, not months.

The AEG supplements and extends beyond the activities of other corporate divisions concerned with developing steel outputs for the auto sector, which comprise just over 20 percent of British Steel's business. But it also represents a radical break (for British Steel) from the normal method of meeting customer needs. As well as using ex-car industry expertise, the group is based close to car company customers in Coventry, rather than at any of the existing R&D centres (one at Swinden and one at Teesside) or mill-sites. While customer services and product development activities continue at these existing divisions, longer term and strategic joint-R&D activities with customers are being moved to the AEG.

The objective in establishing the new division has partly been to by-pass the existing departments and the established ways of learning with customers while at the same time bridging more effectively across the different steel-making divisions ("business silos")(such as Strip Products, Sections and Plates, Tubular Products and Wire Rods) which have tended to service customers separately. Given its success the company is considering extending the model to other core customer industries such as construction, packaging and white goods.

CONCLUSIONS: KNOWLEDGE MANAGEMENT, EMBEDDED CAPABILITIES AND PATH-DEPENDENCY

Managers are now under pressure to strategically think, and continuously rethink in dynamic business environments, about the management of human resources as the organisation of knowledge and expertise that underpins the firm's competitive advantage.

This includes:

- The strategic development of knowledge and expertise. What does the firm need to know now and what will it need to know in the future?

- The distribution and continuous combination of knowledge resources. Where do you put which specialists, and how do you facilitate "knowledge integration" both inside and with outside specialists?
- Decision-making roles and responsibilities. What do they work on and who with? Which specialists, or combination of specialists, have the knowledge and expertise to make which decisions?
- Directing knowledge resources towards the main objectives of the corporation. How do you best motivate and control various experts?

These management challenges were emphasised by the senior managers interviewed in this study who were involved in reorganising links between CR&D, BUs and manufacturing divisions, and with outside organisations, to improve the management of innovation.

There is an increasing competitive premium on knowledge-management and integrative capabilities which stems from a variety of changes in the competitive environment with particularly significant effects on the management of innovation. These changes include the increasing number of technological fields firms have to cope with, the growing specialisation of expertise and the increasing need to combine different technologies to create new products. Other drivers (described previously) are pushing companies to restructure, develop strategic alliances and globalise. Large firms in general are tending to decentralise, delayer, diversify, outsource more and use project structures more often. Alongside this they are particularly investing in IT and in improving intrafirm knowledge-sharing mechanisms and both horizontal and vertical communications.

The case studies presented in this chapter, from a comparative study of large British and Japanese manufacturers, examine some of the ways the British firms have restructured in order to improve their integrative capabilities. The specific organisational mechanisms described include a top-down coordination structure for directing R&D priorities at ICI; an Intranet for linking specialists across various departments at ICI; a cross-functional technology management role at BAE; a team-based structure for managing continuous improvement at British Steel mill sites; and a customer-oriented product development unit at British Steel.

Discussions with managers, engineers and researchers in these firms gives us some indications of how difficult the changes proved to implement and their effects on the management of innovation, given the problems, or "challenges" previously described. In all except the aerospace example we have also compared the firms with Japanese counterparts to identify best practice, as far as possible. In some cases we find a very clear link between different mechanisms and different levels of innovative performance. The steel company comparison is particularly useful in that we have been able to go a step further and trace the direct impact of restructuring, through learning aspects of best practice from the top performer (Nippon Steel Corporation) on clearly defined performance criteria such as mill yield, defect rates, quality improvements and productivity. In most cases, however, this direct link is simply not possible and we have to rely on comparisons of managers own accounts of what makes for good practice. Most of the time managers' recognise when competitors and other firms appear to have developed particular integrative capabilities that promote more efficient and effective management of innovation. This aspect of learning through benchmarking helps direct the restructuring that firms are undergoing, currently in response to the changes taking place in the competitive environment.

The restructuring initiatives in the British firms described above differed substantially in terms of their impact on the integrative capabilities of these firms. They also highlight a number of factors that appear to constrain the restructuring process, contributing to path dependency, and therefore, particularly in the context of substantial and rapid change, influencing competitive advantage.

It is worth emphasising that this research does not conclude that these U.K. firms, or U.K. firms in general, are poor at restructuring compared to their Japanese counterparts. In fact there is every indication that the Japanese firms (particularly those that are least multinationalised), which are relatively inexperienced at restructuring in the face of adversity, face a more difficult task in the current environment. However, the research does conclude, confirming other comparisons with Japanese firms, that they have evolved integrative capabilities that provide a distinct advantage when it comes to managing intrafirm and interfirm knowledge integration for innovation. Whether this is sufficient to outweigh the numerous disadvantages they currently have is not the focus of this study.

Looking at the difficulties encountered by the British firms, there are some similarities in their restructuring experiences and in their accounts of which factors represent the most important barriers to the development of integrative mechanisms.

At ICI, despite establishing a top-level structure for developing R&D strategy and coordinating CR&D-BU collaboration, lower-level interaction and intrafirm knowledge flows seemed to remain weak. The Lotus Notes Intranet has helped fill some of the gaps in the firm's cross-functional science and technology networks, but has so far done much less to bring the R&D personnel and commercial, market-oriented groups and individuals closer together. This is essential for exploring, assessing, selecting and implementing new product development projects, from the huge range of opportunities that arise from the combination of technological potential and market possibilities.

As in most firms, specialists at ICI are divided by differences of organisation culture as well as by their particular area of expertise. Compared to the Japanese chemical company studied, the career paths of R&D personnel and the (mainly contracting) structures in place for financing R&D are less conducive to the evolution of strong intrafirm knowledge networks or for supporting bottom-up, multidivisional project teams. ICI's Japanese counterpart has a number of mechanisms in place which promote the movement of specialists around corporate functions to build their knowledge of where other specialist knowledge is located. These personal knowledge networks provide the basis for temporary knowledge-sharing arrangements or more long-term cross-functional project teams.

Another route to building integrative capabilities as regards CR&D-BU coordination and knowledge-sharing was illustrated by BAE's Technology Programme Managers. These management positions were introduced as "network nodes" both to explore and exploit synergies between different areas of science and technology (across research departments at Sowerby) and to link technological opportunities with commercial objectives as they emerged in the market-focused BUs. TPMs proved to be successful in some respects but once again, as in ICI, a low-density of interactions and weak "knowledge-of-knowledge" across the two functions that form the main axis for product and process innovation still prevails. Indications of this weakness lie in the reportedly low level of development projects initiated from the bottom-up, by CR&D researchers in partnership with commercial managers. Also in implementation problems where projects have evolved with a mismatch between the expectations and/or requirements of either functional group.

The Automotive Engineering Group set up by British Steel showed yet another way of overcoming some of these problems, by bringing technology specialists closer to customers within a separate department, with its own structure and culture. Although this was a solution that applied to one particular customer (car manufacturers buying strip steel for car bodies) it showed in this context how side-stepping embedded organisational structures and entrenched attitudes towards product development can succeed. Here the mechanisms by which CR&D and plant-based personnel built customer requirements into the design, development and quality-assurance activities were seen as inadequate by senior management. The AEG represented a specialist unit, outside the confines of the existing organisation, for bringing product and process technologists closer to customers to understand their current and future steel product requirements.

Finally the Process Enhancement Groups at BSSP were examined as an integrative mechanism for bringing a range of technical specialists to pool their knowledge for process-related troubleshooting and strip steel quality-improvement activities at mill-sites. In this example the link between organisational mechanisms and elements of performance is most clearly made, as described above. The PEGs linked production activities at the mill-sites more closely with outside R&D departments, not least by requiring a significant number of CR&D specialists to relocate to the mill-sites. Following the *jishu kanri* team structure at Nippon Steel Corporation mill-sites, they also required the devolution of responsibility and ability for quality monitoring and quality improvement to mill-level personnel within an integrated total quality management-style production system.

By learning through the technical alliance with its Japanese counterpart BSSP was able to change many aspects of its mill-site management. However, of particular interest are the organisational characteristics at Nippon Steel Corporation, observed by BSSP managers as important elements of innovation best practice, that proved difficult, long-term or impossible to implement in the context of the U.K. firm.

Participating managers realised, for example, that key differences in the kinds of knowledge and expertise available for the process and product development activities in the two firms would take a long time to overcome. This partly reflects how configurations of specialists evolve to meet the strategic priorities of the past and cannot be reconfigured in the short-term. A wide range of routines and management practices such as recruitment patterns, training, rewards and incentive schemes (promoting the development and application of certain kinds of knowledge) and the coordination and interface mechanisms between particular specialist departments were different. These would take time to change, should British Steel wish to alter this wide a range of organisational mechanisms, and it would be even longer before the effects were felt.

Perhaps more fundamentally the *motivation* and *power* of various personnel to develop and apply certain kinds of knowledge for innovation-related activities proved to be very different in the Japanese and British firms with significant implications for performance. In particular the level of involvement in self-initiated continuous improvement activities among plant-level personnel differed significantly and was noted by both Japanese and British interviewees. Employee motivation is clearly rooted in the broader social, cultural and regional context, which underlie the contrast between the lifetime employment, commitment and loyalty on the Japanese side and the "work-as-a-means" to life, "9-to-5" attitude on the British side. Such differences can only ever be partially overcome. (Moreover, most would question the desirability of promoting such fundamental changes, regardless of the corporate and economic consequences.) Similarly the relationship between knowledge and decision-making power differed, with BSSP's restructuring clearly constrained by what many insiders acknowledged to be more hierarchical, territorial and "defensive" management structures compared to Nippon Steel Corporation. Again broader contextual differences help explain this contrast, with Japanese firms in general operating a much more age-related hierarchy, with fewer chances for "leapfrogging" by junior managers and fewer threats (and more career-related incentives) for mentoring, teamwork and knowledge-sharing.

In conclusion, as regards the steel company comparison, BSSP made some significant advances in developing integrative capabilities along the lines demonstrated by Nippon Steel Corporation, including encouraging a greater degree of senior management team-working and plant-level involvement in continuous improvement. However, the senior management on both sides recognised during the process that there were significant constraints preventing the replication of some management practices over the short term and perhaps even over any time scale. Such characteristics that underpin the integrative capabilities identified above are often strongly embedded in the broader context of the organisation and the surrounding socioeconomic infrastructure. This means they represent sustained differences (often conveying competitive advantage) because they are difficult to emulate or transfer to different organisation contexts. This also means they may be difficult to change when new conditions demand a change in strategy and a revised set of capabilities, which is a problem now being faced by many of the Japanese managers interviewed for this study.

Similar factors relating to path-dependency can be seen to be present in the other case studies. Networks for intrafirm and interfirm knowledge integration are central issues in all three examples. The ICI case demonstrates most clearly how difficult it can be to rebuild networks following large-scale restructuring, downsizing and delayering. Despite advances in information technology, such networks are still reliant on trust and credibility and the development of human relationships to underpin knowledge-sharing. The BAE case shows that introducing explicit channels for knowledge integration, in the shape of the TPMs, does improve the capability, but implies again that closer links throughout the organisation may be necessary given the increased emphasis on technology-fusion and cross-functional knowledge flows. British Steel's AEG suggests that building new network nodes or bridging organisations to link product developers and customers, rather than trying to revise existing networks, may succeed in certain cases.

To end it is useful to take a step back and return to some of the themes introduced in the opening part of this chapter. When considering how firms might improve knowledge management capabilities for innovation and competitive advantage it seems that we need to understand more about the nature and function of knowledge within organisations. A common assumption, particularly when our unit of analysis is the firm, is that knowledge is acquired, accumulated, deployed, shared, integrated and exploited or leveraged solely to fulfil corporate objectives—that is, to add value or improve profitability. Other approaches clearly show how knowledge also plays a role in mediating relationships and determining power between individuals and groups in organisations (some of these issues are explored in Collinson, 1999b, drawing on sociological approaches to knowledge management). Moreover, conflicts of interest often exist between knowledge-related activities which benefit the firm and those which benefit particular groups or individuals within the firm. A rational view of the firm might conceptualise knowledge integration as an efficiency issue but there is no perfect market in the valuation and exchange of knowledge within or between firms. A more human-centred approach recognises the social dynamics which sometimes limit this rational efficiency and tend to compromise the adaptive capabilities of firms in general. As a major source of path-dependency these must be taken into account by managers attempting to restructure to build integrative capabilities and by theorists looking to understand this process.

NOTES

1. The research was funded under the UK ESRC (Economic and Social Research Council) Innovation Programme. The project, The Innovative Management of Innovation in UK Companies (Fransman, Collinson and Williams, 1995-1998), compared leading firms in the telecom, chemical, steel and aerospace industries. It was conducted at the

institute for Japanese-European Technology Studies (JETS) at the University of Edinburgh, where the author was Assistant Director. Funding from the ESRC (L125251013) and a Royal Society-Science and Technology Agency (STA, Japanese Government) Fellowship for extended fieldwork in Japan are gratefully acknowledged.

2. M&A activity is particularly interesting in the context of knowledge management because of the huge complexities involved in restructuring to realise the combined value of two sets of knowledge and capabilities. Overlapping capabilities can be cut and new synergies exploited, but the knowledge-mapping, networking and knowledge-sharing that this entails has led the Lotus Development Corporation to explicitly target managers involved in M&A activity for its range of networking and communication technologies (this emerged from a workshop on knowledge management at the Annual European Foundation for Management Development Conference, June 27-29, 1999, in Edinburgh).

3. Recent mergers between Honeywell and Allied Signal in the United States and Siebe and BTR in the United Kingdom (both deals worth over $14 bill.) are examples given in a *Financial Times* analysis (Marsh, 1999) which identifies globalisation and the search for economies of scale in R&D and product development as other key drivers.

4. The INNFORM project, under the ESRC Innovation Programme, surveyed the restructuring taking place between 1992 and 1996 through a questionnaire-based study of the largest U.K., European, U.S. and Japanese firms and 18 detailed case studies. One of the most interesting initial findings of the study is that the best-performing companies are those which tend to manage change across all of these dimensions simultaneously, rather than focusing on just one or two elements of change (Whittington et al., 1999). Highlights can be found in Pettigrew (1999).

5. The U.K. firm has narrowed the gap in its respective capabilities by adopting some specific management practices from the Japanese firm, as illustrated by improvements in defect rates and useable yield (a productivity indicator) at the strip steel mills involved. However, the study shows how some knowledge management capabilities proved more difficult to emulate than others because they were more strongly embedded in the broader organisational practices of the Japanese firm, tied to a range other characteristics that were distinctive. Details of the steel sector comparison are in Collinson (1999a and 1999b).

REFERENCES

Arrow, K., 1974, *The Limits of Organization*. New York: Norton.

Castells, M., 1996, *The Rise of the Network Society*. Oxford: Blackwell.

CBI, 1999, *CBI Innovation Trends Survey*, at http://www.cbi.org.uk/innovation/index.htm.

Cohen, W.M. and Levinthal, D.A., 1990, "Absorptive Capacity: A New Perspective on Learning and Innovation", *Administrative Science Quarterly*, Vol. 35, 1990, pp 128-152.

Collinson, S.C., 1997, "Organising knowledge to manage technology: British and Japanese companies compared", presented at the British Academy of Management (BAM97) conference, September 9, Queen Elizabeth II Conference Centre, London.

Collinson, S.C., 1999a, "Knowledge Management Capabilities for Steel Makers: A British-Japanese Corporate Alliance for Organisational Learning", *Technology Analysis and Strategic Management*, Vol. 11, No. 3, September.

Collinson, S.C., 1999b, "Developing and deploying knowledge for innovation: British and Japanese corporations compared", paper presented at Knowledge, Knowing and Organisations, sub-theme arranged by *Organisation Science* at the 15th European Group on Organisation Studies (EGOS) Colloquium, Warwick, July 4-6, 1999.

Collinson, S.C. and Molina, A.H., 1998, "Reorganising for Knowledge Integration and Constituency-Building in the Era of Multimedia: Product Development at Sony and Philips" in Coombs, R. et al. (eds.), *Technological Change and Organization*. London: Edward Elgar.

Coombs, R. W. and Hull R., 1997, "Knowledge Management Practices and Path-dependency in Innovation", paper presented at the British Academy of Management (BAM97) Conference, London, September.

Coombs, R. and Metcalfe, S., 1998, "Distributed Capabilities and the Governance of the Firm", *CRIC Discussion Paper* No. 16. The University of Manchester: Centre for Research on Innovation and Competition.

Cyert, R.M. and March, J.C., 1963, *A Behavioral Theory of the Firm*. Englewood Cliffs, NJ: Prentice-Hall, Inc.

Dodgson, M., 1991, *The Management of Technological Learning*. Berlin: De Gruyter.

Fransman, M., 1994, "Knowledge Segmentation-Integration in Theory and in Japanese Companies", in Granstrand, O. (ed.), *Economics of Technology*. Amsterdam: Elsevier Science.

Fransman, M., 1999, *Visions of Innovation: The Firm and Japan*, Japan Business and Economics Series. Oxford: Oxford University Press.

Ghoshal, S. and Bartlett, C.A., 1998, *The Individualised Corporation*, London: Heinemann.

Henderson, R., 1994, "The Evolution of Integrative Capability: Innovation in Cardiovascular Drug Discovery", *Industrial and Corporate Change* (Special Issue on Dynamic Capabilities), Vol. 3, No. 3, pp. 607-629.

Ianisti, M., 1995, "Technology Integration: Managing Technological Evolution in a Complex Environment", *Research Policy*, 24, pp. 521-542.

Jackson, T., 1999, "The End of an Empire", *The Financial Times*, March 7, p. 21.

Kodama, F., 1995, *Emerging Patterns of Innovation: Sources of Japan's Technological Edge*. Boston: Harvard Business School Press.

Kusunoki, K., Nonaka, I. and Nagata, A., 1998, "Organizational capabilities in product development of Japanese firms: A conceptual framework and empirical findings", *Organization Science*, Vol. 9, No. 6, pp. 699-718.

Lam, A., 1997, "Embedded Firms, Embedded Knowledge: Problems of Collaboration and Knowledge Transfer in Global Co-operative Ventures", *Organization Studies*, Vol. 18, No. 6, pp. 973-996.

Leonard-Barton, D., 1995, *Wellsprings of Knowledge: Building and Sustaining the Sources of Innovation*. Boston: Harvard Business School Press.

Marsh, P., 1999, "Industry's subtle shift of focus", *The Financial Times*, June 30.

Metcalfe, S. and De Liso, N., 1998, "Innovation, Capabilities and Knowledge: The Epistemic Connection", in Coombs, R. et al. (eds.), *Technological Change and Organization*. London: Edward Elgar.

Metcalfe, S. and Gibbons, M., 1989, "Technology, Variety and Organisation: A Systematic Perspective on the Competitive Process", in Rosenbloom, R. and Bergman, R. (eds.), *Research on Technological Innovation, Management and Policy*, Vol. 4. Greenwich, CT: JAI Press.

Metcalfe, J. S. and James, A., 1998, "Knowledge and Capabilities: A New View of the Firm", *CRIC Mimeo*, University of Manchester (http://les.man.ac.uk/cric/papers.htm).

Miyasaki, K., 1994, *Building Competencies in the Firm: Lessons from Japanese and European Optoelectronics*. New York: St. Martin's Press.

Nelson, R. and Winter, S., 1982, *An Evolutionary Theory of Economic Change*. Boston: Harvard University Press.

Nonaka, I. and Takeuchi, H., 1995, *The Knowledge-Creating Company: How Japanese Companies Create the Dynamics of Innovation*. Oxford: Oxford University Press.

O'Dell, A., and C. J. Grayson, 1998, "If Only We Know What We Know: Identification and Transfer of Internal Best Practices", *California Management Review*, Vol. 40, No. 3, pp. 154-174.

Patel, P. and Pavitt, K., 1998, "The wide (and increasing) spread of technological competencies in the world's largest firms: a challenge to conventional wisdom", pp. 192-213 in Chandler, A.D., Hagstrom, P. and Solvell, O. (eds.), *The Dynamic Firm: The Role of Technology, Strategy, Organization, and Regions*. Oxford: Oxford University Press.

Pavitt, K., 1998, "Technologies, products and organization in the innovating firm: what Adam Smith tells us and Joseph Schumpeter doesn't", *Industrial and Corporate Change*, Vol. 7, No. 3, pp. 433-452.

Penrose, E.T., 1959, *The Theory of the Growth of the Firm*. Oxford: Blackwell.

Pettigrew, A.M., 1999, "Organising to improve company performance", *HotTopics*, Vol. 5, No. 1, February, Warwick Business School.

Teece D.J., 1998, "Research Directions for Knowledge Management", *California Management Review*, Vol. 40, No. 3, pp. 289-294.

Whittington, R. et al., 1999, "Change and Complementarities in the New Competitive Landscape: A European Panel Study, 1992-1996", *Organisation Science*, special issue on "New Forms of Organising".

Winter, S.G., 1987, "Knowledge and Competence as Strategic Assets", in Teece, D.J. (ed.), *The Competitive Challenge*. New York: Harper and Row.

21

Knowledge Assets in Global Services Strategy

Pedro Oliveira, Aleda V. Roth, Michael Von Conley,
and Chris Voss

INTRODUCTION

> One force driving the economy is the trend toward an increasingly
> conceptual content of output—the substitution of ideas for physical
> matter in the creation of economic value.
>
> Alan Greenspan
> Chairman of the Board of Governors of the Federal Reserve System
> Charlotte, NC, 10 July 1999

In the past decades, we have witnessed the emergence of a new economy where
brainpower and knowledge, rather than machine power, are becoming the most
critical economic resources (e.g., Drucker, 1993; Nonaka, 1994; Leonard-Barton
et al., 1994; Roth and Giffi, 1995; Roth, 1996; Teece, 1998). Additionally,
services currently dominate the economies of developed countries and have
faced growing competition, which can be characterized by substantial
deregulation, technological progress, continuous fragmentation of markets,
shorter product life-cycles, and the enormous growth in telecommunications and
inexpensive computing power (Fuchs, 1982; Wyckoff, 1996; Fitzsimmons and
Fitzsimmons, 1997; OECD, 2000). As summarized by the Agility Forum (1994),
the critical market forces that are driving business change today can be broken

into five areas: intensifying competition, fragmentation of mass markets, cooperative business relationships, evolving customer expectations, and the fostering of societal values and pressures. Today high quality and competitive prices are necessary but not sufficient determinants of commercial success. Speed to market and quick, flexible customer response are increasingly pivotal and have created "hypercompetition" (see, e.g., D'Aveni, 1994; Shapiro and Varian, 1999) and "high-velocity markets" (e.g., Eisenhardt, 1989; Eisenhardt and Galunic, 2000).

This chapter explores the role of knowledge assets in global service strategy (see Roth, Gray, Singhal and Singhal [1997] for references on global service strategies). Within the context of the so-called knowledge-based economy, we provide a conceptual framework that presents the key factors underlying the evolution from the industrial era towards a more knowledge-based economy. In particular, we examine a number of interacting forces driving the globalization of services and provide a set of propositions regarding future trends toward global leadership in services. Globalization is the process of building and reinforcing an organization toward establishing and maintaining competitive positions across a set of geographically dispersed markets. Our research discusses how decreasing trade barriers, favorable policies and regulations, limited domestic markets, increasingly common customer needs, and improvements in information and communication technologies (ICT) and transportation infrastructures have created an environment conducive to global services.

We discuss the continual growth in the importance of global services as well as the increasing need of knowledge assets to promote them worldwide. In the International Service Study[1], the very best of services are *global leaders*, defined by Roth, Chase and Voss (1997: 3) as "possessing the enterprise capabilities equal to the best in the world, regardless of the geographic markets in which the firm offers its services." It is no coincidence that the rise of multinational service firms brings a critical mass of what we coin as *customer-pulling* services into the global marketplace. By customer-pulling services, we mean those services where customers increasingly expect similar levels of service quality and ease of access around the world, and therefore, they *pull* the level of service to global standards. Empirical evidence that service practices are converging was found in the International Service Study (Voss et al., 1997; Meyer et al., 1999), although there are some cultural differences in customer's tolerance to lower quality services among countries (Voss et al., 2000) or in the tactics used to customize "culture-based preferences for certain service attributes" (Pullman, Verma, and Goodale, 2000: 4). Arguably, as the degree of customer-pulling expands, the ante for all services is upped, increasing the drive for global service leadership. Customer-pulling, in turn, requires a significant attention to global service strategies and supply chains.

Network externalities and the existence of a significant global customer base also present a significant opportunity for service companies to capture global economies of scale from both traditional and nontraditional services. A particular example is the rise of electronically enabled services (e-services). The new ICT available have enhanced mass services in at least two ways. First, developments in information collection, storage, processing, and distribution technologies have made possible the replacement of paper-based and labor-intensive methods by automated processes. Second, ICT have affected the ways in which customers interact with service providers and define their products. For example, Roth (2000) shows how the changes in technology have influenced service delivery channels.

This chapter explores the strategic influence of knowledge assets and its impact on future trends in the globalization of services. In short, the globalization of services has arrived. Foreign direct investment (FDI) in services is now significantly higher than that of manufacturing and, according to the OECD (2000), important contributions to services are being made by FDI in retailing, banking, business services and telecommunications, and to a more limited extent in the hospitality industry. We contend that the operations strategies of global service providers must link together resources and competitive capabilities in a systematic process of knowledge management. The knowledge perspective of services is also concerned with understanding the way technological change and organizational learning affect a company's success. In developed countries, for example, the efficient production of services relies on information and know-how. In this context, after this current introduction, the next section discusses the positioning of services in the knowledge-based economy. Then, current trends in services are explored and three propositions are set forth regarding the ability to use knowledge assets as a fundamental driver of global services. The importance of service businesses to the economy is discussed and quantified, and a conclusion ends the chapter.

MOVING TOWARDS A KNOWLEDGE-BASED ECONOMY

As global services struggle with seemingly endless challenges to familiar practices that no longer work, they must look to new ways to make knowledge productive. According to Drucker (1992: 95)

> In this society, knowledge is the primary resource for individuals and for the economy overall. Land, labor, capital—the economists' traditional factors of production—do not disappear, but they become secondary. They can be obtained, and obtained easily, provided there is specialized knowledge. At the same time, however, specialized knowledge by itself produces nothing. It can be productive only when it is integrated into a task. And that is why the knowledge society is also a society of organizations: the purpose and function of every organization, business and non-business alike, is the integration of specialized knowledge into a common task.

The new paradigm of the knowledge-based economy emphasizes the role of knowledge for the development of economic activities and contests the orthodox understanding of the firm and the economy (Quinn, 1992; Drucker, 1992; Kogut and Zander, 1992; Leonard, 1995; Spender and Grant, 1996; Roth, 1996). The neoclassical economic perspective views firms as rational entities, choosing among a set of feasible alternatives in order to maximize utility, given internal and external constraints. This vision of the firm, however, is static in that the distribution of knowledge is taken as "given." It does not consider either how knowledge is created in the first place or how its associated dynamic processes are altered over time. Each firm is viewed simply as a homogeneous input-output black box. The traditional view is not concerned with what happens inside the black box.

In contrast, the knowledge perspective that is addressed in this chapter seeks to understand the ways learning, technological change, and organizational behavior affect the success of organizations. The current trend toward a knowledge-based view of the firm recognizes knowledge as the principal source of economic rent (e.g. Quinn, 1992; Drucker, 1992; Spender and Grant, 1996; Leonard, 1995; Shapiro and Varian, 1999; Roth, 1996). Accordingly, the organization is understood essentially as a repository of knowledge assets. Knowledge-based service strategies are translated into routines that guide organizational action and resource allocations. Services are usually sold first and then produced and consumed simultaneously. Moreover, these services cannot be touched, seen, and tasted in the same manner as manufactured goods.

In Figure 21.1, we show the evolution of the economic paradigms in developed countries as a series of overlapping eras. The first era represents the traditional industrial society; the second era, the information society; and the third era, the newly emerging knowledge society. In our conceptual framework, constellations of exogenous forces influence the direction and speed of economic growth and evolution through each era.

Figure 21.1
Key Forces Driving Growth in the Globalization of Services

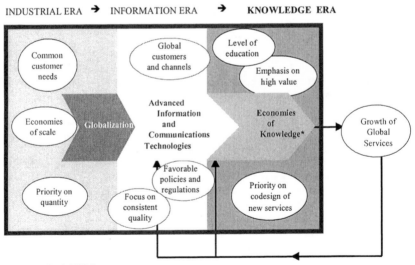

INDUSTRIAL ERA ➜ INFORMATION ERA   ➜   KNOWLEDGE ERA

Source: see Roth (1996).

Driving Forces of the Industrial Era

The industrial era focused on developing physical products to meet local customers' needs and on improving profits through economies of scale and sales revenues. Firms sought to bring down the cost of their products to make them affordable to a larger portion of their domestic markets (Greis and Kasarda, 1997). In the early part of this era, cost advantages were obtained through economies of scale in mass production. In addition, two related factors primary forces define the industrial economy. First the emphasis on ramping up production quantities (or volumes); second, the focus on an common customer needs (versus customization).

Priority on quantity: The industrialized world moved rapidly in the direction of large-scale economies. A focus on gaining cost advantages has led service firms to scale up for global distribution. Overall global trade has tripled in the past 25 years. As a case in point, the McDonald's approach to the globalization of services has enabled them to become the largest global food service retailer. Striving to be the world's best quick-service restaurant and focusing on consistency and volume in the delivery of their core products, McDonald's today has a unique global infrastructure position (25,000 restaurants in 119 countries) and capitalizes on its global economies of scale.

Common customer needs: Markets are becoming global in scope. Customers, regardless of their location in the world, are increasingly demanding the same type and level of services, even if there is some local adaptation. The advent of world markets for services potentially allows service providers to reduce costs through single management systems and common suppliers. For example the global acceptance of inexpensive, fast food has made the McDonald's globalization approach successful. Even multinational manufacturers must be concerned about services. A case in point is Nortel Networks, the telecommunications giant, whose global customers demand reliable services anywhere, anytime. Furthermore their global services must address the additional logistics challenges of distributing goods around the world. As domestic markets became saturated and margins thin, many services like McDonald's saw globalization as a venue for market growth. This phenomena drove market growth and enabled by technological progress gave rise to the information era. Consequently, since the early 1980s, there has been a marked growth and integration of world markets, resulting in a huge flow of goods, information and capital across borders. U.S. exports and imports have more than doubled in the past decade.

Driving Forces of the Information Era

A more global perspective is a hallmark of the information era in Figure 21.1 because of the relatively low cost, mass access to ICT. Because of its user-friendly "anywhere-anytime" access, the Internet is now considered the key enabler of global services and the pivotal factor catapulting society even further toward a knowledge era. Thus, enabled by advanced ICT, the information age is characterized by global customers and multiple channels, increasingly favorable policies and regulations, and expectations of consistent quality.

Global customers and channels: Advances in ICT, and more recently the Internet, became the bridge to worldwide information exchange. Moreover, customers scattered around the globe can now access services through multiple channels. As the relationship between service providers and consumers is radically changing, there are significant implications for service strategies and design. Roth's (2000) P^3 model indicates "proximity" is now as important to service design as *product* and *process* characteristics were a decade ago (Huete and Roth, 1988). Technology now allows providers to produce a single product that is not mass-produced but is capable of being mass-consumed, on either a standardized or a customized basis. Such is the case with online Internet access to dictionaries, encyclopedias, newspapers, museum collections, and so on. Proximity choices are affecting service encounters between providers and consumers in areas previously unthinkable, such as health care, where the need for personal contact to diagnose and treat is becoming less essential. E-banking, real estate, retail and financial services provide other examples where personal, or on-site, contact with service providers is no longer essential (or in some cases even expected) for outstanding performance. Another example from the tourism sector is Marriott's customer information system. Marriott's system allows the company to pamper its clients throughout the world (1,850 hotels and resorts worldwide) (Borrus, 2000). Marriott's customers expect the same level of process capability and customer support worldwide. Financial services can provide detailed information quickly to any client around the world using an array of process channels from full service branches to self-service.

Favorable policies and regulations: The laws of a country have a significant effect on its participation in the global economy. If the policies and regulations stifle industry, they directly impact the growth of services. The world is experiencing a period of increasingly permissive trade rules and regulations unparalleled in recent history. Europe, for example, has recently followed the reduction of internal trade barriers with the introduction of a single currency in most European Union countries. Political changes associated with market-based economic development have been spreading widely and have contributed to a significant increase in world trade and investment. The fact that 90 nations approved the General Agreement on Tariffs and Trade (GATT) is a sign of this trend. Countries such as Brazil, China, India, and Russia are emerging as nations of potential global importance, indicating that a genuinely global economy is starting to take shape in which all countries can participate actively. Under conditions of increasing free trade, further growth in global services is anticipated.

Focus on consistent quality: In the second half of the 20th century, firms began to look more toward product quality and speed to attain competitive advantage (Giffi, Roth, and Seal, 1990). The ability to produce large quantities at low cost (one important competitive focus of the industrial era) diffused across industries and countries, and gave rise to the emergence of consistent quality as a global competitive priority in manufacturing and services (Roth and van der Velde, 1991; Roth et al., 1997; Roth, 1996; Voss et al., 1997; Meyer et al., 1999). The customer-pulling effect, previously mentioned, established heightened expectations for both industrial and individual consumers that they will get comparable service regardless of location. Services, like e-Trade or Amazon.com consolidate their back-office processes to give the consistent quality demanded by their global customers. Also, speed of all kinds of transactions arose as a competitive weapon. Global service providers, whereby similar services are offered across different time zones, adopted a beat-the-clock approach. Take for instance the delivery of financial services worldwide by Citicorp and Merrill Lynch. Similarly, as global firms contract for services in one country, they will want to be able to obtain the same service in other locations as well. Yet by the late 1980s and early 1990s, the ability to produce consistent quality services at competitive prices became a qualifier and not a guarantor of commercial success.

Driving Forces of the Knowledge Era

We posit that as demand for global services increases, the utilization of knowledge assets becomes a limiting factor to production. The knowledge era differs from the traditional industrial economy in several key respects, which have been extensively discussed in the management literature. Some key differences include the fact that the economics of the knowledge era are not one of scarcity, but rather of abundance. Unlike most resources, which are depleted when used, information and knowledge can be shared and actually grow through application. In describing this situation, Roth (1996: 30) coined the term "economies of knowledge." As a key enabler of global competitiveness, economies of knowledge means that "the firm is able to use its business acumen, combined with skilled people and experience with advanced technologies, to create an organization that consistently identifies, assimilates, and exploits new knowledge more efficiently and effectively than the competition".

Higher education level of the work force: The new knowledge era includes an increasingly global workforce, networks, corporations that are simultaneously global and local, and increased decision speed. The transition to a knowledge-based, service-oriented economy is raising the importance of human capital for enterprises. As discussed by Roth and Jackson (1995), the need for workers to acquire a range of skills and to continuously adapt these skills underlies knowledge management in services. One of the characteristics of today's economy in developed countries, however, is the changing nature of employment. An acute shortage of skilled workers already exists as a major problem for some countries and companies (OECD, 2000). World Bank data also show that agriculture in industrialized nations has shifted from being a major employer to a minor one over the last one hundred years, while employment in manufacturing has held almost constant over the same time period. In contrast, service industries have experienced tremendous growth. In the knowledge-based, global economy, more technologically skilled and knowledgeable workers are required for value creation and leveraging the vast amounts of information available.

Emphasis on high value: Global customers will know more, expect more, and demand more services delivered at the right place, the right time, and the right price. They increasingly want high-value services that are defined by more personalization and more features at lower prices. The pursuit of high value is also reflected in the innovativeness and expertise captured in the final delivered offerings, including design, technical assistance, and other "intangibles." The extant management literature generally concludes that knowledge-enhanced products or services command price premiums over comparable products with low levels of embedded knowledge. Thus, pricing and value depend heavily on context, since the same information can have vastly different values to different people at different times and contexts.

In some cases, the push for high value is reflected in a rising demand for goods with a higher service-oriented content. For example, the embedded ICT in mobile phones, automobiles, toys, and appliances has greatly enhanced the value of physical products. This in turn has had an impact on the way that companies view the sources of value-added in their operations and pricing strategies. The convergence between services and manufacturing is making it difficult to classify the value propositions uniquely under either sector category. Take, for instance, GE and IBM. These major "goods" manufacturers are currently generating more than half their revenues from services, reflecting a transition that can be found through different industrial sectors (OECD, 2000). As another example, one of the world's largest steel producers currently considers its service-related activities to drive its business, with its manufacturing operations playing an important but less dominant role. Thus, the emphasis on high-value offerings often leads to an inordinate emphasis on operational agility, defined by Menor, Roth, and Mason (2000) as: "the ability to excel simultaneously on operations capabilities of quality, delivery, flexibility, and cost in a coordinated fashion."

Priority on codesign of new services: Armed with more knowledge and expertise, one hallmark of the new knowledge era is this: Customers will increasingly expect to be included in the codesign of their new services. Information technology directly affects both the speed and the general effectiveness of a firm's efforts in developing new service products (Froehle et al., 2000; Menor and Roth, 2000). Collaboration between businesses and customers in this context becomes an essential element in corporate strategies aimed at speeding up new service development and creating new value for customers. Attention must be paid to how the business landscape is evolving, particularly in high-velocity marketplaces. Neglect and failure to update the collaborative links as markets change can have an adverse impact on performance (Eisenhardt and Galunic, 2000).

Feedback Loops

Growth in global services creates a positive feedback loop, moderated by the strengthening and liberalization of international trade laws. This highlights the need to make enterprise-wide operations and service supply chains more manageable by developing the infrastructures necessary to offer global services effectively. The growth in global services reinforces future growth, since network externalities occur. The three service types described by Lovelock and Yip (1996) are useful in illustrating the reinforcement that occurs, illustrated in our model by feedback loops. First, as "people-processing services" (such as transportation) grow, interest beyond national borders increases, which combined with lowered trade barriers can promote conditions for growth in international business. "Possession-processing services" on a global scale provide manufacturers with the means to manufacture in one country or continent and sell in another. These services include freight transport, equipment installation and service, and waste disposal, among others. Clearly, having access to familiar suppliers with a known reputation makes global expansion easier. This exact pattern can be seen at the British Airport Authority (BAA) and retailers as they expand around the globe (Voss, 1997). "Information-based services" facilitated by advanced ICT, the World Wide Web (WWW), and the collection, manipulation, and storage of data, are essential to linking firms as they expand globally. Shapiro and Varian (1999) provide examples of network externalities in such type of services.

THE MACROECONOMIC CONTEXT FOR GLOBAL SERVICES

Learning Orientation Context

The increasing importance of intangible assets characterizes service as the dominant work sector in the knowledge-based economy. The need for workers to acquire a range of skills and to continuously adapt (and learn) these skills underlies knowledge management in service firms (Roth and Jackson, 1995). The importance of knowledge accumulation and technology diffusion requires better understanding of knowledge networks and systems of innovation (Shapiro and Varian, 1999). Many authors have attempted to conceptualize the success of economic organizations on their knowledge accumulation through the "learning" processes (Argote, 1999; Leonard, 1995; Roth, 1996; Teece, 1998; Shapiro and Varian, 1999; Silverman, 1999). These previous studies conclude that the increase in knowledge accumulation is reflected in workers' improved skills and in the generation, diffusion, and usage of new ideas.

Roth, Marucheck, Kemp and Trimble (1994) provide a model that links a company's predisposition for learning and deliberate learning strategies to accelerated learning. Included in their learning outcomes is organizational learning, which reflects social processes driven by collective cultures and appropriate management attitudes. In a broad characterization of these perspectives, the ability to continuously acquire new skills and ideas (which is to say, to accumulate knowledge through learning) is the ultimate driver of an economy's long-run prospects (World Bank, 1999).

Most important, new macroeconomic issues and questions are being raised regarding the implications of the knowledge-based economy of the new economy for employment and the role of governments in the development and maintenance of the knowledge base (OECD, 2000). A complementary concept to knowledge economy useful for describing the macro-orientation of a nation is the "learning economy" (Lundvall and Borrás, 1997). The concept of learning economy can be used in two different ways. First, it can refer to a specific theoretical perspective on the economy in which the emphasis is on explaining and understanding the process of change in technology, skills, preferences, and institutions. Second, it may refer to specific historical trends that make knowledge and learning increasingly important at all levels of the economy. Lundvall and Borrás (1997) make use of both perspectives and, arguing that world economies have entered a historical period in which the role of knowledge and learning is more important than ever before, they argue that a new theoretical perspective is needed. It is no longer appropriate to operate with a theoretical core that treats technology, skills, and institutions as exogenous. As discussed by Conceição et al. (1998), the minimum level of training should be the one that maximizes an individual's ability to learn. There is, therefore, an increased need for training in learning.

Thus, the learning economy reflects a macroeconomic orientation in which the success of individuals, firms, regions, and national economies depends upon their capability to learn. In the learning economy, change is rapid, and the rates at which old skills become obsolete and new ones are demanded is high. In this context, information technologies play an important role; however, the learning economy is not synonymous with the information society. Information corresponds to the specific elements of knowledge that can be broken down into bits and sent a long distance by means of information infrastructures. Therefore, learning is not simply access to an increasing amount of information, but rather it is fundamentally a process of building competencies.

According to Ghoshall et al. (1999), managers in the learning economy are encouraged to replace the narrow economic assumptions of the past and recognize that modern societies are not market economies but instead organizational economies in which companies are the chief actors in creating value and advancing economic progress. Additionally, they argue that the growth of firms and, therefore, economies is primarily dependent on the quality of their management, and that the foundation of a firm's activity is a new moral contract with employees and society, replacing paternalistic exploitation and value appropriation with employability and value creation in a relationship of shared destiny. The core of the managerial role is giving way to the "3 Ps": purpose, process, and people.

One aspect of the learning economy is that knowledge-intensive activities grow more rapidly than other activities. For developing countries the establishment of processes of learning in traditional sectors as well as new knowledge-based activities is a major challenge, as shown by the case of shipbuilding in Korea cited by Upton and Kim (1998). However, for companies that embrace the knowledge building required by the learning economy, there are great rewards. (Kim 1998) reports how Hyundai started to develop its knowledge base in 1967 by hiring engineers from other auto producers and by serving as an assembler for Ford, which involved the transfer of "packaged" technology and significant interactions between engineers of both companies. In the 1990s Hyundai got caught up with its knowledge base, shifted its learning orientation from imitation to innovation, and increased the intensity of pure research activities. In less than 30 years it became the most dynamic auto producer in developing countries by developing absorptive capacity and building the capabilities necessary to unveil its own designs and produce more than 1 million cars per year.

Propositions for Global Services

We now turn to the implications of the increasing importance of knowledge assets for global services and for the economy in general. We offer three propositions regarding the trends in global services in the knowledge society. The first proposition relatess the codification of knowledge and the globalization of services. Knowledge can be codified or tacit (e.g. Nonaka, 1994; Roth et al., 1994; Conceição et al., 1998). Codified knowledge is explicit knowledge that has been recorded or stored in books, paper, formulas, computer codes, CDs, and so on. Explicit knowledge is more precisely and formally expressed. Tacit knowledge is subconsciously understood and applied, and consequently it is difficult to articulate in a way that is meaningful and complete. Since tacit knowledge is developed from direct experience and actions, it is stored in the human brain and can be represented in the expertise of professionals and craftsman. Tacit knowledge can be codified, if it can be made explicit, usually through interactive conversations, apprenticeship, and story telling (Froehle, Roth and Marucheck, 2000).

There is a relationship between codification of explicit knowledge and the costs of transfer (e.g., Teece, 1998; Nonaka, 1994). The more a given item of knowledge or experience has been codified, the more economically it can be transferred. On the other hand, uncodified or tacit knowledge is slow and costly to transmit. In some situations, existing tacit knowledge is codified into detailed routines that precisely specify steps and subdivide activities among different individuals. Such routines deepen the memory of firms for the routine (Argote, 1999) and enhance the predictability of the process (Nelson and Winter, 1982).

As discussed by Teece (1998), in the transfer of tacit knowledge, ambiguities abound and can be overcome only when communications take place in face-to-face situations. Errors of interpretation can then be corrected by a prompt use of personal feedback. On the other hand, the transmission of codified knowledge does not require face-to-face contact and can often be carried out largely by impersonal means (Froehle et al, 2000). Messages are better structured and less ambiguous if they can be transferred in codified form. However, the use of codified knowledge always requires a certain degree of tacit knowledge, which is deeply rooted in action, commitment, and involvement in a specific context (Nonaka, 1994).

Service businesses that are based upon high levels of codified knowledge are more likely to benefit from economies of scale and to become global, since their knowledge is more easily shared and transferred across countries and is more likely to achieve economies of scale. The rapid worldwide expansion of fast-food chains, like McDonald's described earlier, illustrates this; however, less obvious examples can be drawn from other knowledge-intensive services, such as consulting[2]. For example Pricewaterhouse, Andersen Consulting, KPMG, and other peers have created knowledge centers to improve the capture of explicit knowledge, codification, and dissemination of "best practices" (e.g., the codification of explicit knowledge). Thus, we offer the following proposition:

> *Proposition 1*: Codified knowledge strategies facilitate the efficient globalization of services.

Because personal and group knowledge is expensive to re-create, firms normally develop programs to codify, simplify, and standardize such knowledge to make it accessible to the wider organization (Kogut and Zander, 1992). However, in service sectors that are very dynamic, "hypercompetitive," or what is termed "high-velocity[3]" (e.g., D'Aveni, 1994; Eisenhardt, 1989), change becomes nonlinear and less predictable. Uncertainty cannot be modeled as probabilities, because it is not possible to specify a priori the possible future states. Here there will be a greater reliance on creative, rigorous advice based on individual expertise. Thus, in high-velocity markets, an adequate level of expertise, which often takes the form of tacit knowledge, is essential for pioneering new knowledge. In such environments, service businesses necessarily rely much less on existing knowledge and much more on rapidly creating situation-specific, new knowledge. Existing knowledge can be a disadvantage if managers overgeneralize from past situations (Argote, 1999).

An inordinate focus on existing knowledge can even be a "core rigidity" (Leonard, 1995). As a case in point, Oliveira et al. (2000) analyzed the efficiencies of a group of agile banks and the operations strategies that contribute significantly to achieve efficiency and suggested that those banks that attempted to codify knowledge and promoted the standardization of processes were actually less efficient than those that built human capital and learning culture. In these instances, highly skilled people were available to solve unique and extremely complex problems, while more well-recognized and familiar problems were routinized. This empirical result is in line with our second proposition:

> *Proposition 2:* In "high-velocity markets," global service firms will be required to acquire more expertise that is not codified, and hence leverage higher levels of tacit knowledge in order to compete effectively.

The current convergence of interests of the American, European, and Asian economies in strengthening and liberalizing international trade, increasing investment, and creating financial linkages significantly increases the need for global services. Service businesses that want to play a key role in this new economy will need to define global strategies in order to be integrated into the global economy. The ability to develop transnational organizational capabilities will be the key factor determining a company's performance, and multinational services will need to adjust their strategies to the changing pattern of international competition. Firms may be distinguished according to whether they operate in multidomestic industries (in which competition is independent across countries of operation) or in global industries (in which competition in each country affects competition in other countries).

Particularly interesting is the situation of the "digital dot-coms" (e.g., Internet-based companies, whose services and offerings are totally digital, such as music, news, or many financial services) and are offered on the WWW. Digital dot-coms have an immediate potential to become global. Similar concerns apply to what have been called "physical dot coms," companies that are based entirely on the Internet, but sell physical products. It is essential for these companies to develop global service supply chain strategies. Porter (1986) argues that firms in global industries cannot rely upon country-by-country competitive strategies. Instead, they must form linkages among the various activities in the value chain in order to achieve operational effectiveness. Globally competing services firms must determine the optimal configuration of activities (where activities are to be performed) and coordination of activities (how they are to be linked across countries of operation). Global information alone provides little added strategic value.

One key service strategy that has been understudied is global sourcing, although this practice has become commonplace both in manufacturing and in services. It is difficult to find assembled goods anywhere in the United States made up entirely of domestic parts and components. As pointed out by Apte (1991), the advantages of global sourcing include cost savings and capital market gains, faster cycle time, help in developing and operating global information systems, and access to foreign markets and a skilled labor pool. Drawbacks include problems with communication and coordination, lack of control of quality and timetable, the potential for violation of intellectual property rights, and unclear attitudes toward transborder data flow and ICT services. Apte and Mason (1995) also identify a movement towards the global disaggregation of information services associated with the trend to reformulate and geographically spread the services around the world, as another way of capitalizing from the opportunities of the new economy.

Thus, to excel in making decisions on a global basis rapidly, global service leaders must communicate well (understand and intuit both the local and global needs of their customers), recognize their global workforce as an asset, take advantage of joint ventures and networks to expand their knowledge base and networks economies, and consider outsourcing services globally. To summarize we propose the following proposition:

Proposition 3: The rise in importance of services requires strategies for new service operations that better leverage competitive capabilities and knowledge assets globally.

MACROECONOMIC EVIDENCE

> Services account for over 60% of total economic activity in most OECD countries. Growth has outpaced overall economic growth in the OECD area, a trend which is expected to continue. Services are playing a greater role in business cycles, and knowledge-based services linked to information technology (IT) may be an important engine in overall growth.
>
> OECD, 2000: 13

Since the early 1980s there has been a marked growth and integration of world markets, resulting in a huge flow of goods, information, and capital across borders. U.S. exports and imports have more than doubled in the past decade. But the growing interdependence of the world markets is even more impressive in terms of international information flows. Between 1977 and 1997, international telephone calls to and from the United States (the vast majority for business purposes) increased 8,000 percent, from 375 million minutes in 1977 to nearly 30 billion minutes 20 years later (U.S. Federal Communications Commission, 1997).

Codified Knowledge and Global Expansion

We suggested in proposition 1 that increasingly codified knowledge will lead to greater expansion of global services. This first requires that tacit knowledge be made explicit, as only explicit knowledge can be codified (Froehle et al., 2000). Macroeconomic data provides tentative empirical evidence of the transition. Clearly, the rise of the Internet and the codified information it contains is a case in point. Media adoption curves in the United States (Figure 21.2) illustrate the accelerated pace of change: radio took almost four decades to reach 50 million users, while TV took 13 years, cable TV 10 years, and the Web less than 5 years (Friel, 1998).

Internet commerce has also experienced explosive growth (Figure 21.3). Two recent studies (Barua et al., 1997; Barua and Lee, 1997) suggest that the "Internet economy" exceeded $500 billion in revenues in 1999, representing a 68 percent growth from 1998. The studies also find that the Internet is creating unprecedented opportunities for new businesses—one out of every three companies surveyed did not exist prior to 1996. Watson et al. (1998) identify the following strategic and tactical reasons for firms to invest in e-commerce: (1) to reduce the costs of matching buyers and sellers; (2) to promote the image of a leading-edge corporation and increase visibility; (3) to improve customer service; (4) to enable market expansion; and (5) to lower stakeholder communication costs through on-line transactions and global information distribution. To illustrate the impact of the Internet in the reduction of costs, Figure 21.3 compares the costs of banking transactions over the Internet and other alternative channels (ATM, phone, mail-in, and branch).

Figure 21.2
Adoption Curves of Radio, TV, Cable, and the WWW in the United States

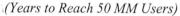

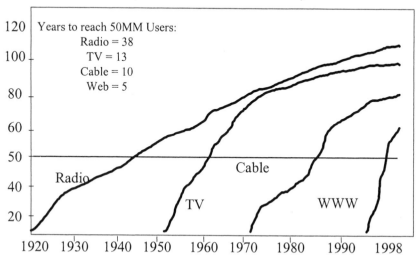

(Years to Reach 50 MM Users)

Source: see Friel (1998).

Figure 21.3
U.S. Banks' Transaction Costs by Channel

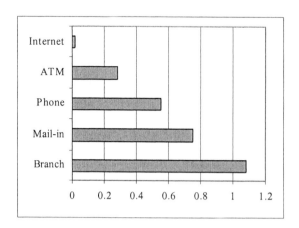

Source: see *The Economist* (2000)—data provided by Jupiter Communications.

Figure 21.4
Estimated sales on the WWW

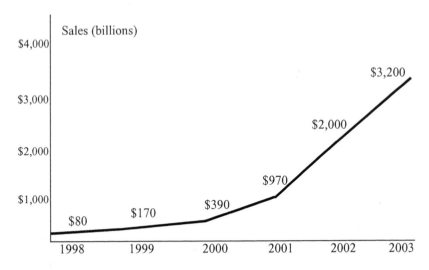

Source: see Friel (1998).

Importantly, unlike the radio, TV, or cable, which offers customers one-way communication flow, the WWW permits two-way, interactive and information rich communications (see Figure 21.4). Thus, since knowledge is socially constructed, the "information technology infrastructure of the web provides a seamless pipeline for the flow of explicit knowledge" (Zack, 1999: 49-50). Zack further suggests that the Web and groupware can build a multimedia repository for rich, explicit knowledge. Organizations capture and store units of knowledge in forms that assign various labels, categories, and indexes to inputs. The Web also facilitates the transfer of less explicit knowledge through e-mail conversations and, chat and electronic bulletin boards, which enhance the conversion of tacit knowledge to explicit. It greatly speeds up the efficient transfer of codified materials, procedures, and documents. As previously indicated, global services like McDonald's gained significant leverage from routinizing its processes and transporting them globally. The WWW tremendously increases the potential to transfer codified process and content knowledge globally.

Arguably, the rise in Internet sales increases the conversations between customers and service providers, expanding the ability to develop new services and knowledge as well. The rise of the new intermediaries is a case in point. Global sourcing has also become a small but rapidly growing sector of the overall outsourcing market (Apte, 1991). Recently corporate executives are showing increasing interest in outsourcing anything that is not considered to be a core competence. The Internet, in particular, is enabling the selective turning over of certain functions of information systems and processing services to subcontractors and consultants, who are greatly expanding global information services. Outsourcing of ICT is seen as an option for leveraging resources, containing costs, and focusing on strategic and value-added services (Apte, 1991). Many countries are able to provide well-trained ICT professionals whose salary expectations are significantly less than those of their U.S. counterparts.

Despite the diffusion of the Internet and ICT, tremendous barriers to the development of global services remain, including legal restrictions, advertisability, standard versus customized service package, technical capabilities, conflicts in distribution channels, cultural and social norms, buyer behavior, language, political stability, and national synergism (McLaughlin and Fitzsimmons, 1996). Emerging market economies are most vulnerable, yet they provide the greatest opportunities.

People in Services

The evolution of U.S. employment (see Figure 21.5 and Table 21.1) has brought about significant changes in the distribution of jobs among the various sectors.

Figure 21.5
U.S. Employment by Sector, 1820-1997

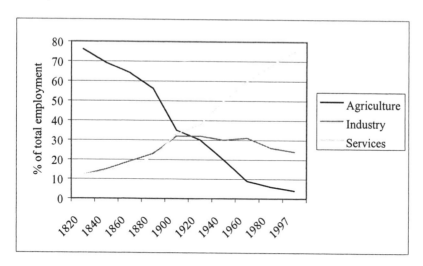

Source: Based on OECD (1998).

At the beginning of the 19th century, more than 75 percent of the workforce was employed in agriculture. In 1995 three-quarters of workers were employed in the much more productive service sector, while agriculture made up only 3 percent of the total. The manufacturing share of employment has also declined in many industrialized countries. However, the losses in manufacturing jobs have been offset by the job growth in the service sector, so that the employment effect of technological change is slightly positive. Figure 21.6 illustrates the significant rise of the share of employment in the service sector in 1950, 1985, and 1995 in five industrialized countries. Table 21.2 provides data on the breakdown of GDP into agriculture, industry, and services for the United States, Japan, and the European Union countries.

Table 21.1
Distribution of Employment (by sector and income level)

Level of income and year	Agriculture (%)	Manufacturing (%)	Services (%)
High-income countries			
1870	49	27	24
1950	25	36	39
1995	5	30	64
Middle-income countries			
1995	30	28	42
Low-income countries			
1995	62	15	23

Source: World Bank (1999).
Note: Each economy is classified as low-income (GNP per capita $785 or less); middle-income, subdivided into lower-middle ($785-$3,125), and upper-middle ($3,126-$9,655); or high-income ($9,655 or more) (World Bank, 1999).

Table 21.2
Share of GDP per Sector in the United States, European Union, and Japan in 1997

Country	% of GDP		
	Agriculture	Industry	Services
US	1.8	26.3	71.9
Japan	1.9	38.0	60.0
European Union:			
Germany	1.1	34.5	64.4
France	3.3	28.5	68.2
Italy	3.6	29.2	67.2
Belgium	1.7	29.2	69.1
Denmark	3.7	27.0	69.3
Austria	2.4	39.0	58.7
Netherlands	3.3	27.3	69.4
U.K.	1.9	29.2	68.9
Sweden	2.2	28.7	69.1
Finland	6.2	32.5	61.3
Ireland	7.5	34.3	58.2
Spain	3.4	31.3	65.3
Portugal	4.3	33.5	62.2
Greece	14.8	26.3	59.0

Source: OECD (1998).

Figure 21.6
Shares of Employment in the Services in 1950, 1985 and 1995 in Five Industrialized Countries

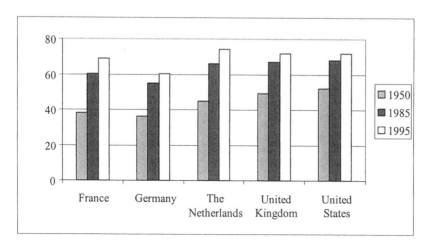

Source: OECD 1998

Wilson (1993) discusses the evolution of the U.S. service-sector workforce from 1967 to 1992, divided into six different categories, classified according to type of demand: (1) distribution of electricity, gas, water, telecommunications, and transport (intermediate services for companies and final services for consumers); (2) services for producers, provided to companies upstream of consumers, including high added-value activities such as consulting (legal, management, engineering, finance, and accounting), insurance, and asset management; (3) retail (direct sales of finished products to consumers); (4) services to the end consumer, similar to category 2 except that the client is the end consumer; (5) education and health; and (6) public administration. According to Wilson the results show that employment in categories 1, 4, and 6 remained at the same proportionate level during the period under analysis. The relative increase of the services workforce was caused by growth/increases in approximately categories 2 (from approximately 7% to 13%), 3 (from 15% to 18%), and 5 (from 14% to 19%).

Wilson argues that a considerable proportion of the employment generated in the retail sector has been in positions with low qualification requirements, from which it could be inferred that in this case the knowledge factor is less significant. However, as discussed by Conceição and Heitor (1999), growth in the retail sector has taken place in franchises, such as fast-food chains, clothing outlets, book and music shops, and department stores, in which there is a great need for codified knowledge such as sales-point instruction manuals, purchasing regulations, promotions, and sales. So also here knowledge is important in the economic activities of the firms that have created employment in the retail sector, although this knowledge is codified.

While the relative proportion of service-sector employment for countries with low income is still very low (Table 21.1), the 1995 levels of employment in the service sector for middle-income and low-income countries correspond to the levels exhibited in the developed countries, in the 1950s and in the late 19th century, respectively. In support of proposition 2 above, OECD data over the last two decades indicate that the key sectors for employment growth in developed countries have been technologically sophisticated industries and services (OECD 1994, 1998). In these sectors, leveraging of knowledge assets is expected to dominate firms' efforts to achieve a competitive edge. This macroeconomic data suggests that there is an increasing demand for highly skilled workers, and, on average, unemployment of workers with a college education is less than half that of workers with below-secondary education.

In the knowledge-based economy the key sectors for employment have been technologically sophisticated, information-intensive services including finance, insurance and real estate, and business services. In the OECD, where unemployment exceeds 36 million people (varying from around 5% in the United States, to around 20% in Spain), individuals with more knowledge are more likely to get jobs. Globalization and intensified competition have led to increased demand for more highly skilled workers, who are able to respond faster to today's changes and challenges. When imagination, analyses, and flexibility are important to competing, then more expertise is required, which is often expressed as tacit knowledge. Roth and Jackson (1995), for example, found that higher skilled workers were critical in financial services for absorbing knowledge about customers and competitors and converting this knowledge into higher levels of service quality and profitability.

Also, individuals with more knowledge are more likely to be better paid since companies can benefit significantly from their knowledge either as a differentiated offering or in improving the effectiveness of backroom operations. Roth (2000) reported: "'Fewer' people can cost considerably more. Despite conventional wisdom that dot coms are cheap to run, many like REI found that their dot.com payroll costs for acquiring and retaining their technical talent are actually very similar to the total payroll costs of their brick-and-mortar network." On average, individuals with a college education can expect to earn 62 percent more than individuals with only a secondary-level education, and individuals not obtaining an upper secondary-level education can expect to earn only 79 percent of those with a secondary school diploma.

Neo-operations Strategies

The driving forces to the new knowledge era suggest that operational effectiveness in services will largely be a function of how they manage knowledge and, to a much lesser extent, capital. Roth (1996) refers to this paradigm shift in competitive priorities, process management, and the primary source of value-added for exploiting knowledge and learning capabilities better than the competition, as *neo-operations strategy*. Thus, the old rules of competing in services need to be revisited in terms of the roles of tacit and codified knowledge, as key resources, essential for superior performance on a global scale. Global services must be able to respond rapidly to changing competitive environments and be sufficiently agile to accommodate the dynamic markets and changing technologies. Clearly the diffusion of the WWW and the technology infrastructure and the macroeconomic forces propelling nations toward global services, provide tentative support for proposition 3, namely, that new service strategies are required to achieve economies of knowledge through accelerated enterprise learning and knowledge transfer. This is no easy task, as the dizzying speeds at which customers, suppliers, and competitors are swapping boundaries, niches, and roles worldwide.

In this chapter we argue that the traditional approach to service operations strategies (Roth and van der Velde, 1991) must be augmented for attaining global leadership in three important ways. First, global services strategies must explicitly and proactively consider the impact of advanced ITC and Internet technologies, as well as "the ability of individuals, organizations, and even society at large to exploit their potential has not kept pace with the new technology" (Roth, 1996). Clearly, there must be a juxtaposition of managerial logic from the industrial era of "mass production" to that of strategic agility (Menor et al., 2000), where quality, delivery, flexibility, and cost are not traded off but rather act in concert as mutually reinforcing capabilities to compete globally. Second, global services strategies must explicitly consider cultural differences in setting their tactics (Pullman et al., 2000; Voss et al., 2000). At the same time, they must be cognizant of the convergence of best practices (Roth et al., 1997). Third, deliberate knowledge management strategies and a culture for learning should be developed as a component of a service operations strategy (Roth et al., 1994). Here managers must focus on the challenge of which knowledge an organization should make explicit (and codified) and which it should leave tacit (Zack, 1999).

CONCLUSIONS

A new economy, knowledge-based and service-oriented, is emerging and is characterized by the increasing importance of knowledge and by an accelerating rate of innovation and change in the industrialized world, including a transition towards a global economy that began as early as the 1970s. Additionally, the service sector currently dominates in developed economies and is likely to become even more important in the future (OECD, 2000). Evidence shows that employment in business services in the OECD has more than tripled since 1970, while manufacturing continues to decline in many industrialized countries.

Economic growth in recent years has become more dependent on the accumulation of intangible assets than on the accumulation of physical capital, as the increase in the ratio of intangible to tangible stock from 0.992 in 1973 to 1.15 in 1990 shows. As a result, traditional knowledge-based sectors such as computing, consulting, pharmaceuticals, and communications tend to increase their share of GDP.

As discussed above, advances in ICT are revolutionizing the way individuals and organizations collect and transmit knowledge and information in both home and work environments. These developments are likely to have profound effects on the role and global impact of services. E-commerce has emerged with the arrival of the WWW and is expected to transform the marketplace by replacing traditional intermediary functions, developing new products and markets, and creating new and closer relationships between business and consumers. As a result, the organization of work will be changed, new channels of knowledge diffusion and human interactivity will be opened, more flexibility and adaptability will be needed, and workers' functions will be refined. In addition E-commerce is expected to increase the interactivity of the economy, with natural implications for global services, since people will have the ability to communicate and transact business anywhere at any time, thereby eroding geographic boundaries. Also, it is altering the relative importance of time by speeding up production cycles, allowing service firms to operate in close coordination and enabling consumers to conduct transactions around the clock.

These observations led us to present three propositions regarding the emergent knowledge-based economy. The first proposition contends that services based upon high levels of codified knowledge are more likely to become global than those based upon tacit knowledge. However, in service sectors that are very dynamic, hypercompetitive, or high-velocity this change will be nonlinear and less predictable. The second proposition suggests that an adequate level of tacit knowledge is essential, since in dynamics environments service businesses necessarily rely much less on existing codified knowledge and much more on rapidly created situation-specific new knowledge. The use of existing knowledge can even be a disadvantage if managers overgeneralize from past situations instead of creating new knowledge to face new situations. The third proposition contends that global services must devise new operations strategies in order to better leverage their knowledge assets. Service business that want to play a role in this new economy must define global strategies in order to be integrated into the global economy. The ability to develop transnational organizational capabilities will be the key factor determining a company's performance. This is of particular importance for the so-called dot-coms.

However, the current analysis leads to a paradox. It is known that about 16 percent of the world population that lives in the developed world is responsible for about 82 percent of total world consumption (World Bank, 1999). While services are expanding globally, the income and knowledge resources available to the poorer 84 percent of the world population limit the number of players able to participate in, and take advantage of the ICT, in the knowledge-based economy. In this context we conclude with a word of caution. The analysis presented here reflects essentially the situation of the industrialized world and, in our view, current changes highlight the potential danger of less-developed countries being left out of the rapid technological transformation of a number of specialized and infrastructural service sectors with potential negative consequences for the economic development of such countries. This observation opens avenues for further research on the role of global services in economic development of less-developed countries aiming to devise policies to promote inclusive socioeconomic development.

NOTES

1. For more details on the International Service Study (ISS), see http://itr.bschool.unc.edu/kmrsrch/ISS/index.html

2. PricewaterhouseCoopers, KPMG, and other consulting firms have benefited from the creation of knowledge centers to improve the capture, codification, and dissemination of "best practices".

3. High-velocity markets are those in which market boundaries are blurred, successful business models are unclear, and market players (i.e., buyers, suppliers, competitors, complementers) are ambiguous and shifting. The overall service structure is unclear.

REFERENCES

Agility Forum (1994), Agile customer-supplier relation. Report series on agility. Bethlehem, PA: Agility Forum.

Apte, U. M. (1991), "Global outsourcing of information systems and processing services," *The Information Society*, 6(4), 287-303.

Apte, U. M. and R. O. Mason (1995), "Global disaggregation of information intensive services," *Management Science*, 41(7), 1250-1262.

Argote, L. (1999), *Organizational learning: creating, retaining, and transferring knowledge*. Boston: Kluwer Academic.

Barua, A., R. Chellappa and A. B. Whinston (1997), "Design and implementation of Internet and Intranet based collaboratories," *International Journal of Electronic Commerce*, 1(2), Winter 1996-97, 32-58.

Barua, A., and B. Lee (1997), "An economic analysis of the introduction of an Electronic Data Interchange system," *Information Systems Research*, 8(4), 398-422.

Borrus, A. (2000), "How Marriott never forgets a guest," *Business Week*, February, 21, 74.

Conceição, P. and M. Heitor (1999), "On the role of the university in the knowledge economy," *Science and Public Policy*, 23, 145-167.

Conceição, P., M. Heitor, and P. Oliveira (1998), "Expectations for the university in the age of the knowledge based societies," *Technological Forecasting and Social Change*, 58(3), 203-214.

D'Aveni, R. A. (1994), *Hypercompetition: Managing the Dynamics of Strategic Manoeuvring*. New York: The Free Press.

Drucker, P. (1992), "The new society of organizations," *Harvard Business Review*, 70(5), 95-104.

Drucker, P. (1993), *Post-Capitalist Society*. New York: HarperCollins Publishers, Inc.

Eisenhardt, K. M. (1989), "Making fast strategic decisions in high-velocity environments," *Academy of Management Journal*, 32(3), 543-576.

Eisenhardt, K. M. and D. C. Galunic (2000), "Coevolving at last, a way to make synergies work," *Harvard Business Review*, January-February, 91-101.

Fitzsimmons, J.A. and M.J., Fitzsimmons (1997), *Service Management: Operations, Strategy and Information Technology.* New York: McGraw-Hill.

Friel, D. (1998), "Technology, Innovation and Economic Growth," (mimeo).

Froehle, C. M., A. V. Roth, R. B. Chase, and C. A. Voss (2000), "Antecedents of new Service development effectiveness: An exploratory examination of strategic operations choices," *Journal of Service Research*, 3:1, 3-17.

Froehle, C. M., A. V. Roth, and A. Marucheck (2000), "Knowledge management and service operations: a synergy exposed," Kenan-Flagler Business School Working Paper, University of North Carolina at Chapel Hill presented at POMS 2000.

Fuchs, V. R. (1982), *The Service Economy.* New York: National Bureau of Economic Research.

Ghoshall, S., C. A. Bartlett, and P. Moran (1999), "A new manifesto for management," *Sloan Management Review*, 40(3), 9-20.

Giffi, C., A. V. Roth, and G. Seal (1990), *Competing in World Class Manufacturing: America's 21st Century Challenge.* Homewood, IL: Business One Irwin.

Greis, N. P. and J. D. Kasarda (1997), "Enterprise logistics in the information era," *California Management Review*, 39(3), 55-78.

Huete, L. and A. Roth (1988), "The industrialization and span of retail banks' delivery system," *International Journal of Operations & Production Management*, 8, 46-66.

Kim, L. (1998). "Crisis construction and organizational learning: Capability building in catching-up at Hyundai Motor," *Organization Science*, 9(4), 506-521.

Kogut, B. (1985), "Designing global strategies: Profiting from operational flexibility," *Sloan Management Review*, Fall 1985, 27-38.

Kogut, B. and U. Zander (1992), "Knowledge of the firm. Combinative capabilities, and the replications of technology," *Organization Science*, 3(3), 383-396.

Leonard D. (1995), *Wellsprings of Knowledge: Building and Sustaining the Sources of Innovation.* Boston: Harvard Business School Press.

Leonard-Barton, D., H. K. Bowen, K. B. Clark, C. A. Holloway, and S. C. Wheelwright (1994), "Regaining the lead in manufacturing: How to integrate work and deepen expertise," *Harvard Business Review* 72(5), 121.

Lovelock, C. and G. Yip (1996), "Developing global strategies for service businesses," *California Management Review*, 38(2), 64-86.

Lundvall, B. and S. Borrás (1997), "The globalising learning economy: implications for innovation policy," DG XII, Commission of the European Union (mimeo).

McLaughlin, C. and J. Fitzsimmons (1996), "Strategies for globalizing service operations," *International Journal of Service Industry Management*, 7(4), 43-57.

Menor, L. A. and A. V. Roth (2000), "Methodological note: an application of the 'fuzzy front end' of survey research—development and validation of multi-item scales in new service development," Richard Ivey Business School Working Paper, The University of Western Ontario.

Menor, L., A. V. Roth, and C. Mason (2000), "Agility in retail service management: A numerical taxonomy", Kenan-Flagler Business School Working Paper, University of North Carolina at Chapel Hill.

Meyer, A., R. Chase, A. V. Roth, C. Voss, K.-U. Sperl, L. Menor, and K. Blackmon (1999), "Service Competitiveness—An international benchmarking comparison of service practice and performance in Germany, UK, and USA," *International Journal of Service Industry Management*, 10(4), 369-379.

Nelson, R. and S. Winter (1982), *An Evolutionary Theory of Economic Change.* Cambridge, MA: Belknap Press.

Nonaka, I. (1994), "Dynamic theory of organizational knowledge creation," *Organization Science* 5(1), 14-37.

OECD (1994), *OECD Jobs Study*. Paris: OECD.

OECD (1998), *The Knowledge-Based Economy*. Paris: OECD.

OECD (2000), *The Service Economy*. Paris: OECD.

Oliveira, P., A. V. Roth, D. S. Rubin, and W. Gilland (2000), "An Imprecise Data Envelopment Analysis (IDEA) framework for the analysis of retail banking strategies," Kenan-Flagler Business School Working Paper, University of North Carolina at Chapel Hill.

Porter, M. (1986), "Changing patterns of international competition," *California Management Review*, Winter 1986, 9-40.

Pullman, M. E., R. Verma, and J. Goodale (2000), "Service design and operations strategy formulation in multicultural markets," *Journal of Operations Management*, 248, 1-16.

Quinn, J. B. (1992), *Intelligent Enterprise: A Knowledge and Service Based Paradigm for Industry*. New York: Free Press.

Roth, A. V. (1996), "Achieving strategic agility through economies of knowledge," *Strategy and Leadership,* March/April.

Roth, A. V. (2000), "Service strategy and the technological revolution: the 7 myths of eServices," *in POM Facing the New Millennium: Evaluating the Past, Leading with the Present and Planning the Future of Operations* (J.A.D. Machuca and T. Mandakovic, eds.), POM Sevilla 2000, ISBN 84-8009-102-9, 2000, pp. 159-168.

Roth, A. V., R. Chase, and C. Voss (1997), *Service in the US: Progress Towards Global Service Leadership*. Birmingham, UK: Severn Trent Plc. (http://itr.bschool.unc.edu/kmrsrch/ISS/index.html)

Roth, A. V. and C. Giffi (1995), "Winning in global markets: Neo-operations strategies in US and Japanese manufacturing," *OM Review*, 10(4).

Roth, A. V., A. E. Gray, J. Singhal, and K. Singhal (1997), "International technology and operations management: Resource toolkit for research and teaching," *Production and Operations Management*, 6 (2), 167-187.

Roth, A. V. and W. J. Jackson (1995), "Strategic determinants of service quality and performance," *Management Science*, 41(11), 1720-1733.

Roth, A .V., A.S. Marucheck, A. Kemp, and D. Trimble (1994). "The knowledge factory for accelerated learning practices," *Planning Review*, May / June: 26-33.

Roth, A. V. and M. van der Velde (1991). "Operations as marketing: A competitive service strategy," *Journal of Operations Management*, 10 (3): 303-327.

Shapiro, C. and H. R. Varian (1999), *Information Rules: A Strategic Guide to the Network Economy*. Boston: Harvard Business School Press.

Silverman, B. S. (1999), "Technological resources and the direction of corporate diversification: toward an integration of the Resource-based View and transaction costs economic," *Management Science*, 45(8), 1109-1124.

Spender, J. C. and R. M. Grant (1996), "Knowledge and the firm: overview," *Strategic Management Journal*, 17, 5-9.

Teece, D. A. (1998), "Capturing value from knowledge assets: The new economy markets for know-how, and intangible assets," *California Management Review*, 40(3), 55-79.

The Economist (2000), *The Virtual Threat—A Survey of Online Finance*.

Upton, D. M. and B. Kim, (1998), "Alternative methods of learning and process improvement in manufacturing," *Journal of Operations Management*, 16, 1-20.

U.S. Federal Communications Commission (1997), *International Traffic Data, 1977-1997*. Washington, DC.

Voss, C. A., (1997), "BAA-International operations," London Business School Centre for Operation Management.

Voss, C. A., K. Blackmon, R. B. Chase, B. Rose, and A. V. Roth (1997), "Service competitiveness—an Anglo-U.S. study," *Business Strategy Review*, 8, 7-22.

Voss, C. A., A. V. Roth, R. B. Chase, E. D. Rosenzweig, K, Blackmon (2000), "Customer behavior and operational performance—A two country service study," International Service Study, Working Paper (http://itr.bschool.unc.edu/kmrsrch/ISS/index.html).

Watson, R., P. Berthon, L. Pitt, and G. Zinkhan (1998), *Electronic Commerce: The Strategic Perspective.* Fort Worth, TX: Harcourt Brace College Publishers.

Wilson, R. (1993), *States and the Economy—Policymaking and Decentralization*, Westport, CT: Praeger.

World Bank (1999), *World Development Report*. New York: Oxford University Press.

Wyckoff, A. (1996), "The growing strength of services," *The OECD Observer*, 200, 11-15.

Zack, M. (1999), "Managing codified knowledge," *Sloan Management Review*, Summer, 45-58.

22

Problems of Learning in Organisations Producing Complex Product Systems

Tim Brady and Gillian Shapiro

INTRODUCTION

Much of the literature and advice on organisational learning assumes a single organisation which carries out repeated processes as typically found in mass production industries. This chapter is concerned specifically with firms who are involved in the design and development of Complex Products Systems (CoPS) which differ from mass-produced goods in a number of ways, which mean that assumptions based on mass-produced goods may be invalid when applied to CoPS. Furthermore the complex nature of the products in CoPS means that they are often developed by a temporary alliance of a number of firms rather than within a single organisation. This means that learning becomes even more difficult than within a single organisation. Furthermore, much of the knowledge needed to produce CoPS is embedded in individuals and teams (Nightingale, 1997a, 1997b; Vincenti, 1990), whereas in mass production the learning becomes embodied in the machines and systems producing the goods. The chapter begins with a brief section describing the characteristics of CoPS and the key differences to mass-produced goods and how this creates specific difficulties for learning in CoPS. The next two sections provide an examination of the literature on organisational learning and knowledge creation as far as it is relevant to the specific problems of CoPS firms related to interproject learning. The final section discusses the implications for learning in CoPS.

WHAT ARE CoPS?

CoPS can be simply thought of as large engineering- and, increasingly, software-intensive business-to-business products, networks and constructs. They are produced on a project basis, often in multifirm alliances, as one-offs or in small customised batches for specific customers and markets. Examples include flight simulators, global business networks, jet engines, civil airliners, power stations, mobile telephone systems and large civil engineering projects.

Many of the innovation and production processes in CoPS do not conform to conventional models derived from research in mass-production industries (Hobday, 1998; Hobday and Rush, 1999). For CoPS, the nature of the production process is very different with a far greater emphasis on software development, systems integration and project management rather than manufacturing and other repeated tasks. Small design changes in one part of the system may have large knock-on effects in other parts of the system, resulting in the need for backward feedback loops from one stage of production to another. Customers frequently change their requirements during the production cycle, leading to unclear goals, uncertainty over best production practices and unpredictable and unquantifiable risks. As a result, many of the tools, techniques and practices derived from mass production may be inappropriate.

In non-CoPS firms, learning tends to take place in functional departments where learning routines have become systematic, and much of what is done is explicit and can be codified. In contrast, in CoPS firms, much of the learning is within the projects, may be fragmented and sporadic, and is more likely to be tacit or implicit. While learning may and often does occur at the level of the individual and teams involved in projects, there are few mechanisms available to firms to allow the exploitation of this learning at the level of the organisation.

The problem is similar to that identified with respect to single and double loop learning (Argyris and Schon, 1978). Within individual projects, new knowledge is created and shared among the project members in order to enable the completion of the project—the development of the particular CoPS. During the lifetime of a project various persons join and leave and once it is completed, the teams disband, individual knowledge is dispersed and the collective learning is often lost. Motivation to reflect on and document the transferable experience for reuse in future projects is low. These factors mean that it is extremely difficult for CoPS firms to develop learning at the level of the organisation. Herein lies the difficulty for CoPS firms. Their core capabilities lie in such areas as systems integration, project management and software development. Much of the knowledge they have which affords these capabilities is created during the course of the projects. But much of this knowledge is tacit in nature and therefore hard to transfer.

ORGANISATIONAL LEARNING AND THE LEARNING ORGANISATION

There is a massive literature on organisational learning, including many reviews of the field. There is not space to go over this vast area here, rather we shall concentrate on selected references which seem most appropriate for the problems of learning in CoPS. The literature discusses the distinctions and relationships between the terms "learning organisation" and "learning within organisations" and addresses the links between individual learning and organisational learning and concepts of organisational memory.

Organisational Learning

As Garvin (1993) points out, there are many different definitions of organisational learning which reveal considerable disagreement as to what it is. Most concur that it is a process that is linked to knowledge acquisition and improved performance over time.

Levitt and March (1988) interpret organisational learning in terms of three observations drawn from behavioural studies of organisations. First, that organisational behaviour is based on routines. Second, that routines are based on interpretations of the past more than anticipations of the future. Third, that organisations are oriented to targets and their behaviour depends on the relation between observed outcomes and aspirations they have for these outcomes. By routines they mean both "the forms, rules, procedures, conventions, strategies, and technologies around which organisations are constructed and through which they operate... [and also] ...the structures of beliefs, frameworks, paradigms, codes, cultures, and knowledge that buttress, elaborate, and contradict the formal routines" (Levitt and March (1988, p. 320). They suggest two ways in which routines and beliefs change: trial and error experimentation, and organisational search. However, they offer little in the way of examples of exactly how to carry out these processes apart from reference to learning by doing, and the creation of stories, paradigms and frames as a means to developing collective understandings of history.

Huber (1990) cites information processing as the means by which learning takes place. He suggests that information and knowledge acquisition takes place via five processes: congenital learning, experiential learning, vicarious learning, grafting and searching.

An organisation's *congenital knowledge* combines the knowledge inherited from its founders at the time of conception with the additional knowledge that has been acquired before the "birth" of the organisation. After its birth an organisation may acquire knowledge as a result of *experiential learning*. This may be as a result of intentional, systematic efforts or it may be acquired unintentionally or in haphazard forms. Huber distinguishes five groupings in terms of organisational experiments, organisational self-appraisal, experimenting organisations, unintentional or unsystematic learning and experience-based learning curves. *Vicarious learning* is about acquiring experience on a second-hand basis by borrowing what other organisations have learned, by imitation of their approaches, and so on. *Grafting* involves acquiring knowledge in the form of new personnel who possess capabilities and knowledge previously nonexistent in the organisation. Learning by *searching* involves scanning the external environment, in a general way or in more focused searches.

Huber concluded that while there were quite extensive literatures on experiential learning and search, there was not much conceptual or cumulative analysis done. Furthermore, despite the importance of organisational experiments, the literature contains very few studies of experimentation by organisations and relatively little has been learned about congenital learning, vicarious learning and grafting other than the fact that they occur.

Shrivastava (1983) recognises that organisations themselves are very different and exhibit different approaches to learning He identifies six types of organisational learning systems representing more or less formalised approaches to learning: one-man institution, mythological learning systems, information-seeking culture, participative learning systems, formal management systems and bureacratic learning systems. In the first a single individual acts as a knowledge broker. In the second much of the learning is the result of stories about activities within the organisation. The third represents an organisation where information is routinely exchanged in informal networks, usually by word of mouth. The fourth reflects an organisation where ad hoc committees, working groups and teams are formed to resolve strategic and management control problems and knowledge is transferred via the members of the committees to the rest of the organisation. The fifth involves the use of systematic procedures developed to guide standard and nonstandard organisational activities and standardising the way knowledge drawn from individuals may be used. The most formal learning system involves establishment of an elaborate system of rigid procedures and regulations which control the format and flow of information and to which all members of the organisation are expected to adhere.

Edmondson and Moingeon (1998) note the propensity for the multiple definitions of organisational learning to create confusion. While recognising that diversity of approach is valuable, they propose another definition of organisational learning synthesised from the literature: "a process in which the organisation's members actively use data to guide behaviour in such a way as to promote the ongoing adpatation of the organisation" (p. 12). This appears to progress us little compared to Garvin's earlier assessment.

The Learning Organisation

Just as organisational learning is subject to many definitions, so too is the learning organisation. It is described by Garvin (1993) as "an organisation skilled at creating, acquiring and transfering knowledge, and at modifying its behaviour to reflect new knowledge and insights" (p. 80).

Stalk et al. (1992) define a successful learning organisation as one which proactively harnesses and modifies its routines, technology, processes structures and cultures in order to maximise and draw on the learning capabilities of its people.

Individual Learning versus Organisational Learning

A common theme among writers within the organisational learning field is that organisational learning is dependent, at least in part, on individuals' learning within organisations. Simon (1991) points out that "All learning takes place inside individual heads" and Kim (1993) says that organisations ultimately learn via their individual members. Kim (1993) and Dodgson (1993) link individual and organisational learning so closely that they describe the latter as a metaphor derived from the former, while Stata (1989) suggests that "organisations can learn only as fast as the slowest link learns (p. 64).

Hedberg (1981) points out that the distinction between the learning organisation and the learning of its people within is important precisely because its members may come and go and some leaders might change. Thus it is important that organisations have the capability to preserve the required behaviours, skills and cultures and so on over time. According to Hedberg: "Although organizational learning occurs through individuals, it would be a mistake to conclude that organisational learning is nothing but the cumulative result of their member's learning. Organizations do not have brains, but they have cognitive systems and memories" (p. 3).

Kim (1993) also suggests the distinction and relations between the two is important to maintain, otherwise: "a model of organisational learning will either obscure the actual learning process by ignoring the role of the individual ... or become a simplistic extension of individual learning by glossing over organisational complexities" (pp. 42-43).

According to Hedberg (1981) organisations frequently know less than their members because of problems in communication. He is skeptical about how applicable laboratory learning experiments are to the real world of organisations. Whereas the former are often conducted in simple, stable environments with unidimensional goal environments, real organisations pursue multiple goals and operate in unstable environments.

KNOWLEDGE CREATION AND ACQUISITION

Earlier it was noted that definitions of organisational learning often thought of it as a process involving knowledge acquisition. This part of the chapter presents a brief exploration of knowledge and its creation. Several definitions of knowledge can be found in the literature, the majority of which encompass a distinction between information and knowledge.

Nonaka (1994), Machlup (1983) and Dretske (1981) each distinguish between information and knowledge, with information defined as a flow of messages and knowledge defined as the creative result of a flow of messages anchored on the commitment and beliefs of its holder—that is, knowledge is related to human action. They further suggest that information is a necessary medium for initiating and formalising knowledge. Information itself can be viewed as syntactic or semantic. Shannon and Weaver (1949) illustrate the syntactic nature of information by using the example of a telephone bill which shows the duration of a cost of a call—not its content, its content being the semantic aspect of the information. The semantic aspect of information is the more relevant for understanding knowledge capture and transfer. Arora and Gambordella (1994) also distinguish between information and knowledge. They define information as "facts" about products, processes and markets, and knowledge as providing the context within which information is interpreted. Davenport, De Long and Beers (1998) define knowledge as: "information combined with experience, context, interpretation, and reflection" (p. 43).

At a second level, definitions of knowledge also distinguish between different types of knowledge, the majority of which refer to distinctions between tacit and explicit knowledge. This is particularly relevant for CoPS producers as has been pointed out; the knowledge required to produce CoPS is largely tacit and more difficult to formalise to the same degree as in mass-produced goods. However, there is some disagreement within the literature over the extent to which tacit knowledge can or indeed should be formalised.

Polanyi (1983/1966) first made the distinction between tacit and explicit knowledge. In essence, Polanyi describes these as two different types of knowledge rather than two forms of the same thing. That is, neither, he argues, can be substituted or turned into the same thing. Tacit knowledge can be defined as things we know, but cannot say. Conversely, explicit knowledge can be said or read and so on. Polanyi (1983) argues that each type of knowledge—tacit or explicit—needs to be learned or acquired in its own right. Explicit knowledge can be learned in a number of ways, such as consulting an "expert", reading books or manuals, learning from videos or group interaction. Tacit knowledge, he proposes, is learned on its own and not made out of explicit knowledge.

In direct contrast to Polyani, Nonaka (1994) suggests that knowledge is created through *conversion* (our emphasis) between tacit and explicit knowledge. He suggests four modes of conversion as shown in Figure 22.1.

The key to acquiring tacit knowledge, according to Nonaka, is experience and he refers to apprenticeships and mentors to note how tacit knowledge can be transferred not necessarily through language, but through observation, imitations and practice—what he calls "socialisation". "Combination", the transfer of explicit to explicit knowledge, is achieved through the use of social processes—such as meetings, telephone conversations and IT systems. The combination mode is triggered by coordination between team members and other sections of the organisation and the documentation of existing knowledge. Meaningful dialogue triggers the externalisation mode and uses "metaphors" to enable team members to articulate what might otherwise be tacit or hidden or hard to communicate. Experimentation with new concepts can then trigger internalisation through a process of learning by doing. That is, teams, for example, share explicit knowledge that can be translated over time, through interaction and trial and error into different aspects of tacit knowledge.

Figure 22.1
Nonaka's Modes of Knowledge Conversion

	To Tacit	To Explicit
From Tacit	'socialisation'	'externalisation'
From Explicit	'internalisation'	'combination'

At the centre of Nonaka's theory of organisational knowledge creation is the argument that "a dynamic interaction" between the four modes of knowledge conversion is crucial. This dynamic interaction can be triggered, Nonaka claims, by different events and interventions. For example, he argues that the socialisation mode is often started with the development of a "team" or "field" of interaction which facilitates the sharing of members' experiences and perspectives.

In contrast to Nonaka, Cook and Brown (1999) take Polyani's view that tacit and explicit knowledge are separate things and refute the assertion that one can be converted to the other. They caution against confusing using one type of knowledge as an aid in acquiring another with one being converted to the other: "Tacit knowledge is not changed or "surfaced" when used as a tool in learning something explicit, nor is explicit knowledge changed or "submerged" when used as a tool for learning something explicit." Further, they suggest that while tacit and explicit knowledge might be used as an aid to learning or discovering the other, there is no guarantee one type will always be a useful aid to acquiring the other and might even be a hindrance.

In addition, Cook and Brown (1999) criticise the tendency for the learning and knowledge literature to heighten the importance of the individual over the organisation and the explicit over the tacit as being theoretically and operationally problematic. They suggest a categorisation of knowledge according to whether it is tacit or explicit and whether it is at the level of the individual or at the level of the group (the group may be a team or it could be a whole organisation). These result in a categorisation of knowledge as shown in Figure 22.2.

The upper left-hand cell of the matrix contains the things individuals can know and learn that are explicit—typically rules, equations, concepts that can be written down. The upper right-hand cell includes those things which are used, expressed or transferred in a group such as stories about how work is done, about famous successes and failures or metaphors that have particular meaning to a group. Things that are known by individuals but cannot be expressed explicitly (Polyani's tacit knowledge) populate the lower left-hand cell. The lower right-hand cell is populated by genres a term that Cook and Brown describe as something which "identifies for a particular group the distinctive and useful meanings that they attach to the objects" (specific terminology and tools, for example) and activities (such as a specific way of doing a task) that are common to a group. According to Cook and Brown, these shared meanings are not explicitly learned or known, they are generated, acquired and evoked as the objects and activities become part of and incorporated in the regular practices of the group.

Figure 22.2
Cook and Brown's Categories of Knowledge

	Individual	Group
Explicit	concepts, rules, equations etc.	stories, metaphors
Tacit	skills etc.	genres

While Nonaka (1994) argues that the practical benefits of tacit knowledge can be reaped only when it becomes explicit, Cook and Brown argue that the different categories of knowledge inherent in the explicit/tacit and individual/group distinctions need to be treated as being of equal standing to each other. Together they label these four types of knowledge as constituting what they call "the epistemology of possession" as they are traditionally seen as things people possess. They argue that in addition to knowledge there is "knowing". By knowing they mean something that is embodied in action.

They argue for a parallel "epistemology of practice" (based on the American philosophical school of pragmatism and in particular on the work of John Dewey, 1922) which has knowing as its focus: "Individuals and groups clearly make use of knowledge in what they do, but not everything they can do...is explicable in terms of the knowledge they possess."

Cook and Brown (1999) see the two parallel streams of knowledge and knowing as complementary and mutually enabling. This approach, they argue, "provides a more robust account of...how individuals and groups can draw on tacit and explicit knowledge simultaneously; how what individuals know tacitly can be made useful to groups; and how explicit instruction can be made more useful aids for the development of tacit skills."

They refer to Dewey's (1922) understanding of knowing as "productive inquiry". That is, to engage in productive inquiry is to be actively pursuing a problem, or puzzle or point of interest. What motivates the action of inquiry is some sense of query—a problem or question. It is productive because it aims to produce an answer or solution. Productive inquiry is not a random search but informed by sets of theories, rules of thumb, concepts and such. The activity of using knowledge in inquiry, Dewey would call "knowing". Here, knowledge is a tool of the activity of knowing.

Cook and Brown (1999) build on Dewey's work and add that knowledge itself does not underlie or enable knowing, just as having a hammer may not mean one knows how to skilfully use it. They suggest that knowing is not the same as "know-how" which they view still as a piece of knowledge. They add that knowing is not "tacit knowledge" as defined by Polanyi (1983) because it is embodied in concrete action. Knowing requires action, whereas tacit knowledge does not. Indeed, they suggest that knowing can make use of tacit knowledge as a tool for action, just as it makes use of knowledge ad know-how.

In addition, Cook and Brown (1999) define knowing as a form of action as being about interaction with the world—social and physical. In short, "The term knowledge is about what we possess, it is a term of predication. In all its forms (explicit, tacit, know-how) we use it to indicate something someone possesses, can possess or needs to possess. The terms knowing is about dyadic relations it is about interaction between the knower and the world."

Through their case study of software developers in the United States and United Kingdom, Cook and Brown (1999) note how through the use of mediating technologies such as e-mail and document-sharing systems and video links, it was possible for the U.S. and U.K. members of the group to "meet" regularly to "do real work". That is, they did more than exchange information; they were able to develop a distributed competency. They suggest that such activities can be successful in generating knowledge by facilitating the productive interaction of existing knowledge and knowing—what they term as the "generative dance."

ORGANISATIONAL LEARNING MECHANISMS

Despite the extensive literature on organisational learning, the discussion of interventions aimed specifically at introducing organisational learning is surprisingly slim (Lipschitz et al., 1996). Popper and Lipschitz (1995) introduce the concept of organisational learning mechanisms—institutionalised, structural and procedural arrangements that allow organisations to systematically collect, analyse, store, disseminate and use information. They claim that it is the existence of these mechanisms that is relevant to the effectiveness of the organisation and that enables it to learn.

Such mechanisms are seen as important in improving organisational performance in relation to developing capabilities in continuous improvement (CI) in manufacturing (Caffyn and Bessant, 1996; Bessant and Caffyn, 1997); by Bartezzaghi et al. (1997) and Caffyn (1997) with respect to improving the new product development (NPD) process; and by Coombs and Hull (1997) in relation to the mechanisms through which knowledge affects possibilities for innovation.

Caffyn and Bessant's capability-based model views CI as a set of "key behaviours", or "routines" which are generic to all organisations and which evolve over a period of time. The building up and subsequent embedding of key behaviours depends on the existence of enabling mechanisms (exemplified by procedures, subsystems, methodologies, etc.). The particular form these enabling mechanisms take and whether they are appropriate or not is contingent on an organisation's history, its structure, its culture, the commercial environment in which it operates and many other factors.

Bartezzaghi et al.'s (1997) emphasis is on trying to understand the inner mechanisms that regulate the process of improvement in NPD and to propose adequate enabling mechanisms to facilitate it. They define interproject learning as the accumulation of knowledge about product development and its transfer to subsequent projects.

They point out the difference in continuous improvement in mass-production operations and NPDs. In particular they refer to the plan, do, check, act (PDCA) model for CI (Deming, 1986) and suggest that for interproject learning the process takes place at a more abstract level than within specific projects because of its cross-project nature. These factors also lead to interproject learning being characterised by specific peculiarities which make the process very complex. For example, there may be significant time gaps between various phases in a project so that problems in an early phase are not revealed until months later during a different phase. This time separation makes it very difficult to determine cause and effect. Furthermore the feedback is collected by different project members in different phases, which means that analysis of variances is neither implicit nor spontaneous. Thus the collection of feedback, the analysis of variances and the identification of the causes of such variances require explicit processes or mechanisms to be put in place.

The last step in the PDCA cycle, the implementation of corrective actions, is particularly complex and articulated for NPD projects. This is because plans and feedback are project-specific and hence analysis of variances between initial plans and final feedback cannot directly result in corrective actions to be taken in future projects.

Bartezzaghi et al. (1997) suggest a number of organisational mechanisms and processes which might enable the development of systematic learning at the interproject level: managing project feedback, using vehicles for embodying and disseminating improvements and adopting project classification schemes. They suggest that the most effective interproject learning mechanism is the analysis of variances during project termination and project audit stages (the former is the final phase of the NPD project, while the latter is carried out about six months after manufacture of the new product has commenced.

Bartezzaghi et al. (1997) propose that the enablers talked of in continuous improvement can also help interproject learning (e.g., a clear strategic vision), the diffusion of the improvement objects, the development of a culture for improvement, the empowerment of human resources and so on. (Bessant et al., 1994).

While literature which specifically looks at interproject learning is scarce, the important relationship between teams (within and projects) and the wider organisation (of which much more is written in relation to learning) should be noted. Indeed, there is widespread research to suggest that teams are the key learning unit in organisations (Argyris, 1992; Kofman and Senge, 1993; Senge, 1990; Stata, 1989; Takeuchi and Nonaka, 1986). However, to realise interteam or project learning, Romme (1997) notes the importance of the wider organisational structure in which teams and projects operate. He and Kim (1993) argue that a hierarchical structure is required to link teams together and disseminate knowledge in large organisations. A challenge therefore is how to link and reconcile team and hierarchical structure. Involvement-oriented, participative management methods as opposed to traditional control-oriented methods have been offered as a solution to this challenge (Argyris, 1977; McGregor, 1960; Likert, 1961; and Ackoff, 1981).

Kilmann (1996) argues that interproject learning is not a new area or concept, but in fact builds on other areas. For example, the themes of describing, controlling and improving processes is derived from quality management literature (e.g., Deming, 1986; Harrington, 1995; Juran, 1991). Kilmann points to Total Quality Management (TQM) and the European Foundation for Quality Management (EFQM) as providing the structure for organisational learning that Garvin (1993) recommends. That is:

- operational definitions that give practical meaning to each step of process management;
- specific guidelines, procedures and tools for managing processes effectively;
- well-developed metrics for measuring process improvements.

Basili and Caldiera (1995) note that software development projects, unlike mass manufacturing, are one-shot items and therefore the challenge they face is how to learn from other projects. Traditionally the software industry is driven by its business units and therefore has little ability to capitalise on experiences and capabilities. More recently, however, Basili and Caldiera suggest a solution is to apply the quality improvement paradigm.

Specific mechanisms which are mentioned in the literature include postproject reviews, manuals, stories and IT-based knowledge repositories.

Postproject Reviews

Bartezzaghi et al. (1997) note the potential of project review stages in providing knowledge and information that can be shared across projects. However, they also note a reluctance of firms to undertake wider sharing until after a project's completion. Due to this they recommend that the preproject team (the planning/proposal team) attends the project termination phase and review as they are able to identify variances between initial plans and final results and may provide the systemic connections between causes and effects.

However, Kransdorff (1996) argues that the problem with postproject reviews, internal audits and/or oral postmortems as a way to learn from experience is that they are undertaken retrospectively, making them susceptible to the characteristics of partial and selective memory recall by managers who, after the event, are rarely neutral or objective.

Manuals

While widely used within organisations, manuals have come under criticism in the learning literature for the extent to which in reality they are able to facilitate interproject knowledge capture and transfer. An important distinction to note in terms of knowledge capture and transfer is the one Bourdieu (1977) makes between modus operandi—a task in progress—and opus operatum—a finished task. Both he and Ryle (1954) note that the modus operandi is unfolding over time, it has options and dilemmas which may remain unsolved. However the opus operatum tends to see the action in terms of the task alone and cannot see the way in which the process of doing the task is actually structured by the constantly changing conditions of work and the world.

Bourdieu's analogy of the map—which provides useful directions, but does not show the details of the route or the incidents which may abstract the journey such as road works, diversion, tiredness, conflicting opinions—illustrates this point. Thus, as a journey becomes more complex, the map increasingly conceals what is actually needed to make the journey. "Thick" (Geertz, 1973) or detailed description, on the other hand, ascends from the abstraction to the concrete circumstances of actual practice, reconnecting the map and the mapped.

Brown and Duguid (1991) argue that "many organisations are willing to assume that complex tasks can be successfully mapped onto a set of simple, Tayloristic, canonical steps that can be followed without need of significant understanding or insight" (p. 61). They suggest that working, learning and innovating are not in fact separate or conflicting but interrelated, compatible and complementary. They argue that the source of perceptions that these three elements are conflicting lies in the gap between precepts and practice and argue that formal descriptions of work (e.g., manuals, procedures) and of learning (e.g., subject matter) are removed from actual practice. In contrast, they argue that actual practice is central to understanding work. They cite Orr's (1990) detailed ethnographic studies of service technicians and their need to tell a story to solve a problem when manuals cannot help to illustrate how an organisation's view of work can overlook and even oppose what and who it takes to get a job done.

Brown and Duguid (1991) label espoused practice as "canonical practice" and argue that it can blind an organisation's core to the actual and usually valuable practices of its members. In terms of learning they note that conventional learning theory, including that implicit in most training courses, tends to endorse the valuation of abstract knowledge over actual practice and as a result separates learning from working and learners from workers. This negative view of canonical practice supports Cook and Brown's (1999) view of the importance of tacit over explicit knowledge mentioned earlier.

Stories

Stories are an important method of transferring knowledge in organisations. Quoted in an article in *Fortune*, David Snowden[1] (1998), an expert on tacit knowledge in IBM, said "stories are the way we communicate complex ideas".

IBM Global Services has a novel method of learning from its past successes and failures in bidding for major global account deals. It reassembles the teams who worked on the bids and gets them to re-create the story of what went on by talking about it, interrupting, correcting, supplementing, reminding each other of who did what, when and why. The whole event is recorded on video and this video is kept as a record of the bid. This contrasts sharply with normal project reviews and manuals or guides as described above.

Brown and Duguid (1991) describe storytelling as reflecting: "the complex social web within which work takes place and the relationship of the narrative, narrator, and audience to the specific events of practice. The stories have a flexible generality that makes them both adaptive and particular. They function, rather like the common law, as usefully underconstrained means to interpret each new situation in light of accumulated wisdom and constantly changing circumstances" (pp. 64-65).

Orr's (1990) study of photocopy service reps referred to above highlighted two important aspects of story telling:

- it helps to diagnose the state of troublesome machines,
- it helps to develop causal accounts of machines which are essential when documentation breaks down.

In their storytelling the service reps develop a causal map out of their experience to replace the impoverished directive route coming from the corporation.

It is also worth noting that Zuboff (1988) in her analysis of the skills people develop working on complex systems, describes similar cases of storytelling and argues that it is a necessary practice for dealing with "smart" but unpredictable machines.

IT-based Knowledge Repositories

Many organisations are treating knowledge as an "it"—that is, an entity separate from the people who create and use it. With such an approach, the goal tends to be to take documents with knowledge embedded in them, such as reports, articles, manuals and sort them in a repository where they can be easily retrieved. Another form of the "it" knowledge management approach is the discussion database where participants record their own experiences on an issue and react to comments from others. Davenport et al. (1998) found three types of repositories: external knowledge (e.g., competitive intelligence), structured internal knowledge (e.g., research reports, techniques and methods), and informal internal knowledge (e.g., databases of know-how or lessons learned).

Davenport et al. (1998) found examples of companies trying to transfer tacit knowledge from individuals into a repository using some sort of community-based electronic discussion. For example, Hewlett Packard's corporate education division was capturing tips, tricks, insights and experiences into a Lotus Notes Database and made them available to over 2,000 trainers and educators across the organisation. Microsoft has developed an expert network for making explicit types of knowledge competencies necessary for software development projects and for matching software development teams that need people with certain expertise with those who have it. The network has described 300 knowledge competencies, both general and technology-specific. It uses a database and Web interface to store the knowledge competency categories and personal profiles. BP Exploration (BPX) is facilitating the exchange of tacit knowledge through installing video conferencing systems, document scanning and sharing tools with the requisite telecommunications networks in each site. This is supported by education and coaching on how people can use the system to solve real BPX problems. An illustration of its use came when a compressor in an oil field in Colombia stopped functioning and the only expert was on the North Slope of Alaska. The problem was solved through video conferencing in a few hours.

IMPLICATIONS FOR LEARNING IN CoPS

Two overall deficiencies appear clear from the literature review above. First, the different interpretations of learning, the learning organisation, knowledge, knowledge management, information, skill and so on certainly do not appear helpful to an organisation attempting to navigate its way around this field. Second, much of the literature contains recommendations for what a learning organisation, for example, should look like and the cultures, structures and processes required to enable knowledge capture and transfer. However, there is a scarcity of studies which analyse and report on what organisations are doing in practice to capture and transfer knowledge or that provide guidance in how to establish the cultures and structures called for.

The majority of literature drawn on in this chapter which might be relevant for interproject knowledge capture and transfer comes from the fields of organisational learning and, more recently, knowledge management. This literature tends to concentrate on either organisational wide learning—(the learning organisation)—or sharing knowledge and learning within projects and/or teams. In addition, the literature concentrates on service-sector or mass-production firms and has not addressed issues of knowledge capture and transfer that may be specific to CoPS. The literature and research which is perhaps of most relevance to the specificity of CoPS can be found in the growing area of research on transfer of learning and improvement within the new product development process.

An important debate that appears of particular relevance for CoPS firms surrounds the distinction between tacit and explicit knowledge. There is evidence above that single approaches to learning in CoPS are inappropriate. A

CoPS project involves numerous actors from different communities of practice, and different organisations who are thrown together for the duration of the project. The recommendations and suggestions for tools, techniques and processes to enable interproject knowledge capture and transfer highlighted within the literature may or may not be relevant to CoPS companies. For example, much of the research on which the CI model is based (and most other work on continuous improvement) refers to the operations side of organisations and very often on mass-produced goods. The nature of mass production means that firms are able to learn by gathering data on routines and improving group practices (Stata, 1989; Garvin, 1993). However, the nature of CoPS production (one-shot or small batch) means that data collection is not possible in the same way. There are some examples of learning-by-doing in CoPS—studies of the airframe industry have shown how the costs of production decline along with labour costs depending on the cumulative number of aircraft manufactured (Wright, 1936 and Asher, 1956 cited in Levitt and March, 1988). But many CoPS are one-shots without the same opportunity to attain economies of scale. Furthermore, the temporary nature of CoPS projects means that there is less scope for routinised learning.

However, the literature review undertaken to date highlights the importance of CoPS firms (as for mass-production and service-sector firms) establishing an organisational environment, with the structures, strategies, processes, policies and cultures to support, encourage and enable interproject knowledge capture and transfer, as a means of learning.

A number of features emerge as important for learning in CoPS:

- Experience is valuable and should be rewarded. Key people throughout the project process from bid development to implementation to service, including bid managers, design engineers, project managers and practitioners hold knowledge which is crucial to successful execution of projects.
- Tacit, uncodified knowledge is important. Much of the knowledge in projects is tacit and can't be codified as it lies in the skill and experience of individuals and groups. Because it can't be codified there are no manuals or documents which record the knowledge. It is important however to try to identify who has what expertise and experience so that it can be called upon as necessary in future projects.
- Learning mechanisms and systems should be appropriate to the people who are expected to use them. Different tools and mechanisms may be required at different stages in a project. Explicit knowledge may require formal procedures, rules and manuals. Such knowledge may be captured on databases. Other forms of mechanism, such as storytelling, face-to-face meetings, or project reviews, may be more appropriate means of learning and understanding from previous projects which cannot be expressed in explicit form. Many of the ways learning takes place may be informal such as meetings outside the workplace. Managers seeking to develop learning mechanisms should not rely simply on their knowledge of espoused practice, but should examine actual practice.
- An open learning culture should be encouraged. The levels of uncertainty in CoPS projects mean that it is inevitable that mistakes are made. Such mistakes must be recognised as part of the process of organisational development and as learning

opportunities rather than to find people to blame. If people aren't willing to try new things, the long-term performance of the company may suffer.

- Learning is not free. Resources have to be made available for learning to take place. This means giving people time to undertake reviews and develop learning tools. There has to be support in terms of infrastructure, whether it is in the form of IT or process support staff. If necessary, incentives should be made available to encourage the sharing of information, to encourage the less experienced to spend time with more experienced people, and for the latter to spend their time explicitly in this mentoring role. The organisation rather than the project should bear the costs associated with this.

- Good records of projects have to be kept. This requirement goes beyond the formal requirements of managing the project. Information which reflects on performance and how to inform future projects (such as lesson-learned reports) should be collected. If this information is not recorded close to the time when events took place, then poor or partial recall and post-hoc rationalisation may result in incorrect interpretations of events. Since project personnel are constantly moving out of the project, real-time collection of this information is important, and they are often not present when postproject reviews are undertaken. New IT systems should enable good archives of past projects to be kept which should be accessible by future projects. Increasingly the technology allows use of video clips to allow people to tell their own stories as a means of communicating complex ideas. Thus it should be possible to develop knowledge repositories which provide an opportunity to learn more than from written documents.

NOTE

1. David Snowden, quoted by Thomas Stewart in *Fortune Magazine*, "The Cunning Plots of Leadership", September 7, 1998.

REFERENCES

Ackoff, R. (1981), *Creating the Corporate Future*. New York: Wiley.

Argyris, C. (1977), "Double Loop Learning in Organizations," *Harvard Business Review*, Vol. 55, No. 5, pp. 115-125.

Argyris, C. (1992), *On Organizational Learning*. London: Blackwell.

Argyris, C. and Schon, D. (1978), *Organizational Learning Reading*. MA: Addison-Wesley.

Arora, A. and Gambardella, A. (1994), "The Changing Technology of Technological Change: General and Abstract Knowledge and the Division of Innovative Labour," *Research Policy*, Vol. 23, pp. 523-532.

Asher, H. (1956), *Cost-Quantity Relationships in the Airframe Industry*. Santa Monica, CA: Rand.

Bartezzaghi, E., Corso, M. and Verganti, R. (1997), "Continuous Improvement and Inter-project Learning in New Product Development," *International Journal of Technology Management*, Vol. 14, No. 1, pp. 116-138.

Basili, V. and Caldiera, G. (1995), "Improve Software Quality by Reusing Knowledge and Experience," *Sloan Management Review*, Vol. 37, No. 1, Fall, pp. 55-64.

Bessant, J. and Caffyn, S. (1997), "High involvement innovation through continuous improvement," *International Journal of Technology Management*, Vol. 14, No. 1, pp. 7-28.

Bessant, J., Caffyn, S., Gilbert, J., Harding, R. and Webb, S. (1994), "Rediscovering Continuous Improvement," *Technovation*, Vol. 14, No. 1, pp. 17-29.

Bourdieu, P. (1977), *Outline of a Theory of Practice*. New York: Cambridge University Press.

Brown, J.S. and Duguid, P. (1991), "Organizational Learning and Communities-of-Practice: Towards a Unified View of Working, Learning and Innovation," *Organization Science*, Vol. 2, No. 1, pp. 40-57.

Caffyn, S. (1997), "Extending continuous improvement to the new product development process," *R&D Management*, Vol. 27, No. 3, pp. 253-267.

Caffyn, S. and Bessant, J. (1996), *A capability-based model for continuous improvement*. London: EurOMA.

Cook, S. and Brown, J.S. (1999), "Bridging Epistemologies: The Generative Dance Between Organizational Knowledge and Organizational Knowing," *Organization Science*, Vol. 10, No. 4, July-August, pp. 381-400.

Coombs, R. and Hull, R. (1997), "Knowledge Management Practices and Path-Dependency in Innovation" Working Paper, UMIST, ESRC Centre for Research on Innovation and Competition.

Davenport, T., De Long, D. and Beers, M. (1998), "Successful Knowledge Management Projects," *Sloan Management Review*, Vol. 39, No. 2, Winter, pp. 43-57.

Deming, W. (1986), *Out of the Crisis*. Cambridge, MA: MIT.

Dewey, J. (1922), *Human Nature and Conduct: An Introduction to Social Psychology*. London: Allen and Unwin.

Dodgson, M. (1993), "Organizational Learning: A Review of Some Literatures," *Organization Studies*, Vol. 14, No. 3, pp. 375-394.

Dretske, F. (1981), *Knowledge and the Flow of Information*. Cambridge, MA: MIT Press.

Edmondson, A. and Moingeon, B. (1998), "From Organizational Learning to the Learning Organization," *Management Learning*, Vol. 29, No. 1, pp. 5-20.

Garvin, D. (1993), "Building a Learning Organization," *Harvard Business Review*, Vol. 71, No. 4, July-August, pp. 78-91.

Geertz, C. (1973), *Interpretation of Cultures: Selected Essays*. New York: Basic Books.

Harrington, H. (1995), *Total Improvement Management: The Next Generation in Performance Improvement*. New York: McGraw Hill.

Hedberg, B. (1981), "How Can Organizations Learn and Unlearn" in P. Nystrom and W. Starbuck (eds.), *Handbook of Organizational Design*, Vol. 1, pp. 3-27. Oxford: Oxford University Press.

Hobday, M. (1998), "Product Complexity, Innovation and Industrial Organisation," *Research Policy*, Vol. 26, No. 6, pp. 689-710.

Hobday, M. and Rush, H. (1999), "Technology Management in Complex Product Systems (CoPS): Ten Questions Answered," *International Journal of Technology Management*, Special Issue "Emerging Trends in Technology Strategy Development," Vol. 17, No. 6, pp. 618-638.

Huber, G. (1990), "A Theory of the Effects of Advanced Information Technologies on Organizational Design, Intelligence and Decision Making," *Academy of Management Review*, Vol. 15, No. 1, pp. 47-71.

Juran, J. (1991), *Juran's New Quality Road Map: Planning, Setting and Reaching Quality Goals*. New York: Free Press.

Kilmann R. (1996), "Management Learning Organizations: Enhancing Business Education for the 21st Century," *Management Learning*, Vol. 27, No. 2, pp. 203-237.

Kim, D. (1993), "The Link Between Individual and Organizational Learning," *Sloan Management Review*, Vol. 35, No. 1, Fall, pp. 37-50.

Kofman, K. and Senge, P. (1993), "Communities of Commitment: The Heart of Learning Organizations," *Organizational Dynamics*, Vol. 22, Issue 2, pp. 5-23.

Kransdorff, A. (1996), "Using the Benefits of Hindsight—The Role of Post Project Analysis," *The Learning Organization*, Vol. 3, No. 1, pp. 11-15.

Levitt, B. and March, J. (1988), "Organizational Learning" in Scott, R. (ed.) *Annual Review of Sociology*, No. 14, pp. 319-340. Palo Alto, CA: Annual Reviews.

Likert, R. (1961), *New Patterns of Management*. New York: McGraw Hill.

Lipshitz, R., Popper, M. and Oz, S. (1996), "Building Learning Organizations: The Design and Implementation of Organizational Learning Mechanisms," *Journal of Applied Behavioural Science*, Vol. 32, No. 3, pp. 292-305.

Machlup, F. (1983), "Semantic Quirks in Studies of Information" in P. Machlup and U. Mansfield (eds.), *The Study of Information*. New York: John Wiley.

McGregor, D. (1960), *The Human Side of Enterprise*. New York: McGraw Hill.

Nightingale, P. (1997a), "Knowledge and Technical Change: computer Simulation in the Changing Innovation Process," Doctoral Thesis, SPRU, University of Sussex, Unpublished.

Nightingale, P. (1997b), "The Organisation of Knowledge in CoPS Innovation," Paper presented at 7th International Forum on Technology Management, Kyoto, Japan, 3-7 November.

Nonaka, I. (1994), "A Dynamic Theory of Organizational Knowledge Creation," *Organization Science*, Vol. 5, No. 1, pp. 14-37.

Orr, J. (1990), "Sharing Knowledge, Celebrating Identity: War Stories and Community Memory in a Service Culture" in D. Middleton and D. Edwards (eds.), *Collective Remembering: Memory in Society*. London: Sage Publications Limited.

Polanyi, M. (1983 [orig. 1966]), *The Tacit Dimension*. Magnolia: MA, Peter Smith.

Popper, M. and Lipschitz, R. (1995), "Organisational learning mechanisms: A structural/cultural approach to organizational learning," Haifa, Israel: University of Haifa.

Romme, A. (1997), "Organizational Learning, Circularity and Double-linkng," *Management Learning*, Vol. 28, No. 2, pp. 149-160.

Ryle, G. (1954), *Dilemmas: The Tarner Lectures*. Cambridge: Cambridge University Press.

Senge, P. (1990), "The Leader's New Work: Building Learning Organizations," *Sloan Management Review*, Vol. 32, No. 1, Fall, pp. 7-23.

Shannon, C. and Weaver, W. (1949), *The Mathematical Theory of Communication*. Champaign: University of Illinois Press.

Shrivistava, P. (1983), "A Typology of Organizational Learning Systems," *Journal of Management Studies*, Vol. 20, No. 1, pp. 7-28.

Simon, H. (1991), "Bounded Rationality and Organizational Learning," *Organization Science*, Vol. 2, No. 1, pp. 125-134.

Stalk, G., Evans, P. and Schulman, L. (1992), "Competing on Capabilities: The New Rules of Corporate Strategy," *Harvard Business Review*, Vol. 70, No. 2, March-April, pp. 57-70.

Stata, R. (1989), "Organisational Learning—The Key to Management Innovation," *Sloan Management Review*, Vol. 30, No. 3, Spring, pp. 63-74.

Stewart, T. 1998, "The Cunning Plots of Leadership," *Fortune*, September 7. Available at http://www.pathfinder.com/fortune/1998/980907/lea.html

Takeuchi, H. and Nonaka, I. (1986), "The New Product Development Game," *Harvard Business Review*, Vol. 64, No. 1, pp. 137-146.

Vincenti, W. (1990), *What Engineers Know and How They Know It*. Baltimore: The Johns Hopkins University Press.

Wright, T. (1936), "Factors Affecting the Cost of Airplanes," *Journal of Aeronautical Sciences*, Vol. 3, No. 2, pp. 122-128.

Zuboff, S. (1988), *In the Age of the Smart Machine*. New York: Basic Books.

Index

About the Contributors

Ismael Aguilar-Barajas is Titular Professor in the Economics Department, Instituto Tecnológico y de Estudios Superiores de Monterrey (ITESM), Mexico. Contact: iaguilar@campus.mty.itesm.mx

Erkko Autio is Professor and Head of the Institute at the Helsinki University of Technology, Institute of Strategy and International Business. Contact: erkko.autio@hut.fi

Tomas Gabriel Bas is about to finish his PhD in Technology Management at the Université de Montréal, specializing in venture finance. Contact: tomas_bas@hotmail.com

Tim Brady is currently a senior member of the CoPS Innovation Centre, a joint venture between SPRU and CENTRIM. He is also director of a small U.K. consultancy company, IPRA Ltd. Contact: T.M.Brady@brighton.ac.uk

Sunyang Chung is Professor of Technology Management and Policy and Director of the Institute for Technological Innovation (ITI), School of Business Administration, Sejong University. Contact: sychung@sejong.ac.kr

Simon Collinson is a Senior Lecturer in International Business, Warwick Business School and is Associate Dean for the MBA program. Contact: s.collinson@wbs.warwick.ac.uk

Pedro Conceição is Assistant Professor at the Instituto Superior Técnico, Technical University of Lisbon, and a researcher at the Center for Innovation, Technology and Policy Research at IST. He is also a Deputy Director and Senior

Policy Analyst, Office of Development Studies, United Nations Development Programme, New York.
Contact: pedroc@dem.ist.utl.pt

Michael Von Conley is a doctoral student at the Kenan-Flagler Business School, University of North Carolina-Chapel Hill.
Contact: Michael.Conley@disney.com

Gabriela Couto works for a technology extension office in the Chamber of Industry and Commerce in Montevideo.
Contact: gcouto@ciu.com.uy

Reid Cramer is a research associate for the International Workshop on Local Governance at the Lyndon B. Johnson School of Public Affairs, The University of Texas, Austin.
Contact: rcramer@uts.cc.utexas.edu

Manabu Eto is the Director of New Visual Industry Office, Machinery and Information Industries Bureau, Ministry of International Trade and Industry (MITI), Japan. Dr. Eto is with the Permanent Delegation of Japan to the OECD in Paris, France.
Contact: eto@deljp-ocde.fr

Kenzo Fujisue is an Associate Professor of the Graduate School of Engineering, the University of Tokyo.
Contact: fujisue@aol.com

David V. Gibson, The Nadya Kozmetsky Scott Centennial Fellow, is Director of Research and Global Programs at IC² Institute, The University of Texas at Austin [www.ic2.org].
Contact: davidg@icc.utexas.edu

Susanne Giesecke is a senior consultant at the VDI/VDE Information Center for Information Technologies GmbH in Berlin-Teltow, Germany.
Contact: Giesecke@vdivde-it.de

Lawrence S. Graham is Associate Vice President for International Programs and Professor of Government at the University of Texas, Austin.
Contact: lsgraham@uts.cc.utexas.edu

Manuel V. Heitor is Full Professor at the Instituto Superior Técnico in Lisbon, and is the director of the Center for Innovation, Technology and Policy Research, IN+. He is a Senior Research Fellow of IC² Institute, The University of Texas at Austin.
Contact: mheitor@ist.utl.pt

J. Adam Holbrook is an Adjunct Professor and Associate Director at the Centre for Policy Research on Science and Technology (CPROST), at Simon Fraser University in Vancouver, BC.
Contact: jholbroo@sfu.ca

John Horrigan is a Senior Research Specialist at the Pew Internet and American Life Project, which conducts research into how the Internet is affecting Americans' day-to-day lives.
Contact: jhorrigan@pewinternet.org

Lindsay P. Hughes is a Research Associate with the Centre for Policy Research on Science and Technology (CPROST) in the School of Communications at Simon Fraser University in Vancouver, Canada.
Contact: lphughes@home.com

Annamária Inzelt is Founding Director of the Innovation Research Center (IKU) of Budapest University of Economic Sciences and Policy Administration, Hungary.
Contact: annamaria.inzelt@iku.bke.hu

Thomas Keil is a Ph.D. candidate at the Institute of Strategy and International Business at Helsinki University of Technology, Finland.
Contact: tom.keil@hut.fi

George Kozmetsky (1917-2003) was Dean of the College and Graduate School of Business at The University of Texas at Austin. He founded IC^2 [Innovation, Creativity, Capital] Institute and continued to serve as Executive Associate for Economic Affairs in The University of Texas System, chairman of the Advisory Board and a senior research fellow of IC^2 Institute, and Professor in the Management and Computer Science Departments, The University of Texas at Austin.

Mikel Landabaso works in the European Commission as a principal administrator responsible for the conception, management and evaluation of pilot actions in the fields of innovation promotion.
Contact: mikel.landabaso@cec.eu.int

Kavita Mehra is a Senior Scientist at the National Institute of Science Technology and Development Studies (CSIR), New Delhi, India.
Contact: kavitamehra@yahoo.com

Robin Miège is Head of Strategic Cooperation and Technology Transfer at the European Commission's Joint Research.
Contact: Robin.Miege@cec.eu.int

Kevin Morgan is Professor of European Regional Development in the Department of City and Regional Planning at Cardiff University.
Contact: MorganKJ@Cardiff.ac.uk

Akio Nishizawa is Professor at the Graduate School of Economics and Management and Deputy Director of New Industry Creation Hatchery Center, Tohoku University.
Contact: Nishiz@econ.tohoku.ac.jp

Julie Nordskog is an IC^2 researcher at the University of Texas, Austin.
Contact: jnordskog@yahoo.com

Pedro Oliveira is a Ph.D. candidate in Operations, Technology and Innovation Management at the Kenan-Flagler Business School, The University of North Carolina at Chapel Hill.
Contact: oliveirp@bschool.unc.edu

Christine Oughton is Reader in Management, in the School of Management and Organizational Psychology at Birkbeck, University of London.
Contact: c.oughton@bbk.ac.uk

Carlos Quandt is Professor at the Graduate School of Business Administration, Pontificia Universidade Catolica do Paraná (PUC-PR), Brazil.
Contact: quandt@rla01.pucpr.br

Paul L. Robertson is Professor in the Department of Management at the University of Wollongong, Australia.
Contact: paulr@uow.edu.au

Nikolay Rogalev is Director of Innovative Technological Centre, Science Park of the Moscow Power Engineering Institute, Russia.
Contact: spark@aha.ru

Everett M. Rogers is Regents' Professor in the Department of Communication and Journalism at the University of New Mexico.
Contact: erogers@unm.edu

Aleda V. Roth is Professor and Area Chair of Operations, Technology and Innovation Management at the Kenan-Flagler Business School, University of North Carolina-Chapel Hill.
Contact: rotha@bschool.unc.edu

Claudia P. Salas is currently working for the Mexican State Government of Querétaro.
Contact: paloma_salas@hotmail.com

Filipe M. Santos is a Teaching Assistant in the Department of Management Science and Engineering at Stanford University.
Contact: fsantos@stanford.edu

Gillian Shapiro is a part-time Research Fellow at the Centre for Research in Innovation Management (CENTRIM) within the University of Brighton and an independent organization development consultant.
Contact: g.shapiro@fastnet.co.uk

Robin E. Sowden is Professor of Academic-Industrial Relations and Technology Transfer at Shibaura Institute of Technology (Tokyo).
Contact: sowden@sic.shibaura-it.ac.jp

Chandler Stolp is the Director of the Inter-American Policy Studies Program, an effort supported by the William and Flora Hewlett Foundation and a joint venture of the LBJ School and the University of Texas, Austin Lozano Long Institute of Latin American Studies.
Contact: stolp@mail.utexas.edu

Tae Kyung Sung is Associate Professor of Management Information Systems at Kyonggi University in Korea.
Contact: tksung@kuic.kyonggi.ac.kr

Gabriela Susunaga is currently working for PEMEX, Mexico's oil para-state company.
Contact: Susunaga_Gabriela/region-sur_admon-finanzas@gas.pemex.com

Shiro Takegami is a career official in the Japanese Ministry of International Trade and Industry.
Contact: takegami-shiro@meti.go.jp

Schumpeter Tamada is an Assistant Professor of Social Sciences at Tsukuba Advanced Research Alliance, University of Tsukuba.
Contact: schumpeter_tamada@ybb.ne.jp

Scott Tiffin is Director of Babson College's Institute for Latin American Business Studies, in Boston.
Contact: stiffin@babson.edu

Chris Voss is Deputy Dean (Programmes) and director of the Centre for Research in Operations and Technology Management at London Business School, United Kingdom.
Contact: cvoss@london.edu

Chuck Wessner is the Director of the Program on Technology and Competitiveness for the National Research Council's Board on Science, Technology, and Economic Policy.
Contact: cwessner@nas.edu

Robert H. Wilson is the Mike Hogg Professor of Urban Policy at the Lyndon Baines Johnson School of Public Affairs, the University of Texas at Austin, where he is also Director of the Urban Issues Program and of the Brazil Center.
Contact: rwilson@mail.utexas.edu

Duane Windsor is the Lynette S. Autrey Professor of Management at Rice University's Jesse H. Jones Graduate School of Management in Houston, Texas.
Contact: odw@rice.edu

Jing Yin is a doctoral candidate at Penn State University.
Contact: jxy159@psu.edu